1977年隨哈佛大學校長巴克（Derek C. Bok）訪問東亞，途經檀香山合影。

1975年在哈佛燕京圖書館。

1982年在哈佛燕京圖書館辦公室。

1987年台塑創辦人王永慶先生
參觀哈佛燕京圖書館。

1988年美國亞洲學會頒贈「傑出
貢獻獎」與（右起）亞洲學會會長
莫菲（Rhoades Murphey）及另一
得獎人魏裴德（Andrew Walder）
教授合影。

1992年司法院院長林洋港參觀哈佛燕京圖書館（左為波士頓北美事務協調辦事
處處長張文中）。

1995 年與哈佛大學校長魯登斯廷（Neil L. Rudenstine）在哈佛校園合影。

1997 年退休晚宴，與哈佛大學文理學院院長諾爾斯（Jeremy R. Knowles）。

1998年與Chinn Ho Reading Room贊助者何清先生合影。

2001年華人圖書館員協會頒贈「傑出貢獻獎」。

美國東亞圖書館發展史及其他

吳文津

序

余英時

　　吳文津先生和我相知已近半個世紀。現在為他的文集寫這篇序文，我實在感到無比的高興，因為這恰好給我提供了一個最適當的機會和方式，藉以表達對老友的敬意。讓我從我們友誼的始點——哈佛燕京圖書館——說起。

　　我初次接觸哈佛燕京圖書館，便得到一次很大的驚異，至今記憶猶新。1955年10月我以「哈佛燕京學社訪問學人」（Harvard-Yenching Visiting Scholar）的資格從香港到哈佛大學進修。那時我正在進行有關東漢士族大姓的專題研究，因此行裝安頓之後立即展開工作。我雖然早已聞哈燕社漢和圖書館之名，但是它藏書之完備還是遠遠超出我的預想之外。我在香港多年遍求不獲的書刊，在此一索即得。這是我受惠於哈佛燕京圖書館之始。第二年我進入研究院，它更成為我求知的一個最重要泉源了。

　　時間稍久，我終於認識到裘開明先生（1898-1977）作為第一任館長對於哈燕圖書館作出的重大貢獻。哈佛的中、日文藏書之所以在美國大學圖書館系統中長期居於領先的地位，裘先生的功勞最大。[1]所以在哈佛從事中國或東亞研究的人，無論是本校人員或外來訪客，也無論是教授或研究生，多少都對裘先生抱有一種感激的意識。1964年費正清、賴世和與克雷格三位哈佛教授將他們合著的《東亞：現代的轉變》獻給裘先生，便清楚地表達了這一意識。[2]我還記得，1960年代初期，我們都非常關注一件大事：裘先生不久將退休了，誰來接替這一重要職位呢？

　　1966年我重回哈佛任教，裘先生已於上一年退休，繼任人則是吳文津先生，於1965年就職。吳文津先生前任史丹佛大學胡佛研究所的東亞圖書館館長，以收藏現代中、日資料獨步北美。由一位現代圖書館專家接替一位古籍權威為第二任館長，這是哈佛燕京圖書館的發展史上一件劃時代的大事。我這樣說絕沒有絲毫故甚其辭的意思。經過深思熟慮之後，我現在可以斷定：這件大事之所以具有劃時代的意義，是因為它象徵著美國的中國研究進入了一個嶄新的歷史階段。下面讓我試對這一論斷的根據略作說明，以求證於文津先生及一般讀者。

首先必須鄭重指出，1928年登記成立的哈佛燕京學社（Harvard-Yenching Institute）自始便以推動國際漢學（Sinology）為它的主要宗旨之一。因此哈燕社最早的一位諮詢人是法國漢學大師伯希和（Paul Pelliot）；他同時也是創社社長的內定人選。但是他最後不肯接受社長的聘約，轉而推薦葉理綏（Serge Elisséeff）作他的替身。葉氏出自帝俄世家。專治日本古典文學，畢業於東京大學。1917年革命後，他移居巴黎，在伯希和門下從事研究，並成為後者的學術信徒。在他的領導下，哈燕社的國際漢學取向便確定了下來。[3]不用說，漢和圖書館為了配合這一取向，書刊的收藏自然也以19世紀以前的傳統中國與日本為重心所在，而且特別注重精本與善本。在這一取向下，裘開明先生的許多特長，如精確的版本知識以及他與當時北平書肆和藏書家的深厚關係等，恰好都得到了最大程度的發揮。哈佛燕京圖書館終於成為西方漢學研究首屈一指的圖書館中心，絕不是倖致的。[4]

但是從20世紀中葉起，中國研究這一領域在美國開始了一個劃時代的轉向。這一轉向包含了兩個層次：第一，就研究的內涵說，專家們越來越重視中國的現狀及其形成的時代背景；相形之下，以往漢學家們所最感興趣的傳統中國就受到比較冷落的待遇。第二，就研究的取徑論，人文與社會科學各門的專業紀律獲得了普遍的尊重，而以往漢學傳統中的文獻考釋則退居次要的地位。

為什麼會有這一轉向呢？這當然是因為二戰後中國的局勢發生了翻天覆地的大變化。美國在東亞的處境受到嚴重威脅，以致當時美國朝野都在爭辯「美國為什麼失掉了中國？」的問題。事實上，1949年8月美國政府頒布的關於中國的《白皮書》是國務院內外的中國專家集體編寫的，主要根據現代史及檔案來解答「為什麼失去中國」的問題。美國許多第一流大學在1950年代群起向現代中國研究的領域進軍，而且成績輝煌，顯然是因為受到了上述政治氛圍的激勵。

我恰好見證了這一轉向在哈佛大學的展開過程。1955年費正清在福特基金會（Ford Foundation）的大力支持下，創建了「東亞研究中心」（Center For East Asian Studies）。我清楚地記得，當年這中心網羅了一批校內外的專家，從事長期或短期研究。他們的專題主要集中在近代和現代中國的範圍之內；其研究成果則往往以專著（Monograph）的形式出版，構成了著名的《哈佛東亞叢書》（*Harvard East Asian Studies*）。[5]

另一方面，由於政府和大學提供了較多的獎學金名額，哈佛研究院（Graduate School）中以現代中國為研究對象的博士生與碩士生也人數激增。他們遍布在人文與社會科學各門之中，因而將中國研究和現代專業紀律有系統地結合了起來。

相應於這一研究轉向，哈佛燕京圖書館的收藏重心也從傳統時期擴展到中國和東亞的現代了。這便是文津先生受聘為第二任館長的時代背景。但為什麼入選的是文津先生，而不是任何別人呢？這是我要接著說明的問題。

事實上，文津先生當時確是最理想的人選，因為在現代中國研究的領域中，胡佛研究所的資料收藏在美國，甚至整個西方，處於遙遙領先的地位，而文津先生的卓越領導則有口皆碑。

胡佛研究所最初以收藏歐洲當代與戰爭、革命與和平相關的資料著名。二戰以後範圍擴大到東亞，分別成立了中文部與日文部。收藏的範圍以20世紀為限。1948年芮瑪麗（Mary C. Wright, 1917-1970）受聘為首任中文部主任，直到1959年移講耶魯大學歷史系為止。她是費正清的大弟子，後來以深研同治中興和辛亥革命為史學界所一致推重。在她任內，現代中國的收藏已極為可觀。其中包括1946-47年她親自從延安搜集到的中共報刊、伊羅生（Harold R. Issacs）在二、三〇年代收羅的中共地下刊物、斯諾（Edgar Snow）夫婦所藏有關文獻等。[6]

但胡佛研究所的一切收藏最終匯為一個完備現代中國研究與日本研究的圖書中心，則顯然出於文津先生集大成之功。限於篇幅，他的輝煌業績在此無法充分展示。但邵東方先生在2010年總結史丹佛大學東亞圖書館發展史，對文津先生的貢獻有一段很扼要的概括，其文略曰：

> 作為美國華人圖書館長的先驅，吳文津對胡佛研究所的中文收藏做出了
> 巨大的貢獻。1951年首任中文藏書館長芮瑪麗聘請他入館工作。1956年
> 他已成為副館長。1959年芮加入耶魯大學歷史系後，吳則繼任館長之職
> （按：「中文藏書館長」也就是「中文部主任」。）1961年胡佛研究所決
> 定將中、日文部合成「東亞圖書館」（"East Asian Collection"），吳則成
> 為第一任館長。在他1967年11月就任哈佛燕京圖書館館長時，吳已將
> 「東亞藏書」轉變為美國收藏現代中、日資料的一個主要中心了。（按：
> 吳文津先生就職哈燕圖書館館長時期為1965年10月。）就現代中國的
> 資料而言，館中所藏之富在中國大陸和台灣之外，更是屈指可數。[7]

這一概括既客觀又公允，不過僅僅呈現出文津先生在事業方面的一個靜態輪
廓。下面我要對他的動態精神略加介紹。

　　自1959年繼任中文圖書館館長，獨當一面以來，文津先生搜求資料的
精神才逐步透顯出來。這個精神我無以名之，只有借用傅斯年先生的名言
「上窮碧落下黃泉，動手動腳找東西」。事實上，無論是傅先生或文津先
生，所發揚的都是中國史學的原始精神，即司馬遷最早揭出的所謂「網羅天
下放失舊聞」。文津先生只要聽說任何地方有中國現代研究所不可缺少的重
要史料，他便不顧一切困難，全力以赴地去爭取。一個最著名的例子是
1960年他在台北拍攝了全部「陳誠特藏」的檔案。所謂「陳誠特藏」是指
「江西蘇維埃共和國」的原始資料，1930年代初由陳誠的部隊在江西瑞金地
區俘獲得來；運到台北以後，陳把這批資料交給下屬蕭作樑等人整理和研
究。1960年4月有兩位美國專家專程到台北，希望獲得閱覽的機會。蕭請示
陳誠，得到的批示是：「反共的人士都可以參觀」。但這兩位專家一向有
「左傾」的聲名，蕭感到為難，因此求教於當時深受陳誠敬重的胡適。最後
胡的答覆是「不妨寬大些，讓他們看看」。[8]

　　此事發生在文津先生赴台北爭取「陳誠特藏」之前6個多月，二者之間有內在的聯繫。文津先生認識到這批原始資料的重要性曾受上面兩位專家越洋「取經」的影響，這是可以斷言的。不但如此，文津先生也同樣得到胡適的助力。他告訴我們：

> 為此事1960年第一次來台灣。當時台灣的條件很差，據說攝製縮影微卷的機器只有兩部。一部在中央銀行，一部在中央研究院。那時胡適之先生任中央研究院院長，我去請他幫忙。他一口就答應了。把機器與操作人員都借給我使用。經過兩個多月的時間，把這批將近1,500多種的資料照成縮微膠卷帶回美國……[9]

但是我相信胡適的幫助並不僅僅限於技術方面。上面提到他關於「不妨寬大些」的主張必曾對陳誠有所啟發，因而無形中也為文津先生開闢了道路。

　　在爭取「陳誠特藏」的整個過程中，文津先生的基本精神特別體現在兩個方面：第一，他初知台北藏有江西蘇維埃資料，但不得其門而入。稍後偶遇史丹佛大學地質系教授申克（Hebert G. Schenk），曾在台灣負責美援工作，與陳誠相熟。他便毫不遲疑地請申克教授介紹，終於得到複印的許可。可見他在「網羅天下放失舊聞」中寓有一種「求道」的精神，不放過任何一點可能的機會。第二，他說爭取這一套極為珍貴的史料，最初是為了「加強胡佛對中共黨史的收藏」，這是忠於職守的自然表現。然而他對於研究資料卻抱著「天下為公」的態度，不存絲毫「山頭主義」的狹隘意識。因此他後來又取得陳誠的許可，「將這批資料再作拷貝以成本供應美國各大學圖書館以作研究之用」。[10]他的職位在胡佛研究所，但是他同時也為全美所有東亞圖書館提供研究資料。

　　另外一個類似的例子是他在1960年代中期繼獲得江西蘇維埃資料後去爭取胡漢民1930年代未刊的來往信札事。早時，他得知胡木蘭女士存有她父親1930年代與中國各政要的私人手札。胡漢民為國民黨元老，且為華南地區舉足輕重之人物，這批資料的重要性不言而喻。但與「陳誠特藏」一樣，他不得其門而入。後多方打聽，經友人介紹，得識胡木蘭女士及其夫婿。經數年之交往，來往美國與香港之間，得木蘭女士之信任，允考慮將胡漢民先生之信札寄存胡佛研究所，並開放予學者使用但不能複印，而個案研究則必須先得其批准。1964年文津先生受聘任哈佛燕京圖書館館長（1965年就職），胡女士得知後，頗為躊躇，因不知接任文津先生者為何人，乃建議將胡漢民先生之信札轉存哈佛燕京圖書館，由文津先生保管，使用條件依舊。文津先生喜出望外，欣然應允。於是這批2,700餘件信札遂寄存哈佛燕京圖書館。這一批極為珍貴的原始資料，是研究民國史所不可或缺的；後經陳紅民教授編注，並得胡木蘭女士家屬的許可，於2005年由廣西師範大學出版社出版名為《胡漢民未刊往來函電稿》15大冊，以惠士林。[11]

　　上述文津先生的基本精神稍後更得到一次大規模的發揮。1964年「美國學術團體協會」（American Council of Learned Societies）及「社會科學研究理事會」（Social Science Research Council）下面有一個「當代中國聯合委員會」（The Joint Committee on Contemporary China）因為感到美國所藏當代中國資料之不足，決定調查世界各國的收藏狀況，以供美國參考。由於文津先生在這領域中的卓異成就，這一重任終於落在他的肩上；1964-65年期間，他花了整整一年的時間在全世界進行調查工作。他對這一件事，作了下面一段簡報：

　　　調查一年時間裡，通過走訪西歐、東歐、斯堪的納維亞、蘇聯、印度、日本、台灣、香港的重要中國研究和圖書中心，還有美國本土圖書館，我發現蘇聯和東歐的部分圖書館，可以通過我們沒有的途徑從中國獲取原始研究資料，西歐和日本也有，但相對較少。大多數這些圖書館都接受與美國進行交換。所以在呈交給JCCC（按：即「當代中國聯合委員會」縮稱）的報告中，我建議成立一個全國性的東亞圖書館服務中心來

確定、獲取（通過館際互借和交換）以及複製分配那些無法獲取的當代
中國書刊和只有少數美國圖書館才能擁有的稀缺研究資料。[12]

這一次調查旅行，地區之廣大和查詢之詳細，真正不折不扣地可稱為「上窮
碧落下黃泉，動手動腳找東西」。他的報告和建議都是為全美各大學的現代
中國研究著想，所以特別強調研究資料必須向所有圖書館開放。更值得指出
的是：「當代中國聯合委員會」接受了他的建議，終於在1968年成立了「中
國研究資料中心」（Center for Chinese Research Materials）。這中心先後複製
了無數難得的資料，不但遍及全美，而且流傳世界各地。正如文津先生所
言，如果沒有這個資料中心，「各地圖書館現在是不可能擁有那麼多中文書
刊的」。

　　總之，1964-65年文津先生的調查旅行不僅是他個人事業的不朽成就，
而且也是美國現代中國研究史和東亞圖書館發展史上值得大書特書的事件。
難怪美國「亞洲學會」（Association for Asian Studies）在1988年頒發每年一
度的「傑出貢獻獎」（Distinguished Service Award）給文津先生時，獎狀中
有下面的詞句：

> 三十年來你是發展現代和當代中國研究資料的中心動力……牢記中國的
> 傳統價值，我們景仰你在旁人心中激起的抱負，你有惠他人的成就，以
> 及傳播與他人共用知識。本學會表彰如此傑出的事業生涯也是為自己增
> 光。[13]

以上舉文津先生在史丹佛大學時代的幾個重要活動為例，旨在透顯他的獨特
精神。通過這幾個事例，哈佛燕京圖書館為什麼非請他繼任第二任館長不
可，便無須再作任何解釋了。

　　文津先生到哈佛之後，雖然面對的具體問題與胡佛研究所不同，但他的

精神則一仍舊貫。哈佛燕京藏書初以漢學取向，這一點前面已說過了。由於
裘先生在這一領域已建立了規模，文津先生大體上蕭規曹隨，但始終維持著
它的領先地位。我對此有親切的體會。因為漢學正是我的工作領域。我和文
津先生共事10年，從來沒有感到研究資料方面有任何不足的地方。但在近
代和現代中國的研究領域中，文津先生則將哈佛燕京的收藏帶到一個全新的
境地。詳情不可能在此陳述，我只想提一下他在收集「文革」資料方面所費
去的時間和精力比他走遍全世界調查現代中國資料更為艱巨，也更有成就。
1965年他到哈佛的時候，正是文革前夕，但資料已極為難求，1966年文革
起始後，中國出版界除《毛澤東選集》及《毛澤東語錄》等外，工作幾乎全
部停頓。但各地紅衛兵小報遍起如雨後春筍，部分帶至香港經書商複印出售
者為唯一可收購之資料，但供不應求，以致洛陽紙貴。當時美國國務院應學
術界的要求，願意公開政府所收集的紅衛兵資料。於是上述的「當代中國聯
合委員會」又邀請文津先生負起這一重任，到國務院閱讀一大批有代表性的
資料。他認為其中紅衛兵小報和周恩來等人與紅衛兵代表的談話記錄等都有
極高的史料價值。因此建議國務院儘快公開於世。但1967年時「中國研究
資料中心」尚在籌建中。於是哈佛燕京圖書館將最早從國務院收到的資料製
成縮微膠捲，以成本計向各圖書館發行。這是他幾年前複製「陳誠特藏」的
故智。直到1975年「中國研究資料中心」才出版了紅衛兵資料20卷，以後
每隔幾年便續刊數十卷。我同意文津先生的話，這也許是「世界上最大的公
開出版的紅衛兵資料集」。[14]最有趣的事是1980年5月考古學家夏鼐第一次
訪問哈佛，也特別記下文津先生給他看的「紅衛兵各小報縮印本20餘冊」。
[15]我猜想夏所見的必是1975年「中國研究資料中心」出版的20卷本。

　　文津先生的精神一以貫之，此其明證。具此精神動力，所以他的成就特
多，而為各方所推崇。上面已提到美國亞洲學會的「傑出貢獻獎」。先生
1997年榮休時，哈佛大學校長魯登斯廷（Neil L. Rudenstine）在他的賀文中
列舉先生對哈佛的貢獻之外，在末尾說：

我非常高興加上我個人以及哈佛全體同仁對他為哈佛作出的示範性的傑出貢獻致謝。文津，你已經發揮了重要的作用，哈佛因之而是一個更好的大學。[16]

　　最後，我要鄭重指出，這部文集具有極高的史料價值，絕不可以一般個人的文字集結視之。無論我們是要認識20世紀中葉以來中國的歷史動向，還是想理解西方人怎樣研究這一動向，《美國東亞圖書館發展史及其他》都能給我們以親切的指引。

2013.10.17於普林斯頓

2016.1.6重新改定

注釋

[1]　參看本書所收〈裘開明與哈佛燕京圖書館〉。

[2]　John K. Fairbank, Edwin O. Reischauer, Albert M. Craig, *East Asia: The Modern Transformation*. Boston: Houghton Mifflin Co., 1965, p. ix.

[3]　陳毓賢，《洪業傳》（北京：商務印書館，2013），頁159-160。

[4]　參看本書所收〈哈佛燕京圖書館簡史及其中國典籍收藏概況〉。

[5]　最早第一本書是2013年4月27日過世的費維凱（Albert Feuerwerker）的名著：*China's Early Industrialization: Sheng Hsuan-huai (1844-1916) and Mandarin Enterprise*, 1958.

[6]　吳文津，〈美國東亞圖書館蒐藏中國典籍之緣起與現況〉收在淡江大學中國文學系主編《書林覽勝》（台北：臺灣學生書局，2003），頁33-35。此文已收在本書中。

[7]　Dongfang Shao in collaboration with Qi Qiu, "Growing Amid Challenges: Stanford University's East Asian Library," in Peter X. Zhou, ed., *Collecting Asia: East Asian Libraries in North America, 1868-2008*, Ann Arbor: Association for Asian Studies, 2010, p. 182.邵先生寫此文時正在史丹佛大學東亞圖書館館長的任內。

[8]　胡頌平，《胡適之先生年譜長編初稿》（台北：聯經出版公司，1984），第9冊，頁3248-9。

[9]　同注[6]《書林覽勝》頁36。1960年11月10日他向胡辭行。見胡頌平，《胡適之先生年譜長編初稿‧補編》（台北：聯經出版公司，2015），頁296。

[10]　同上，《書林覽勝》，頁36。參看本書所收〈《江西蘇維埃共和國，1931-1934──陳誠特藏文件選輯解題書目》前言〉。

[11]　吳文津口述。

[12]　吳文津，〈北美東亞圖書館的發展〉，張寒露譯，《圖書情報知識》，2011年第2期，頁8。該篇英文原文 "The Development of East Asian Libraries in North America" 載 Chen Chuanfu and Ronald Larsen, eds., *Library and Information Sciences: Trends and Research* (Heidelberg: Springer, 2014), pp. 163-177. 參看本書所收〈當代中國研究在美國的資料問題〉，原載《書林覽勝》，頁87-89。

[13]　獎狀頒予1988年3月26日。此段原文為："For three decades you have been the central dynamic force in the development of research sources for modern and contemporary Chinese studies... Remembering traditional Chinese values, we admire you for the aspirations you inspire in others, for your achievements which benefit others, and your dissemination of knowledge shared with others. The Association honors itself in recognizing so distinguished a career." 至今吳文津先生仍為東亞圖書館界得此殊榮譽之唯一人物。

[14]　同注[12]。參看《文集》所收〈《新編紅衛兵資料》序〉。

[15]　《夏鼐日記》（上海：華東師範大學出版社，2011）卷8，頁426。按：夏氏當時還弄不清楚文津先生的姓名，只知道他是哈佛燕京圖書館館長，四川人。

[16]　魯登斯廷校長賀詞結語的原文是："I am very pleased to add my own thanks and the thanks of all of us at Harvard for his exemplary and distinguished service to the Harvard community. Gene Wu, you have made an important difference, and Harvard is a better university because of it."

目 次

一、美國東亞圖書館發展史

二、哈佛燕京圖書館館史及館藏概況

三、人物懷念

五、當代中國研究及研究資料問題

六、國民黨早期政治史：第一次國共合作

卷尾

前言

　　二戰後美國各大學大幅擴張東亞教研項目，因而帶動東亞圖書館的發展。我自1951年開始在東亞圖書館服務，適逢其盛。工作40餘年，於1997年退休，其間頗多見聞，並曾參與多種項目之籌畫。工作之餘曾撰寫若干有關北美東亞圖書館文稿、書評、序言、紀念文等，先後發表於海內外學報。年前哥倫比亞大學東亞圖書館中文部主任王成志先生敦促選輯部分付梓，以為同仁參考，並存史實。王主任的盛意難卻，遂檢出論文及演講稿46篇，並將原為英文稿者，譯為中文。以中英文對照格式出版，以佐參考。本書分下列部分：美國東亞圖書館發展史；哈佛燕京圖書館館史及館藏概況；人物懷念；書評及序言；當代中國研究及研究資料問題；以及國共第一次合作之論文三篇。此書所提信息及數據均非即時資料，僅代表文章發表時之資訊。事過境遷，若干信息均今非昔比，然仍可作史實視之。雪泥鴻爪，或能聊充北美東亞圖書館發展史料。其中個人粗見，尚祈方家指正。

　　此書得以問世，除王主任、聯經出版公司前總經理劉國瑞先生、現任發行人林載爵先生鼎力支持外，聯經出版公司主編沙淑芬女士的細心編輯使本書增色不少。準備過程中並多賴友人協助。首先，我對前哈佛燕京圖書館中文部主任胡嘉陽女士致最深的謝意和敬意。胡主任費時費力收集整理我發表過的文章，分類掃描歸檔，負責主要的翻譯工作，考證資料，以及出版前後如校對的各項細節，以及與聯經出版公司沙主編聯繫，始終如一，不遺餘力。沒有她的這種慷慨相助，本書的出版料不可能。王成志主任、前普林斯頓大學東亞圖書館館長馬泰來先生及其前任馬敬鵬先生亦惠賜譯文數篇（譯者姓名附譯文後。未署名者為作者自譯）。修正論文時，多承就近史丹佛大學東亞圖書館中文部主任薛昭慧女士，及前東亞語文文化系周力女士協助調閱書刊。編輯中在電腦上文章格式以及其他技術問題，多蒙加州門羅公園基督之家李復華長老指導，均一併致謝。

　　前哈佛大學及普林斯頓大學余英時教授惠賜序言，為拙著增光，亦致衷心的謝忱。

吳文津

2015 年 7 月於美國加州門羅公園

一、
美國東亞圖書館發展史

美國東亞圖書館蒐藏中國典籍之緣起與現況

　　這次能到淡江來和大家見面，分享我這幾十年來在圖書館工作上的一些感受與觀察，感到非常榮幸。以前我到淡江來參觀過好幾次，在朱立民教授擔任副校長的時候我也來過。我和朱教授是很好的朋友，我們在重慶中央大學是同班同學，也同時參加青年軍服役，一起派去作翻譯官。我們在昆明服役的時間最長。他在昆明參謀作戰學校任翻譯官隊長，後來調到緬甸，我接他的職位。後來一直沒有見面。直到戰後才知道他在台灣，於是又和他聯絡上了。之後我們來往很密切，不論他在美國念書，或我到台灣，我們都會相聚。所以我覺得因為他，我和淡江也沾上了一些間接的關係。而這次我被邀請到此地來擔任講座，我覺得跟淡江的關係就更密切了。

　　這次我來演講的三個題目，是在淡江指定的範圍內由我選擇決定的。今天要講的是〈美國東亞圖書館蒐藏中國典籍之緣起與現況〉，明天講〈哈佛燕京圖書館簡史及其中國典籍收藏概況〉，後天講〈當代中國研究在美國的資料問題〉。我希望能在這三個主題之下和大家交換意見，還希望大家能夠多多批評指教。我並且希望每一次講完後大家可以提出問題來，我知道的可以立刻答覆，我不知道的回去以後再作書面答覆。

　　美國現在有六十幾個東亞圖書館在收集中文資料，這次我選當中11個最重要的作一個報告。這11個當中有美國國會圖書館、耶魯大學圖書館、哈佛燕京圖書館、哥倫比亞大學圖書館、普林斯頓大學圖書館、康乃爾大學圖書館、芝加哥大學圖書館、西雅圖華盛頓大學圖書館、史丹佛大學胡佛研究院的東亞圖書館，和加州大學圖書館。因為有這許多圖書館，所以我只能為每一個做些簡單扼要的介紹。但是國會圖書館的中文部和胡佛研究院東亞圖書館這兩處我會講得多一些，因為國會圖書館是美國第一個收集中文資料的圖書館，也是現在西方最大的收集中文資料的圖書館；胡佛研究院的東亞圖書館則是因為我在那裡工作了14年，所以我知道比較多，也稍微多講一些。明天則專門講哈佛燕京圖書館，因為像剛剛黃院長所說，我在哈佛燕京圖書館服務了32年，所以知道的也比較清楚。

　　圖書館的發展跟教學及研究的發展有不可分割的關係。美國關於東亞方面的教學及研究雖然在19世紀末期就已經萌芽，但是其真正的發展是在第二次世界大戰後的事。二次世界大戰之前有少數大學開設了一些有關東亞的課程，但是並未受到很大的重視。教授和學生的人數很少，課程也只限於歷史與語文方面而已。第二次世界大戰以後，美國原本以西方文化為中心的教育政策有了基本的轉變，從比較窄礙的西方唯尊的觀點轉變為世界多元文化的觀點。在歐美以外的地區因而受到重視，特別是東亞。主要的原因是從1940年代到1950年代這短短十幾年當中，美國在東亞地區直接或間接地參與了若干歷史上有轉捩性的重大事件，諸如太平洋戰爭，占領日本，協調中國內戰失敗，朝鮮半島分割為南韓、北韓，旋又參加韓戰抵制北韓和中共等。這一連串的事件提高了美國政府和民間對東亞地區的重視，同時也感覺到需要進一步了解東亞各國歷史與文化的迫切性。

　　於是美國各大學在私人基金會與聯邦政府的大力支持之下，陸續擴張或開創了整體性的──包括所有人文科學與社會科學──有關東亞各國教學的課程和研究的項目。在50年後的今天，在這種有系統和加快步伐的發展下，美國在這方面的教學和研究在西方世界是範圍最廣、內容最豐富的。在這個發展過程當中，為支援教學與研究的需要，美國圖書館在東亞圖書方面也跟著有顯著的發展。美國有些大學在第二次世界大戰以前就開始收集中、日文的書籍，其中並有非常珍貴的，一直到現在還是研究漢學不可或缺的典籍文獻。但是全面性的、普遍的、迅速的發展，還是第二次世界大戰以後的事。在二次大戰後的一二十年間，除早期已經成立的圖書館外，另外有些後來成為重要的東亞圖書館也在這個時期先後成立，諸如密西根大學的亞洲圖書館、胡佛研究院的東亞圖書館、加州大學洛杉磯分校的東亞圖書館等都是在1940年代末期建立的。其他如伊利諾、印第安那與威斯康辛大學的東亞館在1960年代才開始運作。所以說美國東亞圖書館的全面和迅速的發展是第二次世界大戰以後的事不是誇大其詞的。

根據西元2000年6月底的統計，全美東亞圖書館的總藏量如下（在準備這份講稿的時候，更新的2001年的統計還未完全發表）：

藏書總量

藏書總量（書籍）1,400萬冊，其中中文書籍720萬冊，占總藏量的51%。現行連續性出版物，97,960種，中文41,110多種，占總藏量的46.22%。非書資料（其中縮微卷、縮微片占絕大多數，其他包括錄音帶、錄影帶、CD ROM、圖像資料等）181萬多種。其中中文的有335,700種，占總藏量31%。

採購經費

1999到2000年會計年度，採購經費共計大約美金11,276,000多元，中文採購的金額不詳，因為統計中不分語言計算，據估計中文採購經費大概占40%。

服務人員

全國60多間東亞館約有500多位圖書館服務人員。

從這些數字中可以見到東亞館對中文資料的重視。這些東亞館是如何開始以及它們如何發展到今天這樣的地步就是我今天所要講的題目。

美國圖書館中收集中文資料最早的是美國國會圖書館，它是在1869年（清朝同治八年）就開始收藏中文典籍，後來耶魯大學在1878年（清光緒四年），哈佛大學在1879年（清光緒五年），加州大學在1896年（清光緒二十二年）也都開始收集。在20世紀上半紀，哥倫比亞大學在1902年開始、康乃爾大學1918年、普林斯頓大學1926年、芝加哥大學1936年也相繼開始收集。今天所要介紹的就是上述這幾個圖書館（哈佛燕京圖書館除外，那是明天的講題）以及在第二次世界大戰之後才成立的胡佛研究院東亞圖書館，西

雅圖華盛頓大學東亞圖書館，和密西根大學亞洲圖書館收集中文資料的起
源、現況及其特徵作一個簡單扼要的敘述。

國會圖書館

美國國會圖書館是美國收藏中文典籍的第一個圖書館，始於1869年。
關於這件事，前芝加哥大學錢存訓教授曾於1965年在《哈佛亞洲學報》
（*Harvard Journal of Asiatic Studies*）第23卷撰文，有詳盡的敘述。文名 "First
Chinese-American Exchange of Publications" 後譯名為〈中美書緣：紀念中美
文化交換百周年〉收錄在台灣文華圖書館管理資訊股份有限公司1998年出
版錢先生所著的《中美書緣》中。另外一份資料也可供參考。就是現任國會
圖書館亞洲部中文部主任王冀教授撰寫的一篇文章〈簡介美國國會圖書館的
中文收藏〉（"The Chinese Collection in the Library of Congress: A Brief
Introduction"），後來由國家圖書館吳碧娟女士譯成中文，發表在《國立中央
圖書館館刊》新16卷第2期（1983年12月）。前些時候，王冀先生又略微修
改了他的原稿，將中英文合刊，用其原來名字印成一部小冊，私人發行。除
了這兩種資料外，關於國會圖書館中文部發展講述得最詳細的一部書，是從
前台大教授胡述兆先生的專著《國會圖書館的中文藏書建設》（*The
Development of the Chinese Collection in the Library of Congress*, Boulder:
Colorado: Westview Press, Inc. 1979）。這三種資料是國會圖書館中文資料建
設的前後過程最有權威性的著作。現在我就根據它們作一個簡要的敘述。

美國國會在1867年通過了一項法案，規定美國政府的出版物每一種需
保留50份，由史密森學院（Smithonian Institution）負責與各國交換。諮會
各國後，中國清朝政府並沒有回應。第二年，美國農業部派了一位駐華代
表，負責收集有關中國農業的資料。這位農業代表到中國的時候，帶了五
穀、蔬菜、豆類的種子，和有關美國農業、機械、礦業、地圖，和測量美國
太平洋鐵路的報告書若干種，贈送給清廷，並且希望能夠得到同等的回禮作
為交換。但是當時的「總理各國事務衙門」，也就是當時清朝的外交部，沒
有予以答覆。

　　過了一年，1869年（清同治八年）美國國務院應美國聯邦政府土地局的要求，令其駐華公使館向中國政府要求中國戶口的資料。美國公使也藉此機會，再向總理衙門提出圖書交換的要求。於是總理衙門才做出了決定，以相當數量的書籍和穀類種子作為交換。這些東西在1869年6月7日（清同治八年四月二十七日）由總理衙門送到美國使館。國務院把其中的10種書籍交給史密森學院處理，史密森學院再轉存國會圖書館，於是完成了第一次中美圖書交換的工作。國會圖書館因而也成為美國收藏中文典籍的第一個圖書館，這次首次交換給美國的書籍，一共有下列10種，共130函：《皇清經解》道光九年（1829），廣東粵雅堂刊本，360冊，80函、《五禮通考》乾隆十九年（1754），江蘇陽湖刊本，120冊12函、《欽定三禮》乾隆十四年（1749），殿本，136冊18函、《醫宗今鑑》乾隆五年（1740），北京刊本，90冊12函、《本草綱目》順治十二年（1655），北京刊本，48冊4函、《農政全書》道光十七年（1837），貴州刊本，24冊4函、《駢字類編》雍正五年（1727），北京刊本，120冊20函、《針灸大全》道光十九年（1834），江西刊本，10冊2函、《梅氏叢書》康熙四十六年（1707），北京刊本，10冊2函、《性理大全》明永樂十四年（1416），內府刊本，16冊2函。

　　在這次交換之後到19世紀末，除了在1879年購得前美國駐華公使顧盛（Caleb Cushing）所收集的滿漢書籍237種約2,500餘冊（其中有太平天國的官書、清刻的多種地方志）以外，國會圖書館沒有添增其他的中國典籍。

　　到了20世紀初葉，在1901到1902年之間，另一位前駐華公使羅克義（William W. Rockhill）將其收藏的漢、滿、蒙文書籍約6,000冊，全數捐贈國會圖書館。1904年中國政府把運到美國參加聖路易斯萬國博覽會展出的198種中國善本典籍也捐贈美國國會圖書館。之後在1908年，中國政府為了表示感謝美國政府退還給中國還沒有動用的庚子賠款1,200多萬美金，特派唐紹儀作為專使到美國致謝，同時贈送給美國國會圖書館一部非常有價值的雍正六年（1728）在北京以銅活字印行的《古今圖書集成》全套，共5,020冊。

　　雖然有上述的這些收藏，當時國會圖書館仍然還是沒有建立一個有系統的收集中國典籍的政策。有系統的收集在1899年普特南（Herbert Putnam）任館長後才開始的。普特南任國會圖書館館長40年（1899-1939），是一位非常有遠見的學者，也是一位非常有能力的行政人才。在他的任內，他全力以赴為國會圖書館積極收集世界各國文獻典籍。在他的領導下，國會圖書館才開始有計畫地收集中國書籍。

　　當時美國的農業部對中國的農業發展頗為仰慕，所以收集了很多有關中國農業方面的資料。因此，普特南也請他們為國會圖書館收集中文書籍。這個任務當時交給農業部一位華裔名叫馮景桂（Hing Kwai Hung）的植物學家。在1913、1914這兩年當中，馮景桂替國會圖書館收集了大約12,000冊的中文書籍，立刻就增加了當時國會圖書館所有中文書籍的一倍。他所收集的典籍包羅萬象，其中叢書的種類特別多。在他之後，為國會圖書館收集中文典籍功勞最大的是另一位農業部的植物學家施永格（Walter T. Swingle）。施永格非常欽慕中國文化，對中國的典籍有很大的興趣。在1917到1927年這十年間，他曾去中國三次，為國會圖書館收集中文典籍文獻，其數量達到68,000冊之多，其中多善本書、地方志、叢書以及很多國會圖書館在經史子集方面缺乏的古籍。

　　施永格很受普特南的信任，1927年普特南接受他的建議在國會圖書館成立中文部（Division of Chinese Literature），並聘請一位年輕的漢學家恆慕義（Authur W. Hummel, 1884-1975）負責管理。恆慕義是清史專家，他所編輯的《清代名人傳略》（*Eminent Chinese of the Ch'ing Period (1644-1912)*），國會圖書館1943年出版，至今為清人傳記的經典著作。這個中文部後來改名為東方部（Orientalia Division），也由恆慕義主持。後又稱亞洲部（Asian Division），一直至今。恆慕義在國會圖書館從1927年任職到1954年，共27年，在他的任內國會圖書館東方部的典藏增加了三倍，大約從10萬冊到30萬冊，這是國會圖書館收藏中文典籍的黃金時代，並使其成為當時漢學研究的重鎮。

　　第二次世界大戰以後，國會圖書館藏書建設政策有了基本上的改變。從埃文斯（Luther Evans）1945年就任館長以來，藏書建設工作的重點轉向新的、當代的出版物。古籍善本的採購當然受到很大的影響，就是新出版物中也限制於在採購時當年和兩年前出版的書籍。因此，近50年來，除了一部分從其他政府機構轉移給國會圖書館的書籍以外，國會圖書館中文部所收集的資料與其他大學東亞圖書館所收集的資料並無不同，不像以前那樣特出了。

國會圖書館現藏中文典籍約797,700冊，新舊期刊共12,000種，縮微卷18,000多卷，包括1,777卷國立北平圖書館在第二次世界大戰時運美由國會圖書館代為保存的2,800種中文善本的縮微卷，305卷北平協和醫院中文醫學圖書654種的微卷，還有46卷由奧地利人洛克（Joseph Rock）收集的地方志所照成的微卷，日本所藏國會圖書館尚付闕如的37種中國方志的37卷微卷，以及近年從大陸購得的367卷代表1,000多種中國家譜的微卷。目前國會圖書館每年收集中文書籍，包括為數不少的交換品，大概有20,000多冊。

國會圖書館所藏中國典籍的特色在於幾方面。第一就是善本。1957年國會圖書館出了一本原由北平圖書館王重民先生編撰，後由袁同禮先生校定的《國會圖書館所藏中文善本圖書目錄》（*A Descriptive Catalog of Chinese Rare Books in the Library of Congress*）共著錄善本1,775種，其中宋刻本11種、金刻本1種、元刻本14種、明刻本1,439種、清刻本（順治、康熙、雍正）69種、套印本72種、活字本7種、抄本119種、稿本6種、日本漢文刻本10種、日本活字本1種、朝鮮漢文刻本3種、朝鮮活字本8種，還有一些日本和朝鮮的抄本以及敦煌寫本。另外還有明人別集226種、清人別集20種（也是清初的），據說國會圖書館還有一些善本沒有收錄在這本目錄裡，所以目前收藏的總數可能在2,000種左右。

第二個特色就是中國方志。國會圖書館現藏的方志大約有4,000種。1942年朱世嘉先生編纂了一本《美國國會圖書館藏中國方志目錄》（*A Catalog of Chinese Local Histories in the Library of Congress*），當時所著錄的僅2,939種，故現在收藏的4,000種的數字可能包括縮微卷和複印本。朱氏目錄中收錄、修於宋代的計23種、元代的9種、明代的68種、清代的2,376種、民國時代的463種。方志中以河北、山東、江蘇、四川和山西的最多，各有230種到280種之多，山東方志共279種，其中將近一半（118種）是從山東藏書家高鴻裁處購得，其中有不少的稀有版本。四川的方志有252種，很多是洛克（Joseph Rock）在四川為國會圖書館購買的。

第三個特色是《永樂大典》。大家都知道《永樂大典》與《古今圖書集成》是中國最著名的兩大類書。《永樂大典》的編纂始於明朝永樂元年（1403），終於永樂六年（1408）工筆手抄，共22,877卷，裝訂為11,095冊。明末火災，幾被焚毀，清末英法聯軍與八國聯軍之役復被掠奪，更所剩無幾。從原來的11,095冊到現在中外共存不到900冊。目前流散在歐洲的集中在英國，有69冊，大英圖書館有45冊、倫敦大學亞非學院有3冊、牛津大學19冊、劍橋大學2冊。美國有52冊，其中國會圖書館最多，有41冊，其餘的在康乃爾大學華生圖書館（Wason Collection）6冊，哈佛燕京圖書館與普林斯頓大學圖書館各有2冊，哈佛大學的善本圖書館（Houghton Library）也有1冊。今年年底大陸要召開關於《永樂大典》的國際會議，想在會議之後我們對於《永樂大典》在世界上各地分散的情形當有更進一步的了解。

第四個特點是叢書。國會圖書館所藏的叢書有3,000餘種，為歐美各東亞圖書館之冠，可以參照的資料很多，如國會圖書館的中文目錄都可用以查詢。

第五個是很特殊的資料，就是中國少數民族語言的典籍，包括滿文、蒙文、藏文的佛經和其他文獻，其中一批最特別的資料就是3,300多冊的納西族象形文字的經典。納西又稱麼些，其部族處於雲南西北部，和緬甸與西藏交界的地方。從第8世紀到18世紀是一個獨立的部落，之後為清朝統治，麗江曾經是他們的首府，現在人口有26萬左右，都已被漢化。納西族只有象形文字，其經典是東巴（巫師）用以求神占卜、用於各種宗教活動使用的，至今已頗少見。國會圖書館這批資料是從洛克（Joseph Rock）與一位名叫昆廷‧羅斯福（Quentin Roosevelt）——美國希歐多爾‧羅斯福（Theodore Roosevelt）總統之孫——處收集來的。中央研究院李霖燦先生曾在《中央研究院民族學研究所集刊》第6期1958年秋季號中介紹了這批資料。三年前國會圖書館聘請了雲南省博物館納西文專家朱寶田教授到美國來整理這批資料，並且依照朱教授前時在哈佛大學為哈佛燕京圖書館所編的納西文經典目錄的格式，替國會圖書館做了一套類似的目錄。這項工作已在去年10月間完成。據稱，國會圖書館現正計畫把這批目錄掃描上網，以供研究使用。

再者，從1953年到1960年這七年當中國會圖書館中文部將其所藏有關中國法律的書籍全部轉移給國會圖書館的法律圖書館保管。同時有關中國農業技術、臨床醫藥的中文書籍，也分別轉移到美國國家農業圖書館與美國國家醫學圖書館收藏。所以，現在，美國國會圖書館中文部已不復再行收集這些方面的資料。

我報告了很多關於國會圖書館收藏中國典籍的歷史和現況，因為國會圖書館中文部是美國東亞館中最重要的一所圖書館，也是美國收集中文典籍的第一個圖書館。所以是值得大書特書的。今天我要介紹的還有另外九個東亞館。我想最好的辦法就是依它們開始收集中文資料的年份來依序作較為簡單的敘述。

耶魯大學

耶魯大學在國會圖書館收集中國政府交換書籍的九年以後，在1878年也收到一批中國的古籍，成為美國第一所收集中文典籍的大學圖書館。這批典籍包括一部光緒二十年（1894）上海同文書局印行的5,040冊的《古今圖書集成》，以及其他34種，一共1,280冊的古籍，這些古籍是耶魯大學一位校友、當時任中國駐美使館的副公使容閎贈送的。

容閎（Yung Wing）是在中美文化交換上一位很重要的人物。他是廣東香山人，於1828年出生，1912年逝世。幼時在澳門和香港教會學校就學，道光二十七年（1847）他18歲的時候，被學校保送到美國念書。他於1854年在耶魯大學畢業，成為中國第一位在美國大學畢業的留學生。後來他受到曾國藩與丁日昌的賞識，採納了他的建議，選派青年學子到美國留學，同治十一年（1872），第一批學生派到美國去，容閎任監督，是中國公費留學生的開始。

　　容閎捐書給耶魯大學圖書館之後，在1884年耶魯大學圖書館又收到前美國駐華公使、耶魯大學第一任中國語文文學教授衛三畏（Samuel Williams）遺贈的他生前所收藏的全部中文古籍。後來又陸陸續續收到其他的贈送書籍。所以耶魯大學收藏中文典籍的工作就慢慢地發展起來了。1961年，耶魯大學成立東亞學術研究委員會（Council on East Asian Studies），中文藏書建設的工作才開始更有系統的、積極的、不斷的增強。

　　耶魯大學現藏中文書籍有413,000冊左右，現行中文期刊1,620種，另外還有中日韓縮微卷與非書資料10,000餘件（中文數字不詳）。現每年入藏中文出版品約6,300餘冊。

　　館藏最特出的資料是太平天國文獻。這批文獻是聞名的太平天國學者簡又文教授所贈。簡教授1964-1965年受聘為耶魯大學歷史系研究學者。之後他將歷年收藏有關太平天國的資料，包括書籍雜誌320種及拓片、銅幣、印章等全部捐贈耶魯大學圖書館，是一批非常珍貴研究太平天國的第一手資料。其他如明清小說，亦頗有特出者，館藏明清刻本59種中有通俗小說20種，其中有罕見者，如明遺香樓刻本《三國志》，明郁郁堂刻本《水滸四傳全書》，清乾隆五十七年程偉元元萃書屋木活字印本《石頭記》，及清初刻本《金瓶梅》等。

加州大學

　　我現在所講的加州大學是指柏克萊分校（Berkeley）。因為加州大學有九個分校，是美國州立大學系統中最大的學校。加州大學在1896年設立中文講座，聘英人傅蘭雅（John Fryer）為講座教授。傅氏原在北京總理衙門創辦的同文館（College of Foreign Languages）任教，後轉上海江南機器製造局（Kiangnan Arsenal）任翻譯工作，從1867到1896年達30年之久。他到加州大學就任時，把他自己私人的中文藏書以及全部江南機器製造局印行的200多種西方著作的中文翻譯，共2,000餘冊——其中包括科學、歷史、地理、國際公法等——全數捐贈加州大學圖書館，這就是加州大學收藏中文典籍的開始。

　　但是在傅蘭雅先生捐贈這批書籍之後的幾十年當中，加州大學並沒有新增的收藏。一直等到1916年，江亢虎先生來加州大學接任中文講座。江亢虎，江西上饒人，是中國最早提倡社會主義的學者，也曾在北洋編譯局任總辦、兼《北洋官報》的總纂。他在加州大學時，將他從中國帶到美國來的他父親收藏的中文典籍13,000多冊捐贈加大圖書館。他的父親江德宣，是光緒十二年（1886）的進士，他的收藏中有不少有價值的古籍善本，這一批資料為加州大學中文藏書奠下了非常好的基礎。

　　續任江亢虎先生職位的是一位名叫衛理（Edward Thomas Williams）的先生，他也捐贈了一批書籍給加州大學，後來管理加州大學中文古籍的邁克爾‧哈格蒂（Michael Hagerty）和迪特爾‧史泰勒（Diether von den Steiner）也採購了一些。雖然有這樣的開始。但是加州大學一直到1947年正式成立東亞圖書館後，才開始積極從事於中文典籍的藏書建設工作，以人文科學方面，尤其是語言、文學、歷史、考古學為其收集的重點。但是1949年以後中國大陸出版的社會科學方面的書籍，收集的就非常有限，主要是由加州大學的中國研究中心的圖書館來收集。東亞館只是負責收集1949年以來大陸出版的人文科學方面的書籍。這種分工合作的藏書建設的工作模式在美國大學圖書館中還是不常見的。關於中國研究中心圖書館的狀況我在下面再行介紹。

　　加州大學現藏的中國典籍約375,000冊，現行中文期刊2,040餘種，縮微卷及非書資料不詳（中日韓文資料總計約71,000種）。近年來每年入藏書籍約15,000冊。

　　館內特藏有下列各種：第一是剛剛已經提到的江南機器製造局翻譯的書籍，這批2,000餘冊的資料，是西方世界中最完整的一套。第二是拓本，加州大學圖書館有3,000多件拓本，是西方圖書館中數量最大的一批。他們前些時候與中央研究院史語所合作，已經完成整理、編目的工作。據稱，這批資料將數位化上網，以供公開使用。第三是善本，加大收藏的善本不多，但其中頗有珍貴的典籍。宋刻本有6種、元刻本有10種、明刻本356種、清初刻本600多種。還有一批抄本，有20餘部，大部分是藏書家劉承幹嘉業堂舊藏，是非常珍貴的一批資料。另外還有滿蒙藏文的典籍，約有10,000冊左右，其中蒙藏文的書籍較多。

　　加州大學中國研究中心的圖書館成立於1957年，與加州大學的東亞館分工合作。他們專門收集1949年以後大陸出版的有關社會科學方面的書籍，特別是中共黨史及有關1949年以來大陸的各種政治運動、經濟社會發展、軍事外交的資料。各種年鑑、新地方志，以及各種《文史資料》等出版物都在收集之內。除了中文書刊報紙外，他們也收集很多英文的關於當代中國的書刊。該館最獨特的收藏是它的2,000多種錄影帶，包括15年來每天兩個鐘頭的北京中央廣播電台的新聞廣播和大陸紀錄片。這些都是研究當代中國非常重要的資料，因為它們的收藏，使這個圖書館成為一個研究當代中國的重鎮。

哥倫比亞大學

　　關於哥倫比亞大學收藏中文資料的起源有一個傳奇的故事。1901年哥大有一位校友卡朋蒂埃將軍（General Horace W. Carpentier）捐給他的母校20萬美元，成立一個「丁良講座」講授中國文化。他捐錢成立這個講座的目的用來紀念他的一位名叫丁良（Dean Lung）的中國傭人。傳說是這樣的：卡朋蒂埃在19世紀美國西部淘金熱的時代致富，後來在紐約從事地產生意又非常成功。可是這個人的脾氣很暴躁，有一次他因故不滿跟隨他多年的中國傭人丁良，一怒之下就把丁良辭掉了，並命令他馬上離開。第二天早上當他起床的時候，丁良已經走了，但是他在走之前還是照常把卡朋蒂埃的早餐做好，放在桌上。卡朋蒂埃看了，大為感動，認為丁良這種忠誠和寬容大度是受了中國文化薰陶的緣故，很值得學習。所以他就決定捐贈一筆基金給哥大來促進哥大在中國文化方面的教學。除了卡朋蒂埃的錢之外，丁良自己也捐出了12,000元，於是就成立了「丁良講座」（Dean Lung Professorship）。第二年，哥大用這筆基金的一部分成立了一個中文圖書館。同年，清朝政府應哥大校長的要求，贈送了一部光緒二十年（1894）上海同文書局印行的《古今圖書集成》一套，是為哥大收藏中文典籍的開始。

　　「丁良講座」成立以後，哥大聘請英國劍橋大學翟理斯（Herbert Allen Giles）教授作短期講學並負責籌備成立中文系的工作。翟理斯介紹了一位德國的漢學家，慕尼黑巴瓦維亞科學院夏德（Friedrich Hirth）教授在1903年該系成立時任第一任「丁良講座」教授。

　　由於這個講座的成立，為教學的需要，圖書館資料的採購遂成為非常迫切的問題，但是在這方面的工作進度非常緩慢。1920年，哥倫比亞請當時在中國為國會圖書館收集書籍的施永格先生也替他們作採購工作，而買入了一些。1929年，哥大王際真教授也替哥大圖書館在中國買了些古籍。1940年代，哥大得到洛氏基金會的補助，又添了不少的中文書籍。經過這幾次的蒐購，哥大的中文藏書在1942年太平洋戰爭開始時，就已經超過10萬冊了。不過之後的十幾年當中，一方面是因為戰爭的關係，一方面是因為經費的不足，哥大的中文書籍採購沒有什麼特別的進展。一直到1960年代，哥大積極擴張關於東亞方面的教學與研究工作，中文書籍的收藏也就跟著活躍起來了。

　　哥大現存的中文藏書約341,000冊左右，現行中文期刊38種，縮微卷18,000卷，現每年入藏的中文書籍8,000餘冊。

　　哥大的特藏是族譜，有1,040多種，這是在西方大學當中最多的一批中國族譜。還有一批與族譜有關，但是一般圖書館不太注意收藏的資料，那就是行述、事略、榮哀錄之類的東西。哥大有一批文獻，稱「傳記行述彙集」，有210種，分裝成19函，時代從清代到民國，有刻印的、也有鉛印的。這類資料的研究價值很高，因為有些不見經傳而在地方上較有地位的人物的傳記在這些資料中大都可以找到。

　　還有一批資料也是哥大館藏的特色，就是清代的曆書。清代避高宗（乾隆）「弘曆」諱，所以曆書就改稱為「時憲書」。這些資料哥大收藏了很多，是從乾隆到宣統朝的。乾隆時期缺的較多，因為時間早。但是在嘉靖朝25年當中只缺兩年，而從道光到宣統這91年當中則一本也不缺，所以這是一批極為罕見的資料。另外還有「會試卷」，哥大藏有《鄉會試朱卷彙集》，約400冊，是其他圖書館所沒有的。哥大所藏的方志、叢書以及明清文集數量也都不少。

哥大還有一批對於研究民國史非常重要的資料，就是哥大的口述歷史檔案。這批資料不在東亞館，而在哥大圖書館的特藏部中。這個口述歷史項目（The Chinese Oral History Project）是1958年開冶，由韋慕廷（C. Martin Wilbur）及何廉教授主持。當時居住在紐約市區的一些民國時代的在政治、經濟、文化方面的名人都是被訪問的對象。訪問口述的稿子由被訪問人過目同意後，再翻譯成英文供學者研究使用。這些稿子長短不等，有幾百頁的，也有一兩千頁的，大部分的現在都可以公開，但有一兩份是被訪者指定在其生前不可發表的，而有些是指定某部分需要暫時保密，因為牽涉的人很多。被訪問的人包括張發奎、張學良、胡適、顧維鈞、孔祥熙、李漢魂、李璜、左舜生、蔣廷黻、吳國禎等。

康乃爾大學

民初時有許多中國學生在康乃爾大學就讀，其中很多人後來成為五四運動的領導人物，諸如胡適之、趙元任、任鴻雋及其妻子陳衡哲、楊銓（楊杏佛）等。這些人在康乃爾做學生的時候，曾捐贈3,350種中文書刊給康乃爾大學圖書館，這是康乃爾大學圖書館收藏中文典籍的開始。

1918年，康乃爾有一位校友華生（Charles William Wason）在康乃爾設立華生圖書館，專門收集有關「中國與中國人」（China and the Chinese）的資料。華生，機械工程師，1884年在俄亥俄州的克利夫蘭市開創電車，因以致富。1903年去中國旅遊，對中國發生了很大的興趣，於是就開始收集關於「中國與中國人」的各種資料，前後共收集約9,000冊，主要是英文的書籍。在當時這是最大的一批關於這方面的資料。他把這些資料全部捐贈康乃爾大學成立華生圖書館，並且捐了5萬元的基金作為繼續採購之用。除了這批書籍，他還捐贈了另外一批非常特別的資料，就是從150種雜誌上所剪下的62,000篇關於中國的文章。這批資料一直到現在還是研究19世紀末期到20世紀初期有關中國問題的重要參考材料。他捐贈給康乃爾大學的書籍中有一些是中國典籍，包括三冊《永樂大典》。後來康乃爾的另一位中國校友，外交家施紹基又捐給康大三冊《永樂大典》，所以目前康乃爾大學是美國大學中擁有最多《永樂大典》的學校，一共有六冊。

華生圖書館的首任主任是古斯・加斯基爾（Gussie Gaskill）女士。在她36年任期以內（1927-1963）她不但繼續收集關於中國的西文書籍，並且大力擴張中文書籍的採購。她曾到中國數次，得當時北平圖書館袁同禮先生的協助，替康大收集了不少資料。到1960年康大得到了美國教育部的補助，成立了一個東亞語文區域研究的專案，後來又得到了基金會的補助加強關於東亞的教學和研究，因為如此，中文書籍的採購也就增加了不少。後來，由於基金會和政府的繼續補助，一個更積極、更有系統的藏書建設工作就開始進行了。在初期收集的重點是20世紀上半期出版的現代文學、藝術、考古、語言學等的資料，後來收集範圍擴大了許多。

華生圖書館現名華生東亞圖書館（Wason Collection on East Asia）。現藏中文書籍約336,000冊，現行中文期刊4,100種，縮微卷數目不詳（中日韓合計有33,000多種），錄影帶與電影片350種──這也是較為特別的，因為別的圖書館通常不大收藏這些。每年入藏中文書籍約6,880冊。

除了剛才提到了《永樂大典》之外，康大還有一些比較特別的資料，就是東南亞華僑的資料，因為康大的東南亞教研項目在美國頗具盛名，所以華生圖書館也隨之收集了不少關於東南亞華僑方面的資料。另一種特別的收藏就是關於中國通俗文學、戲曲的資料，特別是20世紀上半期的出版物。敦煌卷子的縮微卷也是它的特藏。華生圖書館藏有大英圖書館和法國國家圖書館全部敦煌卷子的縮微卷。如眾所周知，這兩個圖書館是西方世界中收集敦煌卷子最多的圖書館，康大所藏的這批縮微卷是美國唯一的全套。

普林斯頓大學

普林斯頓大學的葛思德圖書館（Gest Oriental Library）也有它的一個傳奇故事。19世紀末期有一個加拿大建築工程師葛思德（Guion Moore Gest），患青光眼，久治不癒。後來在北京遇美國大使館海軍武官義理壽上校（Commander Irvin Van Gillis）。這位武官介紹他試用中國很有名的河北定州馬應龍眼藥。他一用之下果然有很大的功效。所以他對中國的醫藥油然起敬。於是交了一筆錢給義理壽，請他代為收集中國的醫書，特別是關於眼疾方面的資料。

　　義理壽精通中文，而且經過長時期的學習與研究，對於中國古籍也頗有心得，所以他就辭掉了武官的工作，留在中國，娶了一位滿洲妻子，專門替葛思德收集中國典籍，除醫書以外，再包括其他的善本古籍。因為收集的範圍擴大，收集品為數眾多，且種類繁雜，所需的經費也愈來愈多。胡適之先生在1950-1952年任普林斯頓大學葛思德圖書館館長時，寫了一本關於葛思德圖書館的小冊子名為〈普林斯頓大學葛思德圖書館〉（"The Gest Library at Princeton University"），原載1954年出版《普林斯頓圖書館紀事》（*Princeton Library Chronicle*），第15冊（有抽印本），其中有一段說：「從作為一個嗜好開始，這個藏書工作變成了一種投資，不久對其創辦人又變成了一個負擔」（譯文）。因為那時義理壽替葛思德購買的書籍已超過8,000冊，需要管理和適當的儲藏空間，所以葛思德就決定把這些書運回加拿大。1926年寄存在蒙特利爾（Montreal）的麥吉爾大學（McGill University）命名為「葛思德中文研究圖書館」（Gest Chinese Research Library）。到1931年它的藏書已經增加到75,000冊。1937年普林斯頓大學得洛氏基金會（Rockefeller Foundation）的資助，把這批書籍買下，在普林斯頓成立了「葛思德東方圖書館」，當時書籍總共有102,000冊，這是普林斯頓葛思德圖書館的開始。

　　從1937年建館到1945年第二次世界大戰結束之間，葛思德圖書館對於中文典籍的收藏並不很積極。戰後由於學校擴充關於東亞的教學和研究範圍，葛思德圖書館採購的工作也就隨之活躍起來，收集的範圍也擴大了，包括近代和現代東亞的社會科學方面的資料。因為收集的範圍擴大，但是為了保持葛思德圖書館的獨特性，普林斯頓的東亞館後改名為「葛思德東方圖書館及東亞文庫」（Gest Oriental Library and East Asian Collections），但仍通稱為葛思德圖書館。

　　該館現藏中文書籍約425,000冊，現行中文期刊2,270種，縮微卷23,000種，每年入藏量約8,700冊。

　　葛思德以中國善本著名。1946年北平圖書館王重民先生應普林斯頓大學的邀請，整理、鑑定了其所藏的善本書籍，完成了一部書志草稿，後來經台灣大學屈萬里教授校正，於1975年由台灣藝文印書館出版了一本《普林斯頓大學葛思德東方圖書館善本書志》，這是一部非常重要的參考書。

　　葛斯德東方圖書館的善本書以明刻本最多，有1,040餘部，計24,500冊，尚有宋刻本2部、元刻本6部、醫書約500種、雍正六年（1728）銅活字版的《古今圖書集成》一套、武英殿聚珍本《二十四史》一套，以及一些蒙文的佛經。葛思德東方圖書館還有一件很有趣的「文物」，就是一件大的綢袍，裡面貼有用蠅頭小楷寫的七百篇八股文，為科舉考試時代夾帶作弊之用的。

芝加哥大學

　　芝加哥大學在1936年成立遠東語文系和遠東圖書館，都由顧立雅（Herrlee G. Creel）教授主持。顧立雅教授是中國上古史專家，所以對中國古籍的收藏特別注意。1939-1940年間他在中國收購了不少的這一類的資料。1943年又從芝加哥的紐伯里圖書館（Newberry Library）購得貝特霍爾德·勞費爾（Berthold Laufer）19世紀末期在中國為該圖書館收集的中日滿蒙藏文的書籍共21,000餘冊，遠東圖書館的收藏遂蔚為大觀。第二次世界大戰結束時，該館的總藏量已達110,000冊左右，其中最多的是中國經學、考古學，和上古史的典籍。錢存訓先生1947年受聘主持該館，並兼任芝加哥大學圖書館學校教授，遠東圖書館的業務乃蒸蒸日上。1958年起更積極擴充，在原有的收藏範圍外，更加上社會科學和近代和當代的資料。

　　該館現已由遠東圖書館改名為東亞圖書館。目前所藏中文書籍有350,000餘冊，現行中文期刊1,800種，縮微卷35,000卷，每年入藏中文書籍約7,000冊。

　　特藏以中國經部經典最多，約1,700多種，是歐美各大學之冠。方志2,700多種，並有明萬曆年間增刻的《大藏經》全套7,920冊，這是相當重要的資料。還有一些關於現代史的零星資料，包括1947-1948年北京天津學生

遊行示威時，反飢餓、反腐敗、反國民政府的原始傳單70餘種，這些都是
少見的資料。

胡佛研究院

　　胡佛研究院的全名是「胡佛戰爭、革命與和平研究院」（Hoover
Institution on War, Revolution, and Peace）。1919年成立於史丹佛大學
（Stanford University），原稱胡佛戰爭、革命與和平研究所與圖書館（Hoover
Institute and Library on War, Revolution, and Peace）。成立初期，以收集資料
為主，均為第一次世界大戰前後有關歐洲政治，經濟，及社會問題的檔案和
其他的歷史文獻，以及俄國十月革命及俄國共產黨初期黨史的資料。收集之
豐富，世界聞名。其大部分均為胡佛先生（後選為總統）第一次世界大戰後
在歐洲及蘇聯擔任救濟工作時所收集者。1960年改為今名，除繼續資料之
收集外，並積極發展研究工作，現為美國著名智庫之一。

　　1945年1月，胡佛研究所所長費希爾（Harold H. Fisher）（史丹佛大學
歷史系蘇聯史教授）宣布該所成立中文部與日文部的決定。收藏資料的時限
為20世紀，範圍則是有關戰爭、革命，以及和平的中國和日本的文獻。

　　當時代表胡佛在中國收集資料的是芮沃壽夫婦（Arthur and Mary
Wright），芮沃壽先生在史丹佛大學時曾是費希爾教授的學生，後去哈佛大
學研究院；他與他夫人當時是哈佛大學的同學，1940年去中國收集資料寫
博士論文，珍珠港事變後，被日軍軟禁在山東濰縣一間拘留所中。日本投
降，他們被釋放以後，接受了胡佛研究所的邀請，就地在中國為胡佛收集中
國文獻。這個工作主要是由芮夫人辦理。在1946和1947這兩年當中她幾乎
跑遍全中國，得到各方幫助，收集了大量的資料。她甚至得到美軍的許可，
搭乘美國軍用機到延安去了一趟，收集延安和當時中國共產黨控制的邊區的
出版物，因此獲得了很多當時外界看不到的資料，其中最寶貴的是一份差不
多完整的從1941年5月創刊到1947年3月中共撤退延安以前出版的中國共產
黨機關報——《解放日報》。

　　1948年芮沃壽夫婦返美。芮先生（Arthur Wright）應聘為史丹佛大學歷

史系的助理教授，芮夫人（Mary Wright 芮瑪麗）即出任胡佛研究所剛成立的中文部的主任。中文部成立以後，又從伊羅生（Harold R. Issacs）處購得一批非常珍貴的中共原始資料。包括1920年代末期和1930年代初期的中共地下出版物，其中有不少當時中共托洛斯基派油印的刊物。伊羅生原來是美國共產黨員，1932-1934年他得中共的支持在上海發行一個小型的報紙叫《中國評論》（*China Forum*）。當時他收集了很多中共的地下刊物，都是非法的，需要沒收法辦的出版物，但是他是美國人，有治外法權的保護，所以中國警察無法干預他。胡佛收得這批資料後稱其為「伊羅生特藏」（Issacs Collection）。

在1959年，胡佛又收到另外一批也是關於中共的原始資料。當時美國名記者斯諾（Edgar Snow）的前妻海倫・福斯特・斯諾（Helen Foster Snow, 1907-1997，筆名尼姆・威爾斯［Nym Wales］）將她和斯諾在1930年代在中國收集的很多中共以及左派的資料文獻全部轉售胡佛研究所。名為「尼姆・威爾斯特藏」（Nym Wales Collection）。這批資料的性質和伊羅生那批資料大致相同，很多都是地下出版物，不同的就是出版的時間。伊羅生的資料是1920年代末期和1930初期的，斯諾他們的是1930年代中期的。所以在時間上它們連接得很好。因為這樣，這兩批資料就更珍貴了。在「尼姆・威爾斯文庫」當中還有一批關於西安事變的資料。這是他們1936年12月在西安事變時在西安收集的，其中有好些是當時西北軍所散發的傳單和小冊子，非常罕見，是十分寶貴的原始資料。

伊羅生和斯諾這兩批資料中的大部分在下列兩部薛君度教授編撰，胡佛研究院出版的書目中有詳細的注釋：（1）《中國共產主義運動，1921-1937：胡佛戰爭、革命與和平研究院中文圖書館藏中國文獻選輯解題書目》（*The Chinese Communist Movement 1921-1937: An Annotated Bibliography of Selected Materials in the Chinese Collection of the Hoover Institution on War, Revolution, and Peace*, 1960）；（2）《中國共產主義運動，1937-1949：胡佛戰爭、革命與和平研究院中文圖書館藏中國文獻選輯解題書目》*The Chinese Communist Movement: 1937-1949: An Annotated Bibliography of Selected*

Materials in the Chinese Collection of the Hoover Institution on War, Revolution, and Peace, 1962）。

　　1959年芮沃壽夫婦應聘去耶魯大學歷史系任教，之後，胡佛合併其中文部及日文部成立東亞部，我被任為東亞部的主任。當時聽說在台灣有一批關於江西蘇維埃共和國（1931-1934）的原始資料，為陳誠副總統所收。我很希望能夠得到這些資料的影本，以加強胡佛對中共黨史的收藏，但不得其門而入，後偶遇史丹佛大學地質系的休伯特・申克（Hubert G. Schenck）教授，他在第二次世界大戰後曾擔任美援在台灣的負責人，和陳誠很熟。經他的介紹後，得到陳副總統的許可，將這批資料攝成縮微卷。為此事我1960年第一次來台灣。當時台灣的條件很差，據說攝製縮微卷的機器只有兩部，一部在中央銀行，一部在中央研究院。那時胡適之先生任中研院院長，我去請他幫忙，他一口就答應了，把機器與操作人員都借給我使用。經過兩個多月的時間，把這批將近1,500多種的資料照成縮微卷帶回美國，我命其名為「陳誠特藏」（Chen Cheng Collection）用以紀念陳副總統對學術界的貢獻。後來又得他的許可，將這批資料再作拷貝以成本供應美國各東亞圖書館以作研究之用。據陳副總統告，這批資料是1930年代國軍「剿匪」時期他屬下的隊伍在江西瑞金地區俘獲來的。當時已經焚毀不少，他得悉後下令禁止，才保留了剩下來的這些文件。前南伊利諾大學（Southern Illinois University）吳天威教授從這批資料中選出600多種文件加以注釋，並附加資料全部的目錄由哈佛燕京圖書館1981年出版一本書目，名為《江西蘇維埃共和國，1931-1934──陳誠特藏文件選輯解題書目》（*The Kiangsi Soviet Republic, 1931-1934: A Selected and Annotated Bibliography of the Chen Cheng Collection*），列為哈佛燕京圖書館書目叢刊第三種。

　　胡佛研究院東亞部由於上面所講的這三批資料的收藏──「伊羅生特藏」（Issacs Collection），「尼姆・威爾斯特藏」（Nym Wales Collection）及「陳誠特藏」（Chen Cheng Collection）──而著名於世界。這些中國共產黨早期黨史的原始文獻，無論在數量上或品質上，在西方沒有任何圖書館可以與其比美的。除了關於中共黨史的資料以外，胡佛尚以民國時代的各種政治、經濟、社會、教育、文化方面的文獻見稱。以其收藏所編纂的書目除上述薛君度教授的著作外，尚有下列數種，可代表其收藏之一斑：

1. 牟復禮（Frederick W. Mote）編，《日本在華成立的偽政府，1937-1945》（*Japanese-Sponsored Governments in China, 1937-1945*）（1954）
2. 吳文津（Eugene Wu）編，《20世紀中國的領導人物》（*Leaders of 20th Century China*）（1956）
3. 易社強（John Israel）編，《中國的學生運動，1927-1937》（*The Chinese Student Movement, 1927-1937*）（1959）
4. 內田直作（Naosaku Uchida）《華僑》（*The Overseas Chinese*）（1959）
5. 陳明銶（Ming K. Chan）編，《中國工人運動史，1895-1949》（*Historiography of the Chinese Labor Movement, 1895-1949*）（1981）
6. 依牧（I-mu）編，《中國民主運動資料》（*Unofficial Documents of the Democracy Movement in Communist China, 1978-1081*）（1986）
7. 華達（Claude Widor）編，《中國各省地下出版物，1979-1981》（*The Samizdat Press in China's Provinces, 1979-1981*）（1987）

除這些資料以外，胡佛還有一批台灣的特別出版物。那就是從1975到1978年在台灣當時被查禁的「黨外」雜誌。這批雜誌共16種，差不多都是全套。已由荷蘭國際文獻公司（Inter Documentation Center）作為縮微片發行。

最後，胡佛研究院還有一批與哥倫比亞大學口述史相類似的資料，那就是一些民國名人的私人檔案。這一批檔案對於研究中國現代史有高度的研究價值，其中包括宋子文、張嘉璈、顏惠慶、陳納德（Claire L. Chennault）等的個人檔案。

胡佛中文藏書約243,000冊，現行中文期刊810種，縮微卷不詳（中日文共30,000餘卷）。現每年入藏中文書籍約4,400冊。

胡佛研究院與史丹佛大學圖書館已簽訂協定，在不久的將來胡佛研究院東亞部將轉屬史丹佛大學圖書館。唯關於中國的檔案仍留胡佛研究院保管。

華盛頓大學

華盛頓大學1946年得洛氏基金會（Rockefeller Foundation）的補助，創立美國第一間大學主辦的東亞研究中心。華大稱其為「遠東研究所」。第二年（1947）成立「遠東圖書館」（Far Eastern Library），現稱「東亞圖書館」（East Asian Library）。最初的收藏著重於19世紀中葉中國政治和社會經濟史方面的文獻，因為那是當時遠東研究所研究的重點。稍後，中國哲學和文學方面的資料也大量的收集。當時，書籍選擇的工作多由梅谷（Franz Michael）、衛德明（Hellmut Wilhelm）和德懷特・斯庫塞斯（Dwight Schultheis）三位教授負責，分別選購清史（梅谷）、中國思想史（衛德明）和中國文學（斯庫塞斯）方面的資料。後來由於東亞教學研究的範圍擴張，圖書館收集的範圍也就跟著更擴大了。

該館現藏中文書籍240,000餘冊，現行中文期刊1,200餘種，縮微卷6,300餘卷。該館為美國最早引進台灣中央研究院建立的《二十五史全文檢索資料庫》的圖書館。現每年入藏中文書籍約3,500冊。

其特藏是中國的西南方志。這些方志是從洛克（Joseph Rock）處購得，共833種，其中雲南方志146種，四川方志143種，為西方圖書館之最。（洛克在中國雲南居住前後達25年，是納西族專家，國會圖書館和哈佛燕京圖書館的納西經典都是從他的收藏中購得。方志也是他在雲南時所收購的。）關於台灣的方志，該館有80餘種。其方志收藏全部著錄於樓珍希（Joseph Lowe）編纂的一部目錄，名為《華盛頓大學藏中國方志目錄》（*A Catalog of Official Gazetteers of China in the University of Washington*），1960年由荷蘭國際文獻公司（Inter Documentation Center）出版。

該館的善本不多，有明本138部，其中子部與經部的書籍較多。李直方（Chik Fong Lee）曾為其編一書志，名為《華盛頓大學遠東圖書館藏明版書錄》（*A Descriptive Catalog of the Ming Editions in the Far Eastern Library of the University of Washington*），1975年由舊金山美國中文資料中心出版。

　　華盛頓大學除了東亞館之外，還有法學院圖書館的東亞部（East Asian Law Department）。成立於1930年代，最初只是收集關於日本法律方面的日文書籍，後來才開始收集關於中國法律方面的中文資料。該部現有中文書籍7,000餘冊，現行中文法律方面刊物80多種，縮微卷180餘卷。

密西根大學

　　密西根大學在第二次世界大戰以前就開始收集一些中日文的出版物，但是比較有系統的收集還是在第二次世界大戰以後。1948年密西根大學成立日本研究中心，日文資料的收集隨之加強。1961年成立中國研究中心，中文資料也跟著很迅速地發展起來。到目前為止，密西根大學亞洲圖書館所藏的中文書籍多於日文，而其中日韓文藏書的總量在北美東亞圖書館排名第四，在僅僅四、五十年當中有這樣的成果；是很不容易的事。僅以中文藏書的數量來說，它也占全美第七名，由此可見他們工作發展的迅速。

　　因為他們發展的時間較晚，所以原版的古籍較少，但是他們收藏中國古籍的複印本和微卷特別多。比如說台灣1960、70年代出版的中國古籍複印圖書，他們差不多全部都有；還有中央圖書館的1,500多種善本的縮微卷，以及他們在日本購入的許多日本收藏的明刻本和中國地方志的微卷等。另外，還有一批研究當代中國的特別重要的資料，就是香港友聯研究所的中國剪報的縮微卷。友聯研究所1949年後在香港成立，為當時頗負盛名的一個研究機構。他們設法收集了很多當時禁止出口的中國大陸的地方報紙、雜誌。由於研究的需要，他們把這些資料做了很有系統的剪報工作。當時因為西方的學者，特別是美國的學者，不能去大陸，也無法在旁的地方看到大陸的地方報紙和雜誌，所以這些剪報就成了在當時最有價值的研究中國問題的資料。後來友聯將這些剪報攝製成2,000多卷的縮微卷。密西根亞洲圖書館所藏的這批縮微卷是美國東亞圖書館中唯一的全套。

　　密西根亞洲圖書館現藏中文書籍有343,000餘冊，現行的中文期刊1,300多種，縮微卷29,000餘卷，縮微片24,000多片。現每年入藏的中文典籍有8,700餘種。他們的網站設計得很好，內容很豐富，恐怕是美國東亞館中做得最好的，大家不妨去參考看看，網址是 http://asia.lib.umich.edu。

　　從上面所講的，我們可以看出，美國圖書館的中國藏書建設工作與美國大學發展關於中國的教學與研究工作有不可分立的關係。在19世紀末期，美國大學對於中國的教學與研究尚在萌芽的時候，圖書館收集中國典籍的工作是被動的，當時收集的資料大都是偶然得來的。稍後，教學和研究的工作漸漸發展，主動的收集才跟著而來。一直到第二次世界大戰結束，區域研究盛行，新的東亞圖書館相繼成立，中文典籍的收藏才達到最高峰。過去不受重視的東亞圖書館，今天已經是美國研究圖書館主流當中的一部分了。

注釋

本文係作者2003年在台北淡江大學「吳文津先生講座」演講之一。收入《書林覽勝——台灣與美國存藏中國典籍文獻概況——吳文津先生講座演講錄》，淡江大學中國文學系主編（台北：臺灣學生書局，2003）。臺灣學生書局慨允轉載，特致謝忱。

美國中文資料書目管理的現狀與前景

在美國東亞圖書館發展過程中一個異常的現象就是對已經收藏的資料至今缺少有效的全國性書目管理。至1970年6月止66個美國圖書館已經收藏了超過300萬冊中文書刊，相當於全美各圖書館收藏的東亞語文資料總數的61%。[1] 然而這批中國大陸之外最好的收藏卻沒有得到有效的書目管理。此篇報告就是嘗試去探討其原因，回顧過去已經採取過的措施，並思考未來尚需做的工作。

美國東亞圖書館書目管理的缺失是基於傳統的思維和疏忽兩個原因而造成。常石道雄（Warren Tsuneishi）簡明地分析道：

> 當然至今最主要的原因是在於美國一向偏向歐洲，因而容易忽略亞洲。直到發生了珍珠港事件、韓戰、越戰、才警覺到國境的最西邊和亞洲的邊緣相接。另外一個原因就是在美國的東亞圖書館和圖書館員數量相對地少。對美國圖書館界很多人來講，我們只是微不足道的一小部分；我們的問題也得不到重視……我還懷疑另外一個原因就是我們這群管理東亞資料的館員不夠積極參加像美國圖書館協會這類可以決定按全國的需要設定目標和計畫的專業組織。因為不夠積極參與，我們就沒有發言權……[2]

常石道雄還指出：「《全國聯合目錄：作者篇》（the *National Union Catalog: Author List*）中收錄的中文資料只限於各東亞圖書館使用國會圖書館編目卡的資料。而各館過去十年間各自編目的中文資料並沒有收錄其中。這些原始編目而沒有收錄的資料的百分率很高，約占全部的85%或更多。」

[3] 不僅如此，圖書館界傾向歐洲以及東亞圖書館員不夠積極參與全國性專業組織還導致其他全國性專案執行時並未將東亞館考慮在內。1965年美國圖書館協會贊助出版的《全國期刊聯合目錄》（the *Union List of Serials*）第三版就只收錄了第一、二版收錄的東亞期刊。因此自1943年後美國各圖書館新收藏的東亞期刊就沒有出現在此聯合目錄中。另外一個例子就是1966年國會圖書館出版的《全國縮微母片目錄》（*National Register of Microfilm Masters*）中包括的東亞資料就不完整。甚至連國會圖書館自己所拍攝善本圖書的縮微母片也沒有收入。更有甚者，最近美國圖書館協會贊助出版的1956年前全國聯合目錄完全沒有包括東亞語文資料。

　　由於缺少全國性的領導和合作，東亞圖書館徒靠各自為政提供給讀者書目方面的服務。使用的工具通常是傳統的卡片目錄和主題目錄。但此僅能滿足讀者部分的需求。下面是我對東亞圖書館在這方面已經作出的努力的回顧，同時我也對未來可能的發展作了些臆測。

　　1. 卡片目錄：東亞圖書館製作維護卡片目錄是一種有效但是成本很高的工作。國會圖書館長期無法提供足夠的東亞語文編目卡更是導致各東亞館的編目和維護卡片目錄的巨大費用的原因。1965年3月美國研究圖書館協會（Association of Research Libraries）作了一次調查：對參加協會的圖書館所收藏的美國出版物國會圖書館可以提供75.6%的編目卡。給英國的出版物53.7%編目卡。但是給中日文出版物只能提供15.8%編目卡。[4] 據哈佛燕京圖書館1969年度的統計，該館該年度的中文編目只有9.4%利用國會圖書館現成編目卡。這也就是說明各東亞圖書館所作的原始編目的百分比異常地高，因而必須要有龐大的經費來作編目和卡片目錄維護的工作。更不用提其間各館對同樣出版物所作的重複編目了。因此目前用卡片目錄作為東亞圖書館書目管理的工具是非常昂貴的方式，各方面都難以自圓其說。作為一個實質的國家圖書館，國會圖書館早應該檢討和改革其對東亞語文資料提供編目卡的專案，以解決東亞圖書館長期緊迫的需求。如此除能協助各館建立更好的卡片目錄以外，還可以為東亞圖書館節省時間和費用去作其他有關書目的工作。

　　1970年9月國會圖書館宣布對中日韓文編目卡的印刷將嘗試一種新的作法。就是把過去用附注的方式印在卡片上的書名的羅馬拼音（Title Romanized Note）放在中日韓文書名前。羅馬拼音書名也將代替中日韓文印在續卡（continuation card）上。[5] 這種改變想必為加速印刷東亞語文編目卡的生產所致。

　　該館編目處理部助理主任薩默‧斯波爾丁（C. Sumner Spalding）先生於次年（1971年）8月26日給我寫信說：「使用目前方式來處理東亞語文編目卡，自編目開始到編目卡印刷出來現在需要的時間是6到7個月……」

　　他並且告訴我：「更值得鼓舞的是我們試著用照像底稿成功地在日本印刷日文編目卡。一俟所有行政手續辦妥並簽訂合約後，這將是國會圖書館今後印刷日文編目卡的辦法。這個辦法會將編目卡分發給各館的時間減少3個月。稍後也會用此法處理中韓文編目卡的印刷。」

　　斯波爾丁先生認為東亞圖書館使用國會圖書館的編目卡所遭遇的困難可能是卡片不能及時供應的問題，而不是國會圖書館收集範圍的問題。他用以下統計數字來作說明：

完成編目	1969/70年度	1970/71年度
日文	14,052	14,932
中文	2,744	2,883
韓文	774	1,065
	17,570	18,880
分發的編目卡	12,746	22,404

　　從以上數字來看，編目的數量很大，印刷編目卡的數量也很大。但是卡片印刷的過程相當複雜，而國會圖書館對美國政府印刷部的控制權力極為有限，以致編目卡的印刷往往有所拖延。1971年以前東亞資料自編目到分發編目卡很少短於一年，通常需要兩年的時間。大致從1971年初開始，情況有了相當大的改善。根據一大批剛剛印刷好的卡片看起來，目前自編目到分

發編目卡只需要6至7個月。」

　　談到在採購地即時編目和收到資料後編目所花成本問題，斯波爾丁先生建議東亞圖書館採用美國一般研究圖書館在他們「合作編目」工作中使用國會圖書館編目卡的辦法。

　　他的理由是：「這些研究圖書館報告說：六個月內收到國會圖書館根據採購地提供的編目卡達70%以上。顯然地如果在採購地編目成本高就沒有好處；反之，這種方法就很好。一般研究圖書館多半滿意這樣的做法。以理推之，此法對解決在美印刷東亞文字的困難更有好處。」

　　斯波爾丁先生提到的國會圖書館能提供70%編目卡的潛力這一點，固然沒錯。對於東亞圖書館當然有利。但是東亞語文資料的編目工作目前並沒有得到統一的管理，特別是中文和韓文至今還沒有納入合作編目的項目。當編目工作有統一管理而使用國會圖書館編目卡的百分率能達到70%時，東亞圖書館的編目工作當會更上一層樓。

　　2. 書本目錄：由於缺少全國中文圖書聯合目錄，各東亞圖書館出版的書本目錄就成了非常重要的查詢工具。最早出版的是1938到1940年間由哈佛燕京圖書館在北平出版的《美國哈佛大學燕京學社漢和圖書館漢籍分類目錄》（*A Classified Catalogue of Chinese Books in the Chinese-Japanese Library of the Harvard-Yenching Institute at Harvard University*）經學類、哲學宗教類、歷史科學類。但是由於太平洋戰爭爆發，只出版了這三冊而沒有繼續。近年霍爾出版公司（G.K. Hall）陸續將加州大學柏克萊分校東亞圖書館、加州大學洛杉磯分校、紐約公共圖書館、史丹佛大學胡佛研究院的卡片目錄出版成冊，極受讀者歡迎。相信即將由該公司出版的芝加哥大學遠東圖書館卡片目錄將同樣嘉惠於圖書館界和學術界。

　　個別圖書館的書本目錄雖然重要，但是卻永遠代替不了全國聯合目錄。何況出版書本目錄的主要東亞圖書館畢竟還是太少。雖然它們是很有用的工具書，但是還得經常修訂更新出版續輯才更加有用。我還應該提一提：最近有些圖書館為了預防天災人禍，已將卡片目錄拍成縮微膠捲。這也許可以作為查詢該館收藏之用。但是真正解決之道還在於出版全國聯合目錄。

　3. 期刊、報紙、縮微膠捲的管理：像中文圖書一樣，中文期刊、報紙、縮微膠捲也需要有全國性的書目管理。前面已經提到在《全國期刊聯合目錄》第三版中沒有包含1943年後美國圖書館採購的中文期刊。而《全國期刊聯合目錄》續篇《新期刊目錄》（*New Serial Titles*）也收錄不全。因此全國期刊管理專案對中文期刊一點幫助也沒有。各東亞圖書館只好為自己的需要製作特別的目錄。因此我們有了好幾個東亞圖書館的期刊目錄，還有三種類似的聯合目錄。但是都不包括所有美國主要東亞圖書館的收藏。這三種類似的聯合目錄中包含最全面的是國會圖書館建立的《東方語文期刊聯合卡片目錄》（*Union Card File of Oriental Vernacular Serials*）包含美國和加拿大13個東亞圖書館收藏的期刊及其期數。但是除國會圖書館本身的收藏外，其他圖書館的收藏只到1961年為止，而況這個目錄也沒有出版。另外兩種是雷蒙德·納恩（Raymond Nunn）編輯的《1949-1960出版的中文期刊聯合目錄》（*Chinese Periodicals, International Holdings, 1949-1960*）共兩冊，和伯納黛特·施（Bernadette Shih）和理查·斯奈德（Richard Snyder）編輯的《共產中國出版期刊國際聯合目錄》（*International Union List of Chinese Communist Serials*）。這兩種僅包括1949年以後的出版品；後者也主要包含科學、技術和醫學期刊。只有100種左右是社會科學類期刊。

　　因此我們希望國會圖書館將《東方語文期刊聯合卡片目錄》儘早修正，增補，以3×5英寸卡片複印或縮微膠捲出版發行。

　　中文報紙也同樣需要聯合目錄。雖然我們知道美國那些東亞圖書館擁有那些主要的中文報紙，但是我們就不知道那些次要的報紙何在。這是一件遺憾的事，因為報紙是對作研究非常重要的資料。國會圖書館出版的《縮微膠捲報紙目錄》（*Newspapers on Microfilm*）和《戰後外國報紙目錄》（*Postwar Foreign Newspapers*）中所包含的中文報紙都不完全。所以我們需要一份完整的，包含縮微膠捲的美國圖書館所藏的中文報紙聯合目錄。在此應該順便提一下的就是西雅圖華盛頓大學遠東圖書館館長盧國邦正在編輯一份在美國出版的中文報紙目錄。

除此之外，所有圖書、期刊、報紙的縮微膠捲也應該有聯合目錄。我上面已經提到《全國縮微膠捲母片目錄》（*National Register of Microform Masters*）甚至沒有包含國會圖書館自己拍攝的中文善本膠捲。應該可能的是各東亞圖書館將他們已經收藏的縮微膠捲製作目錄送交國會圖書館和國會圖書館拍攝的縮微膠捲將一併收入下一版的《全國縮微膠捲母片目錄》中。更實際的做法就是編輯一部單獨的全國中文資料縮微膠捲目錄，除母片外，還包括在美國沒有母片的正片縮微膠捲。像最近美國研究圖書館協會所屬的中國研究資料中心所編輯的各美國主要東亞圖書館收藏的縮微膠捲目錄即可作為此項工作的底本。

4. 主題書目和索引。當聯合目錄解決了尋找書刊的困難。主題書目和索引卻是尋找出版物內容必備的鑰匙。很不幸地在中國研究這個領域，這樣的工具書可謂鳳毛麟角。哈佛燕京學社出版《哈佛燕京學社引得》（*Harvard-Yenching Institute Sinological Index Series*）已經是好多年前的事了。至今還沒有像這樣類似的出版發行。如果有一系列完整的二十五史引得（哈佛燕京引得已出版的四種除外）以及上千的地方志的索引，那將是如何嘉惠士林的事。

中文期刊文章的索引倒有不少，只是很多都不夠完備，很多也過時了。還有不少只是作為其他著作的一部分，沒有單獨成冊，使用不方便。

報紙的索引就比期刊索引少得多了，很多也比不上期刊索引。中國大陸1949年前出版的中文報紙，根本沒有提供索引。1949年後出版的中文報紙只有少數全國性報紙才提供索引。台灣和香港出版的中文報紙1962年後只選擇性地提供索引。因此我們的報紙索引缺失不少。很顯然地這是一件艱巨的工作，必須全國，乃至全世界共同努力來完成的事。

主題書目和研究指南在中國研究這個領域也是非常重要的。胡佛研究院出版的目錄叢書（*Bibliographical Series*）和哈佛大學東亞研究中心出版的《哈佛大學東亞研究中心專刊系列》（*Harvard East Asian Monographs*）中有關書目的部分都是典型的例子；我們還需要包含更多有關中國研究方面的類似的出版物。哈佛燕京圖書館 1971 年開始出版該館的《哈佛燕京圖書館書目叢刊》（*Harvard-Yenching Library Bibliographical Series*）。第一種為《中國史學論文引得續編——歐美所見中文期刊文史哲論文綜錄》（*Chinese History: Index to Learned Articles, Vol.II, 1905-1964*）。史丹佛大學胡佛研究院今年出版了馬大任著《胡佛戰爭、革命與和平研究院東亞文獻目錄》（*East Asia: A Survey of Holdings at the Hoover Institution on War, Revolution and Peace*）。

　　這些有關中國文學、中國歷史、中國經濟、中國政府、國民黨等等專題書目對中國研究都很有幫助。研究指南也有同樣功能。費正清（John K. Fairbank）和劉廣京曾經編輯《現代中國研究指南》（*Modern China: A Bibliographical Guide*）；彼德·伯頓（Peter Berton）和吳文津曾經編輯《當代中國研究指南》（*Contemporary China: A Research Guide*）。這兩部出版品現在都成為它們所涉及時代的標準參考書，但是它們都需要更新以包括未收的資料。同時也有需要出版一本像費正清、劉廣京所編輯的指南來列舉 1949 年後的資料，像伯頓、吳那樣的參考書來詮釋 1949 年前民國時期的資料。不用說，類似這樣的資料指南對研究 20 世紀前的中國也有同等的重要性。

　　以上所提僅僅牽涉中文資料問題，因為中文資料的書目管理缺失比西文資料嚴重得多。在西文中有高第（Henri Cordier）編輯的《漢學書目》（*Bibiliotheca Sinica*），袁同禮編輯的《西文漢學書目》（*China in Western Literature*），約翰·勒斯特（John Lust）的《連續出版品中的中國學論文索引》（*Index Sinicus*），和亞洲學會每年出版的《亞洲研究文獻目錄》（*Bibliography of Asian Studies*）。從這些參考工具書中我們可以看到非常全面的有關中國研究的西文書刊資料。中文書刊就沒有這麼好的書目了。國會圖書館製作中文書刊編目卡也從來沒有像西文書刊編目卡快速完整。雖然編輯西文書刊書目比較簡單，容易處理，但是也不是沒有問題。像賀凱（Charles Hucker）編輯的《中國：參考文獻》（*China: A Critical Bibliography*）那樣有注解的目錄為數頗少。19 世紀晚期以來在中國出版的英文報紙也需要索引。由於索引的缺乏，其中不少研究資料尚待開發。近年香港美國總領事館發行的大陸報紙翻譯，由於沒有良善的索引系統，很難使用。順便要提到的就是美國聯合出版研究服務處（Joint Publications Research Service）發行的類似翻譯除了早期的幾乎都沒有索引可用。目前要輕而易便地使用西方國家的政府檔案作學術研究也不是容易的事。

在此我們可以提出下面這個問題：要解決書目製作方面的問題，傳統的手工方式有何局限性？自動化是否是可以用來解決問題的新方式？一個有效的檢索系統應該要比現在傳統的方法搜索得更為徹底。其產生的資料可以幫忙制定新的假說、新的質詢、新的途徑，和新的研究方法。但是問題是我們要達到那個目的還有多少距離和從手工方式轉化到自動化的過程中，我們還得作些什麼準備工作。

雖然在牽涉到非羅馬字書目管理的某些領域的自動化工作已經有相當的成就（如耶魯大學人類關係區域檔案處〔Human Relations Area File〕的高全惠星夫人〔Hesung Koh〕、哈佛大學久野暲〔Susumu Kuno〕教授、堪薩斯大學卡爾・萊班〔Carl Leban〕教授的貢獻），但是還沒有任何一家圖書館大規模地試驗這些系統來比較其可行性和成本問題。國會圖書館目前使用的機讀編目只限於英文資料，還沒有計畫應用在非羅馬字資料上。史丹佛大學施堅雅（William Skinner）教授用來編輯他的《近代中國社會研究文獻類目解題索引》（*Modern Chinese Society: An Analytical Bibliography*）精心設計的機器編碼系統是用機器來解決書目管理的最好的方式的一種。但是作為圖書館書目管理之用還得要等他的著作出版後再作進一步的研究。以上這些開創性工作足以鼓舞我們，但是他們都還沒有經過充分的測試來判斷其優劣，以及比較其成本的高低。亞洲學會決定應用自動化系統編輯出版其《亞洲研究文獻目錄》（*Bibliography of Asian Studies*）是件受歡迎的事，但是我們希望這本目錄能進一步除西文有關亞洲研究資料以外，還包含亞洲語文的資料。更希望不僅僅包含書目，還包含資料檢索的功能。這不是一個機構就可以勝任的工作。必須由全國有共同興趣者參加來研發。（最近有些出乎意料的發展，亞洲學會下屬的資料資訊管理委員會〔Committee on Information Control〕對《亞洲研究文獻目錄》〔*Bibliography of Asian Studies*〕自動化的可能性正在進行徹底的複審，包括成本分析。）

　　儘管美國圖書館對中文資料的書目管理有所成就，但尚待努力的地方還很多。往後數年東亞圖書館必須專注於解決中文資料最基本的書目管理的需要，也就是編輯和出版中文書刊的全國聯合目錄。

　　關於全國聯合目錄問題我們已經討論過好多年了。除了國會圖書館東方部在有限的財力人力下所主導的專案外，至今沒有一個有組織的全國性的專案去實現討論後所得到的任何建議。特別是1966年亞洲學會美國圖書館遠東資源委員會聯合目錄小組（Union Catalogue Subcommittee of the Committee on American Library Resources on the Far East of the Association for Asian Studies）所作的相關建議（該委員會後更名為Committee on East Asian Libraries東亞圖書館委員會）。在這份傑出的報告中小組成員常石道雄、查理斯・漢密爾頓（Charles Hamilton）、羅伯特・史蒂文斯（Robert Stevens）建議：在所有可能解決之道中最可行的就是以國會圖書館東方部門所存的編目卡為基礎，包括各東亞圖書館為編輯聯合目錄經常送交給國會圖書館聯合目錄部的各館自己的編目卡，編輯一部聯合目錄。該小組還建議此項工作要按部就班去做，首先初步整理中文、日文聯合目錄。亞洲學會會長為這些建議曾致函國會圖書館館長，館長也覆信致謝，但是自此以後，國會圖書館或亞洲學會都沒有進一步的行動。

　　過去兩年，國會圖書館東方部在中文聯合目錄和《東方語文期刊卡片聯合目錄》（*Union Card File of Oriental Vernacular Serials*）的工作方面有了很多實質上的進展。但是此項工作極為艱巨，離完成的日期尚非指日可待。編撰全國聯合目錄之舉應為所有對東亞研究有興趣者所關注。雖然國會圖書館在這方面的工作上有所進展，但是並沒有解除我們對這項工作應有的責任和義務。讓我們共同參與來保證成功地完成此項具有全國性乃至於國際性的任務。

　　最後，在討論書目管理這個問題上已經不是採取零星辦法的時候。由個別或者一個機構試圖去解決問題在經費上也不是可行的事。這項工作的範圍龐大，需要我們以整體的問題和全國性的視野來有系統地討論我們面對的問

題。現在正是時候重新評估我們所需、我們的假設、我們的方法的時候。全
國性領導和全國性計畫是對工作的優先和程式設定不可或缺的要素。這個任
務不是輕而易舉的事，特別在經費方面。但是東亞圖書館正處在能夠提供未
來學術研究具有潛在發展的門檻上。我們成功的程度全賴於我們能否面對書
目管理所帶來的挑戰。

注釋

本文為1970年4月3-5日在舊金山亞洲學會年會「亞洲研究目錄控制」（Bibliographical
Controls for Asian Studies）研討會發表的報告。載《外文資料採訪通訊》（*Foreign
Acquisitions Newsletter*），第32期（1970年10月），頁1-6。經過修訂後，載《哈佛圖書館
館刊》（*Harvard Library Bulletin*），第20卷，第1期（1972年1月），頁38-48。

[1]　錢存訓（Tsuen-shuin Tsien），〈美國圖書館中的遠東資料收藏〉（"Holdings of Far
　　　Eastern Materials in American Libraries"）《東亞圖書館委員會通訊》（*Newsletter of the
　　　Committee on East Asian Libraries, Association for Asian Studies*），第33期（1971年［三
　　　月]），表I。
[2]　常石道雄（Warren Tsuneish），〈書目控制與圖書館專業：戰略問題〉（"Bibliographical
　　　Controls and Professional Librarianship: A Question of Strategy?"）載《東亞圖書館資
　　　料：美國圖書館遠東資料委員會第10屆年會上的工作報告》（*Library Resources on
　　　East Asia: Reports and Working Papers for the Tenth Annual Meeting of the Committee on
　　　American Library Resources on the Far East, Association for Asian Studies, Inc., at the
　　　Palmer House, Chicago, March 21, 1967*）（瑞士［Zug, Switzerland]：國際文獻公司
　　　[Inter Documentation Company AG], 1968），頁58。
[3]　同上，頁57。
[4]　詹姆斯・斯基普（James E, Skipper），〈研究圖書館編目的特性〉（"Characteristics of
　　　Cataloguing in Research Libraries"），研究圖書館協會第68次會議記錄（1966年7月9
　　　日）（*Minutes of the 68th Meeting of the Association of Research Libraries* [9 July,
　　　1966]），頁55-66（附錄I），常石道雄，頁61。
[5]　《國會圖書館編目處理部通訊》（*Library of Congress, Processing Department, Cataloging
　　　Service: Bulletin*），第90期（1970年9月），頁3。

（胡嘉陽譯）

Bibliographical Controls for Chinese Studies
Present Status and Future Developments

One of the anomalies of the development of East Asian library resources in the United States is the lack of effective national bibliographical control over what has been collected. As of June 1970, there was an estimated total of more than three million volumes of Chinese publications in sixty-six American libraries, making up 61% of all East Asian language materials held by libraries in the United States. [1] Yet this combined resource, the best collection of its kind outside mainland China, suffers from a lack of effective bibliographical control. This paper is an attempt to determine why this is so, to review the corrective measures that have been taken, and to consider what remains to be done.

The bibliographical gap in East Asian library development in the United States is the result of tradition and neglect. Warren Tsuneishi has succinctly summarized the reasons as follows:

By far the most important reason, of course, is the natural orientation of America to Europe; it is easy to disregard Asia — until a Pearl Harbor or a Korea or a Viet Nam reminds us that our far western frontier now touches the rimland of Asia. Another reason is the relatively small number of East Asian libraries and librarians in the United States. To many individuals we must appear to constitute a small, and perhaps an insignificant part of the total U.S. library picture: our problems require only minimal attention... Finally, I suspect an additional reason our voices remain unheard is that those of us who deal directly with East Asian language materials are relatively inactive in such professional bodies as the American Library Association, which determine national needs and set plans and objectives to fulfill those needs. Being inactive, we have no voice in such plans... [2]

Thus, as Dr. Tsuneishi also points out, "the *National Union Catalog: Author List*, in recording the locations of Chinese books, carries only those reported on Library of Congress printed cards — and hence omits most Chinese books catalogued in American libraries during the past ten years, since the percentage of original cataloguing by local libraries is very high, approximating 85 percent or more." [3] The European orientation of the library profession and our inactivity in it has also resulted in the execution of other national library projects from which the East Asian interests have been excluded. The third edition of the *Union List of Serials*, published in 1965 under the sponsorship of the American Library Association, includes only those East Asian serials reported in the first two editions. Thus, all East Asian serials acquired by American libraries since 1943 remain unreported in what was supposed to be a national union list. Another example is the *National Register of Microfilm Masters*, published in 1966 by the Library of Congress; it has only an incomplete listing of East Asian language microfilms in the United States, and does not even include the Library of Congress' own master negatives of Chinese rare books. Moreover, the *pre-1956 National Union Catalog* (a recent publication sponsored by the American Library Association) excludes entries for publications in the East Asian languages entirely.

Lacking national leadership, the East Asian libraries have had to improvise, often individually and without coordination among themselves, in order to satisfy, more or less, the call for bibliographical services. This they have done through the use of such conventional tools as the card catalogue and subject bibliographies, but their efforts have been only partially successful in meeting the needs of the field in general. In the course of reviewing these efforts, I shall also speculate on their future prospects.

（1）Card catalogues. The card catalogue is an effective but very costly instrument of bibliographical control for East Asian libraries. The continuing inadequacy of printed card control over materials in the vernaculars scripts of East Asia as provided by the Library of Congress has been directly responsible for the high cost of cataloguing and catalogue-maintenance in East Asian libraries. A survey conducted in March 1965 by the Association of Research Libraries reveals that, while Library of Congress printed cards were available for 75.6% of American publications and 53.7% of British publications received by institutions belonging to the Association of Research Libraries, only 15.8% of Chinese catalogue cards reproduced for use by that library in the calendar year 1969, only Chinese and Japanese receipts by the same libraries had Library of Congress copy available for use. [4] Statistics kept at the Harvard-Yenching Library show that, of the Chinese catalogue cards reproduced for use by that library in the calendar year 1969, only 9.4% were Library of Congress copies. Thus, an unreasonably high percentage of original cataloguing has to be done locally by East Asian libraries, thereby adding considerably to the cost of cataloguing and of catalogue maintenance, to say nothing of the wasteful duplication of effort in the process. The use of the card catalogue as an instrument of bibliographical control in East Asian libraries has therefore become a very expensive proposition, difficult to justify in many instances. The time is overdue for the Library of Congress, as the de facto national library, to review and revamp its printed card program for East Asian language materials in order to deal effectively with a long-standing, urgent national need. Better card catalogues will be only one result of this program because it will also enable us to save time and money that is needed for other bibliographical tasks.

The Library of Congress announced in September 1970 that it was instituting, on a trial basis, a new practice in printing Chinese, Japanese, and Korean cards. In place of the "title Romanized" note, the Romanization of the title now appears in parentheses preceding the transcription of the title. Continuation cards also give the title in Romanized form instead of in characters. [5] This change was presumably made to speed up the production of printed cards in these languages.

Mr. C. Sumner Spalding, Assistant Director for Cataloging, Processing Department, the Library of Congress, in a letter to the author, dated 26 August 1971, states that

Under the up-to-now standard printing method employed for cards in these [East Asian] languages the normal time span between descriptive cataloging and card printing is now running 6 to 7 months.

However, Mr. Spalding also states that

Even more encouraging is the success of our pilot project to print camera copy for Japanese cards in Japan. This will be the method employed by LC once the necessary administrative and contractual formalities can be concluded. This method will shorten the time that elapses before cards are issued by as much as 3 months. We expect to extend this procedure to the printing of Chinese and Korean cards at a later date.

Mr. Spalding is of the opinion that "the utility of Library of Congress cataloging of materials in East Asian languages is probably adversely affected much more by the factor of timeliness than by that of coverage." He provides the following statistics and comments:

Descriptive cataloging completed

	1969/70	1970/71
Japanese	14,052	14,932
Chinese	2,744	2,883
Korea	774	1,065
	17,570	18,880
Printed cards issued	12,746	22,404

From this it can be seen that a lot of cataloging is being done and a lot of cards are being printed. However, the printing process is so involved and the Library's control over work in the GPO Branch Printing Office is so limited that tremendous delays have often occurred with the result that prior to 1971 it was rare that it took less than a year for an East Asian book to get through the cataloging and card printing operations and often it took more than two years. About the beginning of 1971 things took a considerable turn for the better. A large batch of cards just printed were found to have required about 6 to 7 months for cataloging and card printing.

In the matter of immediacy of cataloguing vs. cataloguing costs, Mr. Spalding suggests that East Asian libraries "take a leaf out of the book of U.S. general research library operations with respect to these libraries' use of LC copy for Shared Cataloging imprints generally." He reasons as follows:

These [general research] libraries report that LC copy for 70-plus percent of their receipts of current imprints from Shared Cataloging countries turns up in their depository files of LC cards within six months. Obviously, this is not very helpful if immediacy of cataloguing is at a premium. On the other hand, this can be very helpful if cataloging costs are at a premium. General research libraries are for the most part well satisfied with this situation and fully adapt to it. It seems to indicate that even greater advantage should accrue to East Asian collections because of the special problems posed by ideographic languages.

Mr. Spalding is right about the potential advantages a 70-percent availability of Library of Congress copy could provide to East Asian libraries. Cataloguing control of East Asian language materials, especially Chinese and Korean, which are not under shared cataloguing control at present, will have reached a new phase if that percentage is attained.

（2）Book catalogues. In the absence of a national union catalogue of Chinese books, individual library book catalogues serve an extremely important function for locational purposes. The earliest such publication in the East Asian field was the *Chinese catalogue of the Harvard-Yenching Library* printed in Peking between 1938 and 1940, but the publication was interrupted after the first three volumes by the Pacific War, and it has yet to be resumed. During recent years the G. K. Hall Company has published the card catalogues of the East Asiatic Library of the University of California in Berkeley, of the UCLA Library, of the New York Public Library, and of the East Asian collection of the Hoover Institution Library of Stanford University. These were extremely welcome, and the imminent publication by the same company of the catalogue of the Far Eastern Library of the University of Chicago will also be of great service to libraries and to the academic community.

Important as book-form catalogues of individual libraries may be, they can never take the place of a national union catalogue, especially when they are still far too few in number to cover even the major East Asian collections of the country, Nevertheless, they are useful tools, and will become even more useful if regularly revised and brought up to date with supplements. It may be added that several libraries have recently put their card catalogues on microfilm as a precaution against fire and vandalism. Some use, presumably, may be made of these microfilms for locational purposes. The only genuine solution, however, remains a national union catalogue.

（3）Control over Periodicals, Newspapers, and Microfilms. Like Chinese monographs, Chinese periodicals, newspapers, and microfilms are in need of national bibliographical control. As has been mentioned, the third edition of the *Union List of Serials* does not include Chinese periodicals acquired by American libraries and not reported to the second edition of 1943. Neither does *New Serial Titles*, published as a supplement to the Union List of Serials, serve as a source of up-to-date information; its coverage is incomplete. As a result, East Asian libraries have had no assistance from national projects in the bibliographical control of Chinese-language periodicals. Whatever control there is has been oriented toward meeting local needs or has been provided by *ad hoc* projects. Thus, we have lists of Chinese periodical holdings of several East Asian libraries, and also three "union lists" of sorts. The issuing bodies, however, do not include all the major libraries in the United States. Of the three "union lists" that have been compiled, the most comprehensive, which is the *Union Card File of Oriental Vernacular Serials*, containing information on the periodical holdings of some thirteen major East Asian libraries in the United States and Canada as of 1961 and up-to-date information on the Library of Congress holdings, remains unpublished. The two published volumes, *Chinese Periodicals, International Holdings, 1949-1960*, by Raymond Nunn, and *International Union List of Chinese Communist Serials*, by Bernadette Shih and Richard Snyder, are useful, but they list only post-1949 titles. Furthermore, the latter contains primarily scientific, technical, and medical journals, with only a selection of one hundred titles in the field of social science.

It is hoped, therefore, that the *Union Card File of Oriental Vernacular Serials*, at present available from the Library of Congress only in microfilm or on 3 x 5 copyflo copy, will be revised, edited, and published at the earliest possible date.

Similar projects are also needed for Chinese newspapers. Although we know the location of some of the leading Chinese newspapers in the United States, no one is ever sure of the lesser-known publications. This is regrettable in view of the importance of newspapers to research. Publications such as *Newspapers on Microfilm* and *Postwar Foreign Newspapers*, both published by the Library of Congress, do not help much; their coverage of Chinese titles is incomplete. A true union list of Chinese newspapers available in American libraries, including those on microfilm, is needed. It should be noted that Mr. Karl Lo, Head of the Asiatic Collections, University of Washington Libraries, is compiling a union list of Chinese-language newspapers published in the United States.

Microfilms of all kinds need to be listed. The incomplete coverage of the *National Register of Microform Masters* has already been mentioned. It is possible that East Asian libraries could list their microfilm holdings with the Library of Congress with a view to their inclusion in the next edition of the *Register*, but a more realistic approach would be to compile a national register restricted to Chinese microform reproductions and including, in addition to negative master films, all positives for which no negatives exist in the United States. The recent acquisition by the Center for Chinese Research Materials of the Association of Research Libraries of lists of microfilm holdings in major East Asian libraries in the country might serve as a basis for such a project.

（4）Subject Bibliographies and Indexes. While union control schemes provide a convenient handle to bibliographical problems, indexes and subject bibliographies are necessary keys to the intellectual content of publications. Unfortunately, such reference aids in the Chinese field are still meager. No current publication approaches the scope of the Sinological Index Series published some years ago by the Harvard-Yenching Institute. What a service it would be to scholarship if there were a comprehensive index to the Chinese standard histories following the four in the Harvard-Yenching Series, and to the tens of thousands of local gazetteers!

Indexes to Chinese journal articles are more plentiful, although many of them are incomplete or out of date. Some also appear as parts of other publications rather than in separate volumes, and are therefore scattered on the shelves and inconvenient to use, It would be desirable to re-issue these as individual volumes.

Newspaper indexes are much less numerous and a great deal less satisfactory than the periodical indexes. Pre-1949 Chinese newspapers did not provide their own indexes, nor, with me the exception of a few national publications, do the post-1949 Chinese newspapers. Taiwan and Hong Kong newspapers have been indexed only since 1962 and on a selective basis. So the newspaper index gap continues, and it is obvious that something needs to be done. Given the magnitude of the task, a national, perhaps even an international, effort will be required to achieve satisfactory results.

Subject bibliographies and research guides are also essential for bibliographical control in the Chinese field. The Hoover Institution's Bibliographical Series and the bibliographical volumes in the Harvard East Asian Monographs are typical examples; many additional compilations of this kind are needed to provide more adequate coverage of the field. The Harvard-Yenching Library is now publishing a Bibliographical Series, of which No. 1 (*Chinese History: Index to Learned Articles, vol. II, 1905-1964*) appeared in 1971. The Hoover Institution of Stanford University has issued a survey of its East Asian holdings this year: *East Asia: A Survey of Holdings at the Hoover Institution on War, Revolution and Peace*, by John T. Ma.

Subject bibliographies on Chinese literature, Chinese history, Chinese economy, Chinese government, the Kuomintang, and a host of other subjects will contribute immeasurably to the progress of Chinese studies. The same can be said of research guides. Publications such as *Modern China: A Bibliographical Guide*, by John K. Fairbank and K. C. Liu, and *Contemporary China: A Research Guide*, by Peter Berton and Eugene Wu, have become standard references for the periods they cover. Both of these publications need to be brought up to date. Moreover, there is a definite need for a Fairbank-Liu for the post-1949 period, and a Berton-Wu for the pre-1949 phase of the Chinese Republic. Needless to say, similar compilations for pre-twentieth-century China would be equally important contributions.

Thus far only problems concerning Chinese-language materials have been considered here, mainly because Chinese sources present more serious bibliographical control problems than their Western-language counterparts. For example, we have, in Henri Cordier and T. L. Yuan, in *Index Sinicus*, and in the Association for Asian Studies annual bibliography, a most comprehensive coverage of existing monographic and serial literature on China in Western languages; but there is nothing comparable for Chinese. Printed Library of Congress cards are much more readily available for Western-language publications on China than they have ever been for Chinese. The problems are much simpler and easier to cope with, but this is not to say, of course, that there are no problems with regard to bibliographical control of Western-language sources. There are still too few subject bibliographies with critical annotations such as Charles Hucker's *China: A Critical Bibliography*. There is still a need for indexes to English-language newspapers published in China since the latter part of the nineteenth century; a great deal of information remains buried to this day because ready access has not been provided. Furthermore, the currently published translations of the Chinese mainland press issued by the American Consulate-General in Hong Kong use an inadequate indexing system. Parenthetically, it should be mentioned that a similar translation series, the Joint Publications Research Service reports, suffers from an almost total lack of indexing except for the early years of its publication. Finally, there is the problem of easy and ready access to facilitate utilization for scholarly purposes of the official government archives of Western nations.

One may ask at this point how far the conventional approaches and manual methods in bibliographical research can help us in getting the job done, and whether automation may solve some of our problems. An effective retrieval system could provide searching more thorough than is possible with our present manual methods. The data that it produced, moreover, could assist in the formulation of new hypotheses, new queries, new approaches, and new research techniques. The question, it seems, is how close we are to having an effective and practical system of automated bibliographical control in East Asian studies, and what we ought to do in the interim before we are able to convert our manual system to an automated one.

Although substantial progress has been made in some areas of automation involving bibliographical control of materials written in non-Roman scripts (e.g. the work of Mrs. Hesung Koh of the Human Relations Area File, of Professor Susumu Kuno of Harvard University, and of Professor Carl Leban of the University of Kansas), no large-scale library application has tested any of these systems to determine feasibility and cost. The MARC project of machine cataloguing at the Library of Congress deals exclusively with English-language publications, and no plans have been made for inclusion of material in non-roman scripts. The elaborate machine-coding system employed by Professor William Skinner of Stanford University in his Chinese Society Bibliography Project illustrates one of the most effective ways machines can be employed in a bibliographical control project, but the applicability of his system to general library use remains to be studied after he has published the results of his project. The pioneering work that has been done in the area of automated bibliographical control of East Asian materials, encouraging as it has been, has not yet been tested sufficiently to enable us to judge the merits of different systems, and to compare performances and costs. The decision to automate the Association for Asian Studies bibliography is certainly to be welcomed. It is hoped that the Association will carry the project one step further to include not only Western language sources, but also sources in the Asian vernaculars. It is further hoped that the Association will go beyond an automated bibliography and into the field of information retrieval. No single institution will be able to underwrite such experiments. It must be a national undertaking in which all interested parties can participate. (Recent unforeseen developments have necessitated a thorough review of the Association for Asian Studies Bibliography Project by the Association's Committee on Information Control. The feasibility of automation, including cost analysis, is still being studied.)

Notwithstanding our accomplishments in bibliographical control of Chinese-language materials in American libraries, much remains to be done. Indeed, it is important that East Asian libraries direct their attention in the next few years to finding a solution to what may well be regarded as the most basic of all our bibliographical needs in Chinese studies at this time — namely, the compilation and publication of a national union catalogue of Chinese monographs and serials.

The subject of union catalogue control has been under discussion for a number of years. Aside from what the Orientalia Division of the Library of Congress has been doing on its own initiative with limited manpower and financial resources, thus far there has been no organized national effort to implement any of the recommendations that have emerged from this discussion. Particularly pertinent are the recommendations made in 1966 by the Union Catalogue Subcommittee of the Committee on American Library Resources on the Far East (since renamed Committee on East Asian Libraries) of the Association for Asian Studies. In its excellent report, the Subcommittee, composed of Warren Tsuneishi, Charles Hamilton, and Robert Stevens, recommended that the best possible solution, among all possible approaches to the problem, was the compilation of a union catalogue on the basis of existing catalogues at the Orientalia Division of the Library of Congress, including the "union catalogue reports" sent in regularly by East Asian libraries to the Union Catalogue Division of the Library of Congress. The Subcommittee also recommended that the work be undertaken in stages, and that the Library of Congress be urged to initiate action to bring their Chinese and Japanese union catalogues under preliminary control. These recommendations formed the basis of a letter to the Librarian of Congress from the President of the Association for Asian Studies. The letter was subsequently acknowledged by the Librarian; but no further action was taken at that time by either the Library of Congress or by the Association for Asian Studies.

During the last two years, the Orientalia Division has made substantial progress in bringing under preliminary control the Chinese union catalogue as well as in editing the Union Card File of Oriental Vernacular Serials. But the task is a huge one; and the work is not anywhere near completion. An undertaking such as a national union catalogue should be the concern of all who are interested in East Asian studies. The fact that some progress has been made by the Library of Congress does not relieve us of either the responsibility or the obligation to join efforts to insure the successful completion of an undertaking of national and international significance.

Finally, it is no longer desirable to approach our bibliographical control problems in a piecemeal fashion, nor is it economically feasible to attack them on an individual or institutional basis. The magnitude of our needs and the economics of library operation demand that we look at the whole range of problems systematically and from a national viewpoint. The time has come for us to reassess our needs, our assumptions, and our approaches. National leadership and nation-wide planning are indispensable to the establishment of priorities and procedures. The task is not an easy one, especially in the area of funding. But East

Asian libraries are at the threshhold of potentially larger development during the coming years in service of scholarship. The extent to which we succeed will depend entirely on our ability to meet the challenge of bibliographical control.

Notes

This was prepared originally for the library panel "Biographical Controls for Asian Studies," at the annual meeting of the Association for Asian Studies in San Francisco, April 1970. By agreement between the two periodicals, it was first published in the *Foreign Acquisitions Newsletter.* no. 32 (October 1970), pp. 1-6, and was subsequently revised for publication in the *Harvard Library Bulletin.,* vol. XX, no.1 (January 1972) pp. 39-44.

[1]　Tsuen-hsuin Tsien, comp., "Holdings of Far Eastern Materials in American Libraries," *Newsletter of the Committee on East Asian Libraries*, Association for Asian Studies, No. 33 ([March] 1971), (Table I).

[2]　Warren Tsuneishi, "Bibliographical Controls and Professional for the Librarianship: A Question of Strategy?" in *Library Resources on East Asia, Reports and Working Papers at the Tenth Annual Meeting of the Committee on American Library Resources on the Far East, Association for Asian Studies, Inc., at the Palmer House, Chicago, March 21, 1967* (Zug, Switzerland, Inter Documentation Company AG, 1967), p. 58.

[3]　*ibid.*

[4]　James E. Skipper, "Characteristics of cataloguing in research libraries," *Minutes of the 68th Meeting of the Association of Research Libraries (9 July 1966)*, pp. 55-66 (Appendix I), quoted in Tsuneishi, *op. cit.*, p. 61.

[5]　*Library of Congress, Processing Department, Cataloging Service: Bulletin*, no. 90 (September 1970), p. 3.

美國東亞圖書館裡的破損資料
對成立全國性東亞資料保存與維護中心的芻議

　　美國東亞圖書館應為其在過去幾十年間的成就感到驕傲。經過個別以及集體努力所收集的資料是當今除了東亞當地外其他各地都無法匹比的。這種情況很可能還會持續到將來。但是成功也帶來了一些問題。這篇簡短的報告就是要檢視其中問題之一：那就是東亞資料的保存與維護，並建議一項全國可行的解決之道。

　　眾所周知，20世紀上半葉在東亞印刷的資料，由於紙張酸度過高，已在圖書館書架上加速破碎。再加上經年累月的使用，以及很多圖書館書庫缺乏空調，這種破損的程度日益加劇。在這個時期出版的無論圖書、期刊、報紙，由於破損的程度過高，很多都不能再行使用。因為紙張太脆弱，在使用時每翻一頁都會造成不可挽回的傷害，因此，下一次的使用可能就是它最後一次的被使用。許多圖書館為了保存資料，因此將其拍攝成縮微品。國會圖書館亞洲部、哥倫比亞大學東亞圖書館、加州大學柏克萊分校東亞圖書館、胡佛研究院，還有哈佛燕京圖書館都做了這樣領頭的工作。近年在東亞各地以及歐洲也有些出版商將一些舊資料拍攝成縮微品出售。日本東京的日本マイクロ寫真（Japan Microfilm Service Center）和雄松堂書店（Yushodo）是其中最突出者。荷蘭萊頓國際文獻公司（the Inter Documentation Center）也熱衷將東亞資料拍攝成縮微品。北京中國縮微出版物進出口公司（China National Microforms Import and Export Corporation）、新中國縮微複製公司（New China Microfilm Company）、台北的漢珍圖書縮影股份有限公司（Transmission Books & Microinfo Co., Ltd.）是最近幾年才加入這個行列的。猶他家譜學會（Genealogical Society of Utah）近年來取得美國各東亞圖書館如哥倫比亞大學、哈佛大學的允准將其收藏的中國和韓國的家譜以及一些中國地方志拍成縮微膠捲保存起來。美國研究圖書館協會中國研究資料中心（Center for Chinese Research Materials, Association of Research Libraries）將若干重要的中國研究資料複製以供學者之用也是眾所周知的事。這許多措施都非常可貴，但還是不能解除東亞圖書館在資料保存維護方面的憂慮。

其理由如下：首先是這些措施沒有一個是永久性的。因為如此，要作有系統的長時期的規畫和實施是不可能的事。除了國會圖書館將報紙拍攝成膠捲的項目外，其他學校的保存項目都是臨時性的，完全被有限的經費所支配。由於人力不足和參考工具的缺乏，館際間的協調也不如人意。因之難免有拍攝同樣的資料的現象和圖書館選擇只是將該館所藏的期刊、報紙拍成膠捲，而未設法向他館借用該館所缺者一併拍攝，以求完備。其次，以上提到的各種項目並不都是專門為保存資料而設。中國研究資料中心雖然對資料的保存做出了重要的貢獻，它真正的目的是複製資料以供研究之需。其三，以上列舉的專案有些涉及的資料範圍較為狹隘，僅限於某一類的出版品。猶他族譜學會就是個好例子。最後要提到的是出版商是以盈利為目的，而非以保存為目的而複製資料，其所考慮的完全以複製品的銷售營利為依歸。雖然上述的各種專案已經保存了一些資料。但是保存的基本問題仍然存在。目前我們還沒有一項全國性保存與維護東亞資料的合作專案。現在該是全國為此需要作出一致努力的時候了——來為保存與維護東亞資料作必要的規畫，建立館際的協調合作，人員的調配，以及經費的尋求。這樣一個全國性項目和其他的全國性項目一樣不是一蹴而成的事。但是我們必須要在這個問題還比較容易處理的時候就開始，如果到了像現在我們一般的研究圖書館有了成千上萬頁破碎書刊的時候，再來做挽救處理的工作，恐怕就為時太晚，費用也會比現在就做貴得很多了。

建立一個像這樣的中心，必須設立一個全國性的組織來負責必要的規畫，館際的合作，人員的調配，經費的尋求，和方案的實施等各項工作。這個組織必須回應東亞圖書館的需求，必須要有合格訓練有素的成員來領導和管理，必須得到東亞研究界的信任和支援。但是我們現在正處於財政緊迫時期，需要一大筆啟動資金來安裝設備，雇傭人員，完成方案實在不是時候。很幸運地，我們已經有個現存的機構可以邀請來擔任這項工作。那就是，研究圖書館協會屬下的中國研究資料中心（Center for Chinese Research Materials, Association of Research Libraries）。

眾所周知，中國研究資料中心的目的就是去確認研究中國，特別是研究20世紀中國的學者們所需要的研究資料，用以複製並做分發的工作。中國研究資料中心自1968年成立。15年來成績昭然，已然成為國際間知名的提供研究現代中國的重要資料複印本和縮微品的機構了。其複製的眾多資料，包括已在破損的報紙、期刊和圖書，都因而保存下來，成了該中心附加的功效。但是保存資料並不是成立中國研究資料中心的初衷，為回應學者需要，複製資料才是其主要目的。然而自中國研究資料中心的輝煌成就來看——其和美國東亞圖書館以及國外東亞圖書館的接觸，其複製資料的經驗，又有美國研究圖書館協會的支持——這些條件足夠使其發展和開創成為一個全國保存東亞資料的理想機構。假定中國研究資料中心同意這個建議，該中心就必須擔任一個新的任務，那就是從資料複製轉換到資料保存，同時在該中心的組織方面也會有所變動。這些都必須事先得到研究圖書館協會和中國研究資料中心諮詢委員會的同意。要是我們東亞圖書館都同意這個睿智而可取的建議，向研究圖書館協會提出有力的說明，保證我們全心全意地支持，相信研究圖書館協會也不會忽視的。

假定我們的贊助和研究圖書館協會的同意都不成問題的話，中國研究資料中心首先得在其組織上作某些變動，包括將中心的名稱更改得更合乎它的新任務，比如改為「全國東亞資料保存維護中心」（The National Center for the Preservation of East Asian Materials）；並將其諮詢委員會擴大到包括所有主要東亞圖書館。諮詢委員會也可改稱為管理委員會，負責決策和監督的任務，決定資料保存的先後次序以及方式——影印、拍攝縮微品、脫酸等。同時管理委員會在東亞圖書館協會的支持下應可與研究圖書館協會共同舉辦募款活動以籌募資金，開始執行其新任務。

中心在執行其任務前，必須首先建立一個全美及海外各東亞圖書館已經拍攝成縮微母片的目錄檔。並需要充分地把握出版社已經影印的資料的情報，和他們當前和未來的影印計畫。如此，不僅可以有足夠的資訊用以避免複製同樣的資料，同時這個目錄檔也可以作為一個資訊交換所以供各東亞圖書館查詢之用。

當中心成立後，毫無疑問地中心不能滿足任何圖書館從自己的立場認為應該保存的資料的要求。有些保存工作，特別在修補方面，還是要由各別圖書館自行處理。所期望保存的資料，管理委員會可以經過討論決定資料複製的先後次序。在中心能有效地執行它的工作以前，還有無數的細節必須先行解決。像所有的合作項目一樣，此事的成功還得取決於所有參與者的合作和支援。我們必須認真地面對這件事，否則我們的苦惱只會延長，我們也只有袖手旁觀目睹書庫裡不斷增加破損的資料，最終成為更多的一堆一堆的黃色碎片。

注釋

本文為 1983 年 3 月在舊金山亞洲學會年會中「資料保存與維護：東亞圖書館日漸關心的問題」（Preservation, a Growing Concern of East Asian Library Collections）研討會發表的報告。載《東亞圖書館通訊》（*Committee on East Asian Libraries Bulletin*），第 70/71 合刊（1983 年 2/6 月），頁 49-51。

（胡嘉陽譯）

Yellow Flakes in East Asian Libraries

Some Reflections on a National Preservation Program of East Asian Publications

East Asian Libraries can indeed pride themselves on their achievements during the last few decades. They have, through individual and collective efforts, built up collections of East Asian publications, the combined strength of which is unrivalled anywhere outside of East Asia today, and is likely to remain so in the future. But success has also brought with it problems. This brief paper is a preliminary attempt at examining one of these problems, namely, preservation, and to suggest a way in which a national approach to the problem can be attempted.

As is generally known, East Asian materials published during the first half of this century are rapidly deteriorating on libraries' shelves everywhere due to the high acid content of the paper on which they are printed. The deterioration process of these publications has further been accelerated over the years through use, and in many cases also by the lack of adequate climatic control in the stack areas in which they have been housed. It is not uncommon to see publications of all types — books, newspapers, and periodicals — published during this period rendered unserviceable in our libraries because the deterioration process has gone too far, and the pages as a result have become too brittle to be turned without irreparable damage being done to them. In such cases, the next use of the publication in question will also most likely be its last. Many libraries have taken to microfilming some of these publications for preservation purposes. The Asian

Division of the Library of Congress, the C.V. Starr East Asian Library at Columbia, the East Asiatic Library at the University of California, Berkeley, the Hoover Institution, and the Harvard-Yenching Library at Harvard are chief among them. Commercial publishers in East Asia and Europe have also in recent years undertaken to issue micro-editions of some of these materials. The Japan Microfilm Service Company and Yushodo in Tokyo are probably the most prominent among these publishers; the Inter Documentation Center in Leiden, Holland, has also been increasingly active in the East Asian field; the China National Microforms Import and Export Corporation and the New China Microfilm Company, both in Beijing, and the Transmission's Microforms Company in Taipei are the latest to join the ranks. The Utah Genealogical Society in Salt Lake City also has in recent years received permission from East Asian libraries in the United States such as Columbia and Harvard to have their collections of Chinese and Korean genealogies as well as certain Chinese local gazetteers microfilmed for preservation purposes. The Center for Chinese Research Materials (CCRM) of the Association of Research Libraries (ARL), as we all know, has been successfully engaged in reproducing important Chinese research materials in response to scholars' needs. However, all such efforts, invaluable as they are, have not relieved the East Asian libraries of their preservation worries.

The reasons for this are several: In the first place, none of the efforts made so far are of a permanent nature. This has made systematic planning and implementation over time impossible. With the exception of the newspaper microfilming project at the Library of Congress, all university preservation programs have been temporary in nature, subject entirely to the availability of funds which have not been plentiful. In the latter case, inter-institutional coordination has also left something to be desired due to a shortage of manpower and reference tools. Some duplication of effort has thus been unavoidable, and libraries have often opted for putting incomplete sets of books, periodicals, and newspapers from their own collections on microfilm, without attempting to make sure whether what is being preserved can be made more complete through interlibrary borrowing. Secondly, not all the programs we have seen to date are exclusively designed for preservation purposes. CCRM has significantly contributed to our preservation efforts, but its main objective is in reproduction work. Thirdly, some of the projects have been limited in scope and have concentrated only on certain types of publications. The Utah Genealogical Society's program is a good case in point. Finally, commercial reprinters, being profit-oriented, are guided solely by considerations of sales and not by considerations of preservation. Thus, in spite of all that has been done in the past, the preservation problem is still very much with us. We have no coordinated program on the national level for the preservation of East Asian publications. It seems therefore that the time has come for us to consider a concerted national effort which would provide the necessary planning, coordination, staffing, and funding of the preservation of East Asian publications in service of our needs. Such a national program, as with all national programs, would not be easy to organize, nor can it be expected to be an overnight success. But a start must be made now while the task is still of a manageable size. If and when our problem approaches the magnitude of what is now facing the general research libraries with their millions and millions of pages crumbling on their shelves, it may very well be too late and too expensive for us to do anything about it.

Central to this national approach would be an organization which would be responsible for the planning, coordination, fund-raising, and implementation of programs. This organization must be responsive to the needs of libraries. It must provide the necessary leadership for management with a qualified and trained staff. It must also have the trust and support of the East Asian Studies community. However, the prospect of creating such an organization at a time of financial stringency such as we are experiencing is not encouraging, requiring as it does a sizeable initial capital outlay for physical facilities and personnel, and funds for continuing projects. Fortunately, there is already in place an organization which could conceivably be asked to serve as such a national agency. I am referring to the Center for Chinese Research Materials of the Association of Research Libraries.

As is generally known, the purpose of CCRM is to identify, reproduce, and distribute Chinese research materials needed by scholars, particularly with regard to the study of the 20th century. For fifteen years since its founding in 1968, CCRM has been eminently successful in its mission, and by so doing has become an internationally known organization supplying reprints in book-and micro-form of important research materials for the study of modern China. As an adjunct of the Center's well-known reprint program, a great many titles, including deteriorating newspapers, periodicals, and monographic publications have also been preserved. This preservation function, however, was not the rationale for the founding of the Center, and CCRM's primary purpose remains that of reproducing materials in response to scholarly needs. Given the record of the Center's admirable accomplishments, its contact with East Asian libraries here and abroad, its experience in reproduction work, and the support of the Association of Research Libraries, it stands to reason that it would be the ideal organization to take responsibility for developing and implementing a national program for the preservation of East Asian materials. Assuming such a responsibility would most likely call for a change in CCRM's mandate — from reproduction to preservation — as well as in CCRM's organization as it is presently structured. Both changes would of course have to have the prior approval of ARL and the Center's Advisory Committee. But a strong case can be made to ARL by East Asian libraries if we agree on the wisdom and desirability of such a move and pledge our wholehearted support to it.

Should our endorsement and ARL's approval be forthcoming, it is envisioned that CCRM would first undertake to make certain organizational changes, including the renaming of the Center to something more appropriate to its new mission, such as "The National Center for the Preservation of East Asian Materials," and expanding the membership on its current Advisory Committee to include all the major East Asian libraries. The new Committee might be designated as a Managing Committee with decision-making powers and oversight responsibilities. It should decide what specific programs and in what order and fashion（microfilming, xeroxing, deacidification, etc.）the National Center's projects should be carried out. The Managing Committee together with ARL could at the same time mount a major fund-drive with the endorsement of CEAL in order to carry out its new mission.

As a prerequisite to implementing programs, the National Center would first of all proceed to create a bibliographical file which would contain all available information on existing master negatives in East Asian libraries in this country and abroad. It should also inform itself on reprint editions of East Asian publications that have been issued by commercial publishers, and on their current and future reproduction plans. By so doing, it will not only have at its disposal information it needs to carry out its own work in order to avoid duplication of effort, but it could also serve as a clearing-house of such information from which all East Asian libraries should benefit.

It goes without saying that the National Center, when and if established, cannot carry all the preservation that may be deemed necessary in a given library. A certain amount of preservation, especially in the area of restoration, will still have to be done locally. But the Managing Committee would be expected to establish priorities through discussions and agreements. There are a myriad of other details that would have to be worked out before effective implementation could take place. Suffice it to say here that the success of this venture, as in all cooperative schemes, depends on the cooperation and support of all of its participants. This will indeed be a challenge. I think we should face it squarely as the alternative is the prolongation of our agony as we stand by and witness greater numbers of the books in our libraries ever-increasingly reduced to piles of yellow flakes.

Notes

This paper was presented at the panel on Preservation: A Growing Concern of East Asian Library Collections, at the 35th Annual Meeting of the Association for Asian Studies in San Francisco, March 25-27, 1983, and published in *Committee on East Asian Libraries Bulletin*, no. 70/71 (Feb/June 1983), pp. 49-51.

北美圖書館中文文獻收藏的現狀與前景

　　今天早上我被指定要講的這個題目範圍很大。恐怕在給我的時間裡很難說得具體。時間短促不是唯一的原因，更重要的是缺少過去5年或者10年北美圖書館中文文獻收藏在量和質方面的足夠資料。沒有這樣的資料，只能憑我個人的觀察提供一些印象和揣測的看法。

　　在東亞圖書館委員會主持的北美東亞圖書館1976-1980年的調查分析報告中，90個圖書館收藏的中文資料超過450萬冊。1981-1985年的調查報告還沒有公布。根據康乃爾大學周明之和他的專案小組發表在1989年6月《東亞圖書館委員會通訊》第87期該年度的統計數字（頁44-48），中文資料的總藏量是520萬冊，但這只是根據46個圖書館（占1976-1989年90個圖書館的一半）提供的數字，不過這個數字已經比1976-1980年90個圖書館的數字增長了12%。因為這只是46個圖書館藏書量，因此我們可以假設所有圖書館實際增長的百分率應該要高過12%。雖然如此，在中國研究的領域還在不斷增長的情況下，中文藏書發展的速度，比起過去的快速增長，還算是緩慢的。譬如：1971-1975年的增長是25%，1976-1980年是18%。緩慢增長的原因：一方面是因為中華人民共和國近年來的出版暴增，另一方面是因為美元貶值，大大減低了我們的購買力。同時，基金會和政府提供給大學區域研究的經費減縮，而圖書館又需為自動化工作增加經費，所以在今天如果有任何一個東亞圖書館宣稱其有足夠的經費來支持它所有的開銷，那可是鳳毛鱗角的事。但是值得慰藉的是，在1976-1980年只有12個圖書館的中文資料超過10萬冊，現在超過10萬冊的圖書館已經有17個了。

　　這固然是好消息，但是真正的問題還在：我們的收藏數量趕得上出版的書刊數量嗎？在沒有作深入的研究和分析之前無法準確地回答這個問題。根據去年我對9個大型東亞圖書館採購中華人民共和國的出版物做的分析，範圍雖然有限，但是對這個問題還是可以找出一些答案。這9個圖書館採購的中華人民共和國的出版物一年平均為圖書4,300種（從低的2,500種到高的7,600種，多數大約4,000到5,000種）；期刊840種（自620種到1,270種）；報紙43種（自10種到117種）。以1984年中華人民共和國政府公布的出版數字（最新的有詳細的主題分類的統計）作標準來比較，這9個圖書館，除極少或完全不收購的科技、教科書和圖片之外，其採購有關社會科學和人文科學的中華人民共和國出版物總量占該年出版15,918種圖書的15.7%到47.74%；1,411種期刊的43.94%到90%；1,041種報紙的0.009%到11.24%。（收藏期刊最多的那個圖書館包括了科技方面的期刊。）

除了上述並不收藏的出版物以外，我們也只選擇性地收藏近年激增的當代通俗小說和外國文學的中譯本。很可能還有大量的複印本在早年出版時已被收藏。除去這些，這9個圖書館採購到的中華人民共和國的出版數量還算不差，特別是那些每年可以採購到超過4,000到5,000種的圖書館。但是在他們收藏的資料中顯然缺乏地方出版社出版的限量出版物，以及禁止出口的內部資料。關於內部資料，值得提起的是有些可以在香港買到，有些也可以從曾經到大陸作訪問學者處獲得，並且其中多數已經由中國研究資料中心複製分發。最近新出版的一份期刊《當代中國研究通訊》（*CCP Research Newsletter*）主要內容的一部分就是公布美國圖書館和研究中心收集的內部資料和為它們所作的書評。

今日在中國發行的4,000多種期刊，只有一半不到可從外國訂閱。中國出版對外貿易總公司（CNPITC）1988年提供訂閱的期刊目錄只有1,796種，其中一半以上為科技類期刊。這9個圖書館可以訂閱620到1,270種實在不錯了。但是報紙比較起來就太令人失望。中國國際圖書貿易總公司（國際書店）1988年目錄提供77種報紙給外國訂閱，包括過去屬於機密的《解放軍報》。中國出版對外貿易總公司1988年目錄提供148種。這9個圖書館平均只訂閱了43種報紙（從10到117種），所以可以改善的空間還相當大。以上只對收藏中華人民共和國的出版物的分析。也許對收藏台灣和香港的出版物的狀況要好一些。但是這個假設尚須確認。

　　以上所述都關於藏書建設，因為我相信各位一定同意藏書建設是研究圖書館的主要任務的看法，應該隨時被列為優先考慮的項目。而藏書建設又和我們正在大幅度發展資源分享這個領域有直接的關係。前面已經提到由於出版暴增，美元貶值而造成研究圖書館營運成本不斷上升，要想繼續維持一個自足的研究圖書館已經是件不可能的事。資源分享乃成為發展藏書建設的一個大家樂於使用的方法。圖書館自動化和圖書館網路的開創更加速地促進了這種互助互惠觀念的成長。從東亞圖書館藏書建設的經驗來講，雖然全國性合作採購的辦法並不切實際，但是區域性的合作採購卻頗有可取之處。例如，加州大學柏克萊分校東亞圖書館和史丹佛大學胡佛研究院東亞圖書館成立了合作採購項目。他們在考慮採購某種中文報紙或者方志前，先諮詢對方，再作決定。目前東岸6個東亞圖書館──哥倫比亞大學、康乃爾大學、哈佛大學、普林斯頓大學、耶魯大學、紐約公共圖書館也成立了類似的專案。在這個合作專案下，每個圖書館在被指定的省份中儘量收集在該省份出版的報刊。這種安排很可能用在其他地方性的出版物，包括1949年後出版的縣志（據稱至1990年初期，縣志的出版將以千計）。這6個圖書館已經完成一份他們收藏的中文報紙聯合目錄初稿。可能還會編輯一份中文期刊聯合目錄。

　　談到目前中文文獻收藏情況，我們不得不提到東亞圖書館最近五年來所經歷的大變化──自動化。自從1987年研究圖書館資訊網（RLIN）推出中日韓文系統後，東亞圖書館的操作基本上起了深遠的改變。自動化在圖書館界並不是新東西，但是能夠處理中日韓文字卻是圖書館科技的突破。雖然線上編目已經成了東亞圖書館常規工作，自動化也加強了我們的參考服務，我們還沒有達到可以充分利用科技來為東亞圖書館服務的目的。我現在特別想到的是回溯轉換（recon）這個問題。我知道加州大學洛杉磯分校有計畫將其東亞卡片目錄轉換成機讀格式。這個計畫的發展值得我們注意。如果成功，其他的圖書館也可以仿效。

　　東亞圖書館另外一項重要發展就是資料維護保存的工作。就像自動化一樣，東亞圖書館也追隨一般研究圖書館的步伐發展這個專案。個別的圖書館如哥倫比亞和哈佛過去曾將少數的資料拍攝成縮微膠捲保存起來。幾個參與研究圖書館資訊網的東亞圖書館也正在合作將一些破損的20世紀出版品拍攝成縮微膠捲。但是由於要保存的資料數量龐大，根本解決的辦法是急需全國性大規模地來處理。這個辦法的可行性目前被看好，因為美國國會已經撥款數千萬元給國家人文基金會為各學術研究圖書館的資料作保存維護的工作。在這個框架下，成立一個全國合作專案來保存中文及其他東亞語文資料並不是不可能的事。關於中文資料的保存問題，我們必須要對中國研究資料中心對近代和當代中文資料所作的保存工作表示謝忱。20餘年來該中心雖是以複製出版為主要任務，但是因複製附帶有保存資料的功能，該處也可謂保存中心。該中心複製得越多，也就意味我們要做的保存工作越少。

展望將來，我們會問：中文圖書館的工作是在向那個方向發展？目前有幾個趨勢。第一，除非東亞圖書館的經費增加，我們都會被迫減少我們的採購。如此，我們滿足讀者要求的能力也會因之降低。如果財務困境繼續下去，較小的圖書館受到的影響可能會大於較大的圖書館。因之，它們在資源分享方面就會更需要依賴較大的圖書館。就是較大的圖書館在也不可能採購其所有所需的資料的情況下，它們之間也會發展更多的資源分享項目。第二，選書的館員、採購館員、公共服務館員都得學習自動化技能以適應自動化的圖書館環境。有的圖書館已經全自動化了，相信其他的圖書館不久的將來也將會全自動化。從圖書館行政者的觀點來看，自動化將帶給圖書館組織結構、人事和物質資源配置上一些基本改變。第三，我相信我們還會長期面臨如何培訓與何處尋求具有中國學各方面的必備知識以及在中國學領域內的書目知識，和具有開創性和富有精力的藏書建設者。最後，在我們擴大我們和中國大陸、台灣、香港的圖書館、圖書館同仁、出版商、書商接觸之際，我們和中國大陸的關係會繼續有其挑戰性。雖然我們和中國大陸廣泛的接觸對我們館藏的工作有利，但是美國圖書館在這方面的經驗告訴我們要培養和維護這樣的關係不是一件容易的事，因為費時，並且還要有耐心和毅力。負責東亞圖書館中文部的同仁也必須在各種不同的情況下扮演外交家和主導者。

　　就如我一開始說的，這些都是一些憑我印象和揣測的看法。我歡迎你們的意見和批評。

注釋

本文為1989年3月16日在華盛頓特區亞洲學會東亞圖書館委員會全體會員大會上發表的報告。載《東亞圖書館委員會通訊》（*Committee on East Asian Libraries Bulletin*），第88期（1989年10月），頁1-4。

（胡嘉陽譯）

Current State and Future Prospects of Chinese Collections in North American Libraries

The topic I have been asked to speak on is a very large one for the time allowed this morning. Time is not the only constraint; a more important concern is the lack of sufficient quantitative and qualitative data on Chinese collections in North American libraries for the last five or ten years. Lacking such data, my remarks will necessarily be somewhat impressionistic and speculative, based largely on personal observations.

In the 1976-1980 Committee on East Asian Libraries (CEAL) survey, 90 libraries reported on the extent of their Chinese collections, with a total of over 4.5 million volumes. The 1981-1985 survey has not yet been published, but the latest annual survey, compiled by Min-chih Chou (Cornell University) and his Task Force and published in the June 1989 issue of *CEAL Bulletin* (no. 87, pp. 44-48), lists a total of 5.2 million volumes, but reported by only 46 libraries. This represents an increase of 12 percent over the 1976-1980 figures. Since only about one half of the 90 libraries that reported to the earlier survey responded this time, it is safe to assume that the total increase would indeed be higher than just 12%. While the field continues to grow, the rate of growth has slowed in comparison with previous years. For example, the average percentage of increase for the 1971-1975 period was 25%, and for the 1976-1980 period 18%. What does this signify? This slower growth points to the fact that the combination of the publishing explosion, especially in the People's Republic of China (PRC) in the last several years, and the devaluation of the American dollar has taken a heavy toll on our purchasing power. At the same time, foundation and government support of area studies at universities was being cut back, and claims for support for new library projects such as automation were on the increase. It would be a rare case nowadays indeed when an East Asian library could boast of adequate funding for all its needs. Nevertheless, it is encouraging to notice that today there are 17 Chinese collections with holdings of more than 100,000 volumes as compared to only 12 reported by the 1976-1980 survey.

This indeed is welcome news. But the real question is: are we keeping up with what has been published? This, unfortunately, cannot be answered with any certainty without further study and analysis. A limited study I did last year analyzing 9 large East Asian libraries' acquisitions of PRC materials might be of some relevance. My study, using as a base for comparison the 1984 official PRC publishing data which are the latest available with a detailed breakdown by subject categories, revealed that the average annual number of books acquired from the PRC by these 9 libraries was about 4,300 titles (from a low of 2,500 to a high of 7,600, with most clustering around 4,000 to 5,000); the average number of periodicals was 840 (ranging from 620 to 1,270); and the average number of newspapers was 43 (ranging from 10 to 117). Not counting publications in the natural sciences and technology, textbooks, and pictorial materials, of which little or none is collected by American libraries, we find that these 9 libraries were collecting from 15.7% to 47.74% of the 15,918 titles of books published in the social sciences and humanities; from 43.94% to 90% of the 1,411 periodicals; and from .009% to 11.24% of the 1,041 newspapers. I must hasten to add here that the library that was receiving the largest number of periodicals included in its report many titles in the natural sciences and technology.

In addition to the types of materials excluded from our collecting as mentioned above, there are also areas in which we collect only selectively such as popular contemporary fiction and translations of foreign literature, both of which have proliferated in recent years. Also, it is likely that among the rather large number of reprints that have been issued, many were already collected by American libraries at the time of their first publication. Taking all this into consideration, the nine libraries' coverage of PRC materials is not bad, particularly those whose acquisitions fell around or exceeded the range of 4,000 to 5,000 titles. Of course, among the conspicuous lacunae remain many of the books published by local publishers in small editions, and the *neibu* materials that are not allowed to be exported. Regarding the latter, it should be noted that some continue to be available from Hong Kong, and more have been brought back by visiting scholars; many of these are being reprinted by the Center for Chinese Research Materials. I might also add that a new journal, *CCP Research Newsletter*, has as one of its major functions the review and announcement of PRC *neibu* publications available at libraries and research centers in the United States.

Of the more than 4,000 periodical titles published in China today, less than half are made available for foreign subscription. The 1988 catalog of the China National Publishing Industry Trading Corporation（CNPITC）offered 1,796 periodicals for this purpose, with more than half in the natural sciences and technology. When the nine libraries receive from 620 to 1,270 periodicals, the record is a very good one indeed. But the newspaper collection is, in comparison, rather disappointing. The 1988 catalog of the China International Book Corporation（Guoji Shudian）offered seventy-seven titles for foreign subscription, including the formerly classified *Jiefangjun bao*（Liberation Army News）. The 1988 CNPITC catalog lists 148 newspapers for which they will take foreign orders. Considering that the average number of newspaper subscriptions among the 9 libraries was only 43（ranging from 10 to 117）, that leaves a great deal of room for improvement The analysis above deals with PRC only. Perhaps we are doing better with Taiwan and Hong Kong publications, but that supposition must await confirmation.

I have dwelt at length on collection development because I believe, and I think you will agree with me, that collection development is at the heart of a research library's work and should always be our first priority. Directly related to collection development is the large stride we have made in the area of resource sharing. As already mentioned, the publishing explosion, the devaluation of the American dollar, and the spiraling costs of maintaining research collections have made self-sufficiency of research libraries a thing of the past. Resource sharing has instead become the *modus operandi* in collection development. The introduction of automation in libraries and the creation of library networks have further hastened and facilitated this concept of mutual dependence. The experience of East Asian libraries indicates that while a national cooperative program in acquisitions is impractical, a great deal can be achieved on a regional basis. The example of the University of California at Berkeley (UC-Berkeley) and Stanford is a case in point. The East Asiatic Library at UC-Berkeley and the East Asian Collection of the Hoover Institution at Stanford have instituted cooperative acquisitions programs for Chinese newspapers and local histories, and they consult with each other when considering purchases of expensive materials. A similar program is now in effect among six East Asian libraries on the East Coast — Columbia, Cornell, Harvard, Princeton, Yale, and the New York Public Library. Under this program each takes primary responsibility for collecting all available periodicals and newspapers in a given number of provinces. It is possible that this arrangement can be extended to cover other materials of a local nature, including *xian* (county) gazetteers on the post-1949 period, which are projected to be published in the thousands by the early 1990s. The six libraries have already compiled a preliminary version of a union catalog of their Chinese newspaper holdings, and a similar union list of their periodicals is a distinct possibility.

One cannot comment on the current state of Chinese collections without also mentioning the far-reaching change that has taken place in East Asian libraries during the last five years; that is the adoption of automation. Since the introduction of the Research Libraries Information Network（RLIN）Chinese-Japanese-Korean（CJK）system in 1987, East Asian libraries have undergone a fundamental change that has permanently altered the way they operate. While automation is nothing new to the library world, its application to East Asian libraries with its ability to process Chinese, Japanese, and Korean scripts is a first and represents a major breakthrough in library technology. While online cataloging has become routine in East Asian libraries and our capability to provide reference service has also been greatly enhanced through the use of automation, we have yet to reach the point where available technology is used to our full advantage. I have particularly in mind the question of retrospective conversion. I understand the University of California at Los Angeles has been making plans to convert its East Asian records into machine-readable form. It would be interesting to see how that project develops. If successful, it may very well be something which other East Asian libraries can emulate.

Another important development in our field is preservation. As in automation, East Asian libraries have followed in the footsteps of the academic libraries at large in this development. Individual libraries such as Columbia and Harvard have had modest programs in microfilming preservation in the past, and several RLIN libraries are now engaged in a cooperative effort in getting some of the fragile 20th-century Chinese publications preserved on microfilm. Due to the magnitude of the need, however, a national effort must be made to attack the problem on a massive scale. The feasibility for such a program looks quite good now that the Congress has appropriated tens of millions of dollars through the National Endowment for the Humanities for preservation projects at various academic and research libraries. It is not impossible that within this framework a coordinated national program for Chinese and other East Asian-language materials can be attempted. On the question of preserving Chinese-language materials, acknowledgment must be made for the work that has been done by the Center for Chinese Research Materials（CCRM）. For more than twenty years CCRM, through its reproduction program, has also functioned successfully as a center for preservation. The more in this area CCRM can do, the less the rest of us will have to do.

Looking to the future we may ask; where are the Chinese collections headed? Several trends seem to be shaping up. In the first place, unless financial support for East Asian libraries across the board is increased, we will all be forced to acquire less and thereby become less able to satisfy the demands of our clientele. This financial stringency, if it continues, will probably affect the smaller libraries more than the larger ones, thus making them more dependent upon the larger libraries for the purpose of resource sharing. But even the larger libraries will likely not be able to do all that needs to be done and will want to develop more resource-sharing programs among themselves. Secondly, automation will demand that our bibliographers, order librarians, and public service librarians also acquire certain skills in adapting their work to a completely automated environment which already exists in some libraries and will surely be in others in the not too distant future. From the viewpoint of the library administration, automation also means that there will be some basic changes made in the library's organization and in the allocation of human and material resources. Thirdly, I believe we will continue to struggle with the perennial problems of how to train and where to find qualified book selectors who possess the prerequisite expertise in a wide range of subject matters, extensive bibliographical knowledge of the field, and the energy and creativeness for collection building. Lastly, in our expanding contact with libraries, librarians, publishers, and book dealers in China, Taiwan, and Hong Kong, our relationship with the PRC will continue to offer the most challenge. While our broadening relationship with the PRC offers us a number of opportunities favorable to our collection development work, the experience of

American libraries in this regard so far indicates that the nurture and maintenance of this relationship is by no means an easy task, requiring as it does a great deal of time, patience, and perseverance. Chinese studies librarians will by necessity also have to become diplomats and facilitators in all kinds of situations imaginable.

As 1 mentioned at the outset, these observations are impressionistic and speculative. 1 welcome your comments and criticisms.

Notes

This article is adapted from a talk given at the Plenary Session of the 1989 Annual Meeting of the Committee on East Asian Libraries, Association for Asian Studies, March 16, at Washington, D.C. and published in *Committee on East Asian Bulletin*, no. 88 (October 1989), pp. 1-4.

出版品國際交換
國立中央圖書館與海外中文文獻的收藏

1992 年台灣國立中央圖書館館長曾濟群與該館國際交換處主任汪雁秋參觀哈佛燕京圖書館。

　　世界上各個國家的國家圖書館一直以交換出版品來增進國家間的文化交流。在中國也是一樣，在還沒有成立國家圖書館前，就由政府捐贈出版品給外國政府了。最早就是康熙三十六年（1697）清朝贈送140種圖書給法國。[1] 同治八年（1869）清朝在收到美國政府贈送的一些糧食和植物種子以及和農業、機械、礦業、測量太平洋鐵路有關的圖書、報告、地圖後，同意美國政府的要求，回送了一些植物和花卉的種子以及934冊圖書，其中圖書多為中國儒家經典。[2] 但是和先前贈書給法國一樣，這只是偶發事件，並無意後續。當1912年民國成立以後，1921年國民政府被邀請參加1886年成立的布魯塞爾公約組織才正式開啟了中國出版品國際交換事業。1925年成立了出版物國際交換局，隸屬教育部。但是由於政局不安定，致使該局業務少有進展。[3] 1928年國民政府北伐成功建都南京，出版物國際交換處改由中央研究院接管。最終於1934年歸屬國立中央圖書館（以下簡稱中圖）。[4] 1937年日本入侵中國，中圖隨政府遷往西南內陸重慶。由於戰時交通不便，又缺少足夠的通訊系統，所以難有什麼有意義的國際交換活動。1945年第二次世界大戰結束，該館隨政府遷回南京才恢復和68個外國圖書館的交換工作。[5] 但是差不多同時中國又陷入國共內戰。該館不得不隨政府於1948年再度離開南京，而在次年1949年中國共產黨在大陸全勝後遷移台灣。遷台初期情況艱難，中圖和國立故宮博物院及國立中央博物院聯合辦公，直到1954年才自行獨立作業。[6] 所以自1948年到1954年7年間中圖和海外各圖書館間都沒有任何交換往來。歷經20年的滄桑，中圖決定全力開發其國際交換專案。自1954年中圖復館後其國際交換活動蓬勃發展，只一年工夫，就已經和24個國家86個圖書館建立了交換關係。[7] 到1992年已增長到93個國家1,209個圖書館。[8]

　　由於中圖過去40年提供交換的出版品（僅1992年就近164,000冊 [9]）差不多都是有關中國研究的資料，如政府公報、學術著作的複印本、學術刊物、研究工具書等，其對海外的中國研究和圖書館中文文獻收藏影響至關重大，特別是對採購台灣出版品經費有所限制的一些學校及其他機構。近年中圖提供的交換專案已經不限出版品，更擴大到人員交換，譬如派館員到華盛頓州立大學、俄亥俄大學作1-3個月的短期交流。目前還為英國劍橋大學提供中文編目的協助。中圖還和連線電腦圖書館中心（OCLC）交換數位目錄。1981年教育部成立的漢學研究資料及服務中心（1987年更名漢學研究中心）附屬於中圖，提供獎學金歡迎國外學者到中心作研究，因而又增加了其與國外的交流項目。中心出版的《漢學研究》供台灣學者發表最新研究論著。而《漢學研究通訊》則報導台灣漢學研究動態、學術會議、書評、書目等。除此之外，中圖自1980年以來主持了若干有關圖書館和資訊科學的國際會議，並繼續其自1957年開始參加的世界各地主要的書展，又到國外學術和圖書館協會召開的年會，諸如美國的亞洲學會年會和美國圖書館協會年會組織書展，[10] 並在會後將書展的書刊贈送給當地收藏中文書刊的大學。

由於中圖不斷增加其交換項目，其跟海外圖書館中文書刊的收藏和海外的中國研究間的關係比過去更加確立。美國的東亞圖書館界非常樂見中圖擴展其交換專案。在此，我們冒昧建議中圖考慮將以下項目納入將來的國際交換工作：

1. 增強中文機讀格式：中文機讀格式和美國的機讀格式不同。由於缺少羅馬拼音和國會圖書館標題，中圖跟OCLC交換的書目難於適用於美國圖書館。誠然台灣圖書編目並不使用羅馬拼音和國會圖書館標題，採用它們自然會為中圖增加其工作負擔。但是從另一角度看，如果採用它們，不僅可嘉惠美國圖書館，也可嘉惠歐洲和其他地方使用OCLC資料庫的圖書館。如此，中圖的國際交換工作當就更上一層樓。外國圖書館如果可以直接使用中圖線上目錄，就不必再重新為台灣出版品編目，也就意味著中圖提供的目錄成為台灣出版品的種子目錄，可以嘉惠世界各地的圖書館。也是對海外中文收藏和中國研究的一大貢獻。

2. 資料保存維護工作：近年來全球圖書館界都關注書架上的書刊逐漸破損的現象。脫酸和拍攝縮微品是大家比較喜歡使用的保存方法。也有些資料輸入全文資料庫。還有些人把珍本當作文物來維護。因為需要保存的資料數量過大，不是一個圖書館，乃至一個國家可以把其收藏的所有資料都保存起來。因此，全球性分工合作應該是最合理而有效的解決方式：就是由每個國家負責保存該國的出版品，然後將其複製品（縮微品、膠捲，或者光碟）出售。其實，中圖過去已經把其收藏的善本書拍成縮微膠捲並出售。已經向保存資料這個方向踏出了重要的一步。只是中圖其他的收藏，特別是第二次世界大戰後在台灣出版的資料，含酸量高，都還沒有保存起來。鑑於海外收藏的台灣出版品都為中圖所收藏，如果中圖保存了這些資料，也就等於海外圖書館也保存了這些資料。當這些資料無論用什麼方式保存起來，可以出售給世界上各圖書館時，也就完成了保存全球各圖書館所收藏的台灣出版品的工作。當然我們還要考慮這樣大的工程的經費問題。這項工程可以與有興趣的商家合作。最近東京丸善株式會社和日本國立國會圖書館合作將該館所藏12萬種（16萬冊，3,500萬頁）明治時代出版品拍攝成15,000卷縮微膠捲就是最好的例子。這個非常成功的例子就證明：通過合作可以來完成保存工作的可行性。中圖所收藏的政府公報、地方志、報刊都非常完整，可以作為合作保存工程的主要資料目標。中圖和出版商分享銷售所得，也許可以解決有關版權的問題。

　　國外圖書館一直面臨中國傳統套裝線裝書的維護問題。在台灣和其他東亞講華語的地區還有人會以傳統的方法修補線裝書和函套。可是在這些地區以外地方就是要補上函套上丟掉的骨扣也是一種非同小可的挑戰。有鑑於此，中圖可以派遣其保養線裝書的專家到外國主持研習班訓練當地圖書館書籍維護人員如何維護中國古書的方法。這個項目可以向蔣經國國際學術交流基金會或中華民國行政院文化建設委員會申請贊助。這項創新必定會開啟出中圖國際交換的另一個新天地。

　　3. 設立中華民國政府官報寄存圖書館：台灣出版的政府官報與日俱增。中央、地方政府出版的行政報告、統計、研究報告、調查等等數以萬計。中圖也將一些如政府公報之類的資料作為交換，但是為數很少。其他沒有作為交換的資料多半是非賣品，無法購買。因為在這些出版品中有些是對研究中華民國的現況非常重要的原始資料，所以外國圖書館無法收集它們，學者也無法利用它們來作研究是非常遺憾的事。如果在美國和歐洲可各有一個圖書館被指定作為這些出版品的寄存圖書館，中圖可以把所有在台灣出版的政府出版品寄存。該館又可以免費由館際借閱提供給他地學者使用。如此，台灣研究當有進一步地發展。這種安排已有先例。多年來，美國國會圖書館就是日本國會圖書館指定的所有日本政府出版品的寄存圖書館。加州大學柏克萊分校東亞圖書館也是部分同樣日本政府出版品的另外一個寄存圖書館。

　　4. 協助採購：前面已經提到中圖目前協助英國劍橋大學中文書刊編目。如果中圖還能在採購上，特別是在期刊的訂閱上，給外國圖書館協助當有其同樣的效益。多年來，很多外國圖書館在台灣都找不到一家可靠的書商可以幫忙訂閱期刊。訂閱期刊的繁雜手續和低利潤該是書商不接受訂閱的明顯原因。不知中圖是否可在外國圖書館訂閱台灣期刊工作上助一臂之力，使其成為國際交換專案之一部分。協助辦法或可向外國圖書館引薦中圖使用的期刊供應商，或者身為國家圖書館在不違反國家的法規下為外國圖書館代訂中圖也訂閱的期刊，除訂費和郵費外，也可收取服務費。如這樣的建議可以付之實施，中圖就可以幫忙解決外國圖書館在訂閱台灣期刊上的大難題了。

　　上面已經提到多年來中圖擴大其國際交換項目對國外的中國研究，中文文獻收藏嘉惠良多。中圖作為中華民國的國家圖書館，其主要的任務是促進中華民國教育和文化的發展，我們可以假定國際交換工作對這項使命的完成也會作出貢獻。如果屬實，中圖再度擴張其國際交換項目，或可考慮本文所簡列的建議。

注釋

本文為 1989 年 4 月 24 日在台北「邁向 21 世紀的國家圖書館國際研討會」發表的報告。載《邁向 21 世紀的國家圖書館國際研討會論文集》（*Proceedings of the International Conference on National Libraries — Towards the 21st Century*），1994，頁 954-966。

[1]　資訊由國立中央圖書館出版品國際交換處主任汪雁秋提供。
[2]　錢存訓，〈中美首次圖書交換〉（"First Chinese-American Exchange of Publications"），《哈佛亞洲研究學報》（*Harvard Journal of Asiaic Studies*）第 25 卷（1964-65），頁 19-30。
[3]　蔣復璁，《國立中央圖書館籌備之經過及現在進行概況》（南京，1936），頁 7；辜瑞蘭，〈國立中央圖書館出版品國際交換工作〉，載《國立中央圖書館概況》（台北，1967），頁 31-35。
[4]　同上。
[5]　辜瑞蘭，前引書，頁 32-33。
[6]　同上。
[7]　〈國立中央圖書館概況〉，載《國立中央圖書館館刊》第 5 卷，第 2 期（1972 年 6 月），頁 30。
[8]　資料來自國立中央圖書館出版品國際交換處主任汪雁秋。
[9]　同上。

[10]　中央圖書館自1980年以來主辦的會議和參加的書展，見《中華民國圖書館年鑑，第
　　　二次》（台北，1988），頁156-164；1980年前參加的書展，見〈國立中央圖書館概
　　　況〉，載《國立中央圖書館館刊》新5卷，第2期（1972年6月），頁19-21。

（胡嘉陽譯）

International Exchange
The National Central Library and Chinese Studies Libraries Abroad

International exchange of publications has long been used by national libraries as an instrument to promote intercultural understanding among nations. In the case of China, such exchanges, or, more accurately, presentations of publications by the Chinese government to foreign governments, were taking place long before there was a Chinese national library.The earliest such instance was a gift of 140 items of Chinese books to France in 1697. [1] In 1869, the Chinese government, in response to a request by U.S. government, and in return for the "several" books relating to agriculture, mechanics, and mining, and maps and reports connected with the survey of the Pacific Railroad, together with some grain and plant seeds which the U.S. government had presented earlier to the Chinese government, sent to Washington 934 volumes (fascicles) of Chinese books, mostly Confucian classics, with some plant and flower seeds. [2] But this was, as in the French case, an *ad-hoc* arrangement, without any intention of its being continued. Following the end of imperial rule in China in 1912, the Chinese Republican government responded in 1921 to an invitation to subscribe to the Brussels Convention of 1886, thus marking the beginning of China's official participation in the international exchange of publications. A Bureau of International Exchange was established under the Ministry of Education in 1925, but the unstable political situation in China at that time prevented any significant progress being made in the Bureau's work. [3] When the Nationalist government was finally established in Nanjing in 1928, following the defeat of the warlord government in Beijing, the Bureau of International Exchange was reassigned to the Academia Sinica, and thence to the National Central Library in 1934. [4] However, the Japanese invasion of China in 1937 brought the exchange activities to a halt. The Nationalist government was forced to leave Nanjing and move to Chongqing in the southwestern interior, and the National Central Library went with it. Due to very poor transportation conditions and a lack of an adequate communications system in wartime, there were no meaningful international exchange activities until the end of World War II, when the National Central Library returned with the government to Nanjing in 1945 and resumed exchanges with some 68 foreign libraries. [5] But almost immediately, China was engulfed in a civil war, and once more, in 1948, the National Central Library had to relocate from Nanjing, and, following the Chinese communist victory on the Chinese mainland, eventually to Taiwan in 1949. Times were not easy in Taiwan at the time, and the work of the National Central Library had to be combined with that of the National Palace Museum and the Central Museum until 1954, when the National Central Library was able to resume its independent operation. Thus, for a period of seven years from 1948 to 1954, no international exchanges took place between the National Central Library and libraries in foreign countries. [6] The vicissitudes confronting the National Central Library in the first two decades of its existence thus had a decidedly retarding effect on its ability to sustain a meaningful international exchange program. However, since 1954 it has entered into an unprecedented period of development, and its international exchange activities have been growing by leaps and bounds ever since. By 1955, one year after it resumed its own independent operation in Taiwan, it was exchanging with 86 libraries in 24 countries, [7] and by 1992 the number had increased to 1209 libraries in 93 countries. [8]

Inasmuch as almost all of the exchange items made available by the National Central Library during the last four decades (nearly 164,000 volumes in 1992 alone [9]) have been publications related to Chinese studies, including government documents, scholarly reprints, learned journals, research tools, etc., the impact of the National Central Library's international exchange program on Chinese studies and Chinese library collections in foreign countries has been significant, especially at institutions where budget constraints have tended to limit their purchase of Taiwan publications. In recent years, the National Central Library has broadened the scope of its international exchanges beyond publications. It has instituted short-term（one to three months）personnel exchanges with the libraries of the University of Washington and Ohio University in the United States. It is now offering professional assistance to Cambridge University in England to help catalog its Chinese collection, and is exchanging bibliographical records in electronic format with OCLC（Online Computer Library Center）, the world's largest library network. The establishment in 1981 of the Resources and Information Center for Chinese Studies, a National Central Library affiliate, under the aegis of the Ministry of Education, added another dimension to the Library's international exchange program through fellowships offered by the Center to foreign scholars in Chinese studies to conduct research in Taiwan. The Center's journal, *Chinese Studies*, publishes the latest research by scholars in Taiwan, and its *Newsletter for Research in Chinese Studies* carries news items on research activities and conferences in Taiwan, book reviews, and bibliographies. In addition, the National Central Library has sponsored since 1980 a number of international conferences on library and information science, has continued its participation in all major book fairs around the world which began in 1957, and has organized book exhibits at annual meetings of academic and library associations in foreign countries such as the Association for Asian Studies and the American Library Association in the United States. [10] And as a matter of policy, the books in these exhibits are usually donated afterward to a local university which collects Chinese-language publications. With the accelerated pace of its international exchange activities, the role of the National Central Library in the development of Chinese library collections and Chinese studies abroad has become even more firmly established than previously.

To those of us who are associated with East Asian libraries in the United States, the expanded nature of the National Central Library's international exchange program has been most welcome. At the same time, we venture to suggest the following for the National Central Library's consideration for possible inclusion in the Library's future international exchange program. They are:

（1）Enhancement of the Chinese MARC records

Due to the different requirements of Chinese MARC and U.S. MARC, the records the National Central Library send to OCLC under their exchange agreement cannot be readily adapted for American libraries' use because of their lack of romanization and LC subject headings. It is recognized that neither romanization nor LC subject headings are used for cataloging in Taiwan, and adding them would mean extra work that is not normally required by the National Central Library. On the other hand, in view of the enormous contribution this added work will be not only to American libraries, but to European and other libraries as well which have access to the OCLC database, the extra efforts will push the National Central Library's international exchange program to a new height. Ready-for-use Chinese MARC records will mean that foreign libraries need no longer catalog any Taiwan imprints themselves, and that the National Central Library will become the source of cataloging information for Taiwan publications from which all the libraries in the world can benefit. This will surely be a lasting contribution of major proportions to the development of Chinese library collections and Chinese studies abroad.

（2）Preservation

The "slow fire" phenomenon of books deteriorating on library shelves has been a major concern to the global library community in recent years. Mass de-acidification and microfilming have been the preferred methods of preservation of library materials; some materials have been electronically transformed into full-text databases; and attention has also been given to conserving rare editions as artifacts. Since the magnitude of preservation work is such that no single library, or even a country, can afford to undertake the preservation of all the printed materials it possesses, it seems that the most logical and efficient way to accomplish the goal of preservation on a world-wide basis is through a division of labor, that is, that each country be responsible for preserving its own publications and for making copies of the final product, be it microfilm, tapes or CD-ROMs, available for purchase. If this is done, it will certainly move us closer to a real solution to the preservation problem. In a sense, the National Central Library has already taken an important step in this direction by undertaking some years ago to microfilm it's rare books collection and offer copies of the microfilm for purchase. But the remainder of the National Central Library's collection, most of which are post-World-War-II publications printed in Taiwan on paper with a high acid content, have not been preserved. Inasmuch as Taiwan publications in foreign libraries are all represented in the National Central Library's collection, their preservation at the National Central Library will also mean the preservation of those materials in foreign libraries' collections. When copies of the items so preserved, in whatever formats, are made available for purchase, the preservation of Taiwan publications in libraries around the world will have been satisfactorily accomplished. Naturally, the costs of mounting such a large-scale preservation project will be considerable, but the job could be done in cooperation with one or more commercial firms interested in such an undertaking. The best example of this is the recent microfilming of the Meiji Era publications at the National Diet Library in Tokyo by the Maruzen Publishing Company. The collection, numbering some 120,000 titles in 160,000 volumes, totaling 35 million pages, was preserved on more than 15,000 reels of microfilm. This monumental accomplishment is proof of what can be achieved through such collaborative efforts. There may or may not be collection of a similar distinct nature at the National Central Library, but long runs of government gazettes, local gazetteers, periodicals and newspapers are all prime candidates for such collaborative ventures.

The problem of copyright of course enters into the picture. But some kind of arrangement for sharing the proceeds of sales between the National Central Library and the publisher(s) in question might be one way of dealing with this problem.

Conserving Chinese stitch-bound fascicles kept in traditional cloth wrappers (cases) presents another aspect of the preservation problem facing East Asian libraries in foreign countries. While this presents no problems in Taiwan or any other parts of the Chinese-speaking world in East Asia where traditional techniques of conserving such items are still practiced, it represents a major problem in other countries where local conservators are not skilled in such techniques. Thus, not only they cannot repair torn or damaged pages, even the simple matter of replacing a missing bone clasp on the cloth cases becomes a major challenge. Perhaps such a preservation training program can be underwritten by the Chiang Ching-kuo Foundation for International Cultural Exchange and/or the Commission on Cultural Planning and Development of the Executive Yuan of the Republic of China. This innovative approach will surely break new ground in the National Central Library's international exchange program.

(3) Establishing depositories of Chinese government documents

The quantity of government documents issued in Taiwan in recent years has been on a sharp increase. There are literally tens of thousands of such publications issued regularly by government ministries, commissions, bureaus, agencies, etc. on the central, provincial, and local levels, including administrative reports, statistical compilations, research studies, surveys, and so on. The National Central Library does send some of these, such as government gazettes, on international exchange, but they represent a relatively small portion of what is being published. Unfortunately, the majority of the others are not-for-sale items, and hence not commercially available. Since most of these publications are primary sources important to research on the current development of the Republic of China, it is regrettable that they are not more readily available to foreign libraries and to scholars who need them for research. If a central depository could be established at a library in the United States, and one in Europe, to receive from the National Central Library one copy each of all the government documents published in Taiwan, with the understanding that the depository library will make them freely available to scholars through interlibrary loan without charge, Taiwan studies in foreign countries will have reached a higher plateau in its development. There is already a precedent to this kind of arrangement. For years, the Library of Congress had been the depository library for all Japanese government documents sent by the National Diet library, with the East Asian Library at the University of California in Berkeley also receiving a select number of the same documents.

（4）Acquisitions assistance

It has been mentioned earlier that the National Central Library is currently offering cataloging assistance to Cambridge University in England. It will be equally useful if some assistance can also be offered to other foreign libraries in acquisitions, especially in serial subscriptions. Over the years, many foreign libraries have experienced difficulties in finding reliable vendors in Taiwan for serials. Obviously, the amount of work involved in handling serial subscriptions and the low profit margin have discouraged many a vendor from accepting serial orders. The question has been raised as to whether it would be feasible for the National Central Library to render some assistance in this matter as a part of its international exchange program by acting as a facilitator. This could be done by introducing the local vendors it deals with in serials to libraries abroad, or, if it does not compromise its position as a national library, placing subscriptions for foreign libraries, but limited to those titles to which the National Central Library already subscribes. To meet the costs of subscriptions and postage, a fee should be assessed for this service. If this can be done, the National Central Library will have helped solve a major problem for foreign libraries in their acquisition of serial publications from Taiwan.

As already mentioned, the expansion of the scope of the National Central Library's international exchange program in recent years has been of great benefit to Chinese studies and the development of Chinese library collections in foreign countries. While the National Central Library, as the national library of the Republic of China, has as its primary responsibility the promotion of libraries and library services as an instrument for educational and cultural development in the Republic of China, it is assumed that the returns from its international exchange activities do contribute to the fulfillment of that mission. To the extent that this is true, a further expansion in the National Central Library's international exchange activity, some of which are outlined in this paper, may be worthy of consideration.

Notes

This article is adapted from a talk given at the International Conference on National Libraries — Towards the 21st Century, April 24, 1989 in Taipei and published in *Proceedings of the International Conference on National Libraries — Towards the 21st Century* (《邁向21世紀的國家圖書館國際研討會論文集》), 1994, pp. 954-966.

[1] Information supplied by Ms. Teresa Wang Chang, Chief, Bureau of International Exchange, National Central Library, ROC.

[2] T.H. Tsien, "First Chinese-American Exchange of Publications," *Harvard Journal of Asiatic Studies*, no. 25 (1964-65), pp. 19-30.

[3] Tsiang Fu-tsung, *guoli zhongyang tushuguan choubei zhi jingguo ji xianzai jinxing gaikuang* (Preparatory Work for the Establishment and the Current Status of the National Central Library), [Nanjing, 1936], p. 7. Also, Ku Juilan, "Guoli zhongyang tushuguan chubanpin guoji jiaohuan gongzuo "(International Exchange of Publications of the National Central Library), *Guoli zhongyang tushuguan gaikuang* "(The Current Status of the National Central Library), [Taipei], 1967, pp. 31-35.

[4] *Ibid.*

[5] Ku Juilan, *op. tit.*, pp. 32-33.

[6] *Ibid.*

[7] "Guoli zhongyang tushuguan gaikuang "(Current Status of the National Central Library), *Guoli zhongyangtushuguan guankan* (National Central Library Bulletin), 5:2 (New Series) (June 1972), p. 30.

[8] Figures supplied by Ms. Teresa Wang Chang, National Central Library, ROC.

[9] *Ibid.*

[10] "For a list of the conferences sponsored by the National Central Library and the book exhibits since 1980, see *Zhonghuaminguo tushuguan nianjian,*di 2ci (Library Yearbook of the Republic of China, Second Edition), comp. by National Central Library (Taipei, 1988), pp. 156-164. For an earlier list of international book fairs in which the National Central Library participated, see "Guoli zhongyang tushuguan gaikuang" (Current Status of the National Central Library), *Guoli zhongyangtushuguan guankan* (National Central Library Bulletin), 5:2 (New Series) (June 1972), pp. 19-21.

美國東亞圖書館協會的歷史沿革

1972年在芝加哥亞洲學會年會與（右起）余秉權（中國研究資料中心主任）、簡麗冰（香港大學馮平山圖書館館長）、吳文津、萬惟英（密西根大學亞洲圖書館館長）合影。

　　美國東亞圖書館是自第二次世界大戰之後才開始發展的。雖然二戰前有些大學已經提供東亞課程（那時稱遠東），但是提供全方面，包括人文和社會科學方面的課程還是二戰後的事。經過太平洋戰爭、日本的民主化、中國共產革命，以及韓戰，美國人意識到東亞在這個不斷變化的世界中的重要性，因此需要對其歷史和文化作更深入的認識。各大學得到基金會和政府提供的大量經費增加擴大其東亞教學和研究。50年後的今天，美國的東亞研究可以說是西方世界裡發展得最壯大和最全面的了。

　　隨著這個學術發展而來的就是建立圖書館收藏。雖然有些大學在二戰前就開始收藏東亞語文的書刊：耶魯大學開始於1878年，哈佛大學開始於

1879年，加州大學柏克萊分校開始於1896年，康乃爾大學1918年，哥倫比亞大學1920年，普林斯頓大學1926年，芝加哥大學1936年。但是迅速增長卻是1945年以後的事。如今被認為東亞資料主要收藏的密西根大學、胡佛研究院、加州大學洛杉磯分校都是1940年代才開始的。而伊利諾大學、印第安那大學、威斯康辛大學等等則遲至1960年代才成立。如今總共已經有80幾個東亞圖書館。其中最大的就是國會圖書館。國會圖書館於1869年開始收藏中文資料。到1995年6月為止，共收藏中日韓文圖書共計1,200萬冊，期刊156,000份，報紙3,350種，縮微膠捲562,000卷。[1] 據最新的資料，1994年度採購經費超過1千萬元。[2]

　　雖然認識到圖書館的館藏建設以及技術開發和公共服務的工作應該是各圖書館個別的責任，但是為了促進美國東亞圖書館能往正確的方向發展，有關人士一直都認為需要有全國性的籌畫和合作（後來加拿大也納入在內）。這篇報告就是要詳述為達到全國籌畫和合作的目的所作的努力，致使1967年成立亞洲學會東亞圖書館委員會（Committee on East Asian Libraries〔簡稱CEAL〕of the Association for Asian Studies〔簡稱AAS〕）的經過。

　　早在1948年，有一群東亞學者和圖書館館員組織了一個非正式組織——美國及國外東方圖書館全國委員會（National Committee on Oriental Collections in the U.S.A. and Abroad）來討論圖書館共同關心的事項。[3] 會上所討論的採購、編目、館員培訓的問題也是繼其以後各個不同委員會所關注的問題。這個委員會只持續了一年，於1949年就被遠東學會（Far Eastern Association，亞洲學會的前身）和美國圖書館協會（American Library Association，簡稱ALA）聯合贊助的東方圖書館聯合委員會（Joint Committee on Oriental Collections）取代。[4] 因此，一個正式的組織就成立了來解決美國東亞圖書館發展的問題。這個聯合委員會最大的成就就是得到國會圖書館的同意建立國會圖書館東方編目卡複製計畫（LC's Oriental Card Reproduction Project），將參加合作編目的圖書館送到國會圖書館的編目卡不經編輯審查印刷出售。但是這個聯合委員會，因為出席者少，兩個贊助組織又鮮有其他的共同興趣，所以只維持了三年，於1952年解散。[5] 美國圖書館協會有鑑於圖書館要是沒有作好其最基本功能之一的編目工作，就很難發展其他合作項目，遂於1954年在其編目和分類部設立了東方資料編目特別委員會（Special Committee on Cataloging Oriental Materials, Cataloging and Classification Division, ALA）。在1950年代初，這是一個頗具遠見的決定。雖然當時國會圖書館已經在進行複製中日韓文編目卡出售，但是全國還沒有統一的編目規則。每個圖書館都按照他們各自的格式和規則編目，甚至在主要款目（main entry）這個基本問題上都有不同的看法。這個特別委員會有系統地進行其工作。由於大部分的時間都花在中日韓文資料的編目問題上，因此於1957年便卸除其對其他東方語文資料的責任而改名為遠東資料特別委員會（Special Committee on Far Eastern Materials）。由於其重要性，ALA於1958年將此委員會作為其常務委員會而改稱為遠東資料委員會（Far Eastern Materials Committee, ALA）。[6] 委員會成員多為主要東亞圖書館有編目經驗的館長。該委員會與國會圖書館於1953年成立同樣性質的東方資料處理委員會（Oriental Processing Committee）緊密合作，從1954到1958年四年間仔細修改當時作為全國編目標準的《美國圖書館協會著者和題名款目編目條例》（*ALA Cataloging Rules for Author and Title Entries*）和《國會圖書館編目著錄條例》（*Rules for Descriptive Cataloging in the Library of Congress*）中有關東亞資料編目的所有條目。[7] 這兩個委員會經過四年的討論，包括大量的通信和無數的協調，獲得折衷的辦法，終於完成此項工作。經美國圖書館協會和國會圖書館批准後，經過主要修正後的規則遂被全國採用為中日韓文資料編目標準，一直沿用至今。後來又作了些修正納入《英美編目條例第二版》（*Anglo-American Cataloging Rules II*）。不久這兩個委員會又出版了《中日韓文資料編目羅馬拼音、大寫、標點、欄位手冊》（*Manual of Romanization, Capitalization, Punctuation, and Word Division for Chinese, Japanese, and Korean*）。這在北美東亞圖書館發展史上是個里程碑。因為使用統一的編目標準，便利了相互間編目卡的交換。從此消除了東亞圖書館合作上一個最基本的障礙。

　　這項重大的工作完成後，東亞圖書館將其注意力轉往資源開發和目錄管理方面迫切需要解決的問題上。於是促成遠東學會於1958年成立美國圖書館遠東資料委員會（Committee on American Library Resources on Far East，簡稱CALRFE）之舉。[8] 該委員會提出一份需要開展的工作方案，包括編輯全國東亞語文期刊聯合目錄、全國東亞語文叢刊目錄、全國東亞語文圖書目錄，以及按先後次序將中西文報紙、中韓文檔案資料拍攝成縮微膠捲向基金會和美國教育部申請經費。但是因為預算超過20萬，金額太大而沒有成功。[9] 但是從其他地方申請到一些少數的金額來完成了一些別的方案。美國學術團體協會和社會科學研究理事會合組的中國研究聯合委員會（Joint Committee on China of the American Council of Learned Societies and the Social Science Research Council）提供了經費合作採購了香港友聯研究所攝製的1,000餘卷縮微膠捲，包括1949年後中國出版的100種全國及地方報紙，200種期刊，超過萬件的剪報。這批縮微膠捲存放在芝加哥被稱作「圖書館的圖書館」的研究圖書館中心（Center for Research Libraries），免費提供給該中心的會員圖書館使用。[10] 美國國家科學基金會（National Science Foundation）提供經費編輯和出版了《1949-1960出版的中文期刊國際聯合目錄》（*Chinese Periodicals, International Holdings, 1949-1960*）和《中國的出版事業》（*Publishing in China*）。[11] 該基金會同時還協助國會圖書館完成《東方語文期刊聯合卡片目錄》的計畫（Union Card File of Oriental Vernacular Serials Project）。這個目錄包括美國主要20個東亞圖書館收藏的中日韓文期刊的編目卡片，以影印或膠捲出售。[12] 美國圖書館遠東資料委員會（CALRFE）於1963年向亞洲學會提議在台北成立中文研究資料中心（Chinese Materials and Research Aids Service Center）來從事協調聯絡和複製美國東亞圖書館所需要的已經絕版的書刊工作。該中心在亞洲學會贊助下於1964年成立。後來還得到美國學術團體協會和圖書館資源理事會（Council on Library Resources）聯合補助。[13] 自此之後，該中心（現已獨立經營）成功地為海外圖書館提供了不少他們缺少的資料。

　　美國圖書館遠東資料委員會也關注館員的素質問題。芝加哥大學遠東圖書館館長錢存訓兼該校圖書館學研究院的教授於1964年作了一個調查。在他的報告《美國遠東圖書館館員現狀與需求》（*Present Status and Personnel Needs of Far Eastern Collections in America*）中提出兩點建議：1. 選擇一些大學，由其圖書館學校和遠東語文系聯合設立關於遠東圖書館學的課程來訓練可在遠東圖書館工作的館員；2. 成立短期暑期培訓班，訓練在職的遠東圖書館館員，補充其在校長期進修學位所需的課程。[14] 第二項建議實施起來比較容易。1969年暑期威斯康辛大學和芝加哥大學分別舉辦了暑期班。後者由CALRFE發動。1988年西雅圖華盛頓大學也舉辦了一次。三者都得到美國教育部的經費補助。第一項聯合學位的建議，雖然有亞洲學會推薦，但是很難推行。因為要改變調動博士碩士生必修課程不是那麼容易的事。而況也難聘請到合格的教授。芝加哥大學可以說是唯一的圖書館學校和遠東語文系聯合提供高等學位課程，訓練遠東圖書館員的學校了。自1963到1981年已經有40多位學生得到這樣的碩士學位或者博士學位。也有些得到短期培訓證書的。[15]

　　錢教授於1957年開始還對1930年以來美國和加拿大東亞圖書館的成長作了一份非常有用的調查分析。其中包括各東亞圖書館的館藏，採購現狀，和經費來源。往後改為每五年作一次，直到1974/1975年。1979/1980年後就由東亞圖書館協會圖書館資源與利用專案小組（CEAL Task Force on Library Resources and Access）接任這份調查分析工作。[16] 1987/1988年後以簡單形式，僅包括不加分析的統計數字，在每年2月出版的東亞圖書館協會通訊（CEAL Bulletin，1995年10月第107期後改稱《東亞圖書館學報》〔*Journal of East Asian Libraries*〕）公布。

　　另外一項CALRFE關心的問題就是和外國圖書館的聯繫。1966年在密西根安娜堡舉辦的第27屆國際東方學大會（The 27th Congress of International Orientalists），CALRFE在美國圖書館資源委員會的贊助下舉辦了一場題為「亞洲研究的圖書館資源」（Library Resources in Asian Studies）的研討會。[17] 十幾個國家的代表出席作報告。這還是國際東方學會中第一次有這樣的研討會。國際東方學圖書館員協會（International Association of Orientalist Librarians）也是在那時成立的。往後每次大會都有舉辦這樣類似的研討會。

雖然十年來有以上的成就，CALRFE並沒有設立章程確定其功能、會員資格，或投票程序。所有工作都由亞洲學會董事會指派的會長一手包辦，甚至還要負責發行通訊。隨著東亞圖書館的增長，特別在1960年代，大家同意需要一個更正式的組織。因此1963年由亞洲學會指派七個會員作為執行組，及除會長以外另外一個沒有指定成員的總務委員會。[18] 但是像會員的性質（機關對個人），或投票程序仍舊沒有定奪。

新成立的執行小組對這些問題作了詳盡地討論於1967年草擬了一份《章程》，在當年芝加哥CALRFE年會上通過。[19] 也就是在那次年會上將CALRFE改稱為Committee on East Asian Libraries（CEAL）。《章程》明確宣稱CEAL的宗旨如下：1. 作為學者和圖書館員的論壇：討論共同關心的問題，並建議如何改善圖書館的設施；2. 促進圖書館館藏建設和書目管理；3. 改善館際和國際間的合作。《章程》也規定開放CEAL會員籍給「美國擁有東亞語文資料的圖書館以及亞洲學會會員」。在這種團體和個人的雙重會員建構下，每一個圖書館僅能有一人對圖書館合作方面的提案投票。「個別會員可以參加該委員會的所有討論，也可以被推舉指派為執行小組成員」。除了需要圖書館館方同意的提案外，個別會員可以在任何提案上投票。會長可以指派小組成員「負責長久計畫或者臨時任務，去調查特定的問題，並向執行小組提出建議為執行小組的參考和採取行動的基礎」。會長、執行小組成員（三位學者、三位圖書館員）以及小組成員的任期不得超過三年。還規定執行小組每年必須有三分之一成員要更換。「會長和執行小組成員不得繼任。必得等三年後再參選。」卸任的會長「必須任執行小組當然成員一年」，但「小組成員，如有需要，可以連任」。執行組長則是所有小組的當然成員。小組成員由會長指派。而會長和執行小組成員則由亞洲學會董事會指派。

在這裡應該注意到的就是《章程》宣示的宗旨正是CALRFE早已邁向的目標，只是現在將其明文宣布而已。《章程》還闡明會員資格，確定在職的任期，並將小組制度化 [20]。因此，清楚地制定CEAL作為一個專業組織該如何開展其業務。當然當時大家都明白《章程》不應該是一成不變的，需要隨著時間及隨著CEAL的需要而修改。所以在1976、1980、1984、1991、

1994年都作了修訂。其中以1980年的修訂最關重要。[21] 那就是改變選舉會長、執行小組成員以及小組組長的方法。這之前CEAL會長是自亞洲學會董事會指派的執行小組成員互選，小組組長則由CEAL會長指派。在CEAL會員越來越多情況下很多人不滿意這樣的方法。因此1979年成立了一個章程小組（Subcommittee on Procedures）來研究這個問題。經過一年研究了各種方案後，最後提議CEAL會長、小組組長，還有執行小組中圖書館員均由全體會員投票選舉。執行小組中學者成員繼續由亞洲學會中國和中亞研究委員會（China and Inner Asia Council）和東北亞研究委員會（Northeast Asia Council）推薦，然後由亞洲學會董事會指派。過去會員中所設的團體會員則被取消了。凡是訂閱東亞圖書館通訊（*CEAL Bulletin*）的亞洲學會會員就可申請成為CEAL會員，享有選舉權。章程上這樣的修訂遂將CEAL從一個任命的機構變成了一個選舉的機構，在CEAL的歷史上又豎立了一個里程碑。這個選舉制度至今還被遵循，為北美東亞圖書館館員提供更多的參與CEAL的事務的機會。

　　從此，CEAL完成了一連串的成就，我不必在此一一陳述。在這裡僅提一些最重要的。其中有由CEAL主持的，或由CEAL支持，有其會員積極參與的活動。CEAL技術服務小組（CEAL Subcommittee on Technical Processing）一直緊密和國會圖書館合作解決東亞資料編目的問題。上面已提到1958年修改的美國圖書館協會和國會圖書館編目規則使其更能適用於東亞圖書的編目工作就是一個好例子。但是還有些小問題還沒有解決。等到採用機讀格式線上編目時，新的問題又產生了。這個小組和國會圖書館共同花了好多時間來解決這些問題，以惠東亞圖書館界。1983年該小組將《英美編目條例第二版》（AACR II）中有關東亞資料編目的條例挑選出來，出版了《英美編目條例第二版──東亞出版品編目手冊》（*AACR II Workbook for East Asian Publications*）；1987年出版了《國會圖書館日文標題一覽表》（*List of Library of Congress Subject Headings Related to Japan*），1989年出版了《國會圖書館中文標題一覽表》（*List of Library of Congress Subject Headings Related to China*）以及《國會圖書館韓文及一般東亞標題一覽表》（*Library of Congress Subject Headings Related to Korea and East Asia in General*）。這些出版品都是非常方便的工具書，一直沿用至今。另一項CEAL的成就就是該會的通訊（*CEAL Bulletin*）。該通訊為北美東亞圖書館與館員間交流的媒介，也對北美東亞圖書館界有獨特的貢獻。[22] 這份通訊是1963年由當時的CALRFE會長，也是時任國會圖書館東方部日文組主任（後任該部中韓文組主任）埃德文・比爾（Edwin G. Beal, Jr.）開始的。他將CALRFE正在各東亞圖書館進行的項目，以及東亞圖書館界的活動發表在早年都是由現任會長編輯發行的通訊中（*Committee on American Library Resources on the Far East Newsletter*）。1967年協會改名為Committee on East Asian Libraries（簡稱CEAL），通訊也相應改為《東亞圖書館委員會通訊》（*Committee on East Asian Libraries Newsletter*）。由於篇幅的增加，每期除了關於活動的報導，又加上其他文章，因此1976年成立了一個出版小組（Subcommittee on Publications）專門負責編輯和發行這份通訊的工作。通訊名也改名為*Committee on East Asian Libraries Bulletin*，簡稱*CEAL Bulletin*。1995年當CEAL改稱為Council on East Asian Libraries時，通訊採用了一個全新名稱《東亞圖書館學報》（*Journal of East Asian Libraries*），但是還繼續其期數，為第107期。此通訊的歷史正代表北美東亞圖書館的發展過程，其重要性無疑地將隨著東亞圖書館的發展與日俱增。

　　CEAL作為東亞圖書館和館員的全國性組織，其他機構經常向其諮詢有關東亞圖書館的問題。1975年CEAL負責人士與福特基金會代表洽商對東亞圖書館補助經費的可能性後，提出了一份計畫書《支援東亞研究之圖書館發展與資金提供的優先次序》（*Priorities for the Development and Funding of Library Programs in Support of East Asian Studies*）。[23] 其後美國學術團體協會（American Council of Learned Societies，簡稱ACLS）指派一個指導委員會來探討東亞圖書館的問題（Steering Committee for a Study of the Problems of East Asian Libraries）。[24] ACLS邀請CEAL會員常石道雄（Warren Tsuneishi，國會圖書館東方部主任）和吳文津（哈佛大學哈佛燕京圖書館館長）作為指導委員會兩個東亞圖書館代表。指導委員會為了方便工作，委託不少人作了一系列報告。其中包括 CEAL 會員西雅圖華盛頓大學的盧國邦、芝加哥大學的錢存訓、加州大學柏克萊分校的湯涵文、匹茲堡大學的郭成棠、威斯康辛大學的李學博、國會圖書館的理查‧霍華德（Richard Howard），還有常石道雄、吳文津。此委員會於 1977 年提交一份題為《東亞圖書館：問題與展望》（*East Asian Libraries: Problems and Prospects*）的報告。[25] 在書目管理、館藏發展和使用、編目和人事三方面提出了建議，引起圖書館和學術界的深切關注。次年美國學術團體協會（ACLS），美國社會科學研究理事會（Social Science Research Council，簡稱 SSRC），和美國研究圖書館協會（Association of Research Libraries，簡稱 ARL）合組了東亞圖書館專案諮詢委員會（Joint Advisory Committee to the East Asian Library Program）來繼續指導委員會的工作。兩位 CEAL 會員：耶魯大學東亞圖書館館長金子英生（Hideo Kaneko）和吳文津被邀請作為委員。就是這個委員會的工作導致了東亞圖書館往後的線上編目。聯合諮詢委員會在其報告《自動化、合作與學術：1980 年代的東亞圖書館》（*Automation, Cooperation, and Scholarship: East Asian Libraries in the 1980's*）中陳述：「十幾年來東亞圖書館跟隨著國外區域研究發展，而不是跟隨著研究圖書館發展的方向，經歷了空前地快速發展以後……現在正處於一個十字路口」。[26] 在基金會和政府提供的經費減少時，東亞圖書館應該「以自動化作為主要規畫和管理的工具」另闢一條新路去分工合作，資源分享。其基石在於「就是要像一般研究圖書館處理西文圖書一樣將東亞文字輸入、處理、存儲、傳遞，並顯示在自動化系統中」[27]。此份報告所提出來對北美東亞圖書館發展重新定位的主張固然會改變東亞圖書館一貫的根本操作方式，但是卻被所有關心東亞圖書館者歡迎。

　　這項建議立刻被研究圖書館組織（Research Libraries Group，簡稱 RLG）採用。在基金會的贊助下 RLG 於 1983 年在其研究圖書館資訊網上（Research Libraries Information Network，簡稱 RLIN）推出中日韓文編目系統（CJK system）。於是，首創了任何一個圖書館的編目資料，其他圖書館都可以套錄，同時也可以在任何地方查詢的可能。[28] 1986 年連線電腦圖書館中心

（Online Computer Library Center，簡稱OCLC）也建立了其中日韓文編目系統。目前有40個東亞圖書館使用RLIN中日韓系統，47個東亞圖書館使用OCLC中日韓系統。到1996年3月RLIN CJK資料庫已經有1,460,574個編目著錄；同年4月OCLC CJK有1,042,283個編目著錄。[29] 兩系統間有交換編目資料的協定。只要有相應的RLIN CJK或者OCLC CJK軟體，就可以在網際網路上查詢。

CEAL還積極參與1980年研究圖書館中心國際研究委員會東亞研究小組（East Asian Subcommittee of the International Studies Committee, Center for Research Libraries，簡稱CRL）建議在該中心成立的擴大東亞資料採購專案（Expanded East Asian Acquisitions Program）。CEAL會員常石道雄、吳文津是該小組成員。這個專案的目的就是要用福特基金會提供的一筆龐大經費採購東亞研究資料來補充美國主要的東亞圖書館的收藏。CRL指派成立一個諮詢小組來執行這項工作。八位成員都是CEAL會員。

CEAL也協助成立了研究圖書館協會主持的中國研究資料中心（Center for Chinese Research Materials, Association of Research Libraries）。該中心是吳文津接受美國學術團體協會（American Council of Learned Societies）和社會科學研究理事會（Social Science Research Council）合組的當代中國研究委員會（Joint committee on Contemporary China）所委託調查全世界所收藏的當代中國資料後於1965年提出來的建議，在得到福特基金會贊助後於1968年成立，由美國研究圖書館協會管理。其主要任務就是去確認、收集、分發研究20世紀中國的重要研究資料。這些資料或者美國沒有收藏，或者只有少數美國圖書館收藏。該中心過去28年來，在各私人基金會及美國國家人文基金（National Endowment for the Humanities，簡稱NEH）的補助下一直以提供全世界大量稀有難得的出版物為責，為非營利機構。許多CEAL會員都曾經是該中心董事。目前董事會的成員都是CEAL會員。（中心目前已改組為獨立機構。）

近來CEAL直接參與的專案是研究圖書館協會（Association of Research Libraries，簡稱ARL）主持的外國採購專案（Foreign Acquisitions Project）。

這個專案的目的就是要調查主要研究圖書館採購外國資料工作中的優點和缺點，決定優先次序，然後針對所發現的問題提出具體的行動計畫。1992年ARL邀請CEAL參加這項專案，並就中文資料和日文資料採購問題提交報告。CEAL為此成立了兩個專案小組。中文由芝加哥大學的馬泰來主持，日文由密西根大學松戶保子（Yasuko Matsudo）主持。他們的報告和由當時CEAL行政小組（莫琳·多諾萬[Maureen Donovan]為主席）所作題為《東亞圖書館採購工作的一般趨勢》（*East Asian Collections*）調查一併呈交ARL，並陸續發表在CEAL通訊和ARL為此專案的總報告中。[30]

　　以上扼要提到的一些事蹟可以說明CEAL是個充滿活力的專業組織。從1948年幾個對東亞圖書館問題有興趣者非正式聚集在一起討論開始，近半個世紀以來東亞圖書館的發展突飛猛進。在促使東亞圖書館參與全國性計畫和合作專案上，CEAL扮演了舉足輕重的腳色，成為關鍵性的催化劑。前面已經提到CEAL成功地建立了全國編目規則，鼓勵支援了全國或者區域合作計畫，舉辦培訓班和宣導資源分享專案（下列東亞圖書館的書本目錄：加州大學柏克萊分校、芝加哥大學、康乃爾大學、哈佛燕京圖書館、胡佛研究院、密西根大學、國會圖書館，以及今日各圖書館的網上目錄都可用以代替全國聯合目錄，因而可以用達到資源分享的目的）。除此之外，CEAL還在亞洲學會年會中舉辦研討會，讓學者、圖書館員、資訊專家同聚一堂討論有共同興趣的題目。CEAL也是其他團體對有關東亞圖書館問題被諮詢的機構。簡而言之，作為北美東亞圖書館唯一的專業組織CEAL對北美東亞圖書館的發展已經扮演了一個非常重要的腳色，將來也必然如此。東亞圖書館如今已不再處於邊緣，而在北美圖書館主流中發展，不僅是各東亞圖書館及其館員不斷努力的結果，也是因為有CEAL這個組織來領導自願參與全國性的計畫和館際合作的工作。

附錄
東亞圖書館協會及其前身各委員會主席人名錄

1948-1949　美國及國外東方圖書館全國委員會
（National Committee on Oriental Collections in the U.S.A. and Abroad）

查理斯・布朗（愛荷華大學）
（Charles H. Brown, University of Iowa）

1949-1952　遠東學會與美國圖書館協會東方圖書館聯合委員會
（Joint Committee of the Far Eastern Association and the American Library
Associationon Oriental Collections）

查理斯・布朗（愛荷華大學）
（Charles H. Brown, University of Iowa）

1954-1956　美國圖書館協會東方資料編目特別委員會
（Special Committee on Cataloging Oriental Materials, American Library Association）

莫德・莫斯利（華盛頓大學）
（Maud L. Moseley, University of Washington）

1957　美國圖書館協會遠東資料特別委員會
（Special Committee on Far Eastern Materials, American Library Association）

雷蒙德・納恩（密西根大學）
（G. Raymond Nunn, University of Michigan）

1958-1970　美國圖書館協會遠東資料委員會
（Committee on Far Eastern Materials, American Library Association）

查理斯・漢密爾頓（加州大學柏克萊分校）
（Charles E. Hamilton, University of California at Berkeley）

1958-1967　亞洲學會美國圖書館遠東資料委員會
（Committee on American Library Resources on the Far East, Association for Asian Studies）

雷蒙德‧納恩（密西根大學）1958-1963
愛德溫‧比爾（Edwin G. Beal, Jr.）（國會圖書館）1963-1966
錢存訓（芝加哥大學）1966-1967

1967-1995　亞洲學會東亞圖書館委員會
（Committee on East Asian Libraries, Association for Asian Studies）

錢存訓（芝加哥大學）1967-1968
鈴木幸九（密西根大學）1968-1969
萬惟英（密西根大學）1970-1971
湯迺文（加州大學柏克萊分校）1971-1972
童世綱（普林斯頓大學）1973-1974
郭成棠（匹茲堡大學）1974-1976
吳文津（哈佛大學）1976-1979
金子英生（耶魯大學）1979-1982
理查‧霍華德（Richard C. Howard）（國會圖書館）1982-1985
李學博（印第安那大學）1988-1991
莫琳‧多諾萬（Maureen Donovan）（俄亥俄州立大學）1991-1994
肯尼士‧克萊因（Kenneth Klein）（南加州大學）1994-1995

1995-　亞洲學會東亞圖書館協會
（Council on East Asian Libraries, Association for Asian Studies）

肯尼士‧克萊因（南加州大學）1995-1997
馬泰來（芝加哥大學）1997-2000

注釋

本文為1996年8月28日在北京國際圖聯大會中國組委員會和北美亞洲學會東亞圖書館協
會合辦「演進中的學術圖書館與東亞研究專題研討會」發表的報告。原載《演進中的學術
圖書館與東亞研究專題研討會論文集》（北京：萬國學術出版社，1996），頁14-27；並載
《東亞圖書館學報》（*Journal of East Asian Libraries*），第110期（1996年10月），頁1-14。

[1]　〈美國東亞圖書館館藏現況〉（"Current Status of East Asian Collections in American
　　　Libraries"），《東亞圖書館學報》（*Journal of East Asian Libraries*），第110期（1996年
　　　10月），頁38-47。

[2]　同上，A45.缺國會圖書館經費數字。

[3]　伊莉莎白・赫夫（Elizabeth Huff），〈東方圖書館全國委員會，1948-1952〉（"The
　　　National Committee on Oriental Collections, 1948-1952"）載《東亞圖書館資料：美國圖
　　　書館遠東資料委員會第10屆年會上的工作報告》（*Library Resources on East Asia:
　　　Reports and Working Papers for the Tenth Annual Meeting of the Committee on American
　　　Library Resources on the Far East, Association for Asian Studies, Inc., at the Palmer
　　　House, Chicago, March 21, 1967*）（瑞士[Zug,Switzerland]：國際文獻公司[Inter
　　　Documentation Company AG], 1968），頁16-17；埃德文・比爾（Edwin G. Beal）〈東
　　　亞圖書館委員會：簡史〉（"The Committee on East Asian Libraries: A Brief History"）載
　　　《東亞圖書館通訊》（*Committee on East Asian Libraries Newsletter*），第41期（1973年
　　　9月），附錄I，頁42-43。

[4]　Huff，前引書，頁42。

[5]　同上。

[6]　雷蒙德・納恩（G. Raymond Nunn），〈東亞圖書館合作編目之發展，1954-1963〉
　　　（"Development of Cooperative Cataloging for East Asian Libraries, 1954-1963"）載《東
　　　亞圖書館資料：美國圖書館遠東資料委員會的10屆年會上的工作報告》（*Library
　　　Resources on East Asia: Reports and Working Papers for the Tenth Annual Meeting of the
　　　Committee on American Library Resources on the Far East...*），頁18。納恩博士（時任
　　　密西根大學東亞圖書館館長）被任命為該委員會的主席。他的繼任為加州大學柏克萊
　　　分校東亞圖書館的查理・漢密爾頓。

[7]　愛德溫・比爾（Edwin G. Beal, Jr.），〈試論錢存訓〈美洲東亞圖書館〉一文〉
　　　（"Discussion of Tsuen-Hsuin Tsien's paper. 'East Asian Collections in America'"）載錢存
　　　訓、霍華德・溫格（Howard Winger）合編《區域研究與圖書館——芝加哥大學圖書

館學院第13次年會，1985年5月20-22日》（*Area Studies and the Library, The Thirtieth Annual Conference of the Graduate Library School, May 20-22, 1965*）（芝加哥、倫敦：芝加哥大學出版社，1965），頁75-76。

[8]　Nunn, 前引書，頁19；Beal，〈東亞圖書館委員會：簡史〉（"The Committee on East Asian Libraries: A Brief History"），頁46。

[9]　Nunn，前引書，頁19-20。

[10]　錢存訓，〈美洲東亞圖書館〉，頁65-66。

[11]　Nunn，前引書，頁20。

[12]　Beal，〈簡史〉，頁47。

[13]　同上。又見《美國圖書館遠東資料委員會簡訊》（*Committee on American Library Resources on the Far East* Newsletter），第6期（1964年9月），頁4。

[14]　Beal，〈簡史〉，頁47。

[15]　錢存訓，〈遠東圖書館學的教育〉（"Education for Far Eastern Librarianship"）載《東方圖書館學的國際合作》（*International Co-operation in Oriental Librarianship*）（坎培拉〔Canberra〕：澳洲國家圖書館〔National Library of Australia〕，1972），頁108-115。

[16]　第一次調查報告發表在《圖書季刊》（*Library Quarterly*），第32卷，第1期（1959年1月）；更新後發表在同季刊，第35卷，第4期（1965年10月），後續者分別發表於《東亞圖書館委員會通訊》（*Committee on East Asian Libraries Newsletter*），第16期（1966年10月）；22期（1967年12月）；29期（1969年5月）；33期（1970年12月）；41期（1973年9月）；及48期（1976年3月）。最後一次，1974/1975年，以《美國東亞圖書館現況1974/1975》（*Current Status of East Asian Collections in American Libraries 1974/1975*）為名，並加附錄，包括〈美國圖書館東亞資料特藏〉（"Rarities and Specialties of East Asian Materials in American Libraries"）以及〈美國東亞圖書館出版品及有關美國東亞圖書館著作一覽表〉（"Publications by or About East Asian Collections in American Libraries"），由華盛頓特區美國研究圖書館協會中國研究資料中心（Washington, D.C.: Center for Chinese Research Materials, Association of Research Libraries）於1976年出版。這本書的簡化版，包括東亞資料特藏的附錄，以原書名發表於《亞洲學報》（*Journal of Asian Studies*），第36卷，第3期（1977年5月），頁499-514。

　　關於東亞圖書館的介紹可參閱：靳淑怡、郭成棠、弗蘭克·舒爾曼編《美國圖書館藏東亞資料》（Teresa S. Yang, Thomas C. Kuo, and Frank J. Shulman, *East Asian Resources in American Libraries*）（紐約：佳作書局〔Paragon Book Gallery〕，1977）；福田直美（Naomi Fukuda）編《美國日文藏書調查，1979-1980》（*Survey of Japanese Collections* in the United States, 1979-1980）（安娜堡［Ann Arbor］：密西根大學日本研究中心［Center for Japanese Studies, the University of Michigan]，1980）；李學博編《北美東亞圖書館指南》（Thomas H. Lee, *A Guide to East Asian Collections in North America,* New York: Greenwood Press, 1992）。

[17] Beal,〈簡史〉,頁48。

[18] 錢存訓,〈美國圖書館遠東資料委員會1966-1967活動報告〉（Report of CALRFE Programs and Activities for 1966-1967）載《東亞圖書館資料：美國圖書館遠東資料委員會的10屆年會上的工作報告》（*Library Resources on East Asia: Reports and Working Papers for the Tenth Annual Meeting of the Committee on American Library Resources on the Far East...*）,頁28。

[19]《章程》全文見《東亞圖書館通訊》（*Committee on East Asian Libraries* Newsletter）,第40期（1973年6月）,頁35-37；復載第49期（1976年3月）,頁53-54。

[20] CEAL自此成立了各小組和專案小組。當1995年東亞圖書館委員會改為東亞圖書館協會時,小組（subcommittee）改為委員會（committee）。目前有中文資料、日文資料、韓文資料、技術服務、圖書館科技應用、公共服務、出版七個常務委員會。

[21] 1984年修改後的《章程》見《東亞圖書館通訊》（*Committee on East Asian Libraries bulletin*）,第74期（1984年6月）,頁81-83。1980年在華盛頓全體會員大會討論修改《章程》的報告,見《東亞圖書館通訊》（*Committee on East Asian Libraries Bulletin*）,第62期（1980年6月）,頁3。

[22] 見馬庭理（Edward Martinique）,〈東亞圖書館通訊簡史〉（"A Short History of the *Committee on East Asian Libraries Bulletin*）載《東亞圖書館通訊》（*Committee on East Asian Libraries Bulletin*）,第101期（1993年12月）,頁vii-viii.馬庭理先生為通訊1987至1996年之編輯。

[23]《東亞圖書館通訊》（*Committee on East Asian Libraries Bulletin*）,第48期（1975年11月）,頁3。

[24] 同上。

[25]《東亞圖書館：問題與展望》（*Asian Libraries: Problems and Prospects, A Report and Recommendations*）東亞圖書館問題指導委員會的報告和建議書（華盛頓：美國學術團體協會［The American Council of Learned Societies]，1977）。

[26]《自動化,合作與學術：1980年代的東亞圖書館》（*Automation, Cooperation and Scholarship: East Asian Libraries in the 1980's*）,東亞圖書館專案諮詢委員會的終極報告（華盛頓：美國學術團體協會［The American council of Learned Societies]，1981）。

[27] 同上。金子英生（Hideo Kaneko）,〈RLIN中日韓文編目系統的歷史視角〉（"RLIN

CJK: A Historical Perspective"），載《東亞圖書館通訊》（*Committee on East Asian Libraries Bulletin*），第101期（1993年12月），頁37-42有更詳細報導。

[28] 參見金子英生（Hideo Kaneko），〈RLIN中日韓文編目系統與東亞圖書館界〉（"RLIN CJK and the East Asian Library Community"），載《資訊技術與圖書館》（*Information Technology and Libraries*）第12卷，第4期（1993年12月），頁423-426。

[29] 數目根據RLIN和OCLC的報告。這個數目預計在幾個大圖書館完成回溯轉換的工作後將有大幅增長。

[30] 有關日文資料的報告參見《東亞圖書館通訊》（*Committee on East Asian Libraries Bulletin*），第99期（1993年6月），頁97-127；有關中文資料的報告參見通訊第104期（1994年10月），頁101-118。執行小組的報告載《東亞圖書館通訊》，第100期（1993年10月），頁88-100。ARL的報告見朱塔・里德–斯科特（Jutta Reed-Scott）撰《學術，研究圖書館與環球出版》（*Scholarship, Research Libraries and Global Publishing*）（華盛頓：研究圖書館協會［Association of Research Libraries］, 1996）。華盛頓大學東亞圖書館崔允煥個人分別地撰寫了一篇〈美國韓文文獻收藏概況〉報告（"The Condition of Korean Collections in U. S. Libraries"）發表於《東亞圖書館通訊》（*Committee on East Asian Libraries Bulletin*），第99期（1993年6月），頁32-54。這篇報告也被收入Reed-Scott的報告中。

（胡嘉陽譯）

Organizing for East Asian Studies in the United States
The Origins of the Council on East Asian Libraries, Association for Asian Studies

The development of East Asian studies in the United States is basically a post-World War II phenomenon. Although a few universities offered some courses on East Asia (then referred to as the Far East) before World War II, full-fledged study of East Asia, in all the disciplines in the humanities and social sciences, did not develop until after the end of the Second World War. The war in the Pacific, the transformation of Japan into a democracy, the communist revolution in China, and the Korean War contributed to a heightening of American awareness of the importance of East Asia in a changing world, and of the need for better understanding of their histories and civilizations. The universities, with generous foundation and government support, responded by expanding their teaching and research programs on East Asia, and today, after fifty years, East Asian studies in the United States is probably the largest and the most comprehensive in the Western world.

A concomitant development in this academic enterprise was the building of library resources. Although some university libraries collected publications in the East Asian languages prior to World War II (Yale started in 1878, Harvard in 1879, UC-Berkeley in 1896, Cornell in 1918, Columbia in 1920, Princeton in 1926, and Chicago in 1936), they experienced their greatest growth after 1945; and a number of today's major collections, such as those at Michigan, Hoover, and UCLA came into being only in the late 1940s; and others, such as Illinois, Indiana, and Wisconsin, in the 1960s. At present, some 80 libraries, the largest being the Library of Congress which began collecting Chinese materials in 1869, are collecting publications in the Chinese, Japanese, and Korean languages, and had, as of June 1995, a combined holding of over 12 million volumes of books, more than 156,000 periodicals, 3,350 newspapers, and 562,000 reels of microfilm. [1] Their total acquisitions expenditures for fiscal year 1994 exceeded $10 million, according to the latest information available. [2]

While collection development, technical and public services are the responsibility of individual libraries, it was felt from the very beginning that a degree of coordination and planning would be necessary on the national level in order to promote an orderly development of East Asian libraries in the United States (Canada was included at a later date). This paper is an attempt to recount the efforts that eventually led to the formation in 1967 of the Committee on East Asian Libraries (CEAL) of the Association for Asian Studies (AAS) which became the *de facto* association of East Asian libraries and librarians in North America.

As early as 1948 a group of scholars and librarians got together to organize an informal National Committee on Oriental Collections in the U.S.A. and Abroad to discuss library matters of mutual concern. [3] The problems they discussed — acquisitions, cataloging, and training of personnel — were to occupy much of the time of the various successor committees in later years. This group existed for just one year and was replaced in 1949 by the Joint Committee on Oriental Collections, sponsored by the Far Eastern Association (the precursor of the Association for Asian Studies) and the American Library Association (ALA). [4] Thus an official body was established with the specific purpose of dealing with die developmental problems of East Asian Collections in the United States. The Joint Committee lasted for three years. Its principal accomplishment was the agreement by the Library of Congress to reproduce for purchase unedited Chinese and

Japanese catalog cards sent in by cooperative libraries under LC's Oriental Card Reproduction Project. The Joint Committee, for reasons of poor attendance and the fact that the two sponsoring associations had few common members, was abolished in 1952. [5] But the recognition that any cooperative development of East Asian libraries in the United States would be impossible without a satisfactory resolution of one of the basic functions of a library, that of cataloging, prompted the ALA to appoint in 1954 a Special Committee on Cataloging Oriental Materials, under its Cataloging and Classification Division. This was a far-sighted decision because, in the early 1950s, even as LC was proceeding with its Oriental Card Reproduction Project, there was no national standard for cataloging Chinese, Japanese, or Korean materials. Every library was using its own format and following its own rules. Indeed, there was even disagreement on such basic matters as the choice of main entry. The Special Committee went about its work systematically, but since it spent most of its time on materials in the East Asian languages, it dropped responsibility for materials other than East Asian and was renamed in 1957 the Special Committee on Far Eastern Materials. In the following year, because of the importance of its work, it was made a standing committee of the ALA under the name Far Eastern Materials Committee. [6] Members of this committee were mostly heads of major East Asian libraries who had cataloging experience. A parallel body, the Oriental Processing Committee, which had been in existence at the library of Congress since 1953, worked closely with the ALA Committee to amend the *ALA Cataloging Rules far Author and Title Entries* and the *Rules for Descriptive Cataloging in the Library of Congress*, which together comprised at that time the American national standards for cataloging, so that they could be more effectively applied to East Asian materials. [7] The two committees worked through the *ALA Rules* and the *LC Rules* in the most meticulous fashion, and amended every rule that had implications for cataloging East Asian materials. Four years' continuous work, from 1954 to 1958, involving an extremely voluminous correspondence between the two committees and a number of compromises and adjustments, saw the completion of a major series of amendments to the two sets of rules, which were then approved by both the ALA and LC and adopted as national standards; and they remain so to this day, with modifications as incorporated in the *Anglo-American Cataloging Rules II (AACR II)*. Shortly afterwards, the Far Eastern Materials Committee and the Library of Congress also issued a *Manual of Romanization, Capitalization, Punctuation, and Word Division for Chinese, Japanese, and Korean* which has since served as the guide in cataloging East Asian materials. This development is a milestone in the history of East Asian libraries in the United States and Canada, for the adoption of the amendments made possible for the first time a cataloging standard which facilitated the exchange of bibliographical records and solved a basic problem that had until that time inhibited the cooperative development of East Asian libraries.

With this task accomplished, East Asian libraries turned their attention to the other pressing problems of national resource development and bibliographical control. In 1958 the Association for Asian Studies, at the urging of East Asian libraries, established the Committee on American Library Resources on the Far East (CALRFE). [8] CALRFE developed a list of desiderata that included the compilation of a union list of East Asian language serials, a union list of East Asian series, a national union catalog of East Asian books, and a series of priorities for the microfilming of Western and Chinese language newspapers and Chinese and Korean archival materials. The proposal was submitted to foundations and the U.S. Department of Education for funding, but it was unsuccessful because of the size of the request, estimated at $200,000. [9] However, more modest funding was received from other sources for some other projects. The Joint Committee on Contemporary China, of the American Council of Learned Societies and the Social Science Research Council, provided funds for the cooperative acquisition of more than 1,000 reels of microfilm, containing 100

Chinese national and local newspapers, 200 periodical titles, and over one million newspaper clippings which had been prepared by the Union Research Institute in Hong Kong, all from 1949. The microfilms were deposited at the Center for Research Libraries (CRL), the "libraries' library" in Chicago, and have since been available on loan to CRL member libraries free of charge. [10] Funds were also received from the National Science Foundation to support the compilation and publication of *Chinese Periodicals, International Holdings, 1949-1960,* and the researching and publication of *Publishing in China.* [11] The National Science Foundation also supported the Union Card File of Oriental Vernacular Serials Project at the Library of Congress, which was a union list of the holdings of 20 major East Asian libraries in the United States. [12] Microfilm and photocopies of this list, in the form of the contributing libraries' holding cards, were made available for purchase.

In 1963 CALRFE developed a proposal to establish a Chinese Materials and Research Aids Service Center in Taipei, under AAS auspices, for the purpose of coordinating and reprinting out-of-print editions of titles needed by American libraries. With AAS approval and with initial grants from it, as well as from the American Council of Learned Societies and the Council on Library Resources, the Taipei Center was set up and began operation in the fall of 1964. [13] Since then the Taipei Center, now independent, has succeeded in filling a number of gaps on many library shelves around the world.

CALRFE also paid attention to personnel needs. Professor T.H. Tsien, then of the Graduate Library School and Curator of the Far Eastern Library at the University of Chicago, undertook a survey of this problem, and made a report in 1964 under the title "Present Status and Personnel Needs of Far Eastern Collections in America" for CALRFE. He made two recommendations: establishing "a joint program for Far Eastern librarianship between the library school and the Far Eastern language department in each of a number of selected universities," and establishing short-term summer institutes for "Far Eastern personnel to supplement the long-term special program for advanced degrees." [14] The second was easier to implement, as evidenced by the three summer institutes that have been held since then: one at the University of Wisconsin and another at the University of Chicago, both in 1969 (the latter was sponsored by CALRFE), and one at the University of Washington in 1988. All three were funded by the U.S. Department of Education. The joint program proposal, although endorsed by the AAS, proved much more difficult to carry out, as it would have necessitated an adjustment in the course requirements for advanced degrees at most universities, and those requirements were not easily amenable to change. The University of Chicago was the only university where such a program was initiated.

Prof. Tsien also began compiling, in 1957, an extremely useful survey of the growth of East Asian collections in the United States and Canada since 1930, with analysis. The survey, which was later repeated at 5-year intervals, contained information on libraries' holdings, current status of acquisitions, and sources of financial support. The 1974/1975 survey was his last effort; the survey for 1979/1980 was compiled by the CEAL Task Force on Library Resources and Access. [15] It has, since 1987/1988, been continued by a simplified annual statistical compilation, also conducted by CEAL. The compilation contains the same categories of information as collected by the earlier surveys, but without analysis. It has been appearing each year in the February issue of *CEAL Bulletin* (renamed *Journal of East Asian Libraries* with no. 107 (Oct. 1995).

Another CALRFE concern was liaison with foreign libraries. In 1966 it initiated a library panel at the 27th Congress of International Orientalists to be held in Ann Arbor, Michigan, that year. Panelists from a dozen countries were invited, with funds provided by the Council on Library Resources, to present papers on the theme "Library Resources in Asian Studies." [16] It was at this meeting that the International Association of Orientalist Librarians was established. The precedent having been set, similar library panels were held at the later meetings of the Congress.

Notwithstanding its accomplishments, CALRFE for almost a decade operated without a charter setting forth its functions, membership requirements, or voting procedures. The committee was run almost single-handedly by a chairperson, appointed by the board of directors of the Association for Asian Studies, who also was responsible for putting out a newsletter. However, as the number of libraries grew, particularly in the 1960s, it was agreed that a more formal organization was needed. In 1963 CALRFE was reorganized with an executive group of seven members, appointed by the Association for Asian Studies, and a general committee of unspecified membership in addition to the chairperson. [17] But matters such as the nature of membership（institutional vs. individual）and voting procedures remained to be clarified.

The new Executive Group deliberated on these matters at length, and proposed in 1967 a set of *Procedures* which was adopted at CALRFE's annual meeting held in Chicago that year. [18] It was at this time that the name of the organization was changed from Committee on American Library Resources on the Far East（CALRFE）to Committee on East Asian Libraries（CEAL）of the Association for Asian Studies. The *Procedures* set forth the objectives of CEAL as follows:

（1）to serve as a faculty-librarian's forum for the discussion of problems of common concern and to recommend programs for the improvement of library facilities;（2）to promote the development of library resources and bibliographical controls; and（3）to improve inter-library and international cooperation and services.

Membership would be open to "institutions in America with library

collections on East Asia and to members of the Association for Asian Studies."
Under this two-tier membership, each institution would be represented by one
person with one vote on projects involving institutional cooperation. Individual
members would be "eligible to participate in all deliberations of the committee,
and to be nominated and appointed to the Executive Group and subcommittees,"
but could vote only on matters other than those requiring institutional approval,
which right was reserved for institutional members. The subcommittees would be
appointed by the chairperson "for permanent projects or for temporary
assignments" to "investigate specific problems as assigned and present findings
and recommendations to the Executive Group for consideration and action." The
term of office of the chairperson, members of the Executive Group (three faculty
members and six librarians), and the subcommittees was fixed at not more than
three years, with the stipulation that one-third of the Executive Group membership
would be replaced each year, and that "no chairperson or member of the Executive
Group may succeed himself but he may be re-elected after a period of three
years," but the immediate past chairperson "shall serve *ex officio* in the Executive
Group for one year." Members of subcommittees, however, "may be reappointed
to serve more than one term, if necessary," and the chairperson of the Executive
Group "shall serve as an *ex officio* member on all subcommittees." With the
exception of the subcommittee members, who were to be appointed by the
chairperson, all others — the chairperson and members of the Executive Group —
would be appointed by the board of directors of the Association for Asian Studies.

It is important to note that the objectives of CEAL, as stated in the
Procedures, were exactly those which had guided the work of CALRFE, but were
now officially pronounced in a written document. The *Procedures* also clarified
the question of membership, fixed the terms of office of officers, and
institutionalized the subcommittees. [19] It was a clear outline of how CEAL
should conduct its business as a professional organization. It was realized at the

time, however, that the *Procedures* should not remain static, and that revisions would be necessary from time to time in order to keep it up to date to meet CEAL's needs. That is what happened in the following years. A series of revisions and amendments were adopted in 1976, 1980, 1984, 1991, and 1994, of which the 1980 amendments are of the utmost importance. [20] The most significant provision in the 1980 revision was the change of method in selecting the CEAL chairperson, members of the Executive Group, and the chairpersons of subcommittees. Up to that time, the CEAL chairperson was elected by the Executive Group from among its own members, who were appointed by the board of directors of the Association for Asian Studies, and the chairpersons of the subcommittees were in turn appointed by the CEAL chairperson. This method of selection was not satisfactory to the increasingly large CEAL membership, who wanted a change. A Subcommittee on Procedures was appointed in 1979 to study the problem and conduct a full-scale review of the existing *Procedures*. Following a full year's work examining various options, the Subcommittee recommended that the CEAL and subcommittee chairs and the librarian members of the Executive Group be popularly elected by the membership (the faculty members of the Executive Group would continue to be nominated by the China and Inner Asia Council and the Northeast Asia Council of the AAS from among their own members, and to be appointed by the board of directors of AAS), that the category of institutional membership be abolished, and that any AAS member might become a CEAL member by subscribing to the *CEAL Bulletin*, with the option of not becoming one if the person so desired. A subscriber who had elected to join CEAL would be considered a CEAL member in good standing and with voting rights. The adoption of these revisions, which transformed CEAL from an appointive to an elective organization, marked another milestone in the history of CEAL. And elections have been held to this day, making possible a much wider participation in the management of CEAL affairs by librarians from East Asian libraries of all sizes and from all parts of North America.

CEAL has since had a long list of accomplishments, but that is not the focus of this paper. However, a few highlights may be mentioned here. Some of these were under direct CEAL auspices, and some were facilitated and supported by CEAL with the active participation of its members. The CEAL Subcommittee on Technical Processing has been working closely, since even before CEAL days, with the Library of Congress on problems of cataloging East Asian materials. The 1958 amendments to the *ALA Rules* and *LC Rules*, as mentioned earlier in this paper, made the rules more applicable to East Asian publications. However, minor problems remain, and the adoption of on-line cataloging using the MARC format has presented new problems that must also be dealt with. The Subcommittee and the Library of Congress have devoted a great deal of time to addressing these problems, with benefit to the entire East Asian library community. This cooperative work is continuing. The Subcommittee also compiled and in 1983 published the *AACR II Workbook, Far East Asian Publications*, which contains all the rules, selected from AACR II, which are relevant to cataloging East Asian materials. In 1987 it issued a *List of Library of Congress Subject Headings Related to Japan*, and in 1989 a *List of Library of Congress Subject Headings Related to China*, and *Library of Congress Subject Headings Related to Korea and East Asia in General*. These publications have proven to be very handy references, whose usefulness will endure for many years to come. Another service CEAL provides, which has served as an excellent medium of communication among East Asian libraries and librarians and has made a unique contribution to East Asian librarianship in North America, is the publication of the *CEAL Bulletin*. [21] This publication was begun in 1963 by Edwin G. Beal, Jr., formerly head of the Japanese Section and later head of the Chinese and Korean Section of the Orientalia Division of the Library of Congress, as the *Committee on American Library Resources on the Far East* (CALRFE) *Newsletter,* when Dr. Beal was the chairperson of CALRFE. The *Newsletter* reported on ongoing CALRFE projects and activities at individual libraries and in the East Asian library community at large, and was, in the early years, compiled and distributed by whoever was the chairperson at the time. When CALRFE became CEAL in 1967, the name of the *Newsletter* was changed to *Committee on East Asian Libraries Newsletter* accordingly. The increase in copy for each issue, with the addition of articles to reports on activities, prompted CEAL in 1976 to appoint a Subcommittee on Publications to be responsible for the editing and distribution of the publication, and the name was changed to *Committee on East Asian Libraries Bulletin (CEAL Bulletin)*. Again, when CEAL was renamed the Council on East Asian Libraries in 1995, the publication adopted a new name *Journal of East Asian Libraries,* but continued with the numbering system, as no. 107. The history of the publication reflects the growth of East Asian libraries in North America, and its importance will undoubtedly grow as the field develops further.

As the national organization of East Asian libraries and librarians, CEAL has been consulted by other organizations on a range of problems concerning East Asian library matters. In 1975 officers of CEAL met with representatives of the Ford Foundation to discuss possible support of East Asian libraries, and submitted a statement on the "Priorities for the Development and Funding of Library Programs in Support of East Asian Studies." [22] Following that, in the same year, the American Council of Learned Societies (ACLS) appointed the Steering Committee for a Study of the Problems of East Asian Libraries, composed of scholars, librarians, and university officials. [23] Warren Tsuneishi (then Chief, Orientalia Division, Library of Congress) and Eugene Wu (Librarian, Harvard-Yenching Library, Harvard University) were the two CEAL members invited to join the Steering Committee. As a guide to its work, the Steering Committee commissioned a series of papers, a number of them written by members of CEAL, including Karl Lo, (then at the University of Washington), T.H. Tsien (then at the

University of Chicago), Warren Tsuneishi, Weiying Wan (University of Michigan), Raymond Tang (then at the University of California, Berkeley), Eugene Wu, Thomas Kuo (then at die University of Pittsburgh), Thomas Lee (then at University of Wisconsin) and Richard·Howard (then at the Library of Congress). The Steering Committee made a report in 1977 on "East Asian Libraries: Problems and Prospects" with recommendations for bibliographical control, collection development and access, and technical and personnel matters. [24] The report attracted significant attention in library and academic circles. In the following year the American Council of Learned Societies, together with the Social Science Research Council and the Association of Research Libraries, co-sponsored the Joint Advisory Committee to the East Asian Library Program in order to continue the work begun by the Steering Committee. Two CEAL members were again invited to join this new committee: Hideo Kaneko (Curator, East Asian Collection, Yale University) and Eugene Wu. It was the work of this Committee that led to online cataloging in East Asian libraries at a later date. In its report on "Automation, Cooperation, and Scholarship: East Asian Libraries in the 1980's," the Joint Advisory committee stated that "after a decade of unprecedented growth along a course linked primarily to foreign areas studies programs rather than to the development of research libraries in general... East Asian libraries were at a crossroad." [25] With the lessening of federal and foundation funding, they ought to embark upon a new course of sharing work, materials, and access, and of relying "on automation as a principal planning and management tool." The keystone to this, according to the report, "is the capability to input, manage, store, transmit, display and output bibliographic records containing East Asian vernacular characters in exactly the same automated systems already created to perform similar functions for Western language material and general research libraries." [26] This basic reorientation of the course of development of East Asian libraries in North America, as advocated in the report, would fundamentally change the way East Asian libraries operate, but it was welcomed by all concerned.

The immediate result of the Joint Advisory Committee's recommendation was the decision by the Research Libraries Group（RLG）to introduce in 1983, with foundation support, the CJK（Chinese, Japanese, Korean）enhancements to the Research Libraries Information Network（RLIN）, RLG's operating arm. This move made possible for the first time the creation of cataloging records at one library which could then be copied by other libraries and also viewed by researchers anywhere. In 1986 the Online Computer Library Center（OCLC）also established a CJK program, a similar bibliographic utility for cataloging Chinese, Japanese, and Korean materials online. These are the two systems in use today （40 libraries use RLIN; 47 libraries use OCLC）. As of March 1996, the RLIN CJK database contains 1,460,574 unique records; and, as of April 1996, the OCLC CJK database contains 1,042,283 records. [27] There is a CJK records exchange agreement between the two, and the records are accessible on the Internet with the appropriate RLIN CJK or OCLC CJK software.

Another project in which CEAL was actively involved was the establishment by the Center for Research Libraries（CRL）of an Expanded East Asian Acquisitions Program in 1980. The program was recommended by CRL's East Asian Subcommittee of the International Studies Committee; two of its members were CEAL members, Warren Tsuneishi and Eugene Wu. The purpose of the program was to acquire, with a substantial Ford Foundation grant, research materials that would supplement the holdings of the major East Asian collections in the United States. An advisory panel was appointed to implement the program; the eight panel members were all members of CEAL.

Still another project to which CEAL lent its support was the founding of the Center for Chinese Research Materials（CCRM）in 1968 under the auspices of the Association of Research Libraries（ARL）with a Ford Foundation grant. The establishment of CCRM was the principal recommendation in a report made by Eugene Wu in 1965 for the Joint Committee on Contemporary China of the American Council of Learned Societies and the Social Science Research Council, following his world-wide survey of the availability of research materials on contemporary China. The purpose of the Center was to identify, assemble, and distribute important research materials on 20th-century China, which were either unavailable or available only in a few American libraries. This not-for-profit enterprise, now independently incorporated, was generously supported by foundations and the National Endowment for the Humanities (NEH), and has been singularly responsible for making available to libraries world-wide a great quantity of rare and difficult-to-obtain publications during the last twenty-eight years. Many CEAL members have served on CCRM's Advisory Board; and its current board members are all CEAL members.

A more recent development in which CEAL was directly involved was the Association of Research libraries' (ARL) Foreign Acquisitions Project, an effort to assess the current strengths and weaknesses of the major research libraries' foreign acquisitions, to determine their needs and priorities, and to offer concrete action proposals to address the identified problems. In 1992 ARL asked CEAL to participate in the project, with the specific request that CEAL present a report each on Chinese and Japanese materials. Two Task Forces were appointed by CEAL for this purpose. The task force on China was chaired by Tai-loi Ma (University of Chicago), and the one on Japan by Yasuko Matsudo (University of Michigan). Their reports, together with a state-of-the-field survey, titled "East Asian Collections" by the CEAL Executive Group (Maureen Donovan, Chair), were submitted to ARL and subsequently published in the *CEAL Bulletin* and in ARL's final report on its Foreign Acquisitions Project. [28]

These highlights illustrate the vibrant nature of CEAL as a professional organization. During the almost half a century since an informal group of interested parties got together to discuss East Asian library problems in 1948, East Asian libraries in North America have developed by leaps and bounds. In this development CEAL has played a pivotal role as a catalyst in national planning and coordination. As already mentioned in this paper, it has worked successfully on national standards, and encouraged and supported national and regional cooperative projects, training institutes, and resource sharing programs（the printed catalogs of the East Asian libraries at the University of California in Berkeley, University of Chicago, Cornell University, Harvard-Yenching Library, Hoover Institution, University of Michigan, and the Library of Congress, as well as the current online catalogs of all the libraries, serve quite adequately as a national union catalog for this purpose）. It has contributed to scholarship by the panels it organized at the annual meetings of the Association for Asian Studies to bring librarians, scholars, and information specialists together to discuss matters of mutual concern, and it also has been the organization to which others have turned for expert advice on problems concerning East Asian library issues. In short, as the only professional organization of East Asian libraries and librarians in North America, CEAL has played, and will continue to play, a crucial role in the development of East Asian studies in the United States and Canada. The fact that East Asian libraries no longer find themselves in a backwater, but in the mainstream of North American library development is the result not only of the indefatigable work of the libraries and librarians themselves, but, equally importantly, also of the existence of a national organization through which national planning and interlibrary cooperation can be effected through voluntary efforts.

APPENDIX

Chairpersons of the Council on East Asian Libraries and its predecessor committees:

1948-1949　National Committee on Oriental Collections in the U.S.A. and Abroad

　　　　　Charles H. Brown, University of Iowa

1949-1952　Joint Committee of the Far Eastern Association and the American Library Association on Oriental Collections

　　　　　Charles H. Brown, University of Iowa

1954-1956　Special Committee on Cataloging Oriental Materials, American Library Association

　　　　　Maud L. Moseley, University of Washington

1957　　　Special Committee on Far Eastern Materials, American Library Association

　　　　　G. Raymond Nunn, University of Michigan

1958-1970　Committee on Far Eastern Materials, American Library Association

　　　　　Charles E. Hamilton, University of California at Berkeley

1958-1967　Committee on American Library Resources on the Far East, Association for Asian Studies

　　　　　G. Raymond Nunn (University of Michigan), 1958-1963
　　　　　Edwin. G. Beal, Jr. (Library of Congress), 1963-1966

Tsuen-Hsuin Tsien (University of Chicago), 1966-1967

1967-1995　Committee on East Asian Libraries, Association for Asian Studies

Tsuen-Hsuin Tsien (University of Chicago), 1967-1968

Yukihisa Suzuki (University of Michigan), 1968-1969

Weiying Wan (University of Michigan), 1970-1971

Raymond N. Tang (University of California, Berkeley), 1971-1972

Shih-kang Tung (Princeton University), 1973-1974

Thomas C. Kuo (University of Pittsburgh), 1974-1976

Eugene W. Wu (Harvard University), 1976-1979

Hideo Kaneko (Yale University), 1979-1982

Richard C. Howard (Library of Congress), 1982-1985

Thomas H. Lee (Indiana University), 1988-1991

Maureen Donovan (Ohio State University), 1991-1994

Kenneth Klein (University of Southern California), 1994-1995

1995-　Council on East Asian Libraries, Association for Asian Studies

Kenneth Klein (University of Southern California), 1995-1997

Tai-loi Ma (University of Chicago), 1997-2000

Notes

This paper was published in *Proceedings of the Special Conference on the Evolving Research Library and East Asian Studies in Conjunction with the 1996 IFLA Conference in Beijing, August 25-31, 1996, Beijing, China* (Beijing: International Academic Publishers, 1996), pp. 14-27; also published in *Journal of East Asian Libraries*, no. 110（1996）, pp. 1-14.

[1]　"Current Status of East Asian Collections in American Libraries, 1994/1995," *Journal of East Asian Libraries*, no. 108（Feb 1996）, pp. 38-47.

[2] *ibid.*, p. 45. The figure does not include expenditures by the Library of Congress which were not reported.

[3] Elizabeth Huff, "The National Committee on Oriental Collections, 1948-1952", Association for Asian Studies, Inc. at the Palmer House, Chicago, *Library Resources on East Asia: Reports and Working Papers for the Tenth Annual Meeting of the Committee on American Library Resources on the Far East..., March 21, 1967* (Zug, Switzerland: Inter Documentation Company, AG, 1968), pp. 16-17. Also Edwin G. Beal, Jr., "The Committee on East Asian Libraries: A Brief History," *Committee on East Asian Libraries Newsletter,* no. 41 (Feb 1973), Appendix 1, pp. 42-43.

[4] Huff, *op cit.*, p. 17; Beal, *op cit.* p. 42.

[5] *ibid.*

[6] G. Raymond Nunn, "Development of Cooperative Cataloging and Resources for East Asian Collections, 1954-1963," *Library Resources on East Asia: Reports and Working Papers for the Tenth Annual Meeting of the Committee on America Library Resources at the Far East..., p. 18. Dr. Nunn, then head of the Asia Library, University of Michigan, was appointed chair of the committee; he was succeeded by Charles E. Hamilton of the East Asiatic Library (now East Asian Library) of the University of California in Berkeley.

[7] Edwin G. Beal, Jr., "Discussion of Tsuen-Hsuin Tsien's paper: East Asian Collections in America," in Tsuen-Hsuin Tsien and Howard W. Winger, ed., *Area Studies and the Library, the Thirtieth Annual Conference of the Graduate Library School, May 2-22, 1965* (Chicago: The University, of Chicago Press, 1965), pp. 75-76.

[8] Nunn, *op cit.*, p. 18; Beal,, "The Committee on East Asian Libraries: A Brief History," p. 46.

[9] Nunn, *op cit.*, pp. 19-20.

[10] Tsuen-Hsuin Tsien, "East Asian Collections in America," pp. 65-66.

[11] Nunn, *op cit.*, p. 20.

[12] Beal, "A Brief History," p. 47.

[13] *ibid.* Also *Committee on American Library Resources on the Far East Newsletter,* no. 6 (Sept 1964), p. 4.

[14] Beal, "A Brief History," p. 47.

[15] The first survey was published in the *Library Quarterly*, vol. 32, no. 1 (Jan 1959); this was updated in vol. 35, no. 4 (Oct. 1965), and further updates were subsequently published in the *Committee on East Libraries Newsletter* nos. 16 (Oct 1966), 22 (Dec 1967), 29 (May 1969), 33 (Dec 1970), 41 (Sept 1973), and 48 (Mar 1976). The last, for 1974/1975, was

also published as a separate volume titled *Current Status of East Asian Collections in American Libraries 1974/75* (Washington, D.C.: Center for Chinese Research Materials, Association of Research Libraries, 1976), with an appendix which includes, among other things, "Rarities and Specialities of East Asian Materials in American Libraries," and "Publications by or About East Asian Collections in American Libraries." A simplified version appeared, under the same title, also with a listing of "rarities and specialities," in The *Journal of Asian Studies*, vol. 36, no. 3 (May 1977), pp. 499-514.

For three other useful guides to East Asian libraries, see Teresa S. Yang, Thomas C. Kuo, and Frank J. Shubnan, *East Asian Resources in American Libraries* (New York: Paragon Book Gallery, 1977); Naomi Fukuda, *Survey of Japanese Collections in the United States, 1979-1980* (Ann Arbor: Center for Japanese Studies, the University of Michigan, 1980); and Thomas H. Lee, *A Guide to East Asian Collections in North America* (New York: Greenwood Press, 1992).

[16] Beal, "A Brief History," p. 48.

[17] Tsuen-Hsuian Tsien, "Report of CALRFE Programs and Activities for 1966-1967," *Library Resources on East Asia: Reports and Working Papers for the 10th Annual Meeting of the Committee on American Library Resources on the Far East...,* p. 28.

[18] For the full text of the *Procedures,* see *Committee on East Asian Bulletin*, no. 40 (June 1973), pp. 35-37. It was reprinted in no. 49 (Mar 1976), pp. 53-54.

[19] CEAL has since established a number of subcommittees and task forces that existed for various lengths of time. When the Committee on East Asian Libraries was renamed the Council on East Asian Libraries in 1995, the designation of "subcommittee" was replaced by that of "committee." At present, there are seven standing committees: Committee on Chinese Materials; Committee on Japanese Materials; Committee on Korean Materials; Committee on Technical Processing; Committee on Library Technology; Committee on Public Services; and Committee on Publications.

[20] The full text of the *Procedures*, as amended in 1984, is reproduced in *Committee on East Asian Libraries Bulletin*, no. 74 (June 1984), pp. 81-83. A report on the discussion of the revised Procedures at the 1980 CEAL Plenum Session, held in Washington, D.C., before its adoption, is available in the *Committee on East Asian Libraries Bulletin*, no. 62 (June 1980), p. 3.

[21] See Edward Martinique, "A Short History of the Committee on East Asian Libraries Bulletin," *Committee on East Asian Libraries Bulletin*, no. 101, (Dec 1993). pp. vii-viii.

Mr. Martinique was the editor of the Bulletin from 1987 to 1996.

[22] *Committee on East Asian Libraries Newsletter*, no. 48（Nov 1975）, p. 3.

[23] *ibid.*

[24] *East Asian Libraries: Problems and Prospects, A Report and Recommendations*, prepared by the Steering Committee for a Study of the Problems of East Asian Libraries（Washington, D.C.: The American Council of Learned Societies, 1977）.

[25] *Automation, Cooperation, and Scholarship: East Asian Libraries in the 1980's — Final Report of the Joint Advisory Committee to the East Asian Library Problem*（Washington, D.C.: The American Council of Learned Societies, 1981）, p. 18.

[26] *ibid.*

[27] Information from RLIN and OCLC. It is expected that the size of these two databases will increase rapidly in the next few years as a number of larger libraries complete their retrospective conversion work.

[28] For the "Report of the Task Force for ARL Foreign Acquisitions Project for Japanese Materials," see *Committee on East Asian Libraries Bulletin*, no. 99（June 1993）, pp. 97-127; for the "ARL Foreign Acquisitions Project Report on Chinese Materials," see *Committee on East Asian Libraries Bulletin*, no. 104,（Oct. 1994）, pp. 101-118. The report by the CEAL Executive Group was published in *Committee on East Asian Libraries Bulletin*, no. 100,（Oct. 1993）, pp. 88-100. For the ARL report, see *Jutta Reed-Scott, Scholarship, Research Libraries and Global Publishing*（Washington, D.C.: Association of Research Libraries, 1996）. Yoon-whan Choe of the East Asian Library. University of Washington, wrote another paper, independent of the ARL project, titled "The Condition of the Korean Collections in U.S. Libraries" which was published *in Committee on East Asian Libraries Bulletin*, no. 99（June 1993）, pp. 32-54. Ms. Choe's paper is also included in Reed-Scott's ARL report.

超越科技

1985年與哈佛大學圖書館館長維巴（Sidney Verba）教授及美國國際圖書館電腦中心（OCLC）亞洲及太平洋副總裁王行仁（Andrew H. Wang）合影。

　　我們今天在此慶祝美國連線電腦圖書館中心（Online Computer Library Center，簡稱OCLC）提供中日韓文服務20周年紀念。當我們在此慶祝時，令我想起過去沒有電腦的時代。那時候所有的業務都是用手工操作。50多年前當我在圖書館學校念書時，我們從來沒有聽說過電腦。放棄打字機用電腦來代替不是件容易的事。學習如何使用電腦也頗費時日。但是我還是學會了，並且對自動化也有了初步的認識。證明老狗還是可以被教耍新把戲的！因為自動化，我們的生活和過去再也不一樣了。

　　美國東亞圖書館自動化作業起步很晚。一直到1970年末，當其他研究圖書館早就開始用電腦作業時，東亞圖書館還滯留在傳統的手工時代。當亞洲學會東亞圖書館委員會於1975年3月向福特基金會申請資助時，所提交的計畫書《支援東亞研究之圖書館發展與資金提供的優先次序》（*Priorities for the Development and Funding of Library Programs in Support of East Asian Studies*）中的方案都是以傳統方式為準。那年年底福特基金會請美國學術團體協會（American Council of Learned Societies，簡稱 ACLS）成立一個「東亞圖書館問題指導委員會」來探討該計畫書所提出的問題（Steering Committee for a Study of the Problems of East Asian Libraries），開啟了一項意義重大的任務。指導委員會包括兩位研究東亞的教授，兩位東亞圖書館館長，一位大學圖書館館長，一位圖書館學教授，兩位大學教務長。經過兩年的討論研究，此委員會於1977年在書目管理，藏書建設，資料使用三個主要專案下作了報告和建議。這份題為《東亞圖書館的問題與展望》（*East Asian Libraries: Problems and Prospects*）的報告是「第一次對第二次世界大戰後幾十年間美國東亞圖書館從蓬勃發展到隨後緊縮的過程作出的一套有系統的分析」。[1] 但是除了概括性地提到「東亞圖書館必須要參加各種已經有的或者正在計畫中的自動化項目，以便融入美國圖書館的主流」外，[2] 很少涉及如何使用科技來解決該委員會報告中所提到的各種問題。

　　次年（1978年）美國學術團體協會（ACLS），繼而和美國社會科學研究理事會（Social Science Research Council，簡稱 SSRC），美國研究圖書館協會（Association of Research Libraries，簡稱 ARL）合組了「東亞圖書館專案聯合諮詢委員會」（Joint Advisory Committee to the East Asian Library Program）來「重新審查指導委員會所作的報告，特別要參考東亞學術及東亞圖書館界在該報告發表後所提出的意見。並且要監督執行對指導委員會的建議所作的任何修正方案」。[3] 有鑑於研究圖書館在自動化上突飛猛進，聯合諮詢委員會改變了其工作重點，期望為東亞圖書館另闢新路。在其1981年的報告中稱：「鑑於研究資訊情報不斷增長，經費永遠不足的情況下」，東亞圖書館應該「分工合作，共用資源。因此得依靠自動化作為計畫和管理的工具。最基本的原則就是要像一般研究圖書館處理西文圖書一樣將東亞文字輸入，存儲，轉換，並顯示在自動化系統中」。[4] 東亞圖書館引進新技術來營運的第一步就因此開始了。其後研究圖書館組織（Research Libraries Group，簡稱RLG）在福特基金會的贊助下於1983年在其研究圖書館資訊網（Research Libraries Information Network，簡稱RLIN）上推出中日韓文編目系統（CJK system）。三年後，美國國際圖書館電腦中心（OCLC）於1986年也推出了其中日韓文編目系統。今天我們在此慶祝它的20周年紀念。

美國國際圖書館電腦中心開始中日韓文編目系統雖然遲緩，但是發展神速。當我們慶祝其推出20年後的今天，其資料庫已經儲存中日韓文書目290萬條。是美國最大的中日韓文書目資料庫。世界各地的圖書館也都使用它。這些都得歸功於OCLC的技術工作人員。他們經年累月無休無止地將中日韓文的功能加進OCLC為其他語文設計的專案中，譬如由最近開始，中日韓文的編目工作也可以使用Connexion軟體了。同時美國國際圖書館電腦中心也為東亞圖書館提供其他方面的服務，特別是書目回溯轉換的工作。這些已經完成或者正在進行中的回溯工作不但對該個別圖書館重要，同時也可以增加美國國際圖書館電腦中心線上聯合目錄（WorldCat）中的中日韓文目錄以利學術研究。

為了提供給東亞圖書館更多更好的服務，OCLC非常配合東亞圖書館的需求。當使用該中心中日韓系統的圖書館想和其他OCLC的用戶團體（Users Group）一樣成立一個類似的組織以方便和OCLC溝通聯繫時，我向OCLC亞太部（OCLC Asia Pacific Services）負責人王行仁（Andrew H. Wang）先生提起這個想法，他馬上同意，並答應只要我們組織好，他們就會盡力支持。旋即由西雅圖華盛頓大學東亞館館長盧國邦（Karl Lo）幫忙起草組織條例，和王負責人商討後，美國國際圖書館電腦中心中日韓系統使用者團體（OCLC CJK Users Group）因而於1991年4月10日在新奧爾良正式成立。當我們在此紀念美國國際圖書館電腦中心中日韓系統成立20周年時，我們要向OCLC的遠見和領導及其20年來對東亞圖書館所作的貢獻致敬。我也趁此機會對王行仁先生和小鷹久子女士（Hisako Kotaka）的寶貴和慷慨的協助致謝。

　　新科技不僅僅改變了書目的管理方法，也改變了圖書館其他方面的工作方式，諸如採訪訂購和讀者服務。高科技還改變了圖書館收藏出版物的形式；因為不少書刊都在迅速地數位化了。因為這些空前的發展，現在已經出現了一批新一代精通科技的圖書館員。他們都在圖書資訊學院接受了科技和資訊管理的訓練。當科技已經而且會繼續影響我們的生活，工作，學習時，包括我們將來如何管理圖書館，這現象是很自然的。雖然科技的應用已經成了圖書館工作的核心，如果我們停下來提出下面這個問題也許也有它的啟發性：單單依靠科技，是否能讓我們達到圖書館存在的目的？

　　我相信沒有人會反對圖書館的核心就在它的收藏這個原理。我曾經在別的地方引用過費正請教授一句話，他說：「傑出的大學都有傑出的圖書館，如果沒有傑出的圖書館就不會有傑出的大學」。他所指的傑出的圖書館就是指有傑出收藏的圖書館。在此我要指出的問題就是在我們使用高科技來提供更好，更有效率的圖書館服務時，我們有沒有同時把足夠的注意力放在圖書館最主要的任務──藏書建設？近年來東亞圖書館界討論最熱烈的都是科技方面的題目。這可以從東亞圖書館協會網路及其年會各語文小組會議討論的題目上得到印證。這並不是說科技這個題目不重要，它實際上是非常重要的。問題是在這些討論中，是否有什麼欠缺的地方？我們是否需要去維護和發展我們的收藏，對我們前輩費了數十年工夫累積的西方最好的東亞圖書文獻給以同樣的關注？值得一提的是現在被數位化的資料大半是多年前收藏的資料，而非當前的出版物。我們是否應該追隨前輩，繼往開來去壯大我們的收藏以惠美國的東亞學術研究？

　　在這方面最關鍵的問題就是人才問題。東亞圖書館自動化作業能夠順利進行的原因是因為有足夠的從圖書資訊學院畢業，精通電腦，又懂得中日韓語文的圖書館員。我認為東亞圖書館還需要深諳東亞文化和文明，訓練有素的學科專家來作為我們的藏書建設者。我們除了需要管理員，電腦專家外，還需要學者型的圖書館員。我們從經驗得知僅憑能聽、說、讀、寫中日韓語文的雇員是不能夠把東亞圖書館的工作做好的。但是很不幸地有些當權者認為一個東亞圖書館員只要懂得本土語言，學科知識無關緊要。最近倫敦大學

亞非學院（SOAS）以只懂中文、日文的文書來代替藏書建設的館員，說後
者的職位是「多餘的」就是一個明顯的例子。幸好該學院最後還是被逼收回
了這個決定，恢復聘用專業人士。我們從此得到的教訓就是圖書館在致力於
管理和技術之外，要同時致力於發揮其學術功能，這樣才不至於被像SOAS
那樣無所根據也不可接受的決定所左右。東亞圖書館員當然也有責任以其專
業來取得大家的尊敬。

注釋

本文為2006年4月8日在舊金山為慶祝美國國際圖書館電腦中心成立中日韓系統20周年紀
念會上的致辭。載《東亞圖書館學報》（*Journal of East Asian Libraries*），第139期（2006
年6月），頁7-9。

[1]　《自動化、合作與學術：1980年代的東亞圖書館——東亞圖書館專案聯合諮詢委員會
　　報告》（*Automation, Cooperation and Scholarship: East Asian Libraries in the 1980's:
　　Final Report of the Joint Committee to the East Asian Library Program*）（紐約：美國學
　　術團體協會〔The American Council of Learned Societies〕，1981），頁1。

[2]　《東亞圖書館：問題與展望——東亞圖書館的問題研究指導委員會的報告與建議》
　　（*East Asian Libraries: Problems and Prospects: A Report and Recommendations. Prepared
　　by the Steering Committee for a Study of East Asian Libraries*）（紐約：美國學術團體協
　　會〔The American Council of Learned Societies〕，1977），頁40。

[3]　見[2] 聯合諮詢委員會雖然是新成立的，但是和指導委員會類似，由兩位研究東亞的
　　教授，兩位東亞圖書館館長（其中一位曾是指導委員會成員），兩位大學圖書館館
　　長。該聯合諮詢委員會主任為當然會員。

[4]　《自動化、合作與學術》，頁18。

（胡嘉陽譯）

BEYOND TECHNOLOGY

We are here to celebrate the twentieth anniversary of the OCLC CJK Service, and that brings me back to the pre-computer days when we did everything manually. When I was in library school more than fifty years ago, we never heard of computers. It was not easy to give up the old typewriter to make room for a computer, and learning how to use one took a while. But I learned, and also acquired rudimentary knowledge about automation, proving that you CAN teach old dogs new tricks! And life was never the same again.

East Asian libraries were late comers to automation. As recently as the late 1970s, when research libraries had already begun introducing new technology in their daily operations, we were still approaching our problems traditionally without reference to technology. For instance, when officers of the Committee on East Asian Libraries (CEAL) initiated talks with the Ford Foundation in March 1975 to discuss East Asian library support, the proposals made were all along traditional lines, and it was on the basis of these proposals, contained in a document entitled "Priorities for the Development and Funding of Library Programs in Support of East Asian Studies," that the Ford Foundation later on that year provided funds to the American Council of Learned Societies (ACLS) to appoint a Steering Committee for a Study of the Problems of East Asian Libraries. It was a significant undertaking with a committee that included two East Asian faculty members, two East Asian librarians, one university library director, one library educator, and two university provosts. Following a two-year study the committee submitted, in 1977, its report with recommendations, covering three major areas of concern: bibliographical control, collection development and access, and technical and personnel matters. The report was "the first systematic and analytical presentation of the extraordinary growth and subsequent retrenchment in the development of America's East Asian collections in the decades following World War II." [1] In the Steering Committee's report titled, *East Asian Libraries: Problems and Prospects*, scant attention was paid to the role technology could play in solving some of the problems the Steering Committee had identified, except the general statement that "it is essential that East Asian libraries become involved in the various ongoing and proposed automated programs in order to become part of the mainstream of American library development." [2]

A successor committee, The Joint Advisory Committee to the East Asian Library Program, was appointed in 1978 by the American Council of Learned Societies (ACLS) together with the Social Science Research Council (SSRC) and the Association of Research Libraries (ARL) to "review the Steering Committee's report, particularly in the light of comments received from the field since its publication, and to oversee the implementation of such modified recommendations as then seemed appropriate." [3] Witnessing the great strides research libraries were making in automation, the Joint Advisory Committee changed its emphasis and charted a new course for East Asian libraries. In its report issued in 1981 the Advisory Committee recommended that in view of the "growing information volume and perpetually limited resources," East Asian libraries should "share work, materials, and access, and should rely on automation as a principal planning and management tool. The keystone is the capability to input, manage, store, and transmit, display and output bibliographical records containing East Asian vernacular characters in exactly the same automated systems already created to perform similar functions for Western language material and general research libraries." [4] The first step was thus taken to introduce new technology into the operation of East Asian libraries. Subsequently, in 1983, the Research Libraries Group (RLG) introduced a CJK system on its Research Libraries Information Network (RLIN), with funds provided by the Ford Foundation. Three years later, in 1986, OCLC launched its CJK Service, whose twentieth anniversary we are celebrating today.

The OCLC CJK Service began slowly. But progress has been rapid since. As we celebrate the twentieth anniversary of the Service, the total number of East Asian records in its database has reached over 2.9 million, by far the largest such database in the country, and libraries around the world are now its users. The credit for this great achievement goes to the OCLC technical staff. It is they who have been working tirelessly over the years to include CJK functionality in the programs OCLC designed for all languages, including the recent introduction of the Connexion client platform. Meanwhile, OCLC has also helped East Asian libraries in other areas, particularly in retrospective conversion. The work OCLC has done and is still doing in this area has been significant for the libraries involved, and it has also helped the expansion of WorldCat by adding hundreds of thousands of East Asian records to this database for the benefit of scholarship.

On its way to providing more and better services to the East Asian library community, OCLC has been extremely accommodating. When the East Asian library users of the OCLC CJK Service thought there should be some mechanism through which they could better communicate their needs to OCLC, I discussed the creation of an OCLC CJK Users Group, along the lines of other OCLC users groups already in existence, with Andrew Wang. Andrew was immediately receptive to the idea, promising that if we could organize such a group, OCLC would gladly support it. Karl Lo helped draft a set of by-laws, and after consulting with Andrew, the OCLC CJK Users Group was officially established at a meeting on April 10, 1991 in New Orleans. The rest, of course, is history. As we celebrate the twentieth anniversary of the OCLC CJK Service, we salute OCLC for its leadership, vision, and contributions to the East Asian library community for the last twenty years. If I may, I would like to take this opportunity to thank Andrew publicly for the invaluable and generous assistance he, together with Hisako, has given to us. Thank you, Andrew and Hisako!

Revolutionizing bibliographical control is not the only gift new technology has given to libraries. Other equally revolutionary innovations are now at our disposal for other areas of library work, such as ordering and public service. Technology also has altered the form of publications libraries collect. Many genres of books and other materials have been rapidly migrating to digital form. Because of these unprecedented developments, there has emerged a new generation of librarians who are technologically savvy, having been trained in library and information schools where library technology and information management have been given heavy emphasis in their curriculum. This phenomenon is natural, as technology has defined and will continue to define the way we live, work, and study, including of course how libraries will be managed in the future. The centrality of technology in library work notwithstanding, it might be instructive to pause and ask: Will technology alone help us achieve the purposes for which libraries exist?

I don't think anyone would disagree that the heart of the library is its collections. I have quoted John K. Fairbank elsewhere that: "Great universities all have great libraries. Without a great library there would be no great university." By "great libraries" he meant libraries with great collections. The question I want to pose here is that in the process of applying technology to provide better and more effective library service, are we in the meantime paying enough attention to the most important mission of libraries: that is, collection building? In the East Asian library community the nature of the discourse among colleagues these days revolves mostly around technical issues. The postings on Eastlib and the discussions that have taken place at the meetings of CEAL's language committees are a good indication of that. It is not that technical issues are unimportant.

Certainly, they are important, but is there something missing in our discussion? Do we not need to pay equal attention to the question of how to maintain the vitality and health of our collections, built over many decades by our predecessors, that have made America's East Asian libraries the best in the Western world? It's worth noting that most, if not all, of the books and other materials that have migrated or are migrating to the digital form, or being reprinted, are not recent acquisitions but collections that were built long ago. Should we not follow in the footsteps of our predecessors to keep our collections strong and viable so that East Asian libraries can continue to play a key role in the development of East Asian studies in this country?

The key consideration here has to be personnel. The reason East Asian libraries are doing so well in the use of technology is that there is available to them a sufficiently large group of library school graduates trained in technology who also know the languages. It seems to me that there is an equal need in our East Asian libraries of well-trained subject specialists who are well versed in the cultures and civilizations of East Asia to serve as collection builders. We need scholar-librarians in addition to business managers and computer specialists. We know from experience that knowledge of the language alone is insufficient to get the job done in East Asian libraries. It takes much more than the ability to speak, read and write the language. Unfortunately, an impression has been left with the powers that be in some quarters that one needs only to know the language to qualify as an East Asian studies librarian; subject knowledge is immaterial. This is nowhere more clearly and sadly demonstrated than in the recent case of the School of African and Oriental Studies replacing their Chinese studies and Japanese studies librarians with Chinese and Japanese-speaking clerks and declaring the librarians' positions "redundant". Fortunately, SOAS was eventually forced to rescind its decision and reinstated its Chinese and Japanese studies librarians. There is a lesson to be learned from this sad affair, which is that East

Asian libraries, while preoccupied with management and technology, must not forget to give equal due to their scholarly function so that they will not leave themselves vulnerable to uninformed and unacceptable decisions such as that made at SOAS. East Asian librarians have the burden to prove they deserve the respect due to learned professionals.

I cannot emphasize enough the marvelous things technology has done and will continue to do for libraries. The benefit that has accrued to librarians and library users alike has been tremendous. With the help of organizations such as OCLC we are now able to do things that could not be imagined ten or fifteen years ago. But we would be remiss if our reliance on technology made us forget that technology is the means and not the end. Looking beyond technology is not to deny the importance of technology, but to remind ourselves that if we are committed to building or maintaining great collections there are other considerations we must also take into account.

Notes

This talk was originally delivered at the OCLC CJK Users Group Meeting celebrating the 20th anniversary of the OCLC CJK Service, April 8, 2006, in San Francisco, California.

[1] *Automation, Cooperation and Scholarship: East Asian Libraries in the 1980's. Final Report of the Joint Committee to the East Asian Library Program.* [New York] : The American Council of Learned Societies, 1981. p.1.

[2] *East Asian Libraries: Problems and Prospects: A Report and Recommendations.* Prepared by the Steering Committee for a Study of East Asian Libraries.[New York] : The American Council of Learned Societies, 1977, p. 40.

[3] See note 1. The make-up of the Joint Advisory Committee was new but similar to the Steering Committee, with two East Asian faculty members, two East Asian librarians（one also served on the Steering Committee）, and two university library directors. The director of the East Asian Library Program served as an ex-officio member.

[4] *Automation, Cooperation and Scholarship, op. cit.*, p. 18.

二、
哈佛燕京圖書館
館史及館藏概況

哈佛燕京圖書館簡史及其中國典籍收藏概況

19世紀美國「中國貿易」（China Trade）的中心是在波士頓。當時有一位做中國貿易的商人鼐德（Francis P. Knight）在1877年（光緒三年）提倡中文教學，發起募捐，籌畫基金，一共募到8,750美元，在當時是相當大的一筆數目。因此他於1879年（光緒五年）託人在中國請了一位秀才戈鯤化先生（寧波人）到哈佛大學教授中文，這是哈佛大學中文教學的開始。戈鯤化先生到美國的時候，帶來了一批書籍，包括他自己的著作，後來他都捐給了哈佛學院圖書館（Harvard College Library），同時他也替哈佛大學買了一些另外的書籍，以作教學之用。這就是哈佛大學收集中文典籍的開始。

戈鯤化先生於1879年的秋天，帶著他的家人到哈佛大學開始中文教學的工作，但不幸兩年後患肺炎，於1882年逝世。他逝世後，哈佛大學中文教學後繼無人，已經是非常有限的書籍採購工作也就停止了。

1914年，東京帝國大學的兩位教授，姉崎正治和服部宇之吉，來到哈佛大學講學。姉崎教授專治佛學與東方哲學，服部教授則是當時的漢學權威。他們到哈佛的時候送了一批關於佛教與漢學的日文書籍給哈佛學院圖書館，是哈佛大學收藏日文典籍的開始。

1921年，趙元任先生應聘至哈佛大學教中文，1924年辭職。後由南京東南大學（中央大學的前身）梅光迪先生接任。這兩位教授從1921到1926年替哈佛大學蒐集了一些中文方面的書籍，也放置在哈佛學院圖書館，但無人管理。1925年，裘開明先生到哈佛大學研究院就讀。裘先生原在廈門大學任圖書館館長，後來被送到美國來進修，到紐約公共圖書館所辦的圖書館訓練班（後來哥倫比亞大學的圖書館學校）受訓。結業後，他到哈佛大學研究院攻讀農業經濟。因為裘先生是圖書館的專業人員，所以他到哈佛大學後，就到哈佛學院圖書館當義工，希望能學得一些實際的經驗。1927年，他得到農業經濟的碩士學位後，又開始念博士班的課程。當時哈佛學院圖書館館長柯立芝（Archibald C. Coolidge）教授問他是否願意在圖書館正式工作，替他們整理館藏的中文、日文書籍。裘先生因為從未在美國圖書館工作過，所以有些猶豫。但是柯立芝教授告訴他：「你不用擔心，你在中國怎麼做，在這裡就怎麼做，不用管在美國有沒有經驗。」於是他就接受了這個任務，當時他的職稱是哈佛學院圖書館中日文書籍總管（Custodian of Chinese and Japanese Books, Harvard College Library）。就這樣，開始了他在哈佛大學從1927到1965年總共38年的有聲有色的圖書館事業。

裘開明先生，字闇輝，浙江鎮海人。1898年出生，1977年逝世。先生啟蒙的時候，念的是三字經、千字文、百家姓與四書五經等等，後來他被送到漢口文明書局（中華書局的前身）做學徒。他在那裡工作了一年半的時間，對中國古籍發生了極大的興趣，同時也約略地知道了一些商業管理方面的基本知識。1911年辛亥革命，先生被送到湖南長沙一間教會學校學習「西學」，之後他又到湖北武昌文華大學（Boone College）圖書科第一屆就讀，1922年卒業。全班共六人。

文華學院圖書科為一美籍教師韋棣華（Mary Elizabeth Wood）女士於1920年創辦，為中國第一間圖書館專業學校。1929年獨立設校稱為「文華圖書館專科學校」（1953年該校併入武漢大學；1984年擴充為武漢大學圖書館情報學院）。裘先生在校時多利用暑假時期在當時頗有名氣，由商務印書館主辦的涵芬樓（後改名為東方圖書館）做見習工作。耳聞目睹，在專業知識方面頗有裨益。

裘先生畢業之後，廈門大學延聘他為該校圖書館館長。當時日本在廈門的勢力很大，日語非常流行，所以裘先生遂學習日文。在校時並結識當時在該校執教的歐洲漢學泰斗戴密微（Paul Demieville），中國名人作家魯迅、林語堂，及廣雅書局經理徐信符先生等。廣雅書局以其刻本著名。先生謂自徐信符先生處學到不少關於版本和目錄學的知識，對他後來的工作有極大的幫助。

　　1924年廈門大學送裘先生赴美深造。1925年他從紐約公共圖書館（New York Public Library）主辦的圖書館訓練班結業後，去哈佛大學研究院就讀，主修農業經濟學。1927年得碩士學位，1933年得博士學位。從1927年裘先生接掌哈佛學院圖書館中日文書籍總管的職務，一直到1965年他在哈佛燕京圖書館館長的職務上榮退，前後共38年，創北美東亞圖書館館長任期的紀錄。先生是北美東亞圖書館的開路先鋒，在1930年代初期曾為很多大學圖書館擔任有關東亞圖書的採購和編目的顧問工作。第二次世界大戰後，胡佛研究院成立中文部，也邀請他去協助籌備的事宜。先生退休後，應聘到明尼蘇達大學設立東亞圖書館；之後香港中文大學又邀先生去擔任中文大學的首任圖書館館長。返美後，任哈佛燕京圖書館顧問，於1977年逝世，享年79歲。裘先生博學多才，平易近人，有高度的服務精神，被東亞學術界深深敬重。誠如他榮休時，哈佛燕京學社董事會所言：開明先生「為一位例證中西傳統之精華及成就的儒者」（A scholar who exemplifies the best in the traditions and accomplishments of both East and West）。

　　說到裘先生的成就，就必須介紹一下他和哈佛燕京學社的關係。哈佛燕京學社成立於1928年，是一個私人的基金會。設立於哈佛大學，但與哈佛大學無行政上的關係，只有工作上的關係。其基金來自一位查理斯・馬丁・霍爾（Charles Martin Hall）先生的遺產。霍爾先生是一位工程師，他發明了將鋁從鋁礦中抽取出來的技術，創辦了美國鋁業公司（Aluminum Company of America），非常富有。他於1914年去世。他在世時，對於教會在亞洲的高等教育事業頗有興趣。為繼承其遺志，他的遺產管理人得到哈佛大學與中國燕京大學的同意和支援，於1928年在波士頓以美金兩百萬元成立一個基金會，成立時就採用這兩個大學的聯名稱為「哈佛燕京學社」（哈燕社）。

　　此學社成立的目的有二：一是協助當時在東亞的教會大學，特別在中國的教會大學，發展當地的高等教育，並且提升東亞各國對於該國歷史與文化的教學研究。第二、協助哈佛大學發展關於東亞的研究和教學。由於第二專案的關係，哈佛燕京學社成立後就接管了哈佛學院圖書館已經收藏的中日文書籍6,194冊，計中文4,526冊、日文1,668冊。裘先生留任，仍稱「哈佛學院圖書館中日文書籍總管」。1931年哈燕社正式成立「哈佛燕京學社漢和圖書館」（Chinese-Japanese Library of the Harvard-Yenching Institute）。

漢和圖書館在1965年改名為「哈佛燕京圖書館」（Harvard-Yenching Library）。因為當時圖書館收集的書籍已經超過了中日文的範圍，包括韓文和與東亞有關的西方文字的書籍。1976年哈佛燕京圖書館由哈佛燕京學社轉屬哈佛學院圖書館。它的經費不再由哈佛燕京學社全部負擔，而由哈佛學院圖書館負大部分的責任。但是哈佛燕京學社每年仍然提供相當大的一筆經費供哈佛燕京圖書館使用。從1928到1976年這麼長一段時間裡，如果沒有哈佛燕京學社在經費上的支持，哈佛燕京圖書館不可能有今天這樣的發展。

哈佛燕京圖書館成立以後，需要解決的問題很多。在1931年東亞圖書館在美國就像是一塊沒有被開墾的處女地。中日文圖書分類法及編目規則全付闕如，也無法從中國或日本引進，因為當時在中國與日本也還未有一套被大家公認為標準的分類法和編目規則。所以裘先生的第一個工作就是要編出一套中日文書籍的分類法，這個分類法一方面要滿足美國圖書館的需要，一方面也要顧慮到東亞目錄學最基本的要求和法則。裘先生最後推出的《漢和圖書分類法》，基本上是依據四庫的分類，然後再加以擴充，一共分為九類，每一號碼以下再加上阿拉伯數字，依此類推可作無限制的擴充；而作者的號碼就用四角號碼。這是一個非常實用的折衷辦法。這部劃時代的巨著不單是裘先生對哈佛燕京圖書館的貢獻，也是對北美東亞圖書館的貢獻，是北美東亞圖書館發展的一個重要里程碑。1943年，全美學術團體委員會（American Council of Learned Societies）管轄下的遠東學會（Committee on Far Eastern Studies, Association for Asian Studies，亞洲學會的前身）出版了這部分類法，名叫《漢和圖書分類法》（*A Classification System for Chinese and Japanese Books*）後通稱為「哈佛燕京分類法」（Harvard-Yenching Scheme）。自此以後一直到1970年代的中期這40多年的時間，美國所有的東亞圖書館（國會圖書館除外）都採用這個分類法，同時在加拿大、英國、荷蘭和澳洲一些主要的圖書館也採用來作他們中日文書籍的編目工作。

裘先生另一個重要的貢獻就是在編目卡片上加上作者與書名的羅馬拼

音，以便於卡片的排列。這個辦法在美國已經通用，而且早已為美國全國編目的標準。同時，裘先生決定把這些卡片目錄用語言分開，分為中文目錄、日文目錄（後又加上韓文目錄），以便查詢；書籍在書庫書架上的排列也是依語言而分。因為當時東亞館還沒有主題編目（subject cataloging），裘先生乃建立分類目錄。這一系列的措施大都被很多東亞館效法，以至於今。

　　所以裘先生在東亞館，如我所說的，是開路先鋒，做了很多事情，是大家仿效的對象。還有，為了讓在哈佛大學以外的人便於查詢哈佛燕京圖書館的藏書，裘先生開始哈佛燕京圖書館書目的編纂與出版工作，這在美國東亞館中也是首創之舉。1936年，裘先生到北平與燕京大學引得出版社洽商出版哈佛燕京圖書館中文藏書目錄的事宜。從1938到1940年，這套目錄的前三冊——經學、哲學宗教、歷史科學——已經問世，其餘的部分也有了校樣本。但是珍珠港事變以後，日本人在北平大事破壞與美國有關的機構。燕京大學是美國教會學校，引得出版社因之被毀。已經印就的其餘目錄的校樣本，也就付之一炬。以後也無法再行印刷出版了。已出的這三本目錄，還有一個非常重要的副產品，就是裘先生要求引得出版社把這三本目錄中的單筆的卡片分印出來，以供其他東亞圖書館使用。這是東亞館館際合作的序幕。後來裘先生在這方面還有很多另外的貢獻，比如在抗戰末期到戰後的幾年間，中國大陸不僅出版圖書不易，在大陸買書也很很困難，因為當時國內外的交通都很不方便。因此，美國圖書館協會成立了一個「中國書籍合作購買項目」（ALA China Cooperative Book Purchasing Program），主要是在重慶和其他的地方買書後，空運回美國，由哈佛燕京圖書館負責編目，然後再把編目卡片分送到其他東亞圖書館使用。從1944到1948這四年當中，由哈佛燕京圖書館編製並由哈佛大學印刷部代印分發到各圖書館的書目卡片一共有19,000張，是東亞圖書館合作編目的先聲。再者，從1949到1958年，國會圖書館成立一個東亞語文卡片複印專案，前後總共複印了各個東亞圖書館送去的45,000張編目卡片，再行分發各館以供其編目之用。在這45,000張卡片中哈佛燕京圖書館的就占了28,000張，將近全部書卡總數的三分之二，所以哈佛燕京圖書館在裘先生領導之下對於館際合作有很大的貢獻。

　　剛剛提到哈佛燕京圖書館無法在北平完成出版中文書本目錄的事，裘先生對此一直引以為憾。因此在1980年代，我們決定將圖書館的全部中日文卡片目錄印成書本目錄，以了其願。之後我們仿照有些東亞圖書館的辦法將單筆目錄卡片用照相、影印的方式出版。這項工作前後花了四年的工夫，包括整理、審訂全部的卡片目錄。終於在1985和1986兩年當中，影印出版了72大冊中日文書本目錄。韓文書籍的目錄我們已在1962、1966與1980年出版了三本，因此沒有包括在內。

　　書本目錄出版以後，頗受歐美東亞學術界的歡迎。之後，為更進一步便利學者的查詢，哈佛燕京圖書館決定開始作回溯建檔的工作。但是從卡片格式轉換到機讀格式的費用較大，每一筆需要美金6元，所需預算是220萬美元，是相當龐大的一筆經費。後來，哈佛燕京學社捐贈110萬，哈佛大學也提供110萬。從1997年開始，到2001年10月為止由連線電腦圖書館中心（Online Computer Library Center，簡稱OCLC）承包的全部回溯建檔工作結束。哈佛燕京圖書館成為北美主要東亞圖書館中第一個館藏目錄全部上網的圖書館（館的網址是：http://hcl.harvard.edu/harvard-yenching）。

　　研究圖書館最重要的任務就是藏書建設。哈佛燕京圖書館最初從哈佛學院圖書館接收過來的幾千冊書基本上還是相當凌亂，因為它們並不是有系統蒐集而來的。所幸的是漢和圖書館開館時得到了燕京大學圖書館大力的協助。從1928到1941這十幾年間，燕京大學圖書館在採購書籍時大都購買兩本，一本自留，一本給哈佛燕京圖書館。因為這樣，那個時期出版的有研究價值的著作大都有所收藏。當時在燕京大學圖書館任職的顧廷龍先生（著名的目錄學家，1949年後任上海圖書館館長）和當時燕京大學的文學院院長洪業教授，也替哈佛燕京圖書館選購了不少的古籍善本。同時，裘先生自己也直接從上海中華書局或商務印書館等處買了不少他們當時出版的圖書。在日文書籍方面，大部分都從東京伊勢堂購買。因此，哈佛燕京圖書館的藏書建設工作就上了軌道，開始進行有系統的採購。在1930年代，哈佛燕京圖書館每年購書的經費是美金一萬元，在那時這是一筆很可觀的數字。

　　盧溝橋事變以後，日本入侵中國，華北名望因不願與日人合作而隱居

者，多出讓私藏古籍，以維持生計。其時，北平琉璃廠、福隆寺書肆善本充
溢，在華日人多購之。裘先生當時在北平監督圖書館書本目錄出版的事，他
也就大量地收購了中文善本古籍。目前哈佛燕京圖書館很多的善本書籍就是
當時裘先生購入的。珍珠港事變以後，燕京大學受到日軍的騷擾，漢和圖書
館與燕京大學圖書館的合作採購工作，遂告結束。館方旋轉中國西南各省自
美國直接採購。現哈佛燕京圖書館所藏的多種中國西南地區的方志，就是當
時購入的。第二次世界大戰以後，日本經濟崩潰、民不聊生，不少私人收藏
的中國古籍流於坊間書肆。裘先生遂赴日，後來又委託他人，採購了若干善
本書籍，其中有明刻本百餘部。

　　哈佛燕京圖書館開辦後20年間，採購的範圍限於中日文的典籍文獻，
而其重點是在人文科學方面。但是由於哈佛大學對於東亞教學研究的擴展，
圖書館蒐集圖書的範圍也隨之擴大，藏文、滿文、蒙文的典籍也開始蒐集，
西文關於東亞方面的書籍、參考工具、報紙、雜誌、學報，也大量的增加。
1951年韓戰時，成立韓文部。1975年又成立越南文部（哈佛燕京圖書館並
不收集東南亞語文書籍，越南是例外。因為當時哈佛大學歷史系設立一中越
歷史講座，圖書館有提供資料文獻的責任，而且哈佛燕京圖書館中已經藏有
若干安南時期用漢文出版的官方歷史文獻，如《阮朝實錄》之類等）。1965
年我接任裘先生的職務之後，開始加強近代及當代中國、日本、韓國在社會
科學方面的圖書資料。數十年來，一所當年是以人文科學資料為主的圖書
館，就逐步的轉變成一所包容所有學科的研究圖書館，甚至包括一些關於自
然科學與應用科學方面的文獻。

　　哈佛燕京圖書館除了蒐集工作外，還有出版的工作，主要是《哈佛燕京
圖書館書目叢刊》。現已出版下列九種：

　　1. 余秉權（Ping-Kuen Yu）編《中國史學論文引得》（*Chinese History:*
Index to Learned Articles, Volume II 1905-1964）。麻州劍橋：哈佛燕京圖書
館，1970。

　　2.《哈佛大學哈佛燕京圖書館韓籍簡目三編》（*A Classified Catalogue of*

Korean Books in the Harvard-Yenching Library, Harvard University, Volume III）。麻州劍橋：哈佛燕京圖書館，1980。

3. 吳天威（Tien-wei Wu）編《江西蘇維埃共和國，1931-1934——陳誠特藏文件選輯解題書目》（*The Kiangsi Soviet Republic, 1931-1934: A Selected and Annotated Bibliography of the Chen Cheng Collection*。麻州劍橋：哈佛燕京圖書館，1981。

4. 岡雅彥（Masahiko Oka）、青木利行（Toshiyuki Aoki）合編，《哈佛大學燕京圖書館和書目錄》（*Early Japanese Books in the Harvard-Yenching Library, Harvard University*）。東京：ゆまに書房（Yumani Shobo, Publisher Inc），1994。

5. 朱寶田（Zhu Baotian）編《哈佛燕京圖書館藏中國納西族象形文經典分類目錄》。麻州劍橋：哈佛燕京圖書館，1997。

6. 宋永毅（Yongyi Song）、孫大進（Daijin Sun）合編《文化大革命書目，1966-1996》（*The Cultural Revolution: A Bibliography, 1966-1996*）。麻州劍橋：哈佛燕京圖書館，1998。

7. 沈津（Chun Shum）編《美國哈佛大學哈佛燕京圖書館中文善本書志》（*An Annotated Catalog of Chinese Rare Books in the Harvard-Yenching Library*）（中文）。上海：上海辭書出版社，1999。

8. 尹忠男（Choong Nam Yoon）《哈佛大學韓國研究之搖籃：紀念哈佛燕京圖書館韓文部成立五十周年》（*The Cradle of Korean Studies at Harvard University: Commemoration of the 50th Anniversary of the Korean Collection at Harvard-Yenching Library*）。首爾：乙酉文化社（Eulyoo Publishing Company），2001。

哈佛燕京圖書館迄2001年6月底，圖書館藏書總量為1,018,500餘冊，其中中文書籍約577,000冊，占總藏量的57%；日文260,750冊，占總藏量26.2%；韓文書籍106,170冊，占總藏量10.5%；西文43,310冊，占4%；越南文11,335冊，占1%；滿蒙藏文合計8,211冊，占總藏量0.8%。

　　館藏新舊期刊總數14,000餘種。現行期刊5,784種，其中中文2,859種，占49%；日文1,513種，占26%；韓文924種，占1.6%；西文440種，占0.7%；越南文48種，占0.08%。現行報紙85種，其中中文60種，占70%；日文4種，0.4%；韓文7種，0.8%；西文8種，0.9%；越南文6種，0.7%。

　　哈佛燕京圖書館收藏的縮微卷，共63,192卷，其中中文31,784卷，占50%；日文23,060卷，占36%；韓文5,129卷，占8%；西文2,775卷，占4%；越南文444卷，占百分之0.7%。微片共18,304片，中文占絕大多數，有17,611片，96%；其餘就是西文，有693片，占4%。除此以外還有錄影帶200多種、照片60,000餘張、幻燈片3,000多張、CD ROM 94種。

　　2000-2001年會計年度，哈佛燕京圖書館總預算是3,516,000多元，其中人事費用2,078,000多元，占59%；採購經費972,000，占28%。還有其他的費用466,000，占13%。

　　中文圖書採購的經費共364,330元，占採購經費全部38%；日文圖書378,390元，占39%；韓文179,240元，占18%；西文30,236元，占3%；越南文8,910元，占0.9%；藏文6,260元，占0.6%。

　　從這些數字看來，日文的採購經費比中文多，但是日文書籍每年的入藏量遠不如中文，這是因為日文書籍的價格比中文書要貴得很多。比如說2000到2001年，哈佛燕京圖書館入藏的書大概總共有31,380冊，其中中文有21,365冊，占68%，但是日文只有4,645冊，占15%，但是所花的經費比中文還要高些。韓文的入藏數是4,102冊，占13%，這與日文的入藏量差不了很多，但是日文採購的經費比韓文多一倍。

　　關於收藏方面，哈佛燕京圖書館各部門的藏書有很多類似的地方，有很多共同點，那就是不論是中文部、日文部、韓文部，或越南文部，它們所收集的典籍文獻都是分別有關中國、日本、韓國、越南的歷史、語言、文學、哲學、宗教、美術以及近代和當代的社會科學方面的資料。但是除了這些共同點之外，每一個部門都有它特殊的收藏，譬如說中文部的方志、叢書、文集、別集、善本或當代的一些文獻都很豐富，這個我在下面會做詳細的說明。現在先介紹一些關於其他部門收藏的概況。

　　日文部關於日本近代史，特別是明治維新時代、近代文學、二次世界大戰後的日本政治、經濟、社會發展的資料都非常豐富，日本學者所撰關於漢學的著作收集也相當完整。另外，圖書館中還有布魯諾‧佩佐爾德（Bruno Petzold）先生的藏書6,500餘冊。佩佐爾德先生奧地利人，在日本居住多年，專佛學，他收集的書籍中多為關於佛教的典籍，其中江戶時代的刻本居多，並有200多本手抄本。

　　關於明治維新時代，館藏最特別的、最珍貴的資料，是一套15,000卷的縮微卷。這一套縮微卷是東京丸善書店與日本國會圖書館合作為紀念明治維新200周年而製作的。這批微卷包括日本國會圖書館所藏全部明治時代出版的書籍，約120,000種，為日本現存明治時期出版書籍全部75%。這15,000卷縮微卷數量龐大，售價非常昂貴。當時除日本本國圖書館購買以外，國外圖書館均未採購。因為如是，東京日光證券股份有限公司出資購買一部，贈送哈佛燕京圖書館，是為全美唯一的全套。

　　韓文部所藏的資料中，韓國文集非常豐富，大概有2,600多種。這些都是韓國文人從13世紀到19世紀末期（元明清時代）用漢文撰寫的著作。另外韓文部收藏的在朝鮮時代「李氏王朝」（西元1392到1910年）的「榜目」與「族譜」也非常珍貴。「榜目」就是當時朝鮮模仿中國科舉制度所放的榜。這兩種資料都是研究朝鮮時代韓國社會史不可或缺的文獻。故哈佛大學韓國史教授愛德華‧瓦格納（Edward W. Wagner）先生根據這兩種資料，整理出了14,607位在朝鮮時代曾經在文科、武科中舉的人的名單。並且將每一位的家世資料，整理得清清楚楚，建立檔案，為研究李氏王朝非常重要的原始資料。備受韓國歷史界尊崇，並準備上網以供學術界使用。

　　越南文部所藏的資料不多，但其中亦不乏重要者。如19世紀用漢文編撰的當時稱為安南的歷史、法政和佛教方面的典籍。現代和當代越南的典籍和出版物也是在蒐集範圍之內。

　　西文部的藏書都是關於中國、日本、韓國和越南的西文專著、學報、期刊和報紙。其中大部分均為英文出版物。哈佛燕京圖書館收集西文資料的政策與其他東亞圖書館有異。其他東亞館收集的西文資料大多限於參考工具書及部分書籍或期刊。哈佛燕京圖書館除了參考工具書之外，更收集一般的專著、學報與期刊。因為哈佛燕京圖書館是哈佛大學有關東亞課程的西文指定課外讀物圖書館之一。但這並不是說哈佛燕京圖書館是在收集所有有關東亞的西文出版物。那是哈佛學院圖書館（Harvard College Library）所屬最大的懷德納圖書館（Widener Library）和拉蒙德大學部圖書館（Lamont Undergraduate Library）的責任。哈佛燕京是收藏其中大部分比較重要的而已。

　　在這裡可以附帶補充一句。哈佛大學是一所行政非常不集中的大學，各個學院的自主權很高。因此，哈佛大學大大小小的圖書館差不多有一百個，所以收集的資料有時難免重複。就中國資料方面來講，雖然哈佛燕京圖書館是哈佛大學蒐集中國資料的主要圖書館，但是也有其他的圖書館同時在收集中文資料，而且他們所蒐集的是比較專業的。比如說，費正清東亞研究中心（John King Fairbank Center for East Asian Research）有一個圖書室，他們蒐集的都是當代大陸出版的資料。還有法學院圖書館，他們也蒐集中國大陸和台灣出版的關於法律、司法行政方面的中文資料。

　　下面我就哈佛燕京圖書館的中國典藏作一個比較詳細的報告。剛才我已經提到哈佛燕京圖書館的中文收藏包括書籍577,000多冊、新舊期刊14,000多種、新舊報紙500多種、縮微卷31,700多卷等等。這些資料總合起來占圖書館總藏量一半以上，在北美洲的東亞館中，也僅次於國會圖書館。所以哈佛燕京圖書館的中文典籍是非常豐富的。因此，要做一份有意義的報告比較困難。我想最好的辦法也許就是以文獻的種類分別介紹一些特別有代表性的典籍。這樣大家就可以舉一反三，也許能對哈佛燕京圖書館所收藏的中文典籍有一個比較清楚的概念。

　　我首先介紹哈佛燕京圖書館所藏的中文古籍近二十萬冊，其中善本有宋元刻本30種，明刻本1,400多種，清代順治、康熙、雍正、乾隆四朝刻本2,000多部，抄本、稿本1,200多種，拓片500多張，法帖36種。在刻本當中又有彩色套版、五色套印，還有明代的銅活字與清代木活字的版本。

　　圖書館的善本有書志，名為《美國哈佛大學哈佛燕京圖書館中文善本書

志》，沈津編著，1999年上海辭書出版社出版。沈先生隨顧廷龍先生二十餘
年，精通目錄學及版本學，現任哈佛燕京圖書館善本室主任。書志著錄從南
宋至明末的所有館藏刻本，共1,433種，約一百餘萬字，按經史子集叢五部
排列，同時附有分類書名目錄，以及書名、作者、刻工、刻書鋪的索引，非
常精細，得到學術界一致的肯定。台灣元智大學中文系的吳銘能教授在《國
家圖書館館刊》民國八十八年第二期發表〈沈津《美國哈佛大學哈佛燕京圖
書館中文善本書志》校讀書後〉一文，頗多讚譽。

現在我再分別介紹一些具有代表性的中文藏書。第一種就是地方志，我
們都知道，地方志是研究中國歷史、政治、經濟和社會史不可缺少的資料。
據統計，大陸現存的方志共8,343種，最多是在北京圖書館，大約有6,066
種；台灣的收藏計4,530種。哈佛燕京圖書館有3,858種，其中原版有3,241
種，複印本與縮微卷617種。如僅以原版計算，哈佛燕京圖書館的藏量占大
陸總藏量的39%，占台灣總藏量的72%；若與北京圖書館比較，哈佛燕京的
藏量有其53%。

哈佛燕京圖書館藏方志以縣志為最多．。大陸收藏的縣志計5,441種，其
中北京圖書館有4,111種；台灣藏縣志有3,155種；哈佛燕京圖書館有2,911
種。在比例上，哈佛燕京圖書館的藏量有大陸的54%、北圖的71%、台灣
的92%。館藏方志最多的是山東、山西、河南、陝西、江蘇、浙江各省。就
以浙江一省來講，我們知道現存所有的浙江方志有599種，在北圖有398
種，浙江圖書館有370種，哈佛燕京圖書館有300種。

以方志原版刊行年代計，哈佛燕京圖書館有明刻31種、清刻2,473種、
民國出版者737種；館藏最早的刻本是明正德元年（1506）刊行的《姑蘇
志》六十卷，最近者是民國八十五年（1996）台北中一出版社出版的《台灣
鄉土全志》12冊。

館藏《潞城縣志》八卷，明馮惟賢修，王溥增修，明萬曆十九年
（1591）刻，天啟五年（1625）增修，崇禎年間再增修本，及《江陰縣志》
八卷，明馮士仁修，徐遵湯，周高起纂，明崇禎十三年（1640）刻本，或均
係存世孤本，因大陸所藏，均為清代或民國時代的抄本。明嘉靖年間《廣西

通志》六十卷，明林富、黃佐纂修，藍印本亦值得一提。這本方志是廣西方志中最早的版本，世間所存不多，除哈佛燕京圖書館外，僅北京圖書館與日本內閣文庫有入藏。

關於哈佛燕京圖書館方志藏書的詳盡介紹，可以參考拙著〈哈佛燕京圖書館中國方志及其有關資料存藏現況〉，載《漢學研究》第三卷第二期「方志學國際研討會」論文集專號第一冊（1985年12月）。

在此，另外需要提到的是新方志的出版。從1980年代以來，中國大陸出版了大量的新方志，與舊的方志在體例上有一些相同，但在內容上有很大的差異，因為這些省、市、各級都有的新方志中，他們只蒐羅記載1949年以後的地方史實，但是也包括在1949年以前，各地共產黨的地下組織及其活動。這類的資料在旁的地方很少能看見的，所以這些新方志對研究中共黨史也有很大的用處。據估計，現已出版的新方志約18,000種，哈佛燕京圖書館藏收有14,000種左右。與新方志有關的是大陸近二十年出版的各省、市、縣、自治區，和各種專業的年鑑，估計有1,800多種，哈佛燕京圖書館現藏約1,700種。

除了新舊方志、新舊年鑑以外，哈佛燕京圖書館尚藏有和它們有關的一些地方性的資料，比如說山水志、寺廟志、輿圖、地方載記、土地文書、官書統計等等。在這些地方資料中，輿圖及土地文書特別值得一提。輿圖有明版輿圖十餘種，其中有明嘉靖三十六年（1557）刻，明張天復之《皇輿考》；嘉靖四十五年（1566）刻，元朱思本之《廣輿圖》；以及崇禎年間刻的《今古輿地圖》朱墨套印本。館藏的清代輿圖中，有康熙內府刊的《康熙內府分省分府圖》，為摺裝本，乾隆四十六年（1781）初版，清嘉慶年間廣幅藍色印本；黃澄孫乾隆十五年（1750）繪製之《大清萬年一統地理全圖》。另有乾隆十五年（1750）繪，1940年敵偽時代北京興亞院華北聯絡部複印的《乾隆京城全圖》。以及清初的彩繪本《湖南全省圖》15幅，1冊。其他尚有光緒年間彩繪的40餘幅江蘇、浙江、江西的里釐卡圖，其中除大卡、小卡、旱卡、水卡的位置以外，還注明各卡間的距離及各卡與其附近城鎮間之距離，是研究清代經濟史很有用的一項資料。

　　關於土地文書方面，館藏中最具有研究價值的，有同治七年到光緒三年江蘇吳縣有關佃農正副租簿，共19冊；乾隆二十七到五十八年間的少數田契；光緒三十年到民國十八年間，江蘇21縣同浙江1縣縣長移交的田賦、漕運，以及其他稅收的清單，並公費賑災的收支帳目，這都是非常重要的研究資料。土地文書當中尚有台北成文出版社出版的《民國二十到三十年代中國經濟、農業、土地、水利問題資料》，是當時大陸地政研究所所長蕭錚先生編輯的，一共收羅26,000餘件，有的從報刊選輯而來的，也有實際調查的資料，分5大類65個細類，用縮微片發行。另外一種也是蕭錚先生編輯的，名《民國二十年代中國大陸土地問題資料──1932-1941年間未刊行土地問題調查資料》，也是成文出版社出版，其中包括各地168項的實際調查，以及176種報告，總共200冊，是很大的一套資料。

　　台灣的土地文書為中央研究院史語所張偉仁、王世慶合編的《台灣公私藏古文書影本》，共10輯，收5,600餘件從17 世紀到20世紀間台灣各地地契、土地田賦收據、借約、合同、土地買賣、田地訴訟等各種原始資料文件，內容極豐富，有高度的研究價值。

　　除方志與其他有關的資料以外，哈佛燕京圖書館的中文特藏就是叢書，約1,400種左右，共60,000餘冊，這是《中國叢書綜目》中所著錄的一半。館藏的明刻叢書有34種，其餘大部分都是清刻的，還有一些民國出版的。館藏中最早的一部叢書是《百川學海》，100種，一百七十九卷，20冊，宋左圭編，明弘治十四年（1501）刻本。此書次於南宋俞鼎孫之《儒學警悟》是中國第二部叢書。哈佛燕京圖書館最著名的叢書還是《武英殿聚珍版叢書》。這部叢書是乾隆時代武英殿木活字印本，收錄138種，八百十二卷，是規模最大的木活字本。據統計，現存僅十餘部，大陸有九部，哈佛燕京、普林斯頓大學葛思德圖書館、美國國會圖書館、大英圖書館、台北故宮博物院各有一套。

　　其次就是類書。哈佛燕京圖書館所收藏的明清類書有350種，據《中國古籍善本書目》著錄，明人所刻類書（不包括叢書），現存約三百數十種，其中北京圖書館有110種，台北國家圖書館102種，美國國會圖書館55種，哈佛燕京圖書館75種。館藏明代類書中，除《永樂大典》與其他聞名的如《三才圖繪》、《山堂肆考》、《唐類函》等之外，還有一些規模較小但非常實用的小型類書，其中有十餘種是其他圖書館所沒有收藏的，如《新刻增補音易四書五經志考萬花谷》，明崇禎余開明刻的巾箱本；《新刻增校切用正音鄉談雜字大全》，明末的刻本。關於哈佛燕京圖書館所藏一部分明代類書著錄，可參考裘開明先生撰〈哈佛大學哈佛燕京學社圖書館明代類書概述（上）〉，載《清華學報》新編第二卷第二期（1961年6月）。

　　清代的類書則以雍正六年內府銅活字印本《古今圖書集成》最為著名，共一萬卷，目錄四十卷，共5,020冊，裝訂為503函。哈佛燕京圖書館所藏，每冊的扉頁有乾隆的「皇華宮寶」同「五福五代堂古稀天子寶」的璽印，每冊的末頁也有「皇華宮寶」、「八徵耄念之寶」的璽印。所以這一套也是非常寶貴的文物。

　　其次講到禁書。哈佛燕京圖書館所藏的禁書大部分為乾隆年間編纂《四庫全書》時以「違礙」之名而遭禁毀的書籍。館藏以明刻本的禁書最多，有74部。其中特別珍貴的是《新鍥李卓吾先生增補批點皇明正續合併通紀統宗》十二卷，卷首一卷，附錄一卷，明陳建撰，袁黃、卜大有補輯，李贄批點，明末刻本。是書現僅存兩部，另一部在台北的國家圖書館。大陸有藏，但為殘本。其他稀見的禁書還有《周忠毅公奏議》四卷，明宋建撰，《行實》一卷，明周廷祚撰，天啟刻本《撫津疏草》四卷，明畢自嚴撰，及《皇明資治通紀》三十卷，明陳建撰，明刻本，有明末定西伯張名振的批點。這些都是好書。

　　禁書中除了牽涉到違礙政治嫌疑的書之外，還有內容較為穢褻的小說。哈佛燕京圖書館從戲劇大師齊如山先生哲嗣處於1960年代購得十餘種，包括《兩肉緣》、《妖狐豔史》、《載花船》、《覓蓮記》等這些作品。從齊如山先生處購得的戲曲小說善本共72種。除上述者外，尚有明刻本如明金陵唐氏刻本《新刊全像漢劉秀雲台記》、《長命鏤傳奇》、明吳郡書業堂刻本《邯鄲記》等。故吳曉鈴教授，中國小說戲曲專家，曾至哈佛燕京圖書館閱讀這批書籍，並錄出小說中23種有齊如山手筆跋尾者，發表〈哈佛大學所藏高陽齊氏白舍齋善本小說跋尾〉一文，載《明清小說論叢》第一輯，瀋陽春風文藝出版社1984年出版，有高度學術價值，可供參考。

再其次，就是抄本與稿本。哈佛燕京圖書館所藏的中文抄本是美國之冠，共1,200多種，分訂為4,560冊。除《永樂大典》兩卷以外，還有明朝黑格抄本《明文記類》、《南城召對》，後者為《四庫》底本，明藍格抄本《觀象玩占》（董其昌舊藏，有翰林院大方印）。還有清初毛氏汲古閣抄《離騷草木疏》，為全美僅有之「毛抄」；清東武劉氏（喜海）《宋明賢五百家播方大全文粹》，40冊，道光二十八年抄；嘉靖三年朱絲欄精抄《鑲黃旗滿洲鈕古祿氏弘毅公家譜》，15冊；《八旗叢書》清恩豐光緒年間抄本，35種、28冊，為恩豐私藏，其中有愛新覺羅敦敏撰《樊齋詩鈔》。敦敏為曹雪芹至友，《樊齋詩鈔》中多收其與曹雪芹唱和詩，為研究曹雪芹生平罕見之資料。或許更為珍貴的是文瀾閣《四庫全書》中駱賓王的《駱丞集注》，四卷，與《熬波圖》，二卷，後者是製造海鹽的繪冊。

在稿本當中，最珍貴的就是《楊繼盛彈劾嚴嵩稿》。楊繼盛，字仲芳，號椒山（1516-1555），因彈劾嚴嵩而下獄被斬。稿本是他的親筆，是特別重要的一項文獻。另一本是丁日昌的《炮錄》，也非常寶貴。滿洲皇室敬徵（1785-1851）的《敬徵日記》，也是罕見的資料。

稿本中尚有尺牘。哈佛燕京圖書館所藏尺牘中以《明諸名家尺牘》為最。共753封（其中102封僅存封無函），都是明嘉靖、隆慶、萬曆年間名人及其他人士致徽州方太古的信札。方氏是當時徽州的一位殷商，交遊甚廣，信札來至二百餘人，其中不乏當時名人，如書法家周天球、文人王世禎、戲曲家汪道昆，甚至戚繼光、臧懋循等人。有如此數量的明人手札想或舉世無雙。這批尺牘已由北京社會科學院研究員陳智超教授（陳垣先生的哲嗣）考證著錄，撰寫為《哈佛燕京圖書館藏明代徽州方氏親友手札七百通考釋》，將列為《哈佛燕京圖書館書目叢刊》第八種。

館藏文集以明清最多，明刻本兩百餘種，其中罕見者不少，如明萬曆、崇禎年間遞刻明陳敬宗撰《重刻澹然先生文集》三卷，詩集三卷；隆慶刻本，明侯一麟撰《龍門集》二十卷；明江百榕撰《清蘿館集》五卷，崇禎元年江氏自刻本等，這些都是在大陸的全國聯合目錄《中國古籍善本目錄》中沒有著錄的。館藏清刻詩文集約在1,600種左右。《中國古籍善本書目》中沒有著錄的也不少，如鍾大源撰《東海半人詩鈔》，二十四卷，嘉慶刻本；清王瀠撰《紅鵝館詩鈔》二卷，乾隆吳益高刻本；以及清宋廷桓撰《漱石詩鈔》七卷，乾隆刻本；清潘松竹撰《梅軒遺草》一卷，乾隆十四年（1776）張裕昆刻本等。

剛才已經講到兩部最著名的活字本：雍正六年銅活字本《古今圖書集成》和乾隆時期木活字本《武英殿聚珍版叢書》。哈佛燕京圖書館還有一部最早的銅活字本，即《會通館校正宋諸臣奏議》，一百五十卷，宋趙汝愚輯，明弘治三年（1490）華燧會通館銅活字本，120冊。據沈津先生的調查，現存大陸、台灣者均為殘卷，哈佛燕京圖書館所藏應為孤本。館藏清代木活字本亦有110餘種。

哈佛燕京圖書館藏套印本甚夥，有朱墨套印、三色套印、四色套印及五色的套印本。朱墨套印本中，乾隆五十三年（1788）曹溶聽雨齋朱熹《楚辭集注》，八卷，且為活字本，極為出色。三色套印中有明天啟二年（1622）吳興閔氏刊朱墨綠三色套印梁蕭統編《文選尤》八卷。四色套印中有凌瀛初萬曆間刻朱墨藍黃四色套印劉義慶撰《世說新語》八卷，4冊。館藏本書口有彩繪。第一冊為仇英《秋江待渡圖》，第二冊為王紱《秋江泛艇圖》，第三冊為唐寅《山路松聲圖》，第四冊為文徵明《雪景圖》。所繪極為細緻，一筆不苟，且彩色鮮明，為世所罕見者。五色套印中，乾隆間內府朱墨藍綠黃五色套印《勸善金科》，二十卷，卷首一卷，亦不多見。

套印本中，尚有畫譜，其中《十竹齋書畫譜》及《芥子園畫傳》為代表作。館藏《十竹齋書畫譜》6部，有康熙五十四年（1715），嘉慶二十二年（1817），及日本明治十五年（1882）復刻明崇禎六年（1633）原刊包背裝本等。《芥子園畫傳》館藏8部，有康熙十八年（1679），乾隆四十七年（1782），嘉慶二十二年（1817），民國十年（1921）及日本寬延元年（1748）翻印本等。

館藏法帖共36種，其中以《戲鴻堂帖》與《三希堂法帖》最為知名者。

　　除上述以外，哈佛燕京圖書館還有一些比較獨特的資料，現舉其兩種以為例。一種是基督教傳教士先後在南洋與中國大陸的出版物，一種是中國傳統皮影戲的唱本。前者是在南洋、廣州、澳門、福州、上海各地出版的關於基督教和神學方面的著作，例如教會史、人物傳記與聖經。還有介紹西方文化的書籍，包括西方歷史、地理、人文科學、社會科學的經典，以及科學技術、生理學、醫學方面的資料。就《聖經》一種而言，就有各種不同方言的翻譯版本，有上海話的、有廈門話的、有寧波話的、有廣東話的。這些出版物是從西文翻譯成中文，或是傳教士的中文著作，撰者都是當時很知名的傳教士，包括林樂知（John Young Allen, 1836-1907）、李提摩太（Timothy Richard, 1845-1919）、丁韙良（William Alexander Parsons Martin, 1827-1916）、艾約瑟（Joseph Edkins, 1823-1905）等。其中也有少數作者不是傳教士，像昨天我已經提過的傅蘭雅（John Fryer）。這些著作出版的時期大部分是從清道光初年（1820）到宣統末年（1911），也有一些民國時代的。資料共700多種，其中以《聖經》的全部（新舊約）和新約單獨的部分如《馬太福音》、《約翰福音》等類最多，計169種，其餘就是一般介紹基督教的著作。這批資料由前哈佛燕京圖書館副館長賴永祥教授編目後，由波士頓霍爾出版公司（G.K. Hall）1980年出版書目，名為《哈佛燕京圖書館藏傳教士中文著作目錄》（*Catalog of Protestant Missionary Works in Chinese*）。同時，資料的本身也由荷蘭的國際文獻公司（Inter Documentation Center）攝製縮微片發行，稱為《哈佛燕京圖書館藏傳教士中文著作膠片》（*Protestant Missionary Works at the Harvard-Yenching Library on Microfiche*）。

　　另外一種就是中國民間傳統皮影戲的唱本。這批唱本共118種，都是手抄。1930年代故哈佛大學方志彤教授在北京從吉順班購得，後由方教授遺孀轉讓哈佛燕京圖書館。全部118種唱本戲曲名稱可參見哈佛燕京圖書館線上目錄《皮影戲劇本》書名項下。

　　最後，我介紹一些哈佛燕京圖館所藏相當特別的關於近代和當代中國的資料文獻。首先要介紹的是胡漢民先生的檔案。胡先生（1879-1936）是國民黨的元老，這批檔案是民國二十到二十五年間他私人往來的函稿，有

2,500多件，包括他自己所發函電的底稿與他收到從各方來的原件。收件和寄件人包括當時所有重要人物，諸如蔣中正、汪精衛、閻錫山、馮玉祥、張學良、孔祥熙、李宗仁、鄒魯、白崇禧、陳濟棠、居正、宋哲元、韓復榘、龍雲、劉湘、楊虎城、杜月笙等人，還有胡漢民與日本首相犬養毅和軍事領袖松井石根（當時台灣日本皇軍司令官）來往的信件。

　　胡漢民當時因與蔣中正意見不合，1931年2月辭立法院院長職，旋被軟禁在南京湯山，當年獲釋後，各省軍政人士均欲與其聯盟反蔣，同時南京中央亦竭力邀請他返寧。這是這些函件的時間和政治背景。函件中討論的內容非常廣泛，是研究民國政治史、當時國民黨分裂問題、反蔣問題、福建事件等，非常的重要的一批文獻。（此項檔案已複印出版為《胡漢民未刊往來函電稿》，陳紅民輯注，廣西師範大學出版社，2005，15冊 [哈佛燕京圖書館學術叢刊第4種]）。

　　其次，哈佛燕京圖書館藏有魯迅與茅盾的親筆信件手稿。昨天我講到史丹佛大學胡佛研究所時曾經提到一位美國人伊羅生（Harold R. Issacs）先生。1930年代他在中國時，曾蒐集若干中共地下刊物，後來轉讓給胡佛研究所。他在上海的時候，準備挑選一些有代表性的中國年輕左翼作家的作品，翻譯成英文向西方介紹，並取了一個書名叫 *Straw Sandals: Chinese Short Stories, 1918-1933*（《草鞋腳：英譯中國短篇小說集，1918-1933》）為了這個原故，他請教於魯迅先生和茅盾先生，請他們建議一些作家與小說。這些信件和手稿就是當時魯迅和茅盾給他的。這是1930年代的事，但是伊羅生要翻譯的小說，在40年後的1974年才由麻省理工學院出版部出版。翻譯出版後，伊羅生問我哈佛燕京圖書館是否願意收集這批資料（他當時在麻省理工學院作研究工作），我當然欣然接受了。

　　這批資料包括：（1）魯迅和茅盾給伊羅生的書信手稿6封（魯迅3封，茅盾起草，茅盾和魯迅共同署名的3封）；（2）魯迅、茅盾自傳手稿各一件（魯迅的是由別人代抄的，茅盾的是他的親筆）；（3）茅盾親筆擬的《草鞋腳》選題目錄及對巴金、冰心、吳組湘、歐陽山、草明、張瓴、東平、漣清等人的作品及生平簡介手稿一份；（4）茅盾親筆擬的介紹29種《中國左翼

文藝定期刊編目》手稿一份；（5）魯迅辭1935年9月紐約《小說雜誌》
（Story Magazine）譯載他的小說《風波》的稿費致伊羅生的英文信一封。這
些資料中，除魯迅的〈草鞋腳小引〉收入他的《且介亭雜文》和《魯迅全
集》第六卷，〈魯迅自傳〉收入《魯迅全集》第七卷外，其餘都未收入1976
年出版的《魯迅書信集》。1979年我為美國圖書館訪問中國代表團成員，順
便將這批文獻的影印本分別贈送北京圖書館與上海圖書館。他們喜出望外，
沒有想到還有這批他們不知道的文獻。當年12月，北京圖書館出版的《文
獻叢刊》中，把這一批資料全部複印並加以注釋出版，供諸於世。

　　除了這兩批重要的中文稿件外，還有兩批是英文的，它們對於研究民國
時期西方教會在中國發展高等教育和社會事業是非常珍貴的文獻。第一種是
廣州嶺南大學從1884年（當時叫Canton Christian College）建校到1952年停
校這一段相當長的時間的該校董事會的紀錄。這一批檔案不但對研究嶺南大
學的校史是不可或缺的第一手資料，也是對於教會在中國發展高等教育的歷
史有很高的參考價值。從這批檔案中也可以看到一些當時廣東的社會、政
治、經濟情形，以及當時中國政府一般的高等教育政策，特別是有關教會學
校的措施。另外一種是費吳生（George A. Fitch）先生和他的夫人
（Geraldine Fitch）在中國的檔案。費吳生夫婦在1920年代服務於中國基督教
青年會，二次世界大戰後與大陸國民政府及南韓政府政要頗多往還。這批檔
案對基督教青年會在中國大陸的發展是相當重要的資料。並包括少數他們與
台北及漢城政府要員的函件。費吳生夫人以其反共著作《台灣灘頭堡》
（*Formosa Beachhead*, 1953）聞名。費吳生先生的回憶錄《我在中國八十年》
（*My Eighty Years in China*），由台北美亞出版社1967年出版。

　　哈佛燕京圖書館對應時資料的收集也很重視，比如釣魚台事件、文化大
革命、天安門民運等。1970年代初期，保衛釣魚台運動在中國大陸、香
港、台灣進行得如火如荼時，在美國、加拿大的中國留學生、香港留學生和
台灣留學生也紛紛回應，遊行示威，同時發行了各式各樣的通訊、簡報、宣
言、特刊等。哈佛燕京圖書館收集了150多種這類的出版物，大部分是1971
年發行的。雖然很多都很零星，有些只有一期、兩期，但是總合起來，這批

文件是研究海外中國知識分子對這個愛國運動的反應的非常重要的文獻。

其次就是文化大革命紅衛兵的資料。在文化大革命期間，中國大陸出版界幾乎完全停止了正常的出版工作。《毛澤東選集》和《毛澤東語錄》差不多是唯一的出版物。但是在文革的初期有一個特別的例外，那就是各地紅衛兵小報的發行。從1966到1968這三年間這些小報是當時各地文革新聞的主要來源。它們登載了很多中共領導在這個時期的指示，包括毛澤東的「最高指示」，被清算的人的「反面教材」，其中包括中共高級幹部和領導，甚至於像劉少奇、鄧小平等人。小報上也登載了一些罕見的關於中共黨史的資料。

哈佛燕京圖書館所藏的紅衛兵小報最初來自香港，之後差不多全部都由華盛頓中國研究資料中心（Center for Chinese Research Materials，簡稱CCRM）供應。從1975到1999年CCRM所複印發行的紅衛兵小報及其他相關的紅衛兵資料約1,700多種，裝訂為56大冊。一兩年內將有另40大冊問世。這些資料是研究文革的最重要的原始文獻。

在應時的文獻檔案中，哈佛燕京圖書館所藏最引人注目的還是該館在六四民運被鎮壓後建立的「天安門檔案」。這個檔案在目前是美國大學圖書館中範圍最大、最廣的。當時建立這個檔案的原因是因為有感於天安門事件在中國現代史上的重要性，並且有鑑於當年五四運動時的文獻，由於無人收藏，現已湮滅不存，所以認為有建立這個檔案為歷史存證的必要。之後，募到一筆專款來支援這個工作，達數年之久，這個檔案方得建立。

檔案的主要內容如下：（1）從1989年4月15日（胡耀邦逝世）到6月4日這段時間內在天安門散發的各式傳單680餘件；（2）當時在北京張貼的1,700多張大字報的照片；（3）1,962張北京、上海等地的民運照片，包括175張幻燈片；（4）139卷錄影帶，包括美國主要的幾家電視台，特別是CNN，關於民運的報導，香港電台的粵語報導，以及北京中央廣播電台的報導。錄影帶中的一卷稱為《六四風波紀實》是中國政府在六四不久後，很匆促地製作的為六四天安門武力鎮壓辯護的紀錄片；（5）錄音帶80幾卷，其中大部分是「美國之音」在六四以後兩周內的報導和在1989年有關天安門回顧的廣播討論；而最具歷史性的，是6月3日晚上到6月4日早上，在天安門現場的一卷錄音；（6）六、七份美國學者當時在中國大陸的目擊記，地點包括北京、鄭州和成都；（7）六四不久後在香港、大陸、美國、英國、法國發表的有關天安門民運的中文文章和小冊子64種，包括中共北京市委宣傳部6月5日發表的《北京發生反革命暴亂的事實真相》和解放軍畫報社出版的《北京平息反革命暴亂》，其餘都是反對用武力鎮壓的出版物；（8）92種天安門後在大陸、香港和台灣出版的中文書籍，和34種緊接著六四中國留學生在美國、英國、法國和德國出版的期刊。大都相當零星，但也有二三十期的，內容都是反鎮壓、反中共的；（9）39種英文書籍、小冊子和130餘篇在各地發表的英文文章。在書籍中最有研究價值的是一部兩冊包含當時從海外發到中國民運組織和個人以及他們發到外面的傳真信件和其他有關的資料；（10）中文剪報，來源於大陸、香港、台灣和美國出版的報紙，其中香港的最多，有13種，包括《明報》、《星島晚報》、《文匯報》、《大公報》、《東方日報》、《香港經濟日報》、《信報》等。台灣其次，全部是《中國時報》，時間是從1989年4月11日到7月1日；（11）英文剪報46種，包括美國、英國和泰國出版的報紙。分量最多的是《紐約時報》（*New York Times*），其餘是泰國曼谷出版的《曼谷郵報》（*Bangkok Post*）、《華盛頓郵報》（*Washington Post*）、《亞洲華爾街時報》（*Asian Wall Street Journal*）、《虎報》（*Hong Kong Standard*）等；（12）兩件血衣。

　　哈佛燕京圖書館所藏電子資料中有兩種是比較特別的。一種是中央研究院建立的《二十五史全文檢索資料庫》，這個大家都很熟悉，不必多講。它之所以特別，是因為它是在美國僅有的兩部之一，另一部在西雅圖華盛頓大學東亞圖書館。館藏另一種特別的電子資料是一個數位資料庫。這個資料庫的內容是4,790多張黑白照片，這些照片是一位享有國際盛譽的德國女攝影家赫達‧莫里遜（Hedda Morrison，1908-1991）從1933到1946年在中國各地所拍的，裡面包括建築、街頭景象、服飾、宗教儀式、手工藝等。這批照片不但技術高超，而且非常有歷史價值。數位庫可以上網察看：http://hcl.harvard.edu/harvard-yenching。

　　哈佛燕京圖書館簡史和它的中國典籍蒐藏概況的介紹就此結束。如有任
何問題，請提出來討論。謝謝大家。

注釋

本文係作者2003年在台北淡江大學「吳文津先生講座」演講之一。收入《書林覽勝——
台灣與美國存藏中國典籍文獻概況——吳文津先生講座演講錄》，淡江大學中國文學系主
編（台北：臺灣學生書局，2003）。臺灣學生書局慨允轉載，特致謝忱。

裘開明與哈佛燕京圖書館

1959年與哈佛燕京圖書館首任館長裘開明先生合影。

　　裘開明這個名字長久以來就是美國東亞圖書館的代名詞。他在中國和美國分別接受了圖書館管理學的專業訓練後，就被美國大學聘請作為東亞圖書館的館長近40年之久，是美國大學中被任用的第一位東亞圖書館館長，並且是在位最久的一位。但是他真正的成就不只是這樣獨特而令人羨慕的紀錄，更在於他對美國東亞圖書館的發展作出的傑出貢獻。

　　他1898年出生在寧波附近鎮海的一個商人家庭。從小被送到鄉下叔輩所辦私塾誦讀四書五經。幾年後，他便被送到漢口文明書店（後來成為有名的中華書局）分店當過一年半的學徒。在那一年半中，裘先生說他開始對圖書感到興趣，並且對經濟學和商業管理也有了粗淺的認識。1911年辛亥革命後，他被送到長沙一個教會學校學習西學，然後得到武昌文華大學獎學金入學。在文華，他從自美國、加拿大、英國來的教師學習英文、法文、德文、歷史和數學。因此他早年即接受了西式教育。這種薰陶幫助他擴展了他的視野，並有利於他日後到美國在學術和專業方面的追求。當韋棣華女士（Mary Elizabeth Wood, 1861-1931）於1920年在中國成立第一所圖書館學校——文華大學圖書科時，裘先生是六個首批入學的學生之一。他暑假則在商務印書館的藏書樓涵芬樓（東方圖書館的前身）實習；1922年畢業後就任廈門大學圖書館首任館長。因為當時廈門深受日本影響，他便開始學習日文；同時還旁聽國文系著名詩人陳衍[1] 的課。由於為圖書館採訪圖書，他認識了以出版精良刻本著名的廣東廣雅書局經理徐信符[2]，向他學習了中國目錄學。在廈門大學，他還認識了著名的歐洲漢學家Gustav Ecke（艾鍔風）[3]和Paul Demieville（戴密微）[4]；還有後來在中國文學界著名的魯迅和林語堂。

　　1924年廈門大學派送裘館長至美國紐約公共圖書館圖書館學學校（The Library School of the New York Public Library，哥倫比亞大學圖書館學學院[The School of Library Service at Columbia University]的前身）研讀圖書館學。一年後他入哈佛大學研究院（Graduate School at Harvard University）研讀經濟學；就讀時，每星期到哈佛大學懷德納圖書館（Widener Library）義務工作數小時，以取得編目的經驗。1927年在他已經得到碩士學位，並且完成了一些博士課程後（1933年得博士學位），他接受了懷德納圖書館給他的一份工作，整理該館所收藏的中日文書籍。按照裘館長後來追述，當時哈佛大學圖書館館長柯立芝教授（Archibald C. Coolidge）對他講的話是這樣說的：「你不用擔心，你在中國怎麼做，在這裡就怎麼做，不用管在美國有沒有經驗。」當時美國東亞圖書管理專業尚未開展，對一個開拓者是機會也是挑戰，需要堅定的毅力和不懈的努力。裘館長本著典型的拓荒者精神接受了這份工作；充滿了精力、熱心、想像、謀略，自荊棘中找出出路；用理想和遠見在這片荒蕪的土地上建立了不少重要的里程碑，為後來者遵循。

　　他在哈佛的第一項主要任務就是為美國圖書館中文和日文資料設計一套分類法。因為當時無法自中國或日本借用一套全面並可被美國圖書館接受的分類法，裘館長結合他的創意和知識，設計了一套獨特而創新的分類法。將中國傳統四庫分類延伸到九類，以西方的數目字來代表。書號則取自作者名字的四角號碼。他1927年撰文 "Classification in China" 詮釋四庫要義，發表於《圖書館學刊》（*Library Journal*）。1929年，他又寫了〈裘開明哈佛大學中國圖書分類法凡例〉發表在《文華圖書科季刊》（*Boone Library School Quarterly*）。1933年將此文修改後以〈哈佛燕京圖書館中文圖書分類法〉發表在《燕京大學圖書館報》（*Yenching University Library Bulletin*）上。經過16年的應用，歷經馮漢驥[5]、于震寰[6]進一步的修正，這套分類法終於在1943年以《漢和圖書分類法》（*A Classification Scheme for Chinese and Japanese Books*）由美國學術團體聯合會（American Council of Learned Societies）下的遠東學會在華盛頓特區出版。（遠東學會原名Committee On Far Eastern Studies為亞洲學會 [Association for Asian Studies] 前身）。這套分類法極受歡迎，被美國、加拿大、英國、荷蘭、澳洲22個主要東亞圖書館採用。雖然過去十年間這些圖書館中有一些已經改用國會圖書館分類法，但是過去採用哈佛分類法分類的資料仍然保持原用的編號。正可作為裘開明對美國東亞圖書館做出最重要的貢獻的證物。

　　裘館長在哈佛的另一項創新便是在編目卡上作者和書名除了使用中文、日文外，還加上羅馬拼音，使美國圖書館的中日文編目卡片也能按英文字母排列。這種史無前例的創新如今已成為常規了。裘館長在哈燕館[7]建立的中日文編目卡片目錄均以羅馬拼音排列，往後建立的分類卡目錄亦以此法排列。東亞館使用主題卡是很多年後的事。裘館長當時採用分類目錄提供主題目錄的功能，是開東亞館使用主題檢索之先河。

　　裘館長也是館際合作的開拓者。當哈燕館於1928年開始用舊時藍墨水複印編目卡片時，他在那年的年終報告中寫道：「這種做法可促進中文書籍合作編目的工作。」因此自1935到1938年哈燕館將此種用藍墨水複製的編目卡片提供給其他東亞圖書館使用。自1938到1944年又提供在北平印刷的編目卡片以及一些在劍橋石印的編目卡片給其他東亞圖書館。當1943年美國圖書館協會決定採取自重慶統籌採購中文資料以航空郵寄來美的措施時（The ALA China Cooperative Book Purchasing Program），哈燕館同意接受這

批書刊，將其編目並複製卡片分發給各東亞館。當時在哈佛印刷部
（Harvard Printing Office）印刷的這些中文編目卡片是在美國印刷中文編目卡
片的開端。直到1949年國會圖書館開始複製和分發美國各東亞館東方資料
的編目卡片時（Oriental Card Reproduction Program），哈燕館方結束其供應
編目卡片的工作。在此之前，哈燕館已經分發的編目卡片總數為19,000張。
自1949到1958年國會圖書館從事此項工作時，裘館長總是確保完成哈燕館
分擔的部分，提供了28,000張編目卡片，超過國會圖書館複製分發的卡片總
數的三分之一。

　　裘館長對館際合作的重視還表現在其他方面。早在1928年他剛上任之
後，即開始作與中國和日本圖書館建立交換關係的準備工作；也開始將所藏
期刊呈報國會圖書館聯合期刊目錄。在1942年美國東方學會（The American
Oriental Society）年會上，他呼籲出版東亞資料聯合目錄。為此他於1945年
將哈燕館日文15,000張分類編目卡片拍攝成縮微膠捲提供給國會圖書館，作
為國會圖書館當時籌畫出版日文書籍聯合目錄之用。1952年他再次呼籲出
版聯合目錄一事，建議從中日文期刊開始。但因資金缺乏，他的建議不幸未
能實現。自1953年始他作為遠東學會代表參加美國圖書館協會東方資料編
目特別委員會（ALA's Special Committee on Cataloging Oriental Materials）
和國會圖書館東方資料處理委員會（LC's Oriental Processing Committee）合
作發展建立東亞資料編目規則的工作。為此他發表了修改美國圖書館協會編
目規則的建議（"Harvard Proposals for Modification of ALA Cataloging
Rules"）。自1957年始所有東亞圖書館均一律採用這個特別委員會設定的編
目規則，奠定了美國東亞資料編目的基礎。

　　作為一個圖書館員，裘館長特別重視服務。沒有什麼比讀者能使用他辛
苦收藏來的資料更令他快樂和感到滿足。他不是一個保守的圖書監管員，小
心守護他的寶藏，而是以「服務」為重的圖書館員，認為圖書館本身沒有存
在的價值，其價值在於為讀者提供服務而來。為了讓哈佛之外的學者對哈燕
館收藏有更清楚的認識，他於1936年到中國監督哈燕館所藏中文資料分類
目錄的出版。自1938到1940年出版了《美國哈佛大學燕京學社漢和圖書館

漢籍分類目錄》（*A Classified Catalogue of Chinese Books in the Chinese-Japanese Library of the Harvard-Yenching Institute at Harvard University*）經學類、哲學宗教類、歷史科學類三冊，首創美國東亞館出版目錄的先例。不幸的是，雖然其餘的目錄校定稿已經送往劍橋，這項工作因為太平洋戰爭爆發，隨後在北平印刷目錄的哈佛燕京學社引得編纂處印刷廠被摧毀而停頓。隨著已經出版的三冊目錄，他還將三冊內的個別卡片分別印刷分發給美國各東亞館為其編目所用。

　　本著如上為讀者服務的理念，他於1954年促使《哈佛大學漢和圖書館日本全集叢書目錄》（*Japanese Collected Works and Series in the Chinese-Japanese Library at Harvard University*）的出版。並在1961年發表〈哈佛大學哈佛燕京學社圖書館藏明代類書概述〉（An Annotated Catalog of Ming Encyclopedias and Reference Works in the Chinese-Japanese Library of the Harvard-Yenching Institute at Harvard University），而後又撰〈四庫失收明代類書考〉（"Ming Encyclopedias and Reference Works Unrecorded in the Ssu-k'u ch'uan-shu"）登錄於1969年香港中文大學《中國文化研究所學報》第二卷第一期。

　　裘館長以樂於助人聞名中外。無論是新生或資深的學者，只要向他求教，他都熱心協助。當我初來哈佛時，他就告誡我不要讓讀者空手而去。他就是本著這種精神為讀者服務。

　　裘館長不僅毫不保留地為哈燕館服務，同時也毫不保留地協助其他東亞館的發展。1930年代初他協助哥倫比亞大學發展其東亞館藏，並協助史丹佛大學開始其中文書的編目。二戰後，加州大學柏克萊分校及胡佛研究所成立東亞館時均曾向他求教。1965年自哈燕館退休後，他馬上接受明尼蘇達大學圖書館邀請去重整其東亞收藏；其後又被香港中文大學延聘為該校大學圖書館第一任館長，服務四年，成績卓然。除此之外，他的影響力還間接地延伸到海內外。他曾吸收了不少人才為哈燕館工作。隨後有些人轉移他地，各自發揮其專業才幹。其中包括後來成為普林斯頓大學圖書館助理館長兼主管葛思德東亞圖書館的童世綱 [8] 及與Arthur W. Hummel（恆慕義）、L.

Carrington Goodrich（傅路德，又名富路特）分別合作編纂《清代名人傳略》
（*Eminent Chinese of the Ch'ing Period* [*1644-1912*]）、《明代人名錄》
（*Dictionary of Ming Biography, 1368-1644*）的房兆楹、杜聯喆 [9] 夫婦；這兩
種巨著成為往後漢學研究不可或缺的參考書。其他尚有後來成為燕京大學圖
書館館長的田洪都 [10]、國立北京圖書館參考諮詢館員的鄧衍林 [11]，以及現
在還在北京大學圖書館系任教的陳鴻舜 [12]。

　　任何關於裘館長在東亞圖書館界開創工作的描述，如未提及他在哈燕館
的收藏，均不可稱為完整。而他在哈燕館的典藏史足可另行開章詳述。簡而
言之，裘館長為圖書館界的巨人，他在哈佛幾乎從無開始而建立了西方最豐
富的東亞圖書館之一。他的建樹可謂空前絕後。

　　美國的東亞研究及教學有今日之發展與成就多賴於東亞圖書館的支持與
協助。裘館長在這方面正是其關鍵人物。我們向他在這個領域的領導力，對
專業的奉獻，熱誠的服務和開拓者的眼光致敬。先生退休時，哈佛燕京學社
董事會稱譽他為「融貫東西傳統精華的典型學者。」誠不虛也。

注釋

本文為1984年3月在華盛頓特區亞洲學會年會「美國東亞圖書館開創者」（Building East
Asian Research Collections in America: Pioneers and Their Achievements）研討會發表的報
告。原載《東亞圖書館通訊》（*Committee on East Asian Libraries Bulletin*）第74期（1984
年6月），頁2-6；並載《架起中美文化的橋梁，華人圖書館員協會回眸三十年，1973-
2003》（*Bridging Cultures, Chinese American Librarians and their Organization: A Glance at
the Thirty Years of CALA, 1973-2003*）（桂林：廣西師範大學出版社，2004），頁26-33。譯
注文載《天祿論叢：中國研究圖書館員學會學刊》，第3卷（2013年3月），頁17-24。

[1]　陳衍（1856-1937），近代詩人，字叔伊，號石遺，福建侯官（今福州市）人。清光緒
　　八年（1882）舉人；曾是台灣巡撫劉銘傳、湖廣總督張之洞幕僚；民國後，在南北各
　　大學執教，編有《福建通志》。
[2]　徐信符（1879-1947），名紹棨，字信符（也作舜符），以字行，原籍廣東番禺；1898
　　年考錄為博士弟子員，後為著名藏書家，對嶺南地方文獻的收藏、整理、研究卓有成
　　就。1917年廣東省長李耀漢指令恢復廣雅書局，設立廣雅板片印行所，從屬廣東圖

書館，由徐負責管理。編輯《廣雅叢書》，於1920年出版。

[3] 艾鍔風（Gustav Ecke, 1896-1971），德國漢學家，研究中國藝術，1923-1928年執教廈門大學。

[4] 戴密微（Paul Demieville, 1894-1979），法國漢學家，敦煌學重要學者，1924-1926年執教廈門大學。

[5] 馮漢驥（1899-1977），湖北宜昌人。1919年入武昌文華大學文科，1921年入圖書科，1923年畢業後歷任廈門大學圖書館、河北省圖書館、湖北省圖書館、浙江大學文理學院圖書館主任；1931年10月被哈燕館聘為編目員。1933年8月15日離職，前往賓州大學深造，1936年獲人類學博士。當裘館長1936年夏回中國時，他於9月1日開始代理漢和圖書館館長至1937年7月回國。回國後從事考古研究工作。1949年後歷任西南博物院副院長、四川大學歷史系考古教研室主任兼四川省博物館館長。

[6] 于震寰（Zunvair Yue, 1907-1999），字鏡宇，山東蓬萊人。1933年畢業於私立武昌文華圖書館學專科學校；1927-1935年在國立北平圖書館任職；1935年到國立北京大學圖書館任中文編目主任；1936年開始在南京中央圖書館工作；1939年12月1日以交換館員被邀請到哈燕館協助日文編目工作；1946年7月回到中央圖書館擔任採訪組主任；1948年被哈燕社聘為副館長，主管日文資料；1951年還兼管新成立的韓文收藏；1959年開始負責參考諮詢，兼管滿蒙藏文資料，一直工作到1973年6月退休。

[7] 哈佛燕京圖書館1928年由哈佛燕京學社成立時稱Chinese and Japanese Collection, Harvard College Library（哈佛大學圖書館漢和文庫），1936年改為Chinese and Japanese Library of the Harvard Yenching Institute at Harvard University（哈佛燕京學社漢和圖書館），1965年改為Harvard-Yenching Library（哈佛燕京圖書館）。1976年轉屬哈佛文理學院為Harvard-Yenching Library, Harvard College Library, Harvard University。本文以哈燕館統稱。

[8] 童世綱（James Shih-kang Tung, 1911-1982），湖北漢川人。1933年畢業於私立武昌文華圖書館學專科學校。就讀前在國立北平圖書館工作兩年，畢業後到南京中央陸軍軍官學校圖書館以及國民黨軍政單位工作。1946年8月到哈燕館工作，同時在波士頓大學讀書，得公共管理學碩士。1951年1月辭職，赴普林斯頓大學葛思德東亞圖書館任中文編目。1952年繼胡適為館長，一直到1977年退休。

[9] 房兆楹（Chaoying Fang, 1908-1985），出生於天津。1928年畢業於燕京大學數學系；1930年畢業於私立武昌文華圖書館學專科學校。1930-1932年擔任燕京大學圖書館採購和編目部主任。杜聯喆（Lienche Tu, 1902-1994），天津楊柳青鎮人。1924年畢業於燕京大學歷史系，1926年獲碩士學位，留校參與哈佛燕京學社引得編纂處的工作。1932年兩人合編《三十三種清代傳記綜合引得》。1941年引得編纂處又出版了他

們合編的《增校清朝進士題名碑錄附引得》。1933年兩人先後赴哈燕館工作。1934年8月轉往國會圖書館東方部參與清人傳記寫作計畫，協助恆慕義編纂《清代名人傳略》。1963年9月房兆楹在澳洲國立大學東方圖書館副館長兩年後，重返哥倫比亞大學協助傅路德教授編輯《明代人名錄》。該書於1976年出版。同年哥倫比亞大學授予房、杜夫婦榮譽博士學位。

[10] 田洪都，1903年生，山東安邱人。1924年武昌文華大學圖書科畢業。1929-1941年擔任燕京大學圖書館館長。當裘館長1930年夏回中國收集博士論文資料時，他來美代理漢和圖書館館長一年。

[11] 鄧衍林（1908-1980），江西吉安人。1928-1930年在江西省圖書館任助理館員。1931年私立武昌文華圖書館學專科學校講習班畢業。1931-1937年任國立北平圖書館參考諮詢館員。抗戰時入西南聯大師範學院。1945年赴美在哈燕館擔任中文編目，不久即入哥倫比亞大學，獲教育學碩士。1946年在聯合國擔任中文出版校對工作。1956年10月回國任教北京大學圖書館系。著有《中文參考書舉要》、《中國邊疆圖籍錄》。

[12] 陳鴻舜（1905-1986），江蘇泰州人。1926年畢業於燕京大學經濟系，任燕京大學圖書館秘書。1941年10月到哈燕館工作；1942年9月辭職入哥大圖書館學院；1943年畢業後任哥大東亞館研究員。1947年4月回國任燕京大學圖書館館長。中共建國後，參加創建北京大學圖書館學系。歷任副教授、教授。

（胡嘉陽譯注）

A. Kaiming Chiu and the Harvard-Yenching Library

The name Alfred Kaiming Chiu has long been synonymous with East Asian librarianship in the United States. Having been trained as a professional librarian both in China and in the United States, Kaiming Chiu was the first person to be appointed Librarian of an East Asian collection at an American university, and his tenure of almost four decades at the Harvard-Yenching Library remains to this day the longest among the nation's East Asian librarians. But Dr. Chiu's legacy lies not in these records, however unique and enviable they may be, but rather in what these records represent in terms of the enormous contributions he made to the course of the development of East Asian librarianship in the United States.

Born in 1898 into a modest merchant's family in the town of Zhenhai near the port city of Ningbo, Kaiming Chiu never went to a modern school in his youth. Instead he was sent to a village clan school run by the family of his uncle. There he was given instruction in the basic Confucian teachings, including the Four Books and the Five Classics. After a few years of study at this old-fashioned school, he was sent to be an apprentice in the Hankow branch of Wenming Shuju which later became the famous Zhonghua Book Company. During his year and a half at the bookstore, he, in his own words, "acquired a taste for books, learned the rudiments of economics and the essentials of business management." Following the 1911 Revolution, he was sent to study Western learning (Xi Xue) at the Changsha Mission School. From there he went to Boone College in Wuchang on a scholarship. While at Boone, he studied English, French, German, history and mathematics under professors from England, Canada, and the United

States. Thus, from an early age, he was exposed to the West and Western teachings, an experience which helped broaden his outlook and greatly facilitated his subsequent scholarly and professional pursuits In the United States. When in 1920 Boone established the first library school In China under the guidance of Miss Mary Elizabeth Wood, Dr. Chiu was enrolled in the first class of six students, and worked during the summers as an apprentice librarian in the great Han Fen Lou（later known as the Oriental Library）attached to the Commercial Press. Following his graduation from Boone Library School and Central China College in 1922, he went to Amoy and became the first Librarian of the University of Amoy. While there he studied Japanese, as Amoy at that time was under heavy Japanese influence. He also attended lectures in Chinese literature given at the University by the well-known poet, Chen Yan, and while acquiring books for the library he became a friend of Mr. Xu Xinfu, the manager of Guangya Shuju （Guangdong Provincial Press）, a renowned publisher of fine woodblock editions. From Mr. Xu he learned much about Chinese bibliography. At the University of Amoy, he also was acquainted with such eminent European Sinologists as Gustav Ecke and Paul Demieville, as well as Chinese literary figures who later became famous authors, among them, Lu Xun and Lin Yutang.

In the fall of 1924, he was sent by Amoy University to study library science at the Library School of the New York Public Library（now the School of Library Service at Columbia University）. A year later, he entered Graduate School at Harvard to study economics. While a graduate student at Harvard, he volunteered a few hours a week at Widener Library in order to gain cataloging experience. In 1927, having taken his M.A. and finished some work toward a Ph.D. degree （which he received in 1933）, he accepted an offer by Widener Library to "do something about its Chinese and Japanese books." His charge from Professor Archibald C. Coolidge, then the Director of the Harvard University Library, was, in Dr. Chiu's words, "to organize and catalog the Chinese-Japanese collection as I would do it in China and not to worry about my short American training." What he began to do rivaled a true pioneer's work, as East Asian librarianship in the United States in those days was frontier land in the library profession, offering both opportunities and challenges to the hardy and the determined. He accepted and plunged ahead with the energy, enthusiasm, imagination, and resourcefulness of a typical frontiersman. He cleared some brush, created some passages, and with vision and foresight laid some of the most important landmarks on this uncharted land which were to benefit greatly those who were to follow him.

His first major task at Harvard was the devising of a classification scheme suitable for Chinese and Japanese books in an American library as there were at that time no comprehensive or generally accepted schemes to be borrowed from China or Japan. Combining ingenuity and knowledge he produced a unique and innovative scheme incorporating the features of the traditional Siku division with expansions into nine classes to which he added a Western numerical notation system. For the author number he opted for the use of the Four Corner system. He explained the outline of the Siku division in an article entitled "Classification in China" in *Library Journal* in 1927, and of his own scheme in "Harvard University Chinese Book Classification: An Introduction" published in *Boone Library Journal* in 1929. With further modifications, the scheme appeared in *Yenchlng University Library Bulletin* in 1933 under the title "Harvard-Yenching Institute Library Classification." Finally, in 1943, after some sixteen years of use at Harvard and with further refinement by Professor Feng Hanji and Mr. Zunvair Yue, the scheme was officially published as *A Classification Scheme for Chinese and Japanese Books* by the Committee on Far Eastern Studies (the predecessor of the Association for Asian Studies) of the American Council of Learned Societies in Washington, D.C. His classification scheme became so popular that some 22 major East Asian libraries in the United States, Canada, England, Holland, and Australia adopted it for their collections use. Although some of these libraries have during the last decade changed to the LC Classification Scheme, the great majority of their collections remain cataloged In the Harvard-Yenching Scheme, and they stand today as a visible testimony to one of the most important contributions Kaiming Chiu made to America's East Asian librarianship.

Another innovation Dr. Chiu Introduced at Harvard was the use of romanization for author and title on a library catalog card in addition to the original script. This made possible the arrangement of a dictionary catalog of East Asian publications in an American library, and is now firmly established as standard practice. The separate dictionary catalogs for Chinese and Japanese which Dr. Chiu set up at Harvard were the first of their kind, as was the extensive use of analytics in those catalogs. Subject cataloging was then many years away in an East Asian library, and he opted for the use of a classified catalog as a means of providing a subject approach.

Kaiming Chiu was also a pioneer in interlibrary cooperation. When the Harvard-Yenching Library began making catalog cards in 1928 using the old blue-ink ditto process, he envisaged this, as recorded in his Annual Report for that year, as "a step forward toward cooperative cataloging for Chinese books," and he made these cards available to other libraries from 1935-1938. From 1938-1944 he distributed Chinese cards printed in Peking as well as some lithographed copies made in Cambridge. When the Harvard-Yenching Library agreed in 1943 to receive books for cataloging under the ALA China Cooperative Book Purchasing Program, he instituted the first Chinese printed card program in the United States at the Harvard Printing Office, and distributed cards for the books by air mail from Chongqing from 1944-1948. With the advent of the Oriental Card Reproduction Program at the Library of Congress in 1949, the Harvard-Yenching Library's card distribution work came to an end. By that time, it had already distributed some 19,000 cards. Under LC's Card Reproduction Program from 1949-58, Dr. Chiu made sure that the Harvard-Yenching Library did its share, and contributed more than 28,000 cards, constituting more than one-third of all the cards reproduced by that program.

His belief in the importance of inter-library cooperation also led him to other activities. As early as 1928, soon after his appointment at Harvard, he began making arrangements for exchange with libraries in China and Japan, and started sending reports to the Union List of Serials. At the annual meeting of the American Oriental Society in 1942, he proposed the establishment of a national union catalog of East Asian publications. Toward that goal, he made available in 1945 to the Library of Congress, where work had begun to develop such a union catalog of Japanese books, a microfilm of the Harvard-Yenching Library's classified catalog of some 15,000 Japanese cards. His striving for inter-library cooperation did not end there. In 1952 he renewed his plea for union catalog work, this time proposing the compilation of a National Union Catalog of Chinese and Japanese Serials. Unfortunately, his proposal was not realized at that time because of a lack of funds. Beginning in 1953 he was appointed as the representative of the Far Eastern Association (the immediate predecessor of the Association for Asian Studies) to ALA's Special Committee on Cataloging Oriental Materials which, in cooperation with the Oriental Processing Committee of the Library of Congress, was developing uniform, standard rules for cataloging East Asian materials. He was quite active in the Committee's deliberations and wrote the "Harvard Proposals for Modification of ALA Cataloging Rules." The Committee's recommended rules were adopted by all East Asian libraries in 1957, and have since been the basis for cataloging East Asian works in the United States.

As a librarian, Dr. Chiu placed a high premium on service. Nothing gave him more pleasure or satisfaction than having people use the collections he had painstakingly developed. He was not a conservative custodian who jealously guarded his treasures, but a service-oriented librarian in a very modern sense dedicated to the proposition that libraries do not exist for their own sake but for the purpose of providing services to their users. In order to make the Harvard-Yenching Library's growing collections better known and thereby more accessible to a wider scholarly community outside of Harvard, he went to China in December 1936 to supervise the production of the classified catalog of Harvard-Yenching Library's Chinese Collection. From 1938 to 1940 the first three volumes of this catalog, covering Confucian Classics, Philosophy and Religion, and Historical Sciences, were published, thus pioneering the publication of book catalogs of East Asian libraries in the United States. Unfortunately, publication of the remainder of the catalog was prevented by the outbreak of war in the Pacific and the subsequent destruction of the Index Press at Yenching University in Beijing where the catalog was being printed, even though page proofs had been run off and sent to Cambridge. As a by-product of this catalog publication project, individual cards for the published volumes were also printed and distributed to American libraries which used them in cataloging their own Chinese collections.

With the same purpose of public service in mind, Dr. Chiu initiated the publication of *Japanese Collected Works and Series in the Chinese-Japanese Library at Harvard University* (1954), and authored *An Annotated Catalog of Ming Encyclopedias and Reference Works in the Chinese-Japanese Library of the Harvard-Yenching Institute at Harvard University* (1961), and *Ming Encyclopedias and Reference Works Unrecorded in the Ssu-k'u chuan-shu* (1969).

In Cambridge and elsewhere, Dr. Chiu was widely known and appreciated for the attention he was always ready and willing to give to anyone who came to him for counsel and advice, be the person a first-year student or an established scholar. His advice to me when I first arrived at Harvard was, "Don't let any user go away from the Library empty-handed." And he lived by that spirit of service.

While he gave of himself unselfishly to serve the Harvard-Yenching Library, he was equally unselfish in helping other East Asian libraries in their development.

In the early 1930s he advised the Columbia University Library on its East Asian collection, and also helped the Stanford University Library to initiate a cataloging program for its Chinese books. Following World War II his advice was likewise sought by the University of California in Berkeley and the Hoover Institution at Stanford in establishing their East Asian collections. Following his retirement from Harvard in 1965 he was invited by the University of Minnesota Library to help revitalize their East Asian Collection, and later he was appointed the first University Librarian at the Chinese University of Hong Kong, where he served with great distinction for four years. Indirectly, his influence was also felt in other ways. During his tenure at the Harvard-Yenching Library, he was able to attract a number of very able people to serve on the Library's staff. Some of them subsequently went on to other institutions, both here and abroad, and distinguished themselves in their professional endeavors. They include the late James S. K. Tung, who became Assistant University Librarian and Curator of the Gest Oriental Library and East Asian Collections at Princeton; Mr. and Mrs. Fang Chaoying, known for their impeccable scholarship on Ming and Qing history who collaborated with Dr. Arthur W. Hummel and Professor L. Carrington Goodrich respectively in the compilation of *Eminent Chinese of the Ch'ing Period* and *Dictionary of Ming Biography,* two publications of lasting importance to Chinese studies; Mr. Tian Hongdu who became Librarian of Yenching University Library; Mr. Deng Yanlin who served as Reference Librarian at the National Library of Peking; and Professor Chen Hongshun who now teaches in the Department of Library Science at Beijing University.

While any description of Dr. Chiu's pioneering work in East Asian librarianship would be incomplete without mention of the great collections he built at Harvard, the history of his collection building efforts is nevertheless another story in itself. Suffice it to say here that he will be remembered as a giant in this field who succeeded in building up from almost nothing one of the greatest libraries for East Asian research in the Western world. It is unlikely that his accomplishments will ever be duplicated.

In closing, it can be said that East Asian scholarship in the United States would not have developed the way it did without the support of America's East Asian libraries, and Kaiming Chiu played an extraordinarily large role in that support. We salute him for his leadership in the field, his devotion to his chosen profession, his dedication to service, and his vision as a pioneer. In the words of the Trustees of the Harvard-Yenching Institute who paid him tribute upon his retirement, he was "a scholar who exemplifies the best in the traditions and accomplishments of both East and West."

Notes

A paper presented at the panel on "Building East Asian Research Collections in America: Pioneers and Their Achievements," Association for Asian Studies, Annual Meeting, Washington, D.C., March 1984. This was published in *Committee on East Asian Libraries Bulletin,* no. 74 (June 1984), pp. 2-6.

哈佛大學哈佛燕京圖書館中國古籍

1988年（右起）故宮博物院副院長昌彼得、台大中文系教授潘美月、
張淑香參觀哈佛燕京圖書館。

　　哈佛大學蒐集中文圖書始於1879年（光緒五年）。初由哈佛大學大學部
圖書館管理。1928年（民國十七年）哈佛燕京學社漢和圖書館成立後（後
改名為哈佛燕京圖書館），凡東亞語文圖書資料之收集、管理及服務工作，
均轉由其負責，迄今已56年。其間對中國古籍之蒐集，不遺餘力，成海外
收藏重點之一。

　　哈佛燕京圖書館古籍收藏可分為三個時期：（1）創始時期（1928-
1937）。此期收集工作多與燕京大學圖書館合作進行。同時亦積極自美國逕
向上海、杭州、漢口、成都及廣西各地採購。（2）中期（1937-1945）。自
盧溝橋事件至珍珠港事件四年間，華北名望隱居不願與偽政府合作者，大批
出讓私藏古籍。其時北平琉璃廠、隆福寺書肆善本充溢，在華日人多購之。

前哈佛燕京圖書館館長裘開明先生時亦在北平監督哈佛燕京圖書館目錄出版事，亦大量選購。現館藏中文善本之大部均在此時購來。珍珠港事件爆發後，日軍占領燕大，本館與燕大之合作採購工作遂告結束。旋乃轉向西南各省自美國直接採購。現館藏多種西南方志，即在此時所購進者。（3）後期（1945至現在）。第二次世界大戰後十餘年間，中國古籍在日本書肆出現者甚夥。本館遂開始在日本收購，所獲頗多。後又由齊耀琳、齊耀珊兄弟處購進鈔本500餘種，復由齊如山哲嗣處購來齊氏收藏明清戲曲小說，計72種。內多當時禁書，且多有齊氏跋尾者。（見吳曉鈴輯〈哈佛大學所藏高陽齊氏百舍齋善本小說跋尾〉，載《明清小說論叢》第一輯〔瀋陽：春風文藝出版社，1984〕，頁289-320）。近年大陸禁止古籍出口，間有出沒於日本書肆者，或索價昂貴，或被日本圖書館爭先搶購，本館收進者無幾。雖古籍微卷之採購有大量之增加，然已非原版之善本矣。

　　現館藏中國古籍善本計（1）宋版15種，66冊；（2）元版25種，576冊；（3）明版1,328種，19,527冊；（4）清版（至乾隆朝止）1,964種，20,904冊。此外尚有鈔本1,215種，分訂4,560冊；拓片500餘張；法帖36種，301冊。茲就館藏古籍有代表性者，分別列舉於後，以供參考及指正。

宋版

　　宋代刻書，極一時之盛。初僅許官刻，由國子監及地方官署執行之。監本刊刻謹嚴，每刻必經校印，詳校，再校。神宗熙寧書刻解禁後，私刻、坊刻大興。私刻亦大都精校慎刻，而坊刻則以牟利為目的，品質較劣。其時坊刻以福建建陽之麻沙及崇化兩地為最盛。其書不及浙蜀刻本之精確，但其快速印量多，遂有「建本遍天下」之說。北宋所刻之書較南宋者流傳較少。本館僅藏少數佛經如北宋梵夾本。今就所藏南宋本略舉數種如下：

　　1.《名臣碑傳琬琰之集》一百零七卷，32冊4函。宋杜大珪編，南宋紹熙五年（1194）刊本。15行25字。是書字體恭端，紙色蒼橙。白口，單邊，順魚尾。書中有元明遞修之滲入。商務印書館《四部叢刊》有收此書，但非全本。台北有據國立中央圖書館藏鈔本之影印本。

2.《西山先生真文忠公讀書記》存卷甲之二十一。宋真德秀撰，南宋開慶元年（1259）湯漢等福州刊本。大字9行16字，小雙行24字。是書書法端正，大字如錢。且刀法秀勁，紙墨亦精良。為蝴蝶裝。

3.《纂圖互注揚子法言》十卷，2冊1函。漢揚雄撰，南宋末建安刊本。11行20字。是書為黑口，左右雙邊，順魚尾。有景佑三年（1036）序文，序後有題記稱：「本宅今將監本四子纂圖互注附入重言重意，精加校正，並無訛謬，謄作大字刊行，務令學者得以參考，互相發明，誠為益之大也。建安謹啟」。有「雙劍樓收藏宋本」、「鐵琴銅劍樓」、「傅沅叔藏書記」等印記，並傅增湘1930年手跋。

4.《漢書》存卷五十三。漢班固撰，唐顏師古注，南宋嘉定間建安蔡琪一經堂刊本。8行16字。小字雙行21字。此書原一百二十卷。仿官刻大字。行格疏朗，墨如點漆。卷末題刻：「右將監本、杭本、越本及三劉宋祁諸本參校其有同異並附於古注之下」。繼有大字：「景十三王傳第二十三」。末行刻「正文伍仟捌佰三拾玖字注文三仟肆佰柒拾陸字」。有「寒雲秘笈珍藏之印」、「與身共存亡」、「後北宋一廛」、「克文」等印記。寒雲手題稱此卷係乙卯年（1915）以宋黃善夫刻《史記河渠書》殘冊與傅沅叔換得者。

5.《廣韻》五卷5冊1函。不著編者姓名，南宋建陽坊刻，明修巾箱本。12行字數不等，小字雙行約30字。是書或為宋陳彭年等編。有陳州司法孫愐唐韻序。每卷卷首有子目，分刻三排。細黑口，雙邊，順魚尾。

元版

元初設興文署於京師，繼中書省主掌刊刻事宜。地方刻書則多由書院主其成，私刻、坊刻亦盛。元代書院群立，刻書標準甚高。顧亭林曾謂書院刻書有三善：「山長無所事，而勤於校讎，一也。不惜費，而工精，二也。板不儲官，而易印行，三也。」元刻多黑口，字亦多仿趙體，紙墨遠不如宋刻，然亦有不在此例者。宋刻多用諱字，元刻則無諱字。元刻牌記有助於版本之鑑定，而因此後世翻刻偽裝者，亦復不少。今檢出館藏元版較佳者數種如後。

　　1.《通志》二百卷，320冊40函。宋鄭樵撰，元至治二年（1322）福州三山郡庠刊本。9行21字。此書紙張寬大，字大而秀美，墨蹟清朗，為元刊中之上乘。白口，單邊，雙魚尾。書口頂端有字數，下端有刻工姓名。有「楊氏家藏書畫印」、「王印士禎」等印章。

　　2.《宋史》存卷一百七十至一百七十二，一百八十七至一百八十八共3冊2函。元托克托等修，元至正間刊本。10行20字。是書為《宋史志》職官卷一百二十三至一百二十五，兵卷一百四十至一百四十一。卷一百七十缺頁16至17；卷一百七十一頁18係抄補。黑口，四周雙邊，順魚尾。下魚尾下有刻工姓名。紙質粗黃，但刻工極佳。

　　3.《圖繪寶鑑》五卷，補遺一卷，4冊1函。元夏文彥輯，元至正二十六年（1366）刊本。12行20字。此書為黑口巾箱本。左右雙欄，對魚尾。「補遺」末頁有「至正丙午新刊」牌記。紙質粗糙，然版刻頗精，字體及刀法亦極嚴整。卷四第17、第25頁，及卷五第1至第2、第6至第7頁抄補。

　　4.《增廣事聯詩學大成》三十卷，10冊2函。宋毛直方編，元至正十四年（1354）浙江鄞江書院刊本。14行字數不等。小字雙行32字。是本黑口，四周雙邊。牌記云：「至正甲午中秋鄞江書院重刊」。

　　5.《新編事文類聚翰墨大全》一百三十四卷，60冊8函。宋劉應李編，元大德十一年（1307）序，刊本。12行26字。小字14行28字。此書黑口，四周雙邊，順魚尾。總目後14頁為「混一諸道之圖」。趙體字跡秀潤，板刻刀法極靈活。

明版

　　明內府刻書由司禮監領其事。監中設漢經廠、番經廠及道經廠，所刻世稱經廠本。多黑口，白紙，趙字，然多校讎不精。南北國子監亦有刊刻，但遠不及司禮監之夥。其時宋元舊版多藏南監，有補刻印行者，皆善本也。藩府及地方官刻亦盛。藩府多精刻，地方官刻書帕本則不如之。私刻、坊刻亦至多。初多精校，尤以吳中刻本為著。明中葉後，書坊蔚起，但刻本妄作臆改，割補屢見。然亦有佼佼者如毛晉汲古閣刻書，至今為世人所推崇。下列舉本館所藏明本，以供參考指正。

1.《十三經注疏》173冊21函。明嘉靖間李元陽，福建刊本。9行21字。是書為明代私刻之上乘。白口，右雙邊，無魚尾。書口有刻工姓名「余伯環、余清、陸榮、陸文、張元隆等」。有「鵝湖亭藏書」印記。

2.《十三經注疏》160冊20函。明崇禎元年（1628）至十二年（1639）海虞毛氏汲古閣刊本。9行21字。此書為汲古閣之精刻本。白口，四周單邊，無魚尾。書口下端刻「汲古閣」。

3.《書傳大全》十卷，卷首一卷，10冊20函。明胡廣等撰，明永樂間經廠刊本。10行22字。此書大字本，黑口，四周雙邊，對魚尾。紙質瑩潔，書法雕刻精美，為經廠本中之上乘

4.《詩傳大全》二十卷，綱領一卷，圖一卷，詩序辯說一卷。明胡廣等撰，明永樂十三年（1415）內府刻本。10行22字。是書板式如《書傳大全》。書法、紙質及刀法精美，為內府刻本之典型。

5.《六子全書》38冊3函。明顧春輯，明嘉靖十二年（1533）吳郡顧氏世德堂刊本。8行17字。此書大字本。字體端方，紙墨優良。白口，四周雙欄，白魚尾。缺扉頁及序跋。書口上端題「世德堂刊」。有「御書樓印」、「橄欖軒」印記。

6.《重修宣和博古圖錄》三十卷，7冊1函。宋王輔等撰，明萬曆間于承祖刊本。8行17字。是書有崇禎九年（1636）于道南跋。白口，單欄，無魚尾。紙色淡黃，字用顏體。圖繪雕刻亦甚工。本館藏本每冊書沿均有一仿明名畫家之山水彩色圖，秀麗奪人，當係後人所作。本館尚有此書明萬曆三十一年（1603）吳公弘刊本，三十卷，30冊4函，8行17字。首卷卷端題東書堂重修，餘卷均題泊如齋重修。疑為吳氏據萬曆十六年（1588）泊如齋本重刻。

7.《史記鈔》九十一卷，22冊3函。明茅坤選閔振業輯評，明泰昌元年（1620）吳興閔振業校刊朱墨套印本。9行19字。此書為明閔氏朱墨套印本，且刊於泰昌元年，頗具文物價值。蓋神宗崩於萬曆四十八年（1620）七月，光宗八月即位，改元泰昌，然九月即崩，故僅在位一月。是本刻於此

年，或為稀書也。缺卷四十四至四十七及卷六十一至六十六。有「白石樵」、「糵公」、「鹿門山中人」、「司訊小勳之章」等印記。

8.《大明仁孝皇后勸善書》二十卷，10冊2函。明仁孝皇后撰，明永樂五年（1407）內府刻本。14行28字。是書紙韌墨精，字體雋秀。黑口，四周雙欄，對魚尾。有「出經堂印」、「厚載之記」等印記。缺第一、二卷。

9.《大明仁孝皇后內訓》二十卷，2冊，與《明章聖慈仁皇太后女訓》同函。明仁孝皇后撰，明嘉靖九年（1530）內府刊本。8行17字。此書精刻大字，格式與前書同。同函《章聖慈仁皇太后女訓》，為嘉靖九年原刊，日本昭和六年（1931）復刻本。十二卷，3冊，1函，8行16字。有「中宮之寶」、「欽文之璽」等印記。

10.《歷代名臣奏議》三百五十卷，320冊40函。明楊士奇等編，明永樂十四年（1416）內府刊本。12行26字。是書黑口，左右雙欄，對魚尾。紙白墨黑，字體秀勁。有「夢翔珍秘」、「五橋珍藏」、「慈谿馮氏醉經閣圖籍」等印記。本館尚有另一刻，乃崇禎八年（1635）太倉張溥刪正本。三百二十卷，80冊8函。9行18字。

11.《元史》二百十卷，36冊4函，明宋濂等撰，明洪武三年（1370）原刊，嘉靖萬曆天啟南監修補刊本。10行20字。明洪武二年開局修元史，次年七月書成，十月刻工完竣，為元史之祖本。館藏本為嘉靖九年（1530）至十年（1531），萬曆二十八年（1600）、三十七年（1609）、四十四年（1616）及天啟三年（1623）南監修補刊本。黑口，對魚尾，有上下雙欄，亦有四周雙欄者。綿紙精字。卷六十至六十五為鈔配。有「島原秘藏」、「對藏靚樓」印記。

12.《大明一統志》九十卷，64冊8函。明李賢等撰，明天順五年（1461）內府刊本。10行22字。此書為內府精刻，有「廣運之寶」御印。大字，黑口，四周雙邊，對魚尾。紙質綿韌，墨色均勻，字體亦雋秀。缺第1冊。館藏尚有明弘治十八年（1505）建陽慎獨齋刻本，48冊8函，10行22字，及明萬曆十六年（1588）建陽書林楊氏歸仁齋原刻本，16冊2函，10行22字。扉頁題劉雙松重梓。

13.《廣西通志》六十卷，30冊3函。明黃佐、林富撰，明嘉靖十年（1531）至十五年（1536）劉士奇刻藍色印本。10行20字。小字雙行。是書為現存廣西全省最早之通志。白口，四周雙邊。白紙藍印。行格頗為疏朗。

14.《汾州府志》十六卷，10冊2函。明王景符等撰，王道一等修，明萬曆三十七年（1609）修刊本。9行18字。

15.《武功縣志》三卷，3冊1函。明康海撰，明正德十四年（1519）刊本。10行24字。

16.《百川學海》100種，20冊3函。南宋左圭輯，明弘治十四年（1501）無錫華成埕刊本。12行20字。

17.《寶顏堂秘笈》正集20種，續集50種，廣集51種，普集49種，彙集42種，秘集（眉公雜著）15種，100冊20函，明陳繼儒輯，明萬曆泰昌間繡水沈氏尚白齋，亦政堂刊本。8行18字。是書正集續集及秘集為萬曆三十四年（1606）刊；廣集萬曆四十三年（1615）刊；普集泰昌元年（1620）刊。

18.《津逮秘書》存70種，69冊10函。明毛晉輯，明末葉虞山毛氏汲古閣刊本。9行19字。是書有崇禎三年（1630）毛晉序。原140種，館藏僅70種。內有刊於胡震亨《秘冊匯函》者。有「毛氏正本」、「汲古閣」、「秋廚齋藏書記」等印記。館藏《秘冊匯函》存17種（原22種），明海監胡氏原刊，海虞毛氏補刊本。9行18字。32冊4函。

19.《集千家注批點杜工部詩集》二十卷，年譜一卷，10冊2函。唐杜甫撰，宋劉辰翁評點，明嘉靖八年（1529）靖江懋德堂刊本。8行18字。此書為靖江藩刊本。黑口大字。注小字。四周雙欄，對魚口。有「靖江王章」印。首尾缺頁。

20.《分類補注李太白詩》二十五卷，年譜一卷。唐李白撰，宋楊齊賢注，元蕭士贇補注明萬曆間刻本。9行20字。本書扉頁有「合刻李杜詩集序」，並太史劍華道人吳廣霈光緒三十四年及民國二年校讀朱墨批注。並有「字余白軾澄」、「振軻」、「軾澂」、「劍華藏書印章」、「吳印廣霈」等印記。館藏另部有「佐藤文庫」章。

21.《朱文公校昌黎先生文集》四十卷，外集十卷，集傳一卷，遺詩文一卷，12冊2函。唐韓愈撰，宋朱熹校異，王伯大音釋，明嘉靖十三年（1534）建陽縣校刊本。10行24字。是書為建陽坊刻。白口，四周雙欄，順魚尾。有「葉德輝煥彬甫藏閱書」印記。

22.《歐陽文忠公全集》一百五十三卷，附錄六卷，24冊4函。宋歐陽修撰，附錄宋何柯編，明嘉靖三十九年（1560）吉州郡學何遷刊本。10行20字是書為歐集舊刻。後刻均無一百五十三卷者。白口，四周雙欄，白魚尾。字體仿趙。有「永清朱樨之字淹頌號玖聃滂喜堂經籍金石書畫記」，「華陽高氏蒼茫齋收藏金石書籍記」等印記。

23.《苑洛集》二十一卷，16冊2函。明韓邦奇撰，明嘉靖間刊本。10行20字。是本有嘉靖三十一年（1552）序。為四庫《苑洛集》之底本。卷首有翰林院關防。卷中有四庫編修注。

24.《第五才子書施耐庵水滸傳》七十五卷七十回，24冊3函。元施耐庵撰，明金人瑞改定。明崇禎十四年（1641）貫華堂刊本。8行19字。此書為金氏貫華堂刻本。傳世極少，或為海外孤本。聞中國大陸亦僅私藏一部。白口，白魚尾。板心上端刻「第五才子書」，下端刻「貫華堂」。牌記有「本府藏板翻刻必究」字樣。

25.《重廣補注黃帝內經素問》二十四卷，10冊2函。唐王冰注，明嘉靖間翻刻宋本。10行20字。小30字。是書有明嘉靖二十九年（1550）顧從德序。有「抱經樓」印記。

26.《古今醫統一正脈全書》44種，62冊8函。明王肯堂輯明萬曆二十九年（1601）新安吳勉學刊本。10行20字。

27.《方氏墨譜》十六卷，8冊1函。明方于魯撰，明萬曆十一年（1583）汪道昆序，十七年（1589）王穉登序。又李維禎序，不著年月。方氏美蔭堂刊本。白口，四周單欄，白魚尾。有「李氏藏書印」。

28.《樂律全書》14種，19冊4函。明朱載堉撰，明萬曆間藩刊本。12行25字。黑口，四周雙欄，對魚尾。

29.《玄玄棋經集》為前卷，2冊1函。宋晏天章一嚴德甫編，明嘉靖七年（1528）歙縣汪氏堂重刊本。13行24字。敦煌石室出現北周寫本《棋經》，宋有《忘憂清樂集》，元有《玄玄棋經》，但均傳世不多。今通行者多萬曆間翻刻本。似此嘉靖刻本，極不多見。原前後卷，館藏缺後卷。

活字本

中國自北宋畢昇製膠泥活字印書，較西方發明印刷先400年。其後又有錫活字、木活字、銅活字、鉛活字、瓷活字，雖不及板刻之盛，然其對印刷術之貢獻，自不待言。朝鮮日本後均仿中國活字印書。朝鮮尤有過之而無不及處。本館藏朝鮮活字本中最早者為朝鮮太宗四年（1403）之《十七史纂古今通要》銅活字殘葉，及《朱文公校昌黎先生集》存卷三十四至三十七，朝鮮正統三年（1438）銅活字本。館藏日本古籍中有杜預注《春秋經傳集解》三十卷，日本慶長間（1596-1615）木活字本。下再列館藏中國活字本數種，以供佐正。

1.《宋李忠定公奏議選》十五卷，6冊1函。宋李剛撰，明崇禎十二年（1639）序。朝宗書局木活字本。9行24字。此書白口，四周單欄，無魚尾。紙色淡黃，似顏體字。有「好古堂圖書記」章。

2.《會通館校正宋諸臣奏議》一百五十卷，120冊16函。趙汝愚輯，明弘治三年（1490）錫山華氏會通館銅活字本。9行17字。是書黑口，四周雙邊，單魚尾。字體仿宋，唯墨汁不均，小字有顯晦處。開卷有大字印史記溫，孫希瀙淳祐十年（1250），淳熙十三年（1186）「乞進皇朝名臣奏議札」及趙汝愚進「皇朝名臣奏議序」。有「當湖邃江珍藏」、「毗陵陳康審定」、「董康暨侍姬亞奴珍藏書籍記」等印記。

3.《孫可之文集》二卷，4冊1函。唐孫樵撰，明末木活字本。7行15字。是書白口，單魚尾。紙白，字似顏體。活字雕刻頗工。

本館藏清代活字本計117種。今僅列二巨帙如後。

1.《古今圖書集成》一萬卷，目錄四十卷，5,020冊503函。清陳夢雷修，蔣廷錫等重修，清雍正四年（1726）武英殿銅活字本。9行20字。此帙為中國類書巨著，亦為銅活字之最佳代表品。白口，四周雙欄，單魚尾。紙淡黃而堅韌，用墨均勻，活字尤工。夢雷稿成後於康熙四十四年（1705）繕寫成清本，名《古今圖書彙編》，帝命改稱《古今圖書集成》，但未印行。
雍正即位後，夢雷發遣邊外，帝命蔣廷錫等重修。匯為曆象、方輿、明倫、
博物、理學、經濟六編，分三十二典，6,109部。每部首匯考，次總論，有
圖表、列傳、藝文、選句、紀事、雜錄、外編等項。雍正四年（1726）始
印，一共出64部，館藏即其中之一。光緒十年（1884）上海有鉛印本，印
1,500部；光緒二十一年（1895）上海同文書局復有石印本，印100部。本
館藏本每冊扉頁有「重華宮寶」及「五福五代堂古稀天子寶」御印。每冊末
頁有「重華宮寶」及「八徵耄念之寶」御印。

　　2.《武英殿聚珍版書》138種，602冊74函。清乾隆三十八年（1773）至
四十八年（1783）武英殿木活字本。10行21字。清乾隆三十八年，帝詔儒
臣輯永樂大典散見之書及世所罕見秘帙刻印通行。時朝鮮人金簡管武英殿刻
書事（後升工部侍郎），奏以木活字排印，帝賜名聚珍版。十年書成，並頒
發於東南各省，准於重刊通行。但除光緒二十五年廣雅書局添印為148種
外，餘所重刊者均非全本。

套印本

　　今日所見套印本，以明萬曆及崇禎間吳興閔凌二氏所印者為多，且為世
人所最推崇者。杜信孚輯《明代版刻綜錄》（揚州江蘇廣陵古籍刻印社1983
年5月出版）據舊存及現存藏書目錄（後者屬北京圖書館、南京圖書館、上
海圖書館、北大、北師大及南京大學等圖書館）列閔凌二氏套印書籍共107
種。其中本館藏55種。今檢出閔凌印行及其他套印本，列舉如後：

朱墨套印

　　1.《四書參》十九卷，6冊1函。明李贄評，楊起元批點，張明憲參訂，
明末吳興閔氏朱墨套印本。8行16字。是書朱色眉批圈點，刻工精研。

　　2.《文選》六十卷，16冊2函。梁蕭統編，唐李善注，清何卓評，清乾
隆三十七年（1772）羊城翰墨園重刊，朱墨套印本。12行25字。此書朱色
眉批，極為鮮明。

　　3.《楚辭集注》八卷，卷首一卷，8冊1函。宋朱熹撰，清初曹氏聽雨齋朱墨套印活字本。8行22字。書名頁題「朱文公楚辭集注八十四家評點聽雨齋開雕」。有聽雨齋主人曹溶刊朱熹序，84家姓名，名人評語，司馬遷撰《屈原列傳》，唐沈亞之撰《屈原外傳》。白口，無魚尾。字體恭端，墨色均勻。套印而兼活字，是其出色處。

二、三色套印

　　1.《文選尤》八卷，8冊1函。梁蕭統編，明周思明評，周德延校，明天啟二年（1622）吳興閔氏刊朱墨綠三色套印本。8行18字。是書韓敬序，未署年月。有「韓敬之印」、「求仲氏」及「庚戌會狀兩元」等印記。

　　2.《孟子》二卷，2冊1函。宋蘇洵評點，明萬曆三十三年（1605）吳興閔齊汲刊朱墨藍三色套印本。8行18字。是書眉批圈點為朱藍色。朱得之嘉靖元年（1522）序。本館藏另部為嘉慶元年（1796）慎詒堂重刊康熙朱墨套印本。9行20字，4冊1函。

　　3.《廣金石韻府》五卷，字略一卷，10冊1函。明朱雲輯，林尚葵補，李根校，明崇禎9年（1636）序。閩侯蓮庵藏板朱墨藍三色套印本。6行12字。館藏本缺卷五第24葉後各葉。另部為康熙九年（1670）大業堂刊周氏賴古堂重訂朱墨藍套印本，6行12字，10冊1函。

四色套印

　　1.《世說新語》八卷，4冊1函。南朝劉義慶撰，齊劉孝標注，明萬曆間吳興凌氏刊朱墨藍黃四色套印本。8行18字。是書有劉應登「耘廬」劉會孟（須溪）王世懋（敬美）批。凌瀛初跋云：「……余復合三先生手澤，耘廬綴於黃，須溪綴以藍，敬美綴以硃，分次井然，庶覽者便於識別云」。館藏書沿有仿明四名家彩繪山水：第一冊明仇英秋江待渡圖；第二冊明王紱秋江泛艇；第三冊明唐寅山路松聲；第四冊明文徵明雪景。館藏另二部，同本，無書沿彩繪。一部16冊2函，一部8冊1函。

　　2.《南華經》存十四卷，8冊1函。明萬曆三十三年（1605）吳興凌以棟刊朱墨藍紫四色套印本。8行18字。是書原十六卷，館藏缺十五、十六兩卷。扉頁書名下題：「晉子玄郭象注，輯諸名家評釋，宋林虞齋口義，劉須溪點校，明王鳳洲評點，附陳明卿批註」。用四色以為分別。諸名家用深墨，王鳳洲用硃紅，林虞齋用紫色，劉須溪用藍色。

五色套印

1.《劉子文心雕龍》上下卷，注上下卷，6冊1函。梁劉勰撰，明梅慶生注，楊慎曹學詮評，明萬曆四十年（1612）吳興凌雲校刊。朱墨紫藍黃五色套印本。9行19字。是本首有曹學詮序及朱印。眉端刻楊慎及梅氏等評語，多用墨色。餘四色以評文之意而別，不以人分。有「慎宣軒」及「舒桐鄉民」等印記。

2.《古文淵鑑》六十四卷，24冊2函。清徐乾學編，康熙二十四年（1685）五香齋朱墨紫藍黃五色套印本。9行20字。本書為清聖祖御選。所錄上起春秋下迄於宋。眉批評注以意分用朱藍紫黃四色，墨色用為正文。有「合肥親多堂郭氏珍藏印」章。

3.《勸善金科》二十卷，卷首一卷，二百四十齣，21冊4函，清張照等撰，清乾隆間內府刻朱墨藍綠黃五色套印本。8行22字。此書與眾套印本不同，無圈點眉批，然正文全用五色套印。色彩較閔凌二氏套印本更為鮮明。墨色為說唱文，藍色為押韻或重唱（疊）處，綠色為合曲，朱色示動作，黃色為曲調名稱。字體極為端莊，紙色淺橙，易脆。是本為世所罕見，或為海外孤本。

套印畫譜

明清套印畫譜，用「銅版」及「拱花」方式印刷。其中以《十竹齋書畫譜》及《芥子圖畫傳》為代表作。下列本館藏此二書之各種版本：

1.《十竹齋書畫譜》8種，8冊1函。明胡正言摹，明崇禎十六年（1643）刊包背裝彩色套印本。是譜凡畫傳、墨華、果、翎毛、蘭、竹、梅、石八種。館藏另五部：清康熙五十四年（1715）包背裝本；清嘉慶二十二年

（1817）張學畊重校李氏芥子園重刊套印摺裝本。有「芥子園珍藏」、「李氏圖章」等印記；日本明治十一年（1878）文榮堂翻刻清嘉慶二十二年（1817）原刊包背裝套印本；清光緒五年（1879）重刊包背裝套印本；日本明治十五年（1882）覆明崇禎六年（1633）原刊包背裝套印本。

2.《芥子園畫傳》初集五卷，二集八卷，三集四卷。清王槩等輯，清康熙十八年（1679）至四十年（1701）芥子園刊彩色套印本。此書初集王槩輯，清康熙18年芥子園初印。二集三集與二弟王蓍王臬合輯，康熙四十年芥子園甥館藏套印。館藏初集共三部。全書另七種：清乾隆四十七年（1782）金閶書業堂重刊套印本；清嘉慶二十二年（1817）金陵芥子園煥記重刊套印本（共四集，第四集清丁臬輯）；另部清嘉慶二十三年（1818）本，亦為金陵芥子園重刊套印；清光緒十三年（1887）至二十三年（1897）上海鴻文書局石印本，四集；民國十年（1921）上海十頃堂書局放大鴻文書局本；日本寬延元年（1748）平安書肆河南樓翻刻彩色套印本；另部為日本寶曆三年（1753）同刊印者彩色套印。

法帖

哈佛燕京圖書館明版法帖12種，105冊，清初版7種，150冊，民國複製精印8種，74冊。今僅列三種，以供參考。

1.《絳帖》十二帖4函。據《古今碑傳考》云：「潘師旦以淳化帖增入別帖，重摹刻於山西絳州。」然《集古求真》有云：「按十二絳帖，雖為偽作，然刊刻頗精。紙墨亦有佳者。且發現甚早。大約明初人或元人所為。有以為金人者，亦未可知。」

2.《戲鴻堂帖》十六帖4函。明董其昌審定。《集古求真》云：「原刻於諸帖中字，有以為未善者，另改單字於卷末。亦有改至一二行者，原以備裱裝時割換，用心亦可謂勤且密矣。翻刻本無之。欲求原刻，以此為驗。」

3.《三希堂石渠寶笈法帖》三十二卷，11函。清高宗敕編，梁詩正校刊。此帖始刻於乾隆十二年（1747），三十年（1765）刻竣。《集古求真》謂：「自鍾、王以至明人，俱以內府所藏真跡上石。自淳化閣帖以下，官私法帖，無此巨麗，摹刻楊三手，俱天下之良工。紙墨亦極精良，固非民間寒儉，所可比擬。」

鈔本

館藏鈔本計1,215種，分訂4,560冊。其中除《永樂大典》3冊外（卷之2610-2611；7756-7757；8841-8842），餘大都為清鈔本，亦有民國者，清鈔本中以文瀾閣《四庫全書》之《駱丞集注》四卷及《熬波圖》上下卷為最珍貴。茲在其他鈔本中檢出下列三種，略為介紹。

1.《詩經世本古義》不分卷，35冊3函。明何楷學撰，清鈔本。10行20字。是書傳鈔清禮部原版。本館尚藏此書另部，為嘉慶二十四年（1819）閩漳謝氏文林堂活字本，二十八卷，首末各一卷。

2.《宋名賢五百家播芳大全文粹》一百二十六卷，40冊8函。明魏齊賢、葉芬等編，清道光二十八年（1848）東武劉氏據宋本校鈔。14行25字。書間有「燕庭士杰珍藏」、「東武劉喜海燕庭所藏」等印章。

3.《鑲黃旗滿洲鈕古祿氏弘毅公家譜》15冊1函。清嘉慶三年（1798）修。10行字數不等。是本為朱絲欄精鈔本。大號紙裝訂，書口題：「鈕古祿氏家譜」

4.《八旗叢書》35種，28冊3函。清恩豐輯鈔。此書為清光緒間鈔本。為恩豐本人私藏。中有愛新覺羅敦敏撰〈懋齋詩鈔〉。敦敏為曹雪芹至友，此卷多收其與雪芹唱和詩，為研究雪芹生平少見之資料。恩豐字希臣，光緒十八年（1892）進士。書內有「富察恩豐希臣藏書印」。

注釋

本文為1984年11月於台北中國圖書館學會主辦的「古籍鑑定與維護研習會」發表的報告，載《古籍鑑定與維護研習會專集》（台北：中國圖書館學會，1985），頁341-151。

哈佛燕京圖書館中國方志
及其他有關資料存藏現況

　　哈佛燕京圖書館創建於1928年，隸屬於哈佛燕京學社，稱哈佛燕京學社漢和圖書館。1965年改稱哈佛燕京圖書館。1976年轉屬於哈佛大學圖書館系統，列為哈佛學院圖書館（Harvard College Library）之一部分。哈佛燕京圖書館開建初期，收集範圍僅限於中、日文；後加增滿、蒙、藏及西文資料。1951年建立韓文部；越南文部亦於1973年成立。哈佛燕京圖書館現藏書籍總計641,200冊，其中中文計374,300；日文174,800冊；韓文53,240冊；西文29,150冊；滿蒙藏及越南文共計8,700冊。此外，尚存期刊10,600種，報紙314種，微卷18,000卷，及微片4,000張。[1]哈佛燕京圖書館為今日西方世界各大學中規模最大之東亞研究圖書館。

　　館藏中文典籍中國方志為其特藏之一種。藏量現共3,858種，計70,553卷。本館收集方志多年，起始於1930年代。其時除向北平、上海、廣州、杭州各地書商直接購買外，燕京大學圖書館亦曾多方協助此一採購工作。1949年後，刻本在中國大陸已無法購買，方志之收集遂轉向於台灣之複印本及微卷之製作。微卷來源為東京內閣文庫、台北國立中央圖書館及美國國會圖書館（抗戰時期北平圖書館託存美國國會圖書館之善本，後運返台灣，現存台北故宮博物院）。1940年前收購之方志載於該年出版之《美國哈佛大學哈佛燕京學社漢和圖書館漢籍分類目錄》第三冊「歷史科學類」。現藏方志之全部將收入《哈佛燕京圖書館中日文典藏目錄》（*Chinese and Japanese Catalogue of the Harvard-Yenching Library*），定由紐約加蘭出版公司（Garland Publishing Company）於1986年出版。館藏方志均可在館內使用，亦可供應微卷。[2]

　　方志之收藏，如眾所周知，以中國大陸最為豐富；大陸圖書館中則以北京圖書館所收藏者居其首。據1978年編印之《中國地方志聯合目錄》（初稿）調查，大陸現共藏方志8,343種，計119,687卷；其中以縣志居多，共5,441種，70,904卷。[3] 北京圖書館方志藏量則為6,066種，計93,000卷，占全國種數及卷數總藏量之72.7%及77.5% [4]。茲將哈佛燕京圖書館之藏量與大陸全國及北京圖書館所收藏者，列表比較分析如下。

（一）中國方志存藏現況〔分省〕**

省　　名	中國大陸		哈佛燕京圖書館		哈佛燕京圖書館比較藏量（%）	
	種數	卷數	種數	卷數	種數	卷數
四　　川	699	8,779	265	4,871	38%	55%
江　　蘇	688	10,853	352	7,486	51%	69%
河　　北	665	8,439	345	5,094	52%	60%
浙　　江	599	10,708	297	7,418	50%	69%
山　　東	543	6,954	430	4,867	79%	70%
河　　南	519	6,602	268	4,049	52%	61%
廣　　東	486	6,968	172	3,630	35%	52%
江　　西	481	10,207	152	4,124	32%	40%
山　　西	428	5,180	265	3,883	62%	75%
陝　　西	417	4,061	212	2,847	51%	70%
湖　　南	397	7,755	142	3,842	36%	50%
安　　徽	380	6,605	170	3,829	45%	58%
湖　　北	334	5,253	144	2,684	43%	51%
福　　建	326	7,183	139	4,414	43%	61%
雲　　南	291	3,796	82	1,703	28%	45%
廣　　西	200	2,826	86	1,318	43%	47%
甘　　肅	186	1,587	81	814	44%	51%
貴　　州	125	2,013	39	807	31%	40%
遼　　寧	123	1,297	54	978	44%	75%

新　疆	116	516	23	291	20%	56%
吉　林	94	551	13	224	14%	41%
黑龍江	50	320	12	126	24%	39%
台　灣	47	423	37	311	79%	74%
西　藏	44	86	8	42	18%	49%
青　海	42	144	8	67	19%	47%
內蒙古	38	415	51*	731*	134%	176%
寧　夏	25	166	11	103	44%	62%
	8,343	119,687	3,858	70,553	46%	59%

** 中國大陸資料統計，見上引吳景熙文。哈佛燕京圖書館統計包括複印本及微卷。第
　一、二、三表種數統計不計重本或不同版本（纂修人及內容相同者均以一種計）。全國
　性方志及專志輿圖古跡之類，不在收錄之例。

* 包括綏遠、熱河、察哈爾。

（二）中國方志存藏現況〔分省〕

省　名	北京圖書館		哈佛燕京圖書館		哈佛燕京圖書館 比較藏量（%）	
	種數	卷數	種數	卷數	種數	卷數
河　北	564	7,440	345	5,094	61%	68%
江　蘇	476	8,274	352	7,486	74%	90%
四　川	458	6,431	265	4,871	58%	76%
山　東	458	6,238	430	4,867	94%	78%
河　南	434	5,800	268	4,049	62%	70%
浙　江	398	8,084	297	7,418	75%	92%
山　西	375	4,627	265	3,883	71%	84%
江　西	342	7,476	152	4,124	44%	55%
陝　西	331	3,516	212	2,847	64%	81%
廣　東	295	4,676	172	3,630	58%	78%
安　徽	261	4,849	170	3,829	65%	79%
湖　南	260	5,536	142	3,842	55%	69%
湖　北	260	4,195	144	2,684	55%	64%

福　建	205	4,670	139	4,414	68%	95%
雲　南	192	3,057	82	1,703	43%	56%
甘　肅	142	1,279	81	814	57%	64%
廣　西	117	2,066	86	1,318	74%	64%
貴　州	98	1,677	39	807	40%	48%
新　疆	87	436	23	291	26%	67%
遼　寧	79	1,104	54	978	68%	89%
吉　林	60	408	13	224	22%	55%
台　灣	44	394	37	311	84%	79%
黑龍江	41	311	12	126	29%	41%
西　藏	36	78	8	42	22%	54%
內蒙古	19	148	51*	731*	268%	494%
寧　夏	19	147	11	103	58%	70%
青　海	15	92	8	67	53%	73%
	6,066	93,009	3,858	70,553	64%	76%

* 包括綏遠、熱河、察哈爾。

（三）中國方志存藏現況〔分類〕

	中國大陸		北京圖書館		哈佛燕京圖書館		哈佛燕京圖書館比較藏量（%）			
	種數	卷數	種數	卷數	種數	卷數	中國大陸		北京圖書館	
縣　志	5,441	70,904	4,111	54,329	2,911	43,474	*54%	61%	71%	80%
府　志	731	19,456	583	16,170	343	11,338	47%	58%	59%	70%
州　志	657	7,450	526	5,889	302	4,271	46%	57%	57%	73%
通　志	308	14,212	235	11,429	150	10,062	49%	71%	64%	88%
鄉土志	603	1,233	233	581	57	158	9%	13%	24%	27%
其　他*	603	6,432	378	4,611	95	1,250	16%	19%	25%	27%
合　計	8,343	119,687	6,066	93,009	3,858	70,553				

* 包括道志，廳志，市志，鎮志，關志。

　　由上表觀之，哈佛燕京圖書館所藏方志種數占中國大陸所藏種數46%，卷數59％；如與北京圖書館比較，種數則占64％，卷數76％。哈佛燕京圖書館所藏種數最多者為山東、山西、河南、陝西、江蘇及浙江各省；最少者為吉林、西藏、青海及新疆。收藏最大部分為縣志，占全館方志藏量75％。

　　以纂修或刊行年代計，哈佛燕京圖書館所藏方志（包括複印本及微卷）可歸納如下：宋——38種（複印本34種，微卷4種）；元——19種（複印本12種，微卷7種）；明——579種（包括複印本107種，微卷411種，餘為原刊本）；清——2,483種（包括微卷10種，餘為原刊本）；民國——739種（除兩種為微卷外，其餘均為原本）。館藏刊本中最早者為《姑蘇志》六十卷，明正德元年（1506）刊本；最近者為《台南縣志》，民國六十七年（1978）印行。此外，尚有鈔本五種。[5]

　　台灣存藏中國方志亦復不少。此可由1985年3月台北漢學研究資料及服務中心出版王德毅教授主編之《中華民國台灣地區公藏方志目錄》見之。該書包括台灣12所圖書館典藏之中國方志，內容詳盡。今就所登錄者與哈佛燕京圖書館所藏作分省分類比較，列表如下。

（四）中國方志存藏現況〔分省〕*

省　　名	台灣		哈佛燕京圖書館		哈佛燕京圖書館比較藏量（％）	
	種數	卷數	種數	卷數	種數	卷數
河　北	397	5,756	345	5,094	87％	88％
山　東	350	5,205	430	4,867	123％	94％
河　南	317	4,801	268	4,049	85％	84％
山　西	289	4,431	265	3,883	92％	88％
浙　江	364	8,201	297	7,418	82％	90％
江　蘇	369	7,480	352	7,486	95％	100％
陝　西	261	3,233	212	2,847	81％	88％
四　川	327	5,226	262	4,856	80％	93％
廣　東	235	4,384	172	3,630	73％	83％
湖　北	197	3,932	144	2,684	73％	68％

江　西	173	3,991	152	4,124	88%	103%
安　徽	173	3,656	170	3,829	98%	105%
湖　南	156	3,678	142	3,842	91%	104%
福　建	184	4,899	139	4,414	76%	90%
雲　南	123	2,213	82	1,703	67%	77%
廣　西	104	1,747	86	1,318	83%	75%
甘　肅	110	1,235	81	814	74%	66%
遼　寧	65	969	54	978	83%	101%
台　灣	91	752	37	311	41%	41%
貴　州	52	936	39	807	75%	86%
察哈爾	38	560	30	406	79%	73%
新　疆	41	378	23	291	56%	77%
西　康	23	133	3	15	13%	11%
黑龍江	16	190	12	126	75%	66%
寧　夏	14	178	11	103	79%	58%
綏　遠	16	86	11	60	69%	70%
吉　林	13	191	13	224	100%	117%
青　海	12	118	8	67	67%	57%
西　藏	12	49	8	42	67%	86%
蒙　古	5	28	5	12	100%	43%
熱　河	3	242	5	253	167%	105%
	4,530	78,878	3,858	70,553	85%	89%

* 台灣存藏方志計算方法大致與中國大陸相同（見第一表注腳），所異者台灣有輿圖及見
於叢書中方志之收錄。方志殘卷亦多另計為一種。

（五）中國方志存藏現況〔分類〕

	台灣		哈佛燕京圖書館		哈佛燕京圖書館 比較藏量（％）	
	種數	卷數	種數	卷數	種數	卷數
縣　志	3,155	44,995	2,911	43,474	92%	97%
府　志	445	13,774	343	11,338	77%	82%

州　志	394	5,161	302	4,271	77%	83%
通　志	322	12,133	150	10,062	47%	83%
鄉土志	96	280	57	158	59%	56%
其　他	118	2,535	95	1,250	81%	49%
	4,530	78,878	3,858	70,553		

　　哈佛燕京圖書館除上述之方志外，尚藏有多種其他有關地方資料諸如山水志、寺廟志、輿圖、地方載記、土地文書、官書、統計及年鑑等。此類資料中，以地方載記為最多，計2,000餘種。今就檢出較為獨特之館藏輿圖及土地文書，作一簡略之敘述。

　　館藏輿圖有明版十餘種，如朱思本之《廣輿圖》（嘉靖四十至四十五年刊本）；張天復之《皇輿考》（嘉靖三十六年刊本）及《廣皇輿考》（天啟六年刊本）。清代輿圖中有蔣廷錫等撰《康熙內府分省分府圖》（康熙內府刊，摺裝本）；黃千人繪製《大清萬年一統地理全圖》（乾隆四十六年初版；嘉慶間廣幅藍色印本）；《乾隆京城全圖》（乾隆十五年繪製，1940年北京興亞院華北連絡部複印）；《湖南全省圖》（清初彩繪本，15幅，1冊，摺裝本）；《鄂省州縣驛傳全圖》（光緒間湖北官書局編製，墨印本）；《陝西全圖》（清刊，墨印本）；《南陽府南陽縣圖》（光緒間彩繪本）。此外，尚有罕見光緒間彩繪之40餘幅江蘇，浙江及江西之釐卡圖。此批圖中，除大卡、小卡、旱卡及水卡之位置外，尚注明各卡間之距離及各卡與其附近城鎮間之距離，為珍貴之研究資料。

　　土地文書亦為哈佛燕京圖書館特藏之一部。其中最具研究價值者有同治七年至光緒三年（1868-1877）間江蘇吳縣有關佃農正副租簿，共19冊；乾隆二十七至五十八年（1762-1793）間之少數田契；光緒三十年至民國十八年（1904-1929）間江蘇21縣及浙江1縣各縣長移交之田賦，漕運及其他稅收之清單，並公費收支之賬目；光緒十至三十年間（1884-1904）江蘇甘泉縣（屬揚州府）蠲除或緩徵田賦之經過（見《甘泉縣續志》鈔本）；民國十年（1921）江蘇常熟縣荒地及熟地蠲徵之清冊；及江蘇〔丹徒縣捕蝻設局總冊〕（民國間）自三月二十日至七月九日收買大小跳蝻及蝻子之付出細目工作人員開支。此外，館藏土地文書中尚有關於台灣及中國大陸1930及1940年代之各種資料。其中以下列數種為著。中央研究院張偉仁、王世慶合編之《台灣公私藏古文書影本》，共10輯，收5,600餘件自17世紀至20世紀間台灣各地地契、土地田賦收據、借約、合同、土地買賣、田地訴訟以及水道、山地居民及宗教儀式之各種原始文件，內容極為豐富。台北成文出版社出版之《民國20-30年代中國經濟農業土地水利問題資料》為當時中國地政研究所所長蕭錚先生編輯，共收26,000餘件自報刊選輯及實地調查之資料，分5大類，65細類，用微片方式印行。另一種亦為蕭錚先生編輯，名《民國二十年代中國大陸土地問題資料，1932至1941年間未刊行土地問題調查資料》，亦為台北成文出版社出版，包括各省各地168項實地調查及176種報告，共200冊。

　　上述僅為哈佛燕京圖書館存藏中國方志及其他有關資料之初步報告。較全面性之介紹尚須進一步之調查與分析。文中所提僅供讀者之一般參考而已。

注釋

本文為1985年4月1-4日在台北漢學研究資料及服務中心與國立中央圖書館合辦之「方志國際研討會」發表的報告。載《漢學研究》第3卷第2期（總號第6號）（1985年12月）〈方志學國際研討會論文專號〉，頁369-376。

[1]　關於哈佛燕京圖書館早期存藏狀況，見裘開明著〈哈佛燕京學社圖書館〉（The Harvard-Yenching Institute Library）載《遠東季刊》（*Far Eastern Quarterly*）第14卷，第1期（1954），頁147-152；及葉理綏（Serge Elisseeff）著〈哈佛燕京學社漢和圖書館〉（The Chinese-Japanese Library of the Harvard-Yenching Institute at Harvard University）載《哈佛圖書館館訊》（*Harvard Library Bulletin*）第10卷，第1期（1956年），頁73-93。

[2]　美國猶他州族譜學會（Genealogical Society of Utah）曾選館藏約1,200種方志攝為微卷。此項資料可在鹽湖城（Salt Lake City）該學會圖書館使用。正片可直接由哈佛燕

京圖書館供應。其他館藏方志亦可由本館複製。

[3]　此聯合目錄包括185所圖書館存藏方志，由北京天文台根據朱士嘉編《中國地方志綜錄》（增訂本）（上海：商務印書館，1958），於1978年油印發行。見吳景熙，〈國內現存方志，北京圖書館藏方志及其他〉，載《中國地方史志》，第6期（1982），頁43；莊威鳳，〈中國地方志聯合目錄編輯始末及其特點〉，載《中國地方史志通訊》第5/6合期（1981），頁44-46。

[4]　吳景熙，見上。

[5]　《嘉善縣志》（浙江）六卷，倪璣等纂修，明正德十二年（1517）修，傳鈔本。

　　《永康縣志》（浙江）八卷，胡楷纂修，明嘉靖二年至四年間（1523-1525）修，傳鈔本。

　　《寧羌州志》（陝西）八卷，盧大謨、楊堂等纂修，明萬曆二十五年（1597）修。

　　《長熟縣私志》（江蘇）十四卷，姚宗儀撰，明萬曆四十五年（1617）序，傳鈔本。

　　《宛平縣志》（河北）六卷，李開泰等纂，清康熙二十二至二十三年（1683-1684）修，傳鈔本。

三、
人物懷念

芮瑪麗與史丹佛大學胡佛研究所中文圖書館

芮瑪麗（Mary Clabaugh Wright）。

芮瑪麗（Mary Clabaugh Wright）是位卓越的學者兼圖書館的創建者。她1917年生於阿拉巴馬州塔斯卡羅薩（Tuscaloosa）城。以最優異的成績獲得瓦薩學院（Vassar College）的學士學位和哈佛大學博士學位。她成功的事業結合了學術研究與藏書建設兩方面的工作，對美國和西方的中國研究發展和促進深具影響。她費了十餘年致力為史丹佛大學胡佛研究所收集的有關中國共產黨史的原始資料至今在西方還是獨一無二的。她最主要的兩部著作：1957年由史丹佛大學出版，1966年再版的《同治中興：中國保守主義的最後抵抗，1862-1874》（*The Last Stand of Chinese Conservatism: the Tung-Chih Restoration, 1862-1874*），以及1968年由耶魯大學出版的她所編輯的《革命中的中國：第一階段，1900-1913》（*China in Revolution: the First Phase, 1900-1913*）已經成為研究近代中國的經典之作。她在這兩本著作中對儒學在19世紀中國扮演的腳色以及20世紀初中國革命的性質提出了重要而具有爭議的見解。正當她在史學界圖書館界風華正茂時她卻於1970年6月18日因病去世，享年僅52歲。

芮瑪麗1938年到哈佛作研究生時，主修歐洲史。不久之後開始對中國產生興趣。她後來追述說：「世界上沒有一個像中國這樣的國家有那麼多讓歷史學家感到興趣的問題和有那麼豐富的文書檔案。」她開始學習中文，並專注於中國近代史的研究。當她在哈佛讀書時，她認識了另外一位研究生——來自俄勒岡州波特蘭的芮沃壽（Arthur Frederick Wright, 1913-1976）。他致力於漢學，研究中國隋唐史。他們於1940年結婚後到日本京都學習研究。一年後他們不顧中日正處於戰爭中，雙雙去到北京。珍珠港事變後，他們被日本人拘留在山東濰縣。拘留期間芮沃壽在鍋爐房工作，芮瑪麗為醫院洗衣。1945年被釋放後，他們回到北京繼續他們的研究。有一天他們自短波收音機中收聽到史丹佛大學胡佛戰爭、革命與和平研究所（Hoover Institute on War，Revolution and Peace，後來改名為胡佛戰爭、革命與和平研究院——Hoover Institution on War, Revolution and Peace）所長哈樂德‧費希爾（Harold Fisher）教授介紹胡佛研究所，並提到計畫開始收藏有關研究現代中國的文獻資料。費希爾是芮沃壽在史丹佛大學讀書時的老師。經過通信聯繫，芮瑪麗因此被胡佛研究所委託在中國為該所收集資料。這個機遇導致了胡佛研究所建立了中文部獨特的收藏，因而對美國的現代和當代中國研究作出了貢獻。

　　這項在中國收購資料的工作對芮瑪麗是個非常大的挑戰，因為她的任務是從頭開始去建立一個以主要收集關於近代和當代中國的研究資料的圖書館，而當時其他的圖書館都比較注重於收藏近代中國以前的資料文獻。她從容不迫地接受了這個挑戰，以她特有的行事風格立即投入工作。她是那麼的具有精力、技巧、睿智及想像力。她走遍所有的主要城市去採購，向傑出的學者及目錄學家討教，不厭其煩地向政府機關索取官方出版物，並跟一流圖書館和大學協議交換。她從在華美軍處借到一部簡單的縮微相機，學會如何使用，然後把康有為一些沒有出版的手稿拍成膠捲。她費了好多時間在北京琉璃廠各書店仔細搜尋瀏覽。有一次她竟然用斤數計價買到一整套要以廢紙出售的光緒宣統時期出版的政府公報：《諭摺彙存，1892-1907》和《華制存考，1908-1912》！由於她艱苦工作努力不懈，她收集了上噸的對社會科學研究非常重要，而其他的圖書館都還沒有作有系統收集的資料，包括期刊、報紙、短時效資料等。她收集資料的途徑也不限於一般的途徑。1947年她在飛延安的美國軍機上爭取到一個坐位。延安當時是中國共產黨的基地，因此她獲得了一大批在那兒和解放區出版的書刊。這些書刊那時在中國其他地方是無法獲得的，其中包括一套差不多齊全的中國共產黨機關報《解放日報》，到現在這還是西方收藏到的唯一的一份原件。

　　芮瑪麗於1947年底回到美國，馬上開始一個艱巨的工作——整理這批為胡佛收集的資料。胡佛研究所中文圖書館於次年1948年正式成立，芮瑪麗被聘為館長。她既沒有受過圖書館員的專業訓練，又沒有專業人士的幫助，只有一位文書助理來協助日常事務。那時候她只好從胡佛研究所編目部學習一些編目要點，以及和哈佛漢和圖書館（後改名為哈佛燕京圖書館）裘開明館長通了無數計信函討教各種技術細節。當我1951年初從圖書館學校畢業，被胡佛雇傭為第一位中文編目員後，芮瑪麗才得全心全意地專注於採購工作以及參與東亞圖書館全國性發展的計畫。那時候她已經採購了頗負盛名的伊羅生（Harold Robert Isaacs, 1910-1986）在中國治外法權保護下收集的1920年代末和1930年代初出版的被政府禁止發行的早期中國共產黨地下出版物。隨即又取得海倫・福斯特・斯諾（Helen Foster Snow, 1907-1997，筆名尼姆・威爾斯［Nym Wales］）的同意出售給胡佛她和她前夫埃德加・斯諾（Edgar Snow, 1905-1972）於1930年代中期和末期訪問中國西北（包括延安、西安）時收集的中國共產黨那時候出版的原始資料。伊羅生和尼姆・威爾斯兩大特藏（Harold Isaacs Collection and Nym Wales Collection）奠定了日後世界各地學者對中國共產運動作研究的基礎。因為在此之前由於資料的缺乏，這樣的研究是可望而不可即的事。鮮有人知道芮瑪麗於1950年代中期還得到一小批從被俘虜的或者死亡的馬來西亞游擊隊身上獲得的中文共產黨資料。這批資料以售者命名，稱為韋伯斯特特藏（Webster Collection），收藏在胡佛中文圖書館。雖然上述這些資料非常重要，但是芮瑪麗並不僅僅局限於有關中國共產黨的資料的收集。她心目中的胡佛中文圖書館是不僅可以為學者提供研究20世紀中國政治、經濟、社會變遷的資料，還可以提供其他的資料去研究20世紀中國人文傳統的轉變，因此她收藏的範圍廣泛。她和當時主要提供中文書刊的香港書商以及其他美國主要東亞圖書館維持良好關係。胡佛和哈佛燕京圖書館的交換關係特別廣泛，互惠互利。這從1950年初期芮瑪麗和裘開明的頻繁通信中可以證實。

作為圖書館館長，芮瑪麗雷厲風行地為發展胡佛的中文收藏而努力。她是個不知疲倦，全心全力的工作狂。她總是在工作，無法停下來。1959年她離開史丹佛大學到耶魯大學任教的前一天，她還趁等待把電梯修理好的時間，把胡佛研究所的中文收藏作份報告。她也不會讓任何困難阻擋其收藏工作。她在中國收購的書刊，雖然多數通過海關運到加州，但是有十多個大箱，因為到中華人民共和國成立後才運抵海關，被新政府海關扣留。由於美國和新政府當時沒有外交關係，無法由官方交涉放行。但是芮瑪麗不是個容易氣餒的人，她開始用各種方法去搶救這批書刊。當她自己以及胡佛研究所向新政府申訴無效後，她轉向當時和新政府關係良好的印度政府求助。她的努力終於得到回報。那十多箱書刊，雖然其中有一些被扣留，終於通過海關成行，當其運抵帕洛阿爾托（Palo Alto）時還成了當地報紙的頭版新聞。

她深信圖書館不應該是靜態的資料儲藏室，而應該是有動力的服務中心。因此她積極參與東亞圖書館間各種合作專案互惠互利，比如國會圖書館主持的合作複製編目卡項目（Cooperative Card Reproduction Program）；她也首創了在美國東亞圖書館中書目叢刊的編輯和發行。從該圖書館中文資料中選擇一系列主題出版有解說的書目：《日本在華成立的偽政府，1937-1945》；《20世紀中國的領導人物》；《中國的學生運動，1927-1937》；《華僑》；《中國共產主義運動，1921-1937，1937-1949》。這些書目至今還是非常有用的參考工具。

1959年芮瑪麗和她先生都被耶魯大學歷史系聘請去任教。芮瑪麗是耶魯大學研究院第一位女性正教授。為不辜負這項殊榮和她全國各地同行的敬仰（耶魯大學特別授予她榮譽碩士學位，把她的資格「合法化」以同嫡系），芮瑪麗從此全心全意為她的學生、學校和專業努力。她成為了美國中國研究的領導人物之一。

自從她到耶魯大學任教後，她就沒有直接參與圖書館的工作，但是她自願為耶魯大學圖書館擔任顧問。1963年她擔任美國學術團體協會和社會科學研究理事會合組的當代中國研究聯合委員會資料小組組長（Subcommittee on Materials of the Joint Committee on Contemporary China of the American Council of Learned Societies and the Social Science Research Council）。該委員會聘請我和彼得・伯頓（Peter Berton）編輯《當代中國研究指南》（*Contemporary China: A Research Guide*）。她為我們看稿，並給以指點。此書於 1967 年由胡佛研究院出版。同時她又開始籌畫改善美國圖書館研究現代和當代中國資料的品質和數量的問題。她領導的小組決定對全球各地所有的資料以及當前研究狀況作一個全面調查，作為加強美國關於現代和當代中國的資料收藏和研究的基礎。她邀請我去擔任這項調查工作。其後一年間我訪問了西歐、東歐、北歐、蘇聯、東北亞，和南亞研究現代和當代中國的主要機構和圖書館。其間我得到她不少的指點和協助。我的調查報告中最主要的建議是建立一個全國性的中心，通過國際間館際借閱和交換，去確認、收集、複製，和分發美國圖書館未收藏或稀有的有關研究 20 世紀中國的資料。她的小組和當代中國研究聯合委員會（JCCC）接受了這個建議。後來在得到福特基金會的 50 萬元基金，以及美國研究圖書館協會的協助於 1968 年在華盛頓特區成立了「中國研究資料中心」（Center for Chinese Research Materials，簡稱 CCRM）。其後都是有口皆碑的歷史了。因為自中國研究資料中心成立以來它已成為對美國以及海外提供研究現代當代中國資料不可或缺的機構。因為芮瑪麗的開創，今天美國當代中國研究這個領域才得以發展得更為豐盛。

　　芮瑪麗給我們留下了她一生富有眼光和鼓舞人心的成就。作為一個東亞圖書館的開創者，她運用她的眼光和智慧去作藏書建設的工作。她以一個學者和圖書館的經常使用者的觀點來看一個研究圖書館應該是什麼樣，應該怎樣去運作。如果她能活得久點，無疑地她會繼續敦促我們不要忘記一個研究圖書館在學術研究領域裡應該扮演一個什麼樣的腳色。她以著名法國歷史學家馬克・布洛赫克（Marc Bloch）的話提醒我們：「由於對過去無知不免造成對現在的誤解。」所以她要我們重視史實。她說：「歷史的長流在兩岸間暢流。它可能改道，卻不能任意漫遊。」她曾經提出這樣的一個問題：「一個獨特的中國文明如何形成，又如何經過什麼樣的階段引領到今天的中國？」我肯定她的答案會是：「到圖書館去讀中國的歷史文獻。」

注釋

本文為1985年3月22-24日在費城亞洲學會年會「美國東亞圖書館的開創者」（"Pioneers in the Development of East Asian Research Collections in America"）研討會發表的報告。此為修訂稿。

（胡嘉陽譯）

Mary Clabaugh Wright and the Chinese Collection at the Hoover Institution, Stanford University

Mary Clabaugh Wright, scholar and library builder *par excellence*, was born in Tuscaloosa, Alabama, in 1917. A *summa* from Vassar and a Ph.D. from Harvard, Mary Wright developed a career that successfully combined scholarship and librarianship and left a deep impact on the development and advancement of Chinese studies in the United States and the Western world. The Chinese Collection which she spent more than a decade building at the Hoover Institution at Stanford University remains today a unique collection due to the scope and nature of its original documentation on the history of the Chinese Communist Party. Her two major publications, *The Last Stand of Chinese Conservatism: The T'ung-chih Restoration, 1862-1874* (Stanford, 1957; reprint 1966) and *China in Revolution: The First Phase, 1900-1913* (New Haven, 1968) which she edited likewise became classics in the field, in that they raised major and truly controversial questions regarding the role Confucianism played in the history of 19th century China and the nature of the Chinese revolution of the early 20th century. Mary Wright was at the prime of her life as a major historian and a former library curator when she died on June 18, 1970. She was 52 years old.

Mary Wright's interest in China began soon after she arrived at Harvard to do graduate work in 1938. She was to pursue studies in European history, but as she was to remark later, that because "the general problems which historians find exciting are nowhere offered in such profuse and interesting combinations, with such abundant documentation, as in the history of China," she began studying

Chinese and dedicated herself to the study of modern Chinese history. While at Harvard she met another graduate student, Arthur F. Wright, from Portland, Oregon, who was training in Sinology to study the history of Sui and Tang. They got married in 1940 and went to Kyoto to study and do research. A year later they proceeded to Beijing in spite of the Sino-Japanese war. Then came Pearl Harbor. For most of World War II they spent their time in an internment camp at Wei Xian in Shandong. There he worked in the boiler room and she did the hospital laundry. Released in 1945, they returned to Beijing to resume their studies. One day while listening to the short wave radio, they heard a talk by Professor Harold Fisher, then the Director of the Hoover Institute on War, Peace, and Revolution at Stanford University, in which he described the work of the Hoover Institute and mentioned plans to add modern China to its collecting activities. Harold Fisher was one of Arthur Wright's professors at Stanford where he did his undergraduate work. Correspondence ensued, and Mary Wright was commissioned by Hoover to collect materials in China for the Hoover Institute (later changed to Hoover Institution). This chance happening was to lead to the founding of the unique Chinese collection at Hoover, which in turn contributed to the shaping of the course of modern and contemporary Chinese studies in the United States.

The task given to Mary Wright was a tremendous challenge, as she was charged with building from scratch a major research collection on a period in Chinese history which up to that time had not received from most libraries the same kind of attention given to earlier periods. But she took the challenge in stride. In a fashion that was characteristic of Mary, she plunged into immediate action with entrepreneurial energy, skill, resourcefulness, and imagination. She travelled to all the major cities on buying trips, sought out eminent scholars and bibliographers for advice, badgered government agencies for their publications, and negotiated exchange agreements with leading libraries and universities. She learned how to use a simple micro-film camera borrowed from the U.S. Army in

China and preserved on microfilm some of the unpublished manuscripts of Kang Youwei. She spent a great deal of time combing the book shops in Liulichang in Beijing. On one such trip she salvaged a whole set of government gazettes of Emperor Guangxu and Xuantong that a dealer was selling as wrapping paper and paid for the documents by their weight! Her painstaking efforts resulted in the collecting of tons of materials, including quantities of journals, newspapers, and other ephemeral materials which are essential to social science research and which up to that point had not been systematically collected by most other libraries. Mary Wright did not confine herself on her book-buying excursions to just the ordinary channels. In 1947, having wangled a seat on a U.S. military transport, she flew to Yan'an, the base of the Chinese Communist Party, where she succeeded in obtaining a large quantity of Chinese Communist publications issued there and in other communist-controlled areas, which were not available elsewhere in China at that time, including an almost complete file of the *Jie-fang ri-bao* (Liberation Daily), the official organ of the Chinese Communist Party, which remains to this day the only original copy in the Western world.

Mary returned to the United States in late 1947, and began the gigantic task of sorting out what she had collected for Hoover. The following year the Chinese Collection at Hoover was officially inaugurated, and Mary Wright was appointed Curator of the Collection. Not being a trained librarian and without professional help, she barely managed with the help of one clerical assistant. This she did by learning the essentials in cataloging from the Cataloging Department at Hoover and through a lengthy correspondence during that period with Dr. A. Kaiming Chiu of the Harvard-Yenching Library concerning technical details. When I joined Hoover as its first Chinese cataloger in 1951, fresh out of library school, Mary was greatly relieved, as she was able to turn her attention to acquisitions and to participation in national planning for East Asian library development. By that time, she had already acquired the famous Harold Isaacs Collection of early underground Chinese Communist publications of the late 1920's and early 1930's. Mr. Isaacs had collected these materials, forbidden for circulation in China then, under the protection of the extraterritorial rights afforded to foreigners in China in those days. Soon afterwards she reached agreement with Nym Wales (Helen Foster Snow) for the sale to Hoover of the Nym Wales Collection, also containing original Chinese Communist documents but for a later period of the mid to late 1930's. They were collected by Edgar Snow and Nym Wales when they visited Northwest China, including Xi'an and Yan'an, during that period. The Harold Isaacs and the Nym Wales collections together provided the basis for much of the subsequent research on the Chinese Communist Movement by scholars from all parts of the world — a task heretofore impossible for a lack of documentation. Little known to most, Mary Wright also acquired in the mid-1950's a small group of Communist documents written in Chinese that were found on captured or dead guerrillas in Malaysia. This group of documents has been maintained at Hoover as the Webster Collection, named after the person from whom the documents were purchased. Important as these collections were, Mary Wright did not confine herself to the collecting of only Chinese Communist materials. She envisaged the Chinese Collection at Hoover becoming a library where students of modern and contemporary China could come to study, whether their interests lay in the process of political, economic, and social changes in 20th century China, or in the changes in the Chinese humanistic traditions. Accordingly, she collected widely. She developed good working relationships with book dealers in Hong Kong, the principal source of supply during those days, and with other major East Asian libraries in the United States. Hoover's exchange with the Harvard-Yenching Library was particularly extensive and mutually beneficial at that time, as evidenced by the voluminous correspondence between Mary Wright and Kaiming Chiu in the early 1950's.

As a library curator, Mary Wright was an indefatigable worker who always gave her full measure of energy to her work. She always worked hard, and seemed incapable of staying idle. The day before she left Stanford to join the Yale faculty in 1959, she made use of her time waiting for the elevator to be fixed to write a report on the Chinese Collection at the Hoover Institution she was about to leave behind. She was also a ferocious and determined worker, who let nothing stand in her way in building up Hoover's Chinese Collection. Following her return to the United States she persisted for several years through official and unofficial channels in obtaining the release of a dozen or so large crates of books which she had purchased in China but which were subsequently detained by the Chinese Customs. While most of what she had bought in China passed safely through the Chinese Customs and arrived in California, a dozen or so crates arrived too late at the dock to be shipped and were forthwith confiscated by the new authorities. Because of a lack of diplomatic relations between the United States and the People's Republic of China at that time, there was no official recourse to press for the release of the property. Never a person to be easily discouraged, Mary Wright set out to rescue the books. After her own and the Hoover Institute's appeals to the Chinese proved futile, she enlisted the help of the Indian government which at that time enjoyed good relations with the new Chinese government. Eventually her efforts were rewarded, and the crates, although stripped of some of their original contents, were cleared for shipping. Their arrival in Palo Alto made local newspaper headlines.

Convinced that libraries should not be merely static depositories, but dynamic service centers, she saw to it that the Chinese Collection at Hoover collaborated with other East Asian Libraries on projects of mutual benefit such as the Cooperative Card Reproduction Program sponsored by the Library of Congress; she also initiated a bibliographical series, a first in East Asian libraries in the United States, in which holdings of the Chinese Collection were selected for annotation into subject bibliographies. The publications on *Japanese-Sponsored*

Governments in China, 1937-1945; Leaders of 20th-Century China; the Chinese Student Movement 1927-1937, The Overseas Chinese; and *The Chinese Communist Movement, 1921-1937, 1937-1949* remain to this day extremely useful reference aids.

Mary Wright was invited with her husband in 1959 to teach in the History Department at Yale, where she became the first woman to be named a full professor in the Graduate School at that institution. Responding to this singular recognition (Yale also conferred upon her an honorary M.A. degree to make her "legitimate") and to the esteem of her professional colleagues across the country, she gave all she had to her students, her university, and her field. She became a leading figure in Chinese studies in the United States.

Mary did not continue to be directly involved in library matters after she joined the Yale faculty; but she made herself available for consultation to the Yale University Library. In 1963 she chaired the Subcommittee on Materials of the Joint Committee on Contemporary China (JCCC) of the American Council of Learned Societies and the Social Science Research Council. In that capacity she worked closely with Peter Berton and me on the Berton-Wu guide on contemporary China, a project initiated by JCCC, read the manuscript, and offered critical comments. The book was published under the title *Contemporary China: A Research Guide* by the Hoover Institution in 1967. Meanwhile, as the subcommittee chair, she also began laying plans for improving the quality and quantity of research materials in American libraries for the study of modern and contemporary China. Her subcommittee made a decision to conduct a world-wide survey of the availability of such materials and of the status of modern and contemporary China studies, as the basis for strengthening our own library holdings and research. She invited me to make the survey and she subsequently gave generously of her time and advice throughout my assignment. The survey was a year in the making, as I travelled to Western, Eastern, and Northern Europe, the Soviet Union, Northeast and South Asia to visit libraries and research centers. The major recommendation contained in my report was the establishment of a national service center to identify, collect, reproduce, and distribute essential research materials on 20th century China that are either unavailable in American libraries or available only in very limited quantity, through a world-wide interlibrary borrowing and exchange program, as a means to strengthen our own library resources. She and JCCC accepted this recommendation and succeeded in obtaining a five-hundred-thousand-dollar grant from the Ford Foundation and the cooperation of the Association of Research Libraries to set up the Center for Chinese Research Materials (CCRM) in 1968 in Washington, D.C. The rest, of course, is history, as CCRM has become an indispensable support facility in modern China studies both in this country and abroad. The field is richer today because of Mary Wright's initiative.

As a scholar and library builder, Mary Wright left us with a lifetime of work rich in insight and inspiration. As a pioneer in East Asian librarianship, she provided vision and ingenuity in her collection-building efforts. She supplied the necessary perspective as a scholar and active library user on what a research library should be like and how it should function, and went about creating such a research collection. Had she lived longer, she undoubtely would have continued to exhort all of us to keep in mind the role of a research library in scholarship. She heeded closely the famous French historian Marc Bloch's warning that "misunderstanding of the present is the inevitable consequence of ignorance of the past." She also advised us to take heed of the fact that "the stream of history runs between banks; it may shift its channel but it cannot wander at will." She once posed the question: "How did a distinctive Chinese civilization come into existence, and how did it lead, through what stages, to the China of today?" Mary's answer, I am sure, would have been: "Go to the Library and study the historical records."

Notes

A revised version of a paper presented at the panel on "Pioneers in the Development of East Asian Research Collections in America," Association for Asian Studies, Thirty-Seventh Annual Meeting, Philadelphia, PA, March 22-24, 1985

回憶余秉權教授

　　秉權的過世不僅是他們家庭的不幸，也是我們東亞圖書館界的大損失。我們東亞圖書館今天收藏了研究現代中國的文獻比從前豐富，我們的學者因為有這些豐富的資料而能作更好的研究，這都是秉權的功勞。他扮演了一個重要的腳色。當我們哀悼他的時刻，我們要向他感恩，因為他豐富了東亞圖書館和東亞學術界。他留下了許許多多讓我們要感激他的事。

　　我認識秉權30多年了。我們第一次見面是在他從香港大學離休一年，到史丹佛大學來為他的巨作《中國史學論文引得續編──歐美所見中文期刊文史哲論文綜錄》收集資料的時候。這兩冊《引得》已經成了研究中國最基本的無可取代的工具書。

　　1966年當代中國研究聯合委員會（Joint Committee on Contemporary China，簡稱JCCC）由於得到福特基金會慷慨補助成立了一個全國性中心去確認、收集、複製、分發重要的研究現代和當代中國的研究資料時，我們很幸運地得到研究圖書館協會（Association of Research Libraries，簡稱ARL）的同意來主持這個中心。但是很難在美國找到一位對中國出版物熟悉，有作研究的經驗，還與在現代和當代中國研究領域的圖書館員和學者廣泛交遊，並且還具商業頭腦的人。於是我到香港去嘗試說服他擔任這個職務，因為他正具備了這個職位所要求的所有條件。他那時正在香港大學當講師，教授中國歷史，頗受學生歡迎和尊敬。同時還很成功地經營一家頗具盛名的書店──龍門書局。該書店也出版複製品。換言之，他當時對在香港舒適的生活非常滿意。所以他對我說：「謝謝您，不要了，謝謝您」。但是我並不是那麼容易就可被打發掉的人。次年我再到香港時，令我意外驚喜的是他居然對我說他願意考慮了，而終於接受了這個職位。多年後我才知道他和他夫人為他們孩子的教育才作了離開他們生長地方的這個相當困難的決定。另外他自己也覺得他可以在這個工作崗位上為學術界做出更大的貢獻。中國研究資料中心（Center for Chinese Research Materials, Association of Research Libraries，簡稱CCRM）於1968年正式成立，余秉權是第一任主任。以他的勤奮和智慧，從無開始促使CCRM成為國際間聞名遐邇的機構。如今在西歐，在北美，乃至在亞洲沒有一個主要東亞圖書館沒有收藏該中心複製的資料。CCRM在世界各地的中國研究中心和圖書館界已經家喻戶曉。

CCRM在余秉權的領導下不僅成為複製品出版者，中心本身也出版了為學者作中國研究需要的參考資料。這些資料都是他費了很多時間和精力做出來的研究成果。中心所複製的上千種圖書、期刊、報紙都附有他學術性的注解。這些都收錄在中心的通訊（CCRM Newsletter）上，使這個通訊為類似的書目刊物樹立了一個新穎又高標準的典範。

他經常被海內外各種會議邀請去作講演。他總是利用這樣的機會去參觀當地的圖書館，尋找CCRM可以借出複製的資料。記得1979年我們一起作為第一批美國圖書館代表到中華人民共和國訪問期間，每到一個圖書館參觀，他總是在書庫裡流連忘返，代表團其他成員都得等候他。

1982年秉權因病退休。我知道他從來沒能接受他體力上不再能夠繼續他奉獻了大半生他喜愛的專業工作這個事實。我一再告訴他，他過去14年替CCRM所做的貢獻，其他人一生也做不到。生病是由不得自己的事，沒有什麼可恥。他會聽我的勸說，可是我知道我並沒有說服他。他對自己很惱怒。他是個非常驕傲的人。如果他還活著的話，我還會向他說同樣的話。我還會告訴他我有他這樣的朋友，何其榮幸。中國研究的學術界也因為有他，何其幸運。我會非常想念他。

注釋

原載《東亞圖書館委員會通訊》（*Committee on East Asian Libraries Bulletin*）第87期（1989年6月），頁2-3。

（胡嘉陽譯）

Recollections of Professor Yu

P. K.'s passing is not only a tragic loss to his family, but also a tremendous loss to the field. If our libraries today are better stocked with research materials on modern China, and if our research scholars are better able to conduct their research because of the availability of these materials, P. K. played an important part in having made that possible. So, while we mourn P. K's passing, we also give thanks for his life, for his life has enriched ours, and there is much that he has left to us for which we shall remain indebted to him.

P. K. and I go back more than thirty years. We met for the first time when he came to Stanford, on leave from the University of Hong Kong where he was teaching, to do research on the second volume of his monumental work, *Chinese History: index to Learned Articles*. This two-volume work has since taken its place among the most basic research tools in Chinese studies, and it is unlikely that it will ever be replaced by anything of its kind.

In 1966 when the Joint Committee on Contemporary China, with a substantial grant from the Ford Foundation, decided to establish a national center to identify, assemble, reproduce, and distribute important Chinese research materials for the study of modern and contemporary China, we were fortunate enough to have enlisted the help of the Association of Research Libraries（ARL） as the sponsor for such a center, but we had difficulties in finding a person in the United States to be the center's director. We were looking for a person who was knowledgeable about Chinese publications, experienced in research, widely acquainted with librarians and scholars in the field, and who also had a head for business. I went to Hong Kong and tried talking P. K. into taking the job, as he had all the qualifications we were seeking in a candidate. P. K. at that time was a popular and respected lecturer in Chinese history at the University of Hong Kong, and he also was running the successful and highly respected Long Man Book Store which was also a reprint publisher. In other words, he was leading a very contented and comfortable life in Hong Kong. So he said to me, "Thank you, but no thank you." But I wasn't that easily turned away. I was in Hong Kong again the following year, and much to my pleasant surprise, he agreed to consider our offer, and finally accepted the job. I was only to learn years later that he and Mrs. Yu had made the difficult decision to pull up roots to come to the United States partly because they wanted better educational opportunities for their children, and partly because P. K. thought he could better serve the field in this new capacity. The Center for Chinese Research Materials (CCRM) was officially established in 1968, and P. K. became its first director. The rest, of course, is history. P. K., through his diligence, resourcefulness, and plain hard work, succeeded in creating something from nothing, and made CCRM into an internationally renowned institution. Today there is no major library in Western Europe, North America, and, in some cases, in Asia that does not have something that has been reproduced by CCRM. Indeed, CCRM has become a household word, as it were, in Chinese studies centers and libraries throughout the world.

CCRM under P. K.'s leadership not only was a reprint publisher, but also a publisher of research aids for Chinese studies. The introduction P. K. wrote to each of these publications was itself a research piece to which he devoted much time and energy. The scholarly annotations he provided for each of the hundreds of volumes of books, journals, and newspapers reproduced by CCRM were one of a kind, and the *CCRM Newsletter*, in which these annotations were published, set a new and higher standard for such endeavors.

P. K. was often invited as a speaker at meetings and conferences in this country and abroad. On such occasions he never failed to take advantage of the opportunity to visit the local library in search of something CCRM could borrow and reprint. When we travelled together in 1979 as members of the first American Library Delegation to visit the People's Republic of China, delegation members often had to wait for him to catch up with the rest of us on our various visits because P. K. would be lost wandering about in some library's stacks.

P. K. retired in 1982 because of illness. I know he never got over the fact that he was no longer physically able to carry on the work he loved so much, and to which he had devoted a major part of his productive professional life. I would try to tell him from time to time that he already had accomplished so much in just fourteen years at CCRM that many others couldn't even hope to do in a lifetime, and that being ill is something one cannot help and is nothing to be ashamed of. He would listen, but I always knew that he wasn't convinced. He was angry at himself. He was a very proud person. If he were alive today, I would tell him the same thing over again, and I would also tell him how privileged I was to have him as a friend, and how tremendously fortunate the Chinese studies field had been because of him. I will miss him sorely.

Notes

This article was published in *East Asian Libraries Bulletin*, no. 87 (June 1989), pp. 2-3.

紀念費正清教授

1977年隨哈佛大學校長巴克（Derek C. Bok）訪問東亞，途經檀香山訪問哈佛大學校友（左起）巴克、何清先生、費正清（John K. Fairbank）教授、吳文津。

　　1964年我為哈佛燕京圖書館館長的職務來哈佛大學面談時才第一次見到費正清教授，過去只是久聞他的大名而已。那時候哈佛燕京圖書館還隸屬哈佛燕京學社，他並不是館長遴選委員會的一員，但是他卻是被指定要和我面談的人之一。我發現他是個非常優雅端莊的人，對收藏研究現代和當代中國資料的問題頗有見解。對編輯書目可以促使較好地使用研究資料也很感興趣。他對哈佛燕京圖書館未來發展的熱情厚望顯而易見，並頗具感染性，因此我對他留下了深刻的印象。那年稍後哈佛燕京學社再次邀請我到劍橋，還邀請了我的內人雷頌平同來。我們事先知道哈佛學院圖書館人事部的主任戈登・比坎南（Gordon Bechanan）會到羅根機場（Logan airport）來接我們。

但是我們萬萬沒有想到費正清教授也和他同來迎接我們。我們還沒有入住被安排的校方達納帕爾默招待所（Dana Palmer House），費教授就以他一貫主管的方式把我們接到他溫思羅普街41號（41 Winthrop Street）的家。他為我們安排了一個招待會，介紹東亞研究中心的一大批教授和訪問學人還有一些研究生給我們。接下來的兩天，他是我們的嚮導。頌平至今還記得她簡直跟不上他的腳步，還擔心他過街毫不注意紅綠燈的習慣！

1965年秋天我到哈佛燕京圖書館上任後，才更知道費教授是如何關心圖書館的發展。早在1945年他在重慶美國新聞處工作時，他就義務地把書刊寄來母校。我的前任裘開明館長在他那年的年終報告中就提到他贈送了1,400冊戰時在重慶和內地出版的書刊。裘館長說：「我們對他為採購這些書刊，並向當時的中央圖書館和文化機構要求贈書所作的努力十分感謝。」1946年他回國後還是繼續給圖書館幫忙。他介紹中國和香港他認識的書商和朋友給裘館長，並且安排胡佛研究所將其中文收藏創始人芮瑪麗（Mary Wright）早先在中國解放區獲得的書刊複本和哈燕館作交換。

除了收集書刊外，費教授經年累月為圖書館爭取經費斡旋。他為東亞區域研究專案（East Asian Regional Studies Program）曾經向哈佛學院圖書館爭取採購研究現代和當代中國中文出版品的經費，這筆錢供我們使用多年。在1950年代末期費教授代表哈佛向政府申請國防教育法立案有關東亞研究方面經費時，圖書館經費就列為優先需求。由於他的開創，從此圖書館就成為此筆經費的受益者。當他作為東亞研究中心主任期間，他提供哈佛燕京圖書館一筆種子資金出版《哈佛燕京圖書館書目叢刊》（*Harvard-Yenching Library Bibliographical Series*）。在出版了三種書目：《中文期刊索引》、《館藏韓文分類目錄》和《陳誠所收藏有關蘇維埃共和國資料目錄》之後，其銷售盈利已經可作為往後出版的周轉金了。他也全力參與了哈佛燕京圖書館1970年代中期的募款活動。他聯合哈佛大學圖書館視察委員會（University Library Visiting Committee）和東亞研究視察委員會（East Asian Visiting Committee）組成了一個聯合小組（Joint Subcommittee on the Harvard-Yenching Library）來為哈佛燕京圖書館募款。他積極參與計畫，並為募款起草小冊子。我們一塊出訪了有希望可能捐款者多次。他的話總是簡短而有力，就像他在小冊子中所寫的：「如果圖書館失去了功能，學術研究也就無法繼續……當美國人希望和東亞建立和平而穩定的關係時，他們對東亞書刊和知識的需要就會與日俱增。如果圖書館萎縮了，光光聘有教授，有獎學金給學生也是無濟於事。哈佛有第一流的教授就是因為有第一流的圖書館。這兩者生死與共。」夏威夷華人實業家何清捐款致使哈佛燕京圖書館參考室以他為名，約瑟夫‧布亭格（Joseph Buttinger）捐出他所收藏的越南文文件，都是費教授努力的成果。

　　費正清教授是哈佛燕京圖書館的摯友。他是圖書館的支持者，也是我個人的朋友和被尊敬的同事。我會懷念他的。

注釋

原載柯文（Paul A. Cohen）、梅谷（Merle Goldman）編輯之《紀念費正清教授》（*Fairbank Remembered*）（麻州劍橋：哈佛大學費正清東亞研究中心，1992），頁159-161。

費正清（John King Fairbank, 1907-1991），美國漢學家，歷史學家，哈佛大學教授，哈佛大學東亞研究中心創始人。

（胡嘉陽譯注）

Fairbank Remembered

I knew John Fairbank only by name until 1964, when I came to Harvard for an interview about the Librarian's position at the Harvard-Yenching library. He was not on the search committee appointed by the Harvard-Yenching Institute (the Library was still a part of the Institute at that time), but he was one of the people I was scheduled to meet. I found him to be a person of great charm and civility, and also of many insights into the problems of developing a research collection on modern and contemporary China. He also showed a deep interest in providing better intellectual access to research materials through bibliographical research. His enthusiasm about the prospects of the Harvard-Yenching Library was as obvious as it was contagious. I went away from our meeting quite impressed. Later that year, I came back to Cambridge for a return visit, and this time the Harvard-Yenching Institute also invited my wife, Nadine. We knew we were to be met at Logan airport by Gordon Bechanan, the personnel officer of the Harvard College Library, but we were totally surprised to see John Fairbank there as well. In the characteristic Fairbank fashion, John took immediate charge of things, and before we had a chance to check into the Dana Palmer House, where we were going to stay, we were whisked to 41 Winthrop Street. At the Fairbanks' residence, John had arranged a reception for us. There we were introduced to a large group of Harvard faculty, visiting scholars at the East Asian Research Center, and some graduate students. For two days, John acted as our escort. Nadine still remembers her difficulty in keeping up with John's stride, and her fears about his total disregard for traffic lights while crossing Cambridge streets!

After taking up my position at the Harvard-Yenching Library in the fall of 1965, 1 began to learn more about John's involvement with the Library. As early as 1945, when he was posted in Chongqing with the USIS, John was already sending books back to the Library as a volunteer service to his *Alma Mater*. In his annual report that year, Dr. A. Kaiming Chiu, my predecessor, acknowledged that the more than 1,400 volumes of Chinese books received that year were "new publications published in Chongqing and other interior cities during the war years. We are much indebted to Professor John K. Fairbank for his services in purchasing these books, and for his efforts in securing gifts from the National Central Library and other Chinese cultural institutions." Following his return to Harvard in 1946, John continued to offer his assistance to the Library. He introduced book dealers as well as friends in China and Hong Kong to Dr. Chiu, and also arranged an exchange with the Hoover Institution whereby the Harvard-Yenching Library would receive many duplicates of Chinese Communist publications which Mary C. Wright had earlier acquired in Communist-controlled areas in China for the newly established Chinese Collection at Hoover.

In addition to securing books, John also used his good offices to secure financial support for the Library over the years. He obtained funds from the Harvard College Library for the purchase of Chinese-language publications on modern and contemporary China for the East Asian Regional Studies Program, funding which lasted for a number of years. In Harvard's application for government funding of East Asian studies under the National Defense and Education Act（NDEA）in the late 1950s, library support was listed as a priority need. Because of his initial effort, the Library has been a beneficiary of that program ever since. During his tenure as director of the East Asian Research Center, John provided the seed money for the publication of the Harvard-Yenching Library Bibliographical Series. The proceeds from the sales of the three titles already published— one an index to Chinese periodicals, one the Library's Korean catalog, and one an annotated bibliography of the Chen Cheng Collection on the Kiangsi Soviet Republic—have made possible the establishment of a revolving fund for future publications in the series. When the Library began its fund drive in the mid-1970s, John lent his full support to the campaign. He arranged with the University Library Visiting Committee and the East Asian Visiting Committee to form a Joint Subcommittee on the Harvard-Yenching Library, and took an active part in the drafting of a campaign brochure and in planning sessions. We took a number of trips together to visit prospective donors in the country. His message was always simple and to the point. As he wrote in the brochure, "Scholarship cannot be maintained if a library ceases to function.... As the American people turn toward East Asia in the hope of peace and stable relations, their need for books and knowledge will steadily increase. The maintenance of faculty members and of fellowships for students will be of no avail if the library withers and decays. Harvard has a first-rate faculty because it has a first-rate library and the two must sink or swim together." The donation which made possible the naming of the Library's main reading room in honor of Chinn Ho, and the gift of the Joseph Buttinger papers on Vietnam to the Library were the direct result of John's efforts.

John Fairbank was a true friend to the Harvard-Yenching Library, 1 shall miss him as an advocate for the Library, a personal friend, and a respected colleague.

Notes

This was published in Paul A. Cohen and Merle Goldman, comp. *Fairbank Remembered* (Cambridge, MA: Fairbank Center for East Asian Research, Harvard University, 1992), pp. 159-160.

平易近人：賀蔣彥士先生八十壽辰賀文

　　我第一次見到彥士先生是在台北，時間是民國四十九年。他當時給我的印象是一位頗有風度的學者專家。他在農復會的建樹，我早已聞名。認識他以後，才發現他的豪爽、熱心與和藹可親的另一面。同時，他又沒有官架子，所以我對他的欽佩就與日俱增了。這幾年，我每次到台北都要去拜訪他，以表示我的尊敬。除非他的公事太忙，他總會抽出時間來接見我。承他的不棄，我們就慢慢地熟悉了。

　　彥士先生對事，一切都從大處著想，小處著手，看見森林，也看見樹木。是一個注重功效、務實、負責任，但不慕虛名的人。民國六十五年，我隨哈佛大學校長巴克（Derek C. Bok）一行，應中華民國哈佛大學同學會的邀請訪問台灣（其時同學會的會長是中央銀行副總裁李幹先生）。彥士先生當時任教育部長，他認為這是一件中美文化學術交流的大事。從旁鼎力協助同學會辦理招待事宜，結果非常圓滿，促進了同學會和母校關係的進一步發展，也增進了台灣和哈佛在教育文化方面的聯繫。後來李登輝先生被選為總統就職時，巴克校長還去信致賀，這與他去台灣的成功訪問有直接的關係。年前同學會發起籌募基金在哈佛大學公共衛生學院設立「李國鼎講座教授」及「李國鼎經濟社會衛生發展中心」，彥士先生也費了不少的精力來促成這件意義非常重大的事。他對這些事情的熱心是鮮為外人所知的。

　　彥士先生平易近人，且很重交情。民國七十一年我和我內人去台北探望我們當時在台北啟聰學校任教英語和美國手語的小女章玲，彥士先生要請我們吃中飯。他當時擔任中國國民黨中央黨部秘書長職。公務很忙，約定的日期沒有記清楚。在約定的那天中午，他打電話來旅館，說是不是今天我約你們吃中飯。我說是的，他說我以為是下個星期。我說下個星期我們已經離開台灣了，你很忙，我們下次再來看你。他堅持不肯，要我們等他，說讓他調整一下他的時間，立刻就到旅館和我們吃飯。身兼黨國大任他對這些小事還能如此重視，對朋友能如此厚待，實在令人敬佩。用餐時，他知道內人在醫藥界工作，就談到很多關於衛生和保健方面的事。他對生化知識的豐富令我內人十分佩服。雖然內人是第一次見到彥士先生，但是她說她的感覺好像是已經和蔣秘書長是很熟的朋友了。彥士先生的平易近人，由此可見。當日他也問到小女在啟聰學校教書的情形。他說：「特殊教育我們非常需要，我們也急需要改正社會上一般人對殘障人士的看法和歧視。郭為藩先生是特殊教育專家，我要介紹你們的女兒去看他。」如此的熱心和關懷！我們的女兒說，有蔣先生這樣的人，台灣對殘障學生的教育就不愁沒有進一步的發展了。

彥士先生雖然一直都在黨政方面負極其重要的領導工作，但是他對台灣的農業改良從來沒有失掉他的興趣。民國七十四年他卸中央黨部秘書長職，我在台北看見他的時候，他暢談要移植世界所有水果在台灣栽培的計畫。他說以台灣的地理環境和已經成功的移植經驗，這是應該可以辦得到的事，可藉此發展台灣的農業經濟，增進台灣人民的福祉。言語間充滿了信心和熱望。他這種淡泊明志，有一分熱發一分光的精神和情操是足以為我們效法的。

彥士先生任總統副秘書長，日理萬機，但對一些小事也能躬親其事，不假手他人。民國八十年我在台北見到他時，他問我認不認識前哈佛大學經濟系知名教授和前美國駐印度大使 John Kenneth Galbraith 先生。我說認識。他說好極了，因為李登輝總統讀過 Galbraith 新著 *The Age of Pragmatism*（《務實的時代》），很佩服他的見解，想和他交換意見。彥士先生提議請中華民國哈佛大學同學會和台灣大學邀請 Galbraith 教授去台灣訪問作公開講演，並安排與李總統見面。第二天他就約了同學會會長馬英九先生、台大校長孫震先生、外交部次長程建人先生，和我在總統府商談邀請事宜。後來 Galbraith 到了台北訪問，作了公開講演，並和李總統交談，結果非常良好。這都是彥士先生做事周詳，大事小事都不厭其煩的一面。我所認識的彥士先生確實是一位不厭不煩的學者和公僕。他的開朗、豪邁、謙讓、誠直、不諛不苟，和平易近人的美德，足以為我們的模範。我幸與他結識，為我的良師益友，謹記瑣碎，聊申敬意，並以祝賀他的八十壽辰。

注釋

本文原載《至情至性為善最樂：蔣彥士先生八十慶賀文集》（台北：何歌健，民國84年），頁413-415。

追思塞貝爾利克博士

我第一次見到塞貝爾利克（Wolfgang Seuberlich）博士是我1964年為美國學術團體協會和社會科學理事會合組的當代中國研究聯合委員會資料小組（Subcommittee on Materials of the Joint Committee on Contemporary China of the American Council of Learned Societies and the Social Science Research Council）對研究現代和當代中國資料作全球調查去到瑪律堡（Marburg）的時候。雖然是初次見面，可是我早已聞名他是歐洲東方學圖書館界的領導人物。當我計畫到西德的時候，我特別安排到瑪律堡的德國國家圖書館（Staatsbibliothek）參觀訪問。我知道他在那兒負責東方資料的收藏。他非常禮貌地接待我，介紹他們的收藏，並且將我要看的資料拿給我閱覽。我立刻發現他是個學者型的圖書館工作者，專注於他的工作，並樂於幫助他人。他對他多年精心收藏和整理的資料感到非常驕傲——那時候是西歐最大的東亞收藏。像歐洲多數的東方圖書館一樣，他沒有什麼助手幫忙，從採購到編目都親力而為。但是他毫無怨言，反而以為是對他的挑戰。他唯一的抱怨就是西德政府要把該圖書館從瑪律堡搬到西柏林。他認為這是從政治方面來考量，對學術研究不利的決定，因為去瑪律堡在地理上其實比去西柏林方便得多。

塞貝爾利克博士敬崇熱愛中國文化的輝煌，是位中國學專家。我還記得我和他漫步在瑪律堡的街上，他指著一座天主教堂說：「那座天主教堂的設計和建築都十分美觀，但是只是南宋時代的建築而已啊！」

從1964年後我們開始了一段長時期的業務上的往來。因為專業的關係我們在香港和紐約數度重逢。我們也經常通信聯絡。他是個值得尊敬的同事，也是一位善良的人。我會永遠記得他。他的過世是中國研究這個領域裡的損失，當然也是西德的損失。

注釋

原載《東亞學者圖書館員賽貝爾利克（1906-1985）》（*Wolfgang Seuberlich [1906-1985], Ostasienwissenschaftler und Bibliothekar*），柏林：德國國家圖書館（Staatsbibliothrk zu Berlin），1998，頁107。

沃爾夫岡・塞貝爾利克（Wolfgang Seuberlich, 1906-1985），曾擔任德國國家圖書館東亞部主任。著有《十七世紀俄中關係》（*Die russisch-chinesischen Beziehungen im 17. Jahrhundert*）。

（胡嘉陽譯注）

Wolfgang Seuberlich
A Memorial

I first met Dr. Seuberlich in 1964 in Marburg while conducting a worldwide survey of library resources for modern and contemporary China studies for the Joint Committee on Contemporary China of the American Council of Learned Societies and the Social Science Research Council. Although it was our first meeting, I had known him by name for some time, for his reputation as a leading European Orientalist Librarian had long preceded him. When I travelled to West Germany, I made sure that my itinerary included the Staatsbibliothek in Marburg, where Dr. Seuberlich was in charge of the Oriental collection. He received me most cordially, briefed me on the collections, and showed me everything I asked to see. It became immediately clear to me that here was a scholar-librarian who was completely dedicated to his work and was enthusiastic in helping others. He was tremendously proud of the collection he had built over the years; it was carefully selected, organized, and at that time the largest such collection in West Germany. Although he was short of help, as was commonly the case with European Libraries collecting East Asian materials, he did not complain. Indeed, he took it as a challenge and did much of the work himself, from book selection to cataloguing. The one thing he did complain about was the West German government's decision to move the Staatsbibliothek from Marburg to West Berlin, which he regarded as a political decision detrimental to academic research, as West Berlin was geographically more difficult of access than Marburg.

Dr. Seuberlich was a China specialist with a boundless admiration for the grandeur of Chinese civilization. I remember strolling through the streets of Marburg with him, and he pointed to a cathedral and said: "that cathedral is quite beautiful in design and construction, but it dates only from Southern Song times!"

Our meeting in 1964 was the beginning of a long professional relationship between us. We met several times thereafter in Hong Kong and in the United States, and we also kept up with each other's activities through correspondence. I will always remember him as a respected colleague and a good and kind-hearted person. His passing surely was a loss to the Chinese studies field, particularly in West Germany.

December 1989.

Notes

This article was published in *Wolfgang Seuberlich (1906-1985): stasienwissenschaftler und Bibliothekar* (Berlin: Staatsbibliothek zu Berlin, 1998), p. 107.

懷念美國東亞圖書館協會的朋友杜克

1996年國際圖聯在北京召開第62屆大會同時舉行的「演進中的學術圖書館與東亞研究」專題研討會上與前文化部圖書館司司長杜克先生（右一）合影。

　　杜克（1938-2003），前中華人民共和國文化部圖書館司司長，北京圖書館常務副館長，美國東亞圖書館協會的朋友，因病於2003年11月8日在北京逝世，享年66歲。

　　他1938年8月23日生於山西省萬榮縣。他對新中國圖書館事業的發展，特別是對公共圖書館事業的發展做出了傑出的貢獻。他1961年自北京大學圖書館系畢業後，就被分派到北京圖書館（自1998年改名中國國家圖書館）工作。四年後於1965年轉調到文化部服務，直到他1998年退休。最初他先在文化部圖書館、博物館、文物局圖書館處工作。文化大革命期間，1968年他被下放到湖北省咸寧縣文化部的五七幹校受訓。那期間博物館和文物局在國務院管轄下成立了國家文物局（傳說這樣作是為了保護文物免於紅衛兵的摧毀）。國家文物局下也設立了圖書館處。1972年他自五七幹校回來後，就在圖書館處工作。文化大革命後圖書館處升格為圖書館事業管理局，又回屬文化部。杜克先生被指派作文化部圖書館事業管理局公共圖書館處處長。兩年後於1982年他升任為局長。但是1984年他被指派為文化部辦公廳主任。1987年才回到原來的崗位，其時文化部圖書館事業管理局已經改名文化部圖書館司。他任司長一直到他1998年退休。其間1987到1991年他同時擔任北京圖書館常務副館長。

　　杜先生在中國圖書館事業發展上建樹良多。他最主要的貢獻就是領導發展中國公共圖書館系統，奠定了其基礎設施。1970年末他主持圖書館，檔案館及其他有關機構的職稱標準化的工作。他提交的《圖書，檔案，資料專業幹部職稱暫行規定》經國務院批准，於1981年公布作為全國標準。杜先生也參與了文化部1982年向全國發布的《省（自治區、市）圖書館工作條例》的起草工作。由於杜先生深諳中國公共圖書館發展的不同階段及其不同需求，他領導文化部設定了一套評估定級的標準來提高縣級公共圖書館的管理和服務工作。1994年杜先生領導文化部對所有縣級公共圖書館做了首次評估，1997-1998年又做了一次。

　　其間，杜先生還完成了一項最具挑戰性的工作，就是促使全國人民代表大會通過中國第一個圖書館法。他認為有了一套法規，就可以加速中國圖書館事業的發展。因為沒有前車可鑑，他集合了一群圖書館專家尋求最好和最有效的方法去達到這個目的。他們草擬了一份法案，認真地向有興趣的政府機構遊說。經過十幾年竭誠的努力，該草案終於提上議程於2001年提交全國人民代表大會。經過全國人民代表大會初步通過，還經過有關政府機關審查後，文化部正在修改該草案以便再行提交。照目前情況看，通過這個法案是指日可待的事。若是沒有杜先生和他的同事扎實的工作，肯定不會有今天的成果。

　　1980年初文化部決定以圖書館自動化為其重點研究和發展項目之一。作為文化部圖書館司司長，杜先生將其人力物力全部投入支援深圳大學發展的圖書館自動化集成系統（Integrated Library Automation System，簡稱

ILAS）。今天該系統成為中國圖書館最廣泛使用的系統：有800高校圖書館和1,100個公共圖書館使用。

　　1997年，杜先生退休前一年，文化部和其他有關政府機構開始籌畫「知識工程」這個大專案。這個專案以圖書館為基地來促進閱讀，傳播知識的目的。指導該專案的委員會就設在文化部圖書館司。杜先生為此專案的啟動作了不少貢獻。

　　杜先生對學術界最大的貢獻就是1980年代中期開始將全國圖書館文獻拍攝成縮微品以為保存，作為「搶救全國文化產業」計畫的一部分。文化部於1985年成立全國圖書館文獻縮微複製中心。1987年杜先生從文化部辦公廳主任調回為文化部圖書館事業管理局局長後，直接督導該中心的工作。當1996年召開全國圖書館文獻縮微工作會議估量其已經完成和尚待完成之工作時，杜先生報告說公共圖書館的珍藏多數已經拍攝完成，全部完成尚需13年。其時這個在中國圖書館史上的非常巨大而空前的資料保存專案就可大功告成。在其已經拍攝的資料中包括1949年前出版的中國報紙和期刊；中國善本書；1912-1949年民國期間的出版品；清朝（1644-1912）和民國初年出版的地方志。這些都是非常有價值的研究資料，多數只有中國獨有的文獻。舉世學者將為此永遠感激杜先生和中心以惠來者的貢獻。

　　雖然杜先生主要關注的是中國公共圖書館的發展，但是作為中國圖書館學會理事會理事，他也關注學術以及非學術圖書館的發展。自1979年該理事會成立以來，杜先生五次當選連任理事會理事。自1983-2001年他還是該理事會副理事長兼常務理事。後來由於年齡的限制，他才辭去了該理事會所有職務，但還享有榮譽理事之名。

　　杜先生不止活躍於中國圖書館界，也活躍於國際圖書館界。他環遊世界各地，參加了不止十屆國際圖書館協會聯合會會議。他到美國訪問多次。第一次是1973年隨中國圖書館代表團而來。我就是在那次他來時認識他的。文化大革命之後我們見面的次數就增多了，特別是隨著1978年中美建交我們可以去中國訪問的時候。由於這些不斷的接觸，他1995年第一次來參加亞洲學會東亞圖書館委員會CEAL（後改稱亞洲學會東亞圖書館協會）在檀香山召開的年會。次年我們不少會員又在北京舉辦的世界圖聯大會上再次見到他。作為大會秘書長，他把大會辦得非常成功。其中包括他一年前和萬惟英、馬泰來討論後，同意在大會期間，同時召開會議研討與東亞圖書館有關的議題。因此北京國際圖聯大會中國組委員會和北美亞洲學會東亞圖書館協會合辦了「演進中的學術圖書館與東亞研究專題研討會」。研討會上發表的15篇報告收集在北京萬國出版社出版的《演進中的學術圖書館與東亞研究專題研討會論文集》。為了感激他對中國圖書館以及對國際圖書館合作上的貢獻，CEAL會長馬泰來在杜先生退休後於1999年邀請他到波士頓參加年會，並致感激函（見下，原載《CEAL通訊》第120期，2000年2月，頁61-62）。他最後一次來參加CEAL年會是2001年到芝加哥。除了在中文資料小組會議報告中國數位資訊資源的發展（"The Development of Digital Information Resources in China"）外，他還回顧了他和美國圖書館和館員為了中國圖書館的發展交流的美好事項。

其中所提到的之一就是我曾經親自參與的項目：在中國為就讀圖書館學以及資訊科學學生成立韋棣華基金會獎學金，懇請中國圖書館學會代為辦理（韋棣華為美國教育家。1929年在武昌成立中國第一家圖書館學校——文華圖書館專科學校）。1996年我參加世界圖聯大會時向他提到這個想法，他立即表示甚有興趣。儘管他忙著大會事務，還是抽空和我討論，並要我提交一份正式計畫書給中國圖書館學會。由於他的極力支持，我們很快達成協議，三個月後於1996年11月他和我分別代表中國圖書館學會和韋棣華基金會簽訂了一份備忘錄（Memorandum of Understanding）。為了開啟這個項目，中國圖書館學會指派以杜先生為主席成立了一個韋棣華獎學金考核委員會，成員包括圖書館學教授和圖書館館長來考核獎學金的所有申請，從1997年到2002年已經為243位本科生和研究生頒發獎學金。

杜先生不僅留下了豐功偉業，也留下了不朽的言論。他有關圖書館的言論有以下的出版：1. 北京學苑出版社1988年出版的《圖書館事業建設》，與吳慰慈合著；2. 當代中國出版社1995年出版的《當代中國的圖書館事業》；3. 北京書目出版社1996年出版的《中國圖書館發展戰略研討會論文集》；

4. 北京圖書館 2001 年出版的《文獻資訊開發工作》。

　　杜先生的過世不僅是中國失去了一位有遠見、認真、具有使命感的圖書館界領導人。在美國圖書館界，特別是東亞圖書館界也失去了一位好朋友和一位值得尊敬的同事。我們會非常想念他。

注釋

原載《東亞圖書館學報》（*Journal of East Asian Libraries*），第 132 期（2004 年 2 月），頁 67-70。

　　　　　　　　　　　　　　　　　　　　　　　　　　　（胡嘉陽譯）

附件

　　1999年3月10日在波士頓美國東亞圖書館協會全體會員大會上，萬惟英代表該協會向前中華人民共和國文化部圖書館司司長杜克宣讀並呈交感謝函。杜克教授過去20多年不僅是中國圖書館事業發展的推動者，並且還是國際圖書館間合作的促使者。感謝函如下：

　　過去20多年杜克教授是中國圖書館事業發展的推動者。當他1980到1998年擔任中華人民共和國文化部圖書館司長，1987到1989年擔任北京圖書館常務副館長，長期擔任中國圖書館學會理事會理事期間，他為發展中國圖書館系統，建立圖書館法，促進國際交流做出了永恆的貢獻。《當代中國的圖書館事業》一書就廣泛記載了他的事蹟。

　　文化部於1985年成立全國圖書館文獻縮微複製中心。在他的領導下將1870至1949年間出版的主要中文報紙、期刊以及成千上萬的善本書和手稿拍攝成縮微膠捲。這個前所未有，無與倫比的成就不僅保存了人類的紀錄和精神，還方便全國和國際間使用這些資料。

　　他為中國乃至世界在中國圖書館事業發展各個方面所提供的眼光和領導令我們矚目和讚賞。他留給後世的偉大成就讓我們想到一位著名的美國詩人的詩句：

　　千秋萬代遠蜚聲
　　學步金鼇頂上行
　　已去冥鴻猶有跡
　　雪泥爪印認分明 [1]

　　杜教授1973年隨中國圖書館代表團到美國來訪問，開啟了中美圖書館之間合作交流的蓬勃發展。作為世界圖聯大會秘書長，他不僅精心策劃了最成功的國際專業會議，還在大會上以他的智慧和努力第一次籌備了一場與東亞圖書館有關的研討會。本會作為合作者與有榮焉。

　　CEAL以此感激信代表我們對杜教授的欽佩和尊敬。祝願他健康和快樂。

會長馬泰來代表美國東亞圖書館協會致敬

注釋

[1]　美國詩人朗費羅（Henry Wadsworth Longfellow, 1807-1882）（〈人生頌〉）詩中四句，清人董恂譯文。

（胡嘉陽譯注）

Du Ke
A Memorial

Du Ke 杜克, formerly Director of the Library Department of the Ministry of Culture and Chief Deputy Director of the National Library of China, People's Republic of China, and a friend of CEAL, died on November 8, 2003, in Beijing following a short illness. He was 66.

Mr. Du was born on August 23, 1938, in Wanrong 萬榮 County in Shanxi 山西 Province. An outstanding library leader, Mr Du had an illustrious career directing the development of libraries and librarianship in the People's Republic of China, especially relating to public libraries. Following his graduation from Peking University in 1961, with a major in library science, he was assigned to the National Library of Peking 北京圖書館 (from 1998 known as the National Library of China 中國國家圖書館). He stayed four years there until his transfer in 1965 to the Ministry of Culture, where he would remain until his retirement in 1998. At the Ministry of Culture he first served at the Ministry's Library, which together with the Ministry's museum and the library of the Ministry's Bureau of Archaeology formed a larger office known as the 文化部圖書館、博物館，文物局圖書館處. His service was interrupted in 1968 when he was sent down, during the Cultural Revolution, to the May 7th Cadre School sponsored by the Ministry of Culture at Xianning County 咸寧縣 in Hubei 湖北 Province for political study. Meanwhile, the Museum and the Bureau of Archaeology of the Ministry of Culture were placed under the jurisdiction of the State Council 國務院 to form the State Administration of Archaeology 國家文物局. (It was rumored that this was done to protect cultural relics from damage and destruction at the hands of the Red Guards.) A Library Division was also created under that office 國家文物局圖書館. When Mr. Du was returned to work in 1972 from the May 7th Cadre School, he was assigned to this Library Division. After the Cultural Revolution, this Division was upgraded to become the Bureau of Library Administration 圖書館事業管理局, and its jurisdiction was retroceded to the Ministry of Culture. Mr. Du was then appointed Director of the Bureau's Public Library Division 文化部圖書事業管理局公共圖書館處處長.Two years later, in 1982, he was given charge of the entire Bureau and assumed the title of Director 局長，but in 1984 he was transferred to head the Ministry's General Office 文化部辦公廳主任. In 1987 he returned to his previous position as Director of the Bureau of Library Administration, its name having by then been changed to Library Department 文化部圖書館司. During his tenure as head of the new department 司長（1987-1998）Mr. Du also served concurrently as the Chief Deputy Director of the National Library of Peking 北京圖書館常務副館長 from1987 to1991. He retired from government service in 1998.

Mr. Du's accomplishments were many. His primary legacy is the leading role he played in the development of the infrastructure of China's public library system. In the late 1970s he presided over the task of standardizing the appellation of professional positions in the library, archive, and other information-related fields. The proposal his task force submitted, 圖書、檔案、資料專業幹部業務職稱暫行規定, was subsequently approved by the State Council and established in 1981 as the national standard. In 1982 the Ministry of Culture promulgated the regulations governing library work in the provinces, autonomous regions, and municipalities（省、自治區、市圖書館工作條例），drafted by a team that included Mr. Du. Realizing the different stages of development of China's public libraries, and therefore their different needs, the Ministry of Culture introduced a grading system 評估定級 for all public libraries above the county level with a view to providing better supervision, assistance, and service. This work was carried out in 1994 and again in 1997-1998 under Mr. Du's leadership.

While these developments were taking place, Mr. Du began to work on perhaps the most challenging of all the tasks he had faced: i.e. advocating the passage of a Library Act 圖書館法, the first ever in the history of China, by the National People's Congress. He envisioned a new day for China's libraries when their development could be nurtured and expedited by a set of laws. Since there were no precedents to follow, he assembled a group of library specialists and went to work finding the best and most effective way to reach that goal. The result was a draft bill. With that they lobbied in earnest the government agencies having an interest in the matter. After more than a decade of dedicated effort, library legislation finally found a place on the nation's agenda. In 2001 the proposed legislation was officially submitted to the National People's Congress 全國人民代表大會 for consideration. Having received the Congress' initial approval and gone through the necessary reviews by relevant government agencies, the proposed legislation is now being revised by the Ministry of Culture for re-submission. The eventual passage of the Library Act is now assured. There is absolutely no doubt that without the solid work done by Mr. Du and his colleagues this final Act would never have come to pass.

In the early 1980's the Ministry of Culture made library automation one of its key research and development projects. In his capacity as Director of the Ministry's Bureau of Library Administration, Mr. Du placed the resources of his office fully behind this initiative and supported the development of the Integrated Library Automation System (ILAS) by Shenzheng University Library. Today, ILAS is the most popular library automation system developed in China used by Chinese libraries, among them more than 800 academic libraries at institutions of higher learning and some 1,100 public libraries.

A year before Mr. Du's retirement, the Ministry of Culture, in collaboration with other government agencies, launched, in 1997, a huge undertaking known as the "知識工程" ("knowledge dissemination project"). Using the library as its base, the project aims to promote reading and disseminate knowledge for the social good. The office of the committee directing this work was set up at the Library Department of the Ministry of Culture 文化部圖書館司. Mr. Du, as the director of the Library Department, contributed much to getting the project started.

　　Mr. Du's most far reaching contribution to scholarship was the nation-wide preservation microfilming project of library holdings, beginning in the mid-1980's, as part of the national program "to salvage and preserve national cultural property." A National Microfilming Reproduction Center 全國圖書館文獻縮微複製中心 was set up at the Ministry of Culture in 1985 while Mr. Du was Director of the Ministry's General Office 文化部辦公廳主任, and he assumed direct supervision of the Center's work after he returned to his old position as director of the Bureau of Library Administration in 文化部圖書事業管理局局長 in 1987. The Center was a huge success. By the time the Conference on National Library Microfilming 全國圖書館文獻縮微工作會議 was held in 1996 to take stock of what had been accomplished and what remained to be done, Mr. Du was able to report that the Center had finished microfilming most of the treasured collections at China's public libraries. It was his hope that all materials in China's public libraries that should be preserved will be microfilmed in thirteen more years, thus bringing to a successful conclusion the most gigantic preservation program in the history of Chinese libraries. Among the materials that have already been preserved on microfilm are pre-1949 Chinese newspapers and periodicals, Chinese rare editions, publications issued during the Republican period of 1912-1949, and local gazetteers published during the Qing dynasty（1644-1912）and the early Republic. These are invaluable research sources, most of which are available only in China. Scholars around the world will forever remain in Mr. Du and the Center's debt for having preserved them for posterity.

Although Mr. Du was concerned mainly with public libraries, he played an important role in guiding the development of all libraries in China, academic and non-academic, while serving as a member of the Council of the China Society for Library Science 中國圖書館學會理事會, to which position he was elected five times since the founding of the Society in 1979. He also was a member of the Society's Executive Committee 常務理事 and concurrently a Vice President 副理事長 four times, from 1983 to 2001. He resigned from all posts in the Society after 2001 owing to the age requirement, and was then made an honorary member of the Council.

Mr. Du's professional activities were not confined to China. He was also active internationally. He traveled widely abroad, participating in more than ten IFLA (International Federation of Library Associations and Institutions) meetings. He visited the United States a number of times, the first in 1973 as a member of the Chinese Librarians Delegation. That was when we met him for the first time. Our meetings with him became more frequent after the Cultural Revolution, particularly when we were able to travel to China following the normalization of relations between Washington and Beijing in 1978. This increased contact led to his attending his first CEAL meeting in Honolulu in 1995. Many of us saw him again the following year at the Beijing IFLA meeting. As the Secretary-General of that meeting, he was credited with making it one of the most successful in IFLA's history. Credit must also be given him for his agreement to have a conference on East Asian libraries and librarianship held in conjunction with the IFLA meeting, as the result of discussion with Messrs. Weiying Wan and Tai-loi Ma the year before. Thus, a Special Conference on the Evolving Research Library and East Asian Studies was convened during the 1996 Beijing IFLA meeting, jointly sponsored by the Beijing IFLA Organizing Committee and CEAL. Fifteen papers altogether were presented by our colleagues in China and members of CEAL. The proceedings were published under the title 演進中的學術圖書館與東亞研究專

題研討會論文集（*Proceedings of the Special Conference on the Evolving Research Library and East Asian Studies*）（Beijing: International Academic Publishers 萬國出版社 1996.）Following his retirement, Mr. Du was invited to the 1999 CEAL Annual Meeting in Boston to receive a letter of appreciation from Tai-loi Ma, President of CEAL, for his contributions to Chinese libraries and librarianship and to the international cooperation of libraries and librarians.（For a full text of the letter see *Journal of East Asian Libraries*, no.120, Feb. 2000, pp. 61-62.）Mr. Du's last CEAL meeting was in 2001, when he came to Chicago to deliver a talk on "The Development of Digital Information Resources in China" at the meeting of the CEAL Committee on Chinese Materials, at which time he also recalled with much fondness his involvement with American libraries and librarians on matters concerning Chinese library development.

One such matter in which I was personally involved was the establishment of the Mary Elizabeth Wood Foundation Scholarship program in China for students in library and information science.（Mary Elizabeth Wood 韋棣華 was an American educator who established the first library school, the Boone Library School, in Wuchang, China, in 1929.）I broached the idea with Mr. Du during the 1996 Beijing IFLA meeting. He became immediately interested and, busy as he was during the IFLA meeting, he took time to ask questions and then urged me to submit a formal proposal for the consideration of the China Society for Library Science, the organization the Foundation hoped would administer the program. Because of his strong support of the program, an agreement was quickly reached between the China Society for Library Science and the Mary Elizabeth Wood Foundation and a Memorandum of Understanding was signed in November 1996 by him for the China Society for Library Science and by me for the Mary Elizabeth Wood Foundation, a mere three months after we discussed the idea. To implement the program the Society appointed a committee composed of library educators and administrators to review and evaluate applications, with Mr. Du as chair. The program has since been ably administered by the China Society for Library Science for the Mary Elizabeth Wood Foundation. From its beginning in 1997 through 2002, a total of 243 students, both undergraduate and graduate, have been awarded the scholarship.

Mr, Du will be remembered not only for his deeds but also for his words. He published a number of articles on Chinese libraries and librarianship and was editor of four major books: (1)《圖書館事業建設》(*Library Development*) with Wu Weici 吳慰慈 (Beijing: 學苑出版社，1988); (2)《當代中國的圖書館事業》(*Library Development in Contemporary China*)(Beijing: 當代中國出版社，1995); (3)《中國圖書館發展戰略研討會論文集》(*Proceedings of the Conference on a Strategy of Library Development in China*)(Beijing: 書目文獻出版社，1996); and (4)《文獻資訊開發工作》(*The Development of Documentation and Information Services*)(Beijing: 北京圖書館出版社，2001)

With Mr. Du's passing China has lost a library leader with vision, dedication, and a deep sense of mission. The American library community, especially its East Asian component, has also lost a good friend and a respected colleague. We will miss him greatly.

Notes

This article was published in *Journal of East Asian Libraries*, no. 132 (Feb. 2004), pp. 67-70.

DU KE PRESENTED LETTER OF RECOGNITION

On March 10, 1999 at the Plenary Session of the CEAL Annual Meeting in Boston, Mr. Weiying Wan read and presented a letter of appreciation on behalf of CEAL to Professor Du Ke, former Director of the Library Department of the Ministry of Culture of the People's Republic of China. Not only was Professor Du the primary moving force behind the development of Chinese libraries and librarianship for the last two decades, he has also been a major promoter of international cooperation of libraries and library professionals. The letter reads:

> For more than two decades, Professor Du Ke has been the primary moving force behind the development of Chinese libraries and Chinese librarianship. During his tenure as the Director of the Library Department, the Ministry of Culture, from 1980 to 1998, his leadership in the National Library of China as its Executive Deputy Director from 1987 to 1989, and his professional leadership in the Chinese Library Association's Board of Directors, he has made lasting contributions to the development of the infrastructure of the Chinese library systems, the development of library laws and standards, and the promotion of international cooperation of libraries and library professionals. The comprehensive report on Chinese library developments, *Dangdai Zhongguo Di Tushuguan Shiye* bears eloquent testimony to his contributions.
>
> The China National Microfilming Center for Library Resources, which since its establishment in 1985 has been under the guidance of the Library Department, has microfilmed all major Chinese newspapers published between 1870 and 1949,

thousands of major journals, and tens of thousands of rare books and manuscripts. This is unprecedented and unparalleled achievement not only in preserving human records and expressions of inspiration and aspiration, but also in national and international resource sharing.

In all aspects of Chinese library development, one cannot but notice and admire what his vision and leadership has created for the country and for the world. It is the great achievements and legacies such as his that brings to mind the stanza of a well-known American poet:

> Lives of great men all remind us
>
> We can make our lives sublime
>
> And, departing, leave behind us
>
> Footprints on the sands of time

Professor Du was a member of the Chinese Library Delegation that visited the United States in 1973, making the beginning of many splendorous blossoms of Sino-American library-exchange. As the Secretary-General of the Beijing IFLA (International Federation of Library Associations), he not only orchestrated the most successful international professional forum, it was his wisdom and endeavor that created the first IFLA panel devoted to East Asian Studies Librarianship, of which the Council on East Asian Libraries was the proud collaborator.

As a token of our admiration and respect, CEAL is honored to present to Professor Du this letter of appreciation with our best wishes for good health and good cheers.

On behalf of the Council on East Asian Libraries,

Dr. Tai-loi Ma, President

韋棣華與近代中國圖書館發展

　　我今天很榮幸能夠參加貴會2006年的年會。我謹代表韋棣華基金會向貴會的邀請同安排和一些韋棣華獎學金和韋棣華出席國際會議獎助金的得獎人見面表示謝意。基金會得貴會鼎力的協助，十年前在台灣設立獎學金項目，四年前設立出席國際會議獎助金項目，均由貴會全權辦理，成績昭著。我在這裡代表基金會向貴會致最深的謝意和敬意。獎學金專案已經又延長五年，到2011年。今後還希望能夠繼續得到貴會的指教、支持和協助來執行這項工作，以期對台灣圖書館學和資訊學的學子有所鼓勵，藉以對台灣圖書館及資訊學的專業教育及訓練工作有一點些微的貢獻。

　　黃理事長要我講幾句話。我知道年會還有很多節目，不想耽擱大家的時間。不過義不容辭，就用韋棣華與近代中國圖書館發展為題，做一個簡單的報告，還希望大家指教。關於韋棣華其人其事，已經有好些著作，如早期沈祖榮先生、裘開明先生、毛坤先生的文章，後來嚴文郁先生，以及近年程煥文先生、徐鴻女士、黃文宏先生等的著作都可以作為參考。今天我想來簡單的談一談韋棣華女士的遠見和她的成就的意義。

　　如眾所知，韋棣華女士（Mary Elizabeth Wood）於1861年（清咸豐十一年）出生於紐約州巴達維亞（Batavia）附近一個小鎮。她的弟弟聖公會牧師韋德生（Robert E. Wood）回憶他的姊姊說：「她在年輕的時候就喜歡閱讀，手不釋卷，所以對於英國文學很有造詣」。所以當巴達維亞在1889年成立公共圖書館的時候，她就被聘任為館長。雖然那時她沒有圖書館專業的訓練，在任內她不但能勝任她的職務，而且有過之無不及的表現。她的弟弟又說：「她對這些名著的知識幫助了很多人在這方面發生了愛好」。她的這種樂於助人和求知的精神對她後來在中國的工作有很大的幫助。她在巴達維亞公共圖書館任職十年。1899年因中國義和團排外運動，韋棣華女士擔心她在武昌作宣教士的弟弟韋德生的安全，遂隻身赴華探望。在武昌時因為當時聖公會創辦的思文學校（Boone Preparatory School，文華書院的前身）缺乏初級英文教師，由韋德生的推薦，她被聘教授英文。由於該校英文書刊的缺乏，她向美國教會朋友及機構求助，收到不少出版物，於是在該校成立了一個小小的圖書館。因為她在思文學校的表現傑出，美國聖公會在1904年任命她為該會的平信徒宣教士。同時，1903年思文學校設立高等科，改名文華書院。1905年（清光緒三十一年）清政府廢除科舉，倡「新學」力主西學中用，各地興建學校，文華書院遂籌備改組大學。韋棣華女士認為要成立大學，圖書館的建立必須為其要務。於是於1906年回到她已經闊別七年的故鄉，籌募經費在武昌建立新圖書館。由於她的努力，募款的工作非常成功。她1908年再回武昌，開始籌備圖書館營造的工作（她在美時曾在紐約普瑞特學院圖書館學校［Pratt Institute Library School］進修）。1909年年中圖書館的建築動工，次年（1910）春完工。圖書館遂行啟用，命名為「文華公書林」，為中國開創第一所現代新型圖書館。此館的特徵在於其採取開架式及開放政策，與中國傳統的「藏書樓」的性質完全不同。「文華公書林」雖位置於文華書院校園，但非文華書院的圖書館，而是一所獨立的公共圖書館。使用者除文華書院的學生外，還對外開放。「文華公書林」的創立為開近代中國公共圖書館的先河。

　　隨著「文華公書林」業務的發展，韋棣華女士由於專業人才對圖書館發展的重要，於是在美國友人的贊助下，她先後於1914年（民國三年）送沈祖榮先生，1917年（民國六年）送胡慶生先生赴美在紐約公共圖書館學校（New York Public Library School，哥倫比亞大學圖書館學校的前身）攻讀。因而沈、胡兩先生成為中國留美研習圖書館學的先鋒。他們的留美為韋棣華女士在中國創立圖書館學校計畫的第一步。韋女士深信中國圖書館事業有其前途，而圖書館事業的發展必須首先造就圖書館的專業人才，因故贊助他們留美進修。韋棣華女士計畫的第二步是籌募經費，為此她於1918年二次返美進行籌募工作，並在波士頓（Boston）的西蒙斯學院（Simmons College）

進修圖書館學。同年（1919年）重返武昌，在沈、胡兩先生的協助下，開始籌畫圖書館學校的建立（沈、胡兩先生在美學成後分別在1916年及1919年返華）。文華圖書科（Boone Library School）於1920年開辦，收第一班學生共六人（包括哈佛燕京圖書館的前任館長裘開明先生），為中國首創圖書館學校。1929年獲教育部批准為獨立學府，更名為「私立武昌文華圖書館學專科學校」（簡稱「文華圖專」，英文名稱仍舊為Boone Library School）。1953年文華圖專轉屬武漢大學稱「圖書館學專修科」；1984年經教育部批准成立「圖書情報學院」以迄於今。

韋棣華女士除文華圖專外，對中國全國的教育及文化事業尚有很大的抱負。在中國教育文化界的大量支持及美國駐華公使的鼓勵下，她於1923年返美遊說國會籲其通過法案將庚子賠款的剩餘金額退回中國以作教育文化專業之用。據她自己的敘述，她在華府的5個月間曾親自拜會82位參議員同420位眾議員。她這種不辭辛勞的努力終於得到報酬。美國國會在1924年通過法案將庚子賠款600餘萬美元的餘項全部退回中國作為推進教育文化事業之用。因之「中華教育文化基金會」成立，由15名知名教育家主持，其中10名為華人、5名為美籍。基金會首先決定以50萬美元建立「國立北平圖書館」並同意負擔該館十年的維修費。基金會又在各地設立其他六所公立圖書館。此外，並為文華圖專提供三年每年5千美元的贊助，作為教員薪俸及獎學金之用。由此可見，韋棣華女士對於近代中國圖書館運動的貢獻遠超過文華圖專的建立。雖然文華圖專的建立本身已經是一件非常重要的富歷史性的事件，對「近代中國圖書館運動之后」的稱譽，韋棣華女士實在是受之無愧。

1929年當全國各界正在籌備於1930年5月16日舉行「韋棣華女士來華服務30周年紀念大會」，並以慶祝文華公書林成立20周年，文華圖專成立10周年之際，韋女士於1930年5月1日在武昌病逝，享年69歲。

韋棣華女士為一極為虔誠之基督徒。她以她在中國的圖書館教育工作為她蒙召作為宣教士的負擔，且一直忠誠於她的蒙召。在文華公書林的入口有很醒目的刻字：「在基督的後面隱藏著知識與珍寶。」由於她的宗教信仰和她對中國和中國人的愛，她把她的下半生留在中國成為近代中國圖書館運動的先驅。她深信中國必須訓練自己的圖書館專業人才，否則無法建立現代化所需要的圖書館和圖書館能提供的服務。她的遠見是為了社會發展的需要。她深信中國將來一定必須而且也會有由專業人員管理，對公共開放，並且提供服務的圖書館。她的這種遠見鼓舞了她的同仁、學生，以及其他關懷的人，為推動中國圖書館教育和圖書館服務的發展而努力。據統計，從1920到1949年文華圖專的畢業生約500人。這些文華校友就是中國圖書館界繼承韋棣華女士遺志的中堅人物。這就是韋棣華女士留給我們的遺產。

　　在此我們可以提出一個問題：鑑於並不是所有創辦事業的人都是成功的人，為什麼韋棣華女士會如此的成功？我想主要的原因是因為她有眼光，她為她的遠見驅使，並且有決心和毅力去達到她為自己設立的目標。而她也從未轉移過她的目標。同時，她也適逢其會，當時沒有人想到宣導圖書館教育，也鮮有人知道如何進行。她一開路後，跟隨者就不乏其人。我也相信她的獻身是由於她的宗教信仰。因為她認為她在中國的工作是她作為宣教士蒙召的負擔。從一個比較世俗的角度來講，她的成功在於她能鼓舞同激勵她的同仁和學生，並且給他們灌注一種迫切感和使命感。她也是一個有高度文化敏感度的領導者。當文華圖專開辦的時候，她請沈祖榮先生作校長，而自己僅任教務長。文華圖專雖然是仿照美國圖書館學校的方式創辦，但是在它的課程當中設立有不少關於中國目錄學及其他相關的科目。在教學中她給學生灌輸了作圖書館專業的自豪感，同做一個有效的圖書館專業人員必須要廣閱讀才能夠勝任自己的工作的信念。所以，她是老師、啦啦隊和輔導員的三合一的人物。韋棣華女士所告訴我們的是沒有好的圖書館專業人才就不會有好的圖書館。好的圖書館專業人才出自好的圖書館學校。韋棣華獎學金同韋棣華出席國際會議獎助金的目的也就在於此──以微薄的力量協助在台灣訓練為台灣社會服務的圖書館專業人員。

　　多謝大家！

注釋

本文為2006年12月2日在台北中華民國圖書館學會年會致辭。載《中華民國圖書館學會會訊》第15卷，第1/2期（2007年6月），頁4-6。

盧國邦先生追思會上的致辭

1993年美國國際圖書館電腦中心中日韓系統用戶團體（OCLC Users Group）主席吳文津卸任（左），盧國邦（右）接任典禮。

「凡事都有定期，天下萬物都有定時：生有時，死有時；栽種有時，拔除所栽種的也有時……哭有時，笑有時；哀慟有時，跳舞有時……」（傳道書3：1-4）

各位朋友：

今天我們聚集在這裡不是來哀悼Karl，而是來紀念他充滿成就具有意義的一生。Karl在美國東亞圖書館界給大家的印象是個精力充沛，樂於助人的人。對他的專業非常投入並具遠見。Jenny告訴我他不要大家為他舉辦追思會，因為他不要大家談論他。這就是他永遠保持低調的一面。

我在1960年代他在堪薩斯大學開始他的圖書館事業時就認識他，至今已經40多年了。但是我和他較多交往還是1970年代他到西雅圖華盛頓大學工作的時候。華大是他到那裡之前大約25年我念書的地方，我也曾經在華大圖書館打工。時間久了我們從同事關係變成了朋友，後來還成了好朋友。他非常慈祥富有愛心。他的頭腦敏銳，對事總是用嚴謹的分析法去解難。這大概和他早年學習科學有關。我非常佩服他在提出每個議題時所具有的邏輯性和說服力。這是他的特長。他也是個具有信念和眼光的人。有鑑於1970年代研究圖書館自動化的成就，Karl是少數幾個人認為只要東亞文字也能像西文一樣數位化，東亞圖書館也是可以自動化的。他確定這是可以做得到的，因為在東亞，特別是台灣，這方面已經頗有進展。因此他鼓動東亞圖書館界趕快向亞洲同事們學習。從1970年中期直到他過世之前，他從來沒有一刻為宣導東亞圖書館的高科技化懈怠。

　　Karl是個行動者。他自己積極投入自動化這項活動。他成為台灣中央研究院謝清俊博士領導發明的漢字資訊交換碼CCCII（Chinese Character Code for Information Interchange）的顧問。後來1982年研究圖書館組織（RLG）以此交換碼發展成目前全國應用的東亞文獻資料使用的東亞字元代碼（East Asian Character Code for Bibliographic Use，簡稱EACC）。他也給連線電腦圖書館中心（Online Computer Library Center，簡稱OCLC）發展其中日韓系統提供諮詢，並於1991年幫忙成立OCLC CJK使用者團體這個組織（OCLC CJK Users Group）。他還無師自通地發明韋氏拼音、漢語拼音互換軟體。這軟體不僅被許多東亞圖書館使用，更在2000至2003年間被OCLC用來轉換資料庫中大批韋氏拼音的中文資料成漢語拼音，以嘉惠全世界的東亞圖書館。

　　在加州大學聖地牙哥分校他成立了環太平洋數位圖書館聯盟（Pacific Rim Digital Library Alliance）。在國際間尚未廣泛合作分享數位資料前，他就開始作這樣的開放分享數位和其他資料的工作了。他總是無私地和人分享他的知識和才能。1982年他和我一同到中國大陸兩個月，在成都四川大學和西安師範大學主持兩個有關圖書館管理學的培訓班。他專門講授圖書館中科技的應用。那已經是25年前的事了。1988年暑期他在西雅圖華盛頓大學也組織了一個東亞圖書館館員培訓班。簡而言之Karl就是個實踐他所宣揚的，而且總是熱衷他所做的人。任何熟識他的人都知道他總是對現狀充滿疑問，眼睛閃閃發光地問：我們還可以做些什麼？

他在2006年4月8日在舊金山我們慶祝OCLC提供OCLC CJK服務20周年紀念會上說他有四個夢想：「（1）以統一代碼（Unicode）來代替東亞字元代碼（EACC）；（2）超越更換機讀編目格式（MARC）；（3）公平、公正地處理智慧財產權（Intellectual Property）問題；（4）以個人電腦連網以利資源分享和資料交換。」這就是典型的Karl Lo。他總是開風氣之先。這次的講話大概就是他最後一次出現在東亞圖書館的聚會中了。

想到Karl，我就想到羅伯特‧甘迺迪（Robert F. Kennedy）借用蕭伯納（Bernard Shaw）的話：「有些人看已成事實的事，總是問『為什麼？』我夢想一些沒有發生的事，而問『為什麼不？』」Karl，我們愛你，將永遠想念你。

注釋

原載《東亞圖書館學報》（*Journal of East Asian Libraries*），第142期（2007年6月），頁9-10；並載《中華民國圖書館學會會訊》15卷，1/2期（144/145）（2007年6月），頁13-14。

盧國邦（Karl Lo, 1935-2007），祖籍廣東省中山市。1958年畢業於香港崇基學院化學系。1960年獲亞特蘭大大學圖書館碩士。1959-1968年任職堪薩斯大學東亞圖書館，官至館長；1968-1990年任西雅圖華盛頓大學東亞圖書館館長；1990-2002年任加州大學聖地牙哥分校東亞圖書館館長；2002年3月至9月為美國國會圖書館亞洲部代理主任。曾為美國東亞圖書館協會主席（1985-1988）、澳大利亞國家圖書館顧問、環太平洋數位圖書館聯盟執行長，與兩岸三地多所高校圖書館顧問。

（胡嘉陽譯注）

Karl Lo – A Tribute

"There is a time for everything, and a season for every activity under heaven: A time to be born and a time to die, a time to plant and a time to uproot... a time to weep and a time to laugh, a time to mourn and a time to dance..." (Ecclesiastes 3:1-4)

Dear Friends:

We are gathered here today not to mourn Karl's passing, but to celebrate a life that was full of meaning and achievement. Karl was energetic, vibrant, helpful, supportive, dedicated, and a visionary in his chosen profession. Jenny tells me that Karl didn't want to have a memorial service, because he didn't want people to talk about him. That was another aspect of Karl: he was always unfailingly modest.

I knew Karl for more than forty years, since he began his library career at the University of Kansas in the 1960's. I got to know him better when he moved to the University of Washington in the 1970's, where some twenty five years earlier I had been a student helper at the UW Library. As time went by, our professional relationship developed into a personal one as well; I found him to be a very kind and caring person, and we became close friends. Karl had a very keen and questioning mind and was strictly analytical in his approach to problems, perhaps because of his early scientific training. I always admired the conviction and logic with which he would advance an argument. That is what was so special about him. He was a man of conviction and vision. Having witnessed the impressive successes research libraries had in automating their operations beginning in the 1970's, Karl was among the few who saw the potential for the same things happening in East Asian libraries, if East Asian scripts could be machine-processed the same way Roman alphabets were. And he was certain that that could be done, because much progress was already being made in that area at the time in East Asia, particularly in Taiwan. So he urged his colleagues in the East Asian library community that we should hasten to learn from our colleagues in Asia for our own benefit. Ever since that time, from the mid-1970's until his last days, he never ceased to be the spark plug for the role high technology could play in East Asian libraries.

Moreover, Karl was a doer. He took an active part in technological developments himself. He became a consultant to Academia Sinica in Taiwan, where Dr. C.C. Hsieh had earlier invented CCCII (Chinese Character Code for Information Interchange), from which the Research Libraries Group (RLG) in 1982 derived the now national standard EACC (East Asian Character Code for Bibliographic Use). He was also consulted by OCLC on the development of its CJK (Chinese, Japanese and Korean) program, and he helped organize the OCLC CJK Users Group in 1991. The Wade-Giles-to-Pinyin software Karl developed as a self-taught programmer was used by many East Asian libraries and by OCLC in converting its huge file of Chinese records from Wade-Giles romanization to Pinyin between 2000 and 2003, a gigantic achievement that benefited the East Asian studies community world-wide.

While at UCSD Karl was a founder of the Pacific Rim Digital Library Alliance for open sharing of digital and other materials before such international cooperation in the sharing of digital materials became common. Always generous in sharing his knowledge and talents, Karl conducted with me two month-long workshops on library management in China in 1982, one at Sichuan University in Chengdu and one at the Shaanxi Normal University in Xi'an, and he lectured specifically on technology application in libraries. That was twenty-five years ago. He also organized the Summer Institute for East Asian Librarians at the University of Washington in 1988. In short, Karl practiced what he preached, and he was always passionate about what he was doing. Anyone who knew Karl well can tell you that he was always questioning the status quo, and with a twinkle in his eye he would ask, was there anything more we could do?

In a speech given at the celebration of the 20th anniversary of OCLC's CJK Service on April 8, 2006, in San Francisco — perhaps his last public appearance before an East Asian library group — Karl said he had four fantasies: "(1) Replace the EACC (East Asian Character Code) with Unicode; (2) Reach beyond MARC (Machine Readable Cataloging Format); (3) Be fair and square with IP (Intellectual Property) rights; and (4) Put our PCs on a grid." That was vintage Karl Lo. He was always thinking ahead, and always ahead of the wave. Thinking of Karl, I thought of what Robert F. Kennedy once said, borrowing from Bernard Shaw: "There are those who look at things the way they are, and ask, "Why?" I dream of things that never were, and ask, "Why not?" Karl, we love you and will miss you greatly!

Notes

This talk was delivered at Karl Lo's memorial service on March 9, 2007 in San Diego, California, and published in *Journal of East Asian Libraries*, no. 142 (June 2007), pp. 9-10; also in《中華民國圖書館學會會訊》, no.144/145 (June 2007), pp. 13-14.

袁守和先生
中國圖書館的先達

　　20世紀40年代末期我在西雅圖華盛頓大學歷史系就讀。因為需要工讀，在該校東亞圖書館找到一份零工，每週20小時，做些雜事，因而接蝕到一些關於中國現代圖書館發展的資料，也才第一次知道袁同禮（守和）先生是中國圖書館界赫赫有名的領導人物。華大畢業後，我對圖書館事業已經產生了濃厚的興趣，於是進入該校的圖書館學院繼續就讀。因為選定了專業，又打算在東亞圖書館服務，所以就更仔細地閱讀了許多關於現代中國圖書館發展的文獻和當年守和先生編輯的《圖書季刊》之類的專業刊物。從這些出版物中我得到不少的知識，同時也深深地領會到中國現代圖書館的發展是如何艱巨的事業，而守和先生在這方面又是何等偉大的功臣！這種開路創業的精神對一個在圖書館學院念書的學生有莫大的啟發，守和先生所扮演的角色也就成為我心中的模範了！

　　1951年我在圖書館學院畢業後，去加州史丹佛大學胡佛圖書館擔任中文編目的工作。萬萬沒有想到會在史丹佛遇見了我久已欽慕的守和先生！當時他受聘參加史丹佛研究所主持的一項《中國手冊》的編制工作。參加的尚有吳元黎（舊金山大學經濟學教授）、許芥煜（後任舊金山州立大學中國文學教授）、侯服五（後任麻州大學政治學教授）及其他諸位先生。因為他們要使用胡佛圖書館中文部的資料，所以我們見面的時候就很多。守和先生給我的第一個印象就是他是一位文質彬彬，頗具儒家風度，但不多言的長者。我初出茅廬，對這位曾任北平圖書館館長並聞名國際的現代中國圖書館界領導人物當然有相當的敬畏。但是，我慢慢發現，他實在是一位非常和藹可親的人。守和先生在史丹佛的兩年，我們公私都有往來，但因為我的資歷太淺，他沒有跟我談到任何中國圖書館界的掌故和他個人的經歷。但是在工作上他對我總是有求必應，循循善誘。對他的教導，我一直是十分感激的。

守和先生效法西方，特別是美國的現代圖書館管理和發展方式，在擔任國立北平圖書館館長任內奠定了中國國家圖書館的基礎，制定了中國現代圖書館發展的方向，並派員至美國深造，培養圖書館幹部人才，厥功至偉。同時，在工具書的編纂方面，他發揮了帶頭作用。在先生的指導下，這項工作開始發芽生根，諸如《國學論文索引》、《文學論文索引》，以及《地學論文索引》都相繼出版，為學術界所推崇。專題索引之編纂亦成為圖書館主要任務之一，與當時洪業教授在燕京大學主持編纂之《哈佛燕京學社引得》並駕齊驅，開以索引方式查詢中國古今典籍文獻之先河。

1957年守和先生受聘去華盛頓國會圖書館任職，有人說他屈就，但他不以為意。守和先生一生以服務學術與促進中西文化交流為宗旨。事情無論大小、職位無論高低，凡是符合他的宗旨的事，他都樂意去盡一份力量。這種高超的、隨遇而安的精神足以令人肅然起敬而為後世師表。去國會圖書館後，先生修訂王重民先生「二戰」前為該館編輯的《國會圖書館中國善本書目》手稿，於1957年由國會圖書館出版。國際漢學界因之對該館所收藏中國善本首次得以窺其全豹。次年，他的巨著《西文漢學書目》（*China in Western Literature: A Continuation of Cordier's Bibliotheca Sinica*）亦行問世。此書繼高第（Henri Cordier）的大作《漢學書目》（*Bibliotheca Sinica: Dictionnaire bibliographique dès ouvrages relatifs a l'Empire chinois*，*Paris: 1881-1885*）分列18,000種自1921到1957年英、法、德文關於中國的各種專著，至為詳盡。書出後，洛陽紙貴，迄今尚為學者不可或缺的主要參考書。繼此之後，先生又出版《俄文漢學書目》（*Russian Works on China, 1918-1960*），以補《西文漢學書目》的不足。於是，20世紀前半期歐美有關中國的專著始有一有系統的記錄。先生致力於文獻書目之編撰孜孜不倦。1961-1963年前後又出版歐美中國留學生博士論文三種：《中國留美同學博士論文目錄》（*A Guide to Doctoral Dissertations by Chinese Students in America, 1905-1960*）（1961）；《中國留英同學博士論文目錄》（*Doctoral Dissertations*

by Chinese Students in Great Britain and Northern Ireland, 1916-1961）
（1963）；《中國留歐大陸各國同學博士論文目錄》（*A Guide to Doctoral Dissertations in Continental Europe, 1907-1962*）（1964）。此三種目錄除能檢索所列四五千人之專業論文題目外，絕大部分作者之中文姓名亦由先生不辭辛勞，向各方求證加列，對使用者莫大的便利。此亦表現其治學態度之嚴謹，足以為我們的師表。先生學術興趣廣泛，除上列書目外尚撰有《新疆研究叢刊》10種（1962）；《中國經濟社會發展史目錄》（*Economic and Social Development of Modern China: A Bibliographical Guide, 1918-1960*）（1963）；《中國數學書目》（*Bibliography of Chinese Mathematics*）（1963）；《胡適先生西文著作目錄》（*A Bibliography of Hu Shih's Works in Western Languages*）（見《中央研究院歷史語言研究所集刊》，第34本下冊，1963），以及由芝加哥大學美術系教授范德本（Harrie Vanderstappen）完成之先生遺著：《袁同禮中國藝術及考古西文文獻書目》（*The T.L. Yuan Bibliography of Western Writings on Chinese Art and Archaeology*）（1973）。書目工具書不受時限，有裨益學術研究萬年之效。守和先生的遺著正是此類具有不朽價值的著作。

　　守和先生逝世已55年。追思先達，想「前人栽樹，後人乘涼」這句話應該是對他的功績最恰當的形容了！

注釋

本文載國家圖書館編《袁同禮紀念文集》（北京：國家圖書館出版社，2012），頁9-11；據〈憶守和先生〉（載《袁同禮先生百齡冥誕紀念專輯》，台北：中國圖書館學會，1995，頁22-23）修正。

紀念韓南教授

　　我初識Pat是他1961年應聘到史丹佛大學亞洲語言系（現在為東亞語言文化系）執教時。那時候我擔任胡佛研究院剛創立的東亞圖書館館長。數年後我於1965年他於1968年分別轉職哈佛大學。因此我們在哈佛共事達29年之久，於1997同年退休。

　　Pat是個安靜，但非常熱情的人。彬彬有禮，親切善良，長於聆聽。他對晚清俗文學的博學和研究方面的巨大的貢獻廣為他的同行所讚揚。在這裡我僅以他為我曾任職32年的哈佛燕京圖書館之友和支持者向他致敬。

　　哈佛有邀請教授參與圖書館諮詢委員會的傳統，如此可以在其學術專業上給圖書館收藏及其他工作方面提供意見。Pat作為哈佛燕京圖書館諮詢委員會成員多年，並於1977-1982年擔任委員會主席。在他任內，他總是關注圖書館的資料採購，對所收資料是否具有價值、是否對研究有用頗有判斷的眼光。但是他對哈佛燕京圖書館最大的貢獻還不在資料的採購上。當他擔任哈佛燕京學社社長（1987-1995）時，他為維護哈佛燕京圖書館作為全國乃至全世界卓越的東亞圖書館作了兩項重要的決定：一個就是提供經費完成將編目卡轉換成機讀格式；另一個就是邀請上海圖書館中國善本書專家沈津作為哈佛燕京學社的訪問學人。

　　美國圖書館自動化始於1960年代，突飛猛進於1970年代。當研究圖書館利用高科技使圖書館工作自動化，特別是將編目卡片目錄轉換成機讀格式時，東亞圖書館無法跟進，因當時尚無可以處理東亞文字的系統。後來這種系統出現時，又因為費用高昂，東亞圖書館無法負擔得起這筆開銷。這也就是為什麼當哈佛大學所有圖書館編目卡轉換成機讀格式時，哈佛燕京圖書館並未包括在內（當時估價為250萬美元）。但是這項工作必須要做。圖書館自動化不會因為東亞館而緩慢下來。於是哈佛燕京圖書館遂自行一項小型的試驗項目。首先在韓國募得10萬美元，在台灣募得25萬美元，與美國國際圖書館電腦中心（OCLC）簽訂合同，初試這項回溯建檔的轉換工作（retrospective conversion project，簡稱recon project），將17,000韓文編目卡和42,500中文編目卡轉換成機讀格式。其結果相當令人滿意。於是我向Pat提出是否可以按照其他哈佛大學圖書館回溯建檔的預算方式來完成哈佛燕京圖書館回溯建檔的工作，也就是哈佛燕京圖書館應出的費用由哈佛燕京學社出資再由校方配合。其實哈佛燕京學社因已於1976年將哈佛燕京圖書館轉屬哈佛大學文理學院圖書館，故已無任何義務負擔這筆費用。但是Pat看到該項目的重要性，馬上同意我的想法，並答應和當時文理學院院長兼哈佛燕京學社董事會主席亨利·羅梭夫斯基（Henry Rosovsky）交涉。該提案並獲得了東亞研究理事會會長柯偉林（William Kirby），和哈佛大學圖書館館長西德尼·維伯（Sidney Verba）的支持。其後，哈佛燕京學社董事會批准了110萬美元的預算，再由校方配合110萬元。哈佛燕京圖書館從而得以在1995年和美國國際圖書館電腦中心（OCLC）簽訂合同。回溯轉換工作由1996年開始，歷時五年將全館所有323,500種編目卡轉換成機讀格式。這是所有主要東亞圖書館中最大的一項回溯建檔工程，其結果嘉惠於所有的東亞圖書館。因他們不必再自行其個別轉換工作，僅須利用哈佛燕京圖書館資料庫中已經轉換的成果即可。此外，全世界的讀者都可以輕而易舉地線上查詢哈佛燕京圖書館的目錄。要不是Pat的遠見和支持，這項前所未有的項目絕無法完成，東亞研究和現在相比肯定也要差得多了。

　　Pat對哈佛燕京圖書館和全球的東亞研究界嘉惠的第二個決定，就是邀請沈津作為哈佛燕京學社訪問學人來編輯哈佛燕京圖書館中文善本書志。哈佛燕京圖書館卓越的中文善本館藏是前館長裘開明積數十年盡其畢生精力所建立，開明先生的宿願為出版一部完整的書目。但先生於1977年逝世前，此願未得以償，深以為憾。1987年沈津以紐約州立大學石溪分校資助從事調查美國圖書館中文善本書籍的工作，因而來哈佛燕京圖書館考察四週。其時我僅知他曾師從著名的藏書家及版本學家，時任上海圖書館館長顧廷龍先生，而他自己是當時上海圖書館特藏部副主任。經過四個星期的調查，臨走前他慷慨地與我分享他所作的筆記，我才發現他對中文善本書的知識深淵廣博，及其工作效率的快速。四年後於1991年我至香港中文大學參加一個會議，非常驚喜地見到他。才知道他兩年前應香港中文大學中國研究中心邀請來作研究，把家也從上海搬到香港了。我問他有無來哈佛燕京圖書館編輯中文書志的興趣。他答應後，我返劍橋後遂去見Pat，建議他邀請沈津作為哈佛燕京學社訪問學人一年來編輯一部哈佛燕京圖書館館藏中文善本書解題目錄。Pat即刻批准了我的要求。沈津和他的夫人於1992年抵劍橋後，立刻開始工作，不分晝夜，兩年內（他的訪問學人身分延長了一年到1993年），將南宋（1127-1279）至明末（1368-1644）1,433種善本編輯成內容豐富的目錄。除了一般善本書目所提供的注釋資料外，此解題書目尚有其他特點。譬如包含作者傳略、特點源流、刻工書鋪、題跋牌記、遞藏鈐印等。以經史子集叢五部排列，並附分類書名目錄及書名、著者、刻工、出版者（刻書鋪）之索引。此書志無論範圍、格式和其他的注釋均係空前之作。1999年上海辭書出版社出版，書名為《美國哈佛大學哈佛燕京圖書館中文善本書志》（哈佛燕京圖書館書目叢刊第7種，927頁），廣受各方好評。

　　此書出版後沈津被聘為哈佛燕京圖書館善本特藏部主任。此後與陸續來自中國的學者合作將館藏清朝（1644-1911）善本編輯成目，和以上書志稍作修正後接合，2011年由廣西師範大學出版社出版《美國哈佛大學哈佛燕京圖書館藏中文善本書志》（哈佛燕京圖書館書目叢刊第15種），共6冊，也廣受中國學術研究界讚賞。書志出版後，沈津提早退休，現執教於廣州中山大學。

　　Pat還將他在中國收集到的74種112冊寶卷、17種20冊彈詞善本捐贈給哈佛燕京圖書館，並於2003年哈佛燕京圖書館慶祝成立75周年紀念時，編輯了《燕京珍藏》（*Treasures of the Yenching*）一書。書中還收錄了他的大作〈漢語基督教文獻：寫作的過程〉（"Chinese Christian Literature: The Writing Process"），長達18頁。他捐贈的寶卷連同哈佛燕京圖書館原來收藏的13種，由霍建瑜編輯成《美國哈佛大學哈佛燕京圖書館藏寶卷匯刊》，2013年由廣西師範大學出版社出版。

　　Pat作為一個學者，一個行政主管，一個圖書館支持者和朋友，我們大家都會非常懷念他。

注釋

原載哈佛燕京學社網站"A Celebration of the Life and Career of Patrick Hanan, 1927-2014"。

韓南（Patrick Dewes Hanan, 1927-2014），紐西蘭人，1949年獲得紐西蘭大學英國文學碩士，1960年獲得英國倫敦大學中國文學博士學位。1957年曾到中國進修。後執教倫敦大學、史丹佛大學。1968年擔任哈佛大學東亞系中國古典文學教授，於1997年退休。1987-1995年間曾擔任哈佛燕京學社社長。主要著作有《金瓶梅版本及其他》（*A study of the composition and the sources of the "Chin P'ing Mei,"* 1960）《中國的短篇小說：關於年代、作者和撰述問題的研究》（*The Chinese Short Story: Studies in Dating, Authorship, and Composition,* 1973），《中國白話小說史》（*The Chinese Vernacular Story,* 1981），《創造李漁》（*The Invention of Li Yu,* 1988），《中國近代小說的興起》（*Chinese Fiction of the Nineteenth and Early Twentieth Centuries,* 2004）。他還翻譯了不少中國古典小說，包括《肉蒲團》（*The Carnal Prayer Mat,* 1990）、《無聲戲選本》（*Silent Operas,* 1990）、《恨海：世紀之交的中國言情小說》（*The Sea of Regret: The Turn of the Century Chinese Romantic Novel,* 1995），《十二樓選本》（*Tower for the Summer Heat,* 1998），《黃金崇》（*The Money Demon,* 1999），《蜃樓志》（*Mirage,* 2014）。

（胡嘉陽譯注）

Patrick Dewes Hanan
A Memorial

I first met Pat in 1961 when he was invited to teach at the Department of Asian Languages (now Department of East Asian Languages and Cultures) at Stanford. I was then the Curator of the newly formed East Asian Collection at Hoover Institution. It so happened that we both relocated to Harvard a few years after that — I in 1965 and he in 1968. We were colleagues there for twenty-nine years, and as it also turned out we both retired from Harvard in 1997

Pat was a quiet but a very warm person, unfailingly courteous, gracious and kind. He was a good listener. His erudition and enormous contribution to the study of the late Qing vernacular novel is widely known and praised by his colleagues around the world, here I would only like to pay tribute to him as a friend and a strong supporter of the Harvard-Yenching Library of which I had the privilege to serve as director for thirty-two years.

Harvard has the tradition of appointing faculty members to library committees serving as advisory bodies to the directors of the libraries of their academic interest. Pat was for many years a member of the Harvard-Yenching Library Advisory Committee, and served as the committee chairman from 1977-1982. In that capacity he was always alert to what the Library was acquiring, with a sharp eye on the value and usefulness of its new acquisitions. But Pat's contribution to the Harvard-Yenching Library lies far beyond his concern about library acquisitions. Two decisions he made during his tenure as director of the Harvard-Yenching Institute (1987-1995) had significant impact on keeping the

Library as the preeminent library for East Asian studies in this country and abroad. The two decisions were the Institute's funding of the retroactive conversion project (converting the Library's card catalog into machine-readable form) and the inviting of Shum Chun 沈津, a Chinese rare editions expert at the Shanghai Library, to Harvard as a Harvard-Yenching Institute Visiting Scholar.

Library automation began in the late 1960s and it gathered momentum in the following decade. While great strides were being made in the use of library technology in research libraries, especially in the conversion of the card catalogs into machine-readable form, East Asian libraries were unable to do so because of the language problem, as there was no available system that could be used to process East Asian scripts. When such a system did become available later on, the cost of conversion was so high that few East Asian libraries were able to afford it. Indeed when Harvard began to convert its many libraries' card catalogs into machine-readable form, Harvard-Yenching Library was left out because of cost considerations (the estimate for the Harvard-Yenching Library was around two and a half millions dollars). Yet the work must be done somehow. Automation would not wait for East Asian libraries to catch up. The Library raised some funds were in Korea ($100,000) and Taiwan ($250,000) for a pilot retrospective conversion project (known as recon) to convert 17,000 Korean and 42,500 Chinese cards, contracted with OCLC (Online Computer Library Center). The result was quite satisfactory and I talked to Pat about the possibility of Harvard-Yenching Institute underwriting one half of the entire recon cost to be matched by the University, following the funding formula used by other Harvard libraries in the recon project, that was, each of the participating libraries would be responsible for one half of the cost with the other half matched by the University. It will be remembered that at that time the Harvard-Yenchiong Library had already become a part of the Harvard College Library by agreement between the Institute and the University in 1976, which meant the Institute was no longer then obliged to underwrite expenses such as that for the recon project. But Pat, seeing the importance of the project, readily gave his support and agreed to take up the matter with Henry Rosovsky, then Dean of the Faculty of Arts and Sciences and concurrently Chairman of the Board of Trustees of the Harvard-Yenching Institute. The proposal also received the endorsement of William Kirby, then Chairman of the Council of East Asian Studies, and Sidney Verba, then the University Librarian. Consequently, the board of the Harvard-Yenching Institute approved an appropriation of 1.1 million dollars for the project, with the understanding that the amount was to be matched by the University which was done. A contract was signed with OCLC in 1995 and actual work began in 1996. The project was to be completed in five years. When all was done, the recon of the Library's entire card catalog of some 323,500 titles into machine-readable form became the largest such project ever attempted by any major East Asian library and contributed enormously to the work of all East Asian libraries since they no longer had to convert their card catalogues and could simply copy from the Harvard-Yenching Library database for their own use. Additionally, the machine-readable catalogue can also be easily accessed by anyone around the world. Were it not for Pat's foresight and support, this unprecedented project would never have come to pass, and the East Asian studies community would be poorer for it.

The second decision Pat made which also benefited the Harvard-Yenching Library and the East Asian studies community at large was his support in bringing Shum Chun 沈津 to Harvard as a Harvard-Yenching Institute Visiting Scholar for the purpose of compiling an annotated catalogue of Harvard-Yenching Library's rare Chinese editions. The Library's Chinese Rare Books Collection was built up over several decades by my predecessor, Dr. Alfred Kaiming Chiu. It was his wish that someday a good catalogue would be compiled and published of this preeminent collection which he had spent almost all of his professional life building. But he never lived to see his wish realized. He died in 1977. Then Shum

Chun came to the scene. He came to the Harvrad-Yenching Library in 1987 for four weeks as part of his research project on American holdings of Chinese rare books, supported by a grant from SUNY Stony Brook. I knew very little about him then except that he had been under the tutelage of the renowned bibliophile and Chinese rare books expert Gu Tinglong 顧廷龍, then director of the famous Shanghai Library and Mr. Shen was the deputy head of Shanghai Library's Rare Books Collection at that time. After his four-week stay at the Harvard-Yenching Library, he produced several notebooks of notes which he generously shared with me before he left. I was amazed at the breadth and depth of his knowledge and the speed with which he had produced these notes. Four years later in 1991 I was in Hong Kong attending a conference at the Chinese University, and was surprised to see Shum Chun at the University Library there. It turned out that he had accepted an invitation from the Center for China Studies of the Chinese University to conduct research, and moved his family from Shanghai to Hong Kong a couple of years earlier. I inquired of his interest in coming to the Harvard-Yenching Library to compile the Library's Chinese rare books. With his positive response I went to Pat after my return to Cambridge and suggested that Shum Chun be invited to Harvard as a Harvard-Yenching Institute Visiting Scholar for one year for the explicit purpose of compiling an annotated catalogue of the Library's Chinese rare books. Pat gave his approval immediately and Shum Chun and his wife arrived in Cambridge in 1992. He began work immediately and worked almost day and night for two years (his invitation as a visiting scholar was extended in 1993 for another year). What he produced after the two years was a monumental manuscript listing 1,433 titles of editions from the Southern Song (1127-1279) to the end of the Ming Dynasties (1368-1644). The annotated catalogue was unique in many aspects. Beside the standard bibliographic information usually given for each title in standard compilations of its kind, the annotations he provided also include additional information such as a biographical sketch of the author, the unique features of and the rarity of the edition, the name of the carver and the name of the issuing bookshop, brief history of the book's transmission through the ages, any postscripts, the seals of the successive owners. Organized into the traditional 經史子集叢 categories, the catalogue also provides a title index, an author index, and indexes to the names of copyists, illustrators, carvers, and issuing bookshops. The catalogue was unprecedented both in scope, format, and other bibliographical details. It received wide acclaim following its publication by the 上海辭書出版社 in 1999 under the title《美國哈佛大學哈佛燕京圖書館中文善本書志》as *Harvard-Yenching Library Bibliographical Series VII*, 927 pp.

It should be added here that following the completion of his manuscript Shum Chun was invited to join the Harvard-Yenching Library as head of its Rare Books Collection. In that capacity he collaborated with a succession of scholars from China and completed a manuscript on the Library's rare Chinese editions of the Qing Dynasty（1644-1911）and published it together with the listings in the above-mentioned 書志 with some revisions under an almost identical title《美國哈佛大學哈佛燕京圖書館藏中文善本書志》by the 廣西師範大學出版社 in 2011 as *Harvard-Yenching Library Bibliographical Series XV*, in six volumes. Like its predecessor volume, this catalogue was also received by the Chinese studies community with applause. Shum Chun took early retirement from Harvard and joined the faculty at the Sun Yat-Sen University in Guangzhou, China.

Pat made other contributions to the Harvard-Yenching Library. He donated 74 寶卷 titles in 112 volumes and 17 彈詞 titles in 20 volumes which he had collected in China to the Library's Rare Books Collection, and he served as editor of an exhibition catalogue entitled *Treasures of the Yenching* celebrating the 75th anniversary of the Harvard-Yenching Library published by the Library in 2003 in which he also contributed an eighteen-page article entitled "*Chinese Christian Literature: The Writing Process*". The 寶卷 he donated were placed together with the thirteen other titles the Library already had and published in 2013 under the editorship of 霍建瑜 by the 廣西師範大學出版社 entitled《美國哈佛大學哈佛燕京圖書館藏寶卷匯刊》。

　　As a scholar, administrator, library supporter, and friend, Pat will be sorely missed by all of us.

Notes

This article was published on the website of Harvard-Yenching Institute: "A Celebration of the Life and Career of Patrick Hanan, 1927-2014".

向錢存訓先生致敬

　　論圖書館服務年資，T.H.比我早了20年。1932年當他自金陵大學（現在的南京大學）畢業開始在圖書館工作時，我還沒有進中學。儘管我一直把他當作長輩來尊敬，年齡的差距並沒有妨礙我們日後成為好朋友。我不確切記得我們是什麼時候初次見面，總應該是上個世紀50年代中期在亞洲學會年會上認識的。那時候我只是胡佛研究所圖書館的編目員，他卻已經是芝加哥大學遠東圖書館（後來改為東亞圖書館）的館長，並且是該校圖書館學研究院和遠東語言文化學系（現在的東亞語言文化系）的講師（後來升任教授）。我對他的第一個印象是一個斯文的儒者：謙遜又樸實。後來當我們交往有時，更證實我最初的印象無誤。

　　T.H.集學者、教師、圖書館長於一身。他的 *Bamboo and Silk: The beginnings of Chinese Books and Inscriptions*（芝加哥，1962；中文譯本：《中國古代書史》，又名為《書於竹帛》，香港中文大學出版部，1975），以及他被李約瑟（Joseph Needham）邀約書寫 *Paper and Printing*，收入在 *Science and Civilization in China* 第5卷第1部分（翻譯本：《造紙與印刷》〔《中國之科學與文明》，台灣商務印書館，1995〕）至今還是經典之作。這些開創性的著作早廣為世人讚揚。1941年他在日本人的嚴密注視下，自淪陷區上海大膽並且巧妙地把中國善本圖書三萬冊偷運到美國國會圖書館保存的功績，亦有廣泛的報導。他一手創立了芝加哥大學第一流的東亞圖書館，也是舉世公認的事實。但是鮮為人們注意的卻是他對美國東亞圖書館早期發展的貢獻和對美國東亞圖書館館員培訓工作所作的開拓性的努力。

　　美國東亞圖書館自二次大戰後發展神速，但是一直沒有一個有效的專業組織。時而在遠東學會（Far Eastern Association，亞洲學會 Association for

Asian Studies的前身）下設委員會，時而在美國圖書館協會（American Library Association, ALA）下設委員會，或者在兩個協會下設聯合委員會。當東亞圖書館相繼成立，面臨的問題也愈趨複雜，東亞圖書館從業人員均意識到需要成立一個正式的專業組織，將職能制度化的必要。1963年原來沒有章程由亞洲學會董事會任命的會長一人管理的美國圖書館遠東資源委員會（CALRFE）改組為由亞洲學會董事會任命的七個會員組成的執行組來管理。除了會長以外，另外成立了一個沒有指定成員的總務委員會，但是對會員的性質（機關對個人）以及選票程式還沒有明確的規定。最終這個新成立的執行組於1967年在芝加哥召開年會時提出了一套《章程》，同時也把組織名稱改為Committee on East Asian Libraries（CEAL）of the Association for Asian Studies（AAS）（現名Council on East Asian Librarians, AAS東亞圖書館協會）。[1] 今天很多人不知道的是，T.H.當初作為CALRFE執行小組的積極分子以及1966-1967年擔任CALRFE會長時為組織及其程式所扮演的關鍵角色。他所推動採用的《章程》往後雖有所修改，卻始終為維持CEAL作為一個專業組織運作的規章。中國有句名言「前人種樹，後人乘涼」。我們大家都應該感謝T.H.在這方面所作的努力。

　　T.H.為東亞圖書館還做了一項傑出的貢獻。那就是1967年他開始對美國和加拿大東亞圖書館所做的非常有用的調查分析報告。往後每5年更新一次，直到他退休。誠如他所說，是他在芝加哥大學圖書館學研究院做學生時，從有名的利昂‧卡諾夫斯基（Leon Carnovsky）教授學習到的方法。[2] 調查分析的項目包括各東亞圖書館的館藏、採購現狀和經費來源。所提供的數字本身已經非常有用；而他對這些數字的分析更提供了對這些數字的進一步的了解。譬如：我們自1967年的調查中，除其他資訊外，得知：1966-1967年共採購了30萬冊圖書，比前一年增長了15%，是美國東亞圖書館有史以來增長最多的一年。如果用這個數字和十年前相比，1950-1955年平均每年只增長8萬冊，1967年的總藏書比1955年增加了一倍。這也可與多數東亞館每兩年便會加倍其藏書增長的趨勢相比。[3] 如此罕見的分析和觀點為東亞圖書館提供了在管理和企畫方面非常有價值的參考資料。1974/1975年的調查是他做的最後一次調查。往後就由東亞圖書館協會（CEAL）繼續，各項目只有簡單的統計數字，而沒有分析。每年在2月份出版的《東亞圖書館學報》（*Journal of East Asian Libraries*）公布。

　　T.H.對東亞圖書館另一項貢獻便是倡導東亞圖書館館員的培訓。他是這方面的開創者，其影響深遠。1972年他在澳洲坎培拉舉行的第28屆國際東方學大會上發表〈遠東圖書館員的培訓〉（"Education for Far Eastern Librarianship"）的報告。[4]闡明一個東方圖書館員除了熟悉現代圖書館的系統外，必須具備語言能力，精通東方圖書業、印刷、出版、編目、索引、目錄、參考工具的知識。但是美國的圖書館學校並不提供這方面的課程，不少東亞圖書館員也缺少這方面的知識，因此他認為需要設立專門的課程來培養將來在美國東亞圖書館工作的館員，而有了結合遠東研究和圖書館學建立一種新學科的想法。

　　早在1964年，芝加哥大學圖書館學研究院就與遠東語言文化系（現在的東亞語言文化系）合作設立了遠東圖書館學碩士和博士的課程。這個聯合項目由T.H.主持，是全美唯一訓練遠東圖書館員並授予學位的學校，成績斐然，非常成功。不幸自T.H.1978年退休後，就後繼無人，該項課程因而終止，也無其他學校仿效。其原因想是缺少了創新的領導人，同時又缺少了像當時芝加哥大學那樣適宜而又贊助的學術環境。雖如是，T.H.的成就永遠長存，唯望這樣的項目能有日又敗部復活。從這個跨系在芝加哥大學前後獲得學位的學生大約有40位，目前尚無名單。[5]1983年台北中文研究資料中心以*Studies in East Asian Librarianship*（《東亞圖書館學系列》）出版了三冊該項目畢業生的碩士論文，T.H.並各自為之書寫導言。[6]畢業生中比較知名的有馬泰來（前普林斯頓葛思德東亞圖書館館長）、鄭炯文（哈佛燕京圖書館館長）和馬庭理（Ed Martinique，前北卡羅來納大學東亞圖書選書館員；1989-1996年《東亞圖書館協會學報》編輯）。還有些畢業後，沒有留在美國的，比較不為人所知。如盧秀菊後為台灣大學圖書資訊學系教授；黃世雄為淡江大學資訊與圖書館學系教授，並曾任文學院院長；成露茜（已故）曾任頗具盛名的《傳記文學》社長。[7]T.H.在發展其跨系項目期間，又推動暑期培訓在職東亞圖書館員的計畫。1969年得到美國教育部的經費補助，由T.H.在芝加哥大學舉辦了一個為期六個星期的暑期培訓班 Institute on Far Eastern librarianship，共有31人參加。[8] 同一個暑期從香港大學圖書館館長轉職威斯康辛大學圖書館學院的多蘿西婭·斯科特（Ms. Dorothea Scott）也舉辦了為期兩個星期的東亞目錄學暑期班（Summer Institute on East Asian Bibliographical Services），有20人參加。近20年後，1988年已故盧國邦以教育部經費補助，在西雅圖華盛頓大學主辦為期兩個星期的暑期班 Summer Institute on East Asian Librarianship，有20人參加。第一次教授了如何應用計算機科技的課程。

之後，一直到2004年均無暑期訓練班的設立。但其間東亞圖書館協會中日韓三種語文委員會在暑期分別為其會員舉辦了研討會。2004年匹茲堡大學與東亞圖書館協會中文資料委員會合作申請到魯斯基金會的經費補助，由沈志佳、陳同麗籌畫在匹茲堡大學主辦一個為期三個星期的研討會，名為 Luce Summer Institute for East Asian Librarianship: China Focus。聚焦在提升東亞圖書館館員的核心職能以及培訓圖書館員的領導力。[9] 有12位包括兩位自中國大陸來的教員，教授不同的研討課程，包括中國出版業、印刷史、參考書、目錄學，以至圖書館科技及行政等等。有來自26個圖書館的28人參加。在7月底暑期班開始前有一個星期遠距線上學習，暑期班後，班上有14位學員同年10月到中國大陸會見出版商、資料庫開發商、書商、圖書館員，為期一星期。[10] 最後一次的暑期班是2008年在西雅圖華盛頓大學舉辦的「電子時代的中國研究圖書館學」（Chinese Studies Librarianship in the Electronic Environment）。這是所有暑期班培訓內容最廣泛、最具國際性的培訓班，為期兩星期，有來自30個東亞圖書館的38個成員參加。由東亞圖書館中文資料委員會和西雅圖華盛頓大學合作主辦，實際工作由華大東亞圖書館館長沈志嘉及其管理團隊指導進行。暑期班主要的經費由魯斯基金會、蔣經國國際學術交流基金會、清華同方知網（北京）技術有限公司補助。授課者包括來自中國大陸、台灣、美國資深圖書館員、圖書館學校教員及東亞研究教員。教授內容不僅包括圖書館中科技的應用，還討論中國研究的趨勢。暑期班前，清華同方知網（北京）技術有限公司和華盛頓大學圖書館還合作召開了一個兩天的會議，研討 CNKI（China National Knowledge Infrastructure〔中國國家知識基礎設施的標準〕）以及中國電子書的出版。暑期班後又舉辦了一個隨意參加的考察行。38 個參加暑期班中的 20 個培訓人員參加，參訪了在北京和上海的主要圖書館和電子資源供應公司。[11]

雖然暑期班難以取代 T.H. 在芝加哥大學首創的圖書館學和遠東語文系的聯合項目，但是暑期班還是非常成功地達到了 T.H. 設立它們的目的，那就是幫助在職的東亞圖書館員通過一種嚴格的訓練更好地充實自己。在這裡我們可以提出下面這個問題：什麼影響了 T.H. 的教育思想？為什麼他認為教育圖書館員這麼重要？部分的原因當然是他是出身於教育世家的關係。他來自書香世家，曾祖父十九世紀末官授翰林院編修，父親是研究佛學的學者。但是，他同時代的人也多有來自書香世家的。令他與眾不同的應該是來自他自己的教育背景。他在中國和芝加哥都受教於圖書館這門新興科學的創始大師。在中國，他的老師有劉國鈞、杜定友、李小緣（李國棟）；在芝加哥大學圖書館研究學院，他上過傑西·謝拉（Jesse Shera）、萊斯特·阿什海姆（Lester Asheim）和韓門·富斯勒（Herman Fussler）幾位教授的課。這樣的雙重機遇是可遇而不可求的。他感激這些老師在他成為一個學者／圖書館員中所扮演的角色，因此他希望年輕的一代也能有和他一樣的經驗。

這篇短文在於彰顯 T.H. 對東亞圖書館發展所作貢獻的寬度和深度。他的創造力和領導力對今天美國的東亞圖書館成為西方世界研究東亞最好的資源的貢獻良多。他是個博學多才的學者兼勇於創新的圖書館員。隨著他的過世，學術界會懷念他的博學；東亞圖書館界將感念他的領導。對我而言，我失去了一位摯友和尊敬的長輩。

注釋

原載《東亞圖書館學報》（*Journal of East Asian Libraries*），第 161 期（2015 年 10 月），頁 1-7。本文承馬泰來、艾朗諾（Ron Egan）提供意見；周原、歐凱尼（Gail King）、沈志佳、亓冰峰、鄭炯文、楊麗瑄協助查詢資料，在此一併致謝。

[1] 美國東亞圖書館協會的歷史，請參看本人著〈美國東亞圖書館協會的歷史沿革〉（Organizing for East Asian Studies in the United States）一文，載《東亞圖書館學報》（*Journal of East Asian Libraries*），第110期（1996年10月），頁1-14。此文已收入本書。

[2] 錢存訓，〈在芝加哥大學圖書館學研究院求學時期〉（"My Study at the Graduate Library School of the University of Chicago"）載《東亞圖書館學報》（*Journal of East Asian Libraries*），第130期（2003年6月），頁46。

[3] 《東亞圖書館資料：美國亞洲學會東亞圖書館委員會第10屆年會上的工作報告》（*Library Resources on East Asia, Reports and working papers for the tenth annual meeting of the Committee on American Library Resources on the Far East, Association for Asian Studies, Inc., at the Palmer House, Chicago, March 21, 1967*）（瑞士［Zug, Switzerland］：國際文獻公司［Inter Documentation Company AG], 1968）附錄D，頁91。

[4] 錢存訓，〈遠東圖書館學的教育〉（"Education for Far Eastern Librarianship"）載《東方圖書館學的國際合作》（*International Co-operation in Oriental Librarianship*）（坎培拉：澳洲國家圖書館〔National Library of Australia〕，1972），頁108-115。

[5] 同上，頁116。注8：「自1964/1965年以來有12位以上，包括兩位博士生選讀芝加哥大學圖書館學研究院和東亞語言文明系課程得到遠東圖書館學位。」又見沈志佳、陳同麗的報告（Chinese Studies Librarians Training and the Luce Summer Institute at the University of Pittsburgh）載《東亞圖書館學報》（*Journal of East Asian Studies*），第130期（2003年6月），頁42。此篇報告稱6位博士，35位畢業生。

[6] 這三篇出版的論文是：1. 馬庭理（Edward Martinique），《中國傳統書籍的裝訂術》（*Chinese Traditional Bookbinding: a Study of Its Evolution and Techniques*），2. 米樂（Constance Miller），《中西印刷術發明的技術和文化先決條件》（*Technical and Cultural Prerequisites for the Invention of Printing in China and the West*），3. 盧秀菊（Shiow-jyu Lu Shaw），《清初殿版書籍考，1644-1805》（*The Imperial Printing of Early Ch'ing China, 1644-1805*）。資料由鄭炯文、楊麗瑄提供。

[7] 資料由馬泰來2005年6月提供。

[8] 順便一提的是在31個參加培訓的圖書館員中包括當時在華盛頓特區中國研究資料中心工作的宋楚瑜（James Soong）。他後來回台從政，1994-1998年為台灣省唯一民選省長，2000年創立親民黨並任主席。

[9] 沈志佳、陳同麗的報告，前引文，頁43。因沈志佳自匹茲堡大學離職就任華盛頓大學東亞圖書館館長，該暑期班實際由沈志佳的繼任徐鴻主持。

[10] 見徐鴻、莎拉‧阿爾米，〈魯斯基金會贊助2004年7月26日至8月13日舉辦的中國研

究圖書館員暑期培訓班報告〉（Report of the Luce Summer Institute for East Asian Librarianship: China Focus）（July 26-August 13, 2004）。

[11]　沈志佳，〈迎接數位圖書館的挑戰：電子時代的中國研究圖書館學暑期培訓班報告〉（"Training to Meet the Digital Challenge: Report on the Summer Institute on Chinese Studies Librarianship in the Electronic Environment"）載《東亞圖書館學報》（*Journal of East Asian Libraries*），第147期（2009年2月），頁43-49。

（胡嘉陽譯）

A Tribute to T.H. Tsien

In terms of seniority in library service, T.H. was a couple of decades ahead of me. When, upon his graduation from the University of Nanking, he began his library career in 1932, I was not even in middle school. But that did not prevent us from becoming good friends later, although I always revered him as my senior. I don't remember exactly when we first met. It must have been in the mid-1950s at an annual meeting of the Association for Asian Studies (AAS). I was then a cataloger at the Hoover Institution and he was already the curator of the Far Eastern Library (later East Asian Library) and Lecturer (later Professor) at both the Graduate Library School and the Department of Far Eastern (now East Asian) Languages and Civilizations at the University of Chicago. My first impression of him was that of a quiet Confucian scholar, unassuming and unpretentious, and this was confirmed in subsequent years as I came to know him well.

As a scholar, teacher, and curator, T.H. was one of a kind. His book, *Written on Bamboo and Silk: The beginnings of Chinese Books and Inscriptions* (Chicago, 1962), remains a classic in the field, as is his *Paper and Printing*, written at the request of Joseph Needham and published as Part 1, Volume 5 of the *Science and Civilization in China Series* (Cambridge, 1985). These seminal works have been widely praised elsewhere, as has his daring and imaginative scheme in 1941 sneaking, under the watchful eyes of the Japanese, some 30,000 volumes of rare Chinese books out of Shanghai to the Library of Congress for safekeeping. His success in building up a first-rate East Asian library at the University of Chicago has likewise been widely acknowledged. What has received less attention is his contribution to the early development of East Asian libraries in the United States and his pioneering effort in training East Asian librarians in this country.

East Asian libraries in the United States developed rapidly after WWII. For a number of years, this took place without the benefit of a professional organization, although there was at various times a committee under either the Far Eastern Association (predecessor of the Association for Asian Studies) or the American Library Association (ALA), or under both jointly. But as the number of East Asian libraries grew and problems facing them became more complex, there was a feeling prevailing among East Asian librarians that a formal professional organization ought to be established and its functions institutionalized. In 1963, the Committee on American Library Resources, or CALRFE, which had been operating without a charter and run almost singlehandedly by a person appointed by the Board of Directors of the AAS, was reorganized with an executive group of seven members, also appointed by the AAS, and a general committee of unspecified membership in addition to the chairperson. But matters such as the nature of membership (institutional vs. individual) and voting procedures remained to be clarified. The new Executive Group deliberated on these matters at length, and a set of *Procedures* was adopted at CALRFE's annual meeting held in Chicago in 1967. It was at this time that the name of the organization was changed to Committee on East Asian Libraries (CEAL) of the Association for Asian Studies (AAS) (now Council on East Asian Librarians, AAS). [1] Many people today are unaware of the crucial role that T.H. played as an active member of the CALRFE Executive Group and then as chairperson of CALRFE from 1966-1967 in shaping the organization and its procedures. He facilitated the adoption of the *Procedures* (now *Bylaws*) which, with some modifications and amendments in subsequent years, still govern the function of CEAL as a professional organization today. As the Chinese saying goes, "The earlier generations plant the trees, the later generations enjoy the shade." We should all be very grateful to T.H. for his contributions in this regard.

T.H. rendered another outstanding service to the profession with the analytical survey he conducted in 1967 of East Asian libraries in the United States and Canada, a survey he repeated at five years intervals until his retirement. As he acknowledged, the survey, the first of its kind, was influenced by a course he took earlier from the renowned Prof. Leon Carnovsky at the Graduate Library School at the University of Chicago. [2] It covers the libraries' holdings, current status of acquisitions, and sources of financial support. While the quantitative information presented was in and of itself very useful, the accompanying analysis provided additional insights. For instance, we learned from the 1967 survey that, *inter alia*, "the total acquisition of almost 300,000 volumes during 1966-1967 represent a 15% increase over that for the previous year and are the largest in the history of American acquisition of East Asian materials. This figure may be compared with that of about a decade ago when the average annual increase was 80,000 volumes in 1950-1955. The total holdings in 1967 also are double those in 1955, which is generally comparable to the trends of many individual collections toward doubling their size every two years." [3] Such analyses provide rare perspectives extremely valuable in management and planning. The 1974/1975 survey was the last conducted by him but it has since been ably continued by CEAL as a simple statistical compilation containing the same categories of information as before, but without analysis. It has been appearing each year in the February issue of Journal of East Asian Libraries.

Yet another contribution T.H. made to the profession was the training of librarians for East Asian studies. In this he was the pioneer, and his impact was wide and deep. He laid out the *raison d'étre* for the special training in a paper presented at the 28th International Congress of Orientalists held in Canberra, Australia in 1972 entitled "Education for Far Eastern Librarianship." [4] He maintained that knowledge of the language or languages and of the "Far Eastern library subjects" — the book trade, printing, publishing, cataloging, indexing, bibliographies, and reference tools — should all be required qualifications for East Asian studies librarians, as is knowledge and understanding of the modern library system. But library schools in America did not offer instructions on these subjects, and many East Asian studies librarians were found lacking in their knowledge of them. He believed that a special training program was therefore needed to train future East Asian librarians in this country. The idea of a combined discipline of Far Eastern studies and librarianship was thus born.

In 1964, the University of Chicago established a Joint Program on Far Eastern Librarianship leading to the MA and Ph.D. degrees, offered by its Graduate Library School in cooperation with its Department of Far Eastern (now East Asian) Languages and Civilizations, and T.H. was appointed director. The program, another first in this country, was eminently successful, but it came to an end with T.H.'s retirement in 1978. It was unfortunate that the program was not continued, and no other university has taken it over, most likely because the combination of an innovative leader and a congenial and supportive academic environment such as that existed in Chicago did not exist elsewhere. But the legacy of T.H.'s accomplishment lives on. Hopefully, the time will come one day for the program to be revived somewhere. No list of all the graduates under the joint program exists, but the number is estimated to be about 40. [5] Three of the MA theses written under this program were published in 1983 by the Chinese Materials Center in Taipei under the series title Studies in East Asian Librarianship, with an introduction by T. H. to each. [6]Among well-known graduates from the program are Tai-loi Ma (formerly Director of East Asian Library of Princeton University), James Cheng (Librarian of Harvard-Yenching Library of Harvard University), and Ed Martinique (formerly Bibliographer of East Asian Library of the University of North Carolina, who was also the editor of *CEAL Bulletin* from 1987-1996). Much less known are those who did not remain in the United States, such as Ms. Lu Shiow-jyu 盧秀菊 who became a professor in the Department of Library and Information Science at the National Taiwan University, Mr. Huang Shih-hsiung 黃世雄, University Librarian and Professor in the Department of Library and Information Science at Tamkang University in Taiwan and later Dean of the Faculty of Arts at that university, and the late Lucie Cheng 成露茜, the publisher of the prestigious *Biographical Literature* 傳記文學 also in Taiwan. [7]

While developing the joint program, T.H. also promoted the idea of summer institutes as in-service training programs for working East Asian librarians. In 1969, with the support of the U.S. Office of Education, an intensive six-week institute on Far Eastern librarianship, organized by T. H., was offered at the University of Chicago and attended by 31 people. [8] In the same year, a two-week "Summer Institute on East Asian Bibliographical Services" attended by 20 people also took place at the University of Wisconsin, organized by Ms. Dorothea Scott, University Librarian at Hong Kong University before she moved on to the University of Wisconsin Library School faculty. Following a long pause, a two-week "Summer Institute on East Asian Librarianship" attended by 20 people took place in 1988 at the University of Washington, under the direction of the late Karl Lo, with funding also from the Department of Education. Lectures on the use of computer technology in libraries were given for the first time at that institute.

While no more summer institutes were held until 2004, the three language committees（Chinese, Japanese and Korean）of CEAL did, in the interim period, hold workshops for their respective members. In 2004 the University of Pittsburg, with funding from the Luce Foundation and in cooperation with the Committee on Chinese Materials of CEAL, offered a three-week "Luce Summer Institute for East Asian Librarianship: China Focus," organized by Zhijia Shen and Karen Wei, to "provide professional training for Chinese studies librarianship to enhance the core competency of Chinese studies librarians and to develop leadership for East

Asian librarians." [9] 12 faculty, including 2 from China, taught seminars on a number of subjects from Chinese books, printing, reference works, bibliography to library technology, library administration, etc. 28 people from 26 libraries attended that institute. There was a one-week web-based distance learning prior to the start of the institute in late July, and a one-week follow-up trip to China in October of that year in which 14 of the institute attendees participated. The group met with publishers, database developers, vendors and librarians. [10] The last summer institute held was at the University of Washington in 2008. The two-week institute named "Chinese Studies Librarianship in the Electronic Environment" was the most comprehensive and the most international of all the summer institutes. Attended by 38 people from 30 East Asian libraries, it was sponsored jointly by the University of Washington and the CEAL Committee on Chinese Materials, with funding for the most part from the Luce Foundation, the Chiang Ching-kuo Foundation for International Scholarly Exchange, and the Tongfang Knowedge Network Technology Group, and was directed by Zhijia Shen and her management team. The lecturers included senior librarians and library school faculty from mainland China, Taiwan as well as the United States. East Asian studies faculty and senior librarians from the University of Washington and elsewhere in the United States also spoke on trends in Chinese studies and on the use of technology in the library. There was a two-day pre-conference, symposium on "CNKI Standards and Chinese e-Publishing", co-sponsored by the Tongfang Knowledge Network Technology Group in Beijing and the University of Washington Libraries（CNKI stands for China National Knowledge Infrastructure）, and an optional post-curriculum field trip to Mainland China where some 20 of the 38 institute participants visited major libraries and electronics resource providers in Beijing and Shanghai. [11] While the summer institutes were a poor substitute for the Joint Program T.H. directed at the University of Chicago, they did fulfill admirably the purpose for which T.H.

created them, that is, helping working East Asian studies librarians to better equip themselves through a rigorous in-service training program. The question might be asked here: what influenced T.H.'s education philosophy and why library education was so important to him? The fact that he came from an academic family is of course part of that influence. His great grandfather served in the Hanlin Academy in late 19th century China and his father was a Buddhist scholar. But many of T.H.'s contemporaries also came from similar scholarly family background. What sets him apart, I believe, is his own education experience. He studied under pioneering giants in the emerging new field of library science both in China and the United States. In China his teachers and supervisors included Liu Kuo-chun 劉國鈞, Doo Ding-u 杜定友 and Li Xiaoyuan（Li Kuo-tung）李小緣 （李國棟）, and at the Graduate Library School in Chicago, he took courses from Jesse Shera, Lester Asheim and Herman Fussler. This kind of experience is unique and can hardly be duplicated. He appreciated the role his teachers played in his growth as a scholar-librarian, and he wanted the younger generation to have the same experience.

This brief account is an attempt to illustrate the width and depth of T.H.'s contributions to the development of East Asian libraries. His ingenuity and quiet leadership have contributed much to shape East Asian libraries in the United States as they are today, a strong and vibrant source for teaching and research on East Asia which may be the best in the Western world. He was erudite as a scholar and innovative as a librarian. With his passing his erudition will be missed by the scholarly community and his leadership by the East Asian library community. Personally, I have lost a good friend and a revered senior colleague.

Notes

This article was published in *Journal of East Asian Libraries*, no. 161（Oct 2015）, pp. 1-7.

Comments and suggestion on this article by Tai-loi Ma and Ron Egan as well as help in locating materials from Gail King, Yuan Zhou, Zhijia Shen, Pingfeng Chi, James Cheng and Sharon Yang are gratefully acknowledged.

[1]　For a study of the history of CEAL, see Eugene W. Wu, "Organizing for East Asian Studies in the United States," *Journal of East Asian Libraries*, no. 110（Oct. 1996）, pp. 1-14.

[2]　Tsuen-hsuin Tsien, "My Study at the Graduate Library School of the University of Chicago," *Journal of East Asian Libraries*, no. 130（June 2003）, p. 46.

[3]　*Library Resources on East Asia, Reports and working papers for the tenth annual meeting of the Committee on American Library Resources on the Far East, Association for Asian Studies, Inc., at the Palmer House, Chicago, March 21, 1967*（Zug Switzerland: Inter Documentation Company AG, 1967）, Appendix D, p. 91.

[4]　Tsuen-hsuin Tsien, "Education for Far Eastern Librarianship," *International Cooperation in Oriental Librarianship, Papers presented at the Library Seminar, 28th International Congress of Orientalists, Canberra, 6-12 January 1972*（Canberra: National Library of Australia, 1972）, pp, 108-116.

[5]　*Ibid.*, p. 116. Note 8 reads: "Since 1964/65, over a dozen students including two in the Ph.D. program have graduated under the Joint Program on Far Eastern Librarianship at the University of Chicago." Also, Zhijia Shen and Karen Wei, "Chinese Studies Librarians Training and the Luce Summer Institute at the University of Pittsburgh," *Journal of East Asian Studies*, no. 130（June 2003）, p. 42. The number here is given as "six PhDs and about 35 graduates." The three are（1）Edward Martinique, *Chinese Traditional Bookbinding: a Study of Its Evolution and Techniques*,（2）Constance Miller, *Technical and Cultural Prerequisites for the Invention of Printing in China and the West*, and（3）Shiow-jyu Lu Shaw, *The Imperial Printing of Early Ch'ing China, 1644-1805*. Information by courtesy of James Cheng and Sharon Yang.

[7]　Information from Tai-loi Ma, June 2015.

[8]　It might be mentioned in passing that among the 31 participants was James Soong（宋楚瑜）then on the Center for Chinese Research Materials（CCRM）staff in Washington, D.C. He later returned to Taiwan and entered politics. He was elected Governor of Taiwan in 1994 and served in that capacity until 1998. He founded the People First Party and has been serving as its chairman.

[9]　Zhijia Shen and Karen Wei, op. cit., p. 43. The Luce Summer Institute was held under the direction of Hong Xu, successor to Zhijia Shen at Pittsburg, following Zhijia Shen's

departure from the University of Pittsburgh to the University of Washington.

[10] Hong Xu and Sarah Aerni, *Report of the Luce Summer Institute for East Asian Librarianship: China Focus (July 26-August 13, 2004)*

[11] Zhijia Shen, "Training to Meet the Digital Challenge: Report on the Summer Institute on Chinese Studies Librarianship in the Electronic Environment," *Journal of East Asian Libraries*, no. 147（Feb 2009）: 43-49.

四、
圖書評論及序言

安・本威克著，《英國圖書館中的亞洲和非洲文獻收藏：問題與展望》（圖書館與資訊研究系列），英國斯蒂夫尼奇：彼得・帕雷葛蘭納斯有限公司，1974（在美國加拿大由俄勒岡州波特蘭國際學術出版物服務社銷售）。139頁。17美元。（書評）

　　本書是作者在英國謝菲爾德大學圖書館和資訊研究學院（Postgraduate School of Librarianship and Information Science, Sheffield University）的碩士論文的修訂版。內容就如緒言所說：「詳述英國收藏亞洲、非洲資料的組織結構的發展」以及「嘗試詳述關於英國收藏處理區域出版品的特有問題及其對英國圖書館的影響」。有關前者作者以平鋪直述的方式來介紹英國收藏亞非資料的發展，提供了不少歷史背景和成果的資料，特別是在1947年和1961年發表了〈斯卡布勒報告〉（"Scarbrough Report"）和〈海特報告〉（"Hayter Report"）後的發展情況（該兩項頗受讚賞的全國性調查對英國日後區域研究和區域研究圖書館發展上有極大影響）。有關後者作者以分題的方式來討論，諸如地區圖書館團體、採購和採購技巧方面的問題、區域專家的任務等等。

　　這本書除了提供了最新的資料，並坦率地提出其問題之所在外，我發現它還提供了非常好可以用來作比較的資料。因為英美圖書館有不少類似的經驗，兩個國家的亞洲、非洲收藏都是緩慢地開始，到1950和1960年代由於政府和基金會提供大量經費才快速發展起來。收藏亞洲、非洲資料的圖書館成倍增長，收藏內容也超越原來僅限於有關人文科學的範疇。由於這樣的擴充形成了不少組織、技術、管理上至今尚待解決的問題。譬如：亞洲、非洲地區的出版品應該分別收藏管理，抑或應為大學總圖書館的一部分，至今圖書館使用者和圖書館行政管理者意見還不得一致。要解決只滿足了部分要求的書目管理問題是另一項挑戰。必須親自到還沒有發展圖書貿易的國家採購，或者要靠通過辛苦經營建立的個人關係來進行採購工作，對講求效率的專家還是種很大的挑戰。（作者對此問題作了很好的現身說法，慣於與使用電腦的美國和西歐國家書商作採購工作的圖書館員讀了這章將獲益匪淺。）

　　目前英美兩國收藏亞洲、非洲語文資料的圖書館面臨的最大問題，可能是當我們不能再理所當然得到政府提供高等教育的經費時，要如何鞏固我們過去20年的成果以便更好地為學術服務。作者提出了全英的合作及計畫的呼籲。美國應該也可以作同樣地呼籲。最近美國對區域圖書館間的合作方案討論甚夥，英國的經驗無論正面負面都可以作為我們的借鏡。

　　最後，我建議如果作者下次再修訂此書時，能附上一些英國亞洲、非洲語文文獻收藏的數字統計表。

注釋

原載《大學與研究圖書館》（*College and Research Libraries*）第36卷，第3期（1975年5月），頁242-243。

（胡嘉陽譯）

Anne J. Benewick. *Asian and African Collections in British Libraries: Problems and Prospects* (Librarianship and Information Science) Stevenage, Herts., England: Peter Peregrinus Ltd., 1974. (Distributed in the U.S. and Canada by International Scholarly Book Services, P.O. Box 4347, Portland, OR 97208). 139pp. $17.00. (Book review)

This book is the revised version of the author's MA thesis for the Postgraduate School of Librarianship and Information Science, Sheffield University, England. It is a "history of developments in the organization of British Asian and African collections" and an attempt "to describe in detail many of the problems peculiar to area collections and their impact on British libraries." The former is presented in a straight forward fashion giving much useful information on the historical background of these collections and their achievements, especially in the years following the widely reclaimed Scarbrough Report of 1947 and the Hayter Report of 1960—two national surveys which greatly contributed to the subsequent development of area studies and area libraries in Great Britain. The latter is discussed under headings such as regional library groups, acquisitions problems and techniques, the role of the area specialist, etc.

In addition to being the most up-to-date, informative, and candid account of the subject in hand, this reviewer finds Ms. Benewick's book an excellent source of information for comparative purposes, for there are many similarities in the British and American experience. In both countries Asian and African collections developed from rather modest beginnings. A period of very rapid growth came in the 1950s and the 1980s as a result of substantial financial support from government and private sources. The number of Asian and African collections multiplied, extending the scope of their coverage far beyond their original concern with materials in the humanities. With this expansion came also a different information number of organizational, technical, and management problems, many of which still await satisfactory solutions. For example, the question of whether area collections should be maintained separately or integrated with the main library collections remains a source of disagreement between users and library administrators. The problem of bibliographical control is another challenge which has been only partially met. Dealing with countries with no developed book trade where many desired items can be had only by personal visits and through diligent cultivation of personal contacts is still a problem that defies the solutions of an efficiency expert (Ms. Benewick offers an excellent account of such difficulties which can be read with profit by those who are accustomed to dealing with American and Western European dealers with computerized operations.)

Probably the most important question facing Asian and African libraries in our two countries today, when financial support for higher education can no longer be taken for granted, is how to consolidate the gains of the past two decades in better service to scholarship. Ms. Benewick pleads for more coordination and planning on the national level for Great Britain. The same plea can and should be entered for the United State. Lately in the United State, there has been much discussion of cooperative schemes in library development in area studies. Both the positive and negative aspects of the British experience can serve as a useful guide to our deliberations.

Finally, this reviewer would recommend the inclusion of a few statistical tables giving more quantitative information on British Asian and African collections, when and if Ms. Benewick updates her study. — Eugene Wu, Librarian, Harvard-Yenching Library, Harvard University, Cambridge, Massachusetts.

Notes

This review was published in *College and Research Libraries*, vol. 36, no. 3, pp. 242-243.

倫敦大學亞非學院當代中國研究所編，《歐洲圖書館收藏的中文報刊目錄》，
紐約倫敦：劍橋大學，1975。1025頁。65美元。（書評）

中國研究需要更多基本的參考工具書是長久以來被公認的事實。在這類
參考書仍然缺乏的時候，倫敦大學亞非學院當代中國研究所出版了《歐洲圖
書館收藏的中文報刊目錄》這部目錄實在是件值得注意的事。這是歐洲圖書
館收藏的中文期刊和報紙目錄首次問世。

這是一部歐洲12個國家102個圖書館收藏的6,000種1970年前出版的中
文連續出版物——期刊、報紙（包括紅衛兵小報）、年刊和叢刊——的聯合
目錄。這12個國家是：奧地利、捷克、丹麥、法國、東德、西德、義大
利、荷蘭、蘇聯、瑞典、瑞士和英國。目錄中的報刊是按照中文拼音排列。
每種報刊下注明中文名稱、副題、出版地、編輯者、出版者、創刊停刊日
期、出版週期及其他有關資料。更重要的是各報刊都注明各個圖書館藏有的
期數。在目錄前有圖書館代號一欄，代號下注明該圖書館的全名和地址。並
有詳細的編輯說明。報刊的西文標題有索引可作相關參照之用。

從這份目錄看歐洲圖書館藏有的中文報刊，1949年後發行的比較完
整。雖然編輯者已經說明「歐洲只有少數幾個圖書館收藏的中文報刊可以和
美國、日本最好圖書館的收藏相比」，但是歐洲還是收藏了一些美國沒有的
東南亞及其他地方早期出版的中文報刊。如大英博物館收藏的倫敦1916-
1919年出版的《成報》；檳城1895-1941年出版的《檳城新報》；舊金山
1874-1875年出版的《舊金山唐人新聞紙》。還有一些在歐洲藏有的期數比
美國齊全。如1928-1933年國民黨中央委員會在南京出版的《中央週報》；
1917-1920年巴黎勤工儉學會出版的《華工雜誌》。

值得一提的是這個聯合目錄將法國里昂中法大學、蘇聯、捷克和東德圖
書館的收藏也包括在內，是為創舉。中法大學的收藏以1920、1930年代出
版的中文報刊著名，包括在法國所出版的。另一方面，令人吃驚的是蘇聯收
藏的1949年前出版的中文報刊相當貧乏。捷克的收藏以捷克科學院東方研

究所魯迅圖書館收藏為代表。該館的收藏偏重人文方面的出版品——文學報刊較多，反映了該所研究的重心。東德國家圖書館和科學院圖書館收藏並不多，但是也有一些1949年前後出版的報刊。令人矚目的是蘇聯和東歐各圖書館都沒有收藏台灣出版的報刊。

此部目錄收錄的範圍非常全面是毫無疑問的，但是還有少數歐洲圖書館的收藏並未包括在內以便使用。譬如捷克科學院總圖書館收藏了不少1949年後出版的中文科技報刊，波蘭華沙大學東方研究院與波蘭科學院也有收藏少量中文報刊。藏有「馬林檔案」的荷蘭阿姆斯特丹國際社會主義歷史研究所也有一些1920年代出版的中國無政府主義和社會主義的報刊。這些都未見於這部聯合目錄中。

最後要提到的是，儘管這是一本規模和範圍都很廣大的目錄，其中中文拼音和中文文字的錯誤卻頗罕見。這顯然是細心的準備和校對的結果。不過有些條目還是令人費解。如第134頁1960-1966年北京法律出版社出版的 *Gai Fa Yan Jiu*《改發研究》，目前可以確定北京那時沒有這樣的刊物。是否是《政法研究》之誤？第185頁 *Gui Lin Jian She Bao*《貴林建設報》中的「貴」字是否應為「桂」？第455頁1965年重慶出版的《陪都工商年鑑》，「陪都」是二次大戰時期重慶的稱謂，不可能在1965年仍舊使用，似乎出版年有誤。第662頁《文化圖書館學專科學校季刊》的「化」字應該是「中華」的「華」，而不是「文化」的「化」。

這些小瑕疵不足影響這部目錄的重要性和實用性。中國研究學術界應為這項艱巨任務的完成感恩。

注釋

原載《亞洲學報》（*The Journal of Asian Studies*）第39卷，第1期（1979年11月），頁159-160。

（胡嘉陽譯）

A Bibliography of Chinese Newspapers and Periodicals in European Libraries. Compiled by The Contemporary China Institute (New York and London: Cambridge University Press, 1975. 1025 pp. $65.00.(Book review)

The need for more basic research tools in Chinese studies has been long recognized by the field. In view of what must still be regarded as a dearth of such publications, the appearance of *A Bibliography of Chinese Newspapers and Periodicals in European Libraries*, compiled by the Contemporary China Institute of the School of Oriental and African Studies of the University of London, is an event worthy of note. For the first time we have available to us a catalogue of the holdings of Chinese periodicals and newspapers in European libraries.

The present volume is a union list of over 6,000 Chinese serials — journals, newspapers (including Red Guard publications), annuals, yearbooks, and series — with a cut-off date of 1970 which are available in 102 libraries from 12 European countries. They are Austria, Czechoslovakia, Denmark, France, Germany (East and West), Italy, Netherlands, Soviet Union, Sweden, Switzerland, and United Kingdom. The entries in the *Bibliography* are listed alphabetically by title according to the Pinyin system. Under each entry is given the following information: title in characters, subtitle, place of publication, editor and publisher, periodical life, frequency of issue and any additional information. More important is the information on holdings of individual libraries which completes each entry. The preliminary material includes a "key" to names and addresses of libraries appearing in the *Bibliography*, a detailed section of the "conventions "used in the volume, and an index to western-language subtitles, a useful feature for cross-reference purposes.

In general, European holdings of Chinese serials, as recorded in the present volume, appear to be more complete for the post-1949 period. Although the compiler points out that "Europe has relatively few individual libraries that match the finest collections in U.S.A. and Japan," there are certain titles which are unique to European collections, especially early Chinese periodicals and newspapers published in Southeast Asia and elsewhere which are not available in East Asian libraries in the United States. For example, the British Museum's holdings of the *Cheng Bao* (London, 1916-1919), the *Bincheng xin bao* (Penang, 1895-1941), the *Jiujinshan tang ren xinwen zhi* (The San Francisco China News) (San Francisco, 1874-75) are a case in point. In addition, there are some titles which are more completely represented in European collections, such as the *Zhongyang zhoupao*, a weekly published by the Kuomintang Central Committee in Nanjing from 1928-33, and the *Hua gong zazhi* (Revue chinoise populaire), published by the Work-Study Group in Paris from 1917-20.

It should also be mentioned that the holdings of the Institut Francochinois of the Cite Universitaire in Lyons, France, and those of the libraries in the Soviet Union, Czechoslovakia, and East Germany are published here for the first time. The Lyons collection is particularly noted for its holdings of Chinese periodicals published in the 1920s and the 1930s, including those which originated in France. The Soviet holdings, on the other hand, are surprisingly deficient in titles publish before 1949. The Czech holdings, represented here by those in the Lu Xun Library of the Oriental Institute of the Czech Academy of Sciences, concentrate on the humanities, especially literary publications, reflecting the main research emphasis of the Institute. The holdings of the Deutsche Staatsbibliothek and the Deutsche Akademie der Wissenschraften, all in East Berlin, are not large but they do contain both pre-and post-1949 publications. Parenthetically, it might be noted that none of the Soviet or East European collections show any holdings of publications from Taiwan.

While the coverage of this volume is unquestionably comprehensive, there are several other European libraries whose holdings could have been included with benefit. For example, the Fundamental Library of the Czech Academy of Sciences has a fairly good size collection of post-1949 scientific and technical journals. The Oriental Institute of the University of Warsaw and the Polish Academy of Sciences also have, albeit quite small, collections of Chinese materials. The Institute of Social History (Institut voor Sociale Geschidinis) in Amsterdam, where the famous Sneevliet Archives are kept, possesses a small special collection of Chinese anarchist and socialist journals published in the 1920s.

Finally, this volume, its size and scope notwithstanding, is remarkably free of typographical errors in romanization and mis-writing of Chinese characters in the entries. This is obviously the result of much painstaking care in the preparation and proof-reading of the manuscript. However, there are entries which are somewhat puzzling. On page 134 we find *"Gai fa yan jiu "(Kai-fa yen chiu)* given as a quarterly published by the Legal Publishing House in Peking from 1960-66. There is no such title published in Beijing as far as can be ascertained. Could this be a mis-reading of the well-known legal journal, *Zhengfa yanjiu*? On page 185 the first character in the title *Gui lin jianshe bao (Kwei-lin chien-she pao)* is given as the "gui" in the name of the Guizhou province. Should this be instead the "gui" in the name of the city of Guilin in Guangxi province? On page 455 is the entry *"Peidu gongshang nianjian* (P'ei-tu kung shang nian chien), published in Chongqing in 1965. Chongqing was the "temporary capital" (P'ei-tu) of China during World War II. This term could not have been used for a publication in 1965. It seems likely that the date of publication given for this entry is in error. Also, on page 662 the second characters in the name of the Boone Library School should be "hua" as in "Zhonghua" (China) and not the "hua" in "wenhua" (culture).

These minor errors, of course, do not detract from the enormous importance and usefulness of this volume. The publication of the *Bibliography* is a monumental undertaking deserving the gratitude of all who labor in the field of Chinese studies.

Notes

This article was published in *The China Quarterly*, no. 68 (September, 1976), pp. 866-868.

朴啟弘、桃樂西・安德森、彼德・哈佛－威廉斯編《1976年5月31日到6月5日國際圖聯全球研討會紀錄》，首爾：韓國圖書館協會，1976。565頁。平裝本35美元。（書評）

　　1976年國際圖書館協會聯盟在韓國首爾舉辦專題研討會，議題為「圖書館資源與國家發展：東西方對東方出版品的使用和管理」。此次研討會在歷史上深具意義，因為其為國際圖聯第一次在歐洲之外的地區召開的研討會，也是第一次在亞洲召開，並且是第一次以亞洲出版品為議題。這部會議紀錄分四部分：1. 自開場辭到閉幕辭全部會議紀錄摘要；2. 所有宣讀論文全文為全書主體（頁51-406）；3. 11篇沒有宣讀的書面論文（頁407-502）；4. 附件，如研討會節目、參加者名單等等。兩場全體大會上和四場技術性會議上宣讀的論文都涉及到與研討會主題有關之議題。前者有「圖書館在國家發展上所擔任的任務」、「出版品和出版：比較東西方出版傳統」。後者有：1.「東方出版品的書目管理：全國總書目所扮的腳色」；2.「東方出版品的書目管理：東方資料的編目」；3.「東西方使用東方資料的圖書館使用者」；4.「國際交流：音譯和羅馬拼音」。

　　這本書的價值不在於對國家發展和圖書館資源關係的理論方面的論述，（有好幾篇論文對此已有清晰地說明），而在於它提供了大量原始資料來陳述東西方圖書館收藏亞洲出版物的歷史和當前狀況及其他有關問題。譬如李鳳順（Poonsoon Lee）、李春熙（Choon Hee Lee）、朴啟弘（Ke Hong Park）的論文就簡潔地介紹了韓國的印刷史、出版史、圖書館和圖書館事業史。佐久間信子（Nobuko Sakura）概述了日本國會圖書館採購日本出版物的情形；森六一郎（Rokuichiro Mori）論述了日本國會圖書館的期刊訂購情形，特別強調其目錄和服務方面的工作；中森強（Tsuyashi Nakamori）介紹了日本專門圖書館協議會（Japan Special Libraries Association）的活動。諸家駿（William C. Ju）代表中華民國介紹國立中央圖書館珍藏的善本；胡安彝（Anyi E. Hu）介紹台灣公共圖書館所藏有關台灣和東南亞的資料；張鼎鍾介紹目前台灣出版界的動態。代表香港的有安東尼・賴丁斯（H. Anthony Ridings）介紹香港圖書館所收藏有關香港資料聯合目錄的歷史及現況；譚惠康（Lawrence W.H. Tam）提供了一份加有注釋的在香港採購中文資料可用的各種書目、書商和出版社名錄。

伊妮德・畢曉普（Enid Bishop）、常石道雄（Warren Tsuneishi）、雷納・克雷姆皮恩（Rainar Krempien）分別代表澳洲、美國和德國圖書館以西方的觀點來討論他們採購東方資料的經驗。傑佛瑞・馬里森（Geoffrey E. Marrison）詳細地介紹了大英圖書館有關東方資料的交換方案。除此之外，亞洲各國還報告了其編輯全國總書目的現況以及在編輯出版上面臨的大大小小問題。

由於研討會是個國際會議，參與者自然將其注意力關注在國際合作和國際標準上。研討會最大的收穫也許就在提供了這樣的平台討論這些問題。在「國際編目標準」研討會上，合不合適使用《國際書目著錄標準》（ISBD: International Standard Bibliographic Description）來編亞洲和阿拉伯文資料就得到熱烈的討論。在需要採用統一標準以方便各國交換資料這點上沒有爭議，但是大家，特別是亞洲圖書館員對目前盛行的西方標準還是持有意見的。麥克雷・埃爾羅德（J. McRee Elrod）和薩迪・埃爾－哈格拉西（Saad M. El-Hagrassy）的論文就點明非羅馬文字採用ISBD的諸多困難，並提供建設性的解決方案。

田邊廣（Hiroshi Tanabe）在他的論文中提醒我們：日文、韓文中漢字有其文化特性，在設定國際編目標準時，必須考慮東西方語文的異同和東西方書目傳統與實踐。可能小田泰正（Yasamasa Oda）對這個爭議下的結論最具說服力。他說：「全球書目管理工作除非有國際間的合作，而不是只有西方各國間的合作才能實現。」（頁367）。他勸告他的西方同仁對東方傳統文化要更為敏感，而東方同仁也要更積極參與國際圖書館論壇的討論。我認為小田先生的忠言，值得我們注意。

注釋

原載《圖書館季刊》（*Library Quarterly*）第49卷，第2期（1979年4月），頁237-238。

（胡嘉陽譯）

Proceedings of IFLA Worldwide Seminar, May 31-June 5, 1976. Edited by Ke Hong Park, Dorothy Anderson and Peter Harvard-Williams. Seoul: Korean Library Association,1976. 545 pp. $35.00 (paper). (Book review)

In 1976, IFLA (International Federation of Library Associations) sponsored a Worldwide Seminar in Seoul, Korea, with the theme of "Library Resources and National Development: Use and Control of Eastern Publications by East and West." The seminar was a historic occasion in that it was the first IFLA meeting held outside Europe, the first in Asia, and the first on Asian publications. The volume under review is the proceedings of that seminar arranged in 4 parts: part 1 contains summary reports on all sessions, from opening address to closing remarks; part 2 reproduces all the papers presented at the seminar and forms the main body of the volume (pp. 51-406); part 3 brings together 11 other papers submitted but not read (pp. 407-502); and part 4 is a series of appendices providing such matter as the seminar program, list of participants, etc.

The papers presented to the two general sessions and four technical sessions of the seminar deal with a wide range of topics related to the main theme of the seminar. For the two general sessions, "The Role of Libraries in National Development" and "Publication and Publishing: Comparison between Eastern and Western Publishing Traditions" are discussed. Technical problems are dealt with at length under the following four subthemes: (1) "Bibliographical Control of Eastern Publications: The Role of the National Bibliography," (2) "Bibliographical Control of Eastern Publications: Cataloging Eastern Materials," (3) "The Library User of Eastern Materials in East and West," and (4) "International Communications: Transliteration and Romanization."

The value of this publication lies not so much in the philosophical discourse on the relationship between national development and library resources, the importance of which is made clear in several of the papers, but rather in the vast amount of primary information on both the historical and current collection development of Asian publications and its related problems in libraries in the East and West. Pongsoon Lee's, Choon Hee Lee's, and Ke Hong Park's papers, for example, provide succinct accounts of the history of printing, publishing, libraries, and librarianship in Korea. Nobuko Sakura outlines the National Diet Library's acquisitions activities in Japanese publications; Rokuichiro Mori discusses serials work in that library, emphasizing its services and bibliographical activities; and Tsuyoshi Nakamori reports on the activities of the Japan Special Libraries Association. Useful information on the Republic of China is provided by William C. Ju in his paper on "special collections" (rare books and manuscripts) in the National Central Library, by Anyi E. Hu on the "public collections" on Taiwan and Southeast Asia, and by Margaret Fung on publishing and publications in Taiwan today. For Hong Kong, H. Anthony Rydings traces the history and reports on the current status of a "Union Catalog of Hong Kong Materials," and Lawrence W. H. Tam provides valuable information on acquiring Chinese materials in Hong Kong in an annotated checklist of bibliographic and trade sources.

From the Western perspective, papers by Enid Bishop, Warren Tsuneishi, and Rainer Krempien discuss the experience of and solutions to acquiring Eastern material by Australian, American, and German libraries, respectively, while Geoffrey E. Marrison details the British Library's exchange scheme involving publications from the East. In addition, there are also status reports on the national bibliographies in various countries in Asia and the magnitude of problems encountered in their compilation and publication.

As the seminar was an international conference, the participants naturally turned their attention to matters concerning international cooperation and standards. It is in this area that the seminar probably proved to be most useful as a forum for exchange. In the session on international cataloging standards, for example, much discussion took place on the suitability of the use of the ISBDs in cataloging Asian and Arabic materials. While no one disputes the desirability and indeed the necessity of adopting uniform standards to facilitate information exchange among nations, there remains a persistent concern, especially on the part of Asian librarians, over the predominant Western orientation in such standards now in use. J. McRee Elrod's and Saad M. El-Hagrassy's papers pinpointed a number of problem areas in adapting the ISBDs to publications written in the non-roman scripts and offered constructive solutions. Hiroshi Tanabe reminds us in his paper that there remains a "cultural sphere of Chinese characters" in Japanese and Korean, and that we must, in the formulation of international cataloging standards, take into consideration the linguistic differences between Eastern and Western languages and bibliographical traditions and practices in the East and the West. Perhaps Yasamasa Oda sums up this argument most eloquently when he says that "Universal Bibliographical Control will be realized not by inter-western but international cooperation" (p. 367). He exhorts his Western colleagues to be more sensitive to the cultural traditions of the East and his Eastern colleagues to be more active in the deliberations at international library forums. In my opinion, we will all do well to heed Oda's advice.

Notes

This review was published in *Library Quarterly*, vol. 49, no. 2 (April 1979), pp. 237-238.

《中國：書目提要》，錢存訓、鄭迴文合編，波士頓：霍爾出版社，1978. xxx, 604頁。附引用連續出版物一覽，補遺。作者索引，書名索引，主題索引。45美元。（書評）

《漢學要籍：精選，注解，主題分列書目指南》，駱傳華編。席拉序。台北：中華印刷公司，1978。X，228頁。附中國歷史年表、地圖。未列定價。（書評）

　　很長的時間，才有一本價值顯著的書出現。唯一合理的書評，就是推薦購買此書。錢存訓新出的《中國：書目提要》就是這樣的一本書。錢教授在芝加哥大學講授中國書目學、史學多年。現在他把授課教材連同鄭迴文的補充，著成此書讓我們共用。此書精裝易用，內容極新，涵蓋周全至1977年（包括一些1978年預定出版的書目），以英、中、日文以及有些法、德、俄文書寫的有關中國研究各方面的書目總匯。毫無疑問，在將來很長的一段時間，此書仍會是中國研究參考書中最重要的工具書之一。

　　在此書出版前，最常用的英文中國書目和參考書是鄧嗣禹、畢乃德（Knight Biggerstaff）二位教授所著的《中國參考書目解題》（*Annotated Bibliography of Selected Chinese Reference Works*）（北平1936，劍橋1950第三版，台北1974翻印版）。另外兩本同類的用中文撰寫的是何多源著的《中文參考書指南》（廣州1936，上海1939修訂版，台北1970翻印版）和鄧衍林著《中文參考書舉要》（北平1936，台北1970翻印版）。就它們涉及的時間來說，這兩本書仍然有用，但在西方，知者藐藐。錢教授的書和這三本書的性質不同。它是書目的書目。它也不包括前三本書所記述的百科全書、年鑑、各科字典、各別著作的引得等等。但是這些參考書籍的書目在錢著中都詳盡無遺的搜羅在內。其中列舉的2,500種以上的書目，文獻短論，以及某一時代或某一研究領域的俯瞰就比上列三書任何一本所列的總數還要多。也許錢教授這書的特色在於把分散在147種中文、105種日文期刊中的書目總歸在一起。這對從事中國研究的人來說是了不起的貢獻。因為這些期刊不一定每個圖書館都有，因而有時會被忽略。

　　錢教授的書分為兩大部：1. 綜合及專門書目，2. 主題書目。每部又分十章，所有條目都有簡而精的注解，有述有評。對這樣的巨作要挑出一些主見或遺漏也許不是難事，但是絕對不會降低本書的用處，反而會顯出書目研究工作的艱難。舉例來說，第1421條列有克拉克（Anne B. Clark）所編《中國將領選傳》（*Selected Biographies of Chinese Military Leaders*），但是克拉克和克萊因（Donald K. Klein）合編的《中共黨史人物辭典》（*Biographic Dictionary of Chinese Communism*）卻沒有列入，或許前書本來就不屬於本書的範圍。第244條余秉權所編的《中國研究資料中心出版總目》，這本有注釋的書目是從該中心的每期通訊摘錄出來的。如果把中心通訊單獨另列或在本條注解中附筆提及，想會更有用，因為通訊本身就是很有價值的書目。另外該中心發行的四卷紅衛兵報紙微卷目錄（原係1974年東京亞細亞經濟研究所發行的《紅衛兵報總目》油印本）應該列入第275-277項紅衛兵出版品類中。另外一本日文目錄《日本主要研究機關圖書館所藏中國文新聞雜誌總合目錄》似也應列入。儘管有這些遺漏，錢教授這本書會和高第（Henri Cordier），袁同禮以及其他的書目著作一樣在中國研究中占有極重要的地位。

　　駱傳華先生的《漢學要籍》卻是一本完全不同的書。正如作者在序言中所說他的書主要是為中國學門外漢寫的，列有1,500種書，主要是英文的，也有些中文的。主要的是1958年以後出版的書。1958年也正是袁同禮《西文漢學書目》（*China in Western Literature*）出版的那一年。按18個主題分類，各類中每項有完整的書目資訊，包括已知的作者中文姓名和生卒年代。每一主題有一條簡短的介紹，有些只有一句說明和評估，大部從《書評文摘》（*Book Review Digest*）中摘錄而來。雖然這書照作者的目的來說還是有用，缺點是沒有索引。書名在每類以作者姓名按字母排列而沒有索引易於混亂而不易使用。例如在歷史項下，薛君度（Chun-tu Hsueh）的《中國共產主義運動1937-1949》（*Chinese Communist Movement, 1937-1949*）（這書的前卷1921-1937運動，並未被提及），排在賀凱（Charles O. Hucker｝的《帝制時期之中國》（*China's Imperial Past*）前面，接著就是胡提辛（G.P. Hutheesing）寫的《新中國印象》（*Great Peace*）一本身歷其境者對竹幕內情的報導。

注釋

原載《亞洲學報》（*Journal of Asian Studies*）第39卷，第1期（979年11月），頁159-160。

（馬敬鵬譯）

China: An Annotated Bibliography of Bibliographies. Compiled by Tsuen-Hsuin Tsien in collaboration with James K. M. Cheng. Boston: G. K. Hall, 1978. xxx, 604 pp. List of Serials Cited, Addenda, Author Index, Title Index, Subject Index. $45.00. (Book review)

Notable Books on Chinese Studies: A Selected, Annotated, and Subject-Divided Bibliographic Guide. Compiled and edited, with introductory essays, by C. H. Lowe. Foreword by Jesse H. Shera. Taipei: China Printing, Ltd., 1978. X, 228 pp. Chronological Chart on the History of China, Map. No price listed. (Book review)

Once in a long while a book comes along whose merit is so obvious that the only sensible review is to recommend purchase. T. H. Tsien's latest contribution to the field, *China: An Annotated Bibliography of Bibliographies*, is just such a book. For many years Professor Tsien taught a course on Chinese bibliography and historiography at the University of Chicago; he has now shared with us, through this publication, the materials he used for his class, with additions by James K. M. Cheng. In one handy, handsomely bound volume we now have the most up-to-date and comprehensive compilation of bibliographic works on every aspect of Chinese studies through 1977 (with some projected for publication in 1978) in English, Chinese, and Japanese, as well as some titles in French, German, and Russian. This book will no doubt remain one of the most important reference tools in Chinese studies for years to come.

Prior to the publication of this book, the most widely used work in English on Chinese bibliography and reference works has been the *Annotated Bibliography of Selected Chinese Reference Works*, by Professors Ssu-yu Teng and Knight Biggerstaff (Beijing, 1936; Cambridge, 1950; 3rd ed., 1971; rpt. Taipei,

I974). Two other Chinese-language compilations on the same subject, *Zhongwen cankaoshu zhinan*, by He Duoyuan (Guangzhou, I936; rev. ed. Shanghai, I939; rpt. Taipei, I970); and *Zhongwen cankaoshu juyao,* by Deng Yanlin (Beijing, I936; rpt. Taipei, I970) remained equally useful for the period they cover, but are perhaps less well-known in the West. Professor Tsien's book differs from these three books in that it is a bibliography of bibliographies, and does not cover the other types of reference works the other three describe. For example, encyclopedias, yearbooks, dictionaries of all kinds, indexes to individual works, and so on do not come under the purview of Professor Tsien's compilation, but bibliographies of such reference works are exhaustively represented. Its listings of more than 2,500 bibliographies, bibliographic essays, and surveys of literature on specific periods or fields are more than the total number of listings in any of the other three works. Perhaps the most unique feature of Professor Tsien's compilation is the inclusion of bibliographies selected from periodicals, serial publications, and monographs. The grouping of such scattered sources of bibliographic information-notably from I47 Chinese and I05 Japanese periodicals is a signal service to the field, for the publications in which they appear are not always readily available in a single library collection and, as a result, the information frequently goes unnoticed.

Professor Tsien's book is conveniently arranged in two main parts: General and Special Bibliographies, and Subject Bibliographies, with ten chapters in each part. All entries are annotated, and the annotations are succinct and well written. They are generally descriptive in nature, with occasional evaluative comments. It is easy to fault a publication of such monumental scope with certain commissions and omissions. To point them out is not to detract from the enormous usefulness of the compilation, but rather to show how exceedingly difficult bibliographic research is. For example, item no. 1421 is Anne B. Clark's *Selected Biographies of Chinese Military Leaders*, while Clark and Klein's *Biographic Dictionary of*

Chinese Communism is not included. Perhaps the former does not really belong in this compilation. Item no. 244 is P. K. Yu's *Research Materials on Twentieth-Century China: An Annotated List of CCRM Publications.* Since this is a compilation of the annotated lists which have appeared in the *Newsletter of the Center for Chinese Research Materials*, an additional entry for the *Newsletter*-a most useful source of bibliographic information in its own right-or its mention in the annotation would have been helpful. The four-volume catalogue of the Red Guard newspapers on microfilm distributed by the CCRM, which was compiled and published in mimeographed form in 1974 by the Ajia Keizai Kenkyujo in Tokyo under the title Hongweibing baozongmu could be added to the section on Red Guard publications (pp. 275-77). Another Japanese catalogue, a union list of Chinese newspapers and serials in major Japanese research libraries (*Nihon shuyo kenkyu kikan toshokan shozo Chugokubun shimbun zasshi sogo mokuroku),* published in 1959 by the Seminar on Modern China of the Toyo Bunko, might also have been included. These omissions notwithstanding, Professor Tsien's work ranks with those of Cordier, T. L. Yuan, and others among the most significant bibliographic contributions to Chinese studies.

Mr. C. H. Lowe's *Notable Books on Chinese Studies* is an entirely different kind of bibliographic publication. As the author states in his preface, his book is primarily for the "layman and the uninitiated in the field of Chinese studies." Its listing of over 1,500 titles, mostly in English with some in Chinese, presents primarily books published since 1958, when T. L. Yuan's *China in Western Literature* was published. The entries are arranged under eighteen subject categories, with full bibliographic information given for each, including Chinese characters for names and authors' dates, when known. There is a short introductory essay to each category, and annotations, when given, consist mostly of one-sentence descriptive or evaluative comments, often quoted from the *Book Review Digest.* Although useful for the purpose for which it is designed, the book suffers from a lack of indexes. The alphabetical arrangement by author under each category, without the aid of any index, is confusing and difficult to use. For example, in the History section, Jundu Xue's *Chinese Communist Movement, 1937-1949* (his earlier volume for the 192I-1937 period is not mentioned) immediately precedes Charles 0. Hucker's *China's Imperial Past,* which is followed by G. P. Hutheesing's *Great Peace*, an eyewitness account of the "conditions behind the Bamboo Curtain."

Notes

This review was published in *Journal of Asian Studies*, vol. 39, no. 1 (Nov 1979), pp. 159-160.

《哈佛大學哈佛燕京圖書館韓籍簡目》三編，麻州劍橋：哈佛大學哈佛燕京圖書館，1980。vii，684頁（哈佛燕京圖書館書目叢刊第2種）（序）

　　哈佛燕京圖書館很高興能出版這部《韓籍簡目》第三編。包含繼第二編出版後1964年底至1976年底採編的書籍11,730種，及至1979年6月館藏所有期刊1,400種。北朝鮮出版品不包括在內；計畫將來另出補編。至1979年底，哈佛燕京圖書館典藏韓文書刊共22,360種，計42,500冊。

　　編輯和出版這部目錄共費時三年。韓文採購和參考部主任兼助理館長金聖河先生從開始就負責這個項目，他制定編輯計畫並監督每個階段的出版事宜，包括繁瑣的校對工作。他兩度到韓國首爾籌募出版經費以及安排必要的編輯出版事宜。我們得感謝首爾樂喜金星集團蓮庵文化財團慷慨提供所有出版的經費。我們還得感謝利久商社具滋益先生幫忙監督所有在首爾各種編輯和出版的細節工作，如果沒有他們的幫忙，這部目錄是無法出版的。

　　由於得到多方的建議和支援，哈佛燕京圖書館韓籍典藏才得以發展。哈佛燕京學社於1928年開創哈佛燕京圖書館，又於1951年在該館成立韓文部，往後一直提供採購韓文資料的經費。哈佛大學韓國研究委員會也提供支援。1976年哈佛燕京圖書館移交給哈佛學院圖書館後，哈佛學院圖書館也慨然提供採購經費。在韓文部初創時期，哈佛燕京圖書館得到延世大學閔泳珪教授不少建言和協助。他和哈佛燕京圖書館故前任館長裘開明在一段比較困難的時期緊密合作從事採購並維持本館韓國古籍的品質。哈佛大學愛德華‧瓦格納（Edward Wagner）教授對目錄的編輯以及資料的採購費時費力提供建議。過去以及現在哈佛燕京學社自韓國邀請來哈佛大學訪問的學者也是對本館韓文部提供資訊和采購建議的固定來源。其中不少更餽贈本館韓文書刊。

　　我們還要感謝韓國國會圖書館和國立中央圖書館提供韓國政府出版物。很多大學圖書館也提供我們不少協助，特別是首爾國立大學圖書館、高麗大學圖書館、延世大學圖書館、梨花女子大學圖書館各自提供其大學出版物。

研究機構如韓國經濟企劃院統計局、韓國銀行金融經濟研究院、韓國開發研究院對本館索取他們出版物的要求總是有求必應。我們還要向凡文社的柳益衡先生致謝。多年來他不僅對本館採購提供優良服務，還對我們這部目錄的出版自願提供協助。

館長吳文津

1980 年 7 月 15 日

（胡嘉陽譯）

*A Classified Catalogue of Korean Books in the Harvard-Yenching Library,
Harvard University, Volume III.* 哈佛大學哈佛燕京圖書館韓籍簡目三編.
Cambridge, MA: Harvard-Yenching Library, Harvard University, 1980.
(Harvard-Yenching Library Bibliographical Series II) (Preface)

The Harvard-Yenching Library takes pleasure in presenting the third volume
of its Korean catalogue, listing some 11,730 monographs and 1,400 serials. The
monographic titles are those acquired and catalogued by the Library between the
end of 1964, the cut-off date for the second volume, and December 1976; the
1,400 serial titles represent the entire serial holdings of the Library as of June
1979. North Korean publications are not included in this volume; a supplementary
volume will be issued in the future. The total extent of the Library's Korean
holdings, as of the end of 1979, amounted to 22,360 titles in 42,500 volumes.

The compilation and publication of the present volume was three years in the
making. Mr. Sungha Kim, Assistant Librarian and head of Korean Acquisitions
and Reference, was in charge of the project from the beginning. He laid out the
plans for the compilation and supervised every phase of its production, including
the tedious proofing of the entire volume. He made two trips to Korea during that
time in order to arrange for the necessary editorial services in Seoul where the
catalogue is printed, and to secure funding for publication. In this connection, we
should like to thank the Yonam Foundation of the Lucky Group in Seoul which
generously provided a grant to cover the entire printing cost of the catalogue. We
also wish to thank Mr. Ja Ik Koo and his staff of the Reegu Company, also in
Seoul, for their assistance in supervising the editorial and other publishing details
throughout the entire project. Without their help, the publication of this catalogue
would not have been possible.

The development of the Harvard-Yenching Library's Korean Collection has benefitted from advice and support from a variety of sources. The Harvard-Yenching Institute, which founded the Harvard-Yenching Library in 1928, later established a Korean Collection in the Library in 1951, and it continues to contribute towards the Library's Korean acquisitions program. The Korean Studies Committee at Harvard University has been responsive to the Library's needs and has provided support. The Harvard College Library, of which the Harvard-Yenching Library became a part in 1976, has since then been most generous in support of the Library's Korean Collection. In its formative years, the Harvard-Yenching Library received much help and advice from Professor Young-gyu Minn of Yonsei University who worked closely with the late Dr. A. Kaiming Chiu, former Librarian of the Harvard-Yenching Library, in acquiring and assuring the quality of publications from Korea during a rather trying period. Professor Edward W. Wagner of Harvard University has given much of his time and advice both on the compilation of this catalogue and on acquisitions matters over the years. Past and present Harvard-Yenching Institute Visiting Scholars at Harvard from Korea have been a constant source of information and advice on acquisitions, and many of them have made gifts of books to the Library.

We are grateful to the National Assembly Library and the Central National Library for their assistance in securing Korean government publications. Many university libraries in Korea have also provided invaluable help, and we wish to thank particularly the Seoul National University Library, the Korea University Library, the Yonsei University Library, and the Ewha Womans University Library for their courtesies and cooperation in providing publications of their respective institutions. Research institutes such as the National Bureau of Statistics of the Economic Planning Board, the Research Department of the Bank of Korea, and the Korea Development Institute have all been unfailingly accommodating with regard to our requests for their publications. We are indebted to Mr. Ick H. Liu of the Panmun Book Company, not only for his outstanding services over the years as a supplier of books, but also for his volunteer help in the publication of the present catalogue.

Eugene W. Wu, Librarian

July 15, 1980

吳天威著《江西蘇維埃共和國，1931-1934──陳誠特藏文件選輯解題書目》麻州劍橋：哈佛大學哈佛燕京圖書館，1981。xiii，340頁（哈佛燕京圖書館書目叢刊第3種）（前言）

1960年在台北中央研究院與胡適先生合影。

　　當一大批原始研究資料被發現時，是值得大為慶賀的事；當那些資料揭露異常重要而為學者所不知的資訊的時候，就更加令人興奮。此即為當史丹佛大學胡佛研究院於1960年得知在台灣藏有一大批有關中國共產黨1930至1934年在江西成立的「江西蘇維埃共和國」的原始文獻，而將它們攝製成縮微膠捲以供研究之用時的情況。這批文獻共約1,500餘種，從油印單張到已出版的書刊均為西方學者從未所見。為了解中國共產黨早期活動不可或缺的研究資料。這批文獻為故國民黨將軍、後台灣中華民國副總統陳誠所收藏。包括關於江西蘇維埃共和國期間黨的指示、政府報告、意識形態的辯論、經濟政策、戰役報告以及其他有關資料。經陳副總統的許可，胡佛研究院在台北中央研究院照相部鼎力協助下，將此批資料攝製成21卷縮微膠捲。後又經陳副總統俯允，胡佛研究院將膠捲的拷貝供應給美國、西歐、日本各研究圖書館。

這些原始資料被統稱為「陳誠特藏」，其出現彌補了海外圖書館當時收藏有關中國共產運動原始文獻中一個重要的空白。之前，關於江西蘇維埃時期的原始資料在西方各國甚為罕見，以致無法進行任何有關的研究。例如，胡佛研究院以其收藏大量中國共產黨文獻著名，在此之前僅有全美唯一的一期中國蘇維埃共和國臨時中央政府的機關報《紅色中華》，而「陳誠文庫」就有203期，差不多是《紅色中華》的全部。

雖然研究中國共產運動的學者已經使用過「陳誠特藏」中的部分資料，但由於缺乏引得或書目，此項豐富的文獻尚未能被充分使用。所幸南伊利諾大學吳天威教授有系統地閱讀「陳誠特藏」全部後，選擇其中對江西蘇維埃共和國歷史各方面最具代表性的文件，詳加注釋，編撰此書，以惠士林。我們企望，由於吳教授此書方便大家使用「陳誠特藏」，將會促進對中國共產黨史作永續價值的研究工作。

吳文津

1981年7月於麻州劍橋

（胡嘉陽譯）

Tien-wei Wu, *The Kiangsi Soviet Republic, 1931-1934 – A Selected and Annotated Bibliography of the Chen Cheng Collection,* Cambridge, MA: Harvard-Yenching Library, Harvard Universiy, 1981, xiii, 340 pp. (Harvard-Yenching Library Bibliographical Series III) (Foreword)

The discovery of a large body of primary sources is always cause for celebration, and the excitement of the occasion is heightened when the sources reveal vital information that has long been denied scholars. Such was the case when in 1960 the Hoover Institution on War, Revolution, and Peace at Stanford University learned of the existence in Taiwan of a large number of contemporary Chinese Communist documents on the historic Kiangsi Soviet Republic, 1930-1934, and succeeded in preserving them on microfilm for research use. The documents, numbering some fifteen hundred and appearing in various formats from mimeographed sheets to published volumes, had never before been available to scholars in the West, and contained information absolutely indispensable to an adequate understanding of this early phase of Chinese Communism in action. The documents were collected by the late Mr. Chen Cheng, formerly a Nationalist Army general and later the Vice President of the Republic of China of Taiwan. They included Party directives, government administrative reports, ideological debates, economic plans, military campaign reports, and a host of other materials relating to the Kiangsi Soviet Republic. With the Vice President's permission, the Hoover Institution preserved the documents on twenty-one reels of microfilm; the work was ably assisted by the Photography Department of the Academia Sinica in Taipei. With further permission from the Vice President, the Hoover Institution later made copies of the microfilm available to research libraries in the United States, Western Europe, and Japan.

The availability of these primary sources, which became known as the Chen

Cheng Collection, filled a crucial gap in our library holdings of Chinese Communist documentation of the history of the Chinese Communist movement. Prior to that time, primary sources on the Kiangsi Soviet period were quite scarce in the Western world, and no serious research was possible on this subject. For example, the Hoover Institution, known for its extensive collections of Chinese Communist materials, had until then the only issue of the *Hong-se Zhong-hua* (Red China), official organ of the Provisional Central Government of the Chinese Soviet Republic, in the entire United States. The Chen Cheng Collection has now given us, among other things, two hundred and three issues of this important publication, representing an almost complete file of this journal.

While selected materials from the Chen Cheng Collection have since been utilized by scholars for the study of the Chinese Communist movement, the vast extent of the Collection and the absence of an index or a bibliography have discouraged the full utilization of these rich resources. It is our good fortune that Professor Tien-wei Wu of the University of Southern Illinois, who has made a systematic study of the entire Collection, has now offered us a carefully and critically compiled annotated bibliography of the most representative items selected from the Collection with a view to illuminating the various aspects of the history of the Kiangsi Soviet Republic. It is hoped that the signal service he has performed will facilitate the use of the Chen Cheng Collection, and in so doing, will stimulate further research of enduring value into the history of the Chinese Communist Party.

Eugene W.Wu

July 1981

Cambridge, Massachusetts

《哈佛燕京圖書館中日文典藏目錄》，紐約：加蘭出版公司，1986。72冊。
（緒言）

　　哈佛燕京圖書館是西方東亞研究界最大的大學圖書館。雖然正式創館於
1928年，可是早在1879年一批和中國從事貿易的波士頓商人從浙江寧波聘
請了一位學者戈鯤化到哈佛大學來教授中文時就開始收藏中文書籍了。戈鯤
化為了教學帶來的少量書籍就是哈佛學院圖書館（Harvard College Library）
開始收集中文書籍的開始。而日文收藏也同樣是因為兩位東京大學的教授姊
崎正治和服部宇之吉於1914年來哈佛大學講學，將一些有關漢學和佛教的
重要日文書籍捐贈給哈佛學院圖書館而開始。當1928年在麻州註冊為獨立
機構的哈佛燕京學社成立漢和圖書館（Chinese-Japanese Library），就接管了
哈佛學院圖書館中日文書籍，計中文4,526冊，日文1,668冊。並聘請前一年
已經開始為這批書籍編目的裘開明為館長。裘開明是位知名的目錄學家，當
時正好在哈佛大學攻讀博士學位。
　　由於哈佛燕京學社的財務支持，裘館長對目錄學的專長，還有由洪煨蓮
（洪業）教授主持的哈佛燕京學社駐北平辦事處的協助，漢和圖書館的收藏
激增，十年後增加了18倍達11萬冊。雖然最初只收集中日文有關人文科學
方面的書刊，隨後因為哈佛大學東亞課程範圍的擴大，書刊收集的範圍也隨
之擴大。除了增加了藏文、蒙文、滿文、西文的書刊之外，1951年還成立
韓文部，1973年成立越南文部。第二次世界大戰後社會科學方面的資料收
集受到重視，自1960年中期開始關於這方面的收集量大增。一所當年是以
人文科學資料為主的圖書館，就逐步地轉變成一所包容所有學科的研究圖書
館，甚至包括一些關於自然科學與應用科學方面的資料。1965年為了體現
圖書館收藏範圍擴大的實況，將哈佛燕京學社漢和圖書館更名為哈佛燕京圖
書館（Harvard-Yenching Library）。圖書館的行政也於1976年由哈佛燕京學
社轉移至哈佛學院圖書館。
　　目前圖書館館藏總量為641,200冊。計中文374,300冊，日文175,810

冊，韓文 53,240 冊，西文 29,150 冊，越文、藏文、蒙文、滿文 8,700 冊。另有期刊 10,600 種，報紙 314 種，膠捲 17,840 卷，膠片 3,900 片。

　　各語言部門的收藏都有類似的共同點，即全面收藏了有關歷史、語言、文學、哲學、宗教、美術以及近代當代社會科學方面的主要資料[1]。但是各語言部門收藏也各有其特性。中文特藏有：地方志（約 3,800 種）、叢書（約 1,500 種）、明清文集、善本（宋版 14 種，元版 38 種，明版 1,277 種，清初版 1,880 種，包括齊如山收藏的明代戲劇和小說），還有研究國民黨和中國共產黨的主要資料。日文特藏有：漢學研究資料，有關日本現代和戰後政治、社會、經濟發展的主要資料。還有佩佐爾德特藏（Petzold Collection），其中共計佛教典籍 6,500 冊，德川時期的刻本多種以及 200 件 13、14 世紀的手抄本。韓文部以 17、18 世紀的族譜和榜目為特藏。尚有以漢文撰寫的文集。滿文特藏除了中國儒家經典、文學、歷史、政書的翻譯外，還有初版滿文《欽定八旗則例》以及 1708 年出版的《滿漢蒙藏四體合璧文鑑》。藏文特藏有《大藏經》善本三種：1732 年那塘版《甘珠爾》、《丹珠爾》，1700 年北京版《甘珠爾》，1933（？）年拉薩版《甘珠爾》。蒙文特藏有 1724 年北京赤字版蒙文《甘珠爾》。越南部所藏 19 世紀以漢文撰寫的安南歷史、政法和佛教典籍甚夥。西文部係有關東亞的主要專著和學報以及新舊東亞文學作品的翻譯。館藏還包括如《日本時報》（*Japan Times*）、《字林西報》（*The North China Daily News*）全套膠捲。其他特藏還有納西（中國雲南少數民族）象形文字經典手稿；中文拓本；嶺南大學（廣州教會學校，原名格致書院，Canton Christian College）董事會 1884-1952 年的會議紀錄；基督教傳教士的中文著作；以及包括國民黨元老胡漢民，在中國基督教青年會服務多年的費吳生（George A. Fitch）、越南研究專家約瑟夫・布亭格（Joseph Buttinger）他們的個人檔案。

　　漢和圖書館為使哈佛大學以外的學術界對其所藏有更深的認識，於 1936 年在北京開始其出版中文館藏目錄的工作。排版完成後，於 1938、1939、1940 年先後出版了經學類、哲學宗教類、歷史科學類三冊目錄。很不幸，這項工作因太平洋戰爭爆發而被停止。縱然其餘的目錄已經排版，但當時未能全部印行。原擬在二戰後再繼續出版的計畫亦未能實現。雖然，隨後有些包含部分館藏的書目問世；三冊韓籍簡目亦相繼出版[2]；1975年開始自新採購的資料中選擇其重要者並附以解題出版《不定期參考書目解題》（*Occasional Reference Notes*），但是這都只代表館藏的部分。所以我們極感榮幸現在可以把全部中日文館藏編輯成目召告於世。

在此我要向哈佛燕京學社創辦本館以及其慷慨持續的資助致敬，也要向哈佛大學文理學院、哈佛大學圖書館、哈佛學院圖書館不斷增加經費和專業指導來保證優良典藏和服務致敬。我也要向圖書館中的同仁致敬。在圖書館過去或現在工作的同仁為本館採訪、選購、編目、提供讀者服務均以促進哈佛以及全美，乃至全世界對東亞的教學和研究為目的。全體中文日文編目人員在副館長賴永祥的領導下辛勤工作經年，本目錄方得付梓。哈佛大學東亞研究的先驅費正清（John K. Fairbank）及賴世和（Edwin O. Reischauer）教授欣然同意分別為此目錄惠賜前言。他們多年來不斷的建言和支持，令圖書館受益匪淺。我們將此目錄敬獻給嘉惠於世代研究東亞的學者的本館第一任故館長裘開明博士，以紀念他近四十年建立以及領導哈佛燕京圖書館發展的豐功偉業。

哈佛大學哈佛燕京圖書館

館長吳文津1984年11月

注釋

[1] 早期館藏情況，請參看裘開明著，〈哈佛燕京學社圖書館〉（"The Harvard-Yenching Institute Library"），載《遠東季刊》（*Far Eastern Quarterly*）第14卷，第1期（1954年），頁147-152；及葉理綏（Serge Elisseeff）著，〈哈佛燕京學社漢和圖書館〉（"The Chinese-Japanese Library of the Harvard-Yenching Institute at Harvard University"），載《哈佛圖書館館訊》（*Harvard Library Bulletin*）第10卷，第1期（1956年），頁73-93。

[2] 《哈佛大學漢和圖書館日本全集叢書目錄》（*Japanese Collected Works and Series in the Chinese-Japanese Library at Harvard University*）（劍橋：哈佛燕京學社，1954）；費正清（John K. Fairbank）、劉廣京編，《現代中國研究指南，1898-1937》（*Modern China: A Bibliographical Guide to Chinese Works, 1898-1937*）（劍橋：哈佛大學出版社，1961）；裘開明著，《哈佛大學哈佛燕京學社漢和圖書館藏明代類書概述》（*An Annotated Catalog of Ming Encyclopedias and Reference Works in the Chinese-Japanese Library of the Harvard-Yenching Institute at Harvard University*）（劍橋：哈佛燕京學社，1961）；裘開明著，〈四庫失收明代類書考〉（"Ming Encyclopedias and Reference Works Unrecorded in the Ssu-k'u ch'uan-shu"），載香港中文大學《中國文化研究所學報》第2卷，第1期，1959；賴永祥編《傳教士中文著作目錄》（*Catalog of Protestant Missionary Works in Chinese*）（波士頓：G.K. Hall, 1980）；吳天威著《江西蘇維埃共和國，1931-1934──陳誠特藏文件選輯解題書目》（*The Kiangsi Soviet Republic, 1930-1934 — A Selected and Annotated Bibliography of the Chen Cheng Collection*）（劍橋：哈佛燕京圖書館，1981）；《哈佛大學燕京圖書館韓籍簡目》（*A Classified Catalogue of Korean Books in the Harvard-Yenching Library, Harvard University*）（劍橋：哈佛燕京圖書館，1962-1980，3冊）。

（胡嘉陽譯）

Chinese and Japanese Catalogues of the Harvard-Yenching Library, New York: Garland Pub., 1986. 72 volumes (Introduction)

The Harvard-Yenching Library is the largest university library for East Asian research in the Western world. Although as an organized library it dates only from 1928, the collection can trace its beginnings back to 1879, when Chinese was first offered as part of Harvard University's regular curriculum. In that year a group of Bostonians engaged in the China trade invited Ge Kunhua, a Chinese scholar from the city of Ningbo, Zhejiang Province, to give instruction in Chinese at Harvard. The small collection of books that was bought for his courses, the first acquisitions in any East Asian language at the Harvard College Library, marked the beginning of a Chinese collection. A Japanese collection was similarly launched in 1914 when two Japanese professors, Hattori Unokichi and Anesaki Masaharu, both of Tokyo Imperial University, came to lecture at Harvard and donated several important groups of Japanese publications on Sinology and Buddhism to the Harvard College Library. In 1928 these two collections, then consisting of 4,526 volumes in Chinese and 1,668 volumes in Japanese, were transferred to the newly established Chinese-Japanese Library of the Harvard-Yenching Institute, which had itself been independently incorporated that year in Massachusetts. Dr. A. Kaiming Chiu, a renowned bibliophile and then a Harvard Ph.D. candidate, who had begun cataloguing the collections a year before, was appointed Librarian of the Chinese-Japanese Library.

Thanks to financial support from the Harvard-Yenching Institute, the expert bibliographical knowledge of Dr. Chiu, and the assistance of the Harvard-Yenching Office at Yenching University in Peking, which was under the able direction of the late Professor William Hung, the Library's collections grew rapidly. At the end of its first decade its holdings were more than 110,000 volumes—eighteen times the original size. Although the Library first collected only in Chinese and Japanese, with the major emphasis on the humanities, subsequent expansion in Harvard's East Asian curriculum led to a similar expansion in the Library's scope. Tibetan, Mongolian, and Manchu publications were added, as were Western-language monographs and journals. A Korean collection was officially inaugurated in 1951, and a Vietnamese collection was added in 1973. Social science publications were given increased attention in the post-World War II years, and collecting in this area has been greatly accelerated since the mid-1960s. Thus, a collection that was once predominantly humanistic has gradually evolved into a research library that encompasses East Asian materials in all of the academic disciplines, including, to some extent, the natural and applied sciences. In 1965 the name, Chinese-Japanese Library of the Harvard-Yenching Institute, was changed to Harvard-Yenching Library in order to reflect more accurately the expanded nature of the Library's collections. The management of the Library, which had been under the Harvard-Yenching Institute from the beginning, was transferred in 1976 to the Harvard College Library.

Today the Library's collections stand at 641,200 volumes, of which 374,300 are in Chinese, 175,810 in Japanese, 53,240 in Korean, 29,150 in Western languages, and 8,700 in Vietnamese, Tibetan, Mongolian, and Manchu. There are also 10,600 titles of periodicals, 314 newspapers, 17,840 reels of microfilm, and 3,900 pieces of microfiche.

In general, the collections share certain common characteristics in that for each country they provide comprehensive coverage of history, language and literature, philosophy and religion, fine arts, and primary sources for the study of the modern and contemporary periods. [1] Each collection, however, has its own unique features. The Chinese Collection is strong in local gazetteers (some 3,800 titles), *congshu* or collectanea (1,500 titles), writings of individuals of the Ming and Qing periods, rare books (14 Song, 38 Yuan, 1,277 Ming, and 1,880 early

Qing editions, including the Qi Rushan Collection of Ming drama and fiction), and primary sources for the study of the Kuomintang and the Chinese Communist Party. The Japanese Collection is rich in Sinological studies and in primary sources concerning Japan's modern and postwar political, social, and economic development. It also contains the 6,500-volume Petzold Buddhist Collection, including a number of books published in the Tokugawa period (1603-1868) and some 200 manuscripts dating from the 13th and 14th centuries. The Korean Collection maintains a unique group of genealogies and government examination rosters from the 17th and 18th centuries. It is also strong in collected individual writings in traditional format. The Manchu Collection, in addition to translations of Chinese Confucian classics, literature, history, and works on government, contains such original Manchu publications as *Laws and Regulations of the Eight Banners* and the 1708 edition of the *Imperial Polyglot Dictionary in Four Languages—Manchu, Chinese, Mongol, and Tibetan*. In the Tibetan Collection are three rare editions of the Tripitaka: The Narthang edition (1732) of both the *Kanjur* and the *Tanjur*, the Peking edition (1700) of the *Kanjur*, and the Lhasa edition (1933?) of the *Kanjur*. The Mongolian Collection includes the "red copy" of the Mongolian *Kanjur* printed in Peking in 1724. The Vietnamese Collection includes a number of nineteenth-century publications written in classical Chinese on Vietnamese history, law, political institutions, and Buddhism. The Western-language Collection includes all the major monographs and journals on East Asia plus translations of East Asian literary works, past and present. There are also complete files on microfilm of such important newspapers as The *Japan Times* and The *North China Daily News*. Other unique features in the Library's collections are a group of Naxi (a minority people in China's Yunnan Province) manuscripts in pictographic script; Chinese rubbings; the archives of the Lingnan University Trustees (a missionary university in Canton originally known as the Canton Christian College) 1884-1952; missionary works in Chinese; and collections of personal papers, including those of the late Hu Hanmin, an early Kuomintang statesman, the late George A. Fitch, who was for many years associated with the YMCA and other missionary activities in China, and Joseph Buttinger, author and Vietnam specialist.

In order to make its resources better known to a wider scholarly community outside Harvard, the Library in 1936 undertook to publish a book catalogue of its Chinese holdings. Type was set in Peking, and the first three volumes—Confucian Classics, Philosophy and Religion, and Historical Sciences—came off the press in 1938, 1939, and 1940. Unfortunately, the war in the Pacific put a stop to this project, and the remainder of the catalogue, though typeset, was never published. Although publication of the book catalogue was never resumed after World War II as had originally been planned, several bibliographies based on portions of the Library's holdings were subsequently issued, and three volumes of the Library's Korean catalogue were also published. [2] Another Library publication, the *Occasional Reference Notes*, which was initiated in 1975, lists selected items from the Library's current acquisitions. Nevertheless, all these represent but a portion of the Library's holdings. Thus it is with great pleasure that we now present to the international community the Chinese and Japanese catalogue of the Harvard-Yenching Library in its entirety.

On this occasion, it is only fitting that we pay tribute to the Harvard-Yenching Institute for its founding of the Library and its generous, continuing support and to the Harvard College Library, the Harvard University Library, and the Faculty of Arts and Sciences of Harvard University for their steadfast commitment to superior collections and high-quality service through ever increasing appropriations and professional guidance. We salute the staff of the Library, past and present, for their dedication to the selection, acquisition, cataloguing, and servicing of the Library's collections; they have shared the goal of furthering teaching and research on East Asia — not only at Harvard, but throughout the nation and the world. The Chinese and Japanese cataloguing staff have worked long and hard under the able direction of the Associate Librarian, John Yung-hsiang Lai, to bring the catalogue to fruition. The Library has for many years also benefitted from the advice and support of Professors John K. Fairbank and Edwin O. Reischauer, the pioneers of East Asian studies at Harvard, who also graciously consented to write the Forewords to the Chinese and Japanese sections of this catalogue, respectively. Generations of scholars are indebted to the late Dr. A. Kaiming Chiu, who, as the first Librarian of the Harvard-Yenching Library, built and shaped the Library's collections for almost forty years. We respectfully dedicate this catalogue to his memory.

Eugene W. Wu, Librarian

Harvard-Yenching Library

Harvard University

November 1984

Notes

[1] For an earlier detailed description of the Library's collections, see A. Kaiming Chiu, "The Harvard-Yenching Institute Library," *Far Eastern Quarterly*, vol. 14. no. I (1954), pp. 147-152, and Serge Elisseeff, "The Chinese-Japanese Library of the Harvard-Yenching Institute at Harvard University," *Harvard Library Bulletin.* vol. X, no. I, (1956), pp. 73-93.

[2] *Japanese Collected Works and Series in the Chinese-Japanese Library at Harvard University* (Japanese and English) (Cambridge: Harvard-Yenching Institute. 1954); John King Fairbank and Kwang-Ching Liu, *Modem China, A Bibliographical Guide to Chinese Works, 1898-1937* (Cambridge: Harvard University Press, 1961); A. Kaiming Chiu, *An Annotated Catalogue of Ming Encyclopedias and Reference Works in the Chinese-Japanese Library of the Harvard-Yenching Institute at Harvard University* (1) (in Chinese) (Cambridge: Harvard-Yenching Institute, 1961); Chiu K'aiming, "Ming Encyclopedias and Reference Works Unrecorded in the *Siku quanshu zongmu* "(in Chinese), *Journal of the*

Institute of Chinese Studies of the Chinese University of Hong Kong, vol. II, no. 1（1969）; *Catalog of Protestant Missionary Works in Chinese,* ed. by John Yung-hsiang Lai（Boston: G. K. Hall, 1980）; Tien-wei Wu, *The Kiangsi Soviet Republic, 1931-1934, A Selected and Annotated Bibliography of the Ch'en Ch'eng Collection*（Cambridge: Harvard-Yenching Library, 1981）; *Classified Catalogue of Korean Books in the Harvard-Yenching Library, Harvard University*（Cambridge: Harvard-Yenching Library, 1962-1980）, 3 vols.

《哈佛大學哈佛燕京圖書館和書目錄》，岡雅彥、青木利行合編，東京：ゆまに書房，1994。413頁。（哈佛燕京圖書館書目叢刊第4種）（序）

　　哈佛燕京圖書館很高興能出版這本日文古籍目錄。哈佛燕京圖書館收藏日文書籍可以追溯到1914年當漢學權威姊崎正治教授和著名佛學家服部宇之吉教授自日本來哈佛大學講學的時候。他們將一些有關漢學和佛教的重要日文書籍捐贈給哈佛學院圖書館（Harvard College Library）。其後增長並不顯著。當1928年哈佛燕京學社在麻州註冊為獨立機構以便管理紐約尼加拉瀑布市（Niagara Falls, New York）查理斯・霍爾（Charles Martin Hall）的基金來幫助中國幾個教會大學以及在哈佛大學設立東亞研究課程時，為了哈佛大學東亞課程的教學，哈佛燕京學社於同年成立了漢和圖書館（Chinese-Japanese Library）。其時哈佛學院圖書館將其1,668冊日文書籍自威德納圖書館（Widener Library）轉到新成立的漢和圖書館。

　　其後數十年圖書館由於哈佛燕京學社的支援遂開始有系統地增加館藏。除了中文、日文部以外，1951年成立了韓文部，1973年成立了越南文部。有關東亞研究的西文（主要是英文）、滿文、蒙文、藏文資料也在收藏之列。雖然圖書館最先主要的收藏是關於人文科學的資料，後來隨著東亞課程的擴大，收藏範圍也隨之擴大。第二次大戰後社會科學受到重視，因此自1960年中期以來增加了大量這方面的資料。一所當年是以人文科學資料為主的圖書館，就逐步地轉變成一所包容所有學科的研究圖書館了，甚至還包括一些關於自然科學與應用科學方面的資料。如今，哈佛燕京圖書館成為了美國大學中最大的東亞研究圖書館。1965年為了體現圖書館收藏範圍擴大的實況，將哈佛燕京學社漢和圖書館更名為哈佛燕京圖書館（Harvard-Yenching Library）。圖書館的行政也於1976年由哈佛燕京學社轉移給哈佛學院圖書館。

　　日文部收藏有關歷史、文學、日本現代和戰後政治、社會、經濟發展的資料甚為豐富。此外尚有佩佐爾德佛教典籍特藏（Petzold Buddhist

Collection）。其中江戶時代（1600-1868）的刻本居多。因為布魯諾・佩佐爾德（Bruno Petzold）在日本曾經是天台宗大師，他的收藏有不少天台宗經典，其中還有14世紀的手抄本。有關漢學的日文資料亦復不少。最有研究價值的還數1991年由東京日光證券股份有限公司贈送的一套由東京丸善書店將日本國會圖書館所藏明治時代（1868-1912）出版約12萬種書籍拍攝成的共15,000卷縮微膠捲。

過去在本館查詢日文資料均賴使用圖書館的卡片目錄。1985年由紐約加蘭出版社（Garland Publishing, Inc.）將日文卡片編製成書本目錄出版。分作者／書名、主題、期刊三部分，共33冊，包含1984年前編目的資料。之前於1954年曾出版過《哈佛大學漢和圖書館日本全集叢書目錄》（*Habado Daigaku Kan-Wa Toshokan Nihon zenshu shoho mokoroku*）。自1989年開始採購的日文資料都以連線電腦圖書館中心中日韓文編目系統（Online Computer Library Center, CJK system，簡稱OCLC CJK）編目，並輸入哈佛大學線上公共目錄資訊系統（HOLLIS）。通過OCLC和RLIN（研究圖書館資訊網）的資料交換，使用研究圖書館資訊網中日韓系統（RLIN CJK）的東亞圖書館也可以查詢使用。

東京國文學研究資料館江戶時代文學與版本專家岡雅彥教授於1985年和1989年兩度來訪，對館藏江戶時代刻本作了初步調查。調查結果題名〈哈佛大學燕京圖書館藏和書簡略目錄〉（30頁）登載於該館文獻資料部出版的《調查研究報告》第11期（1990年10月）。雖然該文中約1,000種全集或叢書已包含在書本目錄中，但為便於參考起見，仍覺得有必要將這些刻本單獨出版目錄。因此，哈佛燕京圖書館遂向日本國際交流基金會申請經費邀請岡雅彥教授於1991年重返劍橋，1992年岡雅彥教授又自費來哈佛燕京圖書館完成他初步調查沒有審視的刻本，並且糾正《哈佛大學漢和圖書館日本全集叢書目錄》中的錯誤。其成果就是這本目錄。

這本目錄包含哈佛燕京圖書館收藏的3,300種日本刻本（hanpon）和抄本。刻本多數為江戶末期明治初期出版。（必須要注明的是在縮微膠捲中沒有收入明治初期刻本）。岡雅彥教授在本目錄〈凡例〉中已經詳細說明目錄的編排和使用法。其中一些重要部分還值得重複如下：

1. 目錄分日文、中文、佛教三部分。主題分類按照內閣文庫分類，稍有修改。如將內閣文庫日文部分下佛教類，單獨成一部分，日文和中文都列於下。另外還加上「在日本所刻漢文書」，其下包括「以日文注釋的漢文書」。
2. 叢書名下個別書沒有書目著錄，但收入書名索引中。
3. 多數條目多有注釋，包括不同書名、序、後記、缺失卷數，以及其他有關鑑別資料。
4. 書末附作者索引和書名索引。以羅馬拼音排列，隨後為漢字與該條在目錄中的目號。

　　為此目錄的出版，我們要特別感謝岡雅彥教授，他從頭至尾參與這個專案的構思和監督工作。他的熱心令人鼓舞。他專注細節的方式可以作為目錄學工作的典範。本館日本部主任青木利行先生作為此目錄的合編者，協助岡雅彥教授將全書作者名和書名注入羅馬拼音，解答岡雅彥教授許多疑難問題，並且補充他忽略的書籍。儘管岡雅彥教授在圖書館的時間有限，卻因為有青木主任的幫忙，此目錄才得以這麼快出版。岡雅彥教授還得到東京國文學研究資料館和田先生幫忙排列本目錄中佛教部分的條目。我們也要感謝日本國際交流基金會提供經費給岡雅彥教授於1991年來哈佛燕京圖書館作研究，同時還要感謝日本教育部補助我們由ゆまに書房出版這本目錄。

哈佛大學

哈佛燕京圖書館

館長吳文津

1994年1月

（胡嘉陽譯）

Early Japanese Books at Harvard-Yenching Library, Harvard University, Catalogued and compiled by Oka Masahiko and Aoki Toshiyuki (Tokyo: Yumani Shobo, Publisher Inc. 1994) 413 pp. (Harvard-Yenching Library Bibliographical Series IV) (Preface)

The Harvard-Yenching Library is pleased to present this catalog of its holdings of early Japanese books. The Japanese Collection of the Harvard-Yenching Library can be traced to 1914, when Professor Hattori Unokichi, a leading Sinologist, and Professor Anesaki Masaharu, a well-known Buddhologist, came from Japan to lecture at Harvard University and presented several important groups of Japanese publications in their respective fields of interest to the Harvard College Library. This collection grew only imperceptibly until 1928, when the Harvard-Yenching Institute was independently incorporated in Boston, Massachusetts, to administer a fund established under the will of Charles Martin Hall of Niagara Falls, New York, to assist several Christian universities in China and to create a center for East Asian studies at Harvard University. For the latter purpose, the Chinese-Japanese Library of the Harvard-Yenching Institute was established at Harvard in the same year, and the Japanese books which had been collected by the Harvard College Library, numbering 1,668 volumes at the time, were transferred from the Widener Library to the newly founded Chinese-Japanese Library.

Funds provided by the Harvard-Yenching Institute made possible a systematic strengthening of the Library's collections in the subsequent decades. In addition to the Chinese and Japanese collections, a Korean collection was added in 1951, and a Vietnamese collection in 1973. Western-language publications on East Asia, primarily in English, were also collected, as were materials in the Manchu, Mongolian, and Tibetan languages. Although the Library's original emphasis was on the humanities, subsequent broadening of Harvard's East Asian curriculum led to a similar broadening of the Library's scope. Social science publications were given increased attention in the post-World War II years, and their acquisition has been greatly accelerated since the mid-1960s. Thus, a collection that was once predominantly humanistic has gradually evolved into a research library that encompasses East Asian materials in all of the academic disciplines, including, to some extent, the natural and applied sciences. Today, the Harvard-Yenching Library is the largest library for East Asian studies at any American university. Its name, Chinese-Japanese Library of the Harvard-Yenching Institute, was changed to Harvard-Yenching Library in 1965 in order to reflect more accurately the expanded nature of the Library's collections. The management of the Library, which had been under the Harvard-Yenching Institute since the founding of the Library in 1928, was transferred to the Harvard College Library in 1976.

The Library's Japanese Collection is rich in history, literature, and Japan's modern and postwar political, social, and economic development. It also contains the Petzold Buddhist Collection, which includes a large number of books printed in the Edo period（1600-1868）, especially those on the Tendai Sect, of which Bruno Petzold（1873-1949）was a high priest in Japan, and some manuscripts dating from the 14th century. Japanese works on Sinology are also well represented in the Library's collection. The collection's research value is further enhanced by the acquisition in 1991 of the 15,000-reel microfilm collection of some 120,000 titles of printed books of the Meiji period（1868-1912）, which was reproduced from the holdings of the National Diet Library by the Maruzen Company of Tokyo, and donated to the Library by the Nikko Securities Co., Ltd.

Access to the Library's Japanese Collection was for many years by the use of a card catalog. In 1985 the Japanese card catalog was photographically reproduced by Garland Publishing, Inc. of New York in book form in three parts: author/title, subject, and serials. Comprising 33 volumes in all, this catalog contains materials cataloged before the end of 1984. Prior to that, the Library published in 1954 a printed checklist of its Japanese *sosho* entitled *Habado Daigaku Kan-Wa Toshokan Nihon zenshu sosho mokuroku* (96+32 pages). Since 1989 all Japanese books have been cataloged online into the OCLC CJK database and the machine-readable records included on HOLLIS, Harvard University Library's online catalog. These same records are also available to other East Asian libraries using the RLIN CJK system, through a record exchange arrangement between OCLC and RLIN.

In 1985 and 1989 Professor Oka Masahiko of the National Institute of Japanese Literature in Tokyo, a specialist on the literature of the Edo period and Edo editions, paid two brief visits to the Harvard-Yenching Library and made a preliminary survey of the Library's collection of Edo printed books. The result was the checklist "Habado Daigaku Enkei Toshokan zo Washo kanryaku mokuroku. 1" (30 pages), published in *Kokubungaku Kenkyu Shiryokan Bunken Shiryobu's Chosa kenkyu hokoku*, no. 11 (October 1990). While the 1,000 or so titles included in the checklist are also recorded in the Library's book catalog, it was thought highly desirable to have these editions grouped together in a separate publication for easy reference. At the invitation of the Library and with a grant from the Japan Foundation, Professor Oka returned to Cambridge in 1991, and again in 1992 (this time on his own funds), to examine the books which were left out of his preliminary survey and to correct some bibliographical errors in the published list. The result is the present catalog.

This catalog contains the listing of approximately 3,300 titles of early Japanese printed books (hanpon) and some manuscripts in the Harvard-Yenching Library's collection. Although most are books printed up to the end of the Edo period, some early Meiji works are also included. (It should be noted, however, that early Meiji publications on microfilm in the Library's possession are excluded from the listing.) The organization and use of the catalog are explained in detail in Professor Oka's "Explanatory Notes" (hanrei). Some of the important features of the catalog may be worth repeating here:

(1) The catalog is divided into three main parts: printed books in Japanese, printed books in Chinese, and Buddhist publications. Subject classification follows that used in the Naikaku Bunko catalog, with slight modification. The "Buddhism" section under "Japanese Books" in the Naikaku Bunko catalog is removed there to form an independent part of the catalog, which lists books on the subject in both Japanese and Chinese. A new classification, "Chinese Books Printed in Japan," is added which also includes "Chinese Books with Japanese Commentary."

(2) Collectanea (sosho) are listed under the title of the sosho, their contents are not given separate bibliographic description. However, individual works in sosho are found in the title index.

(3) A "Notes" section is provided for most entries. It includes information on variant titles, prefaces, postscripts, missing volumes, and other relevant information for the identification of the item.

(4) An author index and a title index are appended at the end of the volume, each arranged alphabetically by romanization, followed by kanji and the assigned item number in the catalog.

In presenting this catalog, we wish to express our enormous gratitude to Professor Oka, who conceived and oversaw the project from beginning to end. His enthusiasm is both contagious and inspiring, and his meticulous attention to detail sets a standard for all to follow in bibliographical research. He was ably assisted in the project by Mr. Aoki Toshiyuki, Assistant Librarian of the Harvard-Yenching Library in charge of the Japanese Collection, Mr. Aoki, as the co-compiler of this catalog, supplied the romanization for the authors names and book titles throughout the catalog, answered many queries from Professor Oka on points of doubt, and added titles which were overlooked by Professor Oka. His contribution to the project made possible the publication of this catalog in a relatively short period of time despite the brevity of Professor Oka's stays at the Library. Professor Oka was also assisted by Mr. Wada Yasuyuki of the National Institute of Japanese Literature, who helped arrange the entries in the part on Buddhism in this catalog. We are equally grateful to the Japan Foundation for the grant it made to Professor Oka for his research trip to the Harvard-Yenching Library in 1991, and to the Japanese Ministry of Education for a subsidy for the publication of the catalog by the Yumani Shobo, Publisher, Inc.

Eugene W. Wu, Librarian
Harvard-Yenching Library
Harvard University
January 1994

《評周恩來》，李天民著，香港：明報出版社，1994，299頁。ISBN 962-357-604-3。（序）

天民先生以半生的時間研究中共問題，從1960年代開始便致力於中共領導人物的研究來闡明中共發展的歷史過程。三十多年來，他陸續出版了劉少奇、周恩來、華國鋒、林彪和鄧小平的專著傳記，其中並有英、日文版。《劉少奇傳》在文革後由大陸湖南人民出版社於1989年再行出版，稱「此書是了解劉少奇生平以及當代中國權力更迭過程的一部難得的好書」。他之所以能得到這樣的評語是因為他的治學態度謹嚴，論事客觀，沒有受到或左或右的八股局限。

先生的《周恩來》一書，先於1970年以英文版由台北國際研究所出版，次年由桑原壽二先生譯為日文在東京由日本時事通訊社出版。1973年略加增補，再由東京實業之世界社發行第二版日文版。後於1975年又重修增訂由香港友聯研究所出版，稱《周恩來評傳》。先生末年，因大陸文革後有大批新的資料出現，決心重寫周傳，歷時五、六年之久，在1993年逝世前不久完稿，是為本書，為先生最後之研究碩果。

此書有兩大特點，第一是取材豐富。本書的論述大都根據大陸在1991年前出版的各種關於中共黨史和周恩來的書刊報紙，特別是文革後所出的前所未見的各種珍貴資料。這種廣徵博引關於中共黨史的著作，還是目前不常見的。這也是天民先生數十年研究中共人物黨史的一貫作法，就是分析論述必須要有資料的根據。第二個特點是本書的寫法。本書一反原《周恩來評傳》的編年論述方式，而以關鍵問題和主導政策等主題下作了依時與事的分章分析。如「在西安事變扮演的角色」、「統一戰線的設計與執行」、「文藝主張及其貢獻」、「對四人幫的忍耐與鬥爭」等。每章可單獨成立，而綜合起來，對周恩來其人其事和他的生平更可以有全面的認識。這種提綱挈領的寫法，除非對所討論問題的來龍去脈有深刻的認識和對資料有全面性的掌握，是不能有像他這樣成功的。

　　先生這本遺著，對研究周恩來是一部非常重要的貢獻。顯然的，在有更多的中共內部資料公開時，還會有其他關於周的著作出現，可能對天民先生的論述或者還有些補充的地方，甚至於提出一些另外的看法。果如是，也不足以為奇，因為這是學術研究的普通現象。但是，先生這部遺著為周恩來研究建立了一個里程碑的事實是不容置疑的。多年來，關於周的著作多注重於他的公開的一面，而少於對他的性格、內涵和抱負的探討。本書對後者首次給我們開了一個窗，讓我們窺見了一些江山的本色。在這一方面，先生為周恩來研究開闢了一條新的途徑。在政治上，周恩來素被稱為「不倒翁」，通常的分析除他做「和事佬」的角色外，很少談到他自身是否還有原則的問題。先生在這方面，以若干史實，以周「功不自居，過不諉人」和「不輕易舉手投足」的論調作了進一步的分析，來闡明周恩來在各種可能的情況下，還是能維持他自己的意識形態和主張。以及和毛澤東「貌合神離」的關係這些論證，頗有啟發性。對將來周恩來和中共黨史的研究當會有它肯定和不滅的價值的。

　　先生逝世前，最掛心的一件事就是本書出版的問題。病中體力不濟，親自委請先生在政大東亞所博士班的高足王振輝和關向光同學共同整理查對校稿，並囑我作一序言。對於致力半生研究中共問題的天民先生，這當是一件最合適的永久紀念品。

吳文津

甲戌年端午節先生逝世周年

寫於哈佛大學哈佛燕京圖書館

朱寶田編，《哈佛大學哈佛燕京圖書館藏中國納西族象形文經典分類目錄》，麻州劍橋：哈佛大學哈佛燕京圖書館，1997。xii，936頁。（哈佛燕京圖書館書目叢刊第5種）（序）

　　納西族是中國邊疆雲南省西北部鄰近西藏和緬甸地方的少數民族。雖然地處偏遠人口只有25萬左右，卻因為一位美籍奧地利探險家，自學植物學家約瑟夫‧洛克（Joseph Francis Rock, 1884-1962）而聞名西方。洛克於1922年到納西族居住地麗江收集植物標本。他為納西族的象形文字和宗教禮儀著迷，從而開始收集為行使禮儀而書寫的象形文經典，並請納西東巴教士作翻譯。他自1922到1949年出入麗江達25年之久。除了收集和學習象形文字外，還學習納西族的禮儀和文化。同時還開始編輯納西文英文字典以及作其他有關研究。發表了20多種著作，有些在他身後才出版。全目可參見傑克遜博士（Anthony Jackson）所著《納西族宗教：解析納西宗教經典》（*Na-khi Religion, an Analytical Appraisal of Na-khi Ritual Text*），海牙：木桐出版社（The Hague: Mouton Publishers），1979，頁343-344。

　　據傑克遜博士調查，現存東巴經典共21,842冊：中國大陸藏12,741冊，美國藏7,288冊，歐洲藏1,513冊，台灣藏300冊（參見傑克遜博士著〈納西族研究的過去、現在和未來〉〔“Naxi Studies: Past, Present & Future”〕載《新亞學術集刊第8期：中國民族關係和民族集團專集》[*New Asia Academic Bulletin, 8: Special Issue on Ethnicity & Ethnic Groups in China*]，1989，頁136），其中洛克收集的就占三分之一：6,000冊藏美國，1,118冊藏歐洲。美國收藏的除了洛克收集的外，還有哈佛1941年畢業生昆亭‧羅斯福（Quentin.Roosevelt）收集的1,861冊。美國收藏的大部分都在私人手中，只有國會圖書館收藏了2,465冊，哈佛燕京圖書館收藏了598冊。

　　哈佛燕京圖書館收藏的598冊（其中510冊來自洛克，88冊來自羅斯福）以及四幅葬禮卷軸是哈佛燕京學社於1945年採購的。當時沒有編目，來自洛克的經典，每冊封面背面注有點收號碼。1956年台北故宮博物院一位納西專家李霖燦教授將該批經典分了大類，重新編號注於封面。一直到1995年初紐約亞洲文化協會為籌備納西展覽邀請雲南省博物館工作的納西專家朱寶田教授到美國檢驗羅斯福家族、國會圖書館、哈佛燕京圖書館收藏的納西經典和文物，哈佛燕京圖書館才計畫將這批經典編目。於是在朱寶田教授完成了紐約亞洲文化協會展覽的項目後，由哈佛燕京學社邀請他來作訪問學人，將這批經典編輯成目錄並加注釋。此書便是其成果。

朱教授對哈佛燕京圖書館收藏的特點已經在他的前言中說明。此目錄按主題分13類，每類條目下有朱教授手書納西象形文書名、羅馬拼音、中文譯名、內容提要、相關注釋、尺寸頁數。如果有日期、作者和地名也都著錄（僅21冊經典有注明日期。最早的為1826年，最晚者為1910年。可參見附錄）。各類下分別編號，在新編號後括弧內有哈燕館舊號以及洛克所編號，如A-1（337；1991）。書後附有兩個交叉引用表：一個為哈燕館舊號和新號對照表，另外一個為洛克編號和哈燕館新號對照表。除了598冊原件外，還將另外23張經典影印件，4幅葬禮卷軸畫，和1張照片的底片一併收入目錄，但在所列入各類下分別編號。

哈佛燕京圖書館為朱教授能夠編輯這部前所未有的目錄感激萬分。同時也感謝哈佛燕京學社首任社長葉理綏（Serge Elisseeff）教授採購了這套文獻，以及現任社長杜維明教授和他的前任韓南教授提供財務和精神上的鼓勵才能完成此目錄的編輯和出版。

因為此目錄包含太多繪圖，只能用朱教授的手稿照相出版。為照相計，本館助理館長暨中文部主任胡嘉陽女士負責整理正文前的中文部分，館長辦公室助理潘蜜拉・德拉（Pamela Dellal）女士負責製作書名頁和序言打字，圖書館行政助理裘蒂・莫里森（Judy Morrison）女士與印刷公司密切合作有關出版事宜。均一併在此致謝。

吳文津

哈佛大學哈佛燕京圖書館館長

1997年12月

（胡嘉陽譯）

Zhu Baotian, *Annotated Catalog of Naxi Pictograph Manuscripts in the Harvard-Yenching Library, Harvard University,* Cambridge, MA: Harvard-Yenching Library, Harvard University, 1997. xii 936 pp. (Harvard-Yenching Library Bibliographical Series V) (Preface)

與雲南省博物館朱寶田先生攝於哈佛燕京圖書館。

The Naxi（Nakhi）are a minority nationality in the northwestern part of Yunnan Province in China, an area close to where the borders of China, Tibet, and Burma converge. Although geographically isolated and with a relatively small population（currently estimated to be around 250,000）, the Naxi people have nevertheless attracted the attention of the West, mainly through the writings of Joseph Francis Rock（1884-1962）, an Austrian-born and naturalized American explorer and self-educated botanist. Rock went to Lijiang, the home of the Naxi, in 1922 to gather specimens. While there he became fascinated by the Naxi pictographic language and Naxi religious rituals. He started collecting the manuscripts written in pictographs, which were used for performing rituals, and engaged the assistance of Naxi *dtombas*（priests）to help translate them. From

1922 to 1949 he stayed in Lijiang off and on for 25 years, all the while collecting and learning the pictographs, and studying Naxi rituals and culture. He also began the compilation of his Naxi-English dictionary and other related research. Altogether he published more than twenty articles and books on the Naxi, several of them posthumously. (A complete list of his writings is found in Anthony Jackson, *Na-khi Religion, an Analytical Appraisal of the Na-khi Ritual Text*, The Hague: Mouton Publishers, 1979, pp. 343-344.)

According to Jackson's survey, 21,842 Naxi manuscripts are extant: 12,741 in the People's Republic of China, 7,288 in the United States, 1,513 in Europe, and 300 in Taiwan (Jackson, "Naxi Studies: Past, Present & Future," *New Asia Academic Bulletin*, v. VIII, 1989, Special Issue on Ethnicity & Ethnic Groups in China, p. 136). Of this total one-third were collected by Rock: 6,000 of them are now preserved in the United States and 1,118 in Europe. The U.S. holdings, in addition to those collected by Rock, also include 1,861 manuscripts collected by Quentin Roosevelt, a Harvard graduate, Class of 1941. The greater part of the U.S. holdings are in private hands, with the rest in the Library of Congress (2,465 manuscripts) and the Harvard-Yenching Library (598 manuscripts).

The Harvard-Yenching Library's holdings (510 from Joseph Rock and 88 from Quentin Roosevelt together with four long funereal scrolls) were acquired by the Harvard-Yenching Institute in 1945. There was no catalog made at the time, but the manuscripts from Rock's collection had his own accession number marked on the verso of the cover of each. In 1956 Li Lincan, a Naxi specialist from the National Palace Museum in Taipei, rearranged the manuscripts by broad topics and renumbered them. The number was marked on the cover of each item. It was not until 1995, however, that a catalog project was organized. Earlier that year Professor Zhu Baotian, a Naxi specialist from the Yunnan Provincial Museum, was invited by the Asian Cultural Council in New York to come to the United States to examine the Naxi artifacts and manuscripts in the possession of the

Quentin Roosevelt family and at the Library of Congress and the Harvard-Yenching Library, in preparation for a Naxi exhibit. Following that, Professor Zhu came to Harvard as a Harvard-Yenching Institute Visiting Scholar to begin the compilation of an annotated catalog of the Library's Naxi collection. The present volume is the result of his work.

The significance of the Harvard-Yenching Library's collection, including the unique items, is explained in Professor Zhu's foreword. The arrangement of the catalog is by subject, in thirteen categories. Within each category, the following information is given for each entry: the title of the manuscript in pictographs (redrawn by Professor Zhu), the title in romanization, a Chinese translation of the title, brief contents, notes, date, dimensions, number of leaves, name of author, and place. The date, author, and place are noted only when that information is found in the manuscript. It might be mentioned that only twenty-one manuscripts are dated, with the earliest being 1826 and the latest 1910; see Appendix.）All manuscripts are renumbered consecutively within each of the thirteen subject categories. Accompanying the new number and in parentheses is the old Harvard-Yenching Library number, followed by Rock's accession number, e.g. "A-l (337; 1991)." Two cross reference tables are appended at the end of the volume; one from the old Harvard-Yenching Library numbers to the new numbers, and one from Rock's accession numbers to the new numbers. In addition to the 598 original manuscripts, the catalog also lists the twenty-three photographs of other manuscripts, four funereal scrolls, and one photographic negative that are in the Library's collection. They are listed after the main body of the catalog and numbered separately within each group.

The Harvard-Yenching Library is enormously grateful to Professor Zhu Baotian for having compiled this catalog, the first of its kind ever published. The Library is also deeply indebted to the Harvard-Yenching Institute for having acquired this collection during the tenure of its first director, Professor Serge

Elisseeff, and for the generous financial and moral support given to the catalog project by its current director, Professor Tu Wei-ming, and his predecessor, Professor Patrick D. Hanan, without which the compilation and publication of this catalog would not have been possible.

Ms. Chia-yaung Hu, Assistant Librarian of the Harvard-Yenching Library for the Chinese Collection, prepared the camera-ready copy of the preliminary matter in Chinese for reproduction; Ms. Pamela Dellal, Staff Assistant in the Librarian's Office, produced the title page and the Preface and prepared the camera-ready copy of the manuscript; and Ms. Judy Morrison, Administrative Officer of the Library, worked closely with the printer on the final product. Because of the many pictographs included in the catalog, the catalog itself is photographically reproduced directly from Professor Zhu's manuscript.

Eugene W. Wu Librarian

Harvard-Yenching Library Harvard University

December 1997

宋永毅、孫大進編，《文化大革命書目，1966-1996》，麻州劍橋：哈佛大學
哈佛燕京圖書館，1998。xi, 521頁。（哈佛燕京圖書館書目叢刊第6種）（序）

　　三十多年前全世界目睹了在中國近代史上發生的最具破壞性的反權威運
動，就是所謂的「偉大的無產階級文化大革命」。從1966到1976年整整歷
時十年間，它導致了社會秩序徹底崩潰，成了無法無天的無政府狀態。數百
萬的中國人，包括中國共產黨傑出的領導人都成為這次運動的受害者。這段
慘痛的當代中國歷史因而成為世界各地學者研究的題目，以便更深入地了解
其起源、發展和後果。當大量的著作已經出版，原始資料也可以使用的時候
（如中國研究資料中心複製出版的《紅衛兵資料》）卻還沒有一本這些一手
和二手資料的書目可供學者和圖書館員參考。這部書目就是為滿足這個需要
而作。

　　迪金遜學院（Dickinson College）工作的宋永毅先生和匹茲堡大學工作
的孫大進先生編輯的這部書目收集全面，包括1966至1996年出版的有關文
化大革命的專著，報刊文章，尚未出版的博士、碩士論文，乃至一些視聽資
料。收錄的主要是英文資料，也有中文、日文資料，還包括一些1997年出
版者。是至今以至將來若干年關於這30年間有關此題目最完整的參考書
目。研究當代中國的學者將會自此書目中發現他們忽略的資料，特別是報刊
上的文章。圖書館員會發現這是部很好的工具參考書，能幫助他們收集典藏
中有所遺漏者。我們為其以哈佛燕京圖書館書目叢刊系列出版深感榮幸。

　　宋、孫兩位先生用了兩年多時間走訪美國和中國各主要圖書館收集資料
編輯了這部書目。編輯書目是項耗時又艱巨的工作，即使已經有線上資料
庫，也不是所有的資料，特別是報刊文章被收入其中。他們用了很多時間和
精力搜查包括在這部書目中的出版物，並以主題將其編排以便使用。沒有做
過同樣編輯目錄工作的人很難想像書目編輯所需的各種要求。宋，孫兩先生
給研究當代中國學術界做出了非常重大的貢獻。我們得對他們出版這部具有
永世價值的參考書感恩。

　　當然這部書目如能有解題就更加有利於研究。但是要為範圍如此廣泛的一部書目作個別的解題，費時需年，就會耽擱學者和圖書館界及早分享宋、孫兩位先生所收集的資料。願本書目以大主題的排列，佐以作者、題名索引能為使用本書提供方便，更願此部書目的出版能促使文化大革命的研究更上一層樓。

吳文津

哈佛大學

哈佛燕京圖書館

1997 年 11 月

（胡嘉陽譯）

The Cultural Revolution: A Bibliography 1966-1996, comp. by Yongyi Song and Dajin Sun and edited by Eugene W. Wu (Cambridge, MA: Harvard-Yenching Library, Harvard University, 1997) xi, 521 pp. (Harvard-Yenching Library Bibliographical Series VI) (Preface)

More than thirty years ago the world witnessed the most destructive rebellion against authority in China in recent history, known as the Great Proletarian Cultural Revolution. The rebellion, lasting a full decade from 1966 to 1976, led to a total collapse of social order and created a state of anarchy and complete lawlessness in China. Millions of Chinese, including prominent leaders of the Chinese Communist Party, fell victim to the upheaval. This tragic episode in contemporary Chinese history has since been a subject of intensive study by scholars around the world with a view to gaining a better understanding of its origin, development and consequences. While a very large number of publications have appeared as a result, and many primary sources have also been available, such as the Red Guard Publications reprinted by the Center for Chinese Research Materials, there has not been a comprehensive bibliography of these primary and secondary sources for the benefit of scholars and librarians. The present publication fills that need.

This bibliography, compiled by Mr. Yongyi Song of Dickinson College and Mr. Dajin Sun of the University of Pittsburgh, is a comprehensive listing of monographs, journal and newspaper articles, unpublished dissertations and theses, and some audio/visual materials on the Cultural Revolution, published in Chinese, Japanese and Western languages, primarily English, from 1966 to 1996. It also includes some publications which have appeared in 1997. It is the most complete bibliography available on the subject for the period covered, and it will remain so for years to come. Scholars in contemporary Chinese studies will find listings here they may have overlooked, especially journal and newspaper articles, and librarians will find the *Bibliography* an excellent tool with which to acquire publications to fill in the gaps in their collections. We are pleased to publish it in the *Harvard-Yenching Library Bibliographical Series*.

Messrs. Song and Sun spent more than two years on this compilation, traveling to major libraries in the United States and in China to gather information. Bibliographical research is a time-consuming and arduous task even in this age of on-line databases, as not everything is recorded on them, particularly journal and newspaper articles. The time and effort Messrs. Song and Sun spent searching out publications for inclusion in the present publication were considerable, and much effort went into arranging this unwieldy mass of material in a useable fashion by subject categories. The demands of producing a work of this scope can hardly be imagined by those who have not gone through similar travails. Mr. Song and Mr. Sun have performed a signal service to the contemporary China studies community. We are indebted to them for having produced a reference work of enduring value.

Although the Bibliography would have been even more useful with annotations, annotating such a vast volume of publications would take years, thus preventing the early sharing of information Mr. Song and Mr. Sun have already collected with the scholarly and library communities. It is hoped that the topical arrangement by broad subjects in this *Bibliography*, along with the author and the titles indexes, will facilitate the use of the *Bibliography*, and that the listings presented here will stimulate further research on the Cultural Revolution.

Eugene W. Wu

Harvard-Yenching LibraryHarvard University

November 1997

周原編，《新編紅衛兵資料》，第一部，小報，Oakton, VA：中文研究資料中心，1999。20冊。（序）

　　在美國蒐集研究中華人民共和國的資料一直是件具有挑戰性的事。自從中華人民共和國1949年成立30多年以來，中國政府一直不允許美國圖書館直接自中國採購中文出版物。在交換方面也只能跟國立北京圖書館（現在的國家圖書館）一個圖書館來往，所以採購的工作只能在香港和東京進行，但是地方報紙卻無法訂閱。書商提供的書刊也是經過選擇的，遠遠不及《全國新書目》和《全國總書目》所列。更有甚者，就是這兩種書目也不允許出口國外，只有走私出來由香港和日本的書商複印以高價出售。只要中國政府允許出版物到香港和日本，這種情況還算可以，但是就是那種情況也因為中國不時的政治動盪影響到出版業的正常運作，而遭到中斷。最壞的情況就是發生在1966年開始的文化大革命時期。

　　文化大革命開始不久，中國只出版數百萬冊《毛澤東語錄》和《毛澤東選集》，因此香港和日本沒有其他出版物可以出售。所以當一些複印的紅衛兵小報在香港出現時，它們馬上就成為炙手可熱的暢銷品。造成這種情況不僅是因為沒有另外出版物可採購，更重要的是這些小報是非常有價值的研究資料。這些小報有些頗具爭議性，但是多數包含了不少別處找不到的有價值的情報。如當時黨對各階層的指示和黨領導的講話，其中許多是毛澤東的指示和講話；被清算人物的「負面教材」，其中有沒有發表過的個人資料；有關黨史的文件；以及有關當時人物和事件的新聞短訊。這批新資料是如此珍貴和重要，一時洛陽紙貴，圖書館爭相採購。但是在香港出售的小報有限，不止美國圖書館需求，全世界的圖書館都向香港採購，因此價格越來越高。有鑑於此，學術界決定另闢他途爭取更多的小報以低價提供研究。美國學術團體協會和社會科學研究理事會合組的當代中國研究聯合委員會（Joint Committee on Contemporary China of the American Council of Learned Societies and the Social Science Research Council，簡稱JCCC。當時的主席為約翰‧林德貝克〔John M.H. Lindbeck〕）因此向美國國務院尋求幫助，要求學術界能夠分享其蒐集的紅衛兵資料。國務院慨然答允，要求JCCC派一代表到華盛頓檢視並判斷該處所收集資料是否有利研究之用，JCCC派我擔任此項任務。1967年夏我赴國務院外事研究部（External Research Division of the State Department）。當我閱讀他們提供給我的樣本後喜出望外，因為除小報以外，尚有許多其他重要的資料，諸如當時油印的中共首長像周恩來等在凌晨接見紅衛兵代表的談話紀錄。於是我向國務院和JCCC報告我的發現，並建議盡快公開這些資料。但是首先得決定如何複製和分發這批資料的方法。

那時都認為正在籌建的非盈利組織中文研究資料中心（Center for Chinese Research Materials，簡稱CCRM）可以來擔當此任務，因為其宗旨正為提供學術界研究20世紀中國重要卻難得的資料。但中文研究資料中心一年後才能開始運作，而學術界又急於利用國務院蒐集的這批資料，因此哈佛燕京圖書館答應暫時擔當複製分發的工作。旋由JCCC向福特基金申請到經費後，CCRM於1968年5月在華盛頓特區正式成立，隸屬研究圖書館協會（Association of Research Libraries，簡稱ARL），香港大學歷史系講師余秉權被延請來擔當主任。於是國務院遂將其蒐集的資料直接提供給該中心，哈佛燕京圖書館所拍攝的縮微膠捲也同時移交給該中心。此後CCRM也自他處蒐集到一些紅衛兵出版物。1975年CCRM將所有的資料編輯出版為19冊的《紅衛兵資料》（Red Guard Publications），內容多數為小報，其他還有期刊及雜項近1,000種。1979年出版的第20冊為19冊的細目，因此頭一系列共20冊。1980年出版續編一，1992年出版續編二，各8冊，前者包含76種，後者包含70種。三次出版共有1,100多種，是西方那時出版的最大的一部紅衛兵資料合集。

現在CCRM又出版了這部《新編紅衛兵資料》，共20冊，包含500種小報，其中大多數是第一次複印出現。其特點有：第一，有87種是人民解放軍各單位以及其他軍事機構出版；第二，有36種整套無缺期，如《新北大》、《井岡山》、《東方紅》，有4種近於完整，如《鐵道紅旗》。強調這點並不為過，因為完整無缺期的期刊對研究總是有利，像紅衛兵小報這樣稀有的出版品能夠求得完整更為難得。相信在中國也難得有這麼多完整無缺的紅衛兵小報；第三，此部資料複印品質良好，幾乎是原件的翻版。

這部資料的出版是CCRM繼續提供給學術界研究20世紀中國重要又難得的資料的極好例證。自1968年成立30年來CCRM為學術界提供這種優異的不可或缺的服務。紅衛兵資料系列的出版僅是其比較大的複製工程之一。其巨大性質足以說明為什麼沒有一個研究圖書館可以提供像CCRM提供的這種服務，也證明CCRM的服務對學術界是如何地重要。就是在我們慶祝這部資料的出版時，CCRM已經開始複製最新獲得的類似資料。因為資料的分量太多，預計2001年出版時估計有40冊。其時，CCRM提供給學術界紅衛兵資料數量之多將可以和中國任何一個包括北京的國家圖書館的公共圖書館相比。在此必須說明的是各省的紅衛兵出版品非常難得，CCRM複製了一些，但是還有許多有待發掘。其實，至今尚未有對政府機關，黨史館乃至個人收藏這類地方出版物以及其數量的調查。希望有一天也有大批紅衛兵地方出版品可供研究。毫無疑問，那時候CCRM將會盡其所能將那些資料複製提供給學術界。我向CCRM在現代和當代中國研究上做出的貢獻，以及繼續做出的貢獻致敬。我也要向前故主任余秉權和現任主任亓冰峰的奉獻精神和努力不懈致敬。這個領域的研究者都得向他們感恩。

吳文津

1999年2月

（胡嘉陽譯）

Yuan Zhou, *A New Collection of Red Guard Publications, Part I, Newspapers*.
Oakton, VA: Center for Chinese Research Materials, 1999. 20 v. (Preface)

In the United States collecting research materials on the People's Republic of China has always been a challenge. For three decades after the founding of the People's Republic in 1949, the Chinese government did not allow direct purchase of Chinese-language publications from China by American libraries. Book exchange was possible only with one library, namely, the National Library of Beijing (now the National Library of China). Book orders had to be placed with vendors in Hong Kong and Tokyo, and no subscriptions were accepted to any local newspapers. The offerings of the vendors, however, were selective and contained far less than what was listed in the national bibliographies: the *Quanguo xin shumu* and the *Quanguo zong shumu*. Indeed, even these two bibliographies were not available for foreign subscription. Copies of them smuggled out of China were reprinted by enterprising book dealers in Hong Kong and Tokyo and sold for a good price. The situation was tolerable as long as the supply of publications allowed by the Chinese government continued to flow to Hong Kong and Tokyo. But that flow was interrupted from time to time mainly by political upheavals in China which adversely affected the normal workings of the publishing industry. The worst interruption came with the Cultural Revolution in 1966.

Soon after the start of the Cultural Revolution, normal publishing in China was supplanted by the issuing of millions of copies of the Quotations of Chairman Mao and the Selected Works of Mao Zedong, and the vendors in Hong Kong and Tokyo had little else to offer. So when reprints of a number of Red Guard tabloids (*xiaobao*) began to appear in Hong Kong, they became instant best sellers. This was not only because there was a book drought, but also, and more importantly, it was because the tabloids turned out to be extremely valuable research sources.

Some of these publications are highly polemical, to be sure, but most contain a great deal of valuable information not available elsewhere. Such information includes directives from all levels of the party and speeches by party leaders, with a good many by Mao Zedong, all from this period; "negative materials," containing unpublished personal biographical information on those being purged; documents on party history; and "news flashes" on people and current events. The rarity and importance of these new sources made them the must-have items on everyone's list overnight, and libraries competed with one another to acquire them. However, the number of the *xiaobao* available in Hong Kong was limited, and the already high price charged for them was rising even higher because of the heavy demand. (American libraries were not the only ones competing for these publications; libraries from around the world were in Hong Kong buying them.) It was not long before the scholarly community decided that other avenues must be found in order to gain access to more of these Red Guard tabloids and to make them available for research at less cost. Consequently, the Joint Committee on Contemporary China (JCCC) (Chairman: John M. H. Lindbeck) of the American Council of Learned Societies and the Social Science Research Council was asked for help. JCCC in turn approached the U.S. Department of State and asked the Department to consider sharing its collection of Red Guard materials with the academic community. The State Department responded in the affirmative, and asked JCCC to send a representative to Washington, D.C. to examine the materials and determine whether their release would indeed be as helpful to the academic community as believed. The JCCC delegated me for this mission, and I went to the External Research Division of the State Department and looked over a representative sample of the materials they provided me. I was elated. What 1 saw were not only Red Guard tabloids, but also a number of other important sources, such as the mimeographed minutes of midnight meetings between Red Guard representatives and high government officials including Zhou Enlai. I reported my findings to both the State Department and JCCC, and strongly urged the early release of the materials. But the mechanics of distribution had to be worked out first. The time was the summer of 1967.

At that time preparatory work for the establishment of the Center for Chinese Research Materials（CCRM）was in the final stage, and all agreed that CCRM, a not-for-profit organization designed to provide important but difficult-to-obtain research materials on 20th-century China to the scholarly community, should be the channel for the distribution of the State Department releases. But CCRM was a year away from being operational and the scholarly community was anxious to have early access to the State Department's releases. As an interim measure the Harvard-Yenching Library was asked, and it agreed, to assume temporary responsibility for distribution. In May 1968 CCRM was officially established, under the Association of Research Libraries（ARL）in Washington, D.C., with funding from the Ford Foundation secured by JCCC. P. K. Yu, formerly Lecturer in the History Department of the University of Hong Kong, was appointed director. The State Department releases were then sent directly to CCRM, and the Harvard-Yenching Library also turned over to CCRM the microfilm of the releases it had previously received from the State Department. In the years immediately following, CCRM acquired additional Red Guard publications from other sources. And In 1975 it reproduced all such materials acquired up to that time in a 19-volume set entitled Red Guard Publications, containing almost 1,000 titles, mostly *xiaobao* and the rest being periodicals and other miscellaneous items. An additional volume, comprising a grand table of contents of the 19-volume set, was issued in 1975, thus making this first series a total of 20 volumes. The reception of this publication by the scholarly community was highly favorable, and in 1980 CCRM published Red Guard Publications: Supplement I and in 1992 *Red Guard Publications: Supplement II*, each in eight volumes, containing 76 and 70 titles respectively. These three series thus make up a collection of more than 1,100 titles, making it the largest single such collection in the West at that time.

Now the scholarly community is presented with yet another set of Red Guard materials by CCRM: *A New Collection of Red Guard Publications*. The present set, in 20 volumes, comprises nearly 500 titles of *xiaobao*, the vast majority of which are reproduced here for the first time. There are several features in this collection that are worth noting. First, 87 titles are published by various units within the People's Liberation Army as well as by other military agencies. Second, 36 titles in this collection are represented by complete runs, such as *Xin Beida*, *Jinggangshan*, and *Dong fang hong*, and four by substantial runs, such as *Tiedao hongqi*. The significance of this cannot be overemphasized. Although complete runs of serial publications are always valued in research, the rarity of the publications in this case makes their complete runs even more valuable, as it is not often one has access to such a significant number of complete files of Red Guard tabloids, even in China. Third, the quality of reproduction of the present set is excellent, as the pages are reproduced entirely from original copies

This publication is an excellent illustration of CCRM's continuing efforts in providing the scholarly community with important but hard-to-obtain research materials on 20th-century China. For the past thirty years since its founding in 1968 CCRM has performed his indispensable service with great distinction, the Red Guard series being one of the larger reproduction projects it has undertaken. The sheer volume of the Red Guard publications project alone explains why no research library can perform the kind of service CCRM offers and how essential CCRM's services are to scholarship. Even as we celebrate the publication of the present collection of Red Guard materials, CCRM has already begun work on further reproduction of similar materials it has acquired very recently. The volume of these new acquisitions is so large that it is estimated that they will fill another 40 volumes, to be published probably in the year 2001. When that happens,

CCRM would have provided the scholarly community with as many Red Guard publications as may be available in any such public library collection in China, including the National Library of China in Beijing. It must be mentioned in this connection, however. Red Guard publications from the provinces have been extremely difficult to obtain. CCRM has reproduced some, but many more remain to be discovered. Indeed, no survey has been conducted on the number and type of such local Red Guard publications that may have been preserved by government agencies, Party archives, and individuals in China. It is hoped that somebody the bulk of these local publications too may become available for research. There is no doubt that when and if they do CCRM will be there to do what it does best — to have them reproduced for the benefit of scholarship. For all that CCRM contributed and is continuing to contribute to modern and contemporary China studies, I salute the dedication and indefatigable efforts of its former director, the late P. K. Yu, and its current director, Pingfeng Chi. The field owes them a deep debt of gratitude.

Eugene W. Wu
February 1999

沈津著，《美國哈佛大學哈佛燕京圖書館中文善本書志》，上海：上海辭書出版社，1999。927頁（哈佛燕京圖書館書目叢刊第7種）（序）

　　美國哈佛大學創立於1636年（明崇禎九年），為英屬美洲殖民地之首間高等學府，如今為世界上最重要大學之一。360餘年來，其圖書館藏書總量巳達1,300萬冊以上，其他如檔案、報刊、縮微製品、照片、光碟等亦無計其數。收藏範圍及數量、品質均居美國各大學圖書館之首，並可與大英圖書館、法國國家圖書館及美國國會圖書館相比美。中文書籍之設置始於1879年（清光緒五年），其時哈佛大學設立中文講座，延聘歟人戈鯤化氏來校講學，遂有採購中文圖書之舉，然數量甚少。1928年，哈佛燕京學社成立，在哈佛大學設立「漢和圖書館」，始進行有系統之收集工作，然範圍大都限於有關傳統漢學之中、日文書刊。二次世界大戰後，哈佛大學增設有關近現代東亞之課程，為適應此需要，中、日、韓文社會科學資料之收集亦隨而擴張。1965年改稱「哈佛燕京圖書館」；1976年由哈佛燕京學社轉屬哈佛大學圖書館系統。

　　70年來，哈佛燕京圖書館藏書近90萬冊，新舊期刊14,000餘種，報紙近700種，縮微製品6萬餘件，復有照片、名人檔案及電子資料之收集。館藏數量居歐美各大學東亞圖書館之冠。創館初期，館長裘開明（闓輝）先生，致力於漢學典籍之蒐集，並得北平燕京大學洪業（煨蓮）教授及該校圖書館顧廷龍（起潛）先生之助，在北平書肆代為選購中國古籍經年，中頗多善本。闓輝先生復在各地徵購，致使館藏日豐。太平洋戰爭結束後，中文善本屢見於日本坊肆，闓輝先生託人代購，頗有所獲。旋由日本書商直接郵購者，亦復不少。館藏中文善本遂蔚為大觀，現藏中文善本4,000餘部，始於南宋，迄至清代，均闓輝先生之功績也。

　　昔羅振玉氏，嘗以哈佛燕京藏書之富，贈以「擁書權拜小諸侯」句，葉恭綽氏則推為「海外嬋媛」，皆美譽也。然館藏豐富，外界並不知其詳，闓輝先生任內，時以出版館藏中文善本目錄為念。余接任後，曾編印館藏中、日文書籍目錄，中文部分亦包括善本，然終有未加提要為憾。思之中國古籍目錄之學，肇自西漢，先有劉向《別錄》，後有劉歆《七略》，條流派別，兼具解題。班固《漢書‧藝文志》也因二劉提要鉤玄之功而成。宋晁公武《郡齋讀書志》、陳振孫《直齋書錄解題》，皆為私家藏書目錄傳於今而最有影響者。而錢遵王《讀書敏求記》，略述圖書源流，踵事增華，例益加密。至於考作者之仕履，釋撰人之宗旨，則《四庫全書總目提要》實採古今之大成。1980年代，又有王重民《中國善本書提要》之出版，極具重要之參考價值。如若館藏珍本皆有解題，於讀者當更有裨益。

　　1991年，余在香港中文大學重遇前上海圖書館研究館員沈津君，談及編纂本館中文善本書志，並邀其來美擔任此項工作。沈君慨允。沈君早年從顧起潛先生習流略之學，曾主掌上圖特藏部工作，熟於古籍文獻。翌年沈君抵館，孜孜不倦，廢寢忘食，兩年內撰就館藏自南宋至明末之刻本書志，凡1,433種，計百萬餘字。舉凡書名卷冊、版式行款、全書要旨、著者生平、特點源流、題跋牌記、刻工書鋪、遞藏鈐印以及海內外收藏館名，均有載記。以經史子集叢五部排列，並附分類書名目錄及書名、著者、刻工、出版者（刻書鋪）之索引。其精細前所未見，館藏宋、元、明善本可藉此窺其全貌，研版本學者亦能得以勘校版本異同而藉資考鏡。闇輝先生之遺願，於此得償，實幸事也。本冊定為上編，館藏清初善本2,000餘種，並稿本、抄本數百種之書志將入下編。

　　本書志之編纂出版，多蒙哈佛燕京學社資助。對前社長韓南（Patrick D. Hanan）教授及現任社長杜維明教授之鼎力支持，特致謝忱。上海辭書出版社社長李偉國先生及該社編輯部同仁對本書出版事宜悉盡心力，亦統此申謝。本書即將問世，爰綴數語，尚祈方家指正。

吳文津

識於哈佛大學哈佛燕京圖書館

1997年11月

本文曾蒙當時哈佛燕京圖書館特藏部主任沈津先生指正，特此致謝忱。

沈寧著，《嗩吶煙塵》，台北：聯經出版公司，2002。2冊（序）

序一：那一代的故事

　　香港《明報月刊》1999年1月號和2月號連續登載了沈寧的兩篇文章：〈為了不能忘卻的過去〉和〈無法癒合的心靈創傷〉。這兩篇都是回憶和紀念性的寫作，簡單地敘述了他父母（特別是他的母親）、弟妹和他自己，生活在中國共產統治下的一些悲哀的遭遇。這兩篇文章對我有很大的吸引力。因為沈寧的父母——沈蘇儒、陶琴薰——是我在重慶中央大學外文系的同班同學；他的外公陶希聖先生是我所敬佩的長輩學者，也曾相識；沈寧本人我在文革後不久去西安時也曾見過。讀完這兩篇文章，我有很多感慨，久久不能釋然。蘇儒和他的家人在大陸的情形，我以前略有所聞，但並不知其詳。沈寧這兩篇文章才填補了很多空白，特別是琴薰在文革中，她去世前所受的苦難，也讓我深深地體會到沈寧和他的弟妹們對他們母親的無法替代的愛。

　　在這兩篇文章發表不久後，沈寧給我來信，說他已完成為他母親寫的傳記上部。從他母親出生到1949年獨留上海這一段時間，大約有四五十萬字。下部打算從共產黨進入上海到1978年他母親受迫害而死為止。他問我是否能抽空看看他的稿子。我答應了。收到稿子後，我詳細地看了一遍。沒有想到，除了琴薰的身世資料外，還有很多關於陶希聖先生的敘述，這些都是很珍貴的歷史史料。我給沈寧提供了一些意見。後來又把這篇稿子介紹給台北《聯合報》副董事長劉昌平兄，蒙他們在《聯合報》副刊（題名《嗩吶煙塵》）和美國《世界日報》（題名《陶盛樓記》）連載，現又蒙聯經出版公司發行人劉國瑞兄鼎力支持出書。琴薰坎坷多難的一生藉以公諸於世，非為頌其德，乃為其時代作一見證耳。

　　這本書所記載的事都是屬實。沈寧為了要強化他母親為人女、為人妻，和為人母的情懷，在史實上又加上些創作和想像，用了許多細節來描述補充。所以此書可以說是一本傳記小說。雖然如此，它仍有它的歷史價值。20

世紀上半期，中國經歷了不少的動亂和變遷，琴薰正在這個時期成長，她的經歷多多少少也反映出這個時期中國社會政治的背景，此其一。再者，琴薰和陶希聖先生的父女關係極為親密。書中關於這一點的敘述，引用了希聖先生給琴薰的手書，包括抗戰時期的。這些都是中國近代史上極珍貴的第一手史料，無法在旁的地方看到的。所以，我認為這本書不但是陶琴薰的傳記，也可以說是陶希聖先生的別傳；不但是陶琴薰一個人的經歷，也可以當作她的同輩人的經歷。

1998年，沈寧和他的弟妹（沈熙和沈燕）編輯了一本紀念琴薰逝世二十周年，用來贈送親友，題名為《懷念》的書。在書的〈前言〉裡有幾句話，我轉錄於下，或可以用來描述沈寧這本書的旨趣：

「我們謹以這本小書紀念媽媽，也紀念無數與媽媽同時代，受盡苦難的中國人。我們但願我們的後代不再經歷這種苦難，也不必再書寫如這本小書中所書寫的那種浸淚的文字。」

2001 年 7 月於加州門羅公園

沈寧著，《百世門風──歷史變革中的沈陶家族》，北京：中國青年出版社，2005。284頁（序）

　　家譜或稱族譜或宗譜始於宋代，為記一姓世系及其代表人物事蹟的譜籍，不時修輯，以示後裔，是一種重要的史籍。沈寧這本《百世門風》，雖有些地方採用家譜的格式，但不是傳統的家譜，也不是純粹沈氏的家譜，而是根據沈氏家譜及沈氏近親數種家譜合編，用以表彰以沈氏為主之各家歷代重要人物之事蹟。但本書的宗旨恐不止於此。我想同等重要的是作者借歷代沈氏及其近親之建樹，來闡明珍惜家庭傳統和文化傳統的重要性。沈寧認為，表現在「威武不能屈，富貴不能淫，貧賤不能移」的中國人文傳統精神「只能來自家族歷史的深層積累，代代承傳的家教傳統，潛移默化的文化影響」，如果「沒有深遠的家族傳統，缺乏強固的文化根基，就如浮萍飄葉，東風強了跟東風，西風烈了隨西風」。他的看法在當今社會是具有很大的啟發性的。因之，《百世門風》除了為沈家後世講解沈氏祖宗的豐功偉績和書香世家的家庭傳統外，也是一部醒世良言。

　　這本書還有另外一種教育意義，特別是對一般對中國歷史不十分熟悉的青年人。比如說，書中對中國歷史上的改朝換代通過沈氏祖宗的事蹟都有簡要的敘述，其他如清朝的科舉制度和職官銜名、戊戌變法、民國初年的中國政治環境、北洋軍閥時代等都有相當詳盡的說明。同時，對在中國近代史上具有影響的一些政治和軍事代表人物，如康有為、梁啟超、袁世凱、張勳、于右任、張季鸞、褚輔成、沈鈞儒、陶希聖、萬耀煌等也有扼要的介紹。所以，這本書也有它的參考價值的。

　　書的內容顯示了作者嚴謹的寫作態度。他除熟讀了沈氏、陶氏、褚氏及萬氏的家譜外，還參考了大批有關的資料和他自己訪問的口述紀錄。沈氏浙江紹興的老家、陶氏湖北黃岡的老家他也曾親自走訪，以存敘述的真實性。這種治學的態度是值得青年人學習的。作者尊先賢往聖的精神以及他對文化復興的呼籲，也值得我們深思反省。

2005年10月於美國加州門羅公園

五、

當代中國研究及
研究資料問題

當代中國研究在美國的資料問題

　　什麼是當代中國，在美國，一般的定義就是 1949 年中共執政以後的中國大陸。當代中國研究就是 1949 年以後的中國大陸研究，包括中國共產黨黨史的研究。今天我要講的是下面幾個問題：美國圖書館如何收集當代中國研究的資料？有什麼樣的成就？在收集當中有些什麼困難？

　　從 1949 年末期到 1970 年末期這 30 年間，因為美國和中國沒有外交關係，中國政府不准許美國圖書館向中國大陸直接採購，所以，美國圖書館收集的中國大陸出版物都是從中國大陸以外，主要是香港和日本，間接而來。在那一段時間，採購大陸出版書籍的工作非常艱巨。但是，經過不斷的努力和各方的協助，美國圖書館還是有相當大的成就。這個過程，我在下面會有詳細的敘述。首先，我們要講美國圖書館收集中共黨史和其他有關資料的歷程，因為這是 1949 年以前就開始的事。

　　中共黨史原始資料的收集始於胡佛研究院（Hoover Institution）。前天我已經講過，胡佛研究院 1948 年正式成立中文部以後曾經先後入藏「伊羅生特藏」（Issacs Collection）和「尼姆・威爾斯特藏」（Nym Wales Collection），其中有許多從 1920 年代末期到 1930 年代中期有關中共黨史的原始資料，大部分都是地下出版物。後來又從陳誠副總統處用縮微卷複印來 1931-1934 年江西蘇維埃共和國的檔案，通稱「陳誠特藏」（Chen Cheng Collection）。因此，中國共產黨 1921 年建黨後十餘年間的許多第一手的黨史資料第一次在美國出現，給研究中共黨史的學者提供了不少的方便（詳情可參照我的講稿〈美國東亞圖書館蒐藏中國典籍之緣起與現況〉）。

　　1937-1945 八年抗戰期間，國共合作，中共的出版物可以公開發行，但是為數不多。其中最重要的是先後在漢口、重慶發行的中共機關報──《新華日報》。當時美國的東亞圖書館只有部分的收藏。

抗戰勝利（1945）到中華人民共和國成立（1949）這一段期間，中共和它的外圍組織有好些出版物，例如，在延安出版的《解放日報》（1941-1947）、《解放》週刊（1931-1947）、《群眾》（1938-1947）、剛才提到的在重慶出版的《新華日報》（1938-1947），和其他中共控制的「邊區」（晉察冀、陝甘寧、晉冀魯豫、晉綏、豫鄂等）的出版物。這些資料美國的東亞圖書館當時也有些收藏，其中胡佛研究院由芮沃壽夫人（Mrs. Arthur Wright, Mary Wright 芮瑪麗）第二次世界大戰後在中國收集的最多。它們的內容，可以參照前天我提到的薛君度教授根據胡佛研究院收藏所編輯的關於中國共產黨運動的兩冊書目：《中國共產主義運動：胡佛戰爭、革命與和平研究院中文圖書館藏中國文獻選輯解題書目》（*The Chinese Communist Movement: An Annotated Bibliography of Selected Materials in the Chinese Collection of the Hoover Institution on War, Revolution, and Peace*），上冊包括1921-1937年，下冊1937-1949年。

從1949年末期到1970年代末期，如我剛才所講，在美國收集大陸的資料是一個非常困難的時期。不但我們不能直接向大陸採購，我們甚至於不知道他們有些什麼樣的出版物。因為當時他們每月出版的《全國新書目》，還有每年出版的《全國總書目》，都禁止出口。除零星的走私到香港的一些外，我們都無法窺其全貌。在報刊方面，除了一些全國性的出版物，如《人民日報》、《光明日報》、《歷史研究》、《經濟研究》等外，任何地方報紙和許多刊物，我們也都不能訂閱。雖然我們在香港和日本可以買到大陸准許出口的書刊，但是，它們的供應因為受到大陸政治和經濟的影響，以致時有漲落。在1959-1961年鬧全國大饑荒的時期和文化大革命時期（1966-1976），因為原料缺乏，社會不安，出版物均有大量的下降，以致到出版業差不多全部癱瘓的程度。因此，自然影響到出口的數量。根據《中國出版年鑑》，1958年出書的總數為45,459種，期刊822種，報紙491種。三年後，人民公社和大躍進失敗以後，1961年出版書的總數降到13,529種，期刊降到410種，報紙下降到221種。和1958年比較，書籍下降70%，期刊50%，報紙

47%。在1967年，文化大革命開始的第二年，生產更繼續的下降，當年出版的書籍僅有2,925種，期刊27種，報紙47種。假如把這些數字和1961年出版的統計來比較，書籍下降是78%，期刊下降93%，報紙下降83%。如果跟1958年比，那就更不能比了。這說明了當時中國政治、經濟影響到出版業的程度，和在海外收集大陸資料的困難。

當時，除採購以外，還能和北京圖書館交換（北圖是當時中國政府指定可以作國際交換的唯一圖書館）。但是，因為他們提供作為交換的出版物，都是可以從香港或日本買到的，所以對我們並無特別的好處。同時，在1950年代到1960年代這個時期，他們提供給美國圖書館交換的書刊，在種類和數量方面，都遠不如當時他們給蘇聯和東歐國家的，這是我1964年到蘇聯、東德、波蘭、捷克所發現的。

雖然有上面所講的這些困難，美國的東亞圖書館從各種不同的管道，在1950到1970年代間也收集了一批數量相當大的大陸出版物。這些資料的來源，除在香港和日本購買的以外，還有來自香港、台灣和日本的研究機構以及美國政府。

在香港方面，友聯研究所（Union Research Institute）是一個重要的資料來源。該所1949年後在香港成立，專門研究中國大陸問題。因為他們近水樓台，收集大陸的資料比較容易，所以他們收到一些旁人沒有辦法收到的大陸出版物。特別是報刊，他們剪貼分類，建立了一個很大的資料庫，成為當時西方研究當代中國的學者必經之地。因為當時外國研究大陸的學者，特別是美國學者，無法去大陸查詢資料或進行研究工作。後來，友聯把這些剪報作成2,000多卷的縮微卷，美國密西根大學的亞洲圖書館有收藏全部。友聯研究所1980年代解散後，這批剪報的原件轉讓香港浸會大學（Hong Kong Baptist University）圖書館。

友聯研究所當年也出版兩種期刊，對研究大陸問題非常有用，一種是《友聯研究服務》（*Union Research Service*），每年平均出9期，每期載有從大陸報紙或期刊選出來資料的英文翻譯；另一種是《友聯研究服務》的副刊，《人物傳記資料》（*Biographical Service*），每期載有一名或兩名中共中、高級幹部的傳略，這些傳略對於不見經傳的領導幹部有特別的參考價值。除此之外，友聯研究所也不時得到一些甚至於在大陸都不是公開發行的資料。這些，友聯也供應給研究者使用。並且，友聯下屬的友聯出版社，根據這些資料也出版了一些資料專輯，諸如《劉少奇選集》、《彭德懷案件專輯》、《中共中央委員會文件──1956年9月–1969年4月》、《紅衛兵資料目錄》、《中國大陸佛教資料彙編》等。這些當時都是很重要的參考資料。

在這個時期，台灣從自己的管道，也得到很多非常罕見的中共文件。其中最聞名的就是《連江文件》和《五七一工程紀要》。《連江文件》是台灣蛙人突擊隊在1964年突擊福建連江縣所獲得的一批文獻，其中包括1962到1963年間一些政府重要的指示、生產計畫和當時所謂「社會主義教育」的文件。《五七一工程紀要》是1971林彪計畫反毛澤東的行動計畫大綱，「五七一」是「武起義」的諧音。當時台灣在發表這個文件以後，很多人都不太相信，以為是台灣假造的。因為這個計畫看起來很幼稚，用的文字也很粗淺。假如林彪要用武起義來反毛澤東，而用這種好像小學生寫的一樣的計畫，可信的程度實在是太低。但是，最後林彪逃亡，飛機失事，死在外蒙古後，大陸證實這個文件是林彪造反的罪狀，大家才相信這個文件的真實性。

另外，台灣在相當長的一段時間裡，又發表了很多台北方面所得到的中共中央文件。這些資料經常在《問題與研究》和《中共年報》上登載，並且又有英文的翻譯在 Issues and Studies（《問題與研究》的英文版）上發表。除此之外，台灣也出版了一些資料選輯，諸如《劉少奇問題資料專輯》、《共匪文化大革命重要文件彙編》、《王洪文、張春橋、江青、姚文元反黨集團罪證》等。還有大批從1970年代末期到1980年代初期的大字報和地下刊物，彙集成為《大陸地下刊物彙編》，共20冊，以及六四天安門大量的民運文獻，包括大字報、傳單和其他有關文件，當年（1989）出版，名為《火與血之真相：中國大陸民主運動紀實》，共四、五千頁，是收集六四文獻最多的一個專輯。再有，就是在文革時期紅衛兵印行，台灣再行翻印的《毛澤東思想萬歲》數冊。這些都是紅衛兵在1967到1969年間從各處抄出來的毛澤東1950年代末期和1960年代初期的講演原稿。這些原稿非常重要，因為後來《毛澤東選集》所收的毛澤東講演稿都是經過修正，有些跟原來毫不相同的。有鑑於此，哈佛大學兩位教授和我三個人從這些資料裡選出19篇毛澤東從「百花齊放」時期（1956-1957）到「大躍進」時期（1958-1960）有關鍵性，而與後來官方印行的有差異的講演稿原稿，翻譯成英文，名為《從百花齊放至大躍進期間毛主席的秘密講話》（*The Secret Speeches of Chairman Mao: From the Hundred Flowers to the Great Leap Forward*），哈佛大學出版部1989年出版。中文的原件由華盛頓中國研究資料中心（Center for Chinese Research Materials）複印發行。

　　上面所講的都是從台灣而來的關於1949年以後的資料。其實，台灣也有很多關於1949年以前中共黨史的資料和1920年代國共合作的檔案。這些檔案和資料分別收藏在國民黨黨史委員會、司法行政部調查局和國防部軍事情報局。黨史會收藏的檔案包括關於民國十三年國民黨改組，孫中山先生開始聯俄容共，以至北伐完成後國民黨清共，在南京成立國民政府那一段時期。黨史會的檔案由中央研究院近史所在1968至1969年間出版了一共11大冊的目錄，名為《中國近代史資料調查目錄》，其中第三冊列出該會所藏1924到1936年的全部檔案的細目。

　　調查局的圖書館藏書十餘萬冊，還有大量的檔案，其中包括有相當數量的中國共產黨1949前的原始資料，是台灣收藏這一類文件最多的圖書館。這些資料包括中共各個領導階層──中共中央、省縣市鎮、各級支部──和他們外圍組織的各式文件，其中有內部通訊、他們出版的期刊、標語、傳單等。密西根大學三個研究生──彼得‧多諾萬（Peter Donovan）、卡爾‧多利斯（Carl E. Dorris）、勞倫斯‧沙利文（Lawrence R. Sullivan）──曾經使用過調查局的資料，而且在1976年出了一本小冊子，名為《台灣調查局藏中共資料》（*Chinese Communist Materials at the Bureau of Investigation, Taiwan*）共105頁，可作參考。日本東京書商雄松堂，曾得調查局的許可，從這些資料中選出四百多件，大部分是關於抗戰時期的文件，攝製成20多卷縮微卷，名為《有關中國共產黨資料》公開發行。國防部軍事情報局收藏的中共的原始文件不多，約一千多種左右，很多都是從山東來的。1960年代該局在台灣國際關係研究所召開的第一屆「中美中國大陸問題研討會」時，曾出版一本目錄，名為《共匪二十年代至五十年代原始文件與書刊》，供出席該會的學者專家參考。上面提到的多諾萬、多利斯、沙利文合編關於調查局的藏書目錄中，對情報局的收藏也有簡略的介紹。

在日本方面，剛剛我已講到，在1970年代末期以前，東京是我們採購大陸書刊除了香港以外的第二個地方。當時，東京的神田區是購買大陸出版物最好的地方，其中有三家書店最為有名：大安、極東和內山。內山書店是魯迅先生的日本好友內山丸造創辦，後來由他的兒子經管。這三家常有一些在香港買不到的書刊，所以，它們是很好的採購來源。除了這些書商以外，還有一些日本的研究所，如日本國際經濟研究所，他們也有從大陸來的獨特的資料，可以供應複印本。同時，東洋文庫和日本國會圖書館的資料也可以公開。但是，我想日本方面對當代中國研究最大的貢獻還不是這些書籍的來源，而是竹內實教授所編撰的《毛澤東集》。此書1970至1972年出第一版，10冊；1983年修訂，仍10冊；1983到1985年又出《補卷》9冊；1986年出《別卷》1冊，總共20冊。這部書為什麼如此重要？因為竹內實教授花了多年的工夫，收集了非常零星而又分散的毛澤東1949年以前的著作、講演、通信等，並且把它們和1951年中共官方出版的《毛澤東選集》對照，指出它們不同的地方，並加以注釋。因為這項工作的浩大，和它的研究價值，美國一位世界著名研究毛澤東的Stuart R. Schram教授（大陸譯他的名字為施拉姆）在一個書評上說：「這部書在很多年後，對所有研究1949以前毛澤東言行著作的人，還會是一部不可或缺的標準著作」（譯文）。

美國政府對當代中國研究在資料方面也有特別的貢獻。美國駐香港總領事館，從1950年開始作了很多大陸資料的翻譯工作，除供政府的參考外，並供應大學及其他研究機構使用。主要的有下列幾種：

1. 《中國大陸報紙一覽》（*Survey of China Mainland Press*），日刊。1950年11月1日創刊。每期30到50頁，選自大陸主要的報紙報導、社論、新華社發的新聞稿之類。

2.《中國大陸雜誌選輯》（*Selections from China Mainland Magazines*），週刊，1955年8月1日創刊。每期30到40頁，選譯各種雜誌有關當時問題的文章五、六篇。

3.《時事背景》（*Current Background*），週刊，1950年6月創刊。每期有一專題，10至20頁，分析各種報章雜誌的報導。

美國政府提供學術界的翻譯的資料還有另外幾種。一種是聯合出版研究服務處（Joint Publications Research Service，簡稱JPRS）編譯的資料。1957年開始，JPRS的目的是為美國聯邦政府各部會提供世界性的資料翻譯工作。這些翻譯後來也供應學術界使用。翻譯關於中國大陸的資料來自大陸本身、日本、蘇聯和其他的國家。關於中國的翻譯有下列幾種：

1.《中共文摘》（*Communist China Digest*）

2.《有關中共農業、畜牧業、原料資料》（*Translations on Communist China's Agriculture, Animal Husbandry, and Materials*）

3.《有關中共工業、礦業、燃料、電力資料》（*Translations on Communist China's Industry, Mining, Fuels and Power*）

4.《有關中共貿易、財政、運輸、交通資料》（*Translations on Communist China's Trade, Finance, Transportation and Communication*）

5.《有關中共科技資料》（*Translations on Communist China's Science and Technology*）

美國政府也提供大陸的地方廣播為學術界使用。這些廣播可以補香港總領事館翻譯的不足，因為它的地區範圍很廣，同時它的資料也比較即時。除這些翻譯的資料以外，美國政府也前後轉移了一些重要的報刊給國會圖書館，以供學術界研究之用。在1960年代，國務院轉移給國會圖書館從1949年到1960年的中國地方報紙，共1,200種。雖然這些資料非常零星，很多只有一期兩期的，但是，在當時美國圖書館根本無法收集任何中國地方報紙的時候，就是這些零星的資料也覺得非常寶貴。特別是，因為在它們當中有很多是省級以下的報紙，它們的重要性也就不難想像到了。這批報紙後來都登錄在黃漢柱（Han-chu Huang）和任學勤（Hseo-chin Jen）合編的《國會圖書館藏中文報刊目錄》（*Chinese Newspapers in the Library of Congress*）（國會圖書館，1985）。

　　1963年國務院又移交了一種更重要的資料給國會圖書館。這個資料就是中國人民解放軍總政治部出版的《工作通訊》。是人民解放軍內部的一種機密刊物，只分發到團級以上的幹部。其中如有涉及到極機密的資料的時候，就只分發到師級以上的幹部，可見其機密的程度。國務院轉移給國會圖書館的共29期，出版的時間是1961年1月1日到當年的8月26日，缺第9期。據揣測，很可能是這一期載有極機密的資料的緣故。這份資料不但是極為罕見的大陸軍方的內部刊物，同時也可以幫助我們了解一些當時大陸鬧全國大饑荒的狀況。因為大陸新聞封鎖，當時饑荒的情形外面只是略知其皮毛。從《工作通訊》裡可以看到較多的報導，以及解放軍內士氣低落的問題。這批資料公開以後，受到研究當代中國學術界的普遍歡迎。最後，胡佛研究院把全部29期翻譯成英文，由鄭喆希（J. Chester Cheng）教授主編，名為《中國紅軍的政治：人民解放軍「工作通訊」的翻譯本》（*The Politics of the Chinese Red Army: A Translation of the Bulletin of Activities of the People's Liberation Army*），1966年胡佛研究院出版。出版後，很受學術界的重視，研究中共軍事問題的專家前後在知名的學報如《中國季刊》（*China Quarterly*）、《亞洲調查》（*Asian Survey*）均作了詳盡介紹和分析。

　　上面我已提到，文化大革命開始以後，大陸正常的出版業務受到空前的干預，可以說是到了完全停頓的狀態。當時除了《毛澤東選集》、《毛澤東語錄》之外，差不多沒有任何另外的出版物。正在那個時候，香港複印了一批從大陸走私出來的紅衛兵小報，如《東方紅》、《新北大》、《井崗山》之類。雖然這些小報登載的，有些都是「反動有理」之類的煽動性的文章，但是也有很多在旁的地方看不見的資料，諸如中共中央各級的訓令、首長的指示，特別是毛澤東的「最高指示」，還有當時被清算的人的「反面教材」，包括甚至於鄧小平、劉少奇、葉劍英這些中共領導。這些「反面教材」，主要是鮮有人知的關於這些人過去的一些言行、歷史，紅衛兵從很多地方抄來，作為鬥爭他們的罪狀的。這些小報還經常登載「號外新聞」，其中有各地的消息和紅衛兵的動態。因為這些內容，加上當時沒有其他的書刊可以購買的情形下，歐美和日本的圖書館都在香港搶購這些小報，於是洛陽紙貴，一份本來只要美金5元的，漲到25元，複印商還供不應求。造成了一種非常不正常的現象。

在這種情況之下，美國研究當代中國的學術界，一致認為開發這些資料另外來源是迫不及待的任務。希望一方面能夠收集得更多一些，同時也希望能夠減輕採購的成本，於是就求助於「當代中國聯合委員會」（Joint Committee on Contemporary China，簡稱JCCC）。這個委員會是由各校遴選研究當代中國的學者組成，其目的在促進美國關於當代中國的教學與研究，隸屬於美國學術團體委員會（American Council of Learned Societies）及社會科學研究理事會（Social Science Research Council），故稱為「聯合委員會」。經費主要來源是福特基金會（Ford Foundation）。JCCC一向對研究資料的收集非常關心，於是向美國國務院說項，呼籲他們公開政府所收集的紅衛兵資料，與學術界共用。國務院的反應很肯定，認為原則上可行，但是希望「聯合委員會」有人先去看看這些資料，再決定是否它們的公開真正有益於當代中國研究。「聯合委員會」邀我擔任這個任務。1967年夏，我赴國務院閱讀了一批他們選出來具有代表性的資料。閱讀後，我喜出望外，因為我所見到的不只是紅衛兵小報，而且還有許多其他的資料，諸如當時油印的中共首長像周恩來等在凌晨接見紅衛兵代表的談話紀錄等。之後，我建議國務院把這些資料全部公開，而且愈早愈好。國務院同意以後，如何複製發行這些資料又是一個問題。當時，「中國研究資料中心」（Center for Chinese Research Materials）正在籌建中，咸以為這個中心應該是最理想來負責辦理這件事的機構。但是，當時離開中心建立的時間還有一年，學術界欲先睹為快，於是要求哈佛燕京圖書館暫時代勞。哈佛燕京圖書館收到國務院最初的幾批資料後，把它們作為縮微卷，以成本計向各東亞圖書館發行。這樣，比在香港以25美元購買一份紅衛兵小報的時候，就有天淵之別了。1968年，中國研究資料中心在華盛頓成立，就開始負責繼續辦理這個複印發行的工作。迄今，該中心以國務院供應的，和其歷年向各處收集的類似的資料，已複印發行1,700多種小報和其他紅衛兵的出版物，分訂為56大冊。預計明年將再出40大冊。

中國研究資料中心自開辦以來，已成為美國當代中國研究重要的一環。但此並非出之偶然，因中心成立之目的，就是在於充實美國當代中國的研究資料。1960年代初期，美國學術界深感美國所藏當代中國研究資料之不足，擬他山攻錯來充實自己的收藏。「當代中國聯合委員會」（JCCC）遂有調查世界各國收藏大陸資料之議，冀能吸取教訓，以為美國學術界之參考。聯合委員會旋邀我擔任此項工作。1964年全年，我走訪西歐、東歐、北歐、蘇聯、東亞（中國大陸除外），以及印度的主要研究機構和圖書館，調查他們研究當代中國的情形，資料收集的狀況和來源，和與我們交換資料的可能性等等。之後，在調查報告中，我提出在美國成立一非盈利性的全國性資料中心的建議，其任務為與世界各國圖書館及研究機構建立資料交換關係，以收互利之效。在聯合委員會接受這個建議之後，福特基金會於1968年撥款50萬美元，在位於華盛頓之美國研究圖書館協會（Association of Research Libraries）下成立「中國研究資料中心」。中心成立後，以向國內外圖書館借用或交換的方式，複印了大量的不單是關於1949年以後當代中國的資料，並且包括了從1912年到1949年出版，美國圖書館未曾收藏或收藏不完整的罕見的中文研究書刊。中心成立三十餘年，有口皆碑，厥功至偉，紅衛兵資料的發行即其一例。

文革以後，大陸的出版事業恢復正常。根據官方統計，文革結束後兩年（1978），全年出版的書籍已經恢復到14,987種，期刊恢復到930種，報紙恢復到186種。這比在文革開始後第二年（1967）全年出版的2,925種書籍，27種期刊，47種報紙，實有天淵之別。之後，在1985年，有更顯著的增長。1985年書籍出版的總量達到45,503種，期刊4,705種，報紙1,445種，以後逐年都有增加。根據最新的統計，西元2000年出版的書籍有143,376

種，其中新書84,235種，期刊8,725種，其中中央級的有2,194種，地方出的有6,531種，報紙有2,007種，中央級的206種，地方1,801種。很明顯的，大陸出版事業不但已一日千里，而出版地區的重心也由中央轉移到地方。此一現象，從另一個角度也可以看出。目前大陸出版社共560多家，其中中央級的有210多家，全部集中在北京，占出版社的總數39%，地方出版社卻有340多家，絕大部分在省、市、自治區政府機關所在地，占出版社的總數61%。這個現象和大陸改革開放的政策有密切的關係，中央的絕對控制權，至少是在出版方面，已漸被溶蝕，業已分散到地方上去。

　　還有一點值得我們注意的，就是現在出版事業中，當年意識型態掛帥的情形已不復存在。根據官方統計，2000年全國書籍出版總數143,376種（新書84,235種），馬克思主義、列寧主義、毛澤東思想這一類的書籍只有236種（新出版的168種），其他最多的是關於文化、科學、教育、體育這方面的書籍，這幾種合起來一共是58,513種，當中，除了再版書以外，新書有25,593種。其次就是文學，有10,756種，包括新書8,093種。再其次是工業技術，有16,267種，新書10,123種；經濟，9,207種，新書6,751種；醫藥衛生，6,329種，新書4,080種；語言、文字，6,301種，新書3,667種；政治、法律，5,509種，新書4,103種；歷史、地理，4,402種，新書3,684種。由此類推，可以看出在大陸改革開放和「社會主義市場經濟」政策下，他們書籍出版的優先次序。不但如此，政府從嚴格限制書刊出口到現在專設貿易公司鼓勵出口，也是一個極大的政策上的大轉彎。目前，從國營的三家大公司——中國出版對外貿易公司、中國國際圖書貿易公司、中國圖書進出口公司——和規模比較小的在各大都市的公立或私立的公司都可以直接購買。同時，各大學也積極地發展和美國圖書館的交換工作，到大陸的旅客也可以自由購買書籍。所以，現在收集大陸的資料，可以說是四通八達，目前的問題是不怕沒有東西可以買，就怕自己的經費不夠。根據中國出版對外貿易公司的目錄，2002年可以訂閱的期刊就有5,107種（人文、社會科學和科技約各占一半）、報紙1,366種。並且，很多報紙，包括《解放軍報》，都已經上網，與當年全面禁止出口的情形，如同隔世。大陸也發展了不少的資訊網站。一個最有用的，可以和這些網站鏈路的是香港中文大學中國研究服務中心（Universities Service Center for China Studies）的網站http://www.usc.cuhk.edu.hk。他們和大陸鏈路的有雜誌網站36條、報紙162條、新聞網站39條、和大陸各級政府（中央，地方，全國性組織）的網站570條。

　　50年來，美國東亞圖書館收集當代中國資料的過程已如上所述，他們究竟有些什麼樣的成就？這可以分兩個階段來講。第一個階段是從1949年中共成立政府到1976年文革結束。在這個時期，我上面已經講過，因為不能向大陸直接購買和其他各種原因，美國東亞圖書館採購大陸出版書籍的工作非常艱巨。但是，也如我上面所講的，在這個時期，我們從香港、台灣、日本，以及美國政府方面得到不少非常重要的資料，為當代中國研究作了很大的貢獻。簡言之，在這個階段裡，美國東亞圖書館收集大陸資料的成就還是相當可觀的。這一點，可以在我和南加州大學彼德・伯頓（Peter Berton）教授合著，胡佛研究院1967年出版的《當代中國研究指南》（*Contemporary China: A Research Guide*）求證。因為那本書所著錄的關於研究當代中國的大量書刊、報紙都是根據當時美國東亞圖書館所收藏的資料。第二個階段是從1976年文革結束以後到現在。特別是從1980年代初期開始，因為中國出版業在那個時候才恢復正常作業。在這一段時間裡，美國東亞圖書館收集中國大陸出版物的工作比以前要順利得很多。如上面講到的，現在不是沒有出版物可買，而是採購的經費夠不夠的問題。在這個情況下，他們的收藏，特別是關於當代中國的研究資料，究竟有些什麼樣的成就？關於這個問題，近年還沒有人做過調查。也許可以用我在1989年做過的一次調查來幫助答覆這個問題。雖然這個調查不能完全代表當前的情況，但是，在1989年大陸的出版業恢復正常差不多已經十年，當時的供應和需要的情形，基本上和現在差不多。所以，1989年的資料還是比較有它的代表性的。

　　根據中國官方統計，1989年大陸全年出版的總額是書籍74,974種，其中55,476種是新書，19,498種是再版；期刊6,078種，其中大概有一半是屬於科技方面的，一半是屬於人文和社會科學的；報紙1,576種。我調查問卷的結果顯示（問卷發給國會圖書館和下列九個大學東亞圖書館：哥倫比亞大

學、耶魯大學、普林斯頓大學、芝加哥大學、密西根大學、加州大學、胡佛
研究院、華盛頓大學，加上哈佛燕京圖書館共十個。國會圖書館提供的資料
在分析時沒有使用。原因下面再作解釋），這九個東亞圖書館在1989年入藏
的大陸出版書籍最低的是2,400種，最高的是8,000種，其餘都是在5,000到
6,000種左右；期刊收集最少是496種，最高的1,279種，這九個圖書館中有
四個是在1,000種以上，還有兩個是900種；報紙最低的是42種，最高的
123種。這些數字和大陸出版的總數比較，乍然看來，當然差得很多很多。
但是，如果我們了解美國東亞圖書館收集資料的範圍，這個差異就不會如此
之大了。首先，美國東亞圖書館不收集科技、教科書、兒童讀物、畫片之類
的出版品，文學作品也是選擇性的收集，外國文學的中譯本，也不收集。所
以，如果我們從大陸出版的總數裡減掉這些出版品的數字，據我的統計，美
國東亞圖書館1989年，在它們採購的範圍裡，可能收集大陸當年出版的人
文科學和社會科學方面的書籍大約只是34,100種，可能收集的期刊有3,321
種，報紙1,576種。用這個調整的數字和這九個東亞館的數字來比較的話，
這九個圖書館1989年收藏的書籍是大陸當年出版書籍總量的7%到23%，期
刊是15%到38.5%，報紙是0.6%到7.8%。

　　在看這些百分率的時候。我們也必須要注意到下面幾點：第一，大陸在
人文科學和社會科學方面出版書刊的總數，除了部分是有關當代中國的，其
餘包括近代中國和古代中國，並且有些是完全和中國無關的，比如關於外國
的，或者世界性的，或者在社會科學方面的理論書籍；第二，近年大陸出版
的通俗小說和外國文學的中文翻譯很暢銷。1989年大陸出版的文學書籍近
14,000種，文藝期刊600多種。美國東亞圖書館，除文學作品和文藝期刊有
選擇性的收集外，對其餘的都不收集；第三，大陸每年再版書的數量甚高。
1989年的再版書近19,500種。美國東亞圖書館鮮有收集再版的；第四，大
陸書刊，就是1989年，也並非可以全部出口。1989年出版的期刊6,000餘
種，根據中國出版對外貿易公司的目錄，當年准許出口的僅2,500餘種，而
且其中41%是科技的刊物。在書籍方面，凡是指定為「內部」的出版物，
也是一律不准出口。換句話說，雖然這九個圖書館收藏的百分比不高，但

是，這些百分比不能代表他們實際的成就，因為依照我上述的分析方法，除去在美國東亞圖書館收集範圍以外的書刊，這九個圖書館的收藏是要比這些百分比要好得很多的。也可以說，1989年在東亞圖書館收集範圍內的關於當代中國的書刊，如果不是全部都已收集，至少絕大部分是已經收藏了。所以，如果1989年的資料能夠作代表的話，第二個階段的成就是非常顯著的。

剛剛講到我的問卷也發給國會圖書館，但是，最後沒有用他們提供的資料。原因為何？因為國會圖書館的情形比較特殊，他們收羅萬象，根據他們提供的資料，1989年國會圖書館總共收集（包括購買和交換）中文書籍15,000多冊，期刊1,835種，報紙30種。據我所知國會圖書館所收書籍中包括科技、教科書、少數民族語言，和各種通俗的資料。因為他們提供的總數下沒有分類，所以無法知道這些出版物占他們收集總量多少。因此，如果把這些性質不完全相同的國會圖書館的資料和其他九個圖書館的資料一視同仁來作分析的話，結果就會有很大的偏差，失去了它的代表性。所以，就只有割愛，沒有用他們的資料了。

我們已經提到早期在美國收集大陸出版品的困難，和在文革以後在開放政策下的若干方便。但是，目前還存在一些問題，這些問題恐怕不是短時間，甚至於在可見的將來可以解決的。首先，是我已經提到的「內部」書刊的問題。「內部」在大陸包括的範圍很廣泛，是非官方發行，或者未經官方許可發行的書刊，或者是限制閱讀的文件等都是「內部」。但是，它們並不是「秘密」或者「機密」的文件。「內部」基本上分為兩類：一類是「內部發行」，一類是「限國內發行」。「內部發行」又分好幾種，包括「內部文件」、「內部資料」、「內部參考」、「內部讀物」，還有「內部控制發行」，和「黨校系內部發行」等等，著作出版前的「徵求意見稿」和「試用本」都是「內部」。因為「內部」出版物印刷量有限，而且不能外銷，所以採購就非常困難。但是，有時也可以從香港或他處收購一些走私的原版或複印本。華盛頓「中國研究資料中心」就已經收集到兩百多種「內部」出版品，業經複印發行。例如，《中華人民共和國最高人民法院特別法庭審判林彪江青反革命團案主犯紀實》，北京法律出版社，1982年出版、《中國人民解放軍大事記，1927-1982》，中國人民解放軍軍事科學院編，1984年出版、《廬山會議實錄》，李銳編，北京春秋出版社，1989年出版。廬山會議為什麼重要？因為彭德懷在人民公社和大躍進失敗以後，在廬山會議上給毛澤東上萬言書，不為毛澤東所納，旋被清算。李銳當時是中央政治局高級幹部，廬山會議任記錄，此書為中共黨內領導鬥爭的真實報導，因此，被列為「內部控制發行」的文獻。但是，這些仍然是極小極小的一部分。1988年北京中華書局出版《1949-1986全國內部發行圖書總目》，其中登錄17,754種「內部」初版本和547種增訂版本。可見「內部」種數之多，包括範圍之廣。雖然近年情形漸有好轉，但有「內部」標示的書籍為數仍然眾多，包括學術著作，繼續為採購大陸書刊的一個障礙。

其次，就是圖書交換的問題。雖然美國圖書館目前可以自由和大陸圖書館交換資料，但是，問題依舊，那就是，他們所提供的書刊都是很容易在市面上買到的普通出版物，同時，沒有任何圖書館樂意提供協助代覓另外的書刊以作交換。還有一個更難解決的問題，那就是交換方式，就是說，交換應該以數量計，抑或是以價格計。因為中國和美國書價的差異很大，以數量計，於美國的圖書館不利，如以價格計，則對中國的圖書館不利。所以，在這個情況下，交換的工作並不積極。一般而言，和大陸有交換關係的圖書館通常都在一種君子協定的默契下進行。換言之，這種交換既不以數量計，也不以價格計，而是由雙方主觀判斷什麼是公平的交換。這顯然不是長久之計。如果有更客觀的方式，交換的工作會變得更活躍，對雙方也會有更大的裨益。

再其次，就是關於學術性書籍出版的問題。近年來大陸的出版公司成為自負盈虧的獨立經濟實體以後，再由於市場競爭的衝擊，出版學術性書籍的困難遂與日俱增。因學術性的著作銷路不高，無法盈利，反而比較平庸通俗的書容易進入市場。所以，出版社在制定選題計畫和出書品種時，經濟效益乃為其優先考慮。因此，學術性書籍的出版不易，甚至於在已發出預告後，因預訂不多，遂取消出版之決定者，時有所聞。除非作者津貼，否則無法出書。有鑑於此，大陸有些政府機構，如國家科委、社科院和一些大學，已設立出版基金。據稱，目前全國這類基金的總額有四千餘萬人民幣，用其孳息補助學術性的出版。從需要的角度看，這筆補助並不是很大，但卻是一個良好的開端。所以，大陸學術性著作的出版也是值得繼續觀察的事。

　　今天的報告，就此結束。謝謝大家。

注釋

本文係作者2003年在台北淡江大學「吳文津先生講座」演講之一。收入《書林覽勝——台灣與美國存藏中國典籍文獻概況——吳文津先生講座演講錄》，淡江大學中國文學系主編（台北：臺灣學生書局，2003）。臺灣學生書局慨允轉載，特致謝忱。

美國之外的當代中國研究

　　近年來，美國之外的學術機構的漢學研究已悄悄發生實質性的變化。漢學研究傳統上幾乎全專注於語言和歷史，但由於結合了現當代中國研究，遂擴展了漢學研究的範圍。此打破傳統之現象在歐洲學術機構為最，誠為值得注意的趨勢。此文試圖簡述歐洲、蘇聯和亞洲當代中國研究之現狀，並觀察各個國家隨附而來的支持當代中國研究的圖書館發展。

　　首先，我認為宜給「當代中國」下定義。此詞對不同地區不同的人有不同的時間內涵。在美國，我們已習慣性地認為「當代中國」是指1949年後的中國。但一般來說這並不為歐洲人所接受。對很多歐洲人而言，「當代中國」所指時段比僅僅二十來年要長。很多人認為「當代中國」應該包括1911年至現在的全部時段，因而，用此詞時其意如此。日本人定義與美國人近似。日文「現代中國」意為1949年以後共產黨控制的中國。為確保各國研究亞洲的學者彼此理解此詞所指，注明此詞之異同實屬重要。本文所說的現代中國為1949年以後的中國。

　　歐洲的漢學研究歷史悠久，傳統一直重視語言學和歷史。現當代中國的研究，從不為此傳統之一部分。歐洲漢學享有著名學者：馬伯樂（Henri Maspero）、伯希和（Paul Pelliot）、理雅各（James Legge）、衛禮賢（Richard Wilhelm）等，然而歐洲現當代中國研究尚未出現學術巨人。傳統之力強大，一旦確立，則難撼動。西歐一些人預測，在西歐國家現當代中國研究領域將永遠不會達到其古典漢學研究的水準，並享同樣高的地位。或許確實如此，但是，最近十年，已經悄悄地發生變化。大學開始聘請教授現代中國的人員，一些大學中對現當代中國感興趣的學生在逐漸增多，而且，並設立有關的研究和研討會。

西德的波鴻魯爾大學（Ruhr University at Bochum）是個很好的例子。該大學1965年招收首批學生，為德國高等教育之試驗。組織形式採用美國的系別制，而不是傳統德國的學院制。其東亞研究所旨在訓練跨學科的研究生和學者，以試驗集體研究的新方法。目前離其目標尚遠，但至少已有很好的起點。還有其他的創新：比如，學生可選中國文學為專業，中國歷史為副業。在語言訓練上並不規定所有的學生必修古代漢語。例如，一個經濟學專業的學生在語言訓練上可允許只修現代「白話」。當然，文學和歷史專業的學生則必修古代漢語和現代漢語。

如此不囿於傳統，使得波鴻的東亞研究專業更像美國大學的東亞區域研究專業。但是歐洲大學遠沒有普遍採納美國對每個國家真正的跨學科式的區域研究的理念。我認為，有三個因素導致此現象：如前已提到的傳統制約；受過專業訓練的人員匱乏；以及經費不足。縱使魯爾大學有中國語言和文學、中國歷史，甚至東亞政治學的講座教授，卻沒有明確的當代中國專業專案。將來或許會有。在目前的德國，研究純粹當代中國事務的學術機構只有在漢堡的由德國政府和私人基金會支持的東亞研究所（Institute of Asian Studies）。

或許，西歐最活躍的當代中國研究專業是在英國。（大多數法國現代中國研究的學者，如巴黎索邦大學的謝諾［Jean Chesneaux］教授，他們主要研究的是1949年前的民國時期。至於那些研究共產主義中國的學者，其學術活動的範圍，難比英國學者。）如歐洲其他國家一樣，英國的古典中國研究，傳統悠久。而現當代中國研究，起源很晚。1960年創辦的《中國季刊》（China Quarterly），主要關注共產主義中國和中國共產主義運動史，儘管其主要作者群為非英國人，該刊卻將英國置於研究中國共產主義事務之學術前沿。里茲大學（University of Leeds）六、七年前成立的現當代中國專業也旨在加快英國20世紀民國時期和共產黨時期的研究。

但是，到目前為止最重大的進展是1968年6月由福特基金會（Ford Foundation）資助在倫敦成立的當代中國研究所（Contemporary China Institute）。該所旨在加強英國當代中國（即共產主義中國）研究將來發展的基礎，開展研究並出版成果，以及成為聯繫英國專家學者和全世界同行的紐帶。

該所雖然在行政上是倫敦大學亞非學院（School of Oriental and African Studies）的一部分，但它是構想為一個全國性的機構，向全英有意於研究當代中國的社區提供服務。其所長在政策制定事務上，聽取成立的管理委員會建議。該委員會由英國的大學、政府以及商業界的代表組成。該所的主要項目包括向合格的學者提供研究經費、出版《中國季刊》，以及舉行學術會議。

該所獨特之處是其側重20世紀中國的研究，特別是1949年以後的中國，這與英國漢學傳統大為不同。該所之創建很可能會成為英國當代中國研究發展的分水嶺。其成功的運作肯定會鼓勵歐洲其他國家做類似的試驗。

與英國的嘗試相平行的是荷蘭萊頓大學漢學研究所最近成立的當代中國文獻與研究中心（Center for Documentation and Research on Contemporary China at the Sinological Institute in Leiden）。該中心1969年5月成立，強調當代中國的文獻、研究和教學。該中心現在為萊頓大學漢學學生提供兩門講座課和兩門研討課。其目前研究專案之一是對外國人到共產主義中國旅行後寫的報告，主要是圖書，進行分析。該中心同時與荷蘭新聞媒體合作，也承擔了有關中國的新聞資訊中心的角色。

其他歐洲國家也在傳統漢學研究上增加了現當代中國研究。哥本哈根的斯堪的納維亞亞洲研究所（The Scandinavian Institute of Asian Studies），專注社會科學和當代中國研究，為斯堪的納維亞國家拓寬中國研究包納現當代中國的共同努力的典型。

經費不足和專業人員不足，是阻礙西歐現當代中國研究快速發展的部分因素。這些困難不是西歐國家獨有，我們在美國也面臨同樣的問題。雖然我們起步較早，已花20年培養後備人才以供錄用，但在財政上資助現當代中國研究越來越難。但歐洲必須從零開始。訓練人才需要時間和金錢。不能指望一位社會學家、一位經濟學家，或一位政治學家一夜之間成為中國專家，特別是無人能訓練他的時候，更不可能。一位英國大學成員在1965年有鑑於此坦誠地說：「我們乾脆把我們對當代中國感興趣的學生送到美國。」但是普遍都同意的是，歐洲國家不得不培養自己的學者，讓他們再培訓其他的人。

為此，歐洲大學越來越指望政府和私人基金會資助。雖然大多數歐洲大學專業都得到一定的政府資助，但是遠不能與美國政府通過國防教育法案或國家高等教育法案來資助美國大學相比。很多時候資助額度不足，需求與現有的資源不成比例，特別是需要大量資金啟動專業專案的時候。私人基金會提供一些幫助，但是不能不停地資助長期的專業項目。比如，德國的大眾汽車基金會（Volkswagen Foundation）一直是德國中國研究的慷慨贊助者。福特基金會也對歐洲的現當代中國專業專案有所貢獻，向德國和英國的大學和其他機構提供資助。卡內基基金會（Carnegie Foundation）通過EWA（Education and World Affairs教育和世界事務）提供資金成立和維護香港大學服務中心；該中心歡迎現當代中國國際學者利用其場地和圖書資源進行研究。

這些努力都有助於訓練歐洲的中國當代事務學者。到目前為止，最雄心勃勃的當數美國學術團體委員會（American Council of Learned Societies）、社會科學研究理事會（Social Science Research Council）、英國東方學家協會（The Association of British Orientalists）和英國科學院（British Academy）資助的當代中國研究聯絡委員會（Liaison Committee on Study of Contemporary China）所設計的計畫。該計畫對現代中國研究的發展不僅對英國和美國的學者和機構提供不同種類的資助，並計畫對美國之外的所有國家的研究生提供一系列獎學金。目前正在申請基金的計畫書旨在結合增加對當代中國研究訓練有素的社會科學家和人文學家的數量，與在幾個國家或地區發展能建立和維護培訓和研究中心的小型學者團體。如果該委員會能就此計畫書申請到資助，毫無疑問該計畫將大力推進全世界關於當代中國研究的發展。

以上簡述即為西歐當代中國研究的現狀。在東歐，只有捷克、波蘭和東柏林有傳統漢學的研究。讓人吃驚的是，在東歐和在蘇聯，中國研究仍然滯留在這個歐洲傳統漢學研究的範疇。基本上，學生還只是接受中國語言、文學、歷史方面的訓練。雖然近二十年來莫斯科大學和列寧格勒大學已開設各種學科有關現當代中國的課程，但基本上，學生還只是接受中國語言、文學、歷史方面的訓練。

華沙大學東方研究所（The Oriental Institute），1964至1965年度有研究人員六、七人，主要為高年級研究生，其中只有一人做現代中國研究。他的研究題目是中國共產黨創始人陳獨秀。同年度，東柏林的科學院無一人對現代中國感興趣。波蘭和東柏林，1964至1965年度，對共產主義中國的研究大多由政府來做。

另一方面，在捷克，捷克科學院的東方研究所（Oriental Institute）的現代中國文學的研究專案，生氣勃勃。近年來，招募一些研究現代歷史和當代事務的人員，研究隊伍增強。但鑑於該所歷史和該所所長普實克（Jaroslav Prusek）教授的個人興趣，當代中國文學可能繼續是其最重要的研究方向。

在蘇聯，莫斯科大學和列寧格勒大學也都教授現當代中國課程；列寧格勒大學的著名歷史學家耶菲莫夫（G.V. Efimov）教授開設「美國史學」研討課，主要通過研討費正清（John K. Fairbank）、史華慈（Benjamin I. Schwartz）、費維凱（Albert Feuerwerker）、芮瑪麗（Mary C. Wright）等著名美國學者的著作，來批評分析現代中國史的資本主義的研究方法。

單從研究而言，莫斯科的蘇聯科學院亞洲民族研究所（Institute of the Peoples of Asia）是蘇聯研究現當代中國的主要中心。其中國研究室1965年有25位在編人員。除四位之外所有人都從事19世紀和20世紀研究。雖然強調個人研究，但也多見集體研究。1965年，正在進行的集體研究項目有兩個，一個是自17世紀以來的現代中國歷史，重點是在鴉片戰爭之後的時期。另一個是1917至1949年中國勞工運動史。該所也出版一些1920年代赴華、最近被恢復名譽的蘇聯顧問的回憶錄。蘇聯和東歐的中國研究者的語言能力讓人印象深刻。1960年代之前，這些國家的語言訓練政策是派遣留學生到中國，一般是到北京大學，進行長時期的語言學習，然後回研究所從事好幾年的踏實工作。自中蘇關係交惡後，派遣留學生到中國已經不可能。但是東歐和蘇聯的中國專家都熱切希望與中國恢復文化關係。

　　歐亞之中國研究，既有會通又有分野。亞洲國家如日本和韓國，由於與中國地理上的接近和文化上的契合，數個世紀以來已將其漢學研究發展到很高的程度，著重於經、史、子、集。與歐洲不同，這些國家對現當代中國事務有強烈的學術興趣，日本尤其如此。1949年共產黨掌權後，日本學者很自然地將其注意力轉移到中國大陸的發展情形。此種學術興趣之轉移，無任何不適之處；實際上，這是他們一直在進行的研究工作的繼續。現在所有重要大學都開設一些當代中國課程，很多知名日本學者都是當代中國事務專家。日本當代中國的圖書資源也有豐富的收藏。今日之日本當代中國研究專業，高度發達和活躍，堪與美國相比。日本的現狀不單是歸功於學術興趣，政府和企業機構因其戰略和企業利益也大力資助日本各種各樣的研究所。這些研究所的工作借重學者來推動他們的發展。日本共產黨也對當代中國研究興趣盎然，雖然這種興趣有兩派的聲音，一派親北京，一派親蘇聯。

　　各種跡象表明，日本對當代中國研究的濃厚興趣會繼續發展，而且可供亞洲其他對共產主義中國的學術研究有待發展的國家借鑑者良多。例如，印度並無漢學研究傳統。印度的中國研究只是新近才開始，而著重於當代中國時期。1949年以來，一些印度學生在中國留學，學成歸國的一些畢業生進入政府工作，特別是在外交部；其他一些人到西方國家繼續留學深造。相對來說只有少數在印度擔任教職。中印邊界衝突強烈地刺激印度制定現當代中國研究的系統計畫。在福特基金會的慷慨資助下，德里大學（University of Delhi）的研究中心得以成立。由於洛克菲勒基金會（Rockefeller Foundation）的部分資助，印度國際關係學院（Indian School of International Studies）的現代中國專案繼續開辦。但從實際上來看，德里大學將成為印度中國研究的主要中心。網路師資人才、發展語言訓練專業，以及增強圖書館收藏，都耗時費力，因而要看見該學術事業的碩果，目前為時尚早。

　　與印度相比，韓國的當代中國研究更為發達。但是，儘管韓國傳統漢學研究歷史悠久，其當代中國研究的成果並不是特別引人注目。韓國政府不容許學者輕易接觸中國大陸出版物，結果造成其現代中國研究只能停留在中華民國時期。由福特基金會的資助，韓國大學亞洲研究所從事了一些共產主義中國的研究，但其範圍不廣。迄今，該研究所最為著名的成就是數年前舉行的關於亞洲現代化的國際會議。重要論文的結集已經出版。南韓政府對共產主義中國進行廣泛的情報研究，但其實質，據稱多為非學術性質。

台灣對共產主義中國的興趣濃烈是顯而易見的事。然而，這種興趣卻沒有導致大規模的大學教學或研究專業。過去20年來，對共產主義中國的研究只局限在政府機構之內。研究所和研究室只見於國防部、調查局、國民黨黨部和其他一些政府機構之內。1968年之前，不管是在全國最高研究機構中央研究院或是在任何大學，都沒有對共產主義中國開展有組織的學術研究。對共產主義中國有著述的學者很少，且都與政府有關係，而且他們當中一些是在政府資助的國際關係研究所任職。大學圖書館不購買中國大陸出版物，一般來說，政府圖書館收藏的共產主義資料不對學者開放。

可是，最近幾年慢慢地發生了一些變化。好幾種政府研究出版物已經解密，可公開訂閱，而且研究的品質已經明顯提高。政府的政策是歡迎外國學者來台灣研究共產主義中國，並真誠努力地為他們提供資料和其他設施。1968年秋政治大學東亞研究所成立，著重當代中國研究；其碩士專業現在有二十多位在讀學生。

台灣目前的趨勢似乎是政府繼續進行共產主義中國的研究，同時容許以大學為本的學術教學和科研進行有限的試驗。

香港是英國直轄殖民地，為所有的中國觀察家的神秘家園。目前香港大學和新成立的香港中文大學的當代中國教學和研究專業相當有限。香港大學亞洲研究所和香港中文大學東亞研究所都是新近成立，對現當代中國重視程度如何，有待觀察。香港其他地方，有不少研究共產主義中國的積極的活動，比如美國駐香港總領事館翻譯中國大陸報紙和期刊。香港友聯研究所也對共產主義中國進行研究。該研究所1950年成立，收藏1949年後中國大陸的報紙、期刊和其他出版物，也開展研究和出版項目。該所出版的《友聯研究服務》（*Union Research Service*）為中國大陸出版物的翻譯系列，是重要的研究資料。該所最近重視編輯出版研究指南和參考書，深受研究當代中國人士的歡迎；可以有把握地假設，友聯研究所的書目文獻研究，會是該所將來的主要活動之一。

　　先前提到香港的大學服務中心。該中心獲卡內基基金會資助，由教育和世界事務所主辦。該所沒有自己的教學和研究專業，只向外國個人研究學者提供如圖書館和辦公室等研究場地資源。

　　此乃香港為研究當代中國人士被使用之特徵。他們去香港不僅僅因為當地機構的專業項目能使他們受益，而是因為該地能向他們提供獨特的研究機會。首先，雖然近年來隨著文化大革命的發展，中國大陸的出版物供應幾乎完全枯竭，但是中國大陸的出版物在香港供應還是較為方便。其次，與中國大陸地理上接緣使香港成為一個重要的監聽站。香港和中國大陸之間不斷的往來，大陸難民的湧入、記者和旅行者等的返回，提供了核查事實、猜想乃至學術假設的良機。再次，有機會與世界各地的同行見面，也提供交流思想和彼此互惠的機會。這些因素結合一起，讓香港成為吸引當代中國專家學者前來工作之地，更不必說當地的中國美食和可量身定做的服裝了。毫無疑問，香港，假如不是最重要的研究當代中國的中心，也將繼續保持其作為研究當代中國的一個主要中心。

　　通過考察美國之外的現當代中國研究圖書館資源，可得到幾個廣泛的結論。總體來說，美國現當代中國研究的圖書館資源之總和遠比中國之外的任何國家的現當代中國研究的圖書館資源之總和為強。不管是東歐或是西歐，包括蘇聯和斯堪的納維亞的歐洲中文圖書館發展都延續重視語言和歷史的收藏傳統。雖然主要中心的古典文獻收藏良好，但除了共產主義的國家收藏的一些1949年後的中國出版物外，現當代中國的文獻資料都普遍薄弱。

　　日本的圖書館發展，與戰後現當代中國研究的快速發展同步。台灣自然以收藏1949年前的國民黨和共產黨文獻著稱，1949年後的文獻收藏大都與情報研究的需求有關。香港友聯研究所的1949年後大陸期刊和報紙的縮微膠捲的製作，非常著名；香港大學馮平山圖書館收藏相當數量的1949年前的大陸期刊和香港地方報紙。印度剛剛邁入現代中國研究領域，現在圖書館收藏仍付之闕如。新加坡和吉隆坡的圖書館的現當代中國文獻資源，無足輕重，可是新加坡大學的當地報紙為研究海外華人的重要文獻資源。

　　倫敦大學亞非學院的圖書館為西歐大多數學者尋找現當代中國資料的造訪之地。亞非學院的圖書館收藏1949年前的出版物已有些時日，但其主要重點是語言和文學。廣泛地收藏1949年前和1949年後的社會科學文獻資料則是最近開始，其收藏現由當代中國研究所（Contemporary China Institute）的採購有所增補。1965年，該館收有約10,000冊20世紀書籍，800種期刊，以及全國性報紙數種。中文報紙的主要的收藏地為大英博物館，可是1949年之前的報紙寥寥無幾。1949年之後的報紙主要來自英國外交部向美國政府和其他機構獲得者。除此之外，該館藏有中國政府出版物和東南亞1920年代至1950年代東南亞出版的一些中文報刊的創刊號的特藏。但該館並不廣求現當代中國資料。

　　劍橋和牛津大學傳統文獻資料，收藏豐富，但如里茲大學一樣，尚未創建現當代時期的收藏。

　　法國圖書館收藏當代中文資料比英國圖書館為差。巴黎四所收藏中文資料的圖書館，只有資料中心（Centre de Documentation）明言負責收藏現當代資料，然而其全部收藏卻僅數千冊，尚無關輕重。其餘三個館，國家圖書館（Bibliotheque Nationale）、漢學研究所（Institut des Haute Etudes Chinoises）圖書館和國立東方語言學院（L'Ecole Nationale des Langues Orientales）圖書館，主要收藏現代前出版物。里昂的中法協會（The Chinese-French Association）有20世紀20年代和30年代出版的中國期刊的重要館藏。

　　西德唯一有系統地收藏現當代中文獻的圖書館為瑪律堡（Marburg）的國家圖書館（Staatsbibliothek）。波鴻（Bochum）將來會收藏相同性質的文獻；漢堡（Hamburg）的亞洲研究所也將廣購現代資料。該所最近的收藏為香港友聯研究所的全套縮微膠捲。

　　荷蘭的強大的傳統漢學使得收藏當代社會科學文獻資源不受重視。但新近成立的萊頓大學漢學研究所當代中國文獻與研究中心（Center for Documentation and Research on Contemporary China at the Sinological Institute in Leiden）卻指向一個長遠的規畫，那就是它要成為荷蘭現當代中國出版物的收藏地。自1969年5月成立以來，該中心已經收藏一些圖書和報刊，並將得到香港友聯研究所的全套縮微膠捲。

斯堪的納維亞國家有同樣的發展模式。新成立的哥本哈根的斯堪的納維亞亞洲研究所（The Scandinavian Institute of Asian Studies）開始收藏現當代時期的資料，以補充現時的傳統中文文獻的收藏。

東歐和蘇聯的圖書館情況有些不一樣。東柏林的德國國家圖書館、布拉格的魯迅圖書館、捷克科學院基本圖書館（Fundamental Library）、莫斯科的列寧圖書館、全蘇外國文學圖書館（All Union Library of Foreign Literature）以及亞洲民族研究所（Institute of the Peoples of Asia）圖書館、列寧格勒公共圖書館和亞洲民族研究所圖書館列寧格勒分館，都是1949年後中國大陸出版物的主要收藏地。另一方面，波蘭的圖書館幾乎沒有收藏這些資料。

所有共產主義國家主要是通過與北京圖書館和中國科學院圖書館的交換來獲得中國出版物。雖然自1960年以來，所收到的出版物數量劇烈下降，但是這些國家有一些我們無法得到的1960年以前的出版物。它們包括通常在遠東地區書商管道無法採購的中國科學院各個研究所的出版物、大學學報，以及省級出版社出版的圖書。但在另一方面，1900至1949年出版的圖書在這些圖書館中的館藏，卻非常之少。例外的情況是，布拉格魯迅圖書館有現代中國文學的收藏；莫斯科列寧圖書館也有一些20世紀出版的一些零散期刊。

日本收藏當代中國文獻的主要中心是國會圖書館（National Diet Library）、東洋文庫（Toyo Bunko）、東京大學東洋文化研究所（Toyo Bunka Kenkyujo of the University of Tokyo）和京都大學人文科學研究所（Jimbun Kagaku Kenkyujo of the University of Kyoto）。其他一些大學，如慶應義塾大學、一橋大學和愛知大學都收藏1949年後的資料；另外一些研究所，如亞細亞經濟研究所（Ajia Keizai Kenkyujo），特別是中國研究所（Chugoku Kenkyujo），也都收集這些資料。內閣總理研究室和外務省圖書館都藏有可觀的中國大陸出版物，但這些政府圖書館不向學者開放。此外，有數個書店專營大陸出版品，但遺憾的是其中主要的一家，也從事複印從日本私人學者及其他來源的中文資料的大安書店（Daian Book），最近關張。

　　台灣的政府圖書館不重專著的收藏，其報刊收藏比專著收藏為強。有時國民政府通過現代歷史資料中心，複印發行中國共產黨出版物。這些出版物是國民政府突擊隊所獲取，或是共產黨叛變人員帶來的。著名的《連江文件》和數年前登陸艇131號帶至金門的文件都是很好的例子。台灣另外的重要文獻資源是監聽大陸中文廣播電台的廣播稿。莫斯科向大陸的中文廣播也受台灣監聽，但不幸的是不向政府之外的任何人開放。

　　除友聯研究所的縮微膠捲外，香港圖書館資源包括美國總領事館整理的中國共產黨領導人物傳記文件。該文件對合格的學者開放，去年做了縮微膠捲，美國數個圖書館有收藏。英國區域資訊室（The British Regional Information Office）過去出版《中國地方廣播電台新聞稿》（*News from Chinese Regional Radio Stations*），現在則出版《中國新聞綜述》（*China News Summary*）和《中國報刊新聞稿》（*China News Items from the Press*）。雖然文化大革命之後，除紅衛兵小報外，鮮有出版物流出中國，但香港的書店仍為中國大陸資料的最佳提供地。

　　儘管總體上很多國家的當代中國研究和支援當代中國研究的圖書館資源不如美國發達，但有些地方都有重要的開端，而這些開端假以時日將會發展成重要的專業項目。目前能進行合作的機會良多。在圖書館領域，朝這個方向的重要的一步已經邁出：研究圖書館協會（Association of Research Libraries）的中國研究資料中心（Center for Chinese Research Materials）於1968年成立。該中心旨在加強現當代中國的圖書館文獻資源之建設，而且並不局限於美國學術機構；該中心冀望全世界圖書館關於這方面的收藏有進一步的發展。

　　此合作之道當為當代中國研究領域裡的所有學者和圖書館人員所效。學術研究沒有國界，而且知識是逐漸積累的。我們所得到的發展全賴於他人所取得的進步。

注釋

本文為1969年7月30日在芝加哥大學東亞圖書館學暑期培訓班演講稿的增訂本。文中基本資訊為作者1964年受美國學術團體協會及社會科學研究理事會合組之當代中國聯合委員會（Joint Committee on Contemporary China）委託調查世界各國研究當代中國資料情況所得。載《哈佛圖書館館刊》（*Harvard Library Bulletin*），第18（XVIII）卷，第2期（1970年4月），頁141-154。

（王成志譯）

Studies of Contemporary China Outside the United States

A quiet and significant development has taken place in Chinese studies at academic institutions outside the United States in recent years. Sinology, with its traditional and almost exclusive emphasis on philology and history, has acquired a new dimension by incorporating the study of the modem and contemporary periods. This break with tradition, particularly true in the case of European institutions, is a trend worthy of notice. This paper is an attempt to describe briefly the status of contemporary China studies in Europe, the Soviet Union, and Asia, with some observations on the concomitant library development in support of these studies in the various countries.

First of all, I think it would be well to define "contemporary China." The term carries different temporal connotations to different people at different places. We have become accustomed to thinking in the United States of "contemporary China" as China since 1949. This, however, is not a view generally accepted by Europeans. To many of them "contemporary China" denotes a longer time span than just two decades. Many maintain that "contemporary China" should cover the entire period from 1911 to the present, and they use the term accordingly. The Japanese definition is closer to the American. "Gendai Chugoku" in Japanese writings usually means China under Communist control since 1949. It is important to note such differences and similarities in meaning in order to make sure that Asian scholars of different countries will understand each other's terms of reference. For the purpose of this paper, I shall refer to contemporary China as

China since 1949.

Europe has had a long tradition of Sinological studies, with the emphasis always on philology and history. Studies of the modern and contemporary periods, however, were never a part of that tradition. Sinology in Europe had its eminent scholars — Henri Maspero, Paul Pelliot, James Legge, Richard Wilhelm, and others — but unfortunately European studies of modern China have not as yet their own intellectual giants. Tradition is a powerful thing. Once established, it becomes extremely hard to change. A number of people in Western Europe have predicted that in their respective countries modern and contemporary Chinese studies probably will never reach the level of classical Chinese studies or enjoy the same status. Be that as it may, changes have been slowly taking place during the last decade. University appointments are being made in modern Chinese studies, the number of students interested in modern and contemporary China is gradually increasing at some universities, and research and seminars are being conducted on current affairs.

The Ruhr University in Bochum, West Germany, is a good example. The university, which admitted its first class in the fall of 1965, is an experiment in German higher education. Instead of following the traditional organizational pattern of faculties, the university adopted the American departmental system. There is now an East Asian Institute at the university, whose aim is to form an interdisciplinary body of scholars and advanced students to experiment in new ways of collective research. The goal is still far away, but at least a good start has been made. There are also other innovations: a student may now take Chinese literature, for example, as a major and Chinese history as a minor in a degree program. Training in classical Chinese is no longer mandatory for all students. A student with an economics major, for instance, is allowed to take his language training exclusively in pai hua, the modern form. Of course those who study literature and history will still have to take both classical and modern Chinese.

Such departures from tradition make the Bochum program much like the East Asian area studies programs in American universities. But the American idea of an area or regional studies program, representing a truly interdisciplinary approach to the study of a country, is still far from being generally adopted by European universities. This, I think, can be attributed to three main factors: tradition, as has just been noted; a shortage of trained personnel; and a shortage of funds. Even the Ruhr University, which now has chairs for Chinese language and literature, Chinese history, and even political science of East Asia, has no distinct contemporary China program. This may ultimately come, but in Germany, for the time being, research into purely contemporary Chinese affairs is conducted only by the Institute of Asian Studies (Institut fur Asienkunde) in Hamburg, which is supported by both the German government and private foundations.

Perhaps the most active program in contemporary China studies in Western Europe can be found in Great Britain. (Most of the French scholars working on modern China, such as Professor Jean Chesneaux at the Sorbonne, are primarily interested in the pre-1949 Republican period. Those who do study Communist China cannot compare with the British scholars in the scope of their activity.) England, like other European countries, enjoys a long tradition of classical Chinese studies. Modern and contemporary Chinese studies are of very recent origin. The publication, beginning in i960, of the *China Quarterly,* a scholarly journal devoted to the study of Communist China and the history of the Chinese Communist Movement, put England in the forefront of scholarship on Chinese Communist affairs, although the majority of the contributors are non-British. A program on modern and contemporary China established six or seven years ago at the University of Leeds was also aimed at accelerating the study in Great Britain of the Republican and the Communist phases of twentieth-century China.

By far the most significant development, however, has been the founding of the Contemporary China Institute in London in June 1968 with Ford Foundation support. The Institute aims to strengthen the foundations for the future growth of studies on contemporary China (that is, Communist China) in the United Kingdom, to carry out research in this field and publish the results, and to serve as a link between specialists on China in England and throughout the world.

Although the Institute is administratively a part of the School of Oriental and African Studies of London University, it is conceived as a British national undertaking to serve the entire community interested in contemporary Chinese affairs throughout the United Kingdom. The Committee of Management, which has been set up to advise the Head of the Institute in policy-making matters, is composed of people from universities as well as representatives from the government and from business communities throughout Great Britain. To implement its program, the Institute provides fellowships to qualified scholars, publishes the *China Quarterly*, and plans to hold research conferences.

The unique feature of the Institute is its orientation towards studies on twentieth-century China, particularly the post-1949 period, a sharp departure from traditional British Sinological scholarship. The founding of the Institute may well prove a watershed in the development of Great Britain's contemporary China studies. Its successful operation should certainly encourage similar experiments by others in Europe.

Parallel with the British undertaking is the recent establishment of the Center for Documentation and Research on Contemporary China at the Sinological Institute in Leiden, Holland. Founded in May 1969, the Center stresses documentation, research, and teaching on contemporary China. It currently offers two lectures and two seminars for students of Sinology at Leiden University. One of the research projects under way is an analysis of published reports, mainly books, by foreign travelers in Communist China. The Center also functions as an information center on China in collaboration with the Dutch information media.

Other European countries are also adding modern and contemporary studies to traditional Sinology. The Scandinavian Institute of Asian Studies in Copenhagen, specializing in the social sciences and modern Chinese studies, is an example of concerted efforts made by the Scandinavian countries to broaden their studies on China to include the modern and the contemporary.

A shortage of funds and trained personnel are among the factors inhibiting a more rapid development of modern and contemporary studies in Western Europe. These difficulties are not limited to universities in Europe; we face the same problems in the United States. Although we started earlier and have had twenty years to build up a reservoir of manpower from which to recruit, financing modem and contemporary China studies becomes more and more difficult. But Europeans must start from scratch. Time and money are needed for training. One simply cannot expect a sociologist, an economist, or a political scientist to become a China specialist overnight, particularly with no one to train him. A British university member observed frankly in 1965, "We simply send our students who are interested in modern China to the United States." But it is generally agreed that the nations of Europe will have to train their own scholars, who can in turn train others.

To accomplish this, European universities have looked increasingly to their governments and to private foundations for financial support. Although most European university programs receive some government funding, it does not compare with the subsidy provided to American universities under the National Defense and Education Act or the National Higher Education Act. The amounts are in most cases inadequate, and the demands are out of proportion to available resources, particularly when massive funding is needed to initiate programs. Private foundations have been of some help, but they cannot underwrite sustained long-term programs. In Germany, for instance, the Volkswagen Foundation has been a generous donor to Chinese studies in that country. The Ford Foundation has also contributed to modern and contemporary Chinese programs in Europe, making grants for them to universities and other institutions in Germany and England. The Carnegie Foundation has provided funds through EWA (Education and World Affairs) for the establishment and maintenance of the Universities Service Center in Hong Kong, where international scholars of contemporary China are welcome to use its facilities for research.

Such efforts have all contributed to the training of European scholars in contemporary Chinese affairs. The most ambitious plan so far has been developed by the Liaison Committee on Study of Contemporary China, sponsored by the American Council of Learned Societies, the Social Science Research Council, the Association of British Orientalists, and the British Academy. The Committee plans different types of assistance to scholars and institutions in countries where studies of modern China are less fully developed than in the United Kingdom and the United States, and has proposed a series of fellowships to be offered to advanced students in countries other than the United States. The present proposal, for which funds are being sought, combines the purposes of increasing the number of highly-trained social scientists and humanists of modern China, and of developing in several countries or regions small groups of scholars capable of establishing and maintaining centers of training and research. If the Committee succeeds in securing funds for its proposal, the program will no doubt go far towards accelerating the growth of contemporary China studies throughout the world.

That, briefly, is the state of contemporary China studies in Western Europe. In Eastern Europe, only Czechoslovakia, Poland, and East Berlin have a tradition of Sinological studies. There and in the Soviet Union one is struck by the fact that Chinese studies have retained the traditional European emphasis on Sinology. Basically, students are still being trained in Chinese philology, literature and history, although in the Soviet Union courses on modern and contemporary China related to the various disciplines have been offered by the University of Moscow and the University of Leningrad in the last two decades.

The Oriental Institute at the University of Warsaw in 1964-65 had a research staff of six or seven members, most of them advanced graduate students, but only one of them was working in the modern period. His topic was Chen Duxiu, the founder of the Chinese Communist Party. At the Academy of Sciences in East Berlin in the same year there was no one with an interest in modern China. In Poland and in East Germany, research on Communist China in 1964-65 was mostly undertaken by the government.

In Czechoslovakia, on the other hand, the Oriental Institute of the Czech Academy of Sciences has maintained a vigorous research program in modern Chinese literature, and has in recent years added to its staff members whose interest is modern history and contemporary affairs. But in view of the history of the Institute and the personal interest of its director, Professor Jaroslav Prusek, modern Chinese literature is likely to remain the predominant interest.

In Soviet Russia the University of Moscow and the University of Leningrad both offer courses on modern and contemporary China; Professor G. V. Efimov, an eminent Soviet historian at the University of Leningrad, offers a seminar on American historiography, a critique of the capitalist approach to modern Chinese history as seen from the writings of John K. Fairbank, Benjamin I. Schwartz, Albert Feuer-werker, Mary C. Wright, and others.

On the purely research side, the Institute of the Peoples of Asia of the Soviet Academy of Sciences in Moscow is the main center of research on modern and contemporary China in the Soviet Union. Its Chinese Section had a staff of twenty-five in 1965, all but four engaged in research on the nineteenth and twentieth centuries. Although individual research was emphasized, a great deal of collective research was much in evidence. Two such collective projects in progress in 1965 were a history of modern China from the seventeenth century, with emphasis on the post-Opium War period, and a history of the Chinese labor movement from 1917 to 1949. The Institute has also published the memoirs of some of the Soviet advisers in China in the 1920's who have recently been rehabilitated. The linguistic competence of research workers in China studies in the Soviet Union and in Eastern Europe is impressive. The official policy in these countries on linguistic training before the early 1960's was to send their students to China, usually to Peking University, for extended language study, following several years of solid work at their home institutions. Sending students to China has not been possible since the beginning of the deterioration of Sino-Soviet relations, but China specialists throughout Eastern Europe and in the Soviet Union are eager for the resumption of cultural relations.

Between Europe and Asia there are both similarities and differences in the pattern of Chinese studies. Because of geographical propinquity and cultural affinity with China, countries like Japan and Korea, more than Europe, have in centuries past developed their own Sinological studies to a high degree, with emphasis on the classics, history, philosophy, and belles lettres. Unlike Europe, they have always maintained a strong scholarly interest in modern and contemporary Chinese affairs; this has been particularly true in Japan. When the Communists came to power in 1949, Japanese scholars naturally turned their attention to events taking place on the Chinese mainland. The transition of scholarly interest was painless; indeed, it was a continuation of the work they had been doing all along. At present all major universities offer some courses on contemporary China, and many eminent Japanese scholars are specialists in current Chinese affairs. Japanese library resources on contemporary China are rich. Japan today has a well-developed and active program for the study of contemporary China rivalling that of the United States. What is happening in Japan is not the result of scholarly interest alone; government and commercial interests have greatly assisted. Research institutes of all kinds, sponsored by the Japanese government and the Japanese business community for strategic and commercial interests respectively, have been assisted in their work by Japanese scholars. The Japanese Communist Party has also kept this interest alive, although it speaks now not as one but as two voices, those of the pro-Peking and the pro-Soviet factions.

There is every indication that in Japan this strong interest in contemporary China will continue, and that Japan will have much to offer in experience to other Asian countries where scholarly interest in Communist China is underdeveloped. India, for example, has no tradition of Sinological studies. Chinese studies there are of very recent origin, with the emphasis on the contemporary era. Since 1949 a number of Indian students have studied in China, some of whom have since entered Indian government service, particularly in the Ministry of External Affairs. Others have gone to the West for advanced studies. Only a relatively few have as yet taken teaching posts in India. The Sino-Indian border clashes provided a strong stimulus to develop a systematic national plan for studies on modern and contemporary China. With generous financial support from the Ford Foundation, a center was begun at the University of Delhi. The modern China program at the Indian School of International Studies continues, with some support from the Rockefeller Foundation, but for all practical purposes the University of Delhi will serve in the future as the main center of Chinese studies in India. So much time and energy has had to be spent in gathering a teaching staff, expanding the language training course, and strengthening the library that it is too early for this new academic enterprise to show results.

Korea is more advanced in contemporary China studies than India, but in spite of a long tradition of Sinological studies in that country, the advances in the contemporary field have not been especially notable. The government has denied scholars ready access to Chinese mainland publications, and as a result, modern China studies usually end with the Republican era. Some work, it is true, has been done on Communist China at the Asiatic Research Institute of Korea University, again with Ford Foundation support, but the scope is not large. The most notable accomplishment of the Institute so far has been an international conference on the modernization of Asia which it organized several years ago. A volume containing some of the more important papers has just been published. The South Korean government carries on extensive intelligence research on Communist China, but its substance is believed to be largely non-academic.

In Taiwan a lively interest in Communist China exists for obvious reasons, interest which has not led to a large-scale teaching or university research program. For the past twenty years the study of Communist China has been exclusively within the government's domain. Research institutes and offices are to be found in the Ministry of National Defense, the Bureau of Investigation, the Kuomintang headquarters, and in a number of other ministries of the National Government. Until 1968 no organized academic research on Communist China was carried out either at the Academia Sinica, the nation's highest research organization, or at any universities. The few scholars who have written on Communist China have connections with the government, and some of them are affiliated with the government-sponsored Institute of International Relations. University libraries do not purchase mainland Chinese publications and in general government libraries collecting Communist materials are not available to scholars.

Some changes, however, have been taking place slowly during the last few years. Several government research publications have been declassified for public subscription, and the quality of research has noticeably improved. The government policy is to welcome foreign scholars who wish to conduct research on Communist China in Taiwan, and a genuine effort has been made to supply them with materials and other facilities. An Institute of East Asian Studies was established in the fall of 1968 at the Chengchi University with emphasis on contemporary Chinese studies; this M.A. program currently has an enrollment of about two dozen students.

The trend seems to be towards continuing government-conducted research on

Communist China in Taiwan, while allowing a limited experiment in a university-based program of academic teaching and research.

The crown colony of Hong Kong is the mysterious home of all China-watchers. The University of Hong Kong and the new Chinese University of Hong Kong have only limited programs at present in teaching or research programs on contemporary China. The Institute for Asian Studies at the University of Hong Kong and the East Asian Institute of the Chinese University are both newly established, and it remains to be seen how much emphasis they will place on the modern and contemporary periods. Elsewhere in Hong Kong there is a great deal of activity in the study of Communist China, such as the translation of Chinese mainland newspapers and periodicals conducted by the American Consulate-General. The Union Research Institute also conducts research on Communist China. Founded in 1950, this organization collects post-1949 Chinese mainland newspapers, periodicals, and other publications, and conducts a research and publication program. *The Union Research Service*, a translation series of Chinese mainland publications, is an important source for research. The recent emphasis on the compilation and publication of research aids and reference works has been a welcome service to students of contemporary China, and it is safe to assume that the trend towards bibliographical research at the URI will be one of the Institute's main activities in the future.

Reference was made earlier to the Universities Service Center in Hong Kong, operated by the Education and World Affairs with support from the Carnegie Foundation. The Center has no teaching or research program of its own, merely providing research facilities, such as a library and office space, to foreign scholars doing individual research.

This is characteristic of the way Hong Kong has been used by students of contemporary China. They go to Hong Kong not merely because of programs at local institutions from which they can benefit, but because the place affords them unique opportunities in research. First, there has been a ready supply of publications from mainland China, although in the last few years, following the Cultural Revolution, the supply has almost completely dried up. Second, its geographical proximity to the Chinese mainland makes Hong Kong an important listening post. The constant traffic between Hong Kong and the mainland, the flow of refugees, returning journalists, tourists, and others, has provided opportunities to check facts, speculations, and even scholarly hunches. Third, the opportunity to meet fellow workers from all over the world provides a chance to exchange ideas for mutual benefit. The combination of these factors makes Hong Kong a more attractive place for contemporary China specialists to work, to say nothing of the good Chinese food and custom-made suits. No doubt Hong Kong will retain its importance as a major, if not the major, center for contemporary studies.

A few broad conclusions can be drawn from surveying the available library resources outside the United States for the study of modern and contemporary China. In general, the combined library resources on modern and contemporary China in American libraries are far richer than the combined resources in any country in the world outside China herself. Chinese library development in Europe, both East and West, including the Soviet Union and Scandinavia, has followed the traditional emphasis on philology and history. Although good collections of classical materials are found at the major centers, the collections of modern and contemporary materials are generally poor, with the exception of certain post-1949 materials in Communist countries.

The libraries of Japan have kept pace with the rapid post-war development in modern and contemporary Chinese studies. Taiwan is, of course, known for its collections of pre-1949 Kuomintang and Chinese Communist documents, but its post-1949 collections are acquired with an eye to the needs of intelligence research. The Union Research Institute's microfilms of post-1949 Chinese mainland newspapers and periodicals are outstanding in Hong Kong, and the Fung

Ping Shan Library of the University of Hong Kong maintains a fairly large number of pre-1949 mainland periodicals, as well as locally published newspapers. India is barely beginning to venture into the modern China field, with no library collections to speak of at present. Libraries in Singapore and Kuala Lumpur are insignificant in modern and contemporary materials. The collection of locally published Chinese-language newspapers at the University of Singapore, however, constitutes an important source for the study of the overseas Chinese.

The library of the School of Oriental and African Studies in London is the one to which most scholars in Western Europe turn for modern and contemporary materials. The SOAS library has been collecting pre-1949 publications for some time, but its chief emphasis has been on language and literature. Extensive collections of social science materials on both the pre-and post-1949 periods began only a short time ago, and these are being augmented by the Contemporary China Institute. The library in 1965 had a collection of approximately 10,000 volumes on the twentieth-century period, plus a periodical collection of about 800 titles, as well as several national Chinese newspapers. The major collection of Chinese newspapers is in the British Museum, which, however, has few published before 1949. The holdings of post-1949 newspapers are mostly those acquired by the British Foreign Office from American government and other sources. Aside from these, and its collection of Chinese government documents, as well as a unique collection of the first issues of a number of Chinese-language newspapers and periodicals published in Southeast Asia from the 1920's to the 1950's, the British Museum does not collect modern and contemporary Chinese materials extensively.

Cambridge and Oxford have good collections of traditional materials but, like Leeds, they have not yet built up their collections on the modern and contemporary periods.

French Libraries are much poorer than British libraries in contemporary

Chinese materials. Of the four Paris libraries where Chinese-language materials are collected, only the Centre de Documentation is explicitly responsible for modem and contemporary materials, and its collection of several thousand titles is of little significance yet. The other three — the Bibliotheque Nationale, the library of the Institut des Hautes Etudes Chinoises, and the library of l'Ecole Nationale des Langues Orientales — are primarily collections of pre-modem publications. The Chinese-French Association in Lyon has an important collection of Chinese periodicals published in the 1920's and 1930's.

The only library in West Germany collecting modern and contemporary Chinese materials systematically is the Staatsbibliothek in Marburg. It is expected that Bochum will collect some of the same materials, and that the Institute of Asian Studies in Hamburg will make extensive purchases in contemporary materials. Among the Institute's recent acquisitions is a complete set of the Union Research Institute microfilms from Hong Kong.

The strong Sinological tradition in Holland formerly placed little emphasis on collecting social science materials on the contemporary period, but the recently established Center for Documentation and Research on Contemporary China at the Sinological Institute in Leiden points to a long-range plan to establish a depository of modern and contemporary Chinese publications in the Netherlands. Since its founding in May 1969. The center has already acquired a number of Chinese monographs, newspapers, and periodicals, and expects to receive a complete set of the Union Research Institute microfilms.

The same development pattern may be seen in the Scandinavian countries. The new Scandinavian Institute of Asian Studies in Copenhagen has begun to collect on the modern and contemporary periods as a complement to existing collections of traditional Chinese materials.

In the libraries of Eastern Europe and the Soviet Union the situation is somewhat different. The Deutsche Staatsbibliothek in East Berlin; the Lu Xun

Library in Prague; the Fundamental Library of the Czech Academy of Sciences; the Lenin Library, the All-Union Library of Foreign Literature, and the library of the Institute of the Peoples of Asia (all in Moscow); the Leningrad Public Library; and the Leningrad Branch of the Institute of the Peoples of Asia are all major depositories of post-1949 Chinese mainland publications. The libraries in Poland, on the other hand, contain very little of such materials.

All Communist countries receive Chinese publications primarily through exchanges with the National Library of Peking and the Library of the Chinese Academy of Sciences. Although the number of items received since 1960 has diminished drastically, these countries do have a number of pre-1960 publications denied to us. These include publications of the various institutes of the Chinese Academy of Sciences, university journals, books issued by provincial publishers and other materials not usually available through commercial channels in the Far East. On the other hand, books issued in China between 1900 and 1949 are poorly represented in these libraries, with the exception of the collection on modern Chinese literature in the Lu Xun Library in Prague, and of certain fragmentary runs of periodicals published in the 1920's which are in the Lenin Library in Moscow.

The major Japanese centers collecting contemporary Chinese mainland materials are the National Diet Library, the Toyo Bunko, the Toyo Bunka Kenkyujo of the University of Tokyo, and the Jimbun Kagaku Kenkyujo of the University of Kyoto. Many other universities, such as Keio, Hitotsubashi, and Aichi, are collecting post-1949 materials, as are some research institutes, among them the Ajia Keizai Kenkyujo and particularly the Chugoku Kenkyujo. The libraries of the Prime Minister's Cabinet Research Office and the library of the Ministry of Foreign Affairs contain sizable collections of Chinese mainland publications, but these government libraries are not available to scholars. In addition there are several bookstores specializing in mainland materials, but unfortunately the major one, the Daian Book Company, which was also engaged in reprinting material from China acquired by private Japanese scholars and others, has recently gone out of business.

Government libraries in Taiwan do not emphasize the collection of monographs, their mainland newspaper and periodical collections being much better than their book holdings. Sometimes the Chinese Nationalist government, working through the Modern China Historical Materials Center, makes available Chinese Communist documents either captured by Nationalist raiding parties or carried out by defectors. The well-known Lien-chiang documents and the documents brought to Quemoy by Landing Craft 131 several years ago are good examples. Another important source in Taiwan is monitored mainland radio broadcasts in Chinese. Chinese broadcasts from Moscow beamed to the mainland are also monitored in Taiwan, but these unfortunately are not available to anyone outside the Chinese government.

In addition to microfilms available from the Union Research Institute, Hong Kong's library resources include the biographical file of Chinese Communist leaders maintained by the American Consulate-General's office. The file, available to qualified scholars, was microfilmed last year and is now available in several American libraries. The British Regional Information Office, which formerly issued a *News from Chinese Regional Radio Stations*, now publishes the *China News Summary* and *China News Items from the Press*. The bookstores in Hong Kong still remain the basic source of supply for mainland materials, although with the exception of some Red Guard newspapers, very little has come out of China since the Cultural Revolution.

Even though contemporary China studies and library resources to support them are not, on the whole, as far advanced in other countries as in the United States, significant beginnings are being made at several places, and these promise in time to develop into important programs. There are excellent opportunities for scholarly cooperation and collaboration. In the library field, one important step in this direction has recently been taken with the establishment in 1968 of the Center for Chinese Research Materials of the Association of Research Libraries. This Center has as its objective the strengthening of library resources on modern and contemporary China, and its interest is not restricted to American institutions; it hopes to further the development of library collections on a world-wide basis.

This approach can be commended for all scholars and librarians in the field of contemporary Chinese studies. Intellectual pursuits recognize no national boundaries, and knowledge is cumulative. Each advance that we make depends on the progress made by others.

Notes

This is a revised version of a lecture presented to the Summer Institute for Far Eastern Librarianship, University of Chicago, 30 July 1969, and published in *Harvard Library Bulletin*, vol. XVIII, no, 2 (April, 1970), pp. 141-154.

美國對中國大陸的研究

　　這是一篇關於美國對中國大陸研究狀況的回顧性文章。論述重點放在大學的學術專案上，至於美國政府的贊助專案只在相關資料可以公開獲得的情況下才有所論及。本文論述了研究背景、資金來源、組織機構、專案的性質、簡單介紹圖書館狀況並對未來做出展望。

背景

　　最近十年以來，美國對中國大陸的研究有了巨大的擴張，這是以下因素綜合導致的結果：北京共產黨政府在1949年的建立；採用「區域研究」方法來研究當代中國所存的厚望；和研究工作得到來自私人基金會、聯邦政府和大學當局前所未有的巨大的財政支持。

　　1949年之前很長一段時間內，中國就已經成為美國學者的學術興趣所在。但是，這種興趣主要還局限於歐洲早期的漢學傳統，主要研究中國的歷史和文化，很少注重社會科學。[1]第二次世界大戰使學者們對中國現代與當代事務的學術研究興趣大大增加，同時也目睹了中文教學專案的快速發展，這個快速發展的語言教學專案最初只是為了支援作戰需要的一部分，但隨後就成為許多大學的正規課程。哈佛大學在1946年開始了關於中國的區域研究專案，採用跨學科方法研究中國社會與文化。與此同時，耶魯大學在洛克菲勒基金會的資助下著手一個相同的專案。康乃爾大學在「現代化」的主題下引入遠東研究專案，哥倫比亞大學用洛克菲勒基金會的撥款在1949年9月建立了東亞研究所來準備培養立志從事現代當代東亞研究的研究生。與此同時，史丹佛大學胡佛研究院（當時稱為胡佛研究所和圖書館）創立了中文藏書部，這個藏書部後來成為研究20世紀中國最重要的原始資料庫。但是這些早期的項目基本上是為了教學和圖書館建設，並沒有一個對當代中國進行大規模研究的計畫。在洛克菲勒基金會的贊助下，華盛頓大學遠東和俄羅斯研究所組織了一個研究近代中國歷史的項目，主要是研究清代，重點是太平天國。

　　然而，推動美國當代中國研究的巨大動力，則是1949年中國大陸共產黨政府的成立，就像之前的俄國革命促進了斯拉夫研究一樣。發生在中國的巨變，使得我們有一種緊迫感要去理解那種變化的性質與意義。為了顯而易見的原因，美國政府加速了它的研究工作以便能夠跟得上在中國的迅速變化。此時由政府啟動的一項加速翻譯中國大陸的出版物（主要是報刊雜誌）的項目產生了具有深遠意義的結果，因為政府把成果分發給對當代中國事務感興趣的學者使用，以致學界在以後的這些年裡都受益匪淺。政府監控的來自中國大陸的無線電廣播成為了學者們獲取資料的另一條途徑。與此同時，各大學也開始引入新的關於當代中國的教學和研究專案。但是，這個發展過程卻是緩慢的，因為我們缺乏訓練有素的專業人才和必須的研究資金。截至當時，絕大部分從事中國研究的學者都只接受了歷史學或人文學科的訓練。只有極少數的學者可以既從事社會科學研究又同時是中國問題專家。大學裡的這些項目也才剛剛起步。要訓練出新一代在社會科學學科領域內和中國研究方面接受過雙重訓練，包括語言能力，尚需時日。為此，「區域研究」這個概念就被廣泛採用。

　　「區域研究」──使用包括一系列社會科學在內的跨學科方法來了解一個當代社會的研究方式──其理念基於從各學科的獨特出發點來研究一個特定的社會及其文化的全部，其產生的綜合結果會比從單一學科的觀點要更為平衡。由於從用跨學科方法取得成功的斯拉夫研究得來的鼓勵，越來越多的美國大學轉向「區域研究」來研究1949年以後的當代中國。

　　此後，這一新專案發展迅速，主要因為有來自於私人基金會和隨後聯邦政府的大量財政資助。1955年，福特基金會撥款給哈佛大學，成立中國經濟研究專案。同年，卡內基財團贊助哈佛大學開展了中國政治研究專案，它們成為了後來大量由基金會和政府撥款協助美國主要大學建立類似的中國語言和研究中心專案的先驅。

資金

第二次世界大戰結束後，主要有三家基金會資助美國大學的中國研究，即洛克菲勒基金會、卡內基財團和福特基金會。1950年代的資金主要來自於洛克菲勒基金會和卡內基財團，福特基金會則通過其1952年設立的外國區域獎學金扮演了一個相對較小的角色。然而，整個1960年代，情況卻發生了反向作用，福特基金會通過史無前例的大量資助專案，成為了中國研究的主要贊助者，尤其是在當代中國研究這方面。

1959年，當福特基金會認為為資助斯拉夫研究設計的模式在當代中國研究專案上也行得通的時候，他們便做出了在中國研究領域進行大筆投資的決定。斯拉夫研究資助模式是二戰後由洛克菲勒基金會和卡內基財團聯合設計出來的，專門為資助兩所大學建立蘇聯和東歐研究中心（哥倫比亞大學和哈佛大學被選中），並撥款設立斯拉夫研究聯合委員會，由美國學術團體協會（American Council of Learned Societies，簡稱ACLS）和社會科學研究理事會（Social Science Research Council，簡稱SSRC）掌管，為個人研究、會議的召開和其他活動提供資金。1955年秋季，由福特基金會發起，在一次有中國研究領域內為數眾多的歷史學家和社會科學家參加的會議上做出了成立當代中國聯合委員會（Joint Committee on Contemporary China，簡稱JCCC）的決議，福特基金會支持這個決議並同意資助這個委員會的工作。這個委員會同樣由美國學術團體協會和社會科學研究理事會管理。此外，福特基金會還決定為以下四所大學的中國研究中心提供財政支援：加州大學柏克萊分校、哥倫比亞大學、哈佛大學和華盛頓大學（後來又加上密西根大學和康乃爾大學）。從1959到1968年，福特基金會為上述項目和在其他大學的類似項目一共劃撥了2,400萬美金。[2] 這些資金並不是全部流向當代中國研究領域，其中一部分投給了前現代中國研究領域，但是大量的資金還是花在了現代和當代的研究方面，包括建立研究中心，設立新的教職崗位，獎學金和圖書館資料的收集。在福特基金會承擔了大量資助專案的同時，洛克菲勒基金會和卡內基財團依然為美國的中國研究提供資助，儘管規模小了。從 1960 到 1968 年，卡內基財團共提供了 1,739,000 美金的撥款，包括在紐約的教育和世界事務公司（Education and world affairs, Inc. of New York）監督下，在香港建立的旨在協助學者們在該英國殖民地進行共產主義中國研究的「大學服務中心」[3]。洛克菲勒基金會 1956 到 1968 年也共支付了 84 萬美元作為研究經費。[4]

幾乎與此同時，聯邦政府通過「國防教育法案」（National Defense and Education Act，簡稱 NDEA），開始了對中國和其他地區研究的資助。雖然這項法案的主要目的是語言訓練，但也為各種學科研究生提供獎學金，以及為各有關大學提供補助，用以支付行政管理和其他後勤服務的費用。從 1959 年到 1966 年，中國語言訓練的獎學金總共有 1,013 個，占其間全國所有東亞語言獎學金的 57.7%，和這 8 年裡所有「國防教育法案」補助費的 14.40%[5]。從 1959 到 1968 這 10 年間，為中國語言研訓練獎學金共支出了 5,790,000 美金。[6]除了「國防教育法案」獎學金之外，從 1960 年到 1968 年，國家科學基金會也撥給中國研究 25 萬美金。[7]

這樣一來，基金會和聯邦政府在 1959 到 1968 年這 10 年間一共在美國大學的中國研究領域投入了超過 3,200 萬美金，而這並不包括由美國政府機構進行的內部的和合同制的研究。這些前所未有的大量的財政資助對美國關於 1911 年以來的中國，特別是關於當代中國的研究起到了重要的作用。

組織機構

在美國，當代中國研究的機構組織一直沿著單一機構和多機構聯合兩條道路前行。單一研究機構的結構通常採取在某一大學的研究中心或研究所的形式。這樣的中心或者研究所通常由行政人員和研究人員組成，後者的成員一般是由該中心或者研究所在的大學各院系中有關中國的教授任命。作為研究人員為中心服務的同時，他們還要承擔在各自系裡的日常教學任務。一個研究中心很少會資助一個長時期的全職研究者。短期的全職研究者可能包括離開教學崗位休假的教授；來自國外或其他大學有對某一中心來說具很有吸引力的研究計畫的訪問學者；還有那些高年級的研究生以及需要時間來完成專題論文或修訂論文準備出版的博士後學者。當然也有例外。位於華盛頓的布魯金斯研究所和史丹佛大學胡佛研究院都有固定的全職研究員職位的設施。所有大學研究中心或研究所一般都不負責教學任務。不過有些有他們自己的出版項目。[8]

多機構聯合的組織一般採用全國委員會的形式進行研究和處理與研究有關的問題。這些委員會的主要職責為各在其專業能力範圍內鑑定其不同的研究需要；提供學者個人的研究經費；召開研討會；和出版研究成果。這些委員會自己並不參與任何教學活動。這種類型的委員會有兩個最為重要。一個是由美國學術團體協會（ACLS）和社會科學研究理事會（SSRC）聯合創辦的「當代中國聯合委員會」（Joint Committee on Contemporary China，簡稱JCCC）另一個則是先前由社會科學研究理事會主辦的「中國經濟委員會」（Committee on the Economy of China）。

當代中國聯合委員會的主要職責，在福特基金會撥款支持其工作的條件下，鼓勵各大學研究中心的相互合作，構想發展對1949年以後的中國的研究方式（自1965年開始在時間上已拓展上自1911年）。當代中國聯合委員會的成員由美國學術團體協會和社會科學研究理事會聯合任命，他們來自著名大學裡不同學科並且在從事現代當代中國研究的教授。他們掌管四個方面的工作：（1）提供博士後津貼；（2）資助調查工作和研究會議；（3）資助研究資料的收集和使用；（4）學術交流。社會科學研究理事會負責支援當代中國聯合委員會的行政工作。

從1961年開始，當代中國聯合委員會在全國性的競爭下給人文學科法律和社會科學的學者們提供研究補貼，讓他們研究自己選擇的有關民國時代和共產黨時代的研究專案。至1968年年底為止，當代中國聯合委員會共收到295份申請書，並給予110份共計668,500美金的研究補貼。[9] 從1960年開始，當代中國聯合委員會還召開了多次關於政治、經濟、社會學和人類學、法律、政治、歷史、地理和比較共產主義的會議，並在這些會議後成立了下面幾個隸屬於當代中國聯合委員會的常設小組委員會：（1）中國社會研究小組委員會（1961-）；（2）中國政府和政治小組委員會（1965-）；（3）中國法律小組委員會（1965-）和（4）資料小組委員會（1961-1967）。在福特基金會910,000美金的撥款資助下，於1961年還建立了一個單獨的中國經濟委員會。由這些委員會發起的研究工作的性質將在本文的下一個部分進行討論。這些小組委員會中的前三個，每一個都創辦了一系列的專題論文集。

在資料方面，當代中國聯合委員會贊助購買了一整套香港友聯研究所的剪報縮微膠捲和該所收集的其他關於共產主義中國的資料，這些資料存放於芝加哥的研究圖書館中心（之前的「中西部地區館際互借中心」）。受益於國家科學基金會（National Science Foundation，簡稱NSF）給予社會科學研究理事會的撥款，當代中國聯合委員會以低成本把那些以前美國聯合出版研究服務處（Joint Publication Research Service，簡稱JPRS）只能提供給美國政府部門使用的關於中國的翻譯資料，分發給了美國研究圖書館和其他國家。它還委託彼得·伯頓（Peter Berton）和吳文津編撰了《當代中國研究指南》一書，1964年由胡佛研究院出版。當代中國聯合委員會下屬的資料小組委員會開始了一項世界性的資料普查工作，查明那些可以得到並可使用的關於當代中國的研究資料。其結果就是由美國學術團體協會和社會科學研究理事會向福特基金會申請資金，在華盛頓特區建立一個研究資料中心，任務是複製和發行關於當代中國的檔案文獻和研究資料。為了這個目的，1967年，福特基金會批准了一筆總額50萬美金的撥款給「研究圖書館協會」（Association of Research Libraries，簡稱ARL）於1968年正式成立了「中國研究資料中心」（Center for Chinese Research Materials，簡稱CCRM）。

除了當代中國聯合委員會之外，還有其他有更多特殊功能性的全國委員會。他們包括：當代中國研究聯絡委員會（Liaison Committee on Study of Contemporary China），它由福特基金會根據當代中國聯合委員會的推薦出資創辦，主要職責是鼓勵來自美國、英國和其他國家的學者在當代中國研究領域內進行合作；和美國學術團體協會和社會科學研究理事會下屬的「國外區域研究獎學金專案聯合委員會」（Joint Committee on the Foreign Area Scholarship Program）。從1952到1961年，這個項目由福特基金會主管，

1962年移交給美國學術團體協會和社會科學研究理事會管理。從1952到1967年這15年間，總共有335份獎學金（包括續發的）發給了163位不同學科研究古代及現代中國的研究生。[10]

　　在政府方面，眾所周知，大部分處理國家安全事務和對外事務的機構都有他們自己對當代中國的不斷進行的內部研究，或者是通過合約委託與學術或半學術團體進行的研究。國防部國際安全事務助理部長辦公室（The Office of the Assistant Secretary of Defense for International and Security Affairs，簡稱ISA）「制定並協調在國際政治軍事和對外經濟事務領域內的政策和程式……」ISA的持續不斷的涉外研究的焦點在於鑑別和分析防衛政策的取捨，用以處理與美國國家安全有關的新興的國際問題。雖然大部分ISA的研究工作都由蘭德公司（Rand Corporation）和防禦分析研究所（Institute for Defense Analysis）負責，ISA依然會接受合乎ISA的要求從其他的研究機構和大學關於這方面的研究計畫。[11]同樣的，美國軍方也有內部的或者合同制的研究專案。「美國軍備控制與裁軍署」（U.S. Arms Control and Disarmament Agency，簡稱ACDA）也被授權「去確保獲得一批有關裁軍理論和實踐的知識……和安排對美國私人機構或政府機構或個人在軍控和裁軍領域內，或其他有關方面進行的研究（包括簽署和約、協議）提供經費……」。[12]國家科學基金會下的經濟和人力研究辦公室（Office of Economic and Manpower Studies）領導了一項研究，旨在為世界上關鍵地區的科學技術提供關於資本資源、人力資源和教育設施的全面資訊。他們還出版了一本關於共產主義中國的專業人才及專業教育的專著。[13]上面已提到的美國聯合出版物研究處（JPRS）是商業部下的聯邦科學技術情報交換所（Clearing House for Federal Scientific and Technical Information）的一個組成部分，主要職責是為其他聯邦機構進行翻譯、摘錄外國語文出版品的研究。從1963年開始，該處每年以千數計的報告中的大多數都以成本價格公開發行[14]。其他對共產主義中國進行廣泛研究的政府機構包括中央情報局（Central Intelligence Agency）、國務院情報研究局（Bureau of Intelligence and Research of the Department of State），和美國新聞署（United State Information

Agency）。

　　為了保證「政府研究人員和政策制定者和從事域外區域和國際事務研究
的民間學者之間的穩定的資訊和意見交流」，國務院情報與研究局的外事研
究辦公室（Office of External Research，簡稱XR）成為國務院研究部門與民
間學者聯繫的「主要聯絡點」。外事研究辦公室的主要任務是「甄別在對外
事務的學術研究成果中，哪些對美國執行外交政策有價值，並且安排將這研
究成果給政策制定者作為參考」，安排的方法是通過該辦公室為情報與研究
局設立的研究合約及顧問專案。[15]

　　除了與學術團體進行聯絡的功能之外，外事辦公室還為一個跨部會稱為
「域外區域研究協調小組」（Foreign Area Research Coordination Group，簡稱
FAR）提供類似的秘書處的服務工作。域外區域研究協調小組成立於1964
年，目的是「更好地協調政府發起的在社會科學領域中的域外區域研究和跨
文化的研究工作」。小組成員都是支援有關域外或者國際事務的合約研究或
贊助研究的政府機構。他們的目的是防止機構間的重複研究，鼓勵研究成果
最大程度上的共用，提高政府對非政府研究成果的利用效率。[16]

　　域外區域研究協調小組的成員代表21個政府部門和機構。在成員會
上，小組把關注點放在實質的研究議題，關於選來進行研究的地區的研究專
案，和影響政府與學界關係的若干事件上。有時小組特邀請來自學術團體的
專家們去幫助確定和評估政府的需要，並核審關於被選來做研究對象的地區
的研究成果。「域外區域研究協調小組」的大量實質工作分別由某一特定地
理區域負責提供研究計畫的小組委員會進行。目前，一共有8個常設的小組
委員會和一個專門的小組委員會。8個小組委員會中有7個是區域性的，它
們是：非洲、中國、東亞（不含中國）、拉丁美洲、近東和南亞、西歐、蘇
聯和東歐。第8個是行為科學小組委員會（另一個專門的小組委員會負責關
於出版政策，於1968年成立）。[17] 域外區域研究協調小組發行一份有關域外
和外交事務的雙月刊通訊《域外區域研究協調小組視野》（*FAR Horizons*），
可以向美國政府印務局（U.S. Government Printing Office）訂閱。

研究的性質

　　總的來說，大學對中國大陸的研究以問題為導向，而政府則以政策為導向。在學術圈裡，經濟學家們一向都從數量和非數量兩個方面對共產主義中國的經濟進行研究，出版了關於共產主義中國的國家收入、國民生產總值、社會核算、工業增長的速度和方式、非農勞工、農業和對外貿易方面的專著。對於各工業部門的，像鋼鐵工業、機器製造業、建築業、工業選址及交通運輸、能源利用的研究，也有專題性的論述出現。同樣，在經濟計畫的政策方面，像政府財政預算、市場控制、工作獎金、工業管理和大躍進運動也進行了專題性研究並有出版物面世。經濟學中數量研究的關鍵在於資料。就共產主義中國而言，這個令人捉摸不定的主題已經被美國的經濟學家們做過深刻的研究和分析。其中有一本書就致力於從資料體系發展的角度來看共產主義中國資料的有效性，還有一本中國大陸經濟資料的手冊也已經面世。[18]

　　在1950年代這10年裡，大部分政治學者在對共產主義中國分析的過程中都傾向於對它的總體政治結構給予一個籠統性的描述。但是，越來越多的政治學家在對當代中國的研究中，把注意力轉向到了「有關政治體系的基本性質和政治發展過程這類問題上；也轉向到有關領導性質、政治文化特性、各種各樣政治結構的功能運作、政策規畫和政策實施的過程，以及社會動員的技術、軍隊扮演的角色、溝通體系和官僚機構的運作等類問題上。」[19] 因此，關於共產主義中國的政治領袖、政治參與、官僚機構、意識形態（特別是那些影響行為的）、精英研究、對外關係和比較共產主義的書都出現了。哥倫比亞大學的歐邁格（Michel Oksenberg）把美國政治學家關於當代中國政治的文章比較方便地分成了利用下面七種方法或模式中的一類或幾類的著述：歷史分析模式、現代化模式、綜合複雜官僚機構模式、極權主義模式、比較共產主義模式、革命社會模式、方法論模式。[20] 根據他的分析，「歷史分析模式」可以被稱作「中國就是中國就是中國」模式，聚焦於歷史的延續性和變化。「現代化模式」視「中國為發展中的、在現代化和工業化進程中的國家，和其他不發達國家有許多共同之處」。所以，這種看法可以稱作「中國是印度是奈及利亞」模式。從這種視角看中國的學者的研究興趣傾向於對那些擺在一起被稱為「現代化」的發展會如何影響政治體系，而政治體系又會如何影響到那些所謂的「現代化」的發展問題上。「錯綜複雜官僚機構模式」比較了中國共產黨政府的一個龐大的官僚機構和旁地方的類似的機構的異同。這種觀點可以稱為「中國是通用汽車公司是哥倫比亞大學」的觀點。那就是說，「中國的權力鬥爭以及很多政府面對的問題和解決問題的途徑都與其他任何錯綜複雜的官僚機構相似」。「集權主義」模式建立在「中國最引人注目的是政治體系全面或接近全面地滲透到社會裡」這樣的理念之上。這種模式也許應可以被貼上「中國是史達林主義的蘇聯是納粹德國」的標籤。「比較共產主義」模式根源於「中國共產黨政府最基本的特徵就是它是共產主義」這種設想。因此據此模式，「中國就是蘇聯就是南斯拉夫」。「革命社會」模式傾向於把共產主義中國看成處在殘酷革命之中的社會的範例。它的特徵是普遍的暴力，舊制度的更新，新社會精英奪取和鞏固他們的政權。這些都是所有正在經歷精英和制度猛迅變遷的社會政治體系的共有現象。因此，這種觀點應該可以說是「中國是1789年以後的法國是1959年以後的古巴」的模式。最後，研究大陸中國的「方法論模式」反映了下列的事實：目前的共產黨中國是一個對田野研究「關閉」的社會體系。因此，研究只能在遠距離進行。此外，使用中文原始資料涉及一門如何解讀有深奧意識形態內涵的語言的藝術。這使當代中國研究像釋譯猶太法典《塔木德經》似的。因此，用「方法論模式」來研究中國可稱為「中國是1940年代末的蘇聯是詮釋《塔木德經》式的研究」。

　　歐邁格在他的分析中明確指出，儘管這七種模式相互交叉而且都可以用來理解共產主義中國，然而事實上其中的三種模式在共產主義中國的政治研究中占首要地位。它們是歷史分析模式，比較共產主義模式，和極權主義模式。不過，他看到了現代化模式和革命視角在未來年代中有增長的趨勢。[21]

　　由於沒有進入中國大陸的機會，美國的社會學家和人類學家不能在實地調查的基礎上進行研究共產主義中國的田野工作，除了兩本楊慶堃（C.

K.Yang）的著作：一本是關於一個過渡到共產黨主義的廣東鄉村，另一本是討論共產黨革命時期的中國家庭。兩書都是根據作者在1940年代末期到1950年初期實地考察寫成。其他所有的美國有關共產主義中國社會的著作都是遠距離研究的成果，未能獲益於實地的觀察。在他們的著作中美國社會學家主要關注的是社會組織的變化和控制，和「再社會化」的問題，其中包括「思想改造運動」的方法和過程，和它與社會變遷、家庭和家族體系變化的關係。依據這些研究已出版了兩部大作：一是弗朗茲‧舒爾曼（Franz Schurmann）撰寫的關於意識形態和社會組織的書，另一本是傅高義（Ezra Vogel）完成的共產主義統治下的廣州的作品。另外，當代中國聯合委員會下屬的中國社會研究小組委員會還把注意力放在了對中國社會微觀和宏觀組織的考察上，不僅包括中國大陸，還有台灣地區而且回溯到中華民國以前的時代。中國社會研究小組委員會還花了相當多時間討論當代中國研究的檔案資料，和田野研究方法，並且發起了一項用電腦制作三本加以注釋的書目計畫，包括用各種語文出版的關於1644年以來的中國社會的書籍論文。這套書目由施堅雅（G.William Skinner）主編，計畫在1971年由史丹佛大學出版社出版。

關於共產主義中國的法律和法律體系的研究是比較近來的發展。美國的法律學者對研究共產主義中國主要的興趣是在中國的法律行政，包括民事和刑事。其次，中國共產黨制度的法律體系的背景和發展，以及中國共產黨對國際法和國際協定的看法也是研究的注意力所在。與社會科學研究者一樣，法律學者也花了時間去討論資料的利用和研究方法，比如採訪難民的技巧。此外由菲力浦‧比蘭恰（Philip R. Bilancia）主編的《中國法律術語詞典》的工作已在進行中，有望在近期出版。

心理學家和社會科學領域的同仁們都研究了在共產主義中國用以控制社會的一種獨特的方法：「洗腦」或是「強制教育」的現象。利用教育作為政治思想的灌輸工具也吸引了研究中國的美國教育家的注意。他們還對發生在共產主義中國教育體系的變革和與此相關的勞動力問題感到興趣。同文學史家和社會科學家一起他們參與了關於中國共產黨和知識分子之間的矛盾的研究，比如，百花齊放運動及其後果，就吸引了許多注意。

　　在科學領域，很少有關注中國大陸科技發展的研究。一些數學家、醫生和其他人在各自領域對共產主義中國的科學發展進行了單獨個人的研究，但是在這方面並沒有有組織的和大規模的研究計畫。美國聯合出版物研究處翻譯了科技領域的中國出版物，美國政府為了國家安全的目的，也在同類領域進行自己的研究。在當代中國聯合委員會的財政支持下，將於1971年春天在英國蘇塞克斯大學舉辦一次關於中國科技領域的會議。

　　前邊已經提到過美國政府發起的對共產主義中國研究工作的性質。總的來說，美國政府對共產主義中國的研究定位於滿足政策制訂的需要。也許闡明這些最好辦法就是引用由域外區域研究協調小組提出的30個主題中美國政府最具興趣的部分。[22]

有及時興趣的研究主題

1. 分析研究中國共產黨高層領導之間、下級政工幹部和行政幹部之間、人民解放軍隊高級將領之間、下屬軍隊領導人之間的個人和政治關係（關於上面每一組合的動力的分別研究也很有用）。重點應該放在這些權力結構中不同分子對中國政治、經濟、社會和意識形態領域中的關鍵問題的態度。

2. 關於美國和中國國家利益的重合之處的研究。

有長期興趣的研究主題

15. 對家庭、村鎮、省、個人關係和國家的忠誠的轉變。
16. 對中層官僚、技術人員、管理人員的角色和地位的分析

圖書館

　　美國圖書館豐富的館藏資源是美國當代中國研究得以快速發展的關鍵因素之一。雖然胡佛研究院在這方面的收藏仍然是最好的，但是其他35家美國圖書館，包括政府機構和十餘所主要大學圖書館，從1949年以來也大量地收藏了1949年以後中國大陸出版的書籍、報紙和期刊。20年來的努力加

上大量的財政支持，在美國已經建立起一個圖書館網路，其總和的藏書量要遠大於中國大陸之外的任何一家圖書館的收藏。[23] 政府為大學的工作成果也作了補充，包括分發美國聯合出版物研究處翻譯的大陸中國的報紙和雜誌，和上面提到的監控收聽的中國無線電廣播，由政府間或公布的其他中國方面的材料，比如《工作通訊》（中國人民解放軍的通訊）、大陸的地方報紙以及紅衛兵出版物。這些資料讓許多大學能夠完成它們不少的研究計畫工作。在這方面我們也必須感謝中華民國政府的合作，他們為美國在台灣進行研究的學者以及美國學術界提供了他們收藏的中國共產黨的文獻。

未來展望

　　評估美國對中國大陸研究的發展，毫無疑問的是它的成就很多，但是還有許多工作要做。經過訓練後的新一代專家已經開始嶄露頭角，研究組織的架構已經確定下來，圖書收藏也建立起來。不過，現在就出現了一個明顯不祥的預兆，那就是，對美國當代中國研究的快速發展起到重要作用的財政支持在將來幾年內可能不再像以前我們所熟知的那樣了。基金會將來支援在美國大學裡的區域研究的幅度目前還不確定。主要基金會的資助如有大量減縮，毫無疑問地會使美國的當代中國研究發展放緩，尤其在政府削減預算使許多高等教育的聯邦專案都得不到補助的情況下。「國防教育法案」獎學金專案在財政緊縮的 1970-1971 會計年度削減了大約 16%；1971-1972 年度，又計畫再次削減 50%，並且很有可能整個「國防教育法案」獎學金項目都將會在之後結束。但是，在這困難的條件情形下，福特基金會做出了鼓舞人心的決定，至少在最近幾年裡，將給 6 個主要的現代及當代中國研究中心基本的後勤支持，並且以相當於最近過去的水準，為學術社團繼續提供研究生的獎學金和博士後研究基金，以資助那些研究中華帝國和近代和現代中國的學者，同時對日本和韓國的研究資助也會有增加。然而，除非有額外的資金可用，否則過去十年裡在美國大學裡形成的對中國大陸的研究勢頭，將不可能繼續維持下去。

注釋

* 本文於1970年12月14-19日在中華民國國際關係研究所主辦之「第一屆中美中國大陸問題研討會」發表的報告。載《第一屆中、美「中國大陸問題」研討會專輯》（*Collected Documents of the First Sino-American Conference on Mainland China*），台北：中華民國國際關係研究所，1971，頁29-46；並載《問題與研究》英文版 *Issues & Studies*，第7卷，第4期（1971年1月），頁21-34。國會圖書館埃德文‧比爾（Edwin G. Beal, Jr.）博士；密西根大學費惟凱（Albert Feuerwerker）教授；哈佛大學傅高義（Ezra Vogel）教授對我的初稿都提供了寶貴的意見；負責當代中國聯合委員會行政工作的社會科學研究理事會（SSRC）的布萊斯‧伍德（Bryce Wood）博士提供了關於基金會和該委員會（JCCC）的最新工作報告。均在此表示謝忱。

[1] 關於美國中國學研究的早期歷史的簡明敘述可以參見：賴德烈（Kenneth Scott Latourette）的〈美國的遠東研究：回顧與展望〉（"Far Eastern Studies in the United States: Retrospect and Prospect"）見《遠東季刊》（*The Far Eastern Quarterly*）1955年第14期，頁3-11；錢存訓1951年在夏威夷大學亞洲研究夏季研習班上的講稿——〈美國的亞洲研究：歷史考察〉（"Asian Studies in America: A Historical Survey"）。關於從1930年代末到1940年代初各大學中國研究專案的詳細報告，見《美國遠東研究短訊》（*Notes on Far Eastrern Studies in America*）第1-12期（1937-1943）。自1946年起類似的資訊，見《遠東季刊》和它的後繼《亞洲研究學報》（*The Journal of Asian Studies*）以及《亞洲學會通訊》（*Newsletter of the Association for Asian Studies*）。

[2] 見1968年3月15-16日在紐約由當代中國聯合委員會發起的討論會摘要附錄3——《關於現當代中國研究的現況》，頁1。以下簡稱「JCCC紐約會議」，1968.3.15-16。

[3] 出處同上。又見《亞洲學會通訊》1968年5月第3期，頁5。

[4] 《JCCC紐約會議，1968.3.15-16》附錄3，頁1。

[5] 《東亞研究學會通訊》增刊，第12期，1967年4月，〈國防教育法案下的東亞研究〉，頁8。

[6] 《JCCC紐約會議，1968.3.15-16》附錄3，頁1。

[7] 同上。

[8] 有兩本介紹美國大學區域研究非常有用的手冊，都是由美國國務院外事研究辦公室（原外事研究小組）編纂的。一本是《美國大學的語言和區域研究專案》（*The Language and Area Study Programs in American Universities*），1964年出版，介紹了153項提供給研究生攻讀學位的項目；一本是《大學外國事務研究中心名錄》（*The*

University Centers of Foreign Affairs Research; A Directory），1968年出版，介紹了191所主要對國外事務進行社會科學方面研究的中心，本科生教學中心不包括在內。

[9]　《美國中國學研究，1959-1969：各全國學術協會下屬之各委員會的結構與功能（草稿）》（Studies of China in the United States, 1959-1969. Committees of National Councils — Structures and Functions[Draft]）為當代中國研究聯絡委員會草擬，1969年3月13日，頁2。當代中國聯合委員會（JCCC）的動態經常在社會科學研究理事會（SSRC）的通訊Items上登載。社會科學研究理事會的年終報告也包含當代中國聯合委員會和它下屬的小組委員會該年的活動狀況，並列研究專案撥款數目。

[10]　同上，頁6。根據1967年當代中國聯合會（JCCC）的調查，該年美國各大學總共招收了665名研究中國的研究生（碩士班和博士班）。參見《對從事現當代中國人文社會科學領域的研究生調查》（Survey of Graduate Students in Humanities and Social Sciences Specializing in Modern and Contemporary China, April 1967–Supplement）1967年10月24日增刊，頁1。目前數字可能更大。

[11]　美國國務院外事研究辦公室：《外國事務研究：政府資源名錄》（Foreign Affairs Research: A Directory of Government Resources）（華盛頓特區，1969），頁6。

[12]　同上，頁4。

[13]　同上，頁30。

[14]　同上，頁8。

[15]　同上，頁36。

[16]　同上，頁11。

[17]　同上，頁11-12。

[18]　這裡和以下段落裡列舉的研究主題取自出版的專著和論文，不包括碩士和博士論文所選的題目。自1949年以來，美國大學通過了有關中國大陸和中國共產黨共165篇碩士論文（1949-1964）和112篇博士論文（1949-1970）。參見彼得・伯頓（Peter Berton）和吳文津主編的《當代中國研究指南》（Contemporary China: A Research Guide）（史丹佛：胡佛研究院，1967），頁560-584，和《亞洲學會通訊》（Newsletter of the Association for Asian Studies）自第4期13卷開始（1969年5月））。有關中國大陸各主題，包括發表和未發表的研究論文的詳細目錄，可參見《亞洲學報》每年出版一次的《亞洲研究文獻目錄》（Annual Bibiliography of the Journal of Asian Studies）。

[19]　鮑大可（A. Doak Barnett）主編的《中共的現行政治》（Chinese Communist Politics in Action）（西雅圖和倫敦：華盛頓大學出版社，1969），首頁xiii。

[20]　歐邁格（Michael C. Oksenberg）編，《當代中國政治英文入門書目》（A Bibliography of Secondary English Language Literature on Contemporary Chinese Politics）（紐約：哥

倫比亞大學東亞研究所，〔1970〕），首頁iii-xxxv。

[21]　同上，首頁xiii。

[22]　30個主題的全文見《FAR視野》（*FAR Horizons*）第2卷，第4期（1969年7月），頁4-5。

[23]　吳文津（Eugene Wu），〈美國之外的當代中國研究〉（"Study of Contemporary China Outside the United States"），《哈佛圖書館館刊》（*Harvard Library Bulletin*）第18卷（1970年4月），頁141-154。

（呂傑譯，胡志宏校，吳文津複校，載《美國學者論美國中國學》，朱政惠編，上海：辭書出版社，2009，頁150-162。此文經過作者再修訂。）

Studies of Mainland China in the United States

This paper is a review of the status of the studies of Communist China in the United States. The emphasis is on the academic programs in universities, with references to U.S. Government-sponsored programs being made only when the relevant information is publicly and readily available. The review covers the background, funding, organization, and nature of these programs, with a brief note on libraries and some comments on future prospects.

Background

The enormous expansion in the study of Mainland China in the United States during the last ten years is the result of a combination of factors: the establishment of a Communist regime in Beijing in 1949, the promise of the "area studies" approach to the study of contemporary China, and the unprecedented and massive financial support by private foundations, the Federal Government, and university administrations.

China had been for many years prior to 1949 a subject of academic interest to American scholars. However, the early interest was primarily in the study of Chinese history and culture in the European Sinological tradition, with relatively little attention being paid to the social sciences. [1] World War II generated greater academic interest, in modern and contemporary affairs; it also witnessed the beginning of an accelerated program of instruction of the Chinese language, initially as part of the War effort, and subsequently as a part of the regular curriculum of a number of universities. Harvard initiated in 1946 its Regional

Studies Program on China with an interdisciplinary approach to the study of Chinese society and civilization. Yale embarked upon a similar program about the same time with the support of the Rockefeller Foundation. Cornell introduced a Far Eastern Studies program with a theme of "modernization," and Columbia University, also using a Rockefeller grant, established in September 1949 its East Asian Institute to prepare graduate students for careers dealing with modern and contemporary East Asia. In the meantime, the Hoover Institution (then known as the Hoover Institute and Library) of Stanford University founded its Chinese Collection which was to become the most important depository of source materials for the study of twentieth century China. But these early programs were essentially for training and library purposes, and there were no large-scale research projects on the contemporary period. The Modern Chinese History Project organized by the Far Eastern and Russian Institute of the University of Washington, with a Rockefeller grant, was for the study of the Qing period, with emphasis on the Taiping Rebellion.

However, the establishment of a Communist government on the China mainland in 1949 served as a great stimulant to the development of contemporary China studies in the United States, as did the Russian Revolution to the development of Slavic studies years before. A great upheaval had taken place in China, and there was a sense of urgency to understand the nature and meaning of the cataclysmic changes that were occurring. For obvious reasons, the U.S. Government moved rapidly in its research efforts to keep pace with the fast-changing Chinese scene. The most far-reaching effort initiated by the Government at this time, which was to benefit greatly the academic community in the following years, was its stepped-up program of translation of Chinese mainland publications, mainly newspapers and magazines, and their distribution to scholars interested in contemporary Chinese affairs. Government-monitored Chinese mainland radio broadcasts were another source to which scholars were given access. The universities, in the meantime, also began to introduce new teaching and research programs dealing with the contemporary Chinese scene, especially in the area of research. But the developmental process was a slow one, for a lack of trained personnel and necessary funding. Up to that time, most China scholars were trained either in history or in the humanities. Very few social scientists were also China specialists. The programs already in existence at universities were just beginning to develop. Time was required to produce a new generation of scholars who would be trained both in the social science disciplines and in Chinese studies/ including language competence. The "area studies" concept was widely adopted for this purpose.

The concept of "area studies"—an interdisciplinary approach, encompassing several social sciences, to the understanding of a contemporary society—has its rationale in the belief that by subjecting the whole of a given society and its culture to an investigation from the vantage points of several disciplines, a more balanced perspective of that society could emerge than would be possible when studied within the confines of a single discipline. Encouraged by the success of Slavic studies using the interdisciplinary approach, American universities in increasing numbers adopted the same approach in dealing with contemporary China after 1949.

This new program developed rapidly during the subsequent years mainly because of the generous financial support it received first from private foundations, and later from the Federal Government. The Ford Foundation grant to Harvard in 1955 to set up a Chinese Economic Studies program, and the Carnegie Corporation grant to the same university in the same year to initiate a Chinese Political Studies program were to become the precursors of a large number of similar foundation and government grants to major universities across the United States for the establishment of research and language centers for Chinese studies.

Funding

The three major foundations which have been funding Chinese studies in American universities since the end of World War II are the Rockefeller Foundation, the Carnegie Corporation, and the Ford Foundation. During the 1950's funds came primarily from the Rockefeller Foundation and the Carnegie Corporation, with the Ford Foundation playing a relatively minor role through its Foreign Area Fellowship Program set up in 1952.

However, during the 1960's the roles were reversed, and the Ford Foundation became the principal supporter of Chinese studies, especially on the contemporary period, through an unprecedented and massive funding program.

The decision on the part of the Ford Foundation to invest substantially in the China field was made in 1959 when Ford deemed it feasible to adopt the model designed for Slavic studies for a contemporary China program. The Slavic studies model which was worked out by cooperation of the Rockefeller Foundation and the Carnegie Corporation just after World War II called for grants to two universities (Columbia and Harvard were chosen) to set up research centers on the Soviet Union and Eastern Europe, and the funding of a Joint Committee on Slavic Studies, appointed by the American Council of Learned Societies (ACLS) and the Social Science Research Council (SSRC), to provide research grants to individuals, conferences, and other activities. At a conference convened by the Ford Foundation in the fall of 1955 which was attended by a large group of' historians and social scientists in the China field, a decision was made to set up a Joint Committee on Contemporary China, also to be appointed by the ACLS and the SSRC, and the Ford Foundation agreed to fund the Joint Committee's program. Furthermore, Ford also decided to provide financial support to centers of. Chinese studies at four universities: the University of California in Berkeley, Columbia, Harvard, and the University of Washington (Michigan and Cornell were added later). From 1959 to 1968 Ford contributed $24 million to the above-mentioned programs as well as to similar programs at a number of other universities and elsewhere. [2] The funds did not all go to contemporary China studies, however. Some of the funds were earmarked for the study of pre-modern China; but the bulk of the funds were spent on programs related to the modern and contemporary period, including the establishment of research centers, new teaching posts, fellowships, and library materials. While Ford was undertaking this massive funding program, the Rockefeller Foundation and the Carnegie Corporation con-tinued to make grants to Chinese studies in the United States, although on a reduced scale. From 1960 through 1968 the Carnegie Corporation made grants totalling $1,739,000, including the establishment, under the supervision of Education and World Affairs, Inc. of New York, of the Universities Service Center in Hong Kong for the purpose of helping scholars in their studies of Communist China in that British Colony. [3] The Rockefeller Foundation from 1956 through 1968 made a total grant of $840,000. [4]

Almost simultaneously, the Government, through the National Defense Education Act (NDEA), began to support Chinese and other area studies. Although designed primarily for language training, the NDEA grants also provided graduate fellowships in subject fields as well as grants to institutions to cover administrative and other supporting services. From 1959 through 1966 a total of 1,013 NDEA fellowships were awarded for Chinese language studies, representing 57.7% of all awards made in East Asian languages during those years, and 14.45% of all NDEA awards during the same eight-year period. [5] The total expenditure on these fellowships for Chinese language studies during a ten-year period, 1959-68, amounted to $5,790,000. [6] In addition to the NDEA fellowships, the National Science Foundation also made grants to Chinese studies totalling $250,000 for the years 1960-68. [7]

Thus, the foundations and the Federal Government invested in excess of $32 million in Chinese studies in American universities during a ten-year period, 1959-68, exclusive of in-house and contract research by the U.S. Government agencies. This massive and unprecedented financial support has been central to the rapid development of Chinese studies, especially on the contemporary period, in the United States.

Organization

The organization for the study of contemporary China in the United States is along both institutional and inter-institutional lines. The institutional structure usually takes the form of a research center or a research institute within the framework of a single university. Such a center or institute usually consists of an administrative staff and a research staff. Members of the latter group are in general faculty members in Chinese studies drawn from various academic departments of the university in which the center or institute is located. While serving on the research staff of a center, the faculty members carry on their usual teaching duties in their respective departments. Only rarely does a research center support full-time research scholars on a long-term basis. Full-time researchers for short durations may include faculty members on leave from their teaching duties, visiting scholars from other universities or abroad who are engaged in a special project of interest to that particular center, and advanced graduate students or post-doctoral scholars who need time to finish their dissertations or revise their dissertations for publication. There are of course exceptions to the rule. The Brookings Institution in Washington, D. C. and the Hoover Institution of Stanford University both support full-time research staffs on a regular basis. Some centers or institutes offer instruction, but in general most of them do not, although some do have their own publication programs. [8]

The inter-institutional organization assumes the form of national committees made up of faculty members from a group of universities to deal with problems related to research. Such committees have as their primary responsibility the identification of research needs in their areas of competence, the making of grants to individual scholars to carry on research, and the sponsoring of research conferences and the publication of their results. These committees do not engage in any teaching programs by themselves. The two most important committees of this type are the Joint Committee on Contemporary China (JCCC) sponsored by the American Council of Learned Societies (ACLS) and the Social Science Research Council (SSRC), and the Committee on the Economy of China of the SSRC.

The broad mandate of the JCCC, within the terms of a Ford Foundation grant to support its work, is to encourage cooperation among university centers and to find ways to develop research on China since 1949 (the temporal scope was broadened in 1965 to include the period since 1911). The JCCC, whose members are appointed by the ACLS and the SSRC from among faculty members of major universities who have a research interest in modern and contemporary China in various disciplines, has engaged in activities on four fronts: (1) post-doctoral grants to individuals for research; (2) survey and research conferences; (3) access to materials; and (4) scholarly communication. The SSRC provides staff assistance.

Since 1961, the JCCC has offered research grants in a national competition to scholars in humanities, law, and social sciences to undertake research on topics of their own selection on Mainland China and Taiwan in the Republican and Communist periods. Through 1968 the JCCC has received 295 applications and had made 110 awards for a total of $668,500. [9] Since 1960, the JCCC has also convened a number of research conferences dealing with economics, sociology and anthropology, law, government and politics, history, geography, and comparative Communism. From these conferences have emerged the following standing subcommittees of the JCCC: (1) Subcommittee on Research on Chinese Society

(1961-); (2) Subcommittee on Chinese Government and Politics (1965-); (3) Subcommittee on Chinese Law (1965-); and (4) Subcommittee on Materials (1961-1967). A separate Committee on the Economy of China was established in 1961 with a grant of $910,000 from the Ford Foundation. The nature of research sponsored by these subcommittee will be discussed in the next section of this paper.

In the field of materials, the JCCC has funded the purchase of a complete set of the microfilms of newspaper clippings and other materials on Mainland China collected by the Union Research Institute of Hong Kong and placed it on deposit at the Center for Research Libraries (formerly the Midwest Inter-Library Center) in Chicago; with a grant from the National Science Foundation to SSRC, the JCCC has arranged for distribution at low cost to research libraries in the United States and other countries copies of translations of materials relating to China formerly made available by the U.S. Joint Publications Research Service (JPRS) only to government agencies; it commissioned the compilation of *Contemporary China: A Research Guide* published by the Hoover Institution; and in 1964 its Subcommittee on Materials initiated a worldwide survey of the availability and accessibility of research materials on contemporary China resulting in a request by ACLS and SSRC to the Ford Foundation for funds for the establishment of a center in Washington, D. C. for reproduction and distribution of documentary and research materials on Communist China. In 1967 the Foundation made available the sum of $500,000 to the Association of Research Libraries (ARL) for this purpose, and the Center for Chinese Research Materials (CCRM) of the ARL was officially opened in 1968.

In addition to the JCCC, there are other national committees of a more functional character. They include the Liaison Committee on Study of Contemporary China, funded by the Ford Foundation on the recommendation of the JCCC, which encourages cooperation in studies of contemporary China by scholars in the United States, the United Kingdom, and other countries; and the Joint Committee on the Foreign Area Fellowship Program of the SSRC and the ACLS. This program, administered by the Ford Foundation from 1952 to 1961, was transferred to the joint administration of the SSRC and the ACLS in 1962. In fifteen years, 1952-67, a total of 335 fellowships (including renewals) were awarded to 163 graduate students for research on China, in all disciplines and for all periods and aspects of the Chinese experience. [10]

On the government side, it is known that most agencies and offices having to do with national security and foreign affairs organize their own research on contemporary China either as an on-going "in-house" research activity or through contract research with academic or semi-academic organizations. The Office of the Assistant Secretary of Defense for International Security Affairs (ISA) "develops and coordinates policies and procedures in the fields of international political-military and foreign economic affairs. The continuous ISA external research program focused on identifying and analyzing alternative defense policies for dealing with emerging international problems of relevance to the security of the United States. Although most research for ISA is performed by the RAND Corporation and the Institute for Defense Analyses, research proposals are accepted from other research organizations and universities, if they meet ISA re-quirements." [11] Similarly, the several branches of the U.S. armed forces also maintain such "in-house" and contract research programs. The U.S. Arms Control and Disarmament Agency (ACDA) is likewise authorized "to insure the acquisition of a fund of theoretical and practical knowledge concerning disarmament..... [and] to make arrangements (including contracts, agreements, and grants) for the conduct of research, development, and other studies in the field of arms control and disarmament by United States private or public institutions or persons..." [12] The Office of Economic and Manpower Studies of the National Science Foundation conducts a research program with a view to supplying "comprehensive information on the capital resources, human resources., and educational facilities for science and technology in critical areas of the world." It has published a volume on professional manpower and education in Mainland China. [13] The Joint Publications Research Service, mentioned earlier, is a component of the Clearinghouse for Federal Scientific and Technical Information of the Department of Commerce which translates, abstracts, and performs foreign-language research for other Federal agencies. Since 1963, most of its reports, numbering in the thousands annually, have been made available to university libraries and the general public at cost. [14] Other government agencies which maintain extensive research programs on Mainland China include the Central Intelligence Agency, the Bureau of Intelligence and Research of the Department of State, and the United States Information Agency.

In order to maintain "a steady exchange of information and ideas between government officials, both researchers and policymakers, and private scholars engaged in research on foreign areas and international affairs," the Office of External Research（XR）of the Bureau of Intelligence and Research of the Department of State serves as the "principal contact point between the Department's research arm and outside scholars." The main task of the XR is "to identify academic research in foreign affairs that would be of value in the conduct of U.S. foreign relations and arrange for its results to be made available to the policymaker." This the Office does through its research contract and consultant programs for the Bureau of Intelligence and Research. [15]

In addition to its liaison function with the academic community, the XR also performs a similar service within the government by providing the secretariat for an interdepartmental organization called the Foreign Area Research Coordination Group（FAR）. FAR was founded in 1964 "to improve the coordination of Government-sponsored foreign area and cross-cultural research in the social sciences. The members of the Group are Government agencies which support contract or grant research related to foreign areas and international affairs; they seek to prevent duplication of research among agencies, encourage the maximum exchange of research results, and promote the efficient use in Government of private research." [16]

Twenty-one Government agencies or offices are represented on the FAR. The Group has in general meetings focused its attention on substantive research problems, research priorities in selected geographical areas, and matters affecting Government-academic relations. Specialists from the academic community have occasionally been asked to help review and assess the Government's own needs, and to survey and evaluate research in the area under consideration. "Much of the substantive work of the FAR takes place in the subcommittees which are devoted to research planning on a specific geographical area. At present there are eight regular subcommittees and one *ad hoc* subcommittee. Of the eight regular subcommittees, seven — Africa, China, East Asia (excluding China), Latin America, Near East-South Asia, Western Europe, and the U.S.S.R. and Eastern Europe — are geographic. The eighth is the Behaviora Sciences Committee. (An *ad hoc* group on Publications Policy was also set up late in 1968.) [17] The FAR publishes a bimonthly newsletter about foreign area and foreign affairs research, *FAR Horizons*, which may be subscribed to from the U.S. Government Printing Office.

Nature of Research

Generally speaking, university research on Mainland China is problem-oriented whereas Government research is policy-oriented. Within the academic community, the economists have been concerned with both quantitative and non-quantitative studies of the economy of Communist China. Monographs dealing with Communist China's national income, gross national product and social accounts, rate and pattern of industrial growth, nonagricultural employment, agriculture, and foreign trade have appeared. Studies of a more sectional character, such as studies of the steel industry, machine-building industry, construction industry, industrial location and transportation, the use of energy resources, have also been given monographic treatment. The politics of economic planning, such as financing the government budget, market control, work incentives, industrial management, and the Great Leap Forward Movement, has also been the subject of study and publication. A key to the quantitative studies in economics is statistics. This illusive subject, as far as Mainland China is concerned, has been the subject of intensive study and analysis by American economists. A book was devoted to the discussion of the validity of Chinese Communist statistics from the viewpoint of the development of the statistical system, and a handbook for Mainland China's economic statistics has now appeared. [18]

During the decade of the 1950's, most political scientists in their analyses of Mainland China tended to provide general, descriptive surveys of her overall political structure. However, an increasing number of political scientists doing research on contemporary China have been turning their attention to "questions about the basic nature of the political system and the course of its political development, questions about the nature of the leadership, the character of the political culture, the functions performed by varied political structures, the processes of policy formulation and policy implementation, the techniques of social mobilization, the role of the military, the system of communications, the operation of the bureaucracy, and so on." [19] Thus, books on Mainland China's political leadership, political participation, bureaucracy, ideologies（especially those affecting behavior）, elite studies, foreign relations, and comparative Communism have appeared. Michael Oksenberg of Columbia University has conveniently grouped writings by American political scientists on contemporary Chinese politics as having adopted one or several of the following seven approaches or models: historical, modernization, complex bureaucracy, totalitarian, comparative Communism, revolutionary society, and methodological. [20] According to his analysis, the "historical" approach might be called the "China is China is China" approach. It focuses upon questions relating to continuity and change. The "modernization" approach "views China as a developing, modernizing, industrializing state... [which] has much in common with the rest of the underdeveloped world." As a result, this orientation might be called the "China is India is Nigeria" approach. People who view China from this perspective tend to be particularly interested in how the political system has been affected by and how it has affected the cluster of developments which together have been labeled "modernization". The "complex bureaucracies" approach compares the Chinese Communist governmental apparatus, a huge bureaucracy at heart, with similar complex bureaucracies elsewhere. This perspective might be labeled "China is General Motors is Columbia University" perspective. "That is, struggle for power in China, many of the problems which the government faces, and the way these problems are solved are similar to those of complex bureaucracies anywhere." The "totalitarian" model presents the belief that "the most striking aspect of China is the total or near total penetration of society by the political system." This approach might be labeled the "China is Stalinist USSR is Nazi Germany" perspective. The "comparative Communism" approach is rooted in the assumption that the essential feature of the Chinese Communist government is that it is Communist. Hence this approach might be labeled the "China is the USSR is Yugoslavia" approach. The "Revolutionary Society" orientation considers Communist China as an example of a society in the throes of revolution. The widespread violence, the transformation of old institutions, the seizing and consolidating of power by a new elite are all features common to a political system in any society undergoing rapid and violent change of elites and institutions. Hence, the "Revolutionary Society" perspective might be labeled the "Communist China is France after 1789 is Cuba after 1959" approach. Finally, the "methodological" orientation in the study of Mainland

China reflects the fact that Mainland China at present is a social system "closed" to field study, and must therefore be studied at a distance. "In addition, use of Chinese original sources involves an art of interpreting an 'esoteric' ideological language, and this makes contemporary Chinese studies similar to interpreting the Talmud." Because of this the "methodological" approach might be called the "China is the USSR of the late 1940's is the study of the Talmud" approach.

Mr. Oksenberg makes clear in his analysis that although the seven approaches are interrelated, and all yield understanding of Mainland China. It nonetheless is true that three of them have dominated the study of Chinese Communist politics. These are the historical orientation, the comparative Communist approach, and the use of the totalitarian model. However, he sees an increasing trend toward the use of the modernization and the revolutionary perspectives in the years ahead. [21]

For a lack of access to Mainland China, American sociologists and anthropologists have not been able to base their study of the Peking regime on actual field work. Except for two monographs, one dealing with a Cantonese village in early Communist transition, and the other with the Chinese family in the Communist revolution, both based on the author's field work and covering the period of the late 1940's and the beginning of the 1950's, all other American writings on Chinese Communist society have been done at a distance and without the benefit of on-the-spot observation. In their study, the sociologists have been concerned primarily with changes in social organization and control, resocialization — techniques and processes of "thought reform" in relation to social change, and changes in the family and kinship system. Among the major works published are one on ideology and social organization by Franz Schurmann, and one dealing with Canton under Communism by Ezra Vogel. The Subcommittee on Chinese Society of the JCCC has in addition paid attention to the examination of both micro and macro-organizations in Chinese society, covering not only Mainland China but also Taiwan and going back to the period pre-dating the Republican period. The Subcommittee has also spent considerable time discussing documentary sources for research on contemporary China and field research methods, and has sponsored a computerized bibliographical project on Chinese society, which annotates, by a coding system, secondary sources published on the subject in all languages.

The study of Mainland China's law and legal system is a rather recent development. American legal scholars are engaged primarily in the study of the administration of law in Mainland China, both in the civil and criminal fields. Attention has also been paid to the background and development of the Chinese Communist legal system as well as to the Chinese Communist perception of international law and agreements. As is the case with social scientists, the legal scholars have also found it necessary to devote time to the discussion of the use of documentary sources and research methodologies, such as techniques of interviewing refugees. In addition, a dictionary of Chinese law and government, compiled by Philip R. Bilancia, has been in progress and is expected to be published in the near future.

Psychologists and their social science colleagues have studied the unique phenomenon of "brain-washing" or "coercive persuasion" as a method of social control in Mainland China. Education as an instrument for indoctrination has received the attention of American educators studying Mainland China, who are also interested in the changes occurring in Mainland China's educational system and its related man-power problems. Together with the literary historians and social scientists, the Hundred Flowers Movement and its aftermath, for instance, have received a great deal of attention in this regard.

In the scientific field, there has been little research activity concerning scientific and technological developments on the Chinese Mainland. Some mathematicians, medical doctors, and others have engaged in individual study of scientific developments in their respective fields in Mainland China, but there have been no organized, large-scale projects. The Joint Publications Research Service does translate Chinese publications in the scientific and technical fields, and the U.S. Government is known to be conducting its own research in these fields for national security purposes.

The nature of some of the U.S. Government-sponsored research on Mainland China has been mentioned earlier. In general, Government research on Communist China is oriented toward meeting policy needs. Perhaps the best way to illustrate this is to quote a few of the thirty topics, suggested by the Subcommittee on China of the Foreign Area Research Coordination Group（FAR）, which are judged to be of interest to the U. S. Government.. [22]

Research Topics of Immediate Interest:

1. Analysis of the personal and political relationships among senior Chinese Communist leadership personnel, lower-ranking political and governmental leaders, the PLA high command, and military leaders at the lower echelons. （Separate studies of the dynamics of each group would also be useful.） Stress should be laid on the attitudes of different elements within the power structure toward the key political, economic, social and ideological issues in Mainland China.

2. A study of overlapping areas of Chinese and American national interest:

Research Topics of Low or Long Range Interest

15. Analysis of the shifting pattern of loyalties amongst family, village, province, personal associations, and State.

16. Analysis of the role and status of middle-echelon bureaucrats, technicians, and managers.

Libraries

One of the key factors in the rapid development of studies on Mainland China in the United States is the availability of a rich reservoir of material resources in American libraries. Although the Hoover Institution remains the best depository of such materials, all major American libraries, government and university alike, have been collecting Chinese Mainland books, newspapers, and periodicals since 1949. Twenty years of diligent work, with generous financial support, has built up a network of libraries in the United States, the combined strength of which is far stronger than any library collection outside Mainland China. [23] The efforts made by the universities have been supplemented by those of the Government. The translation and distribution by the Government of Mainland China press and magazines, of the Joint Publications Research Service reports, and of the monitored radio broadcasts have been mentioned previously. The periodic release by the Government of other materials in Chinese, such as the *Gongzuo Tongxun*, Mainland local newspapers, and the Red Guard publications, has been essential to the completion of many a university research project. In this connection, we must also register our gratitude to the Government of the Republic of China for its cooperation in making certain important Chinese Communist documentation available to American scholars doing research in Taiwan and to the American academic community at large.

Future Prospects

Taking stock of the development of Mainland China studies in the United States, there seems little doubt that much has accomplished. But much more remains to be done. A new generation of specialists has been trained, and library collections established. However, there are clear and ominous signs that the most important element which has made possible the rapid development of contemporary China studies in the United States in the past may not be present in a few more years. That is, financial support. Private foundations have given no indication of their willingness to continue to support area studies programs in American universities. Even if foundation support continues, it is doubtful that it will be on the same scale as it has been in the past. On the other hand, Government economizing has left many Federal programs on higher education unfunded. The NDEA fellowship program has already been reduced by 16%, and it is likely that the entire NDEA program will be phased out in another two years. In short, Mainland China studies in American universities are likely to reach a plateau within a few years. Whether they will again rise and accelerate at the same pace as in the past ten years will depend entirely on the availability of funds.

Notes

This article was published in *Collected Documents of the First Sino-American Conference on Mainland China* (Taipei: Institute of International Relations, 1971), pp.29-46; also in *Issues and Studies*, v.7, no. 4 (January, 1971), pp. 22-34.

[1]　For a brief description of the early history of Chinese studies in the United States, see Kenneth Scott Latourette, "Far Eastern Studies in the United States: Retrospect and Prospect," *Far Eastern Quarterly*, vol. xv, no. 1 (Nov 1955), pp. 3-11, and Tsuen-hsuin Tsien, "Asian Studies in America: A Historical Survey," a lecture delivered at the Summer Institute on Asian Studies, University of Hawaii, 1959. For detailed reports on university programs on China from the late 1930's to the early 1940's see *Notes on Far Eastern Studies in America*, Nos. 1-12 (1937-1943). Similar information for later years beginning in 1946 is available in the "News of the Profession" section in *The Far Eastern Quarterly* and its successor, *The Journal of Asian Studies* and its *Newsletter*.

[2]　*The Status of Modern and Contemporary China*; a summary of. discussions of a conference sponsored by the Joint Committee on Contemporary China, New York City, March 15-16, 1968, "Appendix: 3", p. 1. Hereafter cited as *JCCC New York Conference, March 15-16, 1963*.

[3] *ibid.* See also *Newsletter of the Association for Asian Studies*, vol. XIII, no. 4（May 1968）, p. 5.

[4] *JCCC New York Conference, March 15-16, 1968*, "Appendix 3" p. 1.

[5] *Newsletter of the Association for Asian Studies,* XII Supplement（April 1967）, "Asian Studies under the National Defense Education Act," p. 8.

[6] *JCCC New York Conference, March 15-16, 1968*, "Appendix 3," p. 1.

[7] *ibid.*

[8] There are two useful directories of area centers in American universities, both compiled by the Office of External Research（formerly the External Research Staff）of the U. S. Department of State. *The Language and Area Study Programs in American Universities*, published in 1964, describes 153 programs leading to graduate degrees. *The University Centers of Foreign Affairs Research: A Directory*, published in 1968, describes 191 centers having a main focus on social science research in foreign affairs, excluding centers at which a principal emphasis is on teaching at the undergraduate level.

[9] *Studies of China in the United States 1959-69: Committees of National Councils — Structure and Functions (Draft)* prepared by the Liaison Committee on Study of Contemporary China, March 13, 1969, p. 2. The activity of the JCCC is regularly reported in *Items*, a publication of the Social Science Research Council. The annual report of the Social Science Research Council also contains a summary of the activity of the JCCC and of its sub-committees for the year under review, including grants awarded research,

[10] Ibid., p. 6. It might be mentioned in this connection that according to a survey made by the JCCC in 1967, there was a total of 665 students enrolled in graduate studies on China（M.A. and Ph. D.）in American universities in that year. See *Survey of Graduate Students in Humanities and Social Sciences Specializing in Modern and Contemporary China, April 1967*, Supplement, October 24, 1967, p. 1. The number is probably larger today.

[11] U. S. Department of State. Office of External Research, *Foreign Affairs Research: A Directory of Governmental Resources*（Washington, D. C. 1969）, p. 6.

[12] *ibid.*, p. 4.

[13] *ibid.*, p. 30.

[14] *ibid.*, p. 8

[15] *ibid.*, p. 36.

[16] *ibid.*, p. 11.

[17] *ibid.*, pp. 11-12.

[18] The categories of research subjects enumerated here and in the following paragraphs are derived from published monographs and articles. Topics chosen for M.A. theses and Ph. D. dissertations are not included. Since 1949, approximately 165 M.A. theses (1949-64) and 112 doctoral dissertations (1949-70) on Mainland China and the Chinese Communist Party have been accepted by American universities (See Peter Berton and Eugene Wu, *Contemporary China: A Research Guide*, Stanford: The Hoover Institution, 1967, pp. 560-584, and *Newsletter of the Association for Asian Studies* beginning with v. XIV, no. 4,May 1969). For a comprehensive listing of all published and unpublished works in all subject fields concerning Mainland China, see the annual *Bibliography of The Journal of Asian Studies.*

[19] A. Doak Barnett, ed., *Chinese Communist Politics in Action* (Seattle and London: University of Washington Press, 1969) p. xiii.

[20] Michel C. Oksenberg, *A Bibliography of Secondary English Language Literature on Contemporary Chinese Politics* (New York: East Asian Institute, Columbia University [1970]), pp. iii-xxxv. All quotations of Oksenberg in this paragraph are found here.

[21] *Ibid.*, p. xiii.

[22] For a complete text of the thirty topics, see *FAR, Horizons*, v. II, no. 4 (July 1969), pp. 4-5.

[23] Eugene Wu, "Studies of Contemporary China Outside the United States" in *Harvard Library Bulletin*, v. 18, no. 2 (April 1970), pp. 141-154.

中國出版業近況

　　這篇報告主要是討論中華人民共和國最近的出版狀況以及美國圖書館採購中文資料的情形。其中特別提到可能影響將來中國出版物流向的因素。因為過去幾年中國出版業的不穩定，這樣的題目沒有人可以給予確實的評估。但是根據中國政府的公告，最近收到的最新出版物的抽樣，以及這些最新出版物如何提供給西方圖書館的方式，還是可以看出一些端倪。我認為對將來的臆測可以自以下兩個因素來決定。第一是出版業會恢復到文革前什麼程度；其二是中國政府對圖書館交換工作，出版物出口政策，以及對在中國訪客採買和攜帶這些出版物出國的規定。

　　雖然過去兩三年中國的出版業已經由只專注出版發行毛主席著作的文革時期逐漸恢復正常，但是由於缺少最新資料，要精確比較現在和文革前各方面的出版狀況還是件不可能的事。但是根據1972年6月出版的最新一期《全國新書目》，以及美國圖書館已經收到的一些最新出版物，可以看出以下的趨勢：1.出版數量和種類減少；2.新的重點放在通俗閱讀材料方面；3.非常重視出版物內容的實用性。這種改變的原因是根據中國共產黨的宣稱，出版也要像一切其他活動一樣，要為工農兵服務。

　　有關出版數量和種類的減少可以從比較1972年6月出版的《全國新書目》（包含1972年3、4月和部分5月出版的書刊）和1966年同時期出版的《全國新書目》（文革前最後一期）看出[1]。1966年著錄了其包括的兩個半月出版的2,201種書刊（1,931種新出版，270種重印本），而1972年只有出版了490種（436種新出版，54種重印本）。1972年只出版了1966年22.26%的書刊。新舊兩期的《全國新書目》中類目大致相同，可是1972年《全國新書目》類目下的分類卻減少很多。譬如：1966年在「歷史」類目下有12

個分類，「經濟」下有45個，「文化、教育和體育」下有65個，「語言」下5個，「文學」下273個。但是在1972年相對只有「歷史」7個，「經濟」18個，「文化、教育、體育」2個，「語言」4個，「文學」79個。

我們還可自期刊出版上看到出版的減少。根據北京市郵政局出版的《報刊目錄》，估計1960年中國出版了1,300種期刊，文革初減少到648種，1967年減少到132種，到1968年只剩下58種。美國圖書館雖然沒有獲得所有的期刊，但是在文革前還是收集到不少，特別是1949到1960年間當出版比較多，出口法規不太嚴格時。據稱目前出版的期刊大約50種左右。我們收到的大約6種上下，還包括英文期刊。而《歷史研究》、《經濟研究》等等不是不再出版就是還沒有復刊。據稱《新華月報》已經復刊，但是外國圖書館還是不能訂閱或者作交換。

檢視我們收到的200多種1970、1971、1972年中國出版的書刊[2]，再參照1972年6月出版的《全國新書目》所列中國最新出版品，中國大陸的出版物大致可分成下列5大類：

1. 研究毛主席和馬克思思想的通俗讀物；
2. 有關工農兵模範故事的通俗讀物（令人聯想到大躍進時類似的出版物，只是現在著重在選擇正確革命路線的鬥爭上）；
3. 有關革命戲劇的通俗讀物，包括樂譜類；
4. 有關科技的通俗讀物；
5. 各種中醫手冊：包括培訓「赤腳」醫生的手冊，中藥、針灸等等為實用而編的手冊。

根據中國新聞報導的北京政府官方公告，我們可以期盼將有關於歷史、地理、國際事務的書刊出版。其實標點本的《南齊書》（479-502）、《陳書》（557-589）、《周書》（557-581）已經出版了。兩種考古期刊《考古》、《文物》也復刊了。還出版了一種有關國際事務的大眾期刊《國際知識》，以及一些文學刊物。文學刊物還登載一些工農兵所著短篇小說、詩歌和戲劇。

1972年在廣州出版的《廣東文藝》就是一種新嘗試。同樣的刊物可能會緊接著在其他地區出版。我們可以很清楚地發現當前的出版比只發行毛主席著作的文革時期數量上增加了。

這種相對增加的出版數字是否能達到文革前的程度，或者將來是否會像過去一樣看重學術性的出版，我們還不能得到答案。目前政府的政策還是要求所有出版都達到為工農兵服務的目的。因此最近的將來通俗讀物可能會大量增加，這個政策還不會重視學術性的出版。因為文革前學術性的出版已經被定性為資本主義復辟的工具去毒害和腐敗中國青年，並扼殺為無產階級服務的通俗讀物。[3]

目前中國的出版業和早先的另外一個差別就是目前的出版內容注重實用性，特別是有關科技介紹的出版。這大概就是近兩三年大批科普通俗讀物和醫藥手冊出版的原因。強調實用顯然是源於自力更生運動的要求，或者也可能是反映政府反對廣泛的專業教育，而推行知識和實踐整合的政策。

第二個因素可能影響到中國出版的出口，那就是中國政府對圖書館間的交換工作，出版物的出口，以及到中國訪客採買書刊的政策。我們雖然沒有什麼具體資料可以對這個問題作出結論，但是也有一些已經知道的事實可以作為臆測的基礎。首先是我們知道中國對和美國圖書館交換資料感到興趣。自1950年代初到最近的乒乓外交前，中美維持的唯一交流就是圖書館交換。國立北京圖書館，一度還有中國科學院所屬的文獻情報中心是和美國主要的研究圖書館交換的機構。文化大革命時一度聯繫中斷，1971年1月又重新啟動。這種交換關係雖然長久維持，有時可以交換到從書商處買不到的書刊，但是卻達不到1960年前中國和蘇聯或東歐國家圖書館那種交換關係。美國圖書館獲得的交換書刊數量很小，也都是可以從香港日本書商處買到的書刊。1971年以來情況也沒有改善。將來會怎樣，也只能臆測。可能中美間建立文化交流專案對圖書館交換會有有利的影響，但是這種影響在所有可能性下發展到什麼程度、以什麼方式發展、何時付諸行動都隨時要看中美關係發展的情況而定。

其次，我們應該知道中華人民共和國的政策是不允許所有的出版物出口。有些種類的出版物以及地方報紙就是在中國也不能自由流通。最近有報導說有將地方報紙走私到香港的人定了死罪。政府還嚴控某些出版物的流通：像訂閱了《參考消息》這種內部流通資料的人，據說定期要被追究其所在。我相信這種情況還會繼續。

至於到中華人民共和國訪客採購資料方面。據稱，銷售，郵寄，海關的規定各有不同。到中國的訪客可以採買在書店裡的書刊是毫無疑問的，但是是否可以郵寄和通過海關就沒有清楚的條例。我們還有待中國政府設定政策。

總之，雖然中華人民共和國目前的出版物比不上文革前種類豐富，但是出版數量的增加是可以預期的。不過，在出版僅為大眾使用以及內容實用的通俗讀物的雙重前提下，純學術性的書刊的出版會較文革前少。展望我們將來採購中國的出版物，目前的情況顯示可選擇的書刊會比文革前少，而要選擇有學術性的書刊會更少。外國圖書館能獲得多少書刊將主要取決於中國政府決定的圖書館交換範圍，可以准許書商出口的數量，以及允許訪客可以在中國採買的出版物和可以攜帶它們出國的程度。

注釋

本文為1972年3月25-26日在華盛頓特區「中英翻譯協助組織」（Chinese/English Translation Assistance，簡稱CETA）舉辦的研習會上發表的報告。修訂後經CETA執行秘書吉姆・馬賽厄斯（Jim Mathias）同意，載《中國季刊》（*China Quarterly*），第53期（1973年1/3月），頁134-138。

[1]　1966年7月16日出版的《全國新書目》為第286期，1972年6月復刊為第287期。1970年5月出版者由文化部出版局版本圖書館改為北京圖書館。因為版本圖書館併入北京圖書館版本書庫。

[2]　研究圖書館協會中國研究資料中心（Center for Chinese Research Materials of the Association of Research Libraries in Washington, D.C.）複製了這批資料分發給各圖書館。

[3]　楚洪舒：「出版更多更好的普及讀物」，《紅旗》，1971年第9期，頁4。

（胡嘉陽譯）

Recent Developments in Chinese Publishing

This note discusses the current state of publishing in the People's Republic of China and the acquisition of Chinese-language materials by American libraries, with special reference to the factors which are likely to influence the future flow of materials from China. The subject is one about which no one can be very certain in his assessment, given the rather uncertain state of Chinese publishing during the last few years. Nevertheless, some speculations are possible on the basis of Peking's official announcements, a sampling of recent publications from China, and the way in which such publications have been made available to the West. What the future will hold, I believe, depends on two main factors. One, the extent to which publishing activities return to a pre-Cultural Revolution level, and second, the Chinese Government's policy with regard to library exchanges, the export of printed materials and to the purchase and export of such materials by visitors to China.

While it is true that publishing in China during the last two or three years has taken a turn toward normalization following a period of almost exclusive attention during the Cultural Revolution to the publication and distribution of Chairman Mao's works, the lack of sufficient current data still makes it impossible to compare with precision the various aspects of Chinese publishing now with those before the Cultural Revolution. However, on the basis of one current issue of the national bibliography (*Quanguo xin shumu*) published in June 1972 and of some of the recent publications now available in American libraries, certain trends do stand out. (i) There has been a reduction in the volume and variety of publications; (ii) there is a new emphasis on popular reading materials; and (iii) there is a heavy emphasis on the utilitarian aspect of publications. The rationale behind these changes seems to be based on the Party's dictum that publishing, like all other activities in the People's Republic, must be for the sole purpose of serving the needs of workers, peasants, and soldiers.

The current reduction in the volume and variety of publications can best be illustrated by comparing the June 1972 issue of the *Quanguo xin shumu*, which covers publications issued in March, April, and part of May of 1972, with the issues for the corresponding period in 1966, the last year in which *Quanguo xin shumu* was published. [1] The 1966 *Quanguo xin shumu* lists a total of 2,201 items (1,931 new titles and 270 reprints) for the two-and-one-half-month period in 1966, whereas only 490 items (436 new titles and 54 reprints) are listed in the June 1972 issue, representing only 22.26 per cent, of the earlier output. Although both the new and old editions of the *Quanguo xin shumu* use more or less the same subject categories for listing publications, the number of topics on which there are publications has now been greatly reduced. For example, the 1966 issues listed 12 titles under "History," 45 titles under "Economics," 65 under "Culture, Education, and Physical Education," 15 under "Language," and 273 under "Literature" while in the June 1972 issue the number of titles listed under the respective categories are only 7 for History, 18 for Economics, 2 for Culture, Education, and Physical Education, 4 for Language and 79 for Literature.

Another indication of this reduction can be seen in the field of Chinese journal publishing. It is estimated that in 1960 some 1,300 periodicals were published in China. According to the *Baokan mulu* (Catalogue of Newspapers and Periodicals) issued by the Peking Municipal Post Office, this number was reduced to 648 at the beginning of the Cultural Revolution. It dropped to 132 in 1967, and by 1968 only 58 were reported to be still in existence. Although American libraries have never been able to receive every journal that was published, we did manage to acquire a good number of them before the Cultural Revolution, especially during the years from 1949 to 1960, when more titles were being published and the Chinese export regulations were less stringent. The number published now is reported to be around 50, of which we receive only about half a dozen, including English-language publications. Journals such as *Lishi yanjiu* (Historical Research), *Jingji yankiu* (Economic Research), etc. are either no longer being published or have not yet been revived; although *Xin Hua yuebao* (New China Monthly) is reported to have resumed publication, it remains unavailable to foreign libraries for either purchase or exchange.

On the basis of an examination of some two hundred 1970, 1971 and 1972 publications available in the United States, and of the listings in the June issue of the 1972 *Quanguo xin shumu*, [2] current Chinese mainland imprints can be roughly categorized as follows: (i) Popular works on how to study Chairman Mao's thought and Marxism; (ii) Popular stories about model workers, peasants, and soldiers (reminiscent of similar publications during the Great Leap Forward, although the current emphasis is on the struggle to choose the correct revolutionary line); (iii) Popular works on the revolutionary theatre, including musical scores; (iv) Popular scientific and technological publications; and (v) Manuals on Chinese medicine of all types, including training manuals for "barefoot" doctors, handbooks on Chinese herbs, acupuncture handbooks and similar compilations for practical use.

According to Beijing's official announcements and reports in the Chinese press, we can also look forward to the publication of books on history, geography and international affairs. Indeed, punctuated texts of dynastic histories — *Nan Qi shu* (Southern Qi Dynasty, 479-502), *Chen shu* (History of the Chen Dynasty, 557-89), and *Zhou shu* (History of the Northern Zhou Dynasty, 557-581) — have already been released. The two archaeological journals, *Kaogu* (Archaeology) and *Wenwu* (Cultural Relics), have also recently been revived. A popular series on international affairs called *Guoji zhishi* (International Knowledge) has been published, as have a number of literary works — short stories, poems and plays — some of them written by workers peasants and soldiers. An experimental edition of a literary journal published in Canton entitled *Guangdong wenyi* (Guangdong Literature and Art) also made its appearance in 1972. Similar publications may well follow in other regions. It seems clear, therefore, that there is an increase in volume as compared with the period of the Cultural Revolution, when Chinese publishing was preoccupied with the publication and distribution of Chairman Mao's works.

Whether this relative increase in volume will eventually reach the pre-Cultural Revolution level, or whether scholarly publications will be assigned the same kind of priority in the future as in the past, are questions that cannot yet be answered. The current official policy requiring all publications to fulfill the central objective of serving the workers, peasants, and soldiers, may call for an even larger increase in the volume of popular reading materials in the immediate future, but the same policy would seem to argue for a low priority for the publication of academic and scholarly works. Indeed, pre-Cultural Revolution scholarly publications have been characterized as tools for the restoration of capitalism designed to poison and corrupt the Chinese youth and to strangle popular reading materials essential to serve proletarian politics. [3]

Another difference distinguishing current Chinese publications from earlier ones is the present emphasis on the utilitarian aspect of all work, especially in the fields of science and technology. This perhaps accounts for the large number of popular science and technical publications and medical handbooks of all types during the last two or three years. This emphasis on utility apparently stems from the requirements of the self-reliance campaign but it is perhaps also a reflection of the present policy against wide-spread specialized education and in favor of a more integrated system of knowledge and practice.

The second factor which is likely to influence the future flow of materials from China is the Chinese Government's policy with regard to library exchanges, the export of printed materials, and purchases by visitors to the People's Republic. We have little concrete data on this question from which to draw conclusions, but there are some known facts which may serve as a basis for speculation. In the first place, we know that China is interested in the exchange of materials with American libraries. Indeed, the only sustained communication between China and the United States after the early 1950s and before ping pong diplomacy came onto the scene, was through library exchanges. The National Library of Beijing and, for a time, the Institute of Scientific and Technical Information of the Chinese Academy of Sciences, served as the two contact points with major American research libraries. This link was broken during the Cultural Revolution, but reopened by Beijing in January 1971. This exchange relationship, although long lasting and on occasion producing items not available through commercial channels, never reached the level of activity which existed between Chinese and Soviet or East European libraries before 1960. Such publications as did reach American libraries under this arrangement were small in number and most of them were also available from book dealers in Hong Kong and Japan. The situation since 1971 has not improved. What may be in store for the future can only be surmised. It is likely that the establishment of a cultural exchange program between Beijing and Washington will have a favorable impact on library exchanges but to what extent, and in what form, this impact can be translated into action will, in all likelihood, depend on the state of U.S.-China relations at any given moment.

Secondly, with regard to Beijing's policy of exporting printed materials, it should be kept in mind that the People's Republic has never allowed the export of every printed publication to the outside world. Indeed, certain types of publications, local newspapers for example, do not even circulate freely within

China itself and it has been reported in recent years that the smuggling of local newspapers into Hong Kong has been made a capital offence. The Government exercises such strict control over the circulation of certain publications that those subscribing to journals of restricted circulation, such as the *Cankao xiaoxi* (Reference News) for instance, are said to be held accountable at regular intervals for the physical presence of the publications in their possession. It is reasonable to assume that such restrictions will continue.

Finally, the purchase of materials by visitors to the People's Republic. Reports vary on sales, postal and customs regulations. There is no doubt that, as a rule, visitors to China are allowed to purchase such materials as are available in book stores, but there seems to have been no clear rule about whether all such purchases would be cleared for shipment by postal or customs officials. Whether the Chinese Government will make clear its policy in this regard remains to be seen.

In conclusion, it appears that we can now look forward to an increased volume of publishing in the People's Republic of China in the immediate future although the variety of publications is likely to be less rich than it was before the Cultural Revolution. The twin emphasis on popular reading materials for popular use and a strictly utilitarian principle of publication also suggests that there will be fewer purely scholarly works than formerly. So far as future acquisition of Chinese materials is concerned, this would indicate that there will be fewer publications to choose from than there were before the Cultural Revolution and that of this reduced number there will be an even smaller proportion of scholarly publications. How much of this published material foreign research libraries will be able to acquire will depend primarily on the Chinese Government's decision concerning the scope of library exchanges, the amount of material allowed for export through commercial channels, and the degree to which it will permit visitors to China to purchase and export printed materials.

Notes

This is a revised version of a paper presented at the Chinese/English Translation Assistance (CETA) Workshop held in Washington, D.C., March 25-26, 1972. The author is grateful to Mr. Jim Mathias, Executive Secretary of the CETA, for permission to have the paper reproduced in *China Quarterly*, no. 53 (Jan./Mar. 1973), pp. 134-138.

[1] The *Quanguo xin shumu* ceased publication with issue no. 286 (16 July 1966). It resumed publication in June 1972 with issue no. 287. The sponsorship of the publication was transferred in May 1970 from the Editions Library (Banben tushuguan) of the Bureau of Publications of the Ministry of Culture to the National Library of Peking when the Editions Library merged with the latter to become the Editions Collection (Banpen shuku) of the National Library of Peking.

[2] The Center for Chinese Research Materials of the Association of Research Libraries in Washington, D.C., is reproducing these materials for general distribution. Inquiries should be addressed to Mr P. K. Yu, Director of the Center at 1527 New Hampshire Avenue, N.W. Washington, D.C., 20036.

[3] Chu Hongshu, "*Chuban geng duo geng hao de puji duwu* "(Publish more and better popular reading materials "), *Hong Qi* (Red Flag), No. 9, 1971, p. 41.

當代中國研究的圖書館資源

　　第二次世界大戰結束後，四十多年來，主要的美國圖書館都致力於發展和維護研究當代中國的基本資料，包括中國共產主義的歷史。[1] 今日美國搜集的所有資源，在西方無疑是最為完備。本文綜論美國圖書館收藏當代中國研究資料的發展過去成就、目前情況，及將來展望，並提出一些建議。

　　北美圖書館有計畫的搜集供研究中國共產主義運動的原始資料，始於40年代晚期胡佛研究院建立的中文圖書館，及委任已故的芮瑪麗（Mary C. Wright）為其首任館長。芮教授剛從山東濰縣的日本集中營重獲自由，即前往中國各大城市為胡佛研究所搜集研究20世紀中國的重要書刊。她在延安獲得不少罕見的當時發行的中國共產黨出版物，而最有名的應是一份幾乎完整無缺的共產黨喉舌，1941-47年出版的《解放日報》。後來她又在美國得到伊羅生特藏（Issacs Collection）和尼姆·威爾斯（斯諾夫人）特藏（Nym Wales Collection）。前者主要是20年代晚期到30年代早期的中國共產黨地下小冊子和期刊（很多是油印品），而後者包括一些30年代中期的中國共產黨文件原件。1960年，時任胡佛研究所東亞圖書館館長的筆者安排和監督把在台灣的陳誠特藏（Chen Cheng Collection）製成縮微膠捲；這批檔案包括1,500餘件中國共產黨文件，全部來自長征前之江西蘇維埃時期，大大豐富了胡佛研究所的中國共產黨文獻。[2] 這三種特藏，加上其他美國圖書館所藏有關資料，特別是抗日戰爭時期（1937-45）的出版物，組成在美國的第一批研究早期中國共產主義運動的原始資料。

　　1945-49年間，中國共產黨及其外圍組織直接出版了很多書籍，刊物和報紙。雖然這些出版物在美國圖書館的收藏並非一網打盡，但較重要的如共產黨控制下「邊區」出版物，查閱不難。至80年代圖書館又添置了一些30

年代和40年代中國共產黨期刊和報紙的縮微膠捲，和一批首次在中國發行的中國共產黨歷史文獻彙編。而從60年代開始，美國學者可以利用台灣的一些中國共產黨文獻特藏，最重要的是法務部調查局圖書館的10萬冊資料，絕大部分都早於1949年前出版。

　　1949年以來，美國圖書館一直維持了一個緊密規畫的專案來採購中華人民共和國有關當代中國的出版物。為方便討論，茲分為文革前和文革後兩階段。

　　在第一個階段，從1949年末到70年代後期，圖書館不能直接從中國採購書刊。訂單只能發到其他地方的書商，主要是香港和東京兩地。外國圖書館不能訂閱地方報紙，而圖書交換亦只局限於和國立北京圖書館（後改稱中國國家圖書館）。雖然間接採購至為繁瑣，但書商仍皆盡力提供可外銷的書刊。問題是很多地方出版物發行數量不大，雖然可以外銷，仍甚難獲得。「內部」刊物，更是無法取得，至少官方政策如此。由於書商全賴出版商供應，這些年頭中國出版業的盛衰起伏，自然限制了書商所能提供的品種和數量。例如，在50年代中國出版業躍飛猛進，供應品種和數量都甚充裕。可是，當圖書生產下退，如在60年代初期全國原料缺乏，或文革期間政治動盪，起初選擇較少，內容單調，最後出版業更幾乎完全癱瘓。[3] 只賴和國家圖書館交換，亦不盡人意：它所提供書刊，書商供應不難，而且當中國和蘇聯及東歐國家關係尚友好時，它送往這些國家圖書館的書刊數量和品種皆遠超送往美國圖書館者。不過雖然有上述種種困難，在此期間美國圖書館仍建立了令人矚目的研究中華人民共和國的資料。彼得‧伯頓（Peter Berton）和吳文津合編的《當代中國研究指南》（史丹佛：胡佛研究所，1967）所列舉證實這些成就。在這方面美國圖書館受益於香港、台灣和美國公布的一些中國的刊物和文件。香港的友聯研究所維持一份極佳的報紙和刊物剪報檔案，其中有美國圖書館當日無法得見的資料。友聯研究所亦不時提供它所獲得的中華人民共和國文件。在一段很長時間，台灣政府也發布了數量龐大的中國共產黨重要文件，其中不少中央委員會的指令。其中《連江文件》、《571工程紀要》（林彪武裝反毛澤東的粗糙計畫）和《毛澤東思想萬歲》最為知名。1960年初，美國政府移交給美國國會圖書館 1,200 餘種 1960 年前的中國地方報紙，不少是縣和縣以下的。雖然這批報紙絕大部分不全，甚至有些零星至數期，但其重要性不能低估，因為它們當日以至目前國外都不可訂閱。1963 年美國國務院又向國會圖書館發放一批文件。《中國季刊》（*China Quarterly*）稱這些軍事文件是「40 年代中期，胡佛研究所取得延安文件以後，學界所見最耀眼的第一手資料」[4]。這批文獻是 1961 年 1 月 1 日到 8 月 26 日的 29 期機密軍事期刊《工作通訊》。這份刊物由解放軍總政治部編輯和發行給團部以上軍官，其中最機密的只發給師級指揮官。[5]

　　上面已提到文革給出版事業帶來的嚴重破壞。在此期間學術研究的出版幾乎全面停頓，美國圖書館不得不重金收購各種紅衛兵刊物。雖然有些刊物極富爭議性，大部分包括很多當日無法取得的重要訊息，例如共產黨各級的指令、黨領袖的發言，還包括不少當日毛澤東的言論、被清算者的「反動教材」、黨的歷史文獻及事和人的新聞快訊。最初各圖書館力爭在香港所能取得的這些數量有限的資料，以致價格暴漲。基於中國研究學者的要求，美國國務院同意將其所藏紅衛兵資料開放給學術界。這批資料最先交予哈佛燕京圖書館，而在 1968 年中國研究資料中心（Center for Chinese Research Materials）成立後給予後者。1975 年中國研究資料中心複製這批資料，並加入一些從其他來源取得的紅衛兵刊物，共 19 巨冊，命名《紅衛兵資料》公開發行。1979 年，補發目錄。1980 年，又發行《續編》8 冊。這是西方最大的一套紅衛兵刊物。近年中國研究資料中心再獲得一批紅衛兵刊物，將陸續複製發行。

　　70 年代後期以來，中國出版界經歷一次重大的數量和品質改造。在此文革後時期，中國出版界不單再次活力充沛，並開始出版更客觀和具學術性的研究成果。[6] 文件彙編、黨領導人回憶錄、新期刊、專題報紙和從前因某些原因而未能出版的學術著作，都大量面世；很多研究出版物的素質在研究深度和多元化都有明顯進步。新的出版物種類，如年報、統計和法律文獻，大量激增。[7] 值得特別提及的是中國人民大學出版的《複印報刊資料》。這期刊 50 年代面世，開始時僅在國內發售，1978 年接受國外訂閱。這組複印文章最初覆蓋22個課題，目前已過百；文章選自在中國出版的2,000種報紙和期刊。雖然關於當代中國各方面的課題都在收入之例，但與軍事有關的至1989年方公開。這些複印資料，大多是月刊，每一期附有索引。每年有總索引。這個刊物的重要性在其包含範圍廣泛，收入國外不能訂閱的「內部」報紙和期刊的文章。它尤其方便讀者，關於某一命題的文章，來源眾多，收入專冊。不過，挑選過程每受當時政治氣候左右。例如，在1989年民主運動前，《中國政治》分冊，收入嚴家其、蘇紹智等人談政治改革的文章；而在此次運動其間及以後，只選載支持黨和政府的文章。

　　至於直接從中國採購，70年代後期以來，已成常規；中國圖書館可以並十分熱心和外國同行建立交換計畫；一些地方報紙，主要是省級的，首次讓國外訂閱；中國書展在國內和國外舉辦；旅客可以在國營書店和很多大城市路旁的個體戶書攤購買書刊；大多數東道機構皆給予其訪問學者影印權利。

　　在此大幅改善的令人鼓舞背景下，一些採購舊問題苟延不去，而一些新問題又出現。舊問題為「內部」刊物、地方出版物和地方報紙。「內部」的標籤，廣泛及持久的被使用，書刊被訂為「內部」刊物後，即不能見諸書商書目；即使中國圖書館以之作交換，亦每為海關截止，發回發送者。地方出版物的問題在於地方出版社如不是沒有直接外銷的條件，就是因為外匯規條而未為政府批准。外國圖書館只能依賴數家國營圖書出口公司供應。由於地方出版物通常發行量不大，雖然已收進目錄，未必一定可以供應。還有更複雜的情況：在發表出版預告後，假如訂書量不能擔保盈利，出版社可以不出書。至於地方報紙，雖然省級報紙大部分都可購買，省級以下者仍不可外銷，城市報紙也不是全部國外可以訂閱。[8]

　　新問題最主要的是出口書商的服務品質；交換計畫的問題；和獲取絕版書籍的困難。在我們向出口書商發出訂單後，有時毫無資訊，有時要過了半年甚至一年，才被告知無法供貨。而在這一段時間，失去從別處獲得該書的機會。地方出版物發行量少，問題尤為嚴重。交換計畫的問題是美中兩地書價的差異。沒有一家中國圖書館會同意以同等價值交換書籍。同樣，美國圖書館不願意按冊數交換。結果，交換都是「君子協定」，雙方各據自己的判斷，決定什麼是公平交換。雖然一些中國圖書館同意提供當地圖書，一般都只提供容易購得的全國性主要出版社出版物。最後，在中國尋找絕版書籍一向困難，情況並未因目前可以直接和出口商交易而好轉。由於上舉的各種問題，美國圖書館需倚賴一些到中國訪問人士的幫助，和與中國同行建立的個人關係，來補充平常和較正式的採購管道。這些私人聯繫極有成效，可以斷言在將來繼續發展研究當代中國資料時，必仍為一重要因素。

目前，在美國約有60間圖書館收藏從中華人民共和國，台灣和其他漢語區域出版的中文刊物。但不是所有都維持相同的覆蓋程度或收藏的積極性。規模較大和財政較佳的圖書館當然覆蓋面較廣，獲得資料亦較他館多。一般而言，不論大小，各圖書館主要都集中在社會科學和人文科學書刊；並不收集自然科學和工程資料，除了參考書（主要是字典）和贈書及交換所得，後者大多是學報。

我們是否跟得上目前中國出版物的生產量？假如我們只考慮可以外銷的有關當代的出版物，答案是有條件的肯定。根據1989年的官方統計，目前可見的最近的詳細資料，該年度內中國出版74,973種書刊（包括55,476種新版，19,498種重印），分類如下：書籍57,476種（45,432種新版，12,042種重印）；教科書11,706種（4,721種新版，6,985種重印）；和畫冊5,791種（5,320種新版，471種重印）。[9] 此外還出版了6,078種期刊和1,576種報紙。分類見下表。

1989年出版統計	出版數
書籍分類	
哲學與社會科學	12,426
文化與教育	25,541
文學與藝術	13,889
自然科學與工程	14,977
畫冊	5,791
總類	2,349

總數	74,973
期刊分類	
哲學與社會科學	1,359
文化與教育	653
文學與藝術	662
自然科學與工程	3,019
少年讀物	83
畫冊	81
總類	221
總數	6,078
報紙分類	
中央（全國性）	138
省級與大城市	714
縣級與專題	724
總數	1,576

　　根據這些數字，我們如何衡量自己的成績？根據美國9間圖書館（哈佛、哥倫比亞、耶魯、普林斯頓、芝加哥、密西根、加州大學柏克萊分校、胡佛研究院和華盛頓大學）的中文藏書資料，1989年從中國取得的書籍平均為5,300種（最少者為2,400種，最多者為8,000種，而大部分是5,000至6,000種）；期刊平均數字是942種（從496至1,279種，其中四間訂閱過千種，兩間900種）；和報紙平均42種（從10至123種）。[10] 上面已提到東亞圖書館通常並不收藏自然科學和工程的資料和教科書；畫冊的選擇尤為精細。假如刪除這些種類，1989年出版的社會科學和人文學科書刊（包括初刊和再版）為51,856種，期刊為2,674種。根據這些調整過的數字，我們發現在51,856種書籍中，9間圖書館採購比率為4.63%至15.48%；2,674種期刊中的18.54%至47.83%；和1,576種報紙中的0.63%至7.80%。

　　不過我們尚需考慮以下各點：（1）出版數字包括有關當代和前代；（2）書刊並非全部可以外銷；（3）美國圖書館選收當代流行小說和翻譯文學，

至為精細，而在文革後這兩類作品都激增。美國國會圖書館的政策是完全不收翻譯作品；（4）在大量的再版和重印書籍中，其初印本極可能不少早為美國圖書館入藏。由於這些因素，我們的有關當代中國書刊的收藏肯定遠比上面數字所顯示為佳。尚待解決的是內部書刊和地方出版物，下面我們將再討論。

　　期刊的覆蓋極佳。雖然在1989年有超過6,000種期刊，可供國外訂閱的不過半。1989年中國出版對外貿易總公司的目錄提供2,501種可以外銷的期刊，其中約41%屬於自然科學和工程類。上述的9間圖書館，很少甚至根本沒有訂閱科技期刊，它們平均收到的942種期刊，絕大部分是社會科學和人文學科，這個成就值得讚賞。

　　報紙方面，成就不如期刊。1989年中國出版對外貿易總公司的目錄提供136種可以外銷的報紙，包括從前保密的《解放軍報》。[11] 其中一半屬於全國性、省級和城市報紙，另外一半是專題報紙，例如市場、廣告、廣播、健康、海運、紡織、法律、婦女和運動。縣級報紙一直不能訂閱。136種報紙占1989年1,576種報紙中的8.63%。比對之下，9間圖書館平均收到的42種報紙，只可說是差強人意。

　　最後，我們可以說，雖然需要做的事尚多，美國圖書館集體在發展當代中國研究資源的工作方面，成就已很顯著，特別是在資料每受限制，而採購經費不斷收縮的情況下。以下檢討在那些方面我們可以改善和確保藏書建設的健全的發展用以支援當代中國的研究。

覆蓋範圍

　　我們對當代中國出版物的覆蓋範圍，可以並必須擴大。雖然我們的主要供應來源仍將會是出口書商，我們可以採用各種其他途徑擴大覆蓋範圍。和中國圖書館有交換計畫的圖書館，需要堅持對方只提供該地區的出版物，同時假如該交換圖書館所屬的大學有出版社的話，亦應要求提供其大學出版社的出版物。沒有交換計畫的圖書館亦應考慮建立交換計畫來增加其館藏的地方文獻。大規模圖書館的中文文獻專家或採購圖書館員，應該可以常到中國，不單只是訪求書刊，還可以和出版社、書商、學者和圖書館員建立個人關係。經驗顯示一些書商難以提供的書籍，很多時候可以在本地書店或街上小販買到。面對面的交涉一直比書信往來有效。研究所、編輯室和大學圖書館都是提供絕版書刊的富饒來源。很多機構不願意或無法將書刊寄往外國圖書館，但大多樂意接受當面要求，達成交換。

那些尚未作如此嘗試的圖書館會發現這種做法可以從其他地區，特別是日本和台灣，獲取有關當代中國文獻彙編和專著。（這是假定美國圖書館對有關當代中國的西文資料的收藏已經足夠。）一些在日本出版有關當代中國的重要學報和專刊可能未入藏美國圖書館，因為很少中文書目館員翻閱日文書目，而日文書目館員通常亦只留意和日本有關的資料。雖然近年從台灣取得的中華人民共和國的文獻比前減少，但仍可獲得一些重要資料。例如大量1970年代後期和1980年代初期的非官方雜誌和大字報在台灣以《大陸地下刊物彙編》名義發行，目前已出版20冊。這類採購肯定增進我們研究當代中國的能力。

傳統上被忽視的資料還有視聽材料和短暫的出版物。雖然形式有別，這些資料的價值並不比書籍低，有時對研究者更為有用。1989年民主運動時期的相片、視聽磁帶、油印傳單、呼籲和小冊子，都是絕佳例子。這些材料提供書籍難以表達的即時感。哈佛大學、哥倫比亞大學、芝加哥大學、加州大學洛杉磯分校和耶魯大學的東亞圖書館及紐約公立圖書館，都成立了「天安門檔案」收藏這些資料。假如時光可以倒流，讓我們收集1949年後中國發生的各政治運動的現場資料，如文化大革命和反右鬥爭，我們圖書館的當代中國研究資料必更為豐富。

「內部」資料

「內部」刊物不能公開發行，但不是所有「內部」刊物都含有西方保安的「機密」或「保密」含義。很多學術著作、翻譯，甚至參考書，因為繞過官方管道，即被標籤為「內部」。[12] 一些大學出版社使得事情更為複雜。為了不參與政府指派的出口書商集中對外發行，它們用「內部」標籤來取得自已對外發行的權利。

　　一般而言，「內部」刊物有兩大類：「內部發行」和「限國內發行」。前者又可再分為「內部文件」、「內部資料」、「內部參考」、「內部讀物」、「內部控制發行」及「黨校系統內部發行」等等，不過通常都只用較普通的「內部發行」。書籍「徵求意見稿」和其他「試用本」皆屬於「內部發行」。雖然所有「內部」刊物印發時間都很短，並不正式發售，部分仍流通到國外。香港翻印書商每每以高價發售；而在美國和其他國家亦漸多私人來源。當前的問題是不知道那些「內部」刊物已外傳，和如何可以讓學術界更容易得到這些資料。在維吉尼亞州的中國研究資料中心（從前在首府華盛頓特區），是一非牟利機構，已翻印200多種「內部」刊物[13]，但該中心目前人力不足以訪查散處各地的其他「內部」出版物。

　　因此有急切需要建立一種資訊情報傳播機制，讓學者知道有什麼資料可用，和將這些資料複印發行。近日開辦的《中國共產黨研究通訊》（*CCP Research Newsletter*）（主編齊慕實〔Timothy Cheek〕）非常適合這個用途。《通訊》的目的是傳播研究消息和評估資料，主要是「內部」資料，及研究1949年前中國共產主義運動，中華人民共和國的黨國關係，和後毛澤東時期的社會主義改革學者對這些資料的看法。[14]中國研究資料中心已安排翻印《通訊》所提到的出版物。個別學者和圖書館如獲得任何「內部」刊物，亦期望能讓《通訊》發布訊息，和讓中心複製資料，以廣流通。《中國共產黨研究通訊》和中國研究資料中心是分享我們所有「內部」刊物的最佳工具。

資源分享

　　出版業爆發，美元貶值，和研究圖書館維持經費不斷上升，使得研究圖書館獨立營運的日子不再。資源分享成為發展館藏的常規。圖書館自動化和圖書館網路的成立，加快和促進了相互依賴。東亞圖書館的經驗顯示，雖然全國性的合作採購不宜進行，地區性的合作收穫極大。加州大學柏克萊分校和史丹佛大學的合作，就是一個極好的例子。柏克萊分校的東亞圖書館和史丹佛胡佛研究院的東亞圖館制定合作採購中文報紙和方志的計畫，而在考慮購買昂貴書刊時，亦相互知會。東岸的六間東亞圖書館（哥倫比亞、康乃爾、哈佛、普林斯頓、耶魯和紐約公立圖書館）亦有相似計畫，每館負責收集若干地區的期刊，報紙和地方性出版物。這兩案例說明採用現實和實用的區域方式建立資源，可以增加收藏深度，而不用或僅略微增加開支。資源分享需要圖書館有更佳的溝通和協調。幸好自動化使得圖書館能在網路上即時傳遞資訊。

圖書館自動化

目前有兩個全國性的網路可以處理中日韓（CJK）三種文字的資料：RLIN（研究圖書館資訊網），和OCLC（連線電腦圖書館中心）。RLIN CJK是研究圖書館組織（RLG）在1983年創建，目前有超過一百萬條中日韓附有原文的紀錄，包括400,000本中文書籍。目前有33間東亞圖書館採用RLIN CJK系統，其中三間在加拿大，一間在德國。OCLC的CJK資料庫有超過680,000條單獨紀錄，其中328,000條是中文書刊，並且超過235,000條有中文，超過92,000條只有羅馬拼音。現時有34間東亞圖書館採用OCLC系統，其中香港和台灣各有一間，而澳大利亞有兩間。1980年代出版的中文書刊，分占RLIN CJK和OCLC CJK資料的53%和55%。國會圖書館的東亞資料，採用RLIN CJK系統編目，並予OCLC磁帶。RLIN和OCLC直接交換CJK紀錄。

對於當前出版物，兩個系統都能提供優良的書目控制，但對過往刊物，覆蓋皆不足；這也就是說美國東亞圖書館的絕大部分收藏，尚未自動化，研究者仍得翻查傳統目錄。目前技術已到位，應該組織全國力量籌款，把舊有圖書館目錄回溯轉換為機讀目錄。

上文已提到，當前書刊的目錄資料都很容易從資料庫取得。我們可以考慮進一步將整本書「全文處理」，令全書都能以電腦檢索。很多西文出版物，特別是參考書和索引，現在已有機讀光碟（CD-ROM）。至於中文方面，台北中央研究院歷史語言研究所和計算中心共同發展的二十五史資料庫，是一個極好的例子。這個全文資料庫，六千萬漢字，包括二十五史全文，可以檢索人名、地名、詞彙等等。替將來學者所節省的時間和精力，實在無法計算。這個資料庫已在華盛頓大學的東亞圖書館，和哈佛大學的哈佛燕京圖書館安裝。當然我們無法亦無必要將所有典籍全部賦予「全文處理」，但這種技術可以用來處理一些重要的研究當代中國資料。

研究工具

雖然電腦運作的資料庫能提供存藏資訊，和印出分類目錄，但精心編撰的研究工具，如主題注釋書目、研究指南、索引等，其重要性不會因之而降低。例如，彼得‧伯頓和吳文津合編的《當代中國研究指南》，提供資訊至1964年，需要補訂更新。續編可分兩部分，一為文革時期，一為後毛時期。中國研究資料中心翻印的20冊《紅衛兵資料》和8冊續編，需要有一比李鴻永所編，夏普出版社（M.E. Sharpe）出版的對這批資料的內容選輯指南更詳細的分類主題索引。中華人民共和國所出版期刊和報紙的聯合目錄，亦有出版的需要，最好能附有各地詳細收藏資訊。其他值得考慮出版的，還有各種主題的注解書目，和各種不同形式的出版物的清單，例如年鑑、法令和法規、人口統計等。[15]

最後，我們可以這樣說：美國圖書館在過去40年來，收集了為研究當代中國的大量資料，成就至大。前景亦同樣樂觀：中國將繼續增加出版數量，而美國圖書館亦會繼續向前，加強館藏。自民主運動以來，有關研究和出版的活動，都比80年代為少。但除非目前的以思想嚴格控制學術和出版成為永久政策，根據中國的出版歷史，我們相信只要控制一旦放鬆，各種新的和令人興奮的研究資料將再次出現。當這些事情發生，和更多的中國學者敢於重新投入有爭議性的研究領域，如中國共產黨歷史、毛澤東在中國革命中領導地位的評估，和討論改革等等，新的文獻證據和其他原始史料一定會出現，新的出版物也會面世。在80年代，很多這類資料出版，包括遵義會議的新史料、共產運動在各省的歷史文獻、黨領袖傳記、重要事件的目擊記錄，如李銳的《廬山會議實錄》，和一些新公布的毛澤東文章和演講稿。當情況繼續好轉，前述歷史應會重演。當然，我們的期望亦不能過高，例如黨中央檔案在短期內斷不會公開。同樣，公布歷史文獻來支持當前政策的做法，亦不會停止。[16]

　　這些對美國的學術研究有什麼影響？首先，80年代看到的資料所提供的資訊，將有助於填補我們對中華人民共和國人物和事件的認識和理解的差距。這些資訊將會產生一個重新評估過往研究成果的新環境。一些揣測會被確定，或被否定；不可靠的資料將被更正。我們可以探討一些過往因為資料不足而不能研究的項目。現在的問題倒是資料過於豐盛。當研究者面對新資料的大豐收，他們需要細心去蕪求菁，花不少時間和精力。例如有關黨領導人的傳記，增進我們對這些人物的個性和風格的了解，和對涉及這些人物的事件的認識。但由於這類文字的先天偏倚，我們對其中某些記載，還得和其他來源核對。雖然80年代的中國報紙和期刊遠較從前開放，並不只是發表宣傳當前政策的文章，並且有辯論其他途徑的空間，我們仍得知曉主辦單位的編輯政策。一般而言，這時期學術研究機構主辦的刊物，比黨和政府部門主辦的刊物，對於公共政策問題較為獨立和具分析性。後者傾向從意識形態或組織立場和圈子利益看待問題。

　　作為使用報刊的參考，《中國報刊大全》（北京：郵電出版社，1987）一類書籍，極為有用。這兩冊書羅列1987年中國出版的1,600種報紙和5,300種期刊，附有書目資訊，包括主辦單位，簡單出版歷史和範圍，及是否「內部」刊物。

　　在大量可以取得的統計資料中，人口調查報告和其他人口資料，最為可靠。經濟統計，每有詮釋問題。經濟學家發現這些資料，並未提供專案定義，搜集資料的方法和搜集目的。可幸有時省和地方年報提供的詳盡描敘，可以彌補這些缺失。其他法律文獻彙編，和有關外貿、私人企業、工廠管理和其他方面的手冊，都提供不少80年代經濟改革的資訊。不過這些刊物的內容時間短暫，因為法規等常常更動，各地情況亦不一。所以引用這些資料時，需要留意其時地特點。上面只是80年代我們從中國取得的大量研究資料中的一些弱點。雖然根據文獻的當代中國研究仍將會是主流，但是我們需要以實地考察所得的實驗資料作為補充。問題如中央政府的指令在地方執行的程度，民眾和黨幹部的相互關係，細小團體和大群落的社會行為，都需要實地研究，而不能單靠文獻來理解。

美國圖書館面臨的挑戰是如何繼續加強有關當代中國的館藏——不單只是所謂改革十年的80年代，而是自1949年建國以來整個中華人民共和國歷史——和同時使其更易查閱，以支援當代中國研究。

以下強調一些如何達到這個目的標的方法，其中大部分在上面已簡單提及。

採購

為了增強我們館藏的深度和寬度，我們需要有更多的區域性合作採購專案，以利資源分享。加州大學和胡佛研究院，以及哈佛、哥倫比亞、耶魯、普林斯頓、康乃爾和紐約公立圖書館已建立的合作計畫，可為典範。短暫出版物和視聽材料的收藏需要改善。個人學者和圖書館應該借予中國研究資料中心難得的出版物，包括內部書刊，讓其翻印發行。我們要鼓勵負責中國研究的圖書館員，在中國建立職業網路和定時到中國採購來獲得一般方法不能取得的資料。

檢索使用

全國性的圖書館網路使檢索使用各館館藏易如反掌。然其包括資料僅限於1984年以來編目的資料，東亞圖書館館藏大部分並未進入自動化控制。大規模的回溯轉換工程費用昂貴，圖書館無力勝任此項工作。全國性的圖書目錄回溯轉換工程，需要政府和基金會支援，並可以利用科技來提高館際借閱速度和協助文件傳遞。

對美國學者和圖書館而言，最終的檢索使用境界是知道中國圖書館的館藏，和如何可以使用他們所藏。為了這個目標，我們希望中美兩方的圖書館合作，將中國圖書館藏書的記錄數位化，加進美國的資料庫，如RLIN和OCLC。中國國家圖書館和OCLC的協議，將前者收藏民國時期（1911-1949）13萬種書籍的目錄存進OCLC，是一個良好的先例。

書目研究

　　一個有系統的書目研究計畫應該開始，最好是由一個全國性的委員會指導來編撰研究當代中國的一些工具書，例如專題注解書目、報紙和期刊聯合目錄、索引和其他參考工具。

　　從上世紀40年代後期，胡佛研究院開始發展當代中國研究資料，美國圖書館走了一段遙遠的路。成果得來不易，亦非偶然。這是端賴小心計畫，再加上各大學強有力的慷慨財政支持的成果。將來美國當代中國研究的成功，必須有賴於繼續發展圖書館資源。這才是問題的重心。

注釋

本文原發表於《美國之當代中國研究》（*American Studies of Contemporary China*），沈大偉（David Shambaugh）主編（華盛頓特區：威爾遜中心出版社 [The Woodrow Wilson Center Press], 1993），頁264-280。

[1]　本文部分根據作者著《當代中國研究：資料問題》（*Contemporary China Studies: Questions of Sources*）載《毛主席秘密講話：從百花齊放到大躍進》（*Secret Speeches of Chairman Mao: From the Hundred Flowers Movement to the Great Leap Forward*），馬若德、齊慕實、吳文津（Roderick MacFarquar, Timothy Cheek, and Eugene Wu）合編（麻州劍橋：哈佛大學東亞研究委員會，1989），頁59-73。

[2]　所有伊羅生特藏及威爾斯特藏中的文獻均列於薛君度編《中國共產主義運動，1921-1937：胡佛戰爭、革命與和平研究院中文圖書館藏中國文獻選輯解題書目》（*The Chinese Communist Movement, 1921-1937: An Annotated Bibliography of Selected Materials in the Chinese Collection of the Hoover Institution on War, Revolution, and Peace*）（加州帕洛阿托：胡佛研究院，1960）及其續篇《中國共產主義運動，1937-1949：胡佛戰爭、革命與和平研究院中文圖書館藏中國文獻選輯解題書目》（*The Chinese Communist Movement, 1937-1949: An Annotated Bibliography of Selected Materials in the Chinese Collection of the Hoover Institution on War, Revolution, and Peace*）（加州帕洛阿托：胡佛研究院，1962）。

　　有關陳誠特藏書目及其全部文件目錄，見吳天威編《江西蘇維埃共和國，1931-1934：陳誠特藏文件選輯題解書目》（*The Kiangsi Soviet Republic, 1931-1934: A Selected and Annotated Bibliography of the hen Cheng Collection*）（麻州劍橋：哈佛燕京

圖書館，1981）。

[3] 中國出版事業的起伏可以從下列統計數字得見（書籍數字包括新版與重版）。1958年出版總量為書籍45,495種，期刊822種，報紙491種；1961年降低為書籍13,529種，期刊410種，報紙260種。降低率分別為書籍70.26%，期刊50.12%，報紙47.04%。1967年，文革開始後一年，生產量急轉直下，書籍僅2,925種，期刊27種，報紙43種（紅衛兵小報除外）。與1961年的數字比較，代表更進一步的減縮：書籍78.37%，期刊93.41%，報紙83.46%。參見《中國出版年鑑1985》（北京：商務印書館，1986），頁744、750。

[4] 《中國季刊》，第18期（1964年4-6月），頁67。

[5] 《工作通訊》的英文翻譯，見鄭喆希編《中國紅軍的政治：人民解放軍工作通訊的翻譯本》（*The Politics of the Chinese Red Army: A Translation of the Bulletin of Activities of the People's Liberation Army*）（加州史丹佛：胡佛研究院，1966）。有關這批文件的分析，見約翰‧路易斯（John Lewis），〈中國的秘密軍事檔：「連續」與「啟示」〉（"China's Secret Military Papers: 'continuities' and 'revelations' "）載《中國季刊》第18期（1964年4-6月），頁68-78；謝艾莉（Alice Langley Hsieh），〈中國的秘密軍事文件：軍事教條與戰略〉（"China's Secret Military Papers: Military Doctrines and Strategy"）（同上），頁79-99；鄭喆希，〈從秘密軍事檔中看中國軍事領導問題〉（"Problems of Chinese Military Leadership as Seen in the Secret Military Papers"）載《亞洲觀察》（*Asian Survey*）（1964年6月），頁861-872。

[6] 書籍產量自1979年的17,212種上升至1985年的45,063種，同時期，期刊自1,470種上升至4,705種，報紙自69種至698種。參見中國國家統計局編《中國統計年鑑1986》（北京：中國統計出版社，1986），頁781-782。

[7] 見巴里‧勞頓（Barry Laughton），《中國經濟：新資料與數據》（*The Chinese Economy: New Sources and Data*）；雷偉立（William R. Lavely），《中國人口統計數據：主要資料指南》（*Chinese Demographic Data: A Guide to Major Sources*）；夏道泰與溫蒂‧澤爾丁（Wendy Zeldin），〈中華人民共和國立法與法制出版物〉（"Legislation and Legal Publications in the PRC"），載《中國交換通訊》（*China Exchange News*）第15期（1987年9-12月），頁8-16。

[8] 前香港「大學服務中心」，現屬香港中文大學，於1987年自中國獲得39種自1950至1987年（亦有自1949年者）全國性及省市報紙。此為除中國大陸以外最為齊全的中國地方報紙的收藏。該中心現已開始將這批資料拍攝微卷以廣分發。欲訂購者可直接向香港新界沙田香港中文大學大學服務中心詢問。

[9] 資訊由中國出版對外貿易公司提供。最新的《中國出版年鑑》1991年出版，包括資料

僅至1988年。此處所提數字包括新版與重版。無分別數字。

[10] 國會圖書館收藏數字不在包括之例。根據官方的數字，國會圖書館於1990年自中國共收書籍15,070種（9,544種為交換或贈送，5,516種為購買）。所收出版物覆蓋各類，包括大批科技書籍、教科書、少數民族語言資料、日常「修理」手冊等。由於無法查出社會科學與人文科學書籍的資料，故如包括國會圖書館，會使統計發生偏差，而淪資料的分析為無意義，因而未用國會圖書館的資料。

[11] 《解放軍報》自1987年開放訂購，美國圖書館所藏均始自其時。德國海德堡大學最近從中國購得全套。澳洲國立大學也收購了一份，不過只包括1977到1986年時期。

[12] 見李泡光、趙華春合編，《全國內部發行圖書總目1949-1986》（北京：中華書局，1988）。此目錄共列17,754種初版，547種增訂版圖書。書評見傅勒銘‧克里斯琴森（Flemming Christiansen），〈內部書目：書評〉（"The *Neibu* Bibliography: A Review"）載《中國共產黨研究通訊》（*CCP Research Newsletter*），第4期（1989-1990秋—冬季），頁13-19。又見該刊頁20-21，〈社會科學內部資料特點試析〉（"A Preliminary Analysis of the Characteristics of *Neibu* Materials in the Social Sciences"）。此文為劉昌運〈社會科學內部資料特點試析〉之翻譯，原文載《情報資料工作》，1985年3月，頁18-19。

[13] 關於這些複印可直接向中文研究資料中心詢問。郵箱號碼：P.O Box 3090, Oakton. VA 22124。

[14] 中國共產主義研究小組出版。通信處：Chinese Communism Research Group, Colorado College, 14 E. Cache La Poudre, Colorado Springs, CO 80903。

[15] 《現行中國年鑑一覽表》（*Current Yearbooks Published in the People's Republic of China*）包括下列各大學東亞圖書館所收藏：加州大學柏克萊分校、胡佛研究院、哈佛、哥倫比亞、康乃爾、耶魯、紐約公共圖書館，及香港中文大學大學服務中心。此表於1991年由加州大學柏克萊分校中國研究中心圖書館印行。增訂工作現正繼續中。

[16] 第6屆全國人民代表大會常務委員會在其1987年8月28日至9月5日召開之第22次會議上通過一項檔案法，於1988年1月1日實施。該法稱：「中華人民共和國成立以來形成的檔案，自形成之日起滿30年向社會開放。」在其他施行辦法中又稱：「前款所列檔案中涉及國防外交國家安全等重大利益的檔案，以及其他雖自形成之日起已滿30年，但檔案館認為到期仍不宜開放的檔案，經上一級檔案行政管理部門批准，可以延期向社會開放。」見《北京週報》（*Beijing Review*），第30期（1987年9月21日），頁6。《大公報英文週報》（*Ta Kung Pao English Weekly*）（1987年12月24日）又稱：「中國已經將1949年解放前的3,000多件檔案向社會開放。」

（馬泰來譯）

Library Resources for Contemporary China Studies

For more than four decades since the end of World War II, major American libraries have been diligent in their efforts to develop and maintain an essential corpus of research materials on contemporary China, including the history of the Chinese Communist movement. [1] Today, the combined strength of such resources in the United States is undoubtedly the greatest and the most comprehensive in the Western world. This chapter attempts to survey the past achievements, the present status, and the future prospects of the development of research resources on contemporary China in American libraries, and offers some recommendations.

Systematic collecting of primary sources for the study of the Chinese Communist movement by American libraries began in the late 1940s with the establishment of the Chinese Collection at the Hoover Institution and the appointment of the late Mary Clabaugh Wright as its curator. Having just been released from the Japanese internment camp at Weixian in Shandong province, Professor Wright traveled to all major cities in China in search of publications important to the study of twentieth-century China for the Hoover Institution. Her acquisitions in Yan'an yielded many rare contemporary Chinese Communist publications, the best known of which was probably a nearly complete set of *Jiefang ribao* (Liberation daily), 1941-47, the organ of the Chinese Communist Party. Later on, in the United States, she acquired the Harold Isaacs Collection and the Nym Wales Collection. The former consists mostly of underground Chinese Communist pamphlets and journals published (many were mimeographed) from the late 1920s to the early 1930s, and the latter includes a number of original Chinese

Communist documents of the mid-1930s. The Hoover Institution's collection of Chinese Communist documentation was further enriched in 1960 when the present author, then curator of its East Asian Collection, arranged for and supervised the microfilming in Taiwan of the Chen Cheng Collection, consisting of some fifteen hundred Chinese Communist documents relating exclusively to the Jiangxi Soviet period just before the Long March. [2] These three collections and other related materials, especially those published during the Anti-Japanese War of Resistance (1937-45), which had also been collected by other American libraries, constituted the first body of primary sources for the study of the Chinese Communist movement in its early phase to become available in the United States.

The 1945-49 period saw the publication of many books, journals, and news-papers under the direct sponsorship of either the Chinese Communist Party or its front organizations. While the coverage of these publications by American li-braries is by no means comprehensive, many of the more important sources, including those published in the Communist-controlled "border areas," are readily available. To these acquisitions have been added during the 1980s microfilms of some of the Chinese Communist journals and newspapers published in the 1930s and 1940s as well as many documentary compilations on the history of the CCP published for the first time in the PRC. American scholars have also had access since the early 1960s to several repositories of Chinese Communist documentation on Taiwan, the most important of which is the one-hundred-thousand-volume collection at the Library of the Bureau of Investigation of the Ministry of Justice, mostly dating from before 1949.

Since 1949, American libraries have maintained a rigorous acquisitions pro-gram of PRC publications on contemporary China. For purposes of discussion, this can be divided into the pre-Cultural Revolution and the post-Cultural Revo-lution phases.

During the first phase, from late 1949 to the late 1970s, it was not possible to purchase books directly from the PRC; instead orders had to be placed with dealers elsewhere, principally in Hong Kong and Tokyo. Local newspapers were not available by subscription to foreign libraries, and exchange was limited to the National Library of Beijing (since renamed the National Library of China). Although indirect buying was a nuisance at best, the dealers did offer all that was allowed for export. The problem was that many of the local publications were published in small print runs, and even when cleared for export, they were often difficult to obtain; and those having a *neibu* (internal) classification were not available at all, at least not officially. Furthermore, since commercial dealers depended on Chinese publishers for supply, the vicissitudes experienced by the Chinese publishing industry in those years naturally limited what and how much the dealers had to offer. For example, during the 1950s, when the Chinese publishing industry enjoyed a period of rapid expansion, the supply was plentiful in both volume and variety. However, when book production declined, because of either a shortage of material resources such as occurred throughout China in the early 1960s or political upheavals such as took place during the Cultural Revolution, the selection became first smaller and less diverse, and then practically nonexistent. [3] Exchange with the National Library alone proved unsatisfactory, since the items it provided were also easily available from book dealers, and its offering to American libraries never compared in either volume or variety with what it sent to libraries in the Soviet Union and Eastern Europe when China's relations with those areas were still friendly. These problems notwilhstanding, during this period American libraries managed to build up impressive collections of research materials on the PRC. The listings in *Contempornary China: A Research Guide*, by Peter Berton and Eugene Wu (Stanford: Hoover Institution, 1967), attest to this achievement. In this effort American libraries benefited from the release of a number of PRC publications and documents in Hong Kong, Taiwan, and the United States. The Union Research Institute in Hong Kong maintained an excellent file of Chinese newspaper and journal clip pings, which contained materials not then available in American libraries. From time to time the URI also made available PRC documents that had come into its possession. In Taiwan, the government released over a long period of time n large number of important CCP documents it had acquired. Among these releases, the many Central Committee directives, the "Lien-chiang Documents," the famous "571 Engineering Manual" (Lin Biao's crude plan for an armed uprising against Mao), and the Mao Zedong sixiang wansui! (Long live Mao Zedong thought!) volumes are probably the best known. Early in 1960, the U.S. government released its holdings of some twelve hundred pre-1960 Chinese local newspapers, many of them county-and subcounty-level publications, to the Library of Congress. While the great majority of these newspapers were incomplete and many were fragmentary (some containing just a few issues), the significance of this release cannot be overemphasized, since none of the publications were available for foreign subscription at the time, and they still are not today. In 1963, the State Department made another release to the Library of Congress, this one a set of Chinese military papers that the *China Quarterly* described as "the most illuminating first-hand material that scholars have had on the Chinese Communists since the Hoover Institution acquired the Yan'an Documents in the mid-forties." [4] The papers consisted of twenty-nine issues of the secret military journal *Gongzuo tongxun* (Bulletin of activities), covering the period from January 1 to August 26, 1961. Edited and published by the General Political Department of the People's Liberation Army, the bulletin was distributed to officers at the regimental level or above, with the top-secret issues distributed only to divisional commanders. [5]

The severe disruption of the publishing industry brought about by the Cultural Revolution has been noted above. The almost complete halt in the publication of scholarly and research works during those years forced American libraries to place a high premium on the collecting of all kinds of Red Guard publications. Although some of these materials are highly polemical, most contain a great deal of valuable information not available elsewhere at the time. For example, there are directives from all levels of the party and speeches by party leaders, including a good many by Mao Zedong, all from this period; "negative materials" on those being purged; documents on party history; and "news flashes" on people and current events. Initially, libraries competed with each other in the acquisition of the limited amount of such material available in Hong Kong, and prices soared. At the request of China scholars, the State Department agreed to release its collection of Red guard materials to the academic community. The releases were first made through the Harvard-Yenching Library, and then made to the Center for Chinese Research Materials（CCRM）after its establishment in 1968. In 1975, the CCRM reproduced these releases, along with some additional materials acquired from other sources, under the title Red Guard Publications in nineteen volumes for general distribution; in 1979 a general table of contents to the nineteen volumes was also issued. Another eight volumes were published as a supplement the following year. Together they represent the single largest collection of Red Guard publications available in the Western world. A modest amount of additional Red Guard publications has become available during the last few years. They, too, will be reproduced by CCRM for distribution.

Since the late 1970s, Chinese publishing has undergone a remarkable quantitative and qualitative transformation. In this post-Cultural Revolution period, the Chinese publishing industry not only regained its vitality but also began to publish more objective and scholarly research. [6] Documentary compilations, memoirs of party leaders, new journals, specialty newspapers, and scholarly works that for one reason or another could not be published in the past have all appeared in quantity, and the quality of many of the research publications has shown a remarkable improvement in depth of treatment and diversity of approach. New types of publications such as yearbooks, statistics, and legal materials also have proliferated. [7] One serial publication that merits special mention is the *Fuyin baokan ziliao* (Reprints of newspaper and periodical articles) issued by the Chinese People's University. This series began publication in the 1950s for internal use and was made available for foreign subscription in 1978. These facsimile reprints, originally covering only twenty-two topics, have been expanded to cover over a hundred, with articles selected from two thousand newspapers and periodicals published in the PRC. While articles on all aspects of contemporary Chinese affairs are included, those concerning military affairs were omitted from the public offering until 1989. Most volumes in the series are monthly publications, and each issue carries its own index. There is also a cumulative annual index. The importance of this publication lies in its wide coverage, which includes articles selected from *neibu* newspapers and periodicals that are not available for foreign subscription. It is also extremely convenient for users, since articles on a given subject, published in a variety of sources, are grouped together in handy volumes. However, the selection process is subject to the prevailing political climate at any given time. For example, before the 1989 prodemocracy movement, articles selected for the volumes on Zhongguo zhengzhi (Chinese politics) included those by people like Yan Jiaqi and Su Shaozhi on political reform, but, during and since the movement, the selection has been limited to those supporting the party and the government.

On the acquisitions side, since the late 1970s direct purchases from China have become routine; Chinese libraries are now permitted and are eager to enter into exchange arrangements with foreign libraries; some local newspapers, mostly on the provincial level, are available for foreign subscription for the first time; Chinese book fairs have been held in China and abroad; visitors are free to purchase publications in state-run stores as well as at privately managed book stalls that are set up on sidewalks in many major cities; and most visiting scholars are accorded the privilege of photocopying at their host institutions.

　　Yet, against this encouraging background of vast improvement, certain old problems in procurement linger and some new ones have surfaced. The old problems concern *neibu* materials, local publications, and local newspapers. The wide and continuing use of the *neibu* classification on many publications means that once a book is so classified, it does not get listed in dealers' catalogues; and even when sent on exchange by a Chinese library, it is invariably stopped by customs and returned to its sender. The trouble with local publications seems to be that none of the local publishing houses is either equipped to sell directly overseas or is permitted to do so by the Chinese government because of regulations governing foreign-exchange transactions. Foreign libraries have to depend on the few national book-export corporations for supply. Since local publications are usually issued in small editions, even when they are listed in the catalogues, supply is not always guaranteed. A further complication here is that a publisher is free to withdraw a book from publication after announcement, if advance sales are insufficient to guarantee a profit. As for local newspapers, while almost all provincial dailies are now available, the ban against the export of subprovincial-level publications remains; and not all city newspapers are available for foreign subscription. [8]

　　Chief among the new problems are the quality of service provided by the book-export corporations in China, the problems arising from exchanges, and the difficulty of acquiring out-of-print publications. In our dealings with the export corporations, it is not uncommon to place an order only to learn six to twelve months later, if ever, that the order cannot be filled. In the meantime, one often misses the opportunity to obtain a copy from another source while it is still available. This is a particularly serious problem with regard to local publications in limited supply. The problem with exchange is that the price differential between American and Chinese publications is such that no Chinese library would agree to any exchange based on equal value. For the same reason, American libraries are unwilling to enter into any agreement that is purely on a volume-for-volume basis.

Consequently, exchanges are conducted on a "gentlemen's agreement" basis, with each side exercising its own discretion as to what constitutes a fair trade. While some Chinese libraries do oblige requests for publications issued in their respective localities, the standard exchange offerings, more often than not, consist of publications from national publishing houses that are easily available from commercial sources. Last, while it was always difficult to search for out-of-print publications in China, the situation has not improved now that we are able to deal directly with the export companies. Given the problems just described, American libraries have supplemented the usual and more formal channels of acquisition by relying heavily on the assistance of individuals who travel to China and on personal relationships formed with Chinese colleagues. These private contacts have been very productive, and will certainly continue to be a significant factor in the further development of research resources for the study of contemporary China in the years to come.

At present, there are some sixty libraries in the United States that are collecting Chinese-language publications from the PRC, Taiwan, and other Chinese speaking areas. But not all maintain the same degree of comprehensiveness in coverage or the same collecting intensity. The larger and better-funded libraries naturally achieve a wider coverage and acquire more materials than the others. Generally speaking, all libraries, regardless of size, concentrate on publications in the social sciences and the humanities; natural science and technical materials are not collected except reference tools, principally dictionaries, and those publications, mostly journals, that are received as gifts or on exchange.

Are we keeping up with the current output of publications from the PRC? The answer is a qualified yes, if we consider only those publications on the contemporary period that are allowed for export. According to official statistics for 1989, the latest year for which detailed figures are available, the total number of publications in China that year was 74,973 titles (including 55,476 new publications and 19,498 reprints) under the following categories: books, 57,476 titles (45,432 new, 12,042 reprints); textbooks, 11,706 titles (4,721 new, 6,985 reprints); and pictorial materials, 5,791 titles (5,320 new, 471 reprints). [9] In addition, 6,078 periodicals and 1,576 newspapers were published. Table shows their coverage by subject.

Publications, 1989	Number of Titles
Books, by Subject	
Philosophy and Social Sciences	12,426
Culture and Education	25,541
Literature and Arts	13,889
Natural Science and Technology	14,977
Pictorial Materials	5,791
General	2,349
Total	74,973
Periodicals, by Subject	
Philosophy and Social Sciences	1,359
Culture and Education	653
Literature and Arts	662
Natural Science and Technology	3,019
Juvenalia	83
Pictorial Materials	81
General	221
Total	6,078
Newspapers, by Type	
Central (National)	138
Provincial and Municipal	714
County and Specialty	724
Total	1,576

How do we measure up, in view of these figures? On the basis of information from nine Chinese collections in the United States (Harvard, Columbia, Yale, Princeton, Chicago, Michigan, University of California at Berkeley, Hoover Institution, and University of Washington), the average number of books acquired from the PRC in 1989 was around 5,300 titles (from a low of 2,400 to a high of 8,000, with most clustering around 5,000 to 6,000); the average number of periodicals was 942 (from 496 to 1,279, including four subscribing to over 1,000, and two, 900); and the average number of newspapers was 42 (from 10 to 123). [10] As already mentioned, East Asian libraries usually do not collect in the natural sciences and technology, or textbooks; pictorial materials are collected only highly selectively. Excluding these categories, the number of books (new titles and reprints) in the social sciences and humanities published in 1989 would have been 51,856, and of periodicals, 2,674. Using these adjusted figures for a comparison, we find that these nine libraries were collecting from 4.63 percent to 15.48 percent of the 51,856 books; from 18.54 percent to 47.83 percent of the 2,674 periodicals; and from 0.63 percent to 7.80 percent of the 1,576 newspapers.

However, the following should be kept in mind while looking at these comparisons: (1) the publications figures include works on both the contemporary and the earlier periods; (2) not all books published are allowed for export; (3) American libraries collect only selectively in popular contemporary fiction and translations of foreign literature, both of which have proliferated since the Cultural Revolution (the Library of Congress, as a matter of policy, does not collect any translations at all); and (4) among the large number of reprints that were issued, it is very likely that many were already collected by American libraries at the time of their first publication. What all this means is that, as far as books on the contemporary period are concerned, our coverage is definitely far better than the percentage figures here would indicate. But there remains the question of *neibu* material and local publications, to which we shall return shortly.

As far as periodicals are concerned, our coverage is excellent. While more than 6,000 titles were published in 1989, less than half were made available for foreign subscription. The 1989 catalog of the China National Publishing Industry Trading Corporation（CNPITC）offered only 2,501 titles for this purpose, with about 41 percent in the natural sciences and technology. Since few or none of the scientific and technological periodicals were subscribed to by any of the nine libraries surveyed, their average receipt of 942 titles, the vast majority being in the social sciences and humanities, is a worthy record indeed.

As for newspapers, the record is not nearly so good. The 1989 CNPITC catalog lists 136 newspapers for which they will accept foreign orders, including the once-classified *Jiefangjun bao*（Liberation Army news）. [11] About half the titles offered were national, provincial, and city newspapers, and the other half specialty newspapers, each devoted to a single subject such as marketing, advertising, broadcasting, health, shipping, textiles, laws, women, or athletics. County newspapers were not, and still are not, offered at all. The 136 titles represent 8.63 percent of the 1,576 newspapers published in 1989. Compared to this, the nine libraries' average receipt of 42 titles can only be considered fairly satisfactory.

In conclusion, it may be said that while there is much more that can be accomplished, American libraries collectively have done a remarkable job in the development of research resources on contemporary China, given the constraints imposed by the availability of materials and ever-shrinking acquisitions budgets. The following examines the areas in which action could be taken to improve and ensure the continuing health of our collection development programs in support of contemporary China studies.

Coverage

Our coverage of PRC publications on the contemporary period could and should be widened. Even though our basic source of supply will continue to be the export corporations, there are several other ways that we can achieve a wider coverage. Libraries with existing exchange relationships with Chinese libraries should insist that their exchange partners send only local publications from their respective regions, including those published by their own university presses, if such exist. Libraries not engaged in exchanges may wish to do so as a means to increase their acquisition of local publications. Chinese bibliographers or acquisitions libraries of large Chinese collections should be able to make frequent trips to China, not only to search out publications but also to develop personal contacts with publishers, book corporations, and Chinese scholars and librarians. Experience indicates that books that are hard to get from dealers can often be obtained from local bookstores or street vendors. Negotiations conducted in person are always more effective than correspondence. Research and editorial offices as well as university libraries also have proved a rich source for out-of-print book and journals. Many are reluctant or not equipped to send such materials to a foreign library, but most are willing to accommodate personal requests made in situ in return for some form of exchange arrangements.

Libraries that are not already doing so will find it useful to search out and acquire documentary collections and monographs on contemporary China from other countries, especially Japan and Taiwan. (It is assumed that American libraries' coverage of Western-language publications on contemporary China is adequate.) Some important journals and monographs published in Japan on contemporary China may be missed by Chinese collections, since very few Chinese bibliographers look at Japanese catalogues and Japanese bibliographers usually pay attention only to materials related to Japan. While the volume of PRC documentation through Taiwan has been reduced in recent years, some very significant materials continue to be available. For example, a large number of unofficial magazines and wall posters of the late 1970s and early 1980s have been reproduced in Taipei under the title *Da-lu di-xia kan-wu hui-bian* (A collection of

Chinese mainland underground publications), of which twenty volumes have so far been published. Acquisitions of this type should certainly enhance our research capabilities on contemporary China.

Other types of research sources that we have traditionally ignored are audio visual materials and ephemeral publications. While different in form, these materials are no less important than printed books and are sometimes even more valuable to a research scholar. Photographs, video and audio tapes, mimeographed handbills, appeals, and pamphlets of the 1989 prodemocracy movement in the PRC are good examples. These materials lend a sense of immediacy that cannot be easily conveyed by the printed text. The East Asian libraries at Harvard, Columbia, Chicago, UCLA, Yale, and the New York Public Library have each established a "Tiananmen Archives" containing such materials. If the collecting can be extended backward in time to cover other major political movements in the PRC since 1949, such as the Cultural Revolution and the Anti-Rightist Campaign, we will have greatly enriched our library collections for contemporary China studies.

"*Neibu*" Materials

Neibu is a generic term used for publications not meant for public distribution, but not all *neibu* publications are "secret" or "classified" in the Western security sense. Many scholarly publications, translations, and even reference works, the publication of which has circumvented the official channels, bear the *neibu* designation. [12] Some university presses in China have further complicated the situation. In an effort to keep some of their publications away from central distribution abroad by the government-designated export corporations, they have resorted to using the *neibu* label to gain control over their own distribution overseas.

Generally speaking, there are two basic categories of the *neibu* classification:

neibu faxing (internal distribution) and *xian guonei faxing* (for domestic distribution only). Under the first are also subcategories such as *neibu wenjian* (internal documents), *neibu ziliao* (internal material), *neibu cankao* (internal reference), *neibu duwu* (internal reading material), *neibu kongzhi faxing* (controlled internal distribution), and *dangxiao xitong neibu faxing* (internal distribution within the party school system), but in most cases, only the generic term "*neibu faxing*" is used. Preliminary drafts of books marked as *zhengqiu yijian gao* (drafts for the solicitation of comments) also fall under the *neibu* category, as do other *shiyongben* (trial editions) of publications. While all *neibu* publications are issued in short press runs and are not officially available, some of them, as has been mentioned, do find their way to the outside world. Reprint publishers in Hong Kong offer them for sale from time to time (at a not insignificant price) and increasingly more have been available from private sources in the United States and other countries as well. The problem so far has been one of knowing what has been acquired, and of making the materials more readily available to the scholarly community at large. The Center for Chinese Research Materials (CCRM) in Virginia (formerly in Washington, D.C.), a not-for-profit organization, has already reproduced some two hundred titles of *neibu* publications. [13] But at present the CCRM does not have sufficient manpower to search out the many others that are scattered in various places.

　　Therefore, there is an urgent need to establish some sort of clearinghouse of information so that the existence of materials may be made known to scholars and the materials made available for reproduction. The recently launched *CCP Research Newsletter* (editor, Timothy Cheek) serves this purpose admirably. The *Newsletter* is designed to disseminate research information and critical notes on sources, primarily *neibu* publications, and their interpretation among scholars doing research on the pre-1949 Chinese Communist movement, the PRC party/state, and the post-Mao reform of socialism. [14] Arrangements have been made with the CCRM to reproduce publications mentioned in the *Newsletter*. Individual scholars and libraries, having come upon any *neibu* publications, are encouraged to transmit that information to the *Newsletter* for publication and to lend the materials to the CCRM for reproduction and wider distribution. The *CCP Research Newsletter* and the CCRM provide the best vehicle available to us for sharing our collection of *neibu* publications.

Resource Sharing

The publishing explosion, the devaluation of the American dollar, and the spiraling costs of maintaining research collections have made self-sufficiency of research libraries a thing of the past. Resource sharing has now become the cardinal principle in collection development. The introduction of automation in libraries and the creation of library networks have further hastened and facilitated this concept of mutual dependence. The experience of East Asian libraries indicates that, while a national cooperative program in acquisitions may not be practical, a great deal can be achieved on a regional basis. The example of the University of California at Berkeley and Stanford is a good case in point. The East Asian Library at Berkeley and the East Asian Collection of the Hoover Institution at Stanford have instituted cooperative acquisitions programs for Chinese newspapers and local histories, and they consult each other when considering purchases of expensive materials. A similar program is now in effect among the six East Asian libraries on the East Coast, Columbia, Cornell, Harvard, Princeton, Yale, and the New York Public Library. Under this program, each takes primary responsibility for collecting available periodicals and newspapers as well as other publications of a local nature that fall into the respective areas of their collecting responsibility. These cases illustrate the advantage of a realistic and practical regional approach to collection building that will provide more in-depth collecting with little or no increase in budget. Resource sharing calls for better communication and coordination among libraries. Fortunately, automation has made possible the instantaneous transmission of information on access through library networks.

Library Automation

There are now two national networks that are capable of processing Chinese-, Japanese-, and Korean-language（CJK）materials: the Research Libraries Information Network（RLIN）and the Online Computer Library Center（OCLC）. The RLIN CJK system, introduced by the Research Libraries Group（RLG）in 1983, now has more than one million CJK records in its database（all with vernacular scripts）, of which more than four hundred thousand are unique Chinese titles, There are currently thirty-three East Asian libraries using the RLIN CJK system, including three in Canada and one in Germany. OCLC has more than 680,000 unique records in its CJK database, of which more than 328,000 are Chinese titles. Of this total, more than 235,000 records contain Chinese characters, and more than 92,000 in romanization only. There are thirty-four East Asian libraries using the OCLC CJK system, including one each in Hong Kong and Taiwan, and two in Australia. In both databases, records for Chinese books published in the 1980s account for 53 percent and 55 percent respectively of the RLIN CJK and OCLC CJK totals. The Library of Congress catalogues its East Asian materials into the RLIN CJK database and a tape is available to OCLC for the latter's use. RLIN and OCLC exchange their CJK records directly.

The two available systems provide excellent bibliographical control over current imprints, but they do not cover retrospective publications. In other words, the vast majority of American East Asian libraries' holdings remain outside automated control, and researchers by necessity must continue to consult the manual catalogues. Now that the technology is in place, a national effort should be mounted to seek funding for a retrospective conversion project to convert the manual records into machine-readable form.

As mentioned above, bibliographical data of current imprints can now be easily retrieved from the databases. What we might also consider as a further step is "full-text processing" by which entire books are made computer-accessible, which would permit the texts to be searched. Many Western-language publications are now available on CD-ROMs (Compact Disk—Read-Only Memory), especially reference works and indexes. In Chinese, there is the outstanding example of the *Twenty-Five Dynastic Histories Database* jointly developed by the Institute of History and Philology of Academia Sinica in Taipei and the academy's Computer Center. This full-text database, consisting of some sixty million Chinese characters which make up the entire text of the twenty-five dynastic histories, can be searched for personal names, place names, phrases, and so on. The time and effort it will save future generations of scholars is certainly immeasurable. This database has been installed at the East Asian Library at the University of Washington and at the Harvard-Yenching Library at Harvard University. Of course, it would be impossible and unnecessary to computerize everything with "full-text processing," but the technology can be employed to process selective types of materials important to contemporary China research.

Research Tools

While computerized databases can provide valuable information on holdings and print out lists of publications by subject, the importance of carefully compiled research tools such as annotated subject bibliographies, research guides, indexes, and the like will not diminish. For example, Peter Berton and Eugene Wu's *Contemporary China: A Research Guide* should be updated—its coverage ends with 1964, and a supplement should be compiled to cover the later periods, perhaps in two parts, one on the Cultural Revolution years, and another on the post-Mao period. The twenty-volume collection of Red Guard Publications and its eight-volume supplement, both reproduced by CCRM, will require a subject index more detailed than the guide to selected contents compiled by Hong Yung Lee published by M.E. Sharpe. Union lists of PRC periodicals and newspapers likewise should be published, preferably with detailed holdings information. Other annotated subject bibliographies should be considered, as should checklists of special types of publications such as yearbooks, laws and statutes, demographic compilations, and the like. [15]

In conclusion, it may be said that American libraries have accomplished much during the last four decades in building up an impressive amount of research materials for contemporary China studies. Looking to the future, it seems that they should do at least as well, as China continues to publish more and American libraries move forward to further strengthen their collections. It is true that, since the prodemocracy movement, there has been a decrease in the kind of research and publication that we witnessed during the 1980s. But unless the present strict enforcement of ideological control over scholarship and publication becomes permanent policy, it is reasonable to assume, judging from the history of publishing in the PRC, that once that control is relaxed, we will once again witness the appearance of a variety of new and exciting research sources. When that happens, and when more Chinese scholars again venture into the more controversial areas of research, such as those related to the history of the Chinese Communist Party, the assessment of Mao's leadership in the Chinese Revolution, the debates on reforms and so forth, new documentary evidence and other primary sources are bound to be introduced and new publications to appear. During the 1980s, we saw a large group of such materials being published, including new sources on the Zunyi Conference, documentary histories of the Communist movement in various provinces, biographies of party leaders, eyewitness accounts of important historical events such as Li Rui's *Lushan huiyi shilu* (A veritable record of the Lushan conference), and new texts of Mao's writings and speeches. It seems likely that the cycle will repeat itself when more favorable conditions obtain. Of course, it will remain unrealistic to expect, for instance, that the Central Party Archive would be open at any time in the future, but there is also no reason to believe that the practice of releasing historical documentation to justify policy will become a thing of the past. [16]

What is the implication of all this for American scholarship? For one thing, information we already have from such sources made available in the 1980s will be helpful in bridging the gaps in our knowledge and understanding of people and events in the People's Republic. Such information will create a new context in which to reassess our past findings. Surmises may now be confirmed or rejected in some cases, and once unreliable data corrected in others. Research on topics heretofore impossible to undertake for lack of sources may now be attempted. But there is the problem of an embarrassment of riches. When researchers find themselves faced with a huge harvest of new materials, more care will have to be exercised to separate the wheat from the chaff, a task that will take more time and research. For example, the biographical literature of party leaders enables us to gain much insight into the personalities and styles of the people under study, and adds considerable detail to our knowledge of the events in which they had personal involvement. But the inherent bias of this genre of writing requires one to cross-check certain information found in these publications with other sources. While the Chinese newspaper and periodical press of the 1980s became much more open and no longer published just articles publicizing current policies, but also made room for some debates on alternatives, it is important to know the editorial policy of the sponsoring bodies of these publications. Generally speaking, publications sponsored by academic research institutes during this period tended to be more analytical and independent in their approach to public policy questions than publications sponsored by the party or government ministries or agencies. The latter tended to view problems more from ideological or organizational perspectives and parochial interests.

As an aid to the use of newspapers and periodicals, publications such as the *Zhongguo baokan daquan* (Directory of Chinese newspapers and periodicals) (Beijing: Renmin youdian chubanshe, 1987) are very useful. This two-volume publication lists sixteen hundred newspapers and fifty-three hundred periodicals published in China in 1987, complete with bibliographical information for each entry, including the name of the sponsoring organization, a brief account of the history of the publication and its scope, and whether it is a *neibu* publication.

Also, among the large amount of statistical data that has been made available, census reports and other demographic data are found to be most reliable. Economic statistics, however, pose certain problems of interpretation, as economists have discovered that the sources that provide such data do not make explicit such information as the definition of categories, procedures used in data collecting, or the purpose for which the data were collected. In some cases, the rich descriptive materials in the various provincial and local yearbooks can be of help in this respect. Other documentary collections of laws and regulations, and handbooks regarding foreign trade, private enterprises, factory management, and other areas, are very informative on economic reform of the 1980s, but most suffer from the ephemeral nature of their contents, since the laws and regulations and such are subject to change from time to time, and from place to place. Thus, the time-and locale-specific nature of these publications is a very important consideration in their use. The above are merely a few examples of the weaknesses of some of the large outpouring of research materials we have from China during the 1980s. While the documentary basis of contemporary China studies will continue to be the norm, it must be supplemented by empirical data gathered from on-site field investigations. Questions such as the degree to which central government directives are implemented at the local level, the interaction between the masses and party cadres, and the social behavior of small groups or whole communities all have to be studied in situ and cannot be adequately understood merely through documents.

The challenge for American libraries is how to further strengthen their collections on contemporary China—not only on the so-called reform decade of the 1980s, but on the entire period of the People's Republic since its founding in 1949—and how to make them more easily accessible to support contemporary China studies.

The following highlights some of the ways in which this can be accomplished, most of which have been briefly mentioned earlier in this essay:

Acquisitions. In order to increase the breadth and depth of our collections, there should be more regional cooperative acquisitions programs for the purpose of resource sharing. The programs that have already been developed between the University of California and the Hoover Institution and among Harvard, Columbia, Yale, Princeton, Cornell, and the New York Public Library can serve as models. The collecting of ephemeral and audiovisual materials should be improved. Individual scholars and libraries should be willing to lend hard-to-get publications, including *neibu* materials, to the Center for Chinese Research Materials for reproduction and distribution. Chinese studies librarians should be encouraged to develop professional contacts in and to make periodic acquisitions trips to China in order to acquire materials that cannot be obtained otherwise.

Access. National library networks now provide easy intellectual access to library collections. However, currently available databases of Chinese-language materials include only publications catalogued since 1984, at the earliest, and the vast majority of East Asian libraries' collections remain outside automated control. Since this is a massive undertaking requiring substantial funding, and libraries do not have the means to do it, a national retrospective conversion program should be mounted for this purpose with government and foundation support. Technology should also be employed to speed up interlibrary loans and to facilitate document delivery such as facsimile transmission of journal articles.

The ultimate in access for American scholars and libraries would, of course, be the ability to find out what is available in libraries in the PRC, and to have physical access to their collections. For this purpose, it is to be hoped that some cooperative arrangements can be worked out between Chinese and American libraries to produce machine-readable records of the Chinese libraries' holdings that can then be added to American databases such as RLIN and OCLC. The agreement between the National Library of China and OCLC to have the former's 130,000-title collection of books published during the Republican period (1911—49) catalogued into the OCLC database shows how this can be accomplished.

Bibliographical Research. A systematic bibliographical research program should be initiated, preferably under the guidance of a national committee, to produce research tools on contemporary China studies such as annotated subject bibliographies, union lists of newspapers and periodicals, indexes, and other reference aids.

American libraries have come a long way in developing research resources for the study of contemporary China since the Hoover Institution pioneered the way in the late 1940s. What we have accomplished did not come easily or by accident. It is the result of careful planning backed up by a firm commitment by university administrations with generous financial support. The future success of the American study of contemporary China will require, as part of the centerpiece, the continuing and expanded development of library resources. That is the heart of the matter.

Notes

This essay was published in American Studies of Contemporary China, edited by David Shambaugh (Washington, D.C.: Woodrow Wilson Center Press, 1993), pp. 264-280.

[1]　Parts of this essay are based on the author's chapter, "Contemporary China Studies: The Question of Sources," in *The Secret Speeches of Chairman Mao, From the Hundred Flowers to the Great Leap Forward*, ed. Roderick MacFarquhar, Timothy Cheek, and Eugene Wu (Cambridge: Harvard Council on East Asian Studies, 1989), pp. 59-73.

[2]　All items in the Harold Isaacs Collection and those in the Nym Wales Collection are listed in Chun-tu Hsueh, *The Chinese Communist Movement, 1921-1937, An Annotated Bibliography of Selected Materials in the Chinese Collection of the Hoover Institution on War, Revolution, and Peace* (Palo Alto, Calif.: Hoover Institution, 1960), and its sequel, *The Chinese Communist Movement, 1937-1949, An Annotated Bibliography of Selected Materials in the Chinese Collection of the Hoover Institution on War, Revolution, and Peace* (Palo Alto, Calif.: Hoover Institution, 1962).

　　For a bibliography and complete checklist of all the documents in the Chen Cheng Collection, see Tien-wei Wu, *The Kiangsi Soviet Republic, 1931-1934, A Selected and Annotated Bibliography of the Chen Cheng Collection* (Cambridge: Harvard-Yenching Library, 1981).

[3]　The fluctuations in publishing activities in the PRC are shown by the following statistics (book figures include both new and reprint editions): in 1958, a total of 45,495 books, 822 periodicals, and 491 newspapers were published; in 1961, the numbers were reduced to 13,529 books, 410 periodicals, and 260 newspapers, down by 70.26 percent, 50.12 percent, and 47.04 percent respectively; in 1967, one year after the start of the Cultural Revolution, production dropped precipitously to 2,925 books, 27 periodicals, and 43 newspapers (excluding Red Guard tabloids), representing a further reduction of 78.37 percent, 93.41 percent, and 83.46 percent against the 1961 figures. See *Zhongguo chuban nianjian* 1985 (China publishing yearbook 1985) (Beijing: Shangwu yinshuguan, 1986), 744,750.

[4]　*China Quarterly*, no. 18 (April-June 1964): p. 67.

[5]　For an English translation of the papers, see J. Chester Cheng, ed., *The Politics of the Chinese Red Army: A Translation of the Bulletin of Activities of the People's Liberation Army* (Stanford: Hoover Institution, 1966). For analyses of the documents, see John Wilson

Lewis, "China's Secret Military Papers: 'Continuities' and 'Revelations,'" *China Quarterly*, no. 18 (April—June 1964): pp. 68-78; Alice Langley Hsieh, "China's Secret Military Papers: Military Doctrines and Strategy," *ibid.*, pp. 79-99; and J. Chester Cheng, "Problems of Chinese Military Leadership as Seen in the Secret Military Papers," *Asian Survey* (June 1964): pp. 861-72.

[6]　Book production increased from 17,212 titles in 1979 to 45,603 titles in 1985, periodicals from 1,470 to 4,705, and newspapers from 69 to 698 for the same period. See Zhongguo guojia tongji ju, comp., *Zhongguo tongji nianjian 1986* (China statistical yearbook 1986) (Beijing: Zhongguo tongji chuban she, 1986), pp. 781-82.

[7]　See, for instance, Barry Naughton, "The Chinese Economy: New Sources and Data"; William R. Lavely, "Chinese Demographic Data: A Guide to Major Sources"; and Tao-tai Hsia and Wendy Zeldin, "Legislation and Legal Publications in the PRC," *China Exchange News* 15 (September—December 1987): pp. 8-16.

[8]　The Universities Service Centre (USC) in Hong Kong, now a part of the Chinese University of Hong Kong, managed to acquire in 1987 from China complete sets of 39 Chinese national, provincial, and municipal newspapers published from 1950 to 1987 (some date from 1949). This is now the largest and most complete collection of Chinese local newspapers available anywhere outside of China. USC has begun microfilming this newspaper collection for general distribution. Inquiries may be sent directly to the Universities Services Centre, Chinese University of Hong Kong, Shatin, N.T., Hong Kong.

[9]　Information by courtesy of the China National Publishing Industry Trading Corporation (CNPITC). The latest available edition of *Zhongguo chuban nianjian* (China publishing yearbook) was published in 1991, containing information only for 1988. Figures include both new publications and reprints. Separate figures are not available.

[10]　The Library of Congress is excluded from this count because LC figures, if included, would skew the picture and make the tabulation less meaningful. Official LC statistics show that in fiscal year 1990 the LC received a total of 15,070 titles of books from the PRC (9,554 by exchange or gift and 5,516 by purchase). The receipts were in all categories, including a large number of scientific and technical publications, textbooks, minority-language materials, "how-to" types of publications, etc. Since it is not possible to separate these from the social science and humanities publications the LC does keep, and because of the considerable number of duplicates involved, it is wise not to include LC figures in the count here. The LC currently has subscriptions to 1,835 periodicals from the PRC, plus some

additional titles which it received with varying degrees of regularity as gifts or on exchange. The LC also receives 30 newspapers from the PRC.

[11] *The Liberation Army News* was first offered in 1987, and American libraries' holdings date from that time. The University of Heidelberg, Germany, recently acquired a complete set of this newspaper from China, and the Australian National University also has acquired a set covering the period from 1977 to 1986.

[12] See Li Paoguang and Zhao Huachun, comp., *Quanguo neibu faxing tushu zong-mu, 1949-1986* (National bibliography of internally distributed works, 1949-1986) (Beijing: Zhonghua shuju, 1988). The bibliography covers 17,754 first editions and 547 revised editions. For a review of this publication, see Flemming Christiansen, "The *Neibu* Bibliography: A Review Article," *CCP Research Newsletter* 4 (Fall-Winter 1989 90): pp. 13-19. See also Liu Changyun, "A Preliminary Analysis of the Characteristics of Neibu Materials in the Social Sciences," *ibid.*, pp. 20-21. This is a translation of "Shehui kexue neibu ziliao tedian shixi," *Qingbao ziliao gongzuo* (Information and materials work) (March 1985), pp. 18-19.

[13] Inquiries concerning these reproductions may be sent to the Center for Chinese Research Materials, P.O. Box 3090, Oakton, VA, 22124.

[14] Published by the Chinese Communism Research Group, Colorado College, 14 E. Cache La Poudre, Colorado Springs, CO, 80903.

[15] *Current Yearbooks Published in the People's Republic of China, including holdings of East Asian libraries at Berkeley, the Hoover Institution, Harvard, Columbia, Cornell, Yale, the New York Pubic Library, and the Universities Service Centre at the Chinese University of Hong Kong*, was published by the Center for Chinese Studies Library of the University of California, Berkeley, in 1991. An updated edition is in preparation.

[16] The Standing Committee of the Sixth National People's Congress passed an archives law at its 22d meeting, August 28-September 5, 1987, which provides that "state archives will generally be open to the public after 30 years." The law, which became effective on January 1, 1988, also stipulates, inter alia, that "archives related to state security or other major national interests, as well as those unsuitable for the public, can remain confidential after 30 years" (see *Beijing Review* 30 [September 21, 1987]: p. 6). According to another report, "China has already opened to the public more than 3,000 of its archives recording events before Liberation in 1949" (see *Ta Kung Pao English Weekly*, December 24,1987).

六、
國民黨早期政治史：
第一次國共合作

戰略上之分歧
民國十二年蔣中正先生赴俄報聘之研討

　　1923年9月2日至11月29日蔣介石帶領一個孫中山指派的四人代表團赴俄訪問，訪問的目的是爭取蘇聯的支援，和參與一項國民黨擊敗北方軍閥以取得政權的軍事戰略。但是此次訪問並未成功完成使命。因為國民黨的注意力集中在軍事統一中國，而蘇聯卻認為政治動員應在軍事行動之先。這篇論文試圖以蔣介石1923年赴俄報聘來探討廣州與莫斯科之間戰略上的分歧。為了解此次訪問的歷史背景，我們首先回顧訪問前孫中山與蘇聯的關係。

　　孫中山與蘇聯的接觸最早是在1918年致電列寧恭賀俄國革命成功。[1]蘇聯人民外交委員契切林（Georgy Chicherin）覆信讚揚孫中山對「中國北方的和外國的資產階級以及帝國政府」的抗爭，並把蘇聯的命運和中國人民的命運視為一體。[2] 在這次互賀的兩年後，孫中山和蘇聯有了第一次直接的接觸。[3] 1920年11月他在上海接見了共產國際東方部部長維金斯基（Gregory Voitinsky，中文名胡定康）。孫中山問到關於蘇聯和俄國革命的問題，並且向維金斯基說明他準備將革命運動從南方經過中部到北方的軍事計畫。雖然那時他沒有要求蘇聯的協助，他卻向維金斯基提議蘇聯在海參崴或者東北建立一個強大的無線電台，以便廣州與俄國的通訊。[4] 1921年3月他又見了一位到廣州來設立羅斯塔通訊社分社的阿列克謝耶夫（Alexieff），其目的據稱為協助廣州的宣傳工作。[5]

　　此時，孫中山對俄國和俄國經驗的興趣已經相當濃厚。他於1921年8月28日給契切林6月來信的覆函中說：

　　「……我希望與你及你莫斯科的其他友人取得私人的聯繫。我對你們的

工作非常注意，特別是有關蘇維埃、軍隊和教育方面的組織工作。我希
望你和其他友人能在這些方面，特別是有關教育方面，能多多指
教……」[6]

這些初步的接觸為往後他和另外共產國際代表洽商廣州莫斯科聯盟鋪了
路：1921年12月他會晤了亨德里克斯·斯內夫利特（馬林）（Hendrick
Sneevliet；Maring）；1922年6月會晤了沙吉·達林（Serge Dalin）；1923年1
月又與阿道夫·越飛（Adolf Joffe）商談。馬林是斯內夫利特在中國用的名
字，他原是荷蘭籍共產國際在爪哇的代表，被印度尼西亞驅除出境後，於
1921年6月抵中國接替維金斯基為共產國際駐華代表。他1921年12月在桂
林與孫中山的會晤已經有大量的論述。[7]根據這些論述，我們知道馬林當時
敦促廣州與蘇聯聯盟，並且作了另外三項建議：（1）改組國民黨以收納所
有社會階層，特別是工農分子；（2）建立軍事學校以發展革命軍事力量；
（3）與中國共產黨合作。[8]

　　孫中山對這三項建議未置可否。當時廣州已回到革命軍的控制，久望的
北伐亦即將開始，不是中流換馬的時候。關於與蘇聯聯盟的建議，孫中山對
馬林說，北伐的成功，革命軍必須首先控制華中。而華中一帶是屬英國勢力
及利益範圍，國民黨與蘇聯聯盟必使英國投入北方軍閥的懷抱，因而置整個
北伐軍事行動於不利之地。他說：「為安全計，今僅能與蘇聯作道義之聯
絡。」[9]

　　雖然這次的會晤沒有達成具體的協議，但是在其他方面自有其重要性。
會晤使雙方更清楚彼此的立場。孫中山對蘇聯樂於協助國民黨以及其條件有
更多的自信和認識。他對蘇聯的實際情況也有了更多的了解，並且對蘇聯的
新經濟政策感到欣慰，因為他認為新經濟政策和他的振興實業計畫相似。
[10]對馬林這次會晤也同樣的重要。他親自對國民黨的領導人物和國民黨的
活動有了些認識。他對國民黨對地方軍隊的依賴有所批評[11]，也批評孫中
山只是「沿著軍事陰謀」的思維去思考一切。[12]雖然他對國民黨缺乏組織
和宣傳工作感到失望，卻相信「國民黨散漫的組織反而容易在其黨內推展群

眾運動的意識」，並認為在一年前剛成立的共產黨，其黨員應該「加入國民黨」並「設法利用左翼分子（廖仲愷）改變國民黨的策略」，但是他們「應該保留他們自己的組織和報紙，也應該繼續他們在工人階級中成立活動中心和組織」[13]。

1922年沙吉‧達林來廣州參加中國社會主義青年團第一次代表大會，從4月底至6月中與孫中山有長達兩小時以上的多次會晤。[14] 會晤中達林繼續在廣州與莫斯科結盟的問題上催促孫中山採取行動。但是孫中山以他告訴馬林的原因拒絕了這個建議。那就是一個公開的聯盟在當時會激怒英國，因之會採取行動報復，以致發生對北伐不利的影響。他告訴達林他目前的主要任務是軍事行動，等革命軍占領漢口以後，他會承認蘇聯。達林也建議國民黨與中國共產黨合作，孫中山同樣地拒絕了這個建議。[15]

孫中山與達林初次會晤以後，於當年5月開始北伐。起始一切進行順利，但由於次月陳炯明的叛變，北伐不得不中止，而孫中山亦被迫於8月離開廣州經香港去上海。陳炯明的叛變充分暴露了國民黨所處的險境。本來以為為黨忠誠的軍隊，其實並不可靠。孫中山再次把注意力轉向黨務。在去上海途中，他與蔣介石及其他的人討論向俄國學習的問題。[16]

此時孫中山對蘇聯的傾向正在加速發展。他與蘇聯代表的會晤為他的傾向鋪了路，他最近的失敗更推進了這個傾向的發展。還有另外一個因素對形成他親蘇的態度也具有重大的影響。那就是他對西方各國和日本不支持他反對北京政府的奮鬥日益失望。[17] 因之，他抵達上海時，對與外國聯盟的選擇已經非常明白。蘇聯是唯一可能和他合作來為中國革命運動重整旗鼓的盟友。雖然這是出於迫切的需要，孫中山對於這個選擇並無不安之處。從他的立場看來，俄國目前是一個「非侵略國家」，會以平等眼光對待中國[18]，而且與俄國聯盟和他利用外國援助來發展中國的計畫相符。[19] 此外，誠如他在赴上海途中告訴蔣介石和其他人士，國民黨有模仿俄國革命成功的必要。

不過，他對於這個聯盟也有設限。聯盟不能危及國民黨在中國革命運動中的領導地位，簽盟也並不代表承認共產主義適合於解決中國的問題。他拒絕達林的建議成立一個與中國共產黨的兩黨聯盟就是前者的例證。在舉世皆知的 1923 年 1 月的「孫文越飛宣言」中所提到的共產組織及蘇維埃制度都不能適用於中國，因中國並無可以讓它們實施成功的條件那一段是後者的例證。總而言之，孫中山雖然真正希望的是能得到蘇聯的援助，特別是軍事援助，但他是在對他領導的革命運動有最少傷害的條件下去進行。

　　阿道夫·越飛於 1922 年 8 月抵達中國，與北京政府商議條約。他於 1923 年 1 月 17 日乘火車自北京到上海，次日晚赴孫中山寓所拜會洽談 5 個小時。1 月 21 日他的兩位隨員又赴孫府 1 小時又 20 分鐘，大概是為後來聞名的「孫文越飛宣言」定稿。該宣言於 1923 年 1 月 26 日公布。[20]

　　該宣言的四項聲明中，第一項與廣州─莫斯科協議有最直接的關係。那項聲明對孫中山來講，有一石二鳥之效。第一，其中所謂「共產組織甚至蘇維埃制度，事實上均不能引用於中國」清楚地說明了孫中山對共產主義的立場，而「此項見解，越飛君完全同意」一句，又增強了孫中山聲明的可信度。第二，這兩點聲明加上越飛所宣稱「中國最重要最迫切之問題，乃在民國統一之成功，與完全國家的獨立之獲得」以及「中國當得俄國國民最摯誠之同情，且可以俄國援助為依賴」的立場和保證可以解釋為蘇聯政府的目的無他，旨在支援一個為民族獨立的中國革命，和國民黨在那個革命中正當的領導地位。[21]

　　除此聯合宣言外，不得而知孫中山與越飛是否對蘇聯援助國民黨的方式和實質有無任何協議。很可能他們的會談僅涉及到廣州與莫斯科合作的原則問題，實際執行的細節，尚待往後討論。後來事實的進展就是如此。廖仲愷去日本和越飛在熱海溫泉商談一個月的時間，擬好一套有關國民黨與蘇聯合作的事宜。[22] 根據當時在熱海訪問過越飛的一位日本記者布施勝治的報導，越飛以托洛斯基為紅軍設立的制度為藍本也草擬了一份建立軍事學校的計畫，去訓練國民黨的軍事領導人。[23]

　　緊接著，蘇聯政府在 1923 年 3 月決定「給孫中山援助，並派一些我們的顧問給他。」[24] 同年夏天，第一批包括切列潘諾夫（A.I. Cherepanov）將軍的蘇聯顧問抵達廣州。之後又有另外的軍事和政治顧問相繼來華，包括斯捷潘諾夫（V.A. Stepanov）和羅加喬夫（V.P. Rogachev）。[25] 聯盟於是竟成事實。為這個整體的計畫中的一部分，孫中山遣派蔣介石於1923年9月率領一軍事代表團赴俄報聘。

蔣介石率團訪俄前，孫中山顯然和他的親信和蘇聯顧問有所商討。馬林在他1922年7月給共產國際執行委員會的報告中曾提到孫中山擬派代表訪俄的意願。[26] 孫中山在當年8月30日致蔣介石信稱，他已與「他們的代表」，那就是越飛，取得聯絡，請他派他的軍事隨員來上海「詳談軍事事宜」。並屬蔣介石來上海「準備一切」[27]。11月21日孫中山又致函蔣介石，稱他對蔣前時擬去西方的意願一事，頗有進展。[28] 1923年2月26日廖仲愷，時尚在日本與越飛會談中，致函蔣介石邀他，一俟廖返粵後，去廣州商談「赴歐事」[29]。四個半月後，蔣介石由於政見不合辭大元帥行營參謀長職，遂請求以個人名義赴俄，如廖仲愷或汪精衛同往，則願為代表團之一員。[30] 孫中山批准這個請求，因為這不僅是蔣介石的意願，而在第一批蘇聯顧問已經到達廣州之後，此時訪俄的時機也已經成熟。孫中山遂令蔣介石與馬林和其他幾位黨的領導人在上海會晤，以便準備行程。除指派蔣介石為代表團團長外，沈定一、張太雷（沈、張為加入國民黨的共產黨員）及王登雲亦被指派為團員。代表團於8月16日由上海啟程，9月2日抵莫斯科。在俄訪問三月餘，於11月20日離莫斯科返國。[31]

代表團訪問的目的表面上是「考察俄國革命後的黨部與政治軍事的組織。」[32] 其實，代表團的任務要具體得很多。那就是，爭取蘇聯的支持並參與一項新的推翻北方軍閥的戰略計畫。簡言之，就是將國民黨的軍事活動中心從南方轉移到西北，藉以打破國民黨在地理上的孤立，以免除從南方北伐可能遭遇到外國干預的危險。[33]

這項戰略在孫中山9月17日致蘇聯駐北京大使越飛的繼任加拉罕（Leo Karakhan）的信中已約略地提到：

「以下極為機密。幾個星期以前我發了同樣的信給列寧、契切林及托洛斯基諸同志，介紹我的參謀長及機密代表蔣介石將軍。我已派他赴莫斯科與我們那裡的朋友商討如何可以幫助我在我國的工作，蔣將軍特別是要向貴政府及軍事專家提出關於我的軍隊在西北以及其外地區活動的建議。蔣將軍賦有全權為我的代表。」[34]

代表團抵俄一周後，在9月9日與蘇聯革命軍事委員會副主席斯克良斯基（E.M. Sklyansky）及參謀長加米涅夫（L.B. Kamenov）開始正式商談。[35] 在會議中，蔣介石提出三項建議：（1）革命軍事委員會儘量多派人員至廣州，作為「蘇聯紅軍的模範」；（2）希望代表團有機會了解紅軍實況；（3）達成在中國軍事行動的聯合協議。[36]

不過，國民黨想從蘇聯立刻獲得的大規模援助的期待被潑了冷水。斯克良斯基告訴蔣介石說，蘇聯已經派了軍事顧問到廣州，必須假以時日，看他們對國民黨有什麼樣的用處以後，才能再作派遣。何況革命軍事委員會中並沒有很多會講中國話的人。所以，蘇聯政府那時無法顯著地增加在廣州軍事顧問的人數。

所謂語言問題當然不是真正的問題，因為已經派去中國的人都不會中文。每位顧問必須有兩位翻譯，一個從俄語翻譯成英文，另一位從英文翻譯成中文。[37] 所以，斯克良斯基的婉拒基於蘇聯政府觀看態度的成分居多。但是，他有一個建議，「由於學習中文的困難，不如在俄國建立一所專門訓練中國人的軍事學校。」他也建議很多已經在蘇聯的中國人可以就讀於「東方勞動者大學」或其他已經成立的教育機構。

蔣介石對這個建議的反應無從得知。斯克良斯基的建議可能是代表蘇聯政府的期望來訓練一批被灌注共產主義的軍事和政治幹部，用以增強國民黨黨軍內的共產意識。即使如此，在1924年國民黨改組，莫斯科與廣州致力促成聯盟之事後，有更多的俄國軍事顧問被派遣到廣州，也有更多的中國學生去莫斯科孫逸仙大學就讀。

關於在中國的軍事計畫協議事，蔣介石是指西北計畫。他向斯克良斯基和加米涅夫解釋說，從中國南方北伐有其不可取之處，因為在兩個「堡壘」城市——香港和上海——的外國駐軍，特別是英國和美國，可能嚴重地耽誤國民黨軍隊從揚子江流域北上部隊的調動。目前國民黨軍隊的士氣低落，如果遭到強烈的抵抗，他們是否會瓦解也是不敢保證的事。由於這些因素，蔣介石說，國民黨在考慮轉移其軍事活動於西北。並希望為此能與革命軍事委員會達成一項共同軍事行動的協議。他說：「這就是代表團來訪的原因。」

　　蔣介石為斯克良斯基與加米涅夫進一步說明國民黨為什麼認為這個計畫建議可以成功的理由。他宣稱國民黨在中俄邊境離庫倫不遠的地方已經有在當地居住的中國人，和從中國東北的西部來的另外一批人，在組織一支新的隊伍。這支隊伍正在籌畫對北京的軍事行動。他估計國民黨的軍事力量，包括在西南各省「受廣州指揮」的隊伍，相當於吳佩孚和曹錕的聯合軍事力量，也相當於張作霖的軍事力量，各有八萬人。在華中的所謂「土匪」也已被整編，他們在對吳佩孚的隊伍作宣傳工作和採取破壞行動。他又說，國民黨應該可以整編年前在山西被吳佩孚解散的「游擊隊」。斯克良斯基和加米尼涅夫「要求一份書面的計畫，並且希望能有時間多了解中國的實際情況」[38]。

　　其後，有一連串的活動。4天後，9月13日，蔣介石草就斯克良斯基要求的書面計畫。[39] 9月17和18日晚，他兩次與馬林會談，19日馬林及維金斯基到他的賓館拜會，大概是續商他提出的計畫。10月6日，此項計畫書正式照會蘇聯外交部和革命軍事委員會，其後兩日他繼續與馬林商談。13日他拜會蘇聯外交部；21日見外交部長契切林談蒙古問題。同時，他於18日及21日分別致信斯克良夫斯基及契切林，並且在他與斯克良斯基和加米涅夫11月11日第二次會談前，曾再與馬林會晤兩次，維金斯基（胡定康）一次。[40] 顯然地，他是在為國民黨的西北軍事戰略贏得支持，並表達國民黨關於蒙古問題的立場。

　　第二次與斯克良斯基和加米涅夫見面是一次關鍵性地會晤。因為蔣介石希望得知蘇聯官方對他提出的計畫的回覆。但是他所聽到的結果令他很是失望。據稱，斯克良斯基是這樣對他說明蘇聯的立場：

　　「目前在中國，政治方面的準備看起來至為重要。雖然軍事行動不能放棄，大規模的軍事行動只能在政治工作完成以及在中國內部有足夠能協助軍事行動的條件以後開始……儘管情況困難，國民黨必須在群眾中發展革命工作，以期成功地達到其他的目的。到群眾中去，和他們站在一起——這才是一個中國革命黨的口號……一俟內部的條件有利，軍事行動自然可行。如果從建議書上所提的軍事行動開始，那就無異於是一種注定失敗的冒險……」[41]

就這樣，不但國民黨請求蘇聯對其西北軍事策略協助的希望破滅，同時其整個以武力為優先統一中國的戰略也被質疑。

蔣介石對蘇聯的回答大失所望。雖然他當時對斯克良斯基的回應不見諸文獻，他幻想破滅的心情，在他的日記中躍於紙上。[42]

蘇聯這個決定可能是基於兩種考慮。第一，中國共產運動的前途；第二，蘇聯所視為它在蒙古的利益。共產國際的領導早已認識在殖民地和半殖民地國家裡，共產黨和資產階級民族革命合作的重要性。在1920年召開的共產國際的第二次代表大會已經在這個問題上建立了理論的基礎。而在1923年1月共產國際執行委員會通過的「關於所期望的中國共產黨對國民黨的態度」決議中也稱國民黨是中國唯一的重要的民族革命的黨派，並且指令中國共產黨黨員加入其中以便從中活動。[43] 由此，中國共產黨可望通過群眾動員來擴張其在中國革命中的影響。[44] 至於蒙古問題，國民黨的西北軍事戰略，從蘇聯控制烏蘭巴圖的觀點來講，它的含義也是顯而易見的事。如艾倫‧惠廷（Allen S. Whiting）教授指出：「在消除中國在這個地區的競爭後，俄國並不希望國民黨的旗幟來代替清朝的旗幟。」[45]

蔣介石與斯克良斯基和加米諾夫第二次會談後，在莫斯科又逗留了三個星期。其間，他被邀參加11月25日共產國際執行委員會的會議，並在會議中發表講演。他說「中國國民黨以三民主義為革命最高目標，自信其在兩三年內必有成功的把握。並指出共產國際對於中國革命的實際情形及實際工作，還有隔膜，希望國際共產幹部多到中國來考察。」[46] 在這次會議中，共產國際執行委員會通過了「關於中國人民解放與國民黨」的決議。此項決議使蔣介石大為不悅，因為他認為決議的動機是在「分化中國社會成為互抗的階級社會，其本意就是為煽動他們之間的矛盾。」[47] 他離俄前拜訪托洛斯基時，托洛斯基曾告說，在不派軍隊直接參與的前提下，蘇俄當提供武器及經援盡量協助中國的民族革命。[48] 蔣介石與其代表團團員11月29日離開莫斯科，於12月15日抵達上海，結束了3個月報聘蘇俄的行程。[49]

　　蔣介石率團訪俄爭取蘇俄支援國民黨的西北戰略，說明了孫中山當時最關心的問題，就是如何能找到一種最急速能統一中國的軍事策略。無論蔣介石對蘇聯政府提出的西北計畫的價值如何，那個計畫真實地反映了國民黨長久持有的以武力統一中國的信念。[50] 這個戰略與蘇聯認為政治動員是國民黨能獲得任何成功的關鍵的立場截然不同。這個戰略上的分歧，在蔣介石與斯克良斯基和加米諾夫在莫斯科會談的時候已經顯示出來。在1923年12月4日蘇聯外交人民委員會主席契切林致孫中山的信中表示得更明白：

　　「我非常感謝你的友好的來信和通過你們的代表團所轉達的友好感情。你們代表團的到達，這使我們非常高興。我們確信他們的訪問會取得有益的效果……我們認為國民黨的根本目的在於開展中國人民的偉大的強有力的運動，所以國民黨首先需要的是進行最廣泛的宣傳和組織工作。我們的榜樣是值得重視的：我們的軍事活動是成功的，因為很多年過去了，在這些年代裡，我們組織和領導了我們的群眾，用這種方法在全國範圍內建立了一個偉大的、有組織的政黨，一個能戰勝一切敵人的政黨。整個中華民族一定看到國民黨——這個廣泛而有組織的政黨——同中國各個地區軍事專政之間的區別。國內各民族，如蒙古族、藏族以及中國西部各民族，需要清楚地知道國民黨是支援他們自決權的。所以，你們不許在這些地區使用武力。這就是我們在這些問題上所考慮的一些想法。我們一定要繼續交換意見和進一步討論問題。當我們達到圓滿協議時，一切事情將進行得更好。」[51]

　　契切林在這封信中沒有提到的是通過群眾活動的政治動員對中國共產黨未來發展的特別重要性。早在1922年馬林給共產國際執行委員會的報告中已經為新成立的中國共產黨在政治上的無力深感歎息。他敦促中國共產黨員「放棄他們排斥國民黨的態度，開始在國民黨內活動。通過這些活動可以更容易接觸南方的工人和軍隊。」[52] 之後，國際共產指令中國共產黨員加入國民黨，但是附帶一個警告：「加入的代價不能是中國共產黨的消滅。」[53] 因此，鮑羅廷才可以說，中國共產黨會通過國民黨在中國革命運動中最終發揮更大的影響力。[54]

　　蘇聯的立場誠然一部分如契切林信中所提基於蘇聯本身政治動員的成功經驗，以及維護蘇聯認為其在蒙古的國家安全利益。但是，發展一個強大的能從國民黨手中獲取中國革命領導權的中國共產運動，對蘇聯也應當是一個同等重要的考慮，同時這也正是蘇聯當時在東亞的整體戰略上的一部分。因之，國民黨與蘇聯對中國革命持有不同的觀點；那種不同的觀點是他們在戰略計畫上有所分歧的根本原因。這個分歧排除了蔣介石1923年報聘蘇聯能有任何成功的可能性。

注釋

本文於1986年10月26-30日在台北中國歷史學會、國史館、中央研究院近史所、中國國民黨中央委員會黨史委員會聯合主辦之「蔣中正先生與現代中國學術討論會」發表的報告，載《蔣中正先生與現代中國學術討論集》（台北，1986）第2冊，頁38-53（中文）。修正後轉載《共和中國》（*Republic of China*），厄本那香檳（Urbana-Champaign）：伊利諾大學厄本那香檳分校東亞與太平洋研究中心（Center for East Asian and Pacific Studies, University of Illinois--Urbana-Champaign）第xvi卷，第1期（1990年11月），頁18-34（英文）。現又根據寄存史丹佛大學胡佛研究院之《蔣介石日記》原稿，略加增補重譯。

[1]　引自1918年8月1日契切林致孫中山函，見簡・德格拉斯（Jane Degras）編，《蘇聯外交政策文獻》（*Soviet Documents on Foreign Policy*）（London, 1951），頁92。

[2]　同上，頁93。

[3]　據稱，孫中山在1920年初在上海與以「持有阿莫爾地區布爾什維克軍隊指揮官證書」的一位坡坡夫（Popoff）上校見面，商談國民黨與布爾什維克分子合作計畫。見韋慕庭（C. Martin Wilbur），《孫中山：壯志未酬的愛國者》（*Frustrated Patriot*）（紐約，1976），頁115-116。韋慕庭的敘述根據當時美國駐上海總領事愛德溫・坎寧漢

（Edwin S. Cunningham）發給美國國務院的報告。但是，坡坡夫上校是否蘇聯政府的官方代表不得而知。

[4]　森尼亞・尤丁（Xenia J. Eudin）及羅伯特・諾斯（Robert C. North）編《蘇維埃俄國與東方──文獻綜述》（*Soviet Russia and the East*）（史丹佛，1957），頁218。

[5]　曹錫珍，《中蘇外交史》（北京，1951），頁41；崔書琴，《孫中山與共產主義》（香港：1954），頁21。

　　日本新聞記者及蘇俄問題專家布施勝治稱，在阿列克謝耶夫（Alexieff）到廣州後，共產黨創始人之一的陳獨秀所編輯的《群報》開始登載蘇聯的宣傳，同時廣州政府也在廣州師範學校設立俄語的課程。布施報導，孫中山與阿列克謝耶夫交換關於廣州與莫斯科關係的諒解備忘錄，據稱此備忘錄包括下列幾點：（1）互相尊重主權；（2）即時恢復貿易；（3）允許在廣州政府控制下的地區作宣傳；（4）互相經援；及（5）對彼此公民最優惠待遇。但是，這個報導無法由其他新聞來源證實。無論如何，孫中山似乎不大可能同意在廣州公開宣傳共產主義。見布施勝治著，半粟譯，《蘇俄的東方政策》（上海，1928），頁226-227。

[6]　尤丁及諾斯，上引書，頁219-221。此函未見任何國民黨的官方文件。《孫中山選集》（北京，1956）第1卷，頁434-436收有此函中文翻譯。

[7]　鄧家彥，〈馬丁謁總理實紀〉載《革命文獻》第9輯（台北，1955），頁1409-1411；孫福坤，《共產國際擾亂中國記》（台北，1953），頁11-12；蘇德勇，〈關於馬林謁見總理及其時地之辯正〉載《三民主義半月刊》，第35期（1954年10月），頁45-50；及張繼，《張溥泉先生全集》（台北，1951），頁196。

　　馬林致共產國際關於他訪華的報告的英文翻譯見赫爾姆特・格盧伯（Helmut Gruber）編，《莫斯科控制下的共產國際》（*Soviet Russia Masters the Comintern*）（花園城 ［Garden City］, 1974），頁364-375。此書討論馬林對牽涉國民黨與新創中國共產黨間之關係的中國政治情形，多於他與孫中山會面的報告。其關於後者所提到的最重要的一點，就是孫中山拒絕在那時與蘇聯正式聯盟。有類似這一點的敘述，見伊羅生（Harold R. Isaacs），〈與斯內夫利特談話記錄：關於1920-1923的中國問題〉（"Notes on a Conversation with H. Sneevliet, the Chinese Question, 1920-1923"）載《共產國際與中國革命文獻，第一部》（*Documents on the Comintern and the Chinese Revolution, Part I*），《中國季刊》（*China Quarterly*），第45期（1971年1月/3月），頁102-109。又見道夫・賓（Dov Bing），〈斯內夫利特和初期的中國共產黨〉（"Sneevliet and the Early Years of the CCP"）載《中國季刊》（*China Quarterly*），第48期（1971年10月/12月），頁677-697。這三篇文章的翻譯都收入《馬林在中國的有關資料》（北京，1980），頁11-58。

[8]　孫福坤，頁11-12。

[9]　鄧家彥，頁1411。

[10]　鄒魯，《中國國民黨史稿》（重慶，1944），頁204。

[11]　同上。

[12]　伊羅生（Harold R. Isaacs），頁104。

[13]　同上。

[14]　有關達林與孫中山之會晤，見韋慕庭（C. Martin Wilbur），上引書，頁121-124。韋慕庭教授的敘述根據達林1966年發表的文章〈大轉變：1922年的孫逸仙〉（俄文）（"The Great Turn: Sun Yat-sen in 1922"），見韋慕庭，頁28，注23。關於達林與孫中山會晤，無中文記載。

[15]　陳獨秀，《告全國同志書》，1929年12月10日，頁2。

[16]　蔣中正，〈中國國民黨國民革命和俄國共產黨共產革命的區別〉載《新生命》，第2卷，第5期（1929年5月），頁4。

[17]　關於孫中山與列強關係的詳盡討論，見韋慕庭，上引書，第6章：〈有活力的聯俄背景〉（"The Dynamic Setting for Alliance with Russia"）。

[18]　《字林西報》（The North China Herald），1922年10月7日，頁9。

[19]　同上。

[20]　此項敘述根據1922年1月19日上海市政廳（前工部局）警察署的情報報告。哈佛燕京圖書館藏有複印本，由賽奇教授（Tony Saich）自荷蘭阿姆斯特丹「馬林檔案」得來。

　　此說與廖仲愷夫人及其女兒的回憶有所不同。她們的回憶是1922年越飛與孫中山曾在上海數次會晤，但因英國警察的監視，無法繼續，會晤地點遂轉至東京。同時廖仲愷於當年9月下旬被派為孫中山的代表與越飛繼續談判。他們在東京的會晤同樣地受到日本警察的監視，也無法繼續。當廖仲愷的岳父於12月逝世後，廖旋即返中國。不久後越飛也返中國。見廖夢醒，《我的母親何香凝》（香港，1973），頁13、56-57。另一部相似的敘述，大致基於廖夢醒的著作，見關國煊，〈有關越飛與廖仲愷會談的時間問題〉載《傳記文學》第46卷，第5期（1985年5月），頁57-59。

　　根據慶應義塾大學山田辰雄教授的研究，這些聲稱的廖仲愷與越飛的會晤都不是事實。山田教授，引用現存日本外交史料館的檔案，包括警察及特務報告，建立了如下的說法：廖仲愷及其妻女與許崇清確於1922年9月乘克利夫蘭總統號郵輪離上海，於9月25日到達日本，逗留40日。但檔案中並無任何資料可以建立越飛當時也在日本的事實。因之，所謂當時廖仲愷與越飛會談的說法無法成立。見山田辰雄，〈廖仲愷の兩度の訪日に就いて─1922-23年〉載《法學研究》，第60卷，第1期（1987年1

月），頁79-105。我對山田教授給我介紹他的研究成果表示感謝。

[21] 孫越聯合宣言全文的英文，見《中國年鑑》（*China Year Book*）（天津），頁1318；中譯本可查《國父年譜》（台北，1965），下冊，頁891-893。

[22] 汪精衛1926年〈國民黨第二次全國代表大會政治報告〉。見汪精衛，《汪精衛演講錄》（上海，1927），頁37。

[23] 布施勝治著，半粟譯，《蘇俄的東方政策》（上海，1928），頁229-233。

[24] 卡透諾娃（A.I. Kartunova），〈孫逸仙與蘇俄顧問——根據1923-1924年文獻〉（"Sun Yat-sen i russkie sovetniki. Po documentam 1923-1924"）載《孫逸仙（1866-1966）百周年冥誕：論文、回憶錄及其他文獻集》（*SunYat-sen 1866-1966 K stoleltyu so dyna rozhdeniya: Sbornik statei, vospominanii I materialov*）（莫斯科，1966），頁171。承蒙迪姆夫人（Deidra Deamer）為本文作者譯為英文，深感謝意。

[25] 同上。

[26] 赫爾姆特·格盧伯（Helmut Gruber），上引書，頁372。

[27] 《孫先生致蔣先生手札墨蹟》（曼谷，1939），頁10-11；又《國父全集》（台北，1961）第5卷，頁453-454。

[28] 《孫先生致蔣先生手札墨蹟》，頁3-4；又《國父全集》第5卷，頁495-496。

[29] 毛思誠編，《民國15年以前之蔣介石先生》（出版地不詳，1936），第5冊，頁19上下。此書根據蔣介石日記編成。原20冊2函。
　　［本書原稿業經發現，由中國第二歷史檔案編輯後，於1992年由北京檔案出版社出版，題為《蔣介石年譜初稿》。該書〈編輯說明〉稱，原稿「封面蓋有『秘密』字樣，是蔣介石親自審定修改的原稿秘本。全稿分三編……此稿後又幾經修改……改名為《民國15年以前之蔣介石先生》，並將原來的編目改為八編……我們在輯錄此稿與《民國15年以前之蔣介石先生》一書互校，凡蔣介石刪的重要文字，均照錄原文，並加注釋說明；初稿殘缺部分，則以《民國15年以前之蔣介石先生》的有關記載補足之。」經作者查對後，《蔣介石年譜初稿》對本文中所引《民國15年以前之蔣介石先生》各節並無增添或需修正處。］

[30] 蔣中正，1923年7月13日〈與楊滄白書〉，載《蔣總統言論彙編》（台北：1956）第24卷，頁105-107。

[31] 關於蔣介石赴俄報聘之私人敘述，見毛思誠上引書，第5冊，頁41上-73下。至於英文節略敘述，見蔣介石，《蘇俄在中國》（*Soviet Russia in China*）（紐約，1957），頁19-25。兩書均未提及與蘇聯軍事領導人會談之實質問題。英文節略甚至沒有提及會談之事。

[32] 蔣介石，《蘇俄在中國》（*Soviet Russia in China*），頁18-19。

[33] 此點在中文資料中未有提及。首先的史證由艾倫·惠廷（Allen S. Whiting）在路易士·費雪（Louis Fischer）私人蒐集之孫逸仙與加拉罕通信原件之打字稿中發現。見惠廷，《蘇俄對華政策》（*Soviet Policies in China, 1917-1924*）（紐約，1954），頁323，注16。蔣介石在莫斯科談判詳情，見卡透諾娃（A.I. Kartunova），〈孫逸仙與蘇俄顧問〉，頁175-180。

[34] 路易士·費雪（Louis Fischer），《蘇俄由和平到戰爭之路，1917-1941》（*Russia's Road from Peace to War, 1917-1941*）（紐約，1969），頁73；艾倫·惠廷，頁243。

[35] 毛思誠編，《民國15年以前之蔣介石先生》，第5冊，頁50下。

[36] 蔣介石與斯克良斯基及加米涅夫談判的敘述，引自卡透諾娃（A.I. Kartunova），〈孫逸仙與蘇俄顧問〉，頁27。

[37] 韋慕庭（C. Martin Wilbur）、夏連蔭（Julie Lien-ying Howe）合編，《有關共產主義，民族主義，及在華蘇聯顧問的文件，1918-1927》（*Documents on Communism, Nationalism, and Soviet Advisors in China, 1918-1927*）（紐約，1956），頁197。

[38] 韋慕庭（C. Martin Wilbur），《孫中山：壯志未酬的愛國者》（*Frustrated Patriot*），頁153。

[39] 毛思誠編，《民國15年以前之蔣介石先生》，第5冊，頁51下。此項文件並未公開發表。此書稱此意見書：「共8,200餘言，說明中俄國共兩黨互助關係。甲緒論，乙軍事計畫，丙宣傳計畫，丁結論」。

[40] 會談及其日期均在記載於毛思誠，上引書，第5冊，頁52上-56下。然並未透露會談的內容，唯一的例外就是10月21日與契切林的會談。書中引蔣介石致契切林的信說：「星期天的晤談，雖然沒有討論到什麼具體的問題，我們很感激你抽象的給我們的教益……」信中也說明國民黨對蒙古的態度。蔣10月25日致斯克良斯基的信，據稱已遺失。見毛思誠，上引書，第5冊，頁60下。

[41] 卡透諾娃（A.I. Kartunova），〈孫逸仙與蘇俄顧問〉，頁179-180。

[42] 寄存胡佛研究院之蔣介石日記1923年11月11日有如下之記載：「審查意見書及預備與斯克亮司基談話。下午間斯克亮司基即克西義夫，約談二小時……無論為個人，為國家，求人不如求己。無論親友盟人之如何親密，總不能外乎其本身之利害，而本身之基業，無論大小成敗，皆不能輕視恝置。如欲成功，非由本身做起不可。外力則最不恃之物也。」除此反應外，日記中並無任何關於他與斯克良斯基和加米涅夫會談的實質內容。

[43] 森尼亞·尤丁（Xenia J. Eudin）及羅伯特·諾斯（Robert C. North）編《蘇維埃俄國與東方——文獻綜述》，頁343-344；簡·德格拉斯（Jane Degras）編，《共產國際，1919-1949：文獻篇》（*The Communist International, 1919-1949: Documents*），第2冊

（1923-1928）（倫敦，1960），頁5-6。

[44] 鮑羅廷（Borodin）1923年10月17日對中國共產黨黨員談話時被引述說：「我對新聞記者說國民黨，其實對我們來說，它的意思是我們為穩定國民黨而努力，其目的是為共產勢力最終的增長。絕對不能忘記，我們的工作實際是為穩定共產黨。這個目的應該時時記在心裡。」見米泰羅夫斯基（N. Mitarevsky）《蘇俄世界陰謀》（*World Wide Soviet Plots*）（天津，出版日期不詳），頁133。

[45] 艾倫・惠廷（Allen S Whiting），《蘇俄對華政策》，頁245。

[46] 蔣介石，《蘇俄在中國》（*Soviet Russia in China*），頁22。根據寄存胡佛研究院之蔣介石日記，蔣對維金斯基對其代表團之輕視甚為不悅，故婉拒與國際共產主席團會晤，後因維金斯基之堅持，不得已乃赴會。該日記1923年11月25日稱；「第三國際遠東局長胡定斯基約余會主席團，延宕再三，居為奇貨，而余則實不必與其約會。彼既欲余約會，而又恐余道破其弊。與此三日內，每言約會，而不定時間，視余來此為平常事，且阻礙進行，挾其私見以侮人。而蘇聯幹部以其為曾遊中國，竟為其言所蒙。時至今日，而不定時間來約會，憤激不堪，婉言拒其約會。而彼又來要求赴會，不得已而允之。」

[47] 蔣介石，《蘇俄在中國》（*Soviet Russia in China*），頁22。

[48] 同上，頁24。蔣稱他在蘇聯時「和托洛斯基談話的次數比其他蘇俄領袖為多」。但是，在毛思誠編，《民國15年以前之蔣介石先生》一書中，僅提到這一次和托洛斯基的會談。見第5冊，頁67上。根據寄存胡佛研究院的《蔣介石日記》，他到達蘇聯後曾於10月16日「發托洛斯基信」，並於11月9日「擬托洛斯基函稿」。此事在毛思誠編《民國15年以前之蔣介石先生》及中國第二歷史檔案編《蔣公介石年譜初稿》中均未提及。

[49] 毛思誠編，《民國15年以前之蔣介石先生》，第5冊，頁70上-73下。蔣介石返國後，曾向孫中山提出訪俄的書面報告。此項報告從未公開發表。但是，根據他日後所作關於訪俄的談話來判斷（例如他1924年3月14日致廖仲愷函，見毛思誠，上引書，第6冊，頁28上-31上），他的報告可能不是很肯定的。根據蔣經國的敘述，他父親「在這三個月的期間……更認識了蘇聯的政治制度乃是專制和恐怖的組織，與我們中國國民黨的三民主義的政治制度，是根本不能相容的。」見蔣經國，《沉思在慈湖之畔》（台北，1979），頁7。（此書於1981年由台北黎明出版公司翻印。）

[50] 馬林1935年與伊羅生談話時說：「孫逸仙直到他逝世的時候，從沒有真正地吸收關於群眾運動的理想。他接受這種概念，但並不是真正感到興趣。在1923年他根本是漠不關心。他所關切的僅是軍事問題。」見伊羅生（Harold R. Isaacs），〈與斯內夫利特談話記錄：關於1920-1923的中國問題〉（"Notes on a Conversation with H. Sneevliet, the

Chinese Question, 1920-1923"）載〈共產國際與中國革命文獻，第1部〉（Documents on the Comintern and the Chinese Revolution, Part I），《中國季刊》（*China Quarterly*），第45期（1971年1月/3月），頁108。

[51] 艾倫・惠廷（Allen S. Whiting），《蘇俄對華政策》，頁245-246。引自孫逸仙與加拉罕通信檔案。

[52] 〈馬林同志對執行委員會的報告〉，載赫爾姆特・格盧伯（Helmut Gruber）編，《莫斯科控制下的共產國際》（*Soviet Russia Masters the Comintern*），頁369-370、374。

[53] 共產國際執行委員會1923年1月12日「關於中國共產黨對國民黨的態度」的決議案。見森尼亞・尤丁（Xenia J. Eudin）及羅伯特・諾斯（Robert C. North）編《蘇維埃俄國與東方——文獻綜述》（*Soviet Russia and the East*），頁343-344。關於孫中山對蘇俄和中國共產黨的詳盡研究，參閱李雲漢，《從容共到清黨》（台北，1966）及冷紹銓、諾曼・帕爾默（Norman D. Palmer）合著，《孫逸仙和共產主義》（*Sun Yat-sen and Communism*）（紐約，1960）。

[54] 見上注[45]。

Divergence in Strategic Planning
Chiang Kai-shek's Mission to Moscow, 1923

For three months from September 2 to November 29, 1923, Chiang Kai-shek was in the Soviet Union as head of a four-man military mission appointed by Dr. Sun Yat-sen. The purpose of the mission was to seek Russian support of and participation in a military strategy aimed at the defeat of the northern militarists and the seizing of power by the Kuomintang. But Chiang's mission was not successful. While the Kuomintang focused its attention on unifying China through military means, the Soviet Union favored political mobilization of the masses before military action. This paper attempts to analyze this divergent approach to strategic planning by Canton and Moscow as illustrated by Chiang Kai-shek's mission in 1923. In order to understand the mission in its proper historical context, we shall first examine the relations between Sun Yat-sen and the Soviet Union prior to the mission.

Sun Yat-sen and the Soviet Union

Sun Yat-sen's earliest official contact with the Soviet Union was in 1918, when he sent Lenin a congratulatory message on the success of the Russian Revolution. [1] Georgii Chicherin, Soviet Commissar for Foreign Affairs, in his response, praised Sun for his struggle against "the north Chinese and foreign imperialist governments," and cast the Soviet lot with that of the Chinese. [2] It was two years after this initial exchange of good will that Sun had his first direct contact with a representative of the Soviet Union. [3] This took place in November

1920, when Gregory Voitinsky, head of the Eastern Department of the Communist International, called on him in Shanghai. Sun asked questions about Russia and the Russian Revolution, and explained to Voitinsky his military plans to carry the revolutionary movement from the South to the central and northern provinces. Although not seeking Russian assistance at this time, he did propose that the Russians build a powerful radio station in Vladivostok or Manchuria, so that Canton could communicate with the Russians. [4] In March 1921, Dr. Sun met with one Alexieff, who had come to Canton to establish a branch of the Rosta News Agency, reportedly for the purpose of helping with Chinese propaganda work. [5]

By this time Sun Yat-sen's interest in Russia and Russian experience was deepening. In response to a communication from Chicherin of June 1921, Sun wrote on August 28 of that year:

"I would like to enter into personal contact with you and your friends in Moscow. I am extremely interested in your work, and particularly in the organization of your soviets, your army, and educational system. I would like to know what you and your friends can tell me about these matters, and particularly about education..." [6]

These early contacts paved the way for three subsequent meetings Sun Yat-sen had with representatives of the Communist International on the substance of a prospective Canton-Moscow alliance: his meeting with Hendrick Sneevliet (Maring) in December 1921; with Serge Dalin in June 1922; and with Adolf Joffe in January 1923. Maring, as Sneevliet was known in China, was a Dutch Comintern agent who was active in Java before his expulsion, and arrived in China in June 1921 to succeed Voitinsky as the Comintern agent. Much has been written about his meetings with Sun Yat-sen in December 1921, in Guilin. [7] Based on these accounts, we learn that Maring urged an alliance between the

Kuomintang and the Soviet Union, and that he also put forth three other proposals: (1) reorganizing the Kuomintang to include all social classes, especially the peasants and the workers; (2) establishing a military academy to build up a revolutionary armed force; and (3) cooperating with the Chinese Communist Party. [8]

Sun did not commit himself to any of these proposals. Canton was then back in the hands of the revolutionaries, and the long-awaited Northern Expedition was about to begin. This was not the time to change plans. On the question of an alliance with the Soviet Union, Sun told Maring that the capture of Central China would be essential to the success of a northern expedition, and since Central China was within the British sphere of influence and interest, a Kuomintang-Soviet alliance would undoubtedly provoke the British to come to the northern militarists, thus placing in jeopardy the success of the entire military campaign. He suggested that Canton and Moscow form a "moral fellowship" instead. [9]

The lack of concrete agreements notwithstanding, the Sun-Maring meetings were important in other respects. They provided an excellent opportunity for both sides to have a much better understanding of their respective positions. Sun had a surer sense now of Soviet willingness to assist the Kuomintang and of their conditions. He had also come to know more about actual conditions in Russia, and drew encouragement from Russia's adoption of the New Economic Policy, which he regarded as being similar to his plans for China's industrial development. [10] To Maring, the meetings were equally useful. He gained some personal knowledge of the leaders of the Kuomintang and of the Kuomintang's operations. He was critical of the Kuomintang's reliance on local militarists, [11] and faulted Sun for thinking "purely along lines of military conspiracy." [12] While he was disappointed in the Kuomintang's lack of organization and propaganda efforts, he also believed that "the loose form of organization of the Kuomintang made it very easy to advance the idea of mass activity in that party," and that members of the Chinese

Communist Party, which had been founded the year before, "should enter the Kuomintang," and "try to utilize the left wing（Liao Zhongkai）to change the tactics of the Kuomintang," but that they "should maintain their own organization and their own paper and that they should continue to establish their centers of activity and organization among the workers." [13]

Sun Yat-sen's meetings with Serge Dalin took place in Canton from late April to mid-June, 1922. [14] Dalin had come to Canton to take part in the First Congress of the Chinese Socialist Youth Corps, and saw Dr. Sun a number of times for talks of at least two hours each. He continued to press Sun for a Canton-Moscow alliance, but Sun rejected the idea for the same reason he had given Maring which was an open alliance at that time would arouse the British to take action against him, and would therefore adversely affect his campaign against the North. He told Dalin that his primary task at that time was military, and that he would recognize the Soviet Union after his troops captured Hankow. Dalin also urged an alliance between the Kuomintang and the Chinese Communist Party. This, too, was rejected by Sun. [15]

It will be remembered that the northern campaign was launched in May, after the talks had begun between Sun and Dalin, and that it went well initially. However, the campaign had to be suspended following Chen Jiongming's revolt the following month, and Sun was forced to leave Canton in August for Shanghai *via* Hong Kong. Chen's revolt brought home the precariousness of the party's position, as the army that was supposedly loyal to the party had proved to be unreliable. Sun's mind turned once again to party affairs, and on his way to Shanghai, he discussed with Chiang Kai-shek and others the desirability of learning from the Russians. [16]

Sun's gravitation toward the Soviet Union was now accelerating. His direct contact with Soviet representatives had paved the way, and his latest defeat hastened the process. Yet there was another factor which contributed significantly to his Soviet orientation, that is, his increasing disillusionment with the West and Japan for their unwillingness to support him in his struggle against the Peking government. [17] Thus, when he finally reached Shanghai, his choice was clear insofar as a foreign alliance was concerned. The Soviet Union remained the only potential ally with whom he could join forces to rejuvenate the Chinese revolutionary movement. Although this choice was dictated by dire necessity, Sun Yat-sen did not have any qualms about that choice. In his eyes, Russia was now a "non-aggressive" state which would treat China on terms of equality, [18] and an alliance with Russia was consistent with his plans of developing China with foreign assistance. [19] Furthermore, the Kuomintang needed to emulate the Russian success, as he had told Chiang Kai-shek and others on their way to Shanghai.

However, he did set certain limits to such an alliance. The alliance must not compromise the Kuomintang's leadership of the Chinese Revolution, and it must not be entered into with the notion that communism was suitable as a means of solving China's problems. His rejection of Dalin's proposal to form a two-party alliance with the Chinese Communists is illustrative of the first point, and the famous Sun-Joffe joint declaration of January 1923, which stated, among other things, that neither the Communistic order nor the Soviet system could actually be introduced into China because the conditions for their successful establishment were absent there, is illustrative of the second point. In short, while genuinely interested in Russian aid, particularly military aid, Sun sought to obtain that aid under terms least injurious to his cause.

Adolf Joffe had come to China in August 1922, to negotiate a treaty with the Peking government. He arrived in Shanghai by train on January 17, 1923, and met the next evening with Sun Yat-sen for five hours at Sun's residence. On January 21, his two secretaries, who had accompanied him to Shanghai, visited Sun's home for an hour and twenty minutes, presumably to complete the famous Sun-

Joffe joint statement, which was issued on January 26. [20]

Among the four articles in the joint statement, the first was of immediate importance to the question of a Canton-Moscow entente. By this article in their statement, Sun Yat-sen was able to achieve two basic objectives *vis-a-vis* the proposed Kuomintang-Soviet alliance. In the first place, the declaration that "the Communistic order or even the Soviet system cannot actually be introduced into China" served well to clarify Sun's stand on Communism. The statement that this view was "entirely shared by Mr. Joffe" lent added credence to Sun's position. Secondly, such a disclaimer by both parties, together with Joffe's stated opinion that "China's paramount and most pressing problem is to achieve national unification and attain full national independence" and that "China has the warmest sympathy of the Russian people and can count on the support of Russia" could be interpreted as saying that the interest of the Soviet government was in supporting a Chinese national revolution of independence, as well as the legitimate leadership position of the Kuomintang in that revolution. [21]

Besides the joint statement, it is not known whether any specific understanding was reached in the talks between Sun and Joffe on the form and substance of Soviet assistance to the Kuomintang. It seems likely that they dealt only with the principles of cooperation between Moscow and Canton, and that the details of implementation were to be worked out afterwards. This was done when Liao Zhongkai went to Japan following the Sun-Joffe statement, and spent a month conferring with Joffe at the hot-spring resort, Atami, where he and Joffe worked out a number of problems regarding the proposed alliance [22] According to Katsuji Fuse, the Japanese journalist, who interviewed Joffe at Atami, Joffe also helped to draft a plan for the establishment of a military academy to train party officers, using the system of the Red Army, devised by Trotsky as a pattern. [23]

Almost immediately afterwards, a decision was made by the Soviet government in March 1923 "to give Sun Yat-sen assistance and to send him some of our advisers." [24] In the summer of the same year, the first group of Russian military specialists was sent to Canton, among them General A.I. Cherepanov. Later, other military and political advisers went, including V.A. Stepanov and V.P. Rogachev. [25] The alliance was now fast becoming a reality, and as part of the overall plan Chiang Kai-shek was sent to the Soviet Union in September 1923 as head of a military mission representing Sun Yat-sen.

Chiang Kai-shek's Mission to Moscow

Chiang Kai-shek's mission to Moscow apparently had been discussed among Sun Yat-sen's associates and with Russian representatives long before the mission actually materialized. Maring mentioned Sun's desire to send a representative to Russia, in his report to the Comintern Executive Committee in July, 1922. [26] In a letter dated August 30 of the same year, Sun Yat-sen informed Chiang Kai-shek that he had requested "their representative," i.e., Adolf Joffe, through correspondence, to send his military aide to Shanghai "for detailed discussions on military matters," and asked Chiang to come to Shanghai to make necessary preparations. [27] Sun wrote to Chiang again on November 21 saying that he had already made good progress regarding Chiang Kai-shek's earlier wish to go to the West. [28] On February 26, 1923, Liao Zhongkai, while still conferring with Joffe in Japan, wrote to Chiang suggesting that he and Chiang go together to Canton, upon Liao's return from Japan, so that they could discuss "the European trip." [29] Four-and-a-half months later, Chiang, following his resignation as Chief of Staff to Sun Yat-sen over policy differences, requested permission to go to the Soviet Union, preferably as an individual, or, if accompanied by Liao Zhongkai or Wang Jingwei, as a member of a mission. [30] Sun Yat-sen granted the request, not only because Chiang had requested it, but because the time was now ripe for such a visit, as the first group of Russian military advisers had begun to arrive in China about that time. He also instructed Chiang to meet with Maring and several other leading Kuomintang members in Shanghai to make preparations. In addition to Chiang as the leader, three others were selected for the mission: Shen Dingyi, Zhang Tailei, and Wang Dengyun, the first two being Communists who had joined the Kuomintang. The group left Shanghai on August 16 and arrived in Moscow on September 2. They stayed there for three months, until November 29, when they left Moscow for the trip home. [31]

The mission ostensibly was "to study the Soviet Union's post-revolutionary party system, and its political and military organizations." [32] In fact, the purpose of the mission was far more specific than that. It was to seek Soviet support of and participation in a new military strategy for the overthrow of the northern militarists, namely, the transferring of the Kuomintang's center of military activities from the South to the Northwest — a move designed to break out of Canton's geographical isolation and to eliminate the potential danger of foreign intervention inherent in a military expedition northward from the South. [33]

This new strategy was briefly mentioned in the following letter Sun Yat-sen sent on September 17 to Leo Karakhan, who had just replaced Adolf Joffe as the Russian Ambassador in Peking:

"What follows is rigidly confidential. Some weeks ago I sent identical letters to Comrades Lenin, Tchicherin, and Trotsky introducing General Chiang Kai-shek, who is my chief-of-staff and confidential agent. I have dispatched him to Moscow to discuss ways and means whereby our friends there can assist me in my work in this country. In particular, General Chiang is to take up with your government and military experts a proposal for military action by my forces in and about the regions lying to the Northwest of Peking and beyond. General Chiang is fully empowered to act in my behalf." [34]

One week after Chiang's mission arrived in Moscow, they met on September

9 with E.M. Sklyansky, Deputy Chairman of the Revolutionary War Council, and L.B. Kamenev, Chief of Staff, to begin actual negotiations. [35] At this meeting, Chiang Kai-shek presented three requests: (1) that the Revolutionary War Council send as many people as possible to South China "as models of the Red Army;" (2) that his delegation be allowed the opportunity to acquaint themselves with the Red Army; (3) that a joint agreement be reached on a plan of military action in China. [36]

The Kuomintang's expectation of immediate large-scale help from the Soviet Union was to be quickly dampened. Sklyansky told Chiang Kai-shek that some military advisers had already been sent to Canton, and that it would be necessary to wait until it became known what use they would be to the Kuomintang army before more could be sent. Besides, the Revolutionary War Council did not have many cadres who could speak Chinese under its command. Therefore, the Soviet government could not significantly increase the number of its military advisers in Canton at that time.

The language problem was, of course, not the real problem, as none of the Russian advisers sent to China knew Chinese. Each adviser had to have two interpreters, one Russian-English and one English-Chinese. [37] Sklyansky1s refusal was probably due more to the wait-and-see attitude adopted by the Soviet government than to the alleged language problem. He did suggest, however, that "in light of the difficulties of learning the Chinese language, it would be better to organize a special military academy for the Chinese in Russia." He also suggested that the many Chinese who were already in the Soviet Union could enter the University for the Toilers of the East or other already existing educational establishments.

Chiang Kai-shek's reaction to the last suggestion is not recorded. Sklyansky's proposal might have represented a desire on the part of the Soviets to train a nucleus of Chinese military and political cadres and indoctrinate them in

Communism in order to increase communist influence in the Kuomintang army. Be that as it may, more Russian advisers did eventually go to Canton, following the 1924 Kuomintang reorganization when both Moscow and Canton were firmly committed to an alliance, and more Chinese students also went to Moscow to study at the Sun Yat-sen University.

On the matter of a joint agreement on military action, Chiang was referring to the Northwestern plan. He explained to Sklyansky and Kamenev that a southern military base from which to launch an expedition against Peking had severe disadvantages, as the presence of foreign troops, especially British and American, in the two strategic "fortresses" of Hong Kong and Shanghai, could significantly delay the movement of Kuomintang troops to the North from the valleys of the Yangtze. The morale of the Kuomintang troops was low, he said, and there was no assurance that the soldiers would not break in the face of strong opposition. Based on these considerations, Chiang Kai-shek informed his hosts that the Kuomintang was considering the transferring of its main military activity to China's Northwest, and that the Kuomintang hoped that they could reach an agreed plan of military operation for this purpose with the Revolutionary War Council. According to Chiang, "this is the reason for sending the present delegation."

He described for Sklyansky and Kamenev how, in the opinion of the Kuomintang, this operation could be successfully accomplished. He claimed that a new army was being organized by the Kuomintang near Urga on the China-Mongolian border, consisting of Chinese living in the area and of a number of Chinese brought in from western Manchuria. This force was already mounting an offensive against Peking. Chiang estimated that the Kuomintang's troop strength, including that in the Southwestern provinces "under the command of Canton," was about equal to the combined strength of Wu Peifu and Cao Kun, and also about the same as in the army of Zhang Zuolin, each of which had 80,000 men. The "so-called" bandits in Central China also had been organized, and they were engaged in propaganda and sabotage work against Wu Peifu's forces. He stated further that the Kuomintang should be able to organize the "partisan troops" in Shanxi disbanded by Wu Peifu the year before. Sklyansky and Kamenev listened, "then asked for a plan in writing and time to learn more about the actual conditions in China." [38]

A flurry of activities followed. Four days later, on September 13, Chiang drafted the plan as requested. [39] He met with Maring on the evenings of September 17 and 18, and Maring and Voitinsky paid him a visit at his guest house on the 19th, presumably for further discussions on the proposal. On October 6, the proposal was officially delivered to the Foreign Ministry and the Revolutionary War Council, and Chiang met again with Maring on the two days following. He paid a visit to the Foreign Ministry on the 13th, and met with Foreign Minister Chicherin on the 21st, at which time the question of Mongolia was discussed. In the meantime, he sent a letter to Sklyansky on the 18th, and another one to Chicherin on the 21st, and met twice more with Maring and once more with Voitinsky before his second meeting with Sklyansky and Kamenev on November 11. [40] Apparently, he was trying to win support for the Kuomintang's Northwestern military strategy and to state the Kuomintang's position on Mongolia.

The second meeting with Sklyansky and Kamenev was a crucial one, as Chiang was expecting to hear the official Soviet reply to his proposal. He was to be disappointed, however. Sklyansky is reported to have advised him of the Soviet position that:

"The question of political preparedness seems to be the most important for China at the present time. While it is true that military action must not be forsaken, large-scale military operations may be entered into only when political work is carried out, and those internal conditions which significantly facilitate military action are obtained.... despite difficult conditions, the Kuomintang must carry out revolutionary work among the masses. Other goals may then be realized with success. Go to the masses and stay with them — this is the slogan of the revolutionary party in China.... military operations will be possible when internal conditions have become favorable. Beginning with military action such as that being proposed must be regarded as an adventure and a course that is doomed to failure...." [41]

With that, not only the Kuomintang's hope for Soviet assistance in implementing its Northwestern strategy was dashed, but its entire strategy of military unification of China as the party's first objective was also called into question.

Chiang Kai-shek was bitterly disappointed. While there is no public record of how he replied to Sklyansky, his disillusionment was crystally clear as revealed in his diary. [42]

The Soviet government may have arrived at this position in consideration of two factors: First, the future of the Communist movement in China, and secondly, the perceived national security interest of the Soviet Union in Mongolia. It will be remembered that Comintern leaders had recognized the importance of communist parties cooperating in colonial and semi-colonial countries with bourgeois national liberation movements. The Second Congress of the Communist International had in 1920 laid the theoretical basis for such cooperation, and the resolution adopted by the Executive Committee of the Comintern in January 1923, "On the Expected Attitude of the Chinese Communist Party Toward the Kuomintang," which describes the Kuomintang as the only serious national-revolutionary group in China, had instructed members of the Chinese Communist Party to remain and work within it. [43] Thus, by mobilizing the masses, the Chinese Communist Party could expect to expand its influence in the Chinese Revolution. [44] The implications of the Kuomintang's Northwestern strategy for Soviet control of Urga were also obvious. As Professor Allen S. Whiting has pointed out, "having eliminated Chinese competition from this area, Russia was not anxious to allow the Kuomintang banner to replace the Manchu flag." [45]

Chiang Kai-shek stayed in Moscow for another three weeks following his second meeting with Sklyansky and Kamenev, during which time he was invited to attend a meeting of the Executive Committee of the Comintern on November 25, where he made a speech. He voiced his confidence that "our National Revolution, with the realization of the Three People's Principles as its supreme goal, would succeed in two or three years' time," also pointing out that "the Communist International did not fully understand the actual conditions of our revolutionary movement or what we were doing," and he hoped the Comintern "would send more men to China to see for themselves." [46] At this meeting, the Executive Committee adopted a resolution, "On the National Liberation Movement in China and the Kuomintang Party," which greatly displeased Chiang Kai-shek, as he thought that the idea behind the resolution was to "divide the Chinese society into conflicting classes, and that it was its intention to stir up conflicts among them." [47] Thereupon, he made up his mind to return to China immediately. Before his departure, he called on Trotsky, and the latter told him that, short of direct participation by Soviet troops, Russia would do her best to assist the Chinese National Revolution in the form of weapons and economic aid. [48] Chiang and his delegation left Moscow on November 29 and arrived in Shanghai on December 15, thus concluding a mission which had lasted for three months. [49]

Chiang Kai-shek's mission to Moscow to seek Russian assistance in a Northwestern strategy typified Sun Yat-sen's foremost concern at the time, namely, finding the most expeditious way of achieving national unification through military means. Whatever the merits of the plan presented to the Soviet government by Chiang Kai-shek, the plan was a true reflection of the Kuomintang's consistently held strategy of military unification of China. [50] This military approach contrasted sharply with the Soviet position that political mobilization held the key to any possible Kuomintang success. This divergent approach to strategic planning revealed itself in Chiang's talks with Sklyansky and Kamenev in Moscow, and was made even clearer in a letter from Chicherin, the Soviet Commissar for Foreign Affairs, to Sun Yat-sen, dated December 4, 1923, in which he wrote:

"I thank you very much for your kind letter and for the good feelings transmitted through your delegates. We are all very glad that your delegates have come and we are sure of the beneficial results of their visit.... We think that the fundamental aim of the Kuomintang Party is to build up a great powerful movement of the Chinese people and that therefore propaganda and organization on the biggest scale are its first necessities. Our example was significant: our military activities were successful because a long series of years had elapsed during which we organized and instructed our following, building up in this way a great organized party throughout the whole land, a party capable of vanquishing all its adversaries. The whole Chinese nation must see the difference between the Kuomintang, a popularly organized mass party, and the military dictatorship of the various parts of China. The fraternal nations, such as the Mongolian people, the Tibetans, the various races of Western China, must clearly understand that the Kuomintang supports their right of self-determination. Their territories therefore cannot be used for your armed forces. These are some of the ideas which I nourish in these questions. We must continue our exchange of ideas and discuss the matter further. When we reach a full agreement, everything will go on much better. [51]

What Chicherin did not mention in the letter is the special significance political mobilization through mass activities had for the future of the Chinese communist movement. Maring had lamented in 1922, in his report to the Executive Committee of the Communist international, the political impotence of the newly-established Chinese Communist Party, and urged that Chinese Communists "give up their exclusive attitude toward the Kuomintang and that they begin activity within the Kuomintang through which one can gain access so much more easily to the workers in the South and the soldiers." [52] The Comintern instructed members of the Chinese Communist Party to join the Kuomintang, but cautioned that membership should not be "purchased at the price of effacement of the Chinese Communist Party." [53] Thus, Borodin was able to speak of the increase, in the end, of the influence of the Chinese Communist Party in the Chinese revolution through the Kuomintang. [54]

While the Soviet position can be said to have been partially based on the success of its own experience in political mobilization, as was claimed by Chicherin, as well as on protecting what it regarded as its security interest in Mongolia, the development of a strong Chinese Communist movement capable of wresting the leadership of the Chinese Revolution away from the Kuomintang was certainly an equally important consideration and an integral part of Soviet strategy in China and East Asia at that time. The Kuomintang and the Soviet Union thus viewed the Chinese Revolution differently, and that difference lay at the root of their divergent approach to strategic planning. This divergence precluded any possible success of Chiang Kai-shek's mission to Moscow in 1923.

Notes

This paper was presented at the Conference on Chiang Kai-shek and Modern China, held in Taipei in 1986 and published in the *Proceedings of the Conference on Chiang Kai-shek and Modern China* (Taipei, 1987), vol. 2, pp.58-76. It was later republished with revisions in

Republican China, vol. XVI, no. 1 (November 1990), pp. 18-34. It has now been amended by findings in Chiang Kai-shek's manuscript diary deposited at the Hoover Institution, Stanford University.

[1] Quoted in Chicherin's letter to Sun Yat-sen of August 1, 1918.See Jane Degras, ed. *Soviet Documents on Foreign Policy* (London, 1951), p. 92

[2] *Ibid.*, p. 93.

[3] Sun was said to have met early in 1920 in Shanghai with one Colonel Popoff, "who came with credentials from the Commander of Bolshevik troops of the Amur district," and discussed plans for cooperation between the Kuomintang and the Bolshevists. See C. Martin Wilbur, Sun Yat-sen, *Frustrated Patriot* (New York, 1976), pp. 115-116, quoting from a dispatch from Edwin S. Cunningham, the American Consul General in Shanghai, to the State Department.

However, it is not known whether Colonel Popoff made the visit as an official representative of the Soviet Government.

[4] Xenia J. Eudin and Robert C. North, *Soviet Russia and the East, A Documentary Survey* (Stanford, 1957), p. 218.

[5] Cao Xizhen, *Zhong Su waijiaoshi* (A History of Sino-Russian Diplomatic Relations) (Beijing, 1951), p. 41; Cui Shuqin, *Sun Zhongshan yu gongchan zhuyi* (Sun Yat-sen and Comminism) (Hong Kong,1954), p.21.

According to Katsuji Fuse, a Japanese journalist specializing in Soviet affairs, following Alexieff's arrival in Canton, dissemination of Soviet propaganda began in *Qunbao*, a journal edited by Chen Duxiu, one of the founders of the Chinese Communist Party, and a Russian-language course was also established at the Canton Normal College by the Canton Government. Fuse also reports the exchange of a memorandum of understanding between Sun and Alexieff concerning Canton-Moscow relations, which allegedly contains the following points:(1) mutual respect for each other's sovereignty; (2) immediate' restoration of trade; (3) permission to proselytize communism in areas under the jurisdiction of the Canton government; (4) mutual economic aid; and (5) preferential treatment of each other's citizens. However, this cannot be confirmed by any other source. In any case, it seems unlikely that Sun Yat-sen would have consented to the open preaching of Communism in Canton. See Katsuji Fuse, *Su E di dongfang zhengce* (Soviet Policy in the Orient), trans. by Ban-Su (Shanghai, 1928), pp. 226-227.

[6] Eudin and North, pp. 219-221. This letter does not appear in any of the official Kuomintang publications. An apparent Chinese translation is included in *Sun Zhongshan xuanji* (Selected Works of Sun Yat-sen) (Beijing, 1956), I, pp. 434-436.

[7] Deng Jiayan, "Mading jiejian zongli shiji" (A Record of Mading's Audience with Sun Yat-sen), *Geming wenxian* (Documents of the Revolution) (Taipei, 1953-) IX, pp. 1409-1411; Sun Fukun, *Gongchan guoji raoluan Zhongguo ji* (The Comintern's Subversion of China) (Taipei,1953), pp. 11-12; Su Deyong, "Guanyu Malin jiejian zongli ji qi shidi zhi bianzheng" (Concerning Maring's Audience with Sun Yat-sen and the Time and Place of Their Meetings), *San Min Zhuyi banyue kan* (San-min chu-i Semimonthly), No. 35 (October 1954), pp. 45-50; and Zhang Ji, *Zhang Puquan xiansheng quanji* (Complete Works of Zhang Ji) (Taipei,1951), p. 195.

For an English translation of Maring's report to the Comintern on his visit to China, see Helmut Gruber, ed., *Soviet Russia Masters the Comintern* (Garden City, 1974), pp. 364-375. This document deals more with Maring's assessment of the general political situation in China as it involves the Kuomintang and the nascent Chinese Communist Party, than with his visit with Sun Yat-sen. On the latter, the most important point he made was Sun's rejection of an open alliance with the Soviet Union at the time. For a similar account, see Harold R. Isaacs, "Documents on the Comintern and the Chinese Revolution," Part I, "Notes on a Conversation with H. Sneevliet, the Chinese Question, 1920-1923," *China Quarterly*, No. 45 (January/March, 1971), pp. 102-109. See also Dov Bing, "Sneevliet and the Early Years of the CCP," *China Quarterly*, No. 48 (October/December, 1971), pp. 677-697. All three of these articles have been translated into Chinese. See *Malin zai Zhongguo di youguan ziliao* (Maring in China: Related Materials) (Beijing, 1980), pp. 11-58.

[8] Sun Fukun, pp. 11-12.

[9] Deng Jia-yan, p. 1411.

[10] Zou Lu, *Zhongguo guomindang shigao* (A Draft History of the Kuomintang)(Chongqing, 1944), p.304.

[11] *Ibid.*

[12] Isaacs, p. 104.

[13] *Ibid.*, p. 105.

[14] For Dalin's meetings with Dr. Sun, see Wilbur, pp. 121-124. Professor Wilbur based his account on Dalin's article, "The Great Turn: Sun Yat-sen in 1922," published in Russian in 1966 (Wilbur, p. 329, n. 23.) No Chinese records are available on the Sun-Dalin talks.

[15] Chen Duxiu, *Gao quan dang tongzhi shu*（A Letter to All Comrades of the Party）, December 10, 1929, p. 2.

[16] Jiang Zhongzheng, "Zhngguo guomin geming yu Eguo gongchan geming zhi qubie"（The Difference between China's National Revolution and Russia's Communist Revolution" in *Xin shengming*（New Life）,11:5（May 1929）, p. 4.

[17] For a detailed discussion of Sun's relations with the Powers, see Wilbur, chapter 6, "The Dynamic Setting for Alliance with Russia."

[18] *North China Herald*, October 7, 1922, p. 9.

[19] *Ibid.*

[20] This account is based on the intelligence report of the Commissioner of Police of the Shanghai Municipal Council, dated January 19, 1922. A copy, acquired from the Sneevliet Archives in Amsterdam through the courtesy of Prof. Tony Saich, is available at the Harvard-Yenching Library.

This information contradicts the reminiscences of Liao Zhongkai's wife and daughter, which state that Joffe had met several times with Sun Yat-sen in Shanghai in 1922, but surveillance by the British police there made it difficult for the meetings to continue and the venue was changed to Tokyo, where Liao Zhongkai was sent as Sun's representative in the latter part of September to meet with Joffe. But their meetings there also had to break up because of the surveillance of the Japanese police. Upon the death of Liao's father-in-law in December, Liao returned to China and was soon followed by Joffe. See Liao Mengxing, *Wo di muqin He Xiangning*（My Mother, He Xiangning）（Hong Kong, 1973）, pp. 13 and 56-57. For a similar account, based largely on Liao Mengxing's work, see Guan Guoxuan, "You guan Yuefei yu Liao Zhongkai huitan di shijian wenti"（Concerning the Dates of the Yuefei-Liao Zhongkai Meetings）, *Zhuanji wenxue*（Biographical Literature）, 46:5（May 1985）, pp. 57-59.

However, these alleged meetings between Liao and Joffe in Japan in 1922 have now proven to be non-existent, according to Tatsuo Yamada of Keio University. Professor Yamada, making extensive use of Japanese archival sources, including police and secret service reports now on deposit at the Gaiko shiryokan, established the fact that Liao, accompanied by his wife and Xu Chongqing, did visit Japan for forty days, having arrived from Shanghai aboard the President Cleveland on September 25, 1922, but he could not find anything to establish Joffe's presence in Japan at that time. Thus, the alleged meetings between Liao and Joffe could not have taken place. See Tatsuo Yamada, "Ryo Chu-gai no nido no honichi ni tsuite-1922.23 nen（On Liao Zhongkai's Two Visits to Japan in 1922 and 1923）, *Hogaku kenkyu*, 60:1（January 1987）, p.79-105. I am grateful to Professor Yamada for calling my attention to his findings.

[21] For a complete text in English of the joint statement, see *China Year Book*（Tientsin）, p. 1318. A Chinese translation is available in Guofu nianpu（A Chronological Biography of Sun Yat-sen）（Taipei, 1965）, v. 2, pp. 891-893.

[22] Wang Jingwei's Political Report at the Second National Congress of the Kuomintang, 1926. See Wang Jingwei, *Wang Jingwei yanjiang lu*（Wang Jingwei's Collected Speeches）（Shanghai? 1927）, p.37

[23] Katsuji Fuse, pp. 229-233.

[24] A.I. Kartunova, "Sun Yat-sen i russkie sovetniki. Po documentam 1923-1924"（Sun Yat-sen and the Russian Advisers, based on Documents of 1923-1924）in *Sun Yat-sen 1866-1966. Kstoletiyu so dyna rozhdeniya:Sbornik statei, vospominanii i materialov*（Sun Yat-sen, 1866-1966. For the 100th Anniversary of His Birth: A Collection of Essays, Reminiscences, and Materials）（Moscow, 1966）, p. 171. I am indebted to Mrs. Deidra Deamer for a translation.

[25] *Ibid.*

[26] Helmut Gruber, p. 372.

[27] *Sun xiansheng zhi Jiang xiansheng shouza mo ji*（Facsimile of Sun Yat-sen's Handwritten Letters to Chiang Kai-shek）（Bangkok,1939）,pp.10-11; also *Guofu quanji*（Complete Works of Sun Yat-sen）（Taipei, 1961）, V, pp. 453-454.

[28] *Sun xiansheng zhi Jiang xiansheng shouza mo ji*, pp. 3-4; also *Guofu quanji*, V, pp. 495-49.

[29] Mao Sicheng, ed. *Minguo shiwu nian yiqian zhi Jiang Jieshi xiansheng*（Chiang Kai-shek before 1926）（n.p.,1936）, III, p. 96. This is an edited version of Chiang Kai-shek's diary to 1926 in 20 volumes.

[The original manuscript copy of this book has been found. After some editing by The Second Historical Archives of China, it was published in 1992 by the Archives Publishing Company in Bejing under the title *A Draft Chronological Biography of Chiang Kai-shek*. According to the Editorial Note to the publication, "the manuscript copy has the notation 'Secret' stamped on the cover. It is the version personally approved by Chiang, and the book was divided into three parts... following additional editing... it was given the title *Chiang Kai-shek before 1926*, and the book was rearranged under eight parts... During the editorial process we compared the manuscript copy with the publication *Chiang Kai-shek before*

1926, and restored, with explanatory notes, all the important parts that were deleted by Chiang; for materials lacking in the original manuscript but are in *Chiang Kai-shek before 1926*, the materials in question were copied from the latter publication." This author has made a careful check of these two publications and found nothing from the chronological biography that would alter or add to the information contained in this article taken from the book *Chiang Kai-shek before 1926*.]

[30] Jiang Zhongzheng, "Yu Yang Cangbo shu"（Letter to Yang Shukan）in *Jiang zongtong yanlun huipian*（Collected Speeches and Writing of President Jiang）（Taipei, 1956）,v. 24, pp. 105-107. The letter is dated July 13, 1923

[31] For Chiang's personal account of his mission to the Soviet Union, see Mao Sicheng, *op cit.*, V, pp. 41a-73b. For an abbreviated account in English, see Chiang Kai-shek, *Soviet Russia in China*（New York, 1957）, pp. 19-25. Neither account mentions the substance of his meetings with Soviet military leaders as discussed below. The English version does not even mention the meetings.

[32] Chiang kai-shek, *Soviet Russia in China*, pp. 18-19.

[33] This is not mentioned in any of the Chinese sources. The first evidence was discovered by Allen S. Whiting from typed copies of the original file of the Sun-Karakhan correspondence in the personal collection of Louis Fischer（Whiting, *Soviet Policies in China, 1917-1924*, New York, 1954, p. 323, n. 16）. Chiang Kai-shek's negotiations in Moscow are described in detail in A.I. Kartunova, "Sun Yat-sen and the Russian Advisers," pp. 175-180.

[34] Louis Fischer, *Russia's Road from Peace to War: Soviet Foreign Relations, 1917-1941*（New York, 1969）, p. 73; Allen Whiting, p. 243.

[35] Mao Sicheng, *op cit.*, V, p. 50a.

[36] The account of Chiang's negotiations with Skylyansky and Kamenev is taken from A.I. Kartunova, "Sun Yat-sen and the Russian Advisers", p. 27.

[37] C. Martin Wilbur and Julie Lien-ying Howe, ed., *Documents on Communism, Nationalism, and Soviet Advisers in China, 1918-1927*（New York, 1956）, p. 197.

[38] C. Martin Wilbur, *Sun Yat-sen: Frustrated Patriot*, p. 153.

[39] Mao Sicheng, *op cit.*, V, p. 51b. This document has not been made public. But it is noted here that "it contains more than 8,200 words explaining the relations of mutual assistance between China and Russia, and between the Kuomintang and the Chinese Communist Party," and is divided into:（1）Introduction;（2）Military plans;（3）Propaganda plans; and（4）Conclusion.

[40]　The meetings and their dates are recorded in Mao Sicheng, *op cit,*, V, pp. 52a-65b. However, the substance of the meetings is not revealed, with the exception of the one with Chicherin on 0ctober 21. Chiang records that the question of Mongolia was discussed, but the meeting was "inconclusive." Chiang's letter to Sklyansky of October 25 is reportedly lost（Mao Sicheng, *op cit,* V, p. 60b.）

[41]　A.I. Kartunova, pp. 179-180.

[42]　The entry for Nov. 11, 1923 in Chiang Kai-shek's diary on deposit at the Hoover Institution reads: "Went over the draft proposal in preparation for the meeting with Sklyansky. Met with Sklyansky and Kamenev in the afternoon for approximately two hours...Whether from a personal or from a national viewpoint, it's always better to seek self help than help from others. Regardless of how close the relationship is among one's kindred or allies, it cannot go beyond the concerned party's own interests. This [point] cannot be ignored whatever the nature of one's task is, or one succeeds or fails in that task. If one wishes to succeed, [the effort] has to begin with oneself. Outside help is the most unreliable thing." Except for this reaction, the diary does not reveal any information on the substance of the talks he had with Sklyansky and Kamenev.

[43]　Xenia J. Eudin and Robert C. North, *Soviet Russia and the East*, pp. 343-344, and Jane Degras, *The Communist International, 1919-1943: Documents, v. 2, 1923-1928*（London, 1960）, pp. 5-6.

[44]　Borodin, in a talk on October 17, 1923, with members of the Chinese Communist Party, was quoted as saying: "In the press I spoke of the Kuomintang, but to us it means that I was speaking of the increase, in the end, of the influence of the Communist Party.... while working for the stability of the Kuomintang, it must never be forgotten that in reality the work is done for the stabilization of the Communist Party, which aim should always be kept in mind." See N. Mitarevsky, *World Wide Soviet Plots*（Tianjin, n.d.）, p. 133.

[45]　Allen S. Whiting, *Soviet Policies in China*, p. 245.

[46]　Chiang Kai-shek. *Soviet Russia in China*, p. 22.

According to Chiang Kai-shek's diary on deposit at the Hoover Institution, he was piqued at the slight shown his mission by Voitinsky and had politely declined to attend the meeting, and only because of Voitinsky's insistence, he finally consented to go. The diary entry for Nov. 25, 1923 reads as follows: "The Chief of the Comintern's Far Eastern Bureau Voitinsky has invited me to meet with the Presidium of the Comintern, but has repeatedly postponed arranging a date, viewing this as some rare commodity for hoarding purposes. In fact I don't really have to have such a meeting. While he wants me to go to the meeting, he is also afraid I might point out the shortcomings [of their policy]. During the last three days he has been mentioning such a meeting, but has never set a time, thinking my coming here as something quite ordinary. [He is] throwing road blocks in my negotiations, and showing disrespect. The Soviet officials, thinking he has been to China, have been deceived by what he told them. The fact that until today he has not yet set a date[for the meeting] made me angry and I have politely declined his invitation. But he came to ask me again, I had no choice but to accede to his request and went."

[47] Chiang Kai-shek, Soviet Russia in China, p. 22

[48] *Ibid.*, p. 24. Chiang mentions here that while he was in the Soviet Union he "had more talks with Trotsky than with other Soviet leaders," but this is the only meeting between him and Trotsky mentioned in Mao Sicheng, *op cit.*, V, p. 67a. According to the Chiang Kai-shek diary on deposit at the Hoover Institution, he did write to Trotsky on Oct. 16 after arriving in the Soviet Union, and again "drafted" a letter to him on Nov. 9 while in Moscow. This information is mentioned neither in *Chiang Kai-shek before 1926* edited by Mao Sicheng, nor in *A Draft Chronological Biography of Chiang Kai-shek* edited by the Second Historical Archives of China.

[49] Mao Sicheng, *op cit.*, V, pp. 70a-73b. Following his return to China, Chiang Kai-shek submitted a written report on his mission to Sun Yat-sen. This report has never been made public. However, judging from Chiang's subsequent remarks on the Soviet Union (see, for instance, his letter to Liao Zhongkai dated March 14, 1924, in Mao Sicheng, *op cit.*, VI, pp. 28a-31a), it could be assumed that his report probably was not a favorable one. According to Jiang Jingguo that his father's "three-month stay in the Soviet Union......enabled him to recognize that the Soviet political system is nothing but a dictatorial and terrorist organization, totally different from our political system based on the Three People's Principles, and the two are basically mutually exclusive." See Jiang Jingguo, *Chensi zai Cihu zhi pan* (Reflections by Lake Cihu)(Taipei: 1979), p. 7. This pamphlet was printed by the Liming Company in 1981 in Taipei.

[50] Maring remarked in a conversation with Harold R. Isaacs in 1935 that "Sun Yat-sen up to the very time of his death never really absorbed the idea of mass activity. He accepted it, but was not vitally interested. In 1923 he was indifferent. He was concerned only with military matters." *See* Harold R. Isaacs, "Notes on a Conversation with H. Sneevliet," *China Quarterly*, No. 45 (January/March, 1971), p. 108.

[51] Quoted from the Sun-Karakhan correspondence file in Allen S. Whiting, *Soviet Policies in China*, pp. 245-246.

[52] "Report to the Executive Committee of Comrade H. Maring," in Helmut Gruber, *Soviet Russia Masters the Comintern*, pp. 369-370 and 374.

[53] Resolution of the ECCI "On the Expected Attitude of the Chinese Communist Party towards the Kuomintang," January 12, 1923, in Eudin and North, pp. 343-344. For a comprehensive study of Sun Yat-sen's policy *vis-a-vis* the Soviet Union and the Chinese Communists, see Li Yunhan, *Cong rong gong dao qing dang*（From the Admission of the Communists to the Purification of the Party）（Taipei, 1966）. See also Shao-chuan Leng and Norman D. Palmer, *Sun Yat-sen and Communism*（New York, 1960）.

[54] See note [45].

聯盟政治
國民黨1924年黨章之分析

　　國民黨1924年的改組是一項令人印象深刻的成就。經過改組，國民黨轉變成為一個以民主集中制為原則的高度集權的政黨，加強了黨內嚴格的紀律，建立了有效的宣傳和組織的結構，發動群眾運動以實現黨的政策。因此國民黨其後得以在廣州穩固其基地。組織群眾，建立黨軍，而最終以武力擊敗北方軍閥都證明了1924年改組的成效。但是，這是一段艱巨的成功之路。改組方案之一是容許共產黨員以個人身分加入國民黨，但是由於國民黨內部從改組開始就有的反共情緒，國民黨員與共產黨員間的關係非常緊張和不安。在這個背景下，國民黨改組後經歷了由於內部的異議而引起的三年動盪。本文根據新的史料，試論1924年為國民黨改組所立國民黨黨章的早期異議。

　　孫中山曾稱1924年改組的黨章是他邀請蘇聯顧問鮑羅廷英文起草，由廖仲愷譯為中文。[1] 因此，一般咸認，1924年1月國民黨第一次全國代表大會所通過的黨章即是出於鮑羅廷之手。然而，一篇鮮為人知的鮑羅廷草稿的中譯本，揭示黨章原來有兩個版本。最後通過的黨章與鮑羅廷起草的黨章在多處關鍵地方有明顯的不同。[2] 作者認為這是由於追隨孫中山的資深國民黨員對共產黨員的不信任，設法在鮑羅廷草稿關鍵的地方作了修改，以防共產黨在國民黨政策上散布其影響力。

　　這份黨章基本上是按照蘇俄模式，在民主集中制的架構下，建立一個組織嚴密，又有紀律的政黨。通過一系列執行委員會的錐形結構，下層對其直接上層負責，使國民黨成為一個由選舉產生的少數精英所控制的政黨。在這一個原則上，這兩份草案並無不同。所不同而值得我們注意的是在國民黨第一次全國代表大會所通過的黨章中對原草案作出的增訂和更改。

　　草案的原稿分10章66條，最後通過的黨章分13章84條，並增加了前言和兩條附則。好些更改只是文字的修正，或使其更為精確，或是刪掉重複；還有些也僅牽涉到開會時法定人數的問題。但是以下數處是具有長遠政治意義在實質上的更改：

1. 增加的前言稱，全國代表大會通過黨章之目的是「為促進三民主義之實現，五權憲法之創立。」
2. 增加關於總理位置之條文一章（共6條）。條文中稱「本黨當以創行三民主義，五權憲法之孫先生為總理」……「黨員須服從總理之指導，以努力於主義之進行。」同時它也是全國代表大會及中央執行委員會之主席，且對前者的決議「有交複決之權」，對後者的決議「有最後決定之權。」
3. 原草案中的「審查委員會」改為「監察委員會」，其職權也擴大包括「稽核在黨中央政府任職之黨員其施政治之方及政績，是否根據本黨政綱及本黨制定之政策。」省級縣級的監察委員也賦予同樣的權力。
4. 增加關於黨職人員任期的限制一章。（中央，省，縣，區執行委員會委員，中央監察委員會委員各任期一年；區分部執行委員任期六個月。）
5. 授權中央執行委員會在特別區（內蒙古、市、鎮、及海外華僑地區）設立黨部。
6. 授權黨之「最高機關」全國代表大會解釋黨章之權。

　　表面上看來，這些更改好像是無足輕重。但是，仔細比較這兩個版本，特別是在當時改組方案的爭議的背景下，看起來就不同了。改組起始時是孫中山與鮑羅廷以及孫的少數親信在廣州籌畫。不但沒有向全黨諮詢，甚至改組的範圍，黨員在1923年11月黨章的草案公布後才知道，其時改組的計畫已經開始執行。[3] 當時國民黨的最高的執行機構——在上海的中央幹部會議，對改組計畫的實質也毫不知情。由於中央幹部會議沒有得到廣州方面的官方消息，於是主動請廣州方面說明該改組計畫。

　　謝持，代表中央幹部會議，於 1923 年 10 月 13 日致電孫中山請示幹部會議是否仍有職權召開會議。孫次日回電認可。[4] 再次日幹部會議又電孫中山請示現行黨章將來的情形如何，以及改組後，可能派駐上海的新人選。二日後，孫作覆稱，現行黨章當有大規模的修訂和擴充。至於新派駐滬人員，孫中山說無此計畫。[5] 顯然地，中央幹部委員會急於知道關於國民黨改組的謠言的真偽。孫中山的電報證實了他們的恐懼。更甚者，孫中山在 11 月 7 日下令解散中央幹部會議及國民黨上海支部，以準備在該地依據新的黨章設立一個新的國民黨執行部。[6] 次日，幹部會議召開特別會議。討論的主題是共產黨員的國民黨籍。[7] 會議上的共識是「黨內不應有黨」，因為共產黨員以個人名義加入國民黨是一回事，如果改組是用來促進共產黨的發展，那就完全是另外一回事了。他們認為兩黨應該各自保持自己的特性。在會議上，中央幹部會議未作任何決議，等待譚平山來上海報告改組情形後再議。[8] 11 月 23 日，中央幹部會議在其例行的會議上再次討論這個問題。從討論中可以見到該時幹部會議已經得知改組宣言與改組黨章草案的內容。[9] 張繼表示他對於黨政策中「反帝」和「反軍閥」的立場。他說：「我們所作必有先後。如果我們跟隨社會主義者去作他們所倡議的事，一方面在國內反軍閥，另方面在國外反國際帝國主義，那必定會產生很多疑慮和混淆，因為在執行那種政策時會發生很多實際上的困難。」也就意味國民黨在國內外都會被孤立起來。張秋白對選舉制度的隱患提出警告。他說：「如果改組後，到處都有選舉，其後果當不利於建黨的精神」，那就是，否定孫中山委派人員的權力。彭述民，另外一位中央幹部會議的成員，懷疑共產黨員是否會受國民黨的領導，因為「社會主義者有他們自己的原則。」會議決定把這些顧慮和意見通告廣州。

　　當廖仲愷在 12 月 9 日到上海與中央幹部會議成員見面時，他的目的是平息他們的恐懼，同時也爭取他們對改組的支持。他對幹部會議的成員解釋國民黨如何迫切地需要加強組織來擴大支援的基礎。他認為國民黨只有上層幹部，而無下層黨員來執行工作。由於沒有群眾的支持，國民黨要完全依靠軍

隊，但是軍隊一而再地為追求本身的利益轉過來反對國民黨。他說，這就是
國民黨過去為什麼不能奪權的主要原因。因此，國民黨必須擺脫軍隊的控
制，而建立成為一個強有力的足以控制自己將來的政治勢力。他警告中央幹
部會議說：「吾黨情形，目下除少數幹部並無黨員，雖亦有力量，然不過一
部奮鬥之歷史而已。此種力量固可張羅於一時，恐日久必窮倒……改造中國
之責既在吾黨，倘非從下層多做功夫，而徒拘泥於上層之幹部，必不足以負
此偉大責任。」他並為中央幹部會議解說在廣州已經開始進行的改組工作，
包括訓練一支有政治意識的黨軍，他也為改組的大綱有所說明。[10]

　　值得注意的是，廖仲愷並沒有提到共產黨員的國民黨籍問題。關於這一
點，他的話中最與這個問題有關的是：「當時以團體加入之黨軍，即為日後
攻總統府之人，可見加入黨者需用個人，不可用團體也」。[11] 顯然地，他的
動機是要讓中央幹部會議放心，讓他們了解孫中山並非不知道「黨中有黨」
的內在危機．於是才作出只允許共產黨員以個人身分參加國民黨的決定。更
值得注意的是，在會議中，沒有人向廖仲愷提出質問。會議記錄的文件顯
示，向廖提出的問題僅僅是一些技術上的問題，包括如何設立上海臨時執行
部來舉辦次年1月出席全國代表大會的選舉代表的程式；以及延期召開全國
代表大會，以便有更富裕的時間作選舉工作的可能等。廖仲愷很可能在和中
央幹部會議成員正式見面之前，就已經成功地，雖然只是暫時的，在共產黨
員的國民黨籍的問題上，與幹部會議的個別成員取得一致的意見。廖仲愷於
11月29日在和中央幹部會議成員正式見面9天前就到達上海。我們有理由
假設，他曾利用這段時間，分別和幹部會議成員會面，提出孫中山改組國民
黨的理由。這些會面的內容並無文獻可查。不過，差不多可以肯定地說，廖
仲愷傳達了孫中山的保證，他沒有讓共產黨取國民黨而代之的意圖，而且資
深國民黨員還會繼續控制一切。因為，幾乎不可能是巧合，中央幹部會議的
四位成員——戴季陶、葉楚傖、居正、丁維汾——在全國代表大會上成為第
一屆中央執行委員會委員，而另外兩位——彭述民和張秋白——成為候補委
員。還有另外3位——鄧澤如、謝持和張繼——成為第一屆中央監察委員會
委員。同時很有意思的是只有3位共產黨員——譚平山、李大釗、于樹

德——被選上有24位委員的中央執行委員會，而在中央執行委員會上的17位候補委員中，只有6位共產黨員——林祖涵、毛澤東、于方舟、瞿秋白、韓麟符，及張國燾。中央監察委員會5位委員，以及其5位候補委員中，無一共產黨員。[12]

在廣州，反共的情緒也很強烈。廣東國民黨支部主任鄧澤如（國民黨元老，多年為孫中山在東南亞籌款奔走，並被孫中山指派與廖仲愷同為召開改組特別會議的召集人）及支部其他10位委員在11月29日上書孫中山表達他們對改組方向的關切。[13] 在呈文中，他們提出一些如果改組按照計畫進行，共產黨取國民黨而代之的黯淡的遠景的問題。雖然他們沒有對改組本身提出質疑（他們稱改組的動機是「出自我總理之乾綱獨斷」），他們卻懷疑共產黨加入國民黨的動機和共產黨在幕後操縱改組計畫的落實。他們認為黨章之草擬雖「多出於俄人鮑羅廷之指揮，然此表面文章，尚無大害。為探聞俄替我黨訂定之政綱政策，全為陳獨秀之指導共產黨所議定。」他們斷言，陳獨秀曾經公開批評國民黨和孫中山是「過時的」，並倡言三民主義和五權憲法毫無學理根據，現在反而領導共黨員加入國民黨，可見其別有用心。其最終的目的是「借國民黨之軀殼，注入共產黨之靈魂……是我黨隱為被共產所指揮。」他們力諍孫中山不要陷入這個陷阱。當在攻擊共產黨時，他們很謹慎地沒有公開牽涉到蘇聯。他們說：「至蘇俄政府之協助我黨改組，與陳獨秀是否同一鼻孔出氣，黨員等未敢斷定之。」但是他們確信，中國共產黨是在廣州與莫斯科友好關係的氣氛下，從中取利，激起改組的願望，以使國民黨成為共產黨甕中之鱉。最後，他們對所提議的選舉制度的內在危險提出警告。他們說，根據改組的草案，黨總理一職將變為選舉制，「恐事實隨環境變遷，五年之後，將見陳獨秀被選為總理矣。」至於其他黨的高級職位亦將成為選舉職位，他們認為這是違背已建立的總理的委任制度，不復能行「各局部首領之智愚賢不肖，由總理審定而別擇之，以大公無我之心自收用當其才之效」的慣例。他們也認為這種選舉制度會打開品質不佳的代表被選上的閘門，並且也容易被操縱。不過，他們也提出建議，說如果選舉制度必須採用的話，應該加上一些限制。他們提出一個兩重選舉的建議——初選和複選。初選出來的人數較多，由孫中山在其中提名作複選。如此，「庶幾經過一度之審查，而奸人乃無術施其運動。」呈文者稱，既然「奸人謀毀吾黨，其計甚毒，不可不防，黨員等心所謂危，不得不揭發其詭計。」

然而，孫中山的看法和他們這種危機意識不同。他非常有把握，黨紀足以制裁共產黨的軌外行為，而他可以「採取蘇聯制度的優點，避免其有害之處。」[14] 他在收到呈文的當天，嚴厲地訓斥了上呈文的人。在呈文的批示上，他逐一地答覆了呈文中的每一要點。[15] 他說，陳獨秀並未參加黨章起草的工作，並且把陳獨秀前時對他和國民黨的誹謗歸罪為「中國少年學生自以為是，及一時崇拜俄國革命過當之態度，所以竭加排擠而疵毀吾黨。」他認為中國共產黨員加入國民黨的動機是：「初欲包攬俄國交際，並欲阻止俄國不與吾黨往來，而彼得以獨得俄助，而自樹一幟與吾黨爭衡也。乃俄國之革命黨皆屬有黨政經驗之人，不為此等少年所愚，竊窺破彼等伎倆，於是大不以彼為然，故為我糾正之。並要彼等加入國民黨，與我一致動作……俄國欲與中國合作者，只有與吾黨合作，何有於陳獨秀。陳如不服從吾黨，我亦必棄之。」至於委派與選舉制度之優劣，他強調這不是所倡議的選舉制度是否完美，而是國民黨是否應該民主化的問題。他說：「民權主義端於選舉。若因噎廢食，豈不自反其主義乎。若怕流弊。則當人人竭力奮鬥，不可放責任，嚴為監視。如察悉有弊端，立為指出。以後我每兩禮拜與各人會集一次，如遇有問題，當公共解決之。」他給這些異議人士留下這樣的訓誡：「吾黨自革命以後，則日日退步，必有其故，則不圖進步改良也。」[16]

同時，海外華僑對改組的反應也很迅速。海外國民黨支部強烈反對接納共產黨員加入國民黨的措施。美國舊金山國民黨海外總部主任陳耀元上書廣州，對共產主義和國民黨效法蘇維埃制度的危險性提出警告。據孫中山自己說，還有其他類似的函件，質問國民黨是否因此改組為共產黨，果真如此，他們實在不敢苟同。[17] 面對國民黨主要財政支持者海外華僑這樣的反應，國民黨迅速地採取了動作。1924 年 1 月 3 日在孫中山親自主持的臨時中央執行委員會第 22 次會議上討論了陳耀元的信。會議上決議應該有所回覆，旋即通過了一份草稿，其中一部分說：「當俄國革命之初，施行共產制度時，確與吾黨三民主義不同。至俄國現在所行之新經濟政策，即是國家資本主義，與吾黨之三民主義相同。故非吾黨學俄國，實俄國學吾黨。」[18]

雖然無法證明這些國內國外異議的興起是一種有協調的行動，但是，這些持異議者在容共的政策上，他們反對的立場是一致的。既然孫中山已經決心採取容共的政策，那麼問題是他們要如何將反對意識轉化為行動又不挑戰孫中山的領導力。第一次全國代表大會給他們一個機會來繪製一個協調一致的行動策略。這個策略，由後來的事實證明，是一種遷就的策略，即是，接受容共政策的現實，但是設法遏制共產黨員在國民黨事務上的活動。他們採取修訂黨綱這個主要的手段來達到這個目的。

第一次全國代表大會選派了一個19人的小組審查鮑羅廷起草的黨綱。[19] 19人中除譚平山、李大釗、毛澤東三人為共產黨外，其餘均為國民黨的資深黨員，包括六位中央幹部會議的委員，和一位廣東執行部的代表鄧澤如。[20] 在16位國民黨代表中，除竭力在幕後推動改組的廖仲愷外，其餘均不能算是堅定的容共政策的支持者。於是，他們就變成了異議人士擁護的對象。也就是他們，在幕後活動來確保修訂的黨綱包含阻止任何共產勢力在國民黨內占優勢的條文。作者認為他們採取這個策略，是由於孫中山對廣州莫斯科協議的承諾和此項協議所帶來的約束。他們深知他們能夠做到的有所局限。他們的要求不可能違背國民黨與莫斯科協議的基本條件，那就是與俄國和中國的共產黨合作來創立一個全國性的革命運動。他們只能在這個框架下採取行動。否則，就是完全否定廣州與莫斯科的協議，和公開背叛孫中山的領導。後者是他們不可能認真考慮的事。後來黨章的修訂和補充都能在這個框架下得到最好的解釋。

黨章前言的增訂是向普世宣布，雖然黨有改組，國民黨的思想基礎仍舊是孫中山為建國制定的三民主義和五權憲法。而此思想基礎有黨章來確認。指定孫中山不經選舉為黨的總理（原草案中總理一職由全國代表大會選舉產生），以及賦予他對全國代表大會及中央執行委員會決議的否決權使他成為黨的絕對統治者（草案中僅稱總理為中央執行委員會主席）。此項改變顯然是要給孫中山一切黨章所賦予的權力來對付在想像中的共產黨對國民黨的威脅。同樣地，「審查委員會」改名為「監察委員會」並有權監察黨員任職政府的政績這一項，也可以解釋為制止共產黨在政府工作上的激進行為。從這個觀點來講，黨職的限期，和中央執行委員的權力在地方和特區建立黨部，也可以說是減低共產黨的激進行為和影響的預防措施。因為這些條例的含義是被選出者必須對他們在職的作為負責，並且可以在相當短的任期終結時下台。國民黨也絕不會把控制黨的基層組織的機會讓給共產黨。最後，作為一個額外的預防措施，解釋黨章之權歸於黨的「最高機關」全國代表大會，其中國民黨代表人數預計會成為多數，因為孫中山有權指定一半以上的代表。

　　顯然這些都是為了限制共產黨在國民黨內的影響力而設立的措施，為什麼鮑羅廷和中共黨員沒有提出反對？答案得到別的地方去找。我們還記得，中國共產黨對於加入國民黨的問題，最初意見也相當分歧。一直等到共產國際指令他們參加以後，意見才歸於一致。[21] 共產國際的基本理由是「中國唯一的重大的民族革命集團是國民黨」，同時，由於國內「獨立工人運動尚未完全形成為獨立的社會力量來反對帝國主義者及其在中國的封建代理人的民族革命。所以國民黨與年輕的中國共產黨合作是必要的。因此，在目前條件下，中國共產黨黨員留在國民黨內是適宜的」。共產國際也警告說：「但是，這不能以取消中國共產黨獨特的政治面貌為代價」。[21] 所以，在1923年6月中國共產黨第三次代表大會上以共產國際所用的理由通過了一項決議，指令所有黨員加入國民黨，並且強調「依社會各界階級的現狀，很難另造一個比國民黨更大更革命的黨，即能造成，也有使國民革命勢力不統一不集中的結果。」大會並敦促黨員說：「我們須努力擴大國民黨的組織於全中國，使全中國革命分子集中於國民黨，以應目前中國國民革命之需要」。[22] 這裡的基本前提是剛成立兩年的共產黨需要用國民黨來組織群眾以發展其本身在中國民族革命運動中的影響力。[23] 如像鮑羅廷到廣州不久後所說，中國共產黨黨員加入國民黨，不僅是為了要鞏固國民黨，也是為了要鞏固共產黨。[24]他說：「我在報上為國民黨說話，結果卻是為了擴充共產黨的影響力量。」[25]因之，時間是至關重要的。共產主義在中國的勝利，賴於建立和維持一個強大而有活力的國民黨，從那裡共產黨可以來發展它在群眾中的影響力。除了李大釗在國民黨第一次全國代表大會上代表中國共產黨發表跨黨問題的雄辯，而贏得他的觀點外，中國共產黨員，既獻身於與國民黨合作的政策，為了長遠利益起見，顯然覺得要在修改黨章上一戰，要付的代價太高。[26]

　　對鮑羅廷來講，建立一個「中國人民的強有力的運動」，就像契切林早先給孫中山所說的，是他任務的主要目的。以貫徹國民黨改組的工作來開始發動那個運動是至關重要的事。鮑羅廷很快就意識到只有孫中山才能使改組成功。他10月到達廣州，不久後在一次與國民黨人見面時稱：「國民黨有一位民族領袖──孫逸仙博士，他能夠統一中國，並在人民的支持下，把國家從外國帝國主義者和中國軍閥的奴役下解放出來。」[27]

　　兩個月後，他給莫斯科報告時就可以說：

「目前，我和孫的關係已經達到我可以完全開誠布公和他交談他的事務的地步。關於國民黨的改組，我能讓他明白我們的意圖，同時允許他我們真正的幫助。在所有的事情上，我都強調孫逸仙在就中國國民革命中極其重要的領導地位這一點。我向他指出我們要加強他的領導地位的意願。」[28]

　　他最後說：「我不建議沒有孫的改組。」[29] 所以，無論在黨章裡指定孫中山為總理，抑或賦予他對全國代表大會和中央執行委員決議的否決權，這些和有進行改組的機會而使共產黨能最後受益這一點比較起來，恐怕前者對鮑羅廷的重要性要低於後者。就鮑羅廷來說，不管怎樣，孫中山總會是總理。黨章規定與否是次要的問題。既然這個中心問題已不存在，其他修訂加入黨章的條例，對鮑羅廷同中國共產黨來講，顯然更是不相干了。

　　這整個事件可以用來說明聯盟政治的一個基本概念。就是如何維持在一個不安的聯盟政治中的平衡和妥協，因為其中極端的一方總是傾向於控制另外一方。[30] 國民黨異議分子深恐共產黨控制國民黨，致使他們設立黨章的保障來對付想像中共產黨的威脅。但是，國民黨在一方面需要蘇聯的援助，和在另一方面不願與共產黨分權的互動影響之下，異議分子產生了一種對改組的矛盾心理。那種矛盾心理在改組後幾年中一直是造成國民黨內部紛爭的主因，一直等到清黨後才消除。

注釋

本文於1991年8月11-15日在台北中國國民黨中央委員會黨史委員會主辦之「中華民國建國八十年學術討論會」發表的報告，載《中華民國建國八十年學術討論集》（台北：近代中國出版社，1991），第1冊，頁71-87。

[1]　孫中山眉批，見《彈劾共產黨兩大要案》（〔廣州〕：1927）。後刊印為《中國國民黨第一次全國代表大會史料專集》中華民國史料研究中心編輯（台北，1984），頁511-512。部分英文翻譯見康拉德・布蘭特（Conrad Brant）、史華茲（Benjamin J. Schwartz）、費正清（John K. Fairbank）編，《中國共產主義歷史文獻》（*A Documentary History of Chinese Communism*）（麻州劍橋，1959），頁72-73。

[2]　鮑羅廷草稿的中文翻譯最初登載《國民黨週刊》，第1期（1923年11月25日），頁2-3。該週刊為國民黨在廣州發行的機關報。作者在東京東洋文庫發現這一期。雖然這份譯稿後來在《嚮導週報》第50期（1923年9月29日），頁384-388重新發表，但鮮得研究民國史學者的注意。最後通過的黨章條文多處得見，包括《革命文獻》，第8輯（1955），頁1136-1148。

[3]　黨章草稿發表於《國民黨週刊》（見上注）。草稿發表以前，孫中山已於鮑羅廷抵粵後12日，1923年10月18日，指派他為國民黨的「組織教練」。次日（10月19日）孫中山致電上海幹部會議。知會他們他已指派一改組委員會，其成員為廖仲愷、汪精衛、張繼、戴季陶及李大釗（見《國父全集》〔台北，1961〕，第4冊，頁433）。10月24日，孫中山指派廖仲愷及鄧澤如為改組特別會議的共同召集人（同上，頁559）。25日又指派一臨時中央執行委員會，包括九位正式委員，五位候補委員，並以鮑羅廷為顧問，開始籌備改組的工作（見《國父年譜》〔台北，1965〕，第2冊，頁963）。

[4]　幹部會議電報的全文不見文獻。但是，從孫中山的回覆可知幹部會議所關切的大概。孫的覆電，見《國父全集》，第4冊，頁433。

[5]　同上。

[6]　同上。頁437。

[7]　會議記錄存於中國國民黨黨史委員會，題為《中央幹部會議記錄》，（1923年）第4

冊（編號418/9）。

[8]　孫中山原擬派該年已由共產黨加入國民黨的譚平山赴上海與幹部會議會晤，但後改派廖仲愷，顯然是由於幹部會議成員中的反共情緒。

[9]　以下的敘述根據上引《中央幹部會議記錄》，（1923年）第4冊（編號418/9）。

[10]　同上。這次會議的記錄亦收入《革命文獻》，第8輯，頁1084-1087。

[11]　廖顯然是指陳炯明和他的部隊，他們曾於1922年6月炮轟孫中山的總統府。

[12]　全部名單見《革命文獻》，第8輯，頁1105。

[13]　見上注[2]引書《彈劾共產黨兩大要案》。以下敘述據此。

[14]　鄒魯，《中國國民黨史稿》（重慶，1944），第1冊，頁391，注4。

[15]　見上注[2]。

[16]　孫中山1924年1月21日全國代表大會演講，見《國父全集》，第3冊，頁354。

[17]　陳的信不見文獻。不過從臨時中央執行委員會的回信中，可知其信的大概內容。見臨時中央執行委員會第二十二次會議記錄，載《國民黨週刊》，第7期（1924年1月6日），頁5。回信也收入《國父年譜》，第2冊，頁988-989。

[18]　所有委員姓名見《中國國民黨全國代表大會會議錄》（廣州？1924？），頁19。會議錄亦收入《廣東文史資料》第42輯，〈中國國民黨一大史料專輯〉（1984年7月）頁1-94。

[19]　從中央幹部會議指派的六位是：謝持、戴季陶、居正、茅祖權、丁惟汾、于右任。

[20]　關於這一點的論述，見肖甡、姜華宣撰文〈第一次國共合作統一戰線的形成〉，載朱成甲編《中共黨史研究論文選》（長沙，1983），頁396-399。該文最初發表於《歷史研究》，第2期（1981年4月15日），頁51-68。

[21]　見〈共產國際執行委員會關於中國共產黨對國民黨應有的態度的決議〉（"Resolution of the ECCI on the Expected Attitude of the Chinese Communist Party Toward the Kuomintang"）載森尼亞・尤丁（Xenia J. Eudin）及羅伯特・諾斯（Robert C. North）編《蘇維埃俄國與東方——文獻綜述》（*Soviet Russia and the East*）（Stanford, 1957），頁343-344。中文翻譯見《共產國際有關中國革命的文獻資料，1919-1928》第1輯（北京，1981），頁76-77。

[22]　見〈中國共產黨第三次全國代表大會決議案及宣言〉載《「二大」和「三大」：中國共產黨第二、三次代表大會資料選篇》（北京，1985），頁181-182。

[23]　關於這一點的闡述，見韋慕庭（C. Martin Wilbur）、夏連蔭（Julie Lien-ying Howe）合編，《革命的宣教士：蘇聯顧問在中國，1920-1927》（*Soviet Advisors in Nationalist China, 1920-1927*）（New York, 1957），頁82。

[24]　米泰羅夫斯基（N. Mitarevsky），《蘇俄世界陰謀》（*World Wide Soviet Plots*）（天津：

〔1927〕），頁133。

[25] 同上。

[26] 李大釗講演全文收入《革命文獻》，第9輯，頁1243-1254。部分英譯見蔣介石撰《蘇俄在中國：七十自述》（*Soviet Russia in China: A Summing Up at Seventy*）（New York, 1957），頁26-28。

[27] 切列潘諾夫（A.I. Cherepanov），《中國國民革命軍的北伐：一個駐華軍事顧問的箚記》（北京，1984），頁36。這是 *Severnyi Pokhod Natsional'no Revoliutsionno Armiie Kitaya*（*Zapiski Voennogo Sovetnika*）（Moscow, 1976）的翻譯。

[28] 卡透諾娃（A.I. Kartunova），〈孫逸仙與蘇俄顧問——根據1923-1924年文獻〉（"Sun Yat-sen i russkie sovetniki. Po documentam 1923-1924"）載《孫逸仙（1866-1966）百周年冥誕：論文、回憶錄及其他文獻集》（*SunYat-sen 1866-1966 K stoleltyu so dyna rozhdeniya: Sbornik statei, vospominanii I materialov*）（莫斯科，1966），頁181。承蒙迪姆夫人（Deidra Deamer）為本文作者譯為英文，深感謝意。

[29] 同上。

[30] 莫里斯·杜文傑（Maurice Duvenger），《政黨：在現代國家的組織與活動》（*Political Parties: Their Organization and Activity in a Modern State*），芭芭拉和羅柏特·諾斯（Barbara and Robert North）合譯（紐約，1966），頁347。

The Politics of Coalition
An Analysis of the 1924 Kuomintang Constitution

The 1924 reorganization of the Kuomintang was an impressive achievement. It transformed the Kuomintang into a highly centralized party based on the principle of democratic centralism, imposed tight discipline, and created an effective propaganda and organizational apparatus to initiate and harness a mass movement in support of the party's programs. That the Kuomintang subsequently was able to secure a territorial base in Canton, organize the masses, create a party army, and finally achieve a military victory over the northern militarists attests to the efficacy of the effort undertaken in 1924. But the road to success was an arduous one. Against the background of an uneasy and tense relationship with the Chinese communists, who were admitted as individuals into the Kuomintang as a part of the reorganization scheme, the Kuomintang experienced a turbulent three years of internal dissention, rooted in strong anti-communist sentiments, from the start of the reorganization. This essay is an attempt at analyzing, on the basis of new evidence, one early aspect of that dissent involving the new Kuomintang Constitution, the centerpiece of the 1924 reorganization.

Sun Yat-sen stated that the 1924 Kuomintang Constitution was originally drafted in English by Borodin at his request and translated into Chinese by Liao Zhongkai. [1] The Constitution subsequently adopted by the First National Congress of the Kuomintang in January 1924 has therefore been generally regarded as identical with the Borodin draft. However, the discovery of a little-noticed translation of Borodin's original draft reveals the existence of two versions of the Constitution, with the finally adopted version differing significantly in a number of key provisions from the draft. [2] It is submitted here that Sun Yat-sen's followers among the senior Kuomintang leadership, distrustful of the Chinese communists, managed to introduce key changes into the Constitution as a means of circumscribing the spread of communist influence in Kuomintang affairs.

Basically, the Constitution, embodying the concepts of democratic centralism, provided the structural frame for a close-knit and disciplined political party on the Soviet pattern. Through the provision of a pyramidal hierarchy of executive committees, with the lower always subordinate to the next higher organization, the Kuomintang was to be ruled by a small elected party elite at the top. On this basic concept, the two versions do not differ. What merits our attention here are the additions and modifications introduced into the final version of the Constitution that was adopted by the First National Party Congress.

The original version of the Constitution was divided into ten chapters incorporating sixty-six articles, while the final adopted version contained thirteen chapters with eighty-four articles, an added Preamble, and two supplementary articles. A number of the changes are merely in language, either to make it more precise or to eliminate redundancy; and several involve the question of quorum for meetings. But there are other, more substantive changes, with far-reaching political implications, which are radically different from the original version. They are:

1. the addition of a Preamble which states that the Congress adopts the Party Constitution "in order to promote the realization of both the Three People's Principles and the Five-Power Constitution;"

2. the addition of a chapter containing six articles on the position of the Party's zongli（leader）which stipulate that Sun Yat-sen, "the founder of the Three People's Principles and the Five-Power Constitution," is designated as the

Party's zongli, and that "all members must obey the zongli's leadership and exert themselves in the implementation of [the Party's] principles." He is also to be the chairman of both the National Party Congress and the Central Executive Committee, and shall have veto power over decisions of these two important bodies;

3. the change of the name of the "Auditing Committee" (shencha weiyuanhui), as provided in the original version, to "Supervisory Committee" (jiancha weiyuanhui) and the expansion of its authority to include investigating the policies and performance of Party members serving in the Central government so as to ascertain whether they are in accord with the established Party platform. The Supervisory Committees on the provincial and county levels are also invested with the same investigative powers;

4. the addition of a chapter fixing the terms of office of Party officials (one-year terms for members of the Central, Provincial, County, and District Executive Committees, and of the Central Supervisory Committee; six months for members of the sub-district Supervisory Committees);

5. the authorization of the Central Executive Committee to establish Party organizations in Special Areas (Inner Mongolia, municipalities, townships, and overseas Chinese communities), and to set up its Executive Headquarters wherever it may choose; and

6. the authorization of the Party's "supreme headquarters", i.e., the National Party Congress, to interpret the constitution if the need arises.

At first glance these changes may seem rather inconsequential; but a careful comparison of the two versions, keeping in mind the controversy surrounding the reorganization scheme at the time, would indicate otherwise. It will be recalled that the initial planning for the reorganization took place in Canton, where Sun Yat-sen worked closely with Borodin and a small group of Sun's intimate associates. There was no Party-wide consultation; even the scope of the reorganization was not made known to the general membership until the draft Constitution was published on November 25, 1923, when the reorganization plan had already begun to be implemented. [3] The Central Cadre Council (zhongyang ganbu huiyi) in Shanghai, the highest governing body of the Kuomintang at the time, was not privy to the substance of the reorganization plan. In the absence of any official communication from Canton, it was the Council which took the initiative to seek clarification of reorganization plans.

Xie Chi, on behalf of the Council, cabled Sun Yat-sen on October 13, 1923, asking whether the Council was still authorized to call meetings. Sun replied the next day in the affirmative. [4] On the following day, the Council sent another cable to seek information as to the future status of the existing Kuomintang Constitution and the possibility of new appointments in Shanghai under the reorganization plan. Sun Yat-sen replied two days later that the Party Constitution would be revised: indeed it would be extensively revised and enlarged. As to new appointments, he said there would be none. [5] Apparently, the Council was anxious to have the rumored changes either confirmed or denied. Sun's cable confirmed their fears. Worse still, in another cable dated November 7, Sun ordered the dissolution of the Central Cadre Council and the Party's Shanghai Headquarters in preparation for the establishment of a new Executive Headquarters in that city in accordance with the new Constitution. [6] The next day the Council met in a special session. The chief topic of discussion was communist membership in the Kuomintang. [7] The consensus was that there should not be "a party within a party," for it would be one thing to admit communists into the Party as individuals, but another thing altogether if the reorganization were to be used as a means to help promote the Chinese Communist Party. It was important, in their view, that the two parties preserve their own individual identities. The Council adopted no plan for action at the meeting, pending a personal report by Tan

Pingshan on the reorganization. [8] On November 23, the Council discussed this question again at its regularly scheduled meeting. It is clear from the discussion that followed that the Council had by then learned about the substance of the drafts of the reorganization manifesto and the Constitution. [9] Zhang Ji voiced his concern regarding the proposed "anti-imperialism" and "anti-militarism" planks of the Party platform saying that "there must be priorities in what we do. If we do what the socialists advocate, that is, to oppose the militarists at home, on the one hand, and to fight the international imperialists, on the other, there are bound to be doubts and confusion because there will be many practical difficulties [in the implementation of that policy]," meaning that the Kuomintang would stand isolated both at home and abroad. Zhang Qiubai warned of the pitfalls of the proposed election system. "If elections take place everywhere following the reorganization", he said, "[the consequences] will be detrimental to the founding spirit of our Party," that is, it would negate Sun Yat-sen's authority to make appointments. Peng Sumin, another Council member, was skeptical as to whether the Chinese communists would follow the Kuomintang's lead, because "the socialists have their own principles." The Council resolved that Canton should be apprised of the Council's reservations on these points.

When Liao Zhongkai met with the Council on December 9 in Shanghai, his purpose was to calm their fears and to secure their support for the reorganization effort. He told the Council of the Party's dire need to strengthen its organization in order to broaden its base of support. He maintained that the Party had only upper-level members and no lower-level cadres to carry out its work. The lack of mass support had made the Party totally dependent upon the army, and the army had on repeated occasions turned against the Party in pursuit of its own interests. This, he said, was the main cause of the Party's failure to seize power in the past. It was imperative, therefore, that the Party free itself from military control and build itself up into a political force strong enough to control its own destiny. He warned the Council that "to insist on a limited number of upper-level cadres waging a spiritual struggle, as has been the case in the past, would be totally inadequate to meet the task at hand." He went on to describe the reorganizational work that had already been carried out in Canton, including plans to train a politically in-doctrinated Party army, and he presented a brief outline of the proposed organization of the Party. [10]

It is interesting to note that in his meeting with the Council, Liao did not directly address the question of communist membership in the Kuomintang. The closest he came to it was when he said "those who join the Party must do so as individuals and not as a group... The fact that the army units which attacked the Presidential Office were the same army units which had joined the Party earlier as a group attests to the necessity of this requirement." [11] Apparently, the statement was meant to reassure the Council that Sun Yat-sen was not unaware of the inherent danger of having "a party within a party" and was therefore admitting Chinese communists into the Kuomintang only as individuals. Even more remarkable is the fact that no one at the meeting questioned Liao Zhongkai further on this matter. The record shows that the only questions raised were those concerning the mechanics of setting up a Provisional Shanghai Party Executive Headquarters for the purpose of preparing for the election of delegates to the National Party Congress scheduled for the following January; the election procedures; and the possibility of postponing the National Party Congress so as to allow more time for the election of delegates. It seems likely that Liao had succeeded, at least temporarily, prior to his meeting with the Council, in bringing the Council members into line on the question on communist membership in the Kuomintang. Liao had arrived in Shanghai on November 29, nine days before his meeting with the Council took place. It is reasonable to assume that he had used the time to meet with the Council members individually to present Sun Yat-sen's argument for the reorganization. What actually transpired at these meetings cannot be documented, but it is safe to speculate that Liao had conveyed Sun's personal assurances that he had no intention of letting the communists take over the Party and that senior members of the Kuomintang would remain in control. For it can scarcely be coincidental that four members of the Central Cadre Council — Dai Jitao, Ye Chucang, Ju Zheng, and Ding Weifen — subsequently became members of the First Central Executive Committee at the National Party Congress, while two others — Peng Sumin and Zhang Qiubai — became alternates, and three more — Deng Zeru, Xie Chi and Zhang Ji — became members of the First Central Supervisory Committee. It is also significant to note that only three communists — Tan Pingshan, Li Dazhao, and Yu Shude — were elected to the 24-member Central Executive Committee, and the 17 alternates included just six communists — Lin Zuhan, Mao Zedong, Yu Fangzhou, Qu Qiubai, Han Linfu, and Zhang Guotao. No communists were elected either as standing members of the 5-member Central Supervisory Committee, or as the Committee's five alternate members. [12]

In Canton itself, anti-communist sentiment was also strong. The eleven members of the Kuomintang Guangdong Provincial Headquarters, headed by Deng Zeru — a Party veteran who had been a principal fund-raiser for Sun Yat-sen in Southeast Asia for many years and had been appointed earlier by Sun as co-convener, with Liao Zhongkai, of a special conference on the reorganization — petitioned Sun on November 29 to express their serious concern over the direction the reorganization was heading. [13] In the petition, they raised a number of questions concerning the dark prospect of a communist take-over of the Kuomintang if the reorganization took place as planned. While not taking issue with the reorganization as such (they described the idea as Sun's "sovereign and incisive decision"), they questioned the communists' motives in joining the Kuomintang and the alleged masterminding by the communists of the implementation of the reorganization plan. They maintained that the drafting of the new Party Constitution and the Party platform by Borodin would not have mattered greatly by itself were it not for the fact the "his draft was actually prepared by the Chinese Communist Party under Chen Duxiu's guidance." They asserted that Chen Duxiu, having once denounced the Kuomintang and Sun Yat-sen as "obsolete", and the Three People's Principles and the Five-Power Constitution as without any theoretical foundation, was now leading the Chinese communists to join the Kuomintang only out of ulterior motives. "The ultimate purpose of the Chinese Communist Party," the petitioners alleged, was "to place in the body of the Kuomintang a communist soul" and "to subject the Kuomintang to communist control." They urged Sun Yat-sen not to fall into this trap. While attacking the Chinese communists, the protesters were careful not to implicate the Soviet Union explicitly. "We are not certain if the Soviet Union is acting in concert with the Chinese communists," they stated. But they were convinced that the Chinese Communist Party was taking full advantage of the favorable atmosphere created by the Canton-Moscow entente to arouse a desire to reorganize the Party so that the Kuomintang might be made a communist captive. Finally, they warned of the dangers inherent in the proposed election system. They noted that, according to the draft Constitution, the position of the Party's *zong*li would become an elective office. "With changed circumstances, Chen Duxiu may very well be elected zongli in five years." As for making other high Party office also elective posts, they argued that this would be contrary to the established practice of filling these positions by appointment and would therefore deny the Party leader the opportunity of sifting the wheat from the chaff in considering candidates. The elective system, they maintained, would open the floodgates of inferior representation and become easily susceptible to manipulation. They did suggest, however, placing restrictions on the election system if it must be adopted. Here they proposed a primary and a final election, with the number of candidates elected in the primary to be larger than the number of positions to be filled, so that

Sun Yat-sen might nominate his own choices from these names and present them for the final election. "In this way, any attempt to manipulate and control the elections would be effectively frustrated." The petitioners emphasized that since "artful villains" were plotting to destroy the Kuomintang, it was imperative that their "trickery" be exposed. The consequences would be too grave for the Party not to guard against them.

Sun Yat-sen, however, did not share these fears. He was supremely confident that party discipline would be sufficient to check communist misbehavior and that he could effectively "adopt the best features in the Soviet system while avoiding its evils." [14] He sharply rebuked the petitioners on the same day the petition was submitted. In his marginal comments on the petition, he answered the major points raised by the dissidents. [15] He said that Chen Duxiu had no part in drafting the new Constitution, and dismissed Chen's earlier denunciation of him and the Kuomintang as an expression of "bigotry" and the result of "the excessive adoration young Chinese students have for the Russian Revolution." He offered his own assessment of the Chinese communists' motives in joining the Kuomintang. "They wanted to monopolize Russian friendship and prevent Russia from dealing with our Party, hoping to monopolize Russian aid and to compete with our Party as an independent unit..., but the Russians disagreed with them, corrected them on our behalf, and ordered them to join the Kuomintang for the purpose of acting in unison with us... If Russia wants to cooperate with China, she must cooperate with our Party and not with Chen Duxiu. If Chen disobeys our Party, he will be ousted." On the respective merits of the appointive and the elective systems, he emphasized that the question was not whether the proposed election system was perfect, but rather whether there was a need to democratize the Party. "The Principle of Democracy（minquan zhuyi）is rooted in the election system. If we 'give up eating for fear of choking,' would we not be opposing the very principle in which we profess belief? If we are concerned about possible abuse of the system, then everyone should do his best to struggle against such abuses and not shirk his responsibility. Whenever abuses are discovered, they should be brought out in the open immediately. From now on, I will meet with you every other week so that if such problems arise, we may deal with them collectively." He left this admonition with the dissenters: "Our Party has been backsliding ever since the beginning of our Revolution. Why is it so? It is because we do not seek improvements in our way of doing things." [16]

Meanwhile, overseas Chinese reaction to the news of the reorganization was also swift. There was strong opposition, among the Party's overseas branches, to admitting communists into the Kuomintang. Chen Yaoyuan, head of the Kuomintang's San Francisco branch, the Party's main headquarters in the United States, warned in a letter to Canton against the dangers of communism and of Kuomintang emulating the Soviet system. According to Sun Yat-sen, other communications were also received, inquiring whether the Kuomintang was being reorganized into a communist party, and expressing disapproval of such a move. [17] In the face of this kind of reaction from overseas Chinese, who had been the Kuomintang's main financial contributors, the Party acted quickly. The Provisional Central Executive Committee discussed Chen Yaoyuan's letter at its 22nd meeting on January 3, 1924, presided over personally by Sun Yat-sen. The Committee resolved that a reply was in order, and approved a draft which said in part that "the communistic system as adopted by Russia at the beginning of the Russian Revolution was indeed different from the Three People's Principles. However, Russia has now adopted the New Economic Policy, an equivalent to state socialism, which is the same as the Three People's Principles of our Party. Therefore, it is not that we are imitating Russia, but rather it is Russia that is imitating us." [18]

While there is no evidence to suggest that the dissent at home and abroad at this time was a single, coordinated effort, the dissenters were, in a sense, united insofar as their opposition to collaborating with the Chinese communists was concerned. The question was, given Sun Yat-sen's commitment to the collaboration policy, to what extent their opposition could be translated into meaningful action without challenging Sun Yat-sen's leadership. The First National Party Congress provided the opportunity for the dissidents to map out a strategy for a concerted move. That strategy, as it unfolded, was one of accommodation, but with heavy emphasis on the containment of the Chinese communists in Kuomintang affairs. They chose the revision of the Party Constitution as the primary means to achieve this goal.

It will be recalled that the Congress had appointed a committee of nineteen to study the proposed Party Constitution drafted by Borodin. [19] Excepting three communists — Tan Pingshan, Li Dazhao, and Mao Zedong — the committee members were senior Kuomintang figures, including six from the Central Cadre Council and one (Deng Zeru) from the Kwangtung Provincial Headquarters. [20] None of the sixteen Kuomintang members, except Liao Zhongkai, who was a prime mover behind the reorganization, can be considered staunch supporters of the policy of collaboration with the communists. Thus, it was this group of senior Kuomintang leaders around whom the dissenters rallied, and it was they who worked behind the scenes to ensure that the revised Constitution would include provisions to prevent any possible communist ascendancy within the Party. It is argued here that they adopted this strategy because they knew the limits of what they could accomplish, given the constraints of and Sun Yat-sen's commitment to the Canton-Moscow alliance. They knew they could not press their demands beyond the point at which the demands contravened the basic requirement of the alliance, that is, the creation of a national revolutionary movement in collaboration with the communists, Russian and Chinese. This was the framework within which they had to make their move. The alternative would be complete disavowal of the Canton-Moscow entente and an open rebellion against Sun Yat-sen's leadership, which they could not seriously contemplate. The subsequent revisions and additions written into the final version of the Constitution can best be understood in this context.

The addition of the Preamble served notice to all concerned that the ideological foundation of the Kuomintang, the reorganization notwithstanding, was to remain Sun Yat-sen's Three People's Principles and the Five-Power Constitution he had designed for a national government, and that this was to be guaranteed through constitutional sanction. The designation of Sun Yat-sen as the Party's *zongli* without election (in the original version the *zongli* was to be elected by the National Party Congress), and the investment in him of the extraordinary power to veto the decisions of both the National Party Congress and the Central Executive Committee, made him the absolute ruler of the Party. (The original version merely provides that the *zongli* shall be the Chairman of the Central Executive Committee.) This change apparently was made to afford Sun Yat-sen all the necessary constitutional means to deal with the perceived communist threat to the Kuomintang. In the same context, the change of the name of the "Auditing Committee" to "Supervisory Committee," with authority to investigate the policies and performance of Party members serving in the government, can also be interpreted as a means to check communist activism in governmental affairs. Viewed in this way, the fixing of terms of office for Party officials and the authority given the Central Executive Committee to establish Party organizations on local levels and in Special Areas were also precautionary measures to minimize local communist activism and influence. For it means that elected officials must be held accountable for their conduct in office and can be replaced at the end of their relatively short terms, and that the Kuomintang must not cede to the Chinese communists the opportunity of controlling grass-roots Party organizations. Finally, as an added precaution, the right to interpret the Constitution was to be reserved for the "highest Party headquarters," meaning the National Party Congress, where

Kuomintang members were expected to constitute the majority（more than one-half of the delegates to the First National Party Congress were to be appointed by Sun Yat-sen）.

Given this attempt to limit communist influence within the Kuomintang, the question naturally arises as to why Borodin and the Chinese communists did not oppose it. The answer must be found elsewhere. It will be remembered that the Chinese Communist Party was originally split on the question of joining the Kuomintang, and that it was only after the Communist International directed it to do so that it fell in line. [21] The Communist International's rationale was that the Kuomintang was "the only serious national-revolutionary group in China," and in as much as the "independent workers' movement" in the country was still too weak to wage a struggle against "the imperialists and their domestic feudal agents," a "coordinated action is necessary between the Kuomintang and the young Chinese Communist Party. Therefore, it is expedient for the members of the CCP to remain within the Kuomintang." But the Communist International also warned that "membership in the Kuomintang should not be purchased at the price of effacement of the specific political characteristics of the CCP." [21] Thus, when the Chinese Communist Party met at its Third National Congress in June 1923, it adopted a resolution directing all its members to join the Kuomintang, using the same arguments put forth by the Communist International, and with further emphasis on the fact that "it is very difficult, under the existing conditions, to establish a larger and more revolutionary party than the Kuomintang. Even if it were possible to do so, the result would be the dispersion of the national revolutionary force." It exhorted its members to "endeavor to extend the Kuomintang organization throughout China, and gather all the revolutionary elements within the Kuomintang in order to meet the needs of China's national revolution." [22] The basic premise here is that the Chinese Communist Party, then in existence for only two years, needed the Kuomintang as a means to organize the masses and thereby extend its own influence in the Chinese national revolutionary movement. [23] As explained in slightly different terms by Borodin soon after his arrival in Canton, the Chinese communists, by joining the Kuomintang, would be working not only for the stabilization of the Kuomintang, by also for the stabilization of the Chinese Communist Party. [24] "In the press I spoke of the Kuomintang," he said, "but to us it means that I was speaking of the eventual increase of the influence of the Communist Party." [25] Time therefore was of the essence. Communist success in China depended upon the establishment and preservation of a strong and viable Kuomintang through which the Chinese Communist Party could extend its influence among the masses. With the exception of the question of dual party membership, of which Li Dazhao, on behalf of the Chinese Communist Party, gave a spirited and eloquent defense at the First National Party Congress of the Kuomintang, and won his point, the Chinese communists, having committed themselves to a policy of collaboration with the Kuomintang and with a view to the long-term benefits such a policy would bring to their cause, apparently felt that the stakes were too high for them to stage a fight over the revision issue. [26]

For Borodin, the building up of a "powerful movement of the Chinese people," as Chicherin had earlier advised Sun Yat-sen, was the fundamental aim of his mission. The implementation of the Kuomintang reorganization as the means to generate that movement was, therefore, of paramount importance. It did not take Borodin long to confirm his belief that Sun Yat-sen was the only person who could make the reorganization a success. Shortly after his arrival in Canton in October, he told a gathering of Kuomintang members that "in the Kuomintang there is a nationalist leader—Dr. Sun Yat-sen—who is capable of uniting China and can, with the support of the people, free China from the shackles of foreign imperialists and domestic warlords." [27]

Two months later, Borodin was able to report to Moscow that "at this point, my relations with Sun are such that I am able to talk with him in complete openness about his affairs. In the matter of reorganizing the Kuomintang, I was able to show him our intentions and to promise him real support. In all undertakings, I underlined the extreme importance of the leadership role of Sun Yat-sen in the national revolutionary movement in China, and with this I pointed out to him our desire to strengthen his position of leadership." [28]

He concluded by saying that "I do not propose to reorganize without Sun." [29] Thus, whether Sun Yat-sen was designated as the *zongli* in the Constitution or whether he was given veto power over the decisions of the National Party Congress and the Central Executive Committee probably mattered less to Borodin than the opportunity to proceed with the restructuring of the Kuomintang from which the Chinese Communist Party could eventually benefit. For as far as Borodin was concerned, he knew Sun was to be the leader in any case. Whether this was confirmed by the Constitution or not was of secondary importance. This central question not being an issue, all the other revisions written into the final version of the Constitution apparently became even more irrelevant to him and the Chinese Communist Party.

This whole episode serves to illustrate one basic point in coalition politics. That is, how to maintain the equilibrium of an uneasy and compromise alliance in which the most extreme party always tended to dominate. [30] Domination by the communists was the fear of the Kuomintang dissidents, which led them to seek constitutional guarantees against the perceived communist threat. But the interaction between the Kuomintang's need for Soviet assistance, on the one hand, and a determination not to share power with the communists, on the other, produced a sense of ambivalence on the part of the Kuomintang dissidents toward the entire reorganization experiment. That ambivalence was to remain at the heart of Kuomintang's intra-party politics during the next few years until the communists were purged from the Party.

Notes

This paper was published in the *Proceedings of the Conference on the 80th Anniversary of the Founding of the Republic of China* (Taipei: Jindai Zhongguo chubaneshe, 1991), v.1, pp. 71-87.

[1]　See Sun Yat-sen's marginal notes written on *Tan he gongchandang liang da yao an* (Two Proposals for the Impeachment of the Communist Party) ([Canton], 1927). This is a facsimile reproduction of the original manuscript. A printed version can be found in Zhonghua minguo shiliao yanjiu zhongxin (Center for Research Materials on the Republic of China), comp., *Zhongguo guomindang di yi ci quanguo daibiao dahui shiliao zhuanji* (A Collection of Documents of the First National Party Congress of the Kuomintang) (Taipei, 1984), pp. 521-522. A partial English translation is available in Conrad Brandt, Benjamin I. Schwartz, and John K. Fairbank, *A Documentary History of Chinese Communism* (Cambridge, MA, 1959), pp. 72-73.

[2]　The Chinese translation of the original Borodin draft was first published in *Guomindang zhoukan* (Kuomintang Weekly), no. 1 (Nov. 25, 1923), pp. 2-3. The weekly was the official Kuomintang organ published in Canton. The first issue was discovered by the author at the Toyo Bunko in Tokyo. Although this translation was reprinted in *Xiangdao zhoubao* (Guide Weekly), no. 50 (Dec. 29, 1923), pp. 384-388, it has received little attention by scholars working on the history of the Kuomintang. The text of the final adopted version is available in a number of documentary collections, including *Geming wenxian* (Documents of the Revolution) published in Taipei by the Committee for the Compilation of Party Historical Materials of the Central Executive Committee of the Kuomintang, VIII, pp. 1136-1148.

[3]　The draft Constitution was published in *Guomindang zhoukan*, cited in note 3 above. Prior to its publication, Sun Yat-sen had appointed Borodin as "Instructor in Organization" to the Kuomintang on October 18, 1923, twelve days after Borodin's arrival in Canton. On Oct. 19, Sun sent a brief cable to the Central Cadre Council in Shanghai merely informing them of his appointment of a Reorganization Commission composed of Liao Zhongkai, Wang Jingwei, Zhang Ji, Dai Jitao, and Li Dazhao (*Guo fu quanji* [Complete Works of Sun Yat-sen] [Taipei, 1961], IV, p. 433). On October 24, he commissioned Liao Zhongkai and Deng Zeru as co-conveners of a special conference on the reorganization (*ibid.*, V, p. 559). The following day he appointed a Provisional Central Executive Committee consisting of nine

regular and five alternate members to prepare ground for the reorganization, with Borodin as Advisor (*Guofu nianpu* [Chronological Biography of Sun Yat-sen] [Taipei, 1965], II, p. 963).

[4] The text of the Council's cable is not available. Sun's reply, however, makes clear what must have been the Council's concerns. The text of Sun's cable is found in *Guofu quanji*, p. 433.

[5] The text of the Council's cable is not available. However, Sun's reply (*ibid.*) leaves no doubt as to the cable's contents.

[6] *Guofu quanji*, IV, p. 437.

[7] Minutes of this meeting are kept at the Kuomintang Archives in Taipei, under the title *Zhongyang ganbu huiyi jilu*(Minutes of the Central Cadre Council), 1923, v. 4 (no. 418/9).

[8] Apparently, Sun Yat-sen had intended to send Tan Pingshan, a communist who had joined the Kuomintang earlier that year, to Shanghai to meet with the Council. However, it was Liao Zhongkai who was eventually given this assignment, most likely because of the anti-communist sentiments among the Council members.

[9] The following account is taken from the minutes of the meeting on Nov. 23, see *Zhongyang ganbu huiyi jilu, op. cit.*

[10] *Ibid.* The minutes of this meeting are also reproduced in *Geming wenxian*, VIII, pp. 1084-1087.

[11] Liao was obviously referring to Chen Jiongming and his troops, who had attacked Sun Yat-sen's office in June 1922.

[12] For a complete list of names, see *Geming wenxian*, VIII, p. 1105.

[13] See note 2. The following is taken from this source.

[14] Zou Lu, *Zhongguo guomindang shigao* (A Draft History of the Kuomintang) (Chongqing, 1944), I, p. 391, note 4.

[15] See note 2.

[16] Sun Yat-sen's speech to the National Party Congress on January 21, 1924. See *Guofu quanji*, III, p. 354.

[17] The text of Chen's letter is not available. However, the Committee's reply makes clear what must have been the letter's contents. See minutes of the 22nd meeting of the Provisional Central Executive Committee, *Guomindang zhoukan*, no. 7 (January 6, 1924), p. 5. The Committee's reply is also reproduced in *Guofu nianpu*, II, pp. 988-989.

[18] For a list of the members, sec *Zhongguo guomindang quanguo daibiao dahui huiyi lu* (Proceedings of the National Party Congress of Representatives of the Kuomintang) (Canton? 1924?), 19. The Proceedings are reproduced in *Zhongguo guomindang "yi da" shilia zhuanji* (A Collection of Historical Materials on the First National Party Congress of

the Kuomintang), a special issue of *Guangdong wenshi ziliao* (Historical Materials on Guangdong), no. 42 (July 1984), pp. 1-94.

[19] The six were Xie Chi, Dai Jitao, Ju Zheng, Mao Zuquan, Ding Weifen, and Yu Youren.

[20] For a discussion of this point, see Xiao Sheng and Jiang Huaxuan, "Di yi ci guogong hezuo tongyi chanxian di xingcheng" (The Formation of the First Kuomintang-Communist United Front), in Zhu Chengjia, ed., *Zhonggong dangshi yanjiu lunwen xuan* (Selected Essays on the History of the Chinese Communist Party) (Changsha, 1983), pp. 396-399. This article was originally published in *Lishi yanjiu* (Historical Studies), no. 2, 1981 (Apr. 15, 1981), pp. 51-68.

[21] See "Resolution of the ECCI on the Expected Attitude of the Chinese Communist Party Toward the Kuomintang, January 12, 1923" in Xenia Joukoff Eudin and Robert C. North, *Soviet Russia and the East, 1920-1927: A Documentary Survey* (Stanford, 1957), pp. 343-344. For a Chinese translation, see *Gongchan guoji youguan zhongguo geming di wenxian ziliao*, 1919-1928, ti-i chi (Collection of Communist International Documents Concerning the Revolution in China, 1919-1928, Part I) (Beijing, 1981), pp. 76-77.

[22] See "Zhongguo gongchandang di san ci quanguo daibiao dahui jueyi an ji xuanyan" (Resolutions and Manifesto of the Third National Congress of the Chinese Communist Party) reproduced in "*Er da*" he "*San da*": *Zhongguo gongchandang di er, san ci daibiao dahui ziliao xuanpian* (The Second and Third National Congress of the Chinese Communist Party: A Selection of Documents) (Beijing, 1985), pp. 181-182.

[23] For an elaboration of this point, see C. Martin Wilbur and Julia Lien-ying Howe, *Missionaries of Revolution: Soviet Advisors and Nationalist China, 1920-1927* (Cambridge, MA, 1989), pp. 82-85, and Benjamin I. Schwartz, *Chinese Communism and the Rise of Mao* (Cambridge, MA, 1961), pp. 47-50.

[24] N. Mitarevsky, *World-Wide Soviet Plots* (Tianjin, [1927]), p. 133.

[25] *Ibid.*

[26] The full text of Li Dazhao's speech can be found in *Geming wenxian*, IX, pp. 1243-1254, A partial translation is available in Chiang Kai-shek, *Soviet Russia in China: A Summing Up at Seventy* (New York, 1957), pp. 26-28.

[27] A. I. Cherapanov, *Zhongguo guomingeming jun di beifa: yige zhu hua junshi guwen di zaji* (The Northern Expedition of the National Revolutionary Army of China: Notes of a Military Advisor) (Beijing, 1984), p. 36. This is a Chinese translation of *Severnyi Pok-hod Natsional'no Revoliutsionno Armiie Kitaya* (Zapiski Voennogo Sovetnika) (Moscow, 1976).

[28] A. I. Kartunova, "Sun Yat-sen i Russkie Sovetniki. Po Documentam 1923-1924" (Sun Yat-sen and the Russian Advisors. Based on Documents of 1923-1924), in *Sun Yat-sen 1866-1966. K Stoletiyu So Dnya Rozhdeniya: Sbornik Statei, Vospominanii Materialov* (Sun Yat-sen 1866-1966. For the 100th Anniversary of His Birth: A Collection of Essays, Reminiscences, and Materials) (Moscow, 1966), p. 181.1 am indebted to Mrs. Deidra Deamer for a translation.

[29] *Ibid.*

[30] Maurice Duverger, *Political Parties, Their Organization and Activity in a Modem State*, translated by Barbara and Robert North (New York: 1966), p. 347.

異議處理

國民黨改組後黨內早期反共暗潮

　　雖然國民黨第一次全國代表大會通過了共產黨黨員可以以個人身分參加國民黨，黨內反對這個政策的還不乏其人。反共者對共產黨之動機已深存懷疑。共產黨員加入國民黨後之各種活動，以及共產黨對其在國民黨內的黨員在一密件中提出要他們保持他們的政治獨立性，和通過國民黨來發展共產黨的要求，更加深了他們的疑慮。[1] 新設立的中央監察委員會委員張繼與謝持，遂成為反共先鋒。孫中山先生當時雖然能控制這種對黨內團結帶來的威脅，使其並無大害，卻從未能將這個疑慮的根本原因消除，那就是對共產黨控制國民黨的畏懼。這種持久的畏懼遂成為孫中山先生逝世後黨內的分裂，以及最後清黨的前兆。本篇論文將分析孫中山先生及其親信如何處理國民黨1924年改組後黨內的反共暗潮，以處理彈劾在國民黨內的共產黨黨員事件為討論的重點。

　　國民黨1924年1月召開第一次全國代表大會以後，香港和上海的報紙幾乎同時就有對孫中山先生容共的敵對言論。香港《華字日報》在當年2月15-28日間發表了一系列的消息「揭露」國民黨與共產黨的勾結，並指控孫中山與國民黨向共產黨屈服。[2] 2月29日頗具影響力的上海《新聞報》駐廣州的記者報導，自從國民黨新章程容許「跨黨」以來，多數國民黨元老，如胡漢民、廖仲愷、鄒魯及汪精衛，均已加入共產黨，因之，國民黨中央執行委員半數已為共產黨員。兩位資深國民黨黨員，馮自由及謝英伯，以國民黨已被共產黨取代為由請求退黨而被孫中山威脅由廣州驅逐出境。又報導，孫中山先生的長期追隨者，廣州鹽務局局長趙世瑾曾警告孫先生切勿加入共產黨，否則將會辭職並退黨。黨內反共氣焰之高，該報還報導，甚至時任廣州市長，孫中山的兒子，被稱為「太子派」領袖和資本家代表孫科，也在考慮用他私人財產四百萬元來建立一個新的政黨來和他的父親對抗。[3]

　　儘管在這些報導中只有一項是有些根據以外，那就是孫中山要把馮自由從廣州驅逐出境的威脅，這些聳人聽聞的報導在國民黨的領導層仍然引起了極大地不安。[4] 3月4日國民黨上海執行部發表聲明，逐點反駁《新聞報》的報導，並呼籲應以國民黨的言行來判斷它。[5] 同時，在廣州的中央執行委員會也迅速採取行動來消除這些囂張的謠言以爭取支持。在3月15日召開的第14次會議上，中央執行委員會通過了兩件告黨員書，並於次日分別發表為中央執行委員會通告第23號及第24號。[6] 從這兩個文件中可以明白地看出，孫中山及中執會向反共黨員及共產黨員一併提出警告，說他們必須嚴守黨紀，任何對黨內團結有害的活動都一律禁止。所有黨員必須停止內訌以致力於革命大業。通告第23號明確地禁止任何與國民黨無關的組織在其名稱上盜用國民黨的名義，如有黨員牽連，當以章程規定嚴辦。孫中山手擬的通告24號闡明了國民黨對黨員個人活動與黨的集體利益的立場。其中稱革命尚未成功的主要原因之一就是黨員對其與黨的關係缺乏認識。黨員有義務遵循黨的政策，不能參與任何損害黨的集體利益的活動。個人行動必須與黨的行動一致。犧牲個人自由就是保證黨的自由。他告誡黨員必須遵守三民主義，在國民黨第一次全國代表大會宣言的基礎上實行黨的政策，並隨時把人民的福利作為依歸。這個通告最後又提到黨改組的唯一原因就是要建立一個組織緊密有真正實權的政黨來推進國民革命。要達到這個目標全賴於黨員的個人努力。如無統一的目標，黨員各自行其是，改組的工作就歸於全功盡棄。果真如此，不難得到有些人是別有用心地來加入國民黨的結論。最後這一點很明顯地是為共產黨員而發，同時也有對黨內持異議的人士帶來安撫的作用，表明孫中山不會容忍共產黨員在國民黨內的不當行為。

　　從另外一個文件中也可看出當時國民黨領導對黨內異議及其對黨的將來的影響的關注。那就是中央執行委員宣傳部在同月（3月）發布的一篇長文，說明國民黨政策與共產主義的異同。[7] 該文主要的論點就是國民黨政策與蘇聯所追求的政策的唯一相似點就是雙方都認同國家社會主義的原則。雖然國民黨的改組抄襲蘇聯共產黨的委員會制度而改變了黨的組織結構，但並沒有在任何方面改變了黨的原則或黨的工作。以個人身分加入國民黨的共產黨黨員的目的是為國民革命的成功效力。因之，他們成為黨的一分子不能認為是對國民黨的威脅，或國民黨已成為共產黨。畢竟，這個文件指出，國民黨在1912年以前接受了無政府主義者入黨，也並沒有把國民黨變為無政府主義者。這個文件又以英國勞工黨勝選為例：一向被稱為社會主義或布爾塞維克的勞工黨，並沒有導致英國失去了個人自由，產權私有，皇室制度，或大英帝國。這份文件力勸黨員及中國人民不要為對國民黨的不實指控所迷惑，而必須緊密團結來迎接完成國民革命成功的挑戰。

　　孫中山及中央執行委員會對反共異議的處理，從開始就表現了高度的政治技能與機智。他們選擇解釋和說服的方式來代替壓制。他們很明顯地指出國民黨最高的任務是國民革命的順利完成。要達到此目的，黨的團結至關重要。任何黨內的分裂只有加害於黨而不能達到黨的最終目的。

　　雖然對國民黨的挑戰來自右派，黨中央也必須要應付來自左派的壓力。當持異議者在預測大禍臨頭以及倡議從國民黨中開除共產黨員時，左派人士歸罪國民黨未用黨紀來處理引起黨內分裂的右派。有一個事件就是個恰當的例子。廣州一位黨員陳覺先於1924年4月呈文中執會要求處罰在海外散布謠言說國民黨已變為共產黨的馮自由與謝英伯。[8] 他的理由是馮、謝和他們的同夥因為黨的改組不能再把持黨務，故而轉向誹謗國民黨以冀維持其個人利益。因之，為黨的團結起見，他認為此種反黨行為絕不能姑息，馮、謝必須加以紀律制裁以警他人。兩周後，4月18日中執會把他的呈文轉交中央監察委員會調查處理。[9] 4月28日中央監察委員會覆函中執會，稱此案因無證據，應予撤銷。[10] 中央監察委員會的決定是基於技術上的原因。他們說陳覺先未能指定馮、謝二人散布謠言的時間地點來支持他的控告，也沒有指明馮、謝二人散布謠言的對象，以及任何證人。只是說他有不實的反黨言論不能構成足夠的理由來考慮黨紀制裁。中央監察委員會又稱，該會對如此僅有薄弱證據的案件，通常都不予受理。但由於陳覺先指控的嚴重性，牽涉到黨的主要政策問題，故而同意審查，但發現陳的指控並無事實根據。中央監察委員會並懷疑這個呈文的真實性，稱因呈文中並無陳某人在廣州的地址，故無法與他面談，並且在廣州黨員錄內也沒有查到他的名字，因之該委員會建議此案應予撤銷。

中央執行委員會與中央監察委員會對此事的不同態度代表當時黨內對容共政策的主要分歧點。中央執行委員會有24位正式委員和17位候補委員，其中3位正式委員和7位候補委員為共產黨黨員，為中執會全體委員人數四分之一。所有候補委員均有參加中執會會議及投票的權利。[11] 因之，中執會無法忽視對任何黨所制定有關共產黨員政策的挑戰，雖然有些中執會中的國民黨黨員對那種政策還是有些保留。[12] 另外一方面，中央監察委員會的5位正式委員和5位候補委員都是資深的國民黨黨員，正式委員中3位──鄧澤如、張繼、謝持──從開始就反對讓共產黨員加入國民黨的政策。[13] 在這種情況下，不難理解為什麼在孫中山一個月以前已經親自宣告被控告者無罪後，中央執行委員會仍然決定將陳覺先的呈文交中央監察委員會處理，而為什麼中央監察委員會又會建議將此案撤銷。

黨領導中的意見分歧僅有助於此項爭議的蔓延。各省左右派的爭執也不斷發生。[14]

廣州氣氛緊張。國民黨廣州市市黨部執行委員會委員孫科與黃季陸於1924年6月1日向國民黨中央黨部提出彈劾共產黨員的呈文。[15] 另外一位國民黨資深黨員朱和中，也懇求孫中山調查及處罰國民黨在上海主辦的《國民日報》，為其發表由共產黨員執筆與國民黨政策相違背的鼓吹外蒙古獨立的文章。[16] 但是，真正攤牌的是鄧澤如、張繼，和謝持代表中央執行委員會於1924年6月引用共產黨文件來證明共產黨員加入國民黨的目的是要毀滅國民黨的時候。

所引用的文件有兩組：（1）《中國社會主義青年團第二次大會議決案及宣言》（1923年4月25日），附1923年6月共產黨第三次代表大會通過之《關於國民運動及國民黨問題的決議》；（2）《中國社會主義青年團團刊》（第7號）──1924年3月22日至4月1日中國社會主義青年團擴大執行委員會特號（4月11日發表）。這兩組文件都有關於共產黨員在國民黨中應有的工作及態度的特別指示。[17] 這兩組文件的發現讓反共人士得益匪淺，因為它們暴露了共產黨對國共關係所採取的戰略細節。[18]

《中國社會主義青年團第二次大會議決案及宣言》明確地指出「本團團員加入國民黨，當受本團各級執行委員會之指揮，但本團之各級執行委員會，當受中國共產黨及其各級執行委員會對於團員加入國民黨問題之種種指揮」。再者，在國民黨內，他們也必須保持獨立和秘密的青年團組織。1923年6月共產黨第三次代表大會通過之《關於國民運動及國民黨問題的決議》彰顯下面一點：「我們加入國民黨，但仍舊保存我們的組織，並須努力從各工人團體中，從國民黨左派中吸收真有階級覺悟的革命分子，漸漸擴大我們的組織，謹嚴我們的紀律，以立強大的群眾共產黨之基礎。」

中國社會主義青年團擴大執行委員會會議通過的另外兩個決議案：「關於國民黨工作及態度決議案」和「同志們在國民黨工作及態度決議案」。根據中國共產黨第三次代表大會的決議提供了具體的指示如何組織勞工、農民、學生和婦女。當這些文件強調發展與國民黨員的和諧關係的重要性時，共產黨員也被提醒說：「我們所認為必要事項，而國民黨不願用其名義活動的，仍作為本黨獨立的活動……在發展國民黨的組織之時，關於本黨組織之發展，當然也不能停止」。這些說法正是反共人士所渴望得到用來對抗孫中山的證據。張繼和謝持於是抓住了這個機會於6月初從上海到廣州，拉開了反對共產黨人成為國民黨黨員的積極鬥爭的序幕。

張繼6月14日在廣東高等師範學校一篇講演裡把這件事公開提出來。謝持也準備了一份交中央執行委員會討論的呈文。[19] 同日，張繼與于右任晉見孫中山，張指控共產黨人為其黨的利益正在顛覆國民黨。據稱，孫中山的回答是雖然第三國際可能並不可靠，但是他沒有理由去批評俄國人。那時，張繼給孫中山看當年5月31日中俄簽訂互相承認彼此為合法政府的《中俄解決懸案大綱協定》中第六條。[20] 該條稱「兩締約國政府互相擔任，在各該國境內，不准有為圖謀以暴力反對對方政府而成立之各種機關或團體之存在及舉動。並允諾，彼此不為與對方國公共秩序、社會組織相反之宣傳。」[21] 孫中山那時顯然還沒有見到此協定之全文，他對張繼說一俟鮑羅廷北上歸來後再議。[22]

　　張繼和謝持在廣州的出現和他們公開要彈劾共產黨人的號召，使國民黨和共產黨領導積極開始了一系列的活動。據稱，國民黨領導人——汪精衛、廖仲愷、戴季陶——和俄國顧問每日聚會商討迫在目睫的危機；共產黨領導人也日日在進行討論。[23]中央監察委員會委員廣西的李烈鈞為化解危機起見，邀宴國民黨左右派領導人共商黨事冀以消除歧見。被邀者有張繼、馮自由、孫科、汪精衛、胡漢民、廖仲愷及戴季陶。[24]李的此舉，或出於自動，或係孫中山指示，不得而知。所知者，此次聚會，並未達成任何結論。6月18日中央監察委員會五位委員中之三位，鄧澤如、張繼、謝持，正式向孫中山及中央執行員會提出呈文彈劾共產黨員。[25]

　　彈劾條款引用中國共產黨及中國社會主義青年團之各項決議案來證明共產黨員的不忠和顛覆意圖。他們要求此事應求根本解決，否則「不足以維持本黨之存在及發展。」鄧、張、謝也引用社會主義青年團團員在國民黨內領導支援的甫在北京簽訂的《中俄協定》活動，稱其等於承認北京政府為合法的中國政府，是對國民黨的理想一個致命的打擊。他們又引用一位共產黨員崔文成在國民黨上海的機關報《民國日報》上發表題為〈中國國民革命與無產階級〉的文章。該作者稱「無產階級由於他們參加國民革命會勇猛地要求一個無產階級革命，因為國民革命是一個不徹底的革命」。彈劾者認為在國民黨機關報上發表如此反國民黨的言論是自取毀滅，是把《民國日報》淪為共產黨的宣傳口舌。彈劾書中也把李大釗在國民黨第一次全國代表大會上所作的舉世聞名的共產黨對國民黨和國民革命效忠的誓言和現在發現的這些文件資料作了對比，來證明共產黨的「陰謀和欺詐」是如何地可怕和李大釗的誓言是如何地不可置信。彈劾者並指出共產黨在國民黨中央執行委員會上所占的席數和他們組織動員學生、婦女、農民、工人的活動來證明他們想把國民黨改變成共產黨形象的企圖。

　　值得注意的是提案人在彈劾書裡鄭重表明他們並非反對共產黨員以個人身分加入國民黨這個政策本身的問題，而是在他們所得到的文件裡發現共產黨員係以團體的實質參加，因之造成黨中有黨的現象，遂而成為對國民黨生存的嚴重威脅。由於在國民黨內的秘密組織和其他秘密活動,他們違背了黨的紀律,就喪失了他們的國民黨籍。彈劾書中說,縱然他們的活動不從黨的紀律立場而只從合作的立場來判斷的話,他們的行為已經破壞了合作的精神。因之,這些違法者必須懲辦,迅速根本解決爭議,否則其代價很可能就是國民黨本身的生存問題。

在鄧澤如、張繼和謝持心目中的根本解決辦法,當然是開除共產黨員,而終止國民黨與共產黨的合作政策。很顯然的,這樣重大的,代表與國民黨現行政策完全相反的路線絕對不會被孫中山所採納。在等待鮑羅廷回廣州期間,據說孫中山曾經說,允許共產黨員加入國民黨是蘇聯的建議,他們當然應該對後果負責。[26] 不過他仍然贊成中央執行委員會在6月19日召開特別會議討論彈劾事件。[27] 但該會並無任何結果。中執會共產黨員全部缺席,孫中山、胡漢民、戴季陶也沒有參加。[28] 當時國民黨領導中群情激奮,戴季陶在特別會議開會前夕,在一宴會中被張繼大罵,遂於開會數小時前離粵赴滬。[29] 報導又稱當晚張繼的言詞激烈憤怒,和他同簽彈劾書的鄧澤如也不得不阻止他作出更多的謾罵。[30]

鮑羅廷於6月22日返廣州。據稱,在當晚赴孫中山給他接風的宴會之前,他曾與共產黨員會晤。[31] 又據稱,在宴會中他提醒孫中山共產黨員加入國民黨的目的是為建立中蘇友好關係,為此,國民黨必須表示誠意,而不禁止中國共產黨的發展,否則俄國亦當別求蹊徑,以圖進展。[32] 當鮑羅廷這一席話傳出去之後,一般都認為他是影射除非中國共產黨能自行發展,蘇聯會與北京政府另行交涉。

孫中山當然是進退兩難。一方面他不能沒有蘇聯的協助而希望國民黨能執政,另一方面他也不能和黨內的反共分子完全分離而希望國民黨繼續成為一個有為的政黨。所以必須要有一個折衷的辦法。他採取的第一步就是安排提出彈劾的人和鮑羅廷談話。[33] 6月25日談話在鮑羅廷的寓所舉行,一共兩個半小時。參加的有張繼和謝持,孫科做翻譯,但是提議彈劾的另一個人鄧澤如並沒有參加。[34]

談話的中心環繞在國民黨內發展一個獨立的共產黨組織這個問題上。兩方的對答都很直率。談話結束後，彼此都沒有退讓。張繼和謝持的主要論點是黨中有黨不合理，不合適，對國民黨來說也是致命的，因為共產黨已經指明國民黨是他們鬥爭的目標。要是在國民黨內的共產黨員堅持要有他們的身分和組織，兩黨最好分道揚鑣。國民黨絕對不能容許在黨內存在另外一個組織。鮑羅廷則認為共產黨之所以必須要在國民黨內自己組織起來，是因為國民黨的領導沒有能力對付當前主要的問題。國民黨已死，只有新舊黨員之間的競爭才能夠刺激黨的發展與復活。何況，一個黨中分左右派是很自然的現象。國民黨中有這樣的現象可以產生一個中間派作為黨的中心。國共分開是不合適的事，因為那樣會使中國革命的實力分裂而犧牲中國的革命大業。再者，今日兩者本是互相利用，其結果會更多有利於國民黨。當然，用大多數投票國民黨可以把共產黨分出去，但是鮑羅廷說他希望事實不會發展到那個地步。

　　雖然這次的談話並沒有解決什麼問題，但是有一件事卻是極其明白。那就是，廣州和蘇聯的聯盟是否能夠繼續下去全賴於不僅共產黨員能夠加入國民黨，而他們在國民黨內也能夠獨立發展他們自己的組織。因之，國民黨對彈劾案件的處理，必須要在這個框架內進行。從黨內開除共產黨員是絕對不可能的事。任何處理的方式必須要以維護這個新興聯盟的發展為依歸。

　　一個建議是等國民黨第二次全國代表大會後再行處理彈劾案件。[35] 但未被孫中山採納。於是彈劾案件終於1924年7月3日在中央執行委員會的第40次會議上正式提出討論。經過激烈辯論後，得到以下三項決議：（1）需有國民黨對此事件表示態度的宣言，（2）召開中央執行委員會全體會議，（3）呈請總理決定。並推中執會委員汪精衛和邵元沖依據下列起草宣言：

> 以全國代表大會發表之宣言及政綱為準。凡入黨者，如具有革命決心及信仰三民主義之誠意者，不問其從前屬於何派，均照黨員待遇。有違背大會宣言及政綱者，均得以黨之紀律繩之。[36]

中執會於4日後7月7日通過宣言草案，經孫中山修改後，旋即發表。[37]

其大意為國民黨既負有中國革命之使命，即有集中全國革命分子之必要，對規範黨員之措施，惟以其言論行動，能否一依國民黨之主義政綱及黨章為斷。如有違背者必予以嚴重之制裁。黨員必須解除猜疑，奮勇直前，才不至使革命大業中斷。孫中山在宣言中對反共分子也有明確的批評。宣言中稱：

> 黨內黨外，間多誤會，以為加入本黨之共產黨人。其言論行動尚有分道而馳之傾向。於是反對派得藉此而肆其挑撥。同志間遂由懷疑而發生隔閡。社會群眾之莫明真相者，更覺無所適從，減少其同情或贊助全國革命之發展。

在這裡可以說是國民黨第一次全國代表大會關於共產黨員加入國民黨的辯論的重演。當時，國民黨領導在回應共產黨員加入國民黨會導致黨中有黨，而不利於國民黨的現象時，曾以國民革命的需要以及黨紀的神聖不可侵犯的理由為其政策辯護。現時黨的政策與當時黨的政策完全一致。很明顯的，這對提議彈劾的人士是個不祥之兆。孫中山是不想改變他和共產黨合作的政策的。

除此之外，還有些其他對彈劾案不利的因素。其中最重要的就是在廣州的其他的反共人士對彈劾案沒有回應。馮自由、謝英伯、劉成禺、徐清河等並沒有公開的支持彈劾案。先前已提議過彈劾案的孫科和黃季陸也是默默無聲。這和在上海和北京的情形大不相同。在那裡數百國民黨員簽呈中央執行委員會，要求嚴辦共產黨員。[38] 關於廣州保持沉寂的原因只能付諸猜想。首先，孫中山前些時候對馮自由等案件的處理，想必得到它預期的效果。[39] 很可能孫中山從馮自由和其他反對容共政策的人得到承諾，不得再有反對的言行來換取一個「無罪」的決定。其次，張繼和謝持似乎事先沒有和在廣州其他反共人士對彈劾案件作適當協調。顯然認為他們手上所持有的共產黨文件足夠能得到其他反共人士對他們彈劾案件的支持。當他們所期待的支持並沒出現時，他們似乎束手無策，不知道應該如何進行。同時，謝持在返廣州不久後即抱病。張繼雖然口若懸河，但是由於沒有追隨者終究無法掀起這個彈劾運動。[40]

最後，孫中山和他的親信好像在幕後也進行了一項有力的，為彈劾案釜底抽薪的說服工作。假如馮自由、謝英伯、劉成禺，和徐清河真正是為他們給孫中山的承諾而封口，很難解釋為什麼其他的以前支持他們的人也都沒有任何行動。彈劾案簽署人之一的馮自由在張繼、謝持和鮑羅廷會談的時候也沒有出席，他顯然也不認同張繼6月19日在中執會特別會議上所用的戰術。[41] 孫科不僅沒有支持彈劾運動，反而表示它對中央執行委員會的支持。在7月6日國民黨廣州特別市黨部成立典禮的時候，他宣布這個新的黨部是在中央執行委員會直接管轄之下，黨員必須接受中執會的管轄，去執行上級所交代的任務。無論在黨內或黨外都不能進行任何有損害黨的利益的活動。[42] 還值得注意的事就是在6月17日和7月4日劉成禺和謝英伯分別委派為孫中山軍事大本營的參事。[43]

孫中山可能用些什麼理由來使彈劾運動失掉支持？在檔案文獻中找不到答案。但是從他在這個時期的談話中，可以看出他處處強調蘇聯對國民黨援助的重要性，以及他深信假以時日國民黨可以將共產黨員轉變為民族主義者。如果不行，他可以用黨紀的制裁來有效地對付他們。[44] 從這個角度，孫中山是把這件事當作國民黨生死存亡的事來看，並且把他的個人聲望完全放在廣州與莫斯科聯盟的成果上。由於他的反共對手的命運和國民黨本身的命運是緊密在一起，難分難解的，所以我們有理由假設他們可能是同意孫中山的看法，那就是必須先救病人然後才能談到手術的問題。孫中山對他們的保證，說他自有辦法去處理任何共產黨的不妥協的姿態，使他們選擇了對孫中山政策的默許。

在彈劾運動的勢頭足夠冷卻後，國民黨遂決定召開中央執行委員全體會議，依據其7月7日的決議來解決這個爭議。同時，孫中山又處理另外兩件由於彈劾運動而更覺迫切的問題：（1）如何精簡黨中央的決策程式，（2）如何改進與第三國際的聯絡，以冀能跟上共產運動的發展，而能更適當地處理有關黨內共產黨員的問題。

對第一個問題解決的辦法是依照鮑羅廷的建議設立中央政治委員會為黨

之最高決策機構，其成員由中央執行委員會委員中選任。[45] 此委員會，其功能模仿蘇聯的政治局，於7月11日正式成立，計6位成員。孫中山為主席，鮑羅廷為顧問。[46] 與第三國際及其他國民革命聯絡的構想，在國民黨第一次全國代表大會結束後，已由胡漢民及廖仲愷提出。其理由有二：（1）為中國革命求助，以及協助其他國民革命運動；（2）為取得共產國際運動之信息。因此，他們建議成立一個「民族國際」的組織。據稱孫中山對「民族國際」的建立曾得到鮑羅廷的同意，但是這個建議似乎是無疾而終。[47] 隨著彈劾案件的發生，這個構想又被重新提出來。6月16日中央執行委員會成立了一個聯絡部，以胡漢民為部長。[48] 聯絡部的宗旨是將先前交付「民族國際」的任務付諸實行。可是這個聯絡部從未發生什麼作用，因為它的任務被中央政治委員會在其8月13日第五次會議上決定新成立的國際聯絡委員會所代替。[49] 這個聯絡委員會的組成辦法由中央政治委員會同意後由該委員會、第三國際和中國共產黨各舉一人協同商議，然後呈報該委員會。一俟孫中山批准後，指派一代表在兩日後（8月15日）召開之中央執行委員全體大會上陳述。[50] 國際聯絡委員會成立的原因是要為國民黨直接從第三國際獲得中國共產黨有關國民黨的活動，以便更易於處理和解決黨內的衝突和矛盾。

　　中央執行委員會全體大會於8月15日召開，23日休會。關於彈劾案件的辯論從8月19至21日連續三日。中執會12位正式委員及7位候補委員（其中6位共產黨員）出席。張繼及謝持也應邀出席。但是值得注意的是彈劾案件的第三位簽署者鄧澤如卻並未出席。孫中山及鮑羅廷也未出席。[51]

　　彈劾案件經兩日辯論後皆不能取得共識。張繼堅持共產黨員離開國民黨的建議。他說國民黨以俄為摯友則可，以俄的宗旨為宗旨則不可。國民黨對加入國民黨的共產黨員原以信義為指歸，但共產黨員現已證明他們不足以信任。兩者分開足以消除海內外黨內糾紛的根本問題——黨內有黨的現象。分離後，兩黨仍可合作。

　　瞿秋白代表共產黨員發言。他說，所謂黨團作用（一致行動）的嫌疑，實在是惹起這次糾紛的主要原因。國民黨外既然有一共產黨存在，又准跨黨，就是沒有共青團的文件發現，在國民黨內的共產黨派有一致的行動有什麼可疑的地方？共產黨人以個人資格加入國民黨，應視為國民黨黨員，如違背國民黨的黨章，當以黨的紀律制裁之。否則，國民黨當取消跨黨的決議。如此次會議議決分離，大可謂共產派之發展足以侵蝕國民黨。若不分離，則共產黨之發展即係國民黨中一部分之發展，何用疑忌？毫無疑問，瞿秋白的強硬立場代表共產黨的深信國民黨不至於取消跨黨的決議。

　　之後的辯論都是根據這兩種看法進行。遂處中央執行委員會全體大會於僵局。因之，中央政治局於 8 月 20 日召開會議以謀解決之道。孫中山、鮑羅廷、瞿秋白、胡漢民、廖仲愷及伍朝樞均出席此會議，並通過「國民黨內之共產派問題」與「中國國民黨與世界革命運動之聯絡問題」兩項決議之草案。次日，此兩項草案由汪精衛提交中央執行委員會全體大會討論，以為解決之張本。[52]

　　第一項草案的正文並未公開，據稱其主旨為重申黨紀之尊嚴。[53] 第二項決議提出擬設立的國際聯絡委員會的組織與功能的具體方式。汪精衛的報告稱，此聯絡委員會受政治委員會之管轄，其委員由孫中山指派，負責與世界各國國民革命運動及第三國際聯絡。與第三國際聯絡的方式由雙方商議後定之，包括中國共產黨與中國國民黨有關之活動的聯絡方法。最後一點當然就是設立這個委員會最重要的原因。[54]

　　汪精衛在報告中說，現在黨內糾紛情形約有三派：有認為與共產派合作有害者，有認為與共產派合作有益者，有認為共產派跨黨無害，但如有秘密黨團作用則有害。他又稱，共產黨員為共產黨守秘密是當然的。如果國民黨能與第三國際聯絡溝通，則無所謂有其秘密，彼此當不致誤會，那就是國際聯絡委員會所期望能達到的目的。[55]

　　汪精衛報告後的討論簡短。張繼說關於設立國際聯絡委員會提案不在他中央監察委員職權範圍內，無可否意見。也許認為彈劾案不可能得到中執會全體大會的支持，他建議將該案作為懸案處理。孫科的密友傅汝霖支持張繼的建議。他不認為政治委員會的草案可以解決黨內的糾紛，因為草案是在監察委員已經提出彈劾案之後再行提出。其時，汪精衛宣讀一封另一位中央監察委員李石曾的來函，其中李石曾稱他不屬於第三國際，也並未參加最初關於國共合作的討論，但兩黨既然合作在先，萬不能分裂於後。汪的意圖顯然是藉此指出彈劾案件並非中央監察委員會一致通過的決議。[56] 全體大會主席胡漢民遂以政治委員會提出之兩項草案提出表決，並稱雖然共青團決議案中的用詞諸多不妥，他不認為決議案的內容屬於惡意。在國民黨中的共產派不應以陰謀派看待。表決後，孫中山的政策獲勝。中央執行委員會全體大會以多數通過政治局的草案。[57] 於是，關於共產黨派在國民黨內黨籍的爭論就此暫時告一段落。

　　中央執行委員會在全體大會閉幕後發布通告，一再闡述國共合作之基本理由，以及國際聯絡委員會之建立可能有助消除共產派在國民黨內的活動所引起的疑慮。[58]

　　塵埃落定，但國民黨黨內的分裂如舊。1924年10月張繼請求免除所有黨職，並自行退黨。[59] 謝持也於長期因病在粵住院後，以孫科餽贈禮金1,000元為旅費，悄然返滬。[60] 國民黨內公開反共的活動就此停止。一直等到孫中山去世後再行死灰復燃。

　　此次彈劾案件使幾件事變更為明朗化。首先，國民黨內的共產黨員很明顯地無意放棄他們的政治獨立性。關於這一點，瞿秋白在中央執行委員會全體大會上已經說得很明白。誠如羅伯特・諾斯（Robert North）和史華茲（Benjamin Schwartz）所指出，共產黨員由於他們共同的意識形態、組織和紀律的束縛不能以個人的資格，而必須以一個為有高度紀律性團體的一分子的身分，加入國民黨。[61] 其次，孫中山容忍在國民黨內共產黨員的獨立性的原因並非是他不明白共產黨的動機，而是他對外援的需要。當時外援的唯一來源就是蘇聯，雖然他要付出的代價是與共產黨合作。他之所以願意付出那個代價的原因是因為他相信他可以用黨的紀律來有效地制裁共產黨人，使整個情勢變得對國民黨有利。第三，這一事件也突出了當時鮑羅廷在國民黨黨務上的影響。毫無疑問他是共產黨在彈劾案件中採取強硬立場的後援者，因為他對整個事件的態度早已在他與張繼和謝持的對話中明白地顯示出來。在中央政治委員會的設立上，也可以看出他的影響。由他的建議而成立的中央政治委員會，雖然名義上是屬於中央執行委員會，其實它的設立是藉以代替中央執行委員會成為黨內決策的最高機構，為黨章所未有明文規定的超法律的設施。最後，彈劾事件雖然在國民黨內有廣泛的認同，但是終於失敗的原因是由於這些反共的認同並沒有凝聚起來成為一個有組織和有協調的運動。無疑地國民黨人對孫中山的個人忠誠在這事件中起了很大的作用，因為是在孫中山逝世後，北京和上海反共黨員才組織起來公開對抗廣州的政策。

　　1924年國民黨如果只是要處理黨內的紛爭，事情也會比較容易些。黨內的和諧固然重要，但是建黨和鞏固革命勢力所需不僅單是黨內的和諧。1924年國民黨僅僅控制廣州一處，廣州外圍陳炯明和其他的軍隊對廣州仍然構成一種威脅。黃埔軍校剛剛成立，還需要時間訓練一批軍官來發展一支黨軍。甚至於在廣州，國民黨的控制也不完全。在表面上誓言效忠國民黨的將官們繼續爭權，同時與其他既得利益集團聯合，竭力抵制國民黨的集中廣州財政管理的措施。除此之外，還有其他迫切的問題急需處理。當中央執行委員召開全體大會討論彈劾案件之時，正值「商團事件」發生之際。該事件之發生係由國民黨扣留大批廣州商團購買軍火所致。此事件幾乎為國民黨帶來國際危機，不過最後還是由國民黨用武力解決商團。[62] 這些情況使國民黨在1924年所遭遇的問題愈趨複雜化。因之，迅速且有效地解決彈劾案件以維護廣州與莫斯科聯盟，自有它的急迫性。孫中山在彈劾案件中陷於進退維谷的地步。他的任務是在兩個似乎是互相對立的政治現實中取得平衡，而他的選擇是非常有限的。但是值得注意的是，雖然他的容共政策引起爭議，他的領導地位卻從未被質疑。他的領導力使大家能同舟共濟，維持改組的勢頭，得以鑄成一股強大的革命勢力最後終於獲取政權，只是他未能在他有生之年目睹他領導革命的成功。

注釋

本文於1994年11月19-23日在台北中國國民黨中央委員會黨史委員會主辦之「國父建黨革命一百周年紀念學術研討會」發表的報告。載《國父建黨革命一百周年學術討論集》（*Proceedings of Centennial Symposium on Sun Yat-sen's Founding of the Kuomintang for*

Revolution），第2冊（台北，1995），頁1-26。此為修訂本。

[1]　關於國民黨1924年改組後共產黨黨員在國民黨中的活動及關於共黨密件之爭議，見李雲漢，《從容共到清共》（台北：中國學術著作獎助委員會，1966），第5章，頁250-343。

[2]　《華字日報》（*Wah Tze Yat Pao*）創立於1872年，為香港最早華人經營的報紙。為清末改革運動之支持者，並同情於孫中山先生的早期革命活動。見戈公振《中國報學史》（台北：臺灣學生書局，1964，複印版），頁195；方漢奇《中國近代報刊史》（太原：山西教育出版社，1991），頁60-61、201；李家園《香港報業雜談》（香港：三聯書店，1989），頁9；羅茲韋爾‧布里頓（Roswell S. Britton），《中國期刊新聞，1800-1912》（*The Chinese Periodical Press*, 1800-1912）（上海：別發印書館〔Kelly and Walsh〕，1933），頁46-47。《華字日報》極端反對孫中山先生的容共政策。上述2月15-28日間發布的5則報導發表於該報1924年2月15、19、21、23及25日。

[3]　《新聞報》，1924年2月29日，頁2。該報於1893年由一英商創辦，1899年破產後由美人福開森（John C. Ferguson）接辦。最後由一組中國銀行家購買，成為上海三大報紙之一（其餘兩家為《申報》及《滬報》）。見戈公振，前引書，頁110；方漢奇，前引書，頁42-43、47-48；布里頓，前引書，頁74。

[4]　關於馮自由等被威脅從廣州驅逐出境事，《華字日報》也有報導（1924年2月28日，頁3）。根據這篇報導，孫中山在與馮自由、劉成禺、謝英伯當面對持，怒責他們繼續反對國共合作一事時，曾說如果不是他們長久以來對他和國民黨的忠誠，他會把他們拿去做「槍靶」。所以他決定把他們的事交中央執行委員會處理。孫又說處理的辦法至少應該是包括開除黨籍和從廣州驅逐出境。當時在場者尚有徐清河（見下），但是他的名字並不見該篇報導。

孫中山好像確實把這件事交中央執行委員會處理，這四位也出席在2月中該會召開的第六次會議。但是在公開的文獻中無法確認此事。《中國國民黨週刊》在這一段時期經常都登載中央執行委員會會議記錄摘要，但是第六次會議記錄摘要卻付闕如。不過，孫中山在3月1日的信中曾告知中央執行委員會他對於馮、劉、謝、徐的解釋已感到滿意，因之，他認為此事應告結束，並指令該會為此發行通告。此信見《國父全集》（台北：中國國民黨中央委員會黨史委員會，1973），第3集，頁943。中央執行委員會通告見《國父全集》第5集，頁565。

李雲漢稱，馮、劉、謝、徐在國民黨第一次全國代表大會閉幕不久後曾在廣州林森住所召開秘密會議，由鄧澤如主席，參加者有五十餘華僑及各省反共人士，會議議決草擬一封給國民黨內共產黨領袖李大釗的信，警告其切勿試圖篡奪國民黨的領導權。不料警告書尚未發出，消息已被洩露。李大釗等人遂見孫中山，指名控告馮、劉、謝、徐四人「不守黨員紀律及挑撥國共惡感」，請求懲罰。之後，孫中山召見四人。在四人的辯護中，他們曾引李大釗及陳獨秀在《嚮導》和《新青年》發表的文章來證明共產黨既無信實，且對國民黨多有誹謗。據稱孫中山對他們的解釋感到滿意，遂判他們無罪。見李雲漢，《從容共到清黨》（台北：中國學術著作獎助委員會，1966），頁222。李並未涉及孫中山是否有作將四人驅逐出境之威脅事。

[5]　聲明全文見《中國國民黨週刊》，第12期（1924年3月16日），頁4。聲明也轉載《華字日報》1924年3月21日。

[6]　通告發表於《中國國民黨週刊》，第13期（1924年3月23日），頁3-4。通告24號係孫中山草擬，收入《國父全集》，第1集，頁889-890。

[7]　文件全文見《中國國民黨週刊》，第14期（1924年3月30日），頁3-5。

[8]　呈文收藏於國民黨黨史委員會，檔案編號435/300。

[9]　中央執行委員會致中央監察委員會函由戴季陶、廖仲愷及彭述民（中執會候補委員）簽署。此函及中央監察委員會覆函與陳覺先的呈文一併收藏國民黨黨史會。檔案編號同上，435/300。

[10]　同上。

[11]　根據《中國國民黨週刊》公布的中央執行委員會會議摘要，候補委員例行出席參加會議，並且投票。

[12]　胡漢民、戴季陶和邵元沖都持有不同程度的保留。見李雲漢，前引書，頁235-245；又見下注第36與37。

[13]　早在1923年11月，當國民黨即將改組與改組後將允許共產黨黨員加入國民黨的消息傳出後，以黨元老及孫中山在東南亞主要募款人鄧澤如為首的國民黨廣東執行部11位委員於當年11月29日上書孫中山表達如果改組按既定方案進行，他們對共產黨取代國民黨的深切憂慮。（呈文原件與孫中山批示的影印本收入《彈劾共產黨兩大要案》[南京？]中國國民黨中央監察委員會，1927，頁1-12。）同時，中央幹部會議，國民黨改組前指最高決策機構（其成員包括張繼與謝持），在同年11月8日召開討論共產黨員加入國民黨問題的特別會議上也表達了類似的疑慮，見《中央幹部會議記錄》（1923），第4集，藏國民黨黨史委員會，編號418/9。

[14]　李雲漢，前引書，頁287-289。

[15]　鄒魯，《中國國民黨史稿》（重慶：商務印書館，1944），頁368-369。作者未提供彈劾案件之細節。

[16]　李雲漢，前引書，頁302。

[17]　這組文件的摘要（附引文）最初發表在肅清（筆名）《共產黨之陰謀大暴露》（廣

州：三俱樂部，無出版日期。1924年8月27日序）。該摘要與彈劾全文收入下列書籍：《彈劾共產黨兩大要案》（見上）；鄧澤如，《中國國民黨二十年史績》（上海：中華書局，1948），頁298-323；張繼，《張溥泉先生全集》（台北：中國國民黨中央黨史委員會，1951），頁89-96；《革命文獻》第9輯（台北：中國國民黨中央黨史委員會，1955），頁1279-1286。

〈中國社會主義青年團第二次大會議決及宣言〉全文收藏於國民黨黨史委員會（見李雲漢，前引書，頁340，注60）中國共產黨第三次大會通過之〈關於革命運動及國民黨問題〉決議收入《中共中央文件選集》（北京：中共中央黨校，1989），第1冊，頁146-148。

[18] 一說為這組文件係由一曾有半年共產黨黨籍的國民黨員（孫鏡亞？）在上海出示張繼與謝持（蕭清，前引書，頁25、70）。曾琦，中國青年黨故主席，稱他在巴黎時曾見這組文件，也曾試請國民黨資深黨員如王寵惠等轉達孫中山，均未成功。其時正值謝持的女婿曹任遠甫從德國學成經巴黎返國，遂將這組文件託曹在上海轉交謝持。見曾琦，《曾慕韓先生遺著》（台北：中國青年黨中央執行委員會，1954），頁475。

[19] 蕭清，前引書，頁15。

[20] 同上。

[21] 艾倫‧惠廷（Allen S. Whiting），《蘇聯對華政策，1917-1924》（*Soviet Policies in China, 1917-1924*）（紐約：哥倫比亞大學出版社，1954），頁277。

[22] 蕭清，前引書，頁16-17。

[23] 同上。頁18、23、27。

[24] 同上。頁20-21。

[25] 彈劾案呈文，見上注[17]。

[26] 蕭清，前引書，頁21。

[27] 同上。頁24。

[28] 同上。頁24-27。

[29] 同上。頁24、29-30。戴季陶6月20日抵上海後，以不能勝任及同志間的不諒解為由向孫中山提出辭呈請辭國民黨宣傳部部長職。（辭呈見《國民黨週刊》第9期，1924年7月3日，頁4）。半年後，1925年12月13日戴致蔣介石函重申他當時辭職的理由稱，國民黨內部的爭執與共產黨在國民黨內的發展已使國民黨患精神分裂症，因而充滿有雙重紀律的危險及在宣傳工作上必須處理兩種不同的看法的困難。見戴季陶，《戴季陶先生文存》（台北：中國國民黨中央委員會，1959），第3冊，頁982。

[30] 蕭清，前引書，頁25。

[31] 同上。頁32、34。

[32] 同上。頁34-35。

[33] 雖然現有文件中未有提及這次會談係孫中山所安排，但從以下原因觀察，很可能如是：（1）讓鮑羅廷更能體會國民黨一些領導者的反共情緒，（2）給彈劾者機會直接詢問鮑羅廷共產黨人在國民黨內活動的問題。再者，鮑羅廷在當時的情況下如果沒有孫中山的許可不可能去找他們會晤。據稱，孫科是孫中山指派去為張繼及謝持做翻譯。見蕭清，前引書，頁32。

[34] 同上。

[35] 同上。頁3-36。這被認為是胡漢民和廖仲愷的建議。

[36] 會議記錄摘要公布於《國民黨週刊》第30期（1924年7月20日）。《革命文獻》誤稱此次會議為中央執行委員會第四次會議，顯然是排字誤植。（《革命文獻》第9輯，頁1286。）

邵元沖，以候補委員身分出席這次會議，稱在會中「頗多爭執」。見邵元沖，《邵元沖日記》（上海：上海人民出版社，1990），頁26。此書為2,000冊內部發行限定版。有加注釋，並無更改。

[37] 通告全文見《國民黨週刊》第30期（1924年7月20日），頁6；上注[4]；《國父全集》第1集，頁893-894。

通告由邵元沖與汪精衛共同草擬。邵為中央執行委員會在其7月7日議會上對通告草案的隨意修改極為憤怒。他稱：「七時至大本營，開中央執行委員會，中對於發表對共產黨問題之宣言，多方增減，成為以不痛不癢之文字，而表示其欲言而又不敢之態度，嗚呼！余信筆書唐人［朱慶餘］絕句，『含情欲說宮中事，鸚鵡頭前不敢言』一句以解嘲……當此鼠輩縱橫之時，吾亦不得不忍辱負重，以漸收廓清之效耳……」見邵元沖，前引書，頁27-28。

[38] 計15件此類彈劾呈文收入蕭清，前引書，頁59-84。另15件見李雲漢，前引書，頁319-323。

[39] 見上注[4]。

[40] 蕭清，前引書，頁46、50-51。謝持據稱患嚴重糖尿病。

[41] 參見本文頁4-5。

[42] 《國民黨週刊》第29期（1924年7月12日），頁2。

[43] 《國父年譜》（台北：中國國民黨中央黨史史料編輯委員會，1965），第2冊，頁1031-1037。

[44] 馮、謝、劉、徐事件發生後（見本文頁1），據稱一位海外國民黨黨員蕭佛成曾勸告孫中山不必對老同志如此苛嚴，以致旁的同志失望，而失去他們對黨的支持。孫的回答據稱是，除壓制他們的反對外，他無別的選擇。他的理由是鑑於北方軍閥逐漸鞏固

他們的地盤和對政府的控制，因而北方情勢漸趨穩定，而廣東的軍隊又無錢即拒絕上陣，以致整個情勢影響他北伐的計畫。因之，除與共產黨合作外，並無他策。見《華字日報》1924年2月28日，頁3。

1924年7月孫中山告知劉成禺說，他並未察覺蘇聯對中國有任何企圖。但在英、美、日對廣州政府的敵視態度下，他與蘇聯聯盟的目的在於減輕外國對廣州的壓力。如果廣州與外國的關係改善，國民黨就沒有理由只是向蘇聯一邊倒。他也認為他會以誠對待國民黨內的共產黨人，並試圖把他們變成真正的三民主義信徒。如果他們踰矩，他自有辦法處理他們。見劉成禺，〈先總理舊德錄〉，載《國史館館刊》，第1期（1947年12月），頁53-54。

[45] 亞・伊・切列潘諾夫（A.I. Cherpanov），《中國國民革命軍的北伐——一個駐華軍事顧問的札記》（北京：中國社會科學院出版社，1984），頁114。這是作者著 *Zapiski Voennogo Sovetnika v Kitae*（Moscow, 1976）的中文翻譯本，也是作者原著 *Zapiski Voennogo Sovetnika v Kitae: iz Istorii Pervoi Grazhdanskoi Revolutsionanoi Voiny, 1924-1927*（Moscow, 1964）同 *Severnyi Pokhod Natsionalno Revolutsionnoi Armii Kitaia Zapiski*（Moscow, 1968）的合併修正本。

[46] 《國父年譜》，第2冊，頁1039。六位委員是胡漢民、汪精衛、廖仲愷、譚平山、伍朝樞、邵元沖。譚平山旋即退任，餘缺由瞿秋白替補。（《國父年譜》，第2冊，頁1041。）

[47] 蔣永敬，〈胡漢民先生年譜稿〉，載吳相湘編《中國現代史叢刊》（台北：正中書局，1961），第3冊，頁201-202。戴季陶亦支援「民族國際」的想法。見李雲漢，前引書，頁241-244。

[48] 《國父年譜》，第2冊，頁1030。

[49] 同上，頁1040-1050。

[50] 同上。

[51] 李雲漢，前引書，頁324-331。李的敘述根據國民黨黨史委員會尚未公開的中央政治委員會會議記錄。

[52] 《國父年譜》，第2冊，頁1054。

[53] 李雲漢，前引書，頁327。

[54] 同上。頁327-328。

[55] 同上。蔣永敬在《胡漢民先生年譜稿》中稱此節為胡漢民所講，見蔣永敬，前引書，頁204。

[56] 李雲漢，前引書，頁329。中央監察委員第五位委員吳稚暉也婉拒簽署彈劾書。但在國民黨1927年清黨後，他對此事表示遺憾，說：「當張、謝二公要我一同舉發，我則

婉謝之，至今思之，如何蒙昏。但理由無他，即以彼輩亦世界一種之革命黨，仗義而助世局革命，必不我欺。且恃總理尚不斥絕，君子可欺以方，余等亦當姑自受辱，以待其變。」見吳稚暉為《彈劾共產黨兩大要案》寫序。此書為國民黨中央監察委員會1927年9月出版。封面為胡漢民題字。

[57] 李雲漢，前引書，頁330。投反對票人姓名未列出。

[58] 通告草案發表於《國民黨週刊》第40期（1924年9月28日），頁5。經修改後之定稿，收入《革命文獻》，第16輯（1957），頁2773-2776。

[59] 李雲漢，前引書，頁337。

[60] 同上。

[61] 羅伯特‧諾斯（Robert C. North），《莫斯科與中國共產黨人》（*Moscow and the Chinese Communists*（Stanford: Stanford University Press, 1963第2版），頁83；史華茲（Benjamin Schwartz），《中國共產主義與毛澤東的興起》（*Chinese Communism and the Rise of Mao*）（麻州劍橋：哈佛大學出版社，1961），頁52。

[62] 關於「商團事件」的詳細敘述，見韋慕庭（C. Martin Wilbur），《孫中山：壯志未酬的愛國者》（*Frustrated Patriot*）（紐約，1976），頁250-264。

Early Anti-Communism in the Reorganized Kuomintang

The official approval by the First National Congress of the Kuomintang (KMT) of KMT membership for individual communists notwithstanding, opposition to this policy persisted in the party. The anti-communists remained suspicious of communist motives, and their suspicion was only deepened by communist activism in post-reorganizational KMT affairs, and by the revelation of secret Chinese Communist Party (CCP) directives urging its members in the KMT to remain politically independent and to push for the growth of the CCP through the KMT. [1] Zhang Ji and Xie Chi, both members of the newly established Central Supervisory Committee (CSC), became champions of the anti-communist cause. Although Sun Yat-sen succeeded at the time in neutralizing the threat to party unity posed by the dissent, he was never able to remove its root cause, which was the fear of the communists gaining control of the KMT. The persistence of this fear foreshadowed the open rift within the party after Sun Yat-sen's death and the final expulsion of all communists from the KMT. This essay will examine the ways in which Sun Yat-sen and his close associates coped with the anti-communist dissent in the immediate aftermath of the 1924 KMT reorganization, with particular attention paid to their handling of the impeachment movement against the communists.

Almost immediately following the First KMT National Congress, in January 1924, reports hostile to Sun's policy of admitting communists into the KMT began to appear in Hong Kong and Shanghai newspapers. The Hong Kong *Hua zi ribao* led the way with a series of expose, published between February 15 and 28, alleging collusion between the KMT and the CCP and accusing Sun Yat-sen and the KMT of capitulation to communism. [2] On February 29 the influential Shanghai *Xinwen bao* carried a dispatch from its Canton correspondent, alleging that since "Party-straddling" was now permissible under the new KMT Constitution, a number of senior KMT members, including Hu Hanmin, Liao Zhongkai, Zou Lu, and Wang Jingwei, had already joined the Chinese Communist Party, thus making one-half of the 24-member Central Executive Committee (CEC) communist. The dispatch also reported that two veteran KMT members, Feng Ziyou and Xie Yingbo, were threatened with deportation from Canton by Sun Yat-sen because of their request to leave the party on the ground that the party had been captured by the communists. The dispatch further alleged that Zhao Shijing, the Salt Commissioner of Canton and a long-time supporter of Sun Yat-sen, had warned Sun not to join the CCP or else he (Zhao) would resign from his office as well as from the party. The intensity of anti-communist sentiments in the KMT was such, according to the dispatch, that Sun Ke, the Mayor of Canton, son of Sun Yat-sen, and "leader of the 'prince faction' which represents the 'capitalists' in the KMT," was contemplating founding another political party in opposition to his father, using a reported four million dollars of his personal wealth. [3]

In spite of the fact that only one of these allegations — that of Sun's threat to deport Feng Ziyou *et al.* from Canton — had any truth to it, this sensational dispatch caused great concern among the KMT leadership. [4] Four days later, on March 4, the Shanghai Executive Headquarters of the KMT issued a public statement repudiating point by point the charges made in the *Xinwen bao* article, and asking that the KMT be judged by its words and deeds. [5] Meanwhile, the Central Executive Committee in Canton also moved swiftly to dispel the rampant rumors and rally support. At its 14th meeting, on March 15, the CEC approved the drafts of two circulars to the KMT membership, which were made public the next day as CEC circulars no. 23 and no. 24. [6] It is clear from these two documents that Sun Yat-sen and the CEC were serving notice to the anti-communists and communists alike that they must strictly obey party discipline, not engage in any action detrimental to party unity, and cease their internecine warfare in order to get on with the task of waging revolution. Circular no. 23 made explicit that unauthorized use of the name Kuomintang in naming any organization not affiliated with the party was strictly prohibited, and that any party member doing so would be prosecuted to the full extent under the party Constitution. Circular no. 24, drafted by Sun Yat-sen himself, clarified the party's position regarding individual action *vs.* the party's collective interest. It stated that the lack of understanding by KMT members of the proper relationship between a party member and the party had been a main reason for the party's lack of success. A party member had the obligation of obeying party policy and was not free to pursue individual action detrimental to the party's collective interest. Individual action must be in consonance with party action. To sacrifice individual freedom was to insure the party's freedom. He exhorted party members to observe the principles of the party, namely the Three People's Principles, to implement party policy on the basis of the Manifesto of the First National Congress, and to hold always before them the welfare of the people, whom they must strive to serve. The Circular concluded by saying that the only reason for the party's reorganization was to create a political party with a tight structure and real authority in order to move forward the National Revolution. Whether this could be accomplished would depend entirely on the individual efforts of party members. If there were no unity of purpose, and if party members continued to go their separate ways, the reorganization would have been in vain, and it would be difficult not to conclude that those who joined the party had done so only with ulterior motives. This last statement was clearly directed to the communists and meant to reassure the dissidents that Sun would not tolerate any communist misbehavior in the KMT.

The seriousness with which the party viewed the dissent and its possible impact on the future of the party was evidenced by another party document, a long statement issued in March by the Propaganda Department of the CEC explaining the difference between KMT policy and communism. [7] The essence of the statement was that the only similarity between the policy adopted by the KMT and that pursued by the Soviet Union was that they both subscribed to the principles of state socialism. Although the KMT reorganization altered the party's structure by the adoption of a committee system borrowed from the Soviets, it did not change in any way the principles of the party or the party's program. Members of the CCP who joined the KMT did so as individuals and out of a desire to help carry the National Revolution to a successful conclusion. Their presence in the party, therefore, should not be feared as a threat to the Kuomintang or as proof that the Kuomintang had become communist. After all, the statement argued, the admission of anarchists into the KMT prior to 1912 had not made the KMT anarchist. The statement further pointed to the election of a Labor government in England to show that, contrary to charges, the rise to power of the British Labor Party, which had often been described as Socialist or Bolshevik, did not mean for Great Britain the end of individual liberty, private ownership of property, the monarchial system, or the British empire. The statement urged party members and the Chinese people not to be confused by the false charges leveled against the KMT, but to close ranks and rise to the challenge of carrying the National Revolution to a successful completion.

The anti-communist dissent was thus dealt with from the beginning by Sun Yat-sen and the Central Executive Committee with a great deal of political skill and tact. They elected to inform and persuade rather than to suppress and silence the dissidents. By their action they made clear that the party's supreme task was the successful completion of the National Revolution, for which party unity was essential; and that any divisiveness in the party ranks could only be harmful to the party's cause.

Although the challenge had come primarily from the right, the party also had to deal with pressures from the left. While the dissenters were forecasting impending disaster and advocating the expulsion of the communists from the KMT, the leftists in the party were laying the blame on the doorstep of the party for not having disciplined the rightists for causing party disunity. One episode was a typical case in point. One Chen Juexian of Canton submitted a petition to the CEC on April 5, 1924, in which he demanded punishment of Feng Ziyou and Xie Yingbo for spreading rumors among the overseas Chinese that the KMT had turned communist. [8] Chen maintained that Feng, Xie and their ilk, having monopolized party affairs in the past, were no longer able to do so following the party reorganization, and thus turned to scandalizing the party for their own selfish reasons. He demanded that, in the interest of party unity, such anti-party activity not be tolerated, and Feng and Xie be disciplined as a warning to others. Two weeks later, on April 18, the CEC referred the petition to the Central Supervisory Committee（CSC）for investigation. [9] On April 28 the CSC, in a reply to the CEC, recommended that the case be dismissed for a lack of evidence. [10] The CSC based its action on technical grounds. It stated that Chen did not support his case by failing to specify the times and places at which the charges attributed to Feng and Xie were made; nor did he include the names of the people to whom the charges were made, or the name of any witness thereto. The mere claim that Feng and Xie had made false charges against the party constituted insufficient grounds on which to base disciplinary action. The CSC further stated that it ordinarily would not have consented to hear any cases with such flimsy evidence. However, in view of the serious nature of Chen's charges, involving, as they did, major policy matters, it had agreed to review the case; but it found Chen's charges to be without any basis in fact. Indeed, the CSC questioned the authenticity of the petition saying that it was impossible for the CSC to question Chen in person since the petition did not give Chen's local address, and his name was not listed in the Canton party membership register. Based on these findings, the CSC recommended that the case be dismissed.

The different approaches adopted by the CEC and the CSC in this case reflected the major differences of opinion within the KMT regarding its policy of collaboration with the communists. It will be recalled that the CEC had twenty-four regular members and seventeen alternates, and that three of the regular members and seven of the alternates were communists, representing one-quarter of the total CEC membership. All alternates also enjoyed full participation and voting rights in CEC meetings. [11] Thus, the CEC could not overlook any challenge to the party's policy *vis-a-vis* the communists without calling into question the very legitimacy of its own and the party's existence, even though some KMT leaders of the CEC had certain reservations on that policy. [12] On the other hand, all five members and the five alternate members of the CSC were KMT members of long standing, and three of the standing members — Deng Zeru, Zhang Ji, and Xie Chi — had been opposed to admitting communists into the KMT from the beginning. [13] Given such circumstances, it is not difficult to understand why the CEC considered it necessary to refer the Chen Juexian petition to the CSC for investigation, even though Sun Yat-sen had personally absolved the accused from any wrongdoing just a month before, and why the CSC recommended the case's dismissal.

The divisions within the party leadership thus helped to fan the controversy. Numerous partisan disputes developed in the provinces. [14] Tension was high in Canton. On June 1, 1924, Sun Ke and Huang Jilu, both members of the Executive Committee of the Canton Municipal Headquarters of the KMT, petitioned the Central Party Headquarters in a move to impeach the communists. [15] Zhu Hezhong, a veteran KMT member, also implored Sun Yat-sen to investigate and discipline the Shanghai *Minguo ri pao,* a KMT-sponsored newspaper, for publishing articles written by communists advocating, contrary to KMT policy, the independence of Outer Mongolia. [16] But the showdown did not come until June 1924 when Deng Zeru, Zhang Ji, and Xie Chi, acting on behalf of the CSC, produced CCP documentation as evidence to prove their charge that the communists had joined the KMT only to destroy it.

The documentation involved was two sets of publications: (1) *The Resolution and Manifesto of the Second Congress of the Chinese Socialist Youth Corps*, published on August 25, 1923, with an appendix containing the "Resolution on the National Movement and the Kuomintang," adopted by the Third CCP National Congress in June 1923, and (2) a Special Issue (No. 7) of the *Journal of the Chinese Socialist Youth Corps*, devoted to the Enlarged Meeting of the Executive Committee of the Corps, March 22 to April 1, 1924, published on April 11 of the same year. Both contained specific directives governing the work and attitude of communists in the KMT. [17] The discovery of these documents was a boon to the anti-communists, as they revealed the details of the CCP's strategy and tactics in its relationships with the KMT. [18]

The "Resolution and Manifesto of the Second Congress of the Chinese Socialist Youth Corps" stated explicitly that Youth Corps members who join the KMT were to receive supervision from their respective Executive Committees of the Corps, which would in turn receive supervision from the CCP Central. And Youth Corps members in the KMT should support the positions taken by members of the CCP and keep in step with them in action and speech. Also, they should preserve the independent and secret organization of the Corps while in the KMT. The "Resolution on the National Movement and the Kuomintang," adopted by the Third National Congress of the CCP in June 1923, stressed the following:

While joining the Kuomintang we should still preserve our own organization. We should also endeavor to recruit from among the various labor organizations and from the truly class conscious Kuomintang left revolutionary elements in order to gradually enlarge our organization and tighten our discipline for the purpose of laying a firm foundation for a strong communist party of the masses.

Two other resolutions adopted at the Enlarged Meeting of the Executive Committee of the Chinese Socialist Youth Corps — the "Resolution on the Attitude of the Youth Corps in the Kuomintang," and the "Resolution on the Work and Attitude of the Chinese Communist Party in the Kuomintang" — provided guidelines on these questions, based on the CCP resolution at its Third National Congress, with specific instructions on how to organize labor, peasants, students, and women. While the documents emphasized the importance of developing a harmonious working relationship with other members of the KMT, the communists were reminded that "in matters we consider essential and in which the Kuomintang is unwilling to use its name, we will still carry them out as our own independent activity," and that "while developing the Kuomintang organization, we naturally cannot cease the development of own party organization." Such statements gave the anti-communists exactly the kind of evidence they needed to force a confrontation with Sun Yat-sen. They jumped at the opportunity. Zhang Ji and Xie Chi, who were in Shanghai at the time, left for Canton in the early part of June, and the curtain of the first intensive fight against communist membership in the KMT was raised.

Zhang Ji brought the matter into the open in a speech at the Guangdong Higher Normal School on June 14. Xie Chi also prepared a report to be submitted to the Central Executive Committee for discussion. [19] On the same day Zhang, accompanied by Yu Youren, paid a visit to Sun Yat-sen at which time he charged that the communists were subverting the KMT for their own gain. Sun was reported to have pointed out that while the Third International might not be trustworthy, he had no reason to criticize the Russians. It was then that Zhang showed him the text of Article Six of the Sino-Soviet Agreement signed in Peking on May 31 of that year, by which the Soviet Union recognized the Peking government. [20] In Article Six the Soviet Union and the Peking government mutually pledged themselves not to permit within their respective territories "the existence and/or activities of any organizations or groups whose aim is to struggle by acts of violence against the Governments of either Contracting Party." They further pledged themselves "not to engage in propaganda directed against the political and social systems" of the two parties. [21] Sun apparently had not seen the complete text of the Agreement, and upon being shown the text of Article Six, he indicated to Zhang Ji that they had better wait for Borodin's return from the North. [22]

The presence of Zhang Ji and Xie Chi in Canton and their publicized purpose of impeaching the communists set off a flurry of activity among the leadership of both the KMT and the CCP. KMT leaders — Wang Jingwei, Liao Zhongkai, and Dai Jitao — reportedly held daily meetings with the Russian advisors on the impending crisis, and CCP leaders were said to have closeted themselves for daily discussions. [23] Li Liejun of Kiangsi, a member of the Central Executive Committee, in a move obviously designed to head off the crisis, got together the leaders of the KMT on both sides of the question at a dinner in an attempt to smooth out their differences. Those attending were Zhang Ji, Feng Ziyou, Liu Chengyu, Sun Ke, Wang Jingwei, Hu Hanmin, Liao Zhongkai, and Dai Jitao. [24] Li may have done this on his own initiative, or at the request of Sun Yat-sen. But, in any case, nothing came of the meeting. On June 18, Deng Zeru, Zhang Ji, and Xie Chi, three of the five members of the Central Supervisory Committee, placed a formal charge for impeachment against the communists before Sun Yat-sen and the Central Executive Committee. [25]

The articles of impeachment, using the resolutions of the CCP and the

Chinese Socialist Youth Corps as evidence, charged communist disloyalty and subversion. They demanded that the case be severely dealt with lest "the foundation of the party crumble." Deng, Zhang, and Xie also cited the movement led by members of the Chinese Socialist Youth Corps in the KMT to lend support to the Sino-Soviet Agreement just concluded in Peking. They maintained that such support was tantamount to recognizing the Peking government as the legitimate government of China, thus dealing a fatal blow to the Kuomintang's cause. They further cited as evidence articles written by communists in the KMT, including one by Cui Wencheng, entitled "The Chinese National Revolution and the Proletariat," published in the Shanghai *Minguo ribao,* an official organ of the KMT. Cui argued in his article that "the proletariat by their participation in the National Revolution will come to demand vigorously a proletarian revolution because the National Revolution is not a complete revolution." The impeachers charged that such anti-Kuomintang statements, when allowed to be published in the party's official organ, were an invitation to self-destruction as well as to making the *Minguo ribao* an organ of communist propaganda. The impeachment charges also contrasted Li Dazhao's famous statement at the KMT's First National Congress, pledging communist loyalty to the KMT and the National Revolution, with the evidence now pointing to the contrary, and concluded that communist "scheming and treachery" were as frightening as Li Dazhao's statement was incredible. The impeachers drew attention to the number of communists serving on the Central Executive Committee and to communist efforts to organize students, women, peasants, and workers as sure signs of an attempt to re-make the KMT in the communist image.

It is interesting to note that in bringing up these charges the impeachers emphasized that they were not against KMT membership for individual communists per se; but, based on the evidence they had gathered, the communists had shown themselves to have joined the KMT as a group, thus creating a party within a party, and thereby posing a grave threat to the survival of the KMT itself. By engaging in secret organizational and other secret activities in the KMT, the communists had violated party discipline and forfeited their party membership by default. Even if their action were not to be judged by the requirements of party discipline which should apply to all party members, but to be viewed from the standpoint of cooperation, the impeachers argued, communist behavior had indeed damaged the spirit of that cooperation. Thus the offenders must be punished, for in the view of the impeachers, unless the matter was quickly resolved in a fundamental way, the price might very well be the existence of the KMT itself.

The basic solution Deng Zeru, Zhang Ji, and Xie Chi had in mind was, of course, the expulsion of the communists from the KMT, thus putting an end to Sun Yat-sen's policy of collaboration with the communists. That a decision of such import, representing a complete reversal of the party's basic policy, could not have been even considered by Sun Yat-sen is obvious. While waiting for Borodin's return, Sun was reported to have said that it was at the suggestion of the Soviet Union that communists were admitted into the KMT, and that the Soviet Union should, of course, be responsible for the consequences. [26] Nevertheless, he did give permission for the Central Executive Committee to meet in a special session on June 19. [27] The meeting did not produce any results. None of the communist members of the CEC attended. Neither did Sun Yat-sen, Hu Hanmin, or Dai Jitao. [28] In fact, feelings were running so high among the KMT leaders that Dai Jitao left Canton for Shanghai a few hours before the meeting was to be held, following a verbal assault against him by Zhang Ji at a banquet the night before. [29] It was also reported that Zhang Ji spoke with such vehemence at the CEC meeting that even Deng Zeru, one of the three signers of the impeachment charges, had to restraint Zhang from committing any further verbal violence. [30]

Borodin returned to Canton on June 22. He was reported to have met with the communists first and then attended a dinner in his honor given by Sun Yat-sen that evening. [31] Borodin was quoted as having reminded Sun Yat-sen that the communists had joined the KMT for the purpose of establishing friendly relations between China and Russia. Toward that end the KMT must not prevent the development of the Chinese Communist Party in order to show its sincerity of being Russian's partner, or else Russia would have to look for other ways to advance its own interest. [32] When Borodin's remarks became known, they were interpreted as implying that unless the CCP were permitted to advance on its own, the Soviet Union would make separate arrangements with the Peking government.

Sun Yat-sen was clearly in a dilemma. He could not afford to lose Russian aid and still hope to lead his party to power. Neither could he afford to alienate completely the anti-communists in the party and still hope to keep the KMT a viable political force. A compromise was necessary. The first step he took was to arrange a meeting between the impeachers and Borodin. [33] The meeting took place on June 25 at Borodin's residence and lasted for two and one-half hours. Sun Ke acted as interpreter for Zhang Ji and Xie Chi. Deng Zeru, the third signer of the impeachment, interestingly enough, did not attend [34]

Their discussion centered upon one question: the development of an independent communist organization within the KMT. The exchange was blunt on both sides. When it was over, neither side had given in to the other. The theme developed by Zhang Ji and Xie Chi was that the existence of a party within a party was unnatural, undesirable, and, in the case of the KMT, fatal, as the CCP had designated the KMT as the party to be struggled against. Should the communists in the KMT insist on the CCP's having its own identity and organization, it would be best for the two parties to part ways, so that each could develop independently without any hindrance, because the KMT certainly could not tolerate the existence of another party within its own organization. Borodin argued that the reason the communists must organize themselves in the KMT was the inability of the KMT leadership to come to grips with the major issues of the day. The KMT was dead, he said, and only competition between its new and old members could provide the stimulus for the party's growth and survival. Besides, the existence of a right and a left wing in a political party is a natural phenomenon. Such a division in the KMT would produce a center faction to function as the heart of the party. A separation between the KMT and the CCP would be undesirable, as it would split the Chinese revolutionary force at the expense of the Chinese revolution. Furthermore, the KMT and the CCP are using each other, and the result of which would be more advantageous to the KMT. Of course, the KMT could drive out the communists by a majority vote, but Borodin hoped that it would not come to that.

Although the meeting failed to resolve the issue at hand, it did make one thing crystal clear. That is, the continuance of the Canton-Moscow alliance was contingent upon not only the admission of communists into the KMT, but also the independent development of a communist apparatus within the KMT organization. The party's response to the impeachment charges, therefore, had to be made within that frame of reference. Expulsion of the communists from the KMT was out of the question. The matter had to be settled in ways that would preserve the nascent alliance.

One suggestion made was to postpone action on the impeachment until the Second National Congress of the Kuomintang was convened. [35] Sun Yat-sen rejected that advice. The impeachment proposal was formally discussed by the Central Executive Committee at its 40th session held on July 3, 1924. After some heated discussion, the following resolutions were adopted: (1) to issue a proclamation on the party' position regarding this matter, (2) to convene a plenum of the CEC to dispose of the case, and (3) to request SunYat-sen's approval of these two proposals. In addition, Wang Jingwei and Shao Yuanchong, both members of the CEC, were selected to draft the proclamation based on the following:

The party's program and manifesto should serve as the basis [for the drafting of the proclamation.] All those who have joined the party, regardless of their prior political affiliation, shall be treated as party members, if they profess a revolutionary determination and a sincere belief in the Three People's Principles. Those who violate the party's program and manifesto shall be punished by party discipline. [36]

The proclamation was approved by the CEC four days later, on July 7, and issued after being redrafted by Sun Yat-sen. [37] The gist of it was that the KMT, having assumed the task of leading the National Revolution, had the responsibility of gathering together all revolutionary elements under its banner. Those who had joined the party would be judged by their willingness to carry out the party's program, or else face severe discipline. Party members should get rid of their suspicions and carry on with their work so that the revolutionary task would not be interrupted. Sun also criticized the anticommunists in no uncertain terms, as the proclamation also contained the following statement:

During the last few months a great deal of misunderstanding has arisen both within and without the party as regards alleged splitting tendencies in speech and action on the part of the communists in the Kuomintang. The reactionaries have taken advantage of this misunderstanding to create division. Suspicion among our comrades has turned into alienation. Because of this, the masses have become even more confused, resulting in a lessening of their sympathy for and support of the Revolution.

We find here a replay of the scene at the First National Congress, when the question of KMT membership for communists was first debated. To the charge that communist membership in the KMT would create a party within a party at the expense of the KMT, the party leadership justified its policy on the grounds of revolutionary need and stressed the sanctity of the party Constitution. It was the official position then, and it remained the official position now. To the impeachers, the handwriting on the wall was clear: Sun Yat-sen was not about to reverse the policy of collaborating with the communists.

There were other factors which worked against the impeachment drive. The most crucial of them was the lack of response on the part of other anti-communist leaders in Canton. Feng Ziyou, Xie Yingbo, Liu Chengyu, Xu Qinghe *et. al.* did not publicly back the movement. Sun Ke and Huang Jilu, who had earlier submitted an impeachment proposal against the communists, also remained silent. This was in sharp contrast to the outpouring of anti-communist sentiments in Shanghai and Peking, where hundreds of party members signed petitions to the CEC demanding severe disciplinary action against the communists. [38] We can only speculate on the reasons for the absence of support in Canton. In the first place, Sun Yat-sen's earlier disposition of the case involving Feng Ziyou *et al.* must have had its desired effect. [39] It is possible that Sun had exacted a promise from Feng and others not to engage in further public action or statement opposing party policy in return for a "not guilty" verdict. Secondly, the impeachment does not seem to have been coordinated in advance with the anti-communist leaders in Canton. Zhang Chi and Xie Chi, armed with the Chinese communist documents, apparently thought the documentation itself would be sufficient to arouse the local anti-communists to rally around their cause. When that support failed to materialize, they found themselves without a plan for further action. Xie Chi also became ill shortly after he returned to Canton, and Zhang Ji, in spite of his eloquence, could not carry the movement without a following. [40]

Finally, it appears that Sun Yat-sen and his close associates may have carried out a vigorous, behind-the-scenes campaign of persuasion in order to deny support to the impeachment movement. If indeed Feng Ziyou, Xie Yingbo, Liu Chengyu and Xu Qinghe were kept silent by their promise not to engage in further anticommunist activities, it is hard to explain the inaction of the others who had supported them previously. Feng Ziyou, one of the three signers of the impeachment petition, was not present at the confrontation between Zhang Ji, Xie Chi, and Borodin; and he apparently did not approve of Zhang Ji's tactics at the special meeting of the Central Executive Committee on June 19. [41] Sun Ke not only refrained from lending his support to the impeachment movement, but in fact gave his support to the CEC by declaring at the founding ceremony of the Canton Special Municipality Party Headquarters on July 6 that the new headquarters was to be under the direct supervision of the CEC, and that party members must be willing to accept that supervision, carry out the decisions handed down by higher party authorities, and not engage in activities, within or without the party, detrimental to the party's interests. [42] It is also interesting to note that Liu Chengyu and Xie Yingbo were both appointed as Councilors at Sun Yat-sen's Military Headquarters, on June 17 and July 4 respectively. [43]

What kind of arguments could Sun Yat-sen have used to deny support to the impeachment campaign? Available documentation does not provide any direct answer to this question. But judging from his remarks made during this period, it may be surmised that he had stressed the vital importance of Russian aid to the KMT and his deep conviction that in time the KMT could transform the communists into genuine nationalists; or if not, he could deal with them effectively either through the application of party discipline or by other means. [44] Put in these terms, Sun had made the issue a matter of life or death for the KMT, and staked his personal prestige on the outcome of the Canton-Moscow alliance. Inasmuch as the fortunes of his anti-communist antagonists were so inextricably intertwined with the fortunes of the party itself, it is reasonable to assume that they found it possible to agree with Sun that the patient must first be saved before any operation could take place. Their acquiescence in Sun's policy was probably made more palatable by Sun's assurance that he had a plan to deal with any communist intransigence.

Having thus sufficiently slowed down the momentum of the impeachment movement, the KMT prepared to convene a plenary session of the Central Executive Committee to dispose of the dispute in accordance with the CEC proclamation of July 7. In the meantime, Sun attended to two organizational matters which were made urgent by the impeachment drive: (1) how to streamline the decision-making process of the Party Central, and (2) how to improve the party's communications with the Third International in order to keep abreast of the Communist Movement as a means to deal adequately with the Chinese communists in the KMT.

The answer to the first question was the creation, at Borodin's suggestion, of a Central Political Council as the highest decision-making body of the party, with its members selected from the Central Executive Committee. [45] The Council, meant to function similarly to the Soviet Politburo, was officially established on July 11 with six members. Sun Yat-sen was the Chairman, and Borodin the Advisor. [46] The idea of establishing direct contact with the Third International and other national revolutionary movements had first been broached by Hu Hanmin and Liao Zhongkai following the KMT First National Congress. Their reason was two-fold: (1) to seek help in China's revolution and to render help to other national revolutionary movements and (2) to gain access to information relating to the international communist movement. For this purpose they proposed the establishment of a "Nationalities International" (minzu guoji). Sun reportedly had Borodin's agreement to this suggestion, but little seems to have been done to implement it. [47] With the impeachment movement, the idea was revived. On June 16 a Liaison Department was established by the Central Executive Committee, with Hu Han-min as its head. [48] The purpose of the Department was to carry out the mission ascribed earlier to the Nationalities International. However, the

Department never actually functioned, and its mission was soon taken over by an International Liaison Committee set up by the newly formed Central Political Council at the Council's fifth meeting on August 13. [49] The Council agreed that one representative each from the Council, the Third International, and the Chinese Communist Party would meet on the formation of the Committee, report back to the Council, and, after Sun Yat-sen's approval, send a representative to report to the plenum of the Central Executive Committee that was scheduled to meet two days later, on August 15. [50] The idea here was to provide the KMT with direct access to information, through the Third International, on Chinese communist activities related to the KMT, and thus enable the KMT to better cope with and resolve intra-party conflicts.

The plenary session of the Central Executive Committee was convened on August 15 and lasted until August 23. Debate on the impeachment proposal took three days, from August 19 to 21. Twelve members of the CEC and seven alternates were in attendance, six of them communists. Zhang Ji and Xie Chi were also seated, but conspicuously missing was the third signer of the impeachment proposal, Deng Zeru. Sun Yat-sen and Borodin did not attend. [51]

For two days the meeting failed to reach any consensus on how to resolve the questions raised in the impeachment proposal. Zhang Ji persisted in his call for a separation of the communists from the KMT. He argued that although the KMT could treat Russia as a good friend, it could not regard Russia's interests and objectives as its own. The KMT had shown trust in the Chinese communists, but the Chinese communists had proven untrustworthy. A separation of the two would eliminate the problem of a party within a party, which had become the source of conflict among party members at home and abroad. After separation, the two parties could still cooperate.

Qu Qiubai spoke for the communists. He stated that suspicions of a communist faction acting in unison in the KMT were at the bottom of the current dispute. But since there was a Communist Party outside the KMT, and party-straddling was permitted, how could there be any doubt, even without the discovery of the Youth Corps documents, that the communists in the KMT should be united in their action? Communists had joined the KMT as individuals, and should be treated as any other members of the party. If they violated the party's program or Constitution, then they should be subject to party discipline. Otherwise, he said, the only solution was for the KMT to repeal its decision on dual party membership. If the plenum should decide to separate the communists from the KMT, it would be like saying that the mere development of a communist faction within the Kuomintang is sufficient to erode the KMT; if not, there was no cause for suspicions, for the development of the CCP would be nothing more than the development of a part of the KMT itself. There seems little doubt that, in taking this tough stand, the communists were supremely confident that the KMT would not reverse its decision on allowing communists to join as members. The ensuing debate followed the same pattern and the plenum remained in an impasse. The Central Political Council met on August 20 to find a way out. The meeting, attended by Sun Yat-sen, Borodin, and four others — Qu Qiubai, Hu Hanmin, Liao Zhongkai, and Wu Chaoshu — approved the drafts of two resolutions: "The Problem of the Communist Faction in the Kuomintang," and "The Problem of Liaison between the Kuomintang and the World Revolutionary Movements." The resolutions were presented the following day by Wang Jingwei to the plenum for discussion and adoption. [52]

The text of the first resolution is not publicly available, but it is reported that it emphasized the sanctity of party discipline. [53] The second resolution set out, in concrete terms, the organization and function of the proposed International Liaison Committee. Wang reported that the Committee would be under the supervision of the Central Political Council, with its members appointed by the *zongli* (i.e., Sun Yat-sen), and would have the responsibility of maintaining liaison with the world's revolutionary movements and with the Third International. The Committee would consult the Third International to decide on a method of such liaison, including liaison between the KMT and the Third International on those activities of the Chinese Communist Party which were related to the Kuomintang. The last, of course, was the most important reason for the establishment of the Committee. [54]

In presenting the resolutions, Wang Jingwei remarked that party opinion with regard to the current dispute was split three ways: there were those who believed that cooperation with the communist faction would be harmful to the KMT; there were those who believed such cooperation would be beneficial; and there were those who believed party-straddling by the communists was not harmful, but might become so if they functioned as a secret bloc. He further stated that members of the Communist Party had an obligation to keep their party secrets. But if the KMT could keep its lines of communication open with the Third International, then there would be no secrets to speak of, and there would be no more misunderstandings. That is what the resolution on the International Liaison Committee aimed to achieve. [55]

The discussion that followed was brief. Chang Chi disqualified himself from commenting on the establishment of the International Liaison Committee on the grounds that it was not within his competence as a member of the Central Supervisory Committee to do so. Perhaps realizing that the plenum was not going to support the impeachment proposal, he requested that the CEC consider the proposal an unsettled question. He was supported by Fu Rulin, a close associate of Sun Ke, who said that he did not consider the Central Political Council's draft resolutions sufficient to resolve the question at hand, since they had come only after the impeachment charges were made by the Central Supervisory Committee. At that point Wang Jingwei quoted from a letter from Li Shizeng, one of the five members of the Central Supervisory Committee, as saying that he (Li) did not belong to the Third International, and had not participated in the discussions that led to KMT-CCP cooperation; but since that cooperation had become a fact, he thought it unwise for the KMT and the CCP to separate at this point. The intent of Wang's move was obviously to show that the impeachment proposal did not have the unanimous approval of all the members of the CSC. [56] Hu Hanmin, who presided over the plenum, urged the adoption of the Council's resolutions, saying that although much of the wording in the Youth Corps documents was inappropriate, he did not consider their contents malicious. The communists in the KMT should not be regarded as a conspiratorial faction, he said. When the vote was taken, Sun Yat-sen's will prevailed. The plenary session approved the Council's resolutions by a majority vote. [57] Thus, the debate on the controversy of communist membership in the KMT came to an end, at least temporarily.

Following its plenary session, the CEC issued a statement explaining once again the rationale for the KMT-CCP cooperation, and how the establishment of an International Liaison Committee would help eliminate conflicts arising from communist activities in the KMT. [58]

When the smoke had cleared, the KMT was no more united than it had been before the impeachment proceedings. In October 1924 Zhang Ji asked to be relieved of all his party posts, and resigned his party membership. [59] Xie Chi also quietly returned to Shanghai, following a prolonged hospitalization in Canton, with a thousand dollars provided him by Sun Ke as travel funds. [60] Open anti-communist activities in the KMT were to lay dormant until after Sun Yat-sen's death.

This impeachment episode brought several things into sharper focus. In the first place, it became quite clear that the communists in the KMT were not going to give up their political independence. Qu Qiubai made this a point of emphasis in his statement before the CEC plenum. As Robert North and Benjamin Schwartz have pointed out, the communists, on account of their common ideology and organizational and disciplinary ties, could not join the KMT as individuals but only as members of a highly disciplined faction. [61] Secondly, Sun Yat-sen's tolerance of such independence was due not so much to his failure to understand the communists' motives as to his need for outside material aid — and the only source of that aid at that time was the Soviet Union, but the price for that aid was collaboration with the communists. He was willing to pay that price, however, because he believed that he could effectively deal with the communists through party discipline and turn the situation to the KMT's advantage. Thirdly, this episode also revealed the influence Borodin had in KMT affairs. There seems no doubt that he was the person behind the tough stand the communists took during the impeachment debate, his attitude toward the whole question having been revealed in his earlier meeting with Zhang Ji and Xie Chi. His influence can also be seen in the establishment of the Central Political Council. Although the Council, set up at his suggestion, was placed under the nominal control of the CEC, it was designed to take the place of the CEC and function as the highest decision-making body of the party, an extra-legal organ not provided for by the party Constitution. Finally, the failure of the impeachment move indicated that, the spread of anti-communist sentiments in the KMT notwithstanding, those sentiments had not coalesced into an organized and coordinated movement. Personal loyalty to Sun Yat-sen undoubtedly played a big part in this, as it was not until after Sun's death that the anti-communists organized themselves in Peking and Shanghai in open defiance of Canton's policies.

The Kuomintang's task in 1924 would have been much easier if it had merely involved the settling of intra-party disputes. Party-building and the consolidation of a revolutionary force required much more than just internal harmony, important as that was for the KMT. In 1924 the KMT still controlled only Canton, and the military forces of Chen Jiongming and others just outside Canton remained a threat. The Whampoa Military Academy had just been established, and time was needed to train up a corps of officers to develop a party army. Even in Canton, the party's control was not complete. The generals who pledged nominal allegiance to the KMT continued to vie for power, and, together with other vested interest groups, they strenuously resisted the KMT efforts to centralize control of Canton's finances. There were also other pressing concerns. The CEC plenum convened to deal with the impeachment proposal took place amid the Merchants Corps Incident, when a large consignment of arms for the Merchant Corps arrived in Canton and was seized by the KMT. This incident almost precipitated an international crisis for the KMT, but the Merchant Corps was finally suppressed by force. [62] It was these problems that compounded the KMT's task in 1924, after its reorganization. The urgency created by these problems heightened the need to dispose of the impeachment question expeditiously and effectively while preserving the Canton-Moscow alliance. Sun Yat-sen had the unenviable task of having to balance two seemingly irreconcilable political realities in the impeachment episode, and his choices were limited. Although his policy of collaboration with the communists was in dispute, his leadership was never questioned. It was the force of that leadership that kept the party together and the momentum of the reorganization going, which in turn enabled him to forge a revolutionary force that eventually succeeded in seizing political power, even though he did not live long enough to see it.

NOTES

This is a slightly revised version of a paper presented at the Centennial Symposium on Sun Yat-sen's Founding of the Kuomintang for Revolution, November 19-23, 1994, in Taipei, Taiwan and published in *Proceedings of Centennial Symposium on Sun Yat-sen's Founding of the Kuomintang for Revolution*, Taipei, 1995, v. 2, pp. 1-26.

[1]　For a detailed discussion of communist activism in the KMT following the party's

reorganization in 1924, and the controversy over the secret CCP directives, see Li Yunhan, *Cong rong gong dao qing dang*（From the Admission of Communists to the Purification of the Party）（Taipei: 1966）, chap. 5, pp. 250-343.

[2]　The *Hua zi ribao (Wah Tze Yah Pao)*, founded in 1872, was one of the earliest Chinese-owned newspapers in Hong Kong. It had supported the late-Qing reform movement, and was sympathetic to Sun Yat-sen's early revolutionary endeavors. See Ge Gongzhen, *zhongguo bao xue shi*（History of Chinese Journalism）（Taipei:Xuesheng Shuju, 1964 reprint ed.）, p. 105; Fang Hanqi, *zhongguo jindai baokan shi*（History of Modern Chinese Press）（Taiyuan: Shanxi jiaoyu chubanshe, 1991）, pp. 60-61, 201; Li Jiayuan, *Xianggang baoye zatan*（Random Notes on Hong Kong Journalism）（Hong Kong: Sanlian Shudian, 1989）, p. 9;and Roswell Britton, *The Chinese Periodical Press*（Shanghai: Kelly & Walsh, Ltd., 1933）, pp. 46-47. The paper came strongly opposed to Sun's policy of admitting Chinese communists into the Kuomintang. The five articles referred to here were published on February 15, 19, 21, 23 and 28, 1924.

[3]　*Xinwen bao*, Feb. 29, 1924, p. 2. The *Xinwen bao (Sin Wan Pao)* was founded in 1893 in Shanghai by a British businessman. It went bankrupt in 1899 and was acquired by an American, John C. Ferguson. It was subsequently sold to a group of Chinese bankers, and went on to become one of the three major Chinese-language newspapers in Shanghai（the other two being the *Shen Bao* and the *Hu Bao*）. See Ge Gongzhen, *op.cit.*, p. 110; Fang Hanqi, *op.cit.*, pp. 42-43, 47-48; and Roswell C. Britton, *op.cit.*, p. 74.

[4]　The story of Feng Ziyou, *et al.* being threatened with deportation from Canton was also published in *Hua Zi ribao*（Feb. 28, 1924, p. 3）. According to this report, Sun Yat-sen, at an angry face-to-face confrontation with Feng Ziyou, Liu Chengyu, and Xie Chi over their continuing opposition to the KMT-CCP Party cooperation, told them at one point they had not been loyal to the party and to him for so long, he would have had them "used as targets"（i.e. "executed"）. Instead, he was going to refer their case to the CEC for a decision. Such a decision, Sun was quoted as saying, should include, at the least, expulsion from the party and deportation from Canton. Actually, a fourth person, Xu Qinghe, was also present at the meeting（see below）, but his name was not mentioned in the *Hua Zi ribao* article.

It appears that Sun did refer the case to the CEC, and that the four appeared before the CEC at its Sixth Session, held probably in mid-February; but this cannot be documented according to sources that have been made public. The *Zhongguo guomindang zhoukan*（The Kuomintang Weekly）,（hereafter cited as *KMT Weekly*）, which customarily carried a summary of the proceedings of the CEC sessions during this period, did not, for some reason, publish one for the Sixth Session. However, we do know that Sun Yat-sen, in a letter to the CEC dated March 1, 1924, advised members of the CEC that he was satisfied with the explanation given to him by Feng, Liu, Xie, and Xu, and that he considered the case closed. The letter is reproduced in *Guofu quanji* (Collected Works of Sun Yat-sen) (Taipei: Zhongguo guomindang zhongyang weiyuanhui dangshiweiyuanhui, 1973), v 3. p. 943.

Li Yunhan writes that Feng, Liu, Xie, and Xu, soon after the conclusion of the First KMT Party Congress, had called a meeting at Lin Sen's residence in Canton, attended by more than fifty anti-communists, to prepare a letter of warning to Li Dazhao, the leader of the communists in the KMT, not try to usurp the leadership of the KMT. However, before the letter could be sent, the news leaked out, and Li Dazhao and Borodin went to Sun Yat-sen to accuse the four of "disobeying party discipline and sowing discord within the party," and demanded their punishment. Subsequently, Sun summoned the four for a personal hearing. In their own defense, the four cited, among other arguments, the articles published by Li Dazhao and Chen Duxiu in *Xiang dao* (Guide Weekly) and *Xin qingnian* (New Youth) to show the communists' lack of credibility and their slander against the KMT. Sun was said to be satisfied with their defense, and acquitted them of any wrongdoing. See Li Yunhan, *op.cit.*, p. 222. Li does not mention whether Sun had threatened the four with deportation.

[5]　For a complete text of the statement, see *KMT Weekly*, no. 12, March 16, 1924, p. 4. The statement was also published in *Hua zi ribao*, March 21, 1924, p. 3

[6]　The circulars were published in *KMT Weekly*, no 13, March 23, 1924, pp. 3-4. Circular no. 24, drafted by Sun Yat-sen, is also found in *Guofu quanji* v. 1, pp. 889-890.

[7]　The text of this statement was published in *KMT Weekly*, no. 14, March 30, 1924, pp. 3-5.

[8]　Chen's petition is kept in the Kuomintang Archives, no. 435/300.

[9]　The CEC's letter of referral was signed by Dai Jitao, Liao Zhongkai, Peng Sumin,, an alternate member of the CEC. This letter and the CSC's reply are kept together with Chen Juexian's petition in the Kuomintang Archives, no. 435/300, cited above.

[10]　*Ibid.*

[11]　According to the summary of the proceedings of the CEC meetings published in the *KMT Weekly,* alternate members participated regularly in the meetings and voted.

[12]　They include, in varying degrees, Hu Hanmin, Dai Jitao, and Shao Yuanchong. See Li Yunhan, *op. tit.*, pp. 235-245; see also notes 36 and 37 below.

[13]　As early as November 1923, when the news of the impending KMT reorganization became

known and it was also learned that communists would be admitted into the reorganized party, the eleven members of the KMT Guangdong Provincial Headquarters, headed by Deng Zeru, a party veteran who had been a principal fund-raiser for Sun Yat-sen in Southeast Asia, expressed their deep concern over the potential danger of a communist take-over of the KMT if the reorganization went ahead as planned, in a petition to Sun dated Nov. 29, 1923. The text of the petition, reproduced in facsimile with Sun Yat-sen's comments, is included in *Tanhe gongchandang liang da yaoan* (Two Important Cases of Impeachment of the Communist Party)（[Nanjing?] : Zhongguo guomindang zhongyang jiancha weiyuanhui, 1927), pp. 1-12. Meanwhile, the Central Cadre Council, the KMT's highest executive body prior to the reorganization, on which Xie Chi and Zhang Ji both served, also expressed similar fears at a special meeting called on November 8, 1923, to discuss the question of KMT membership for communists. See *Zhongyang kanbu huiyi yijue lu* (Minutes of the Central Cadre Council), 1923, v. 4, in the Kuomintang Archives, no. 418/9.

[14]　See Li Yunhan, *op. cit.*, pp. 287-289.

[15]　Zou Lu, *Zhongguo guomindang shigao*(A Draft History of the Kuomintang)（Chongqing: Shangwu yinshuguan, 1944), pp. 368-369. Zou does not provide details of the impeachment.

[16]　Li Yunhan, *op.cit.,* p. 302.

[17]　These documents were first summarized with direct quotations and published in Suqing （pseudo）, *Gongchandang zhi yinmou da baolu* (Conspiracy of the Communist Party Exposed)（Canton: Sanmin julebu, n.d.）（preface dated August 27, 1924). The same summary is also reproduced with the text of the impeachment proposal in the following publications: *Tanhe gongchandang liang da yaoan* (Two Important Cases of Impeachment of the Communist Party)（cited above）; Deng Zeru, *Zhongguo guomindang ershi nian shiji* (A Twenty-Year Historical Record of the Kuomintang)（Shanghai: Zhengzhong Shuju, 1948), pp. 298-323; Zhang Ji, Zhang *Puquan xiansheng quanji* (Complete Works of Zhang Ji)（Taipei: Zhongguo guomindang zhongyang dangshi weiyuanhui, 1951), pp. 89-96; and *Geming wenxian* (Documents of the Revolution)（Taipei: Zhongguo guomindang zhongyang dangshi weiyuanhui, 1953-), v. 9, pp. 1279-1286. The complete text of the "Resolutions and Manifesto of the Second National Congress of the Chinese Socialist Youth Corps" is kept at the Kuomintang Archives （Li Yunhan, *op. cit.*, p. 340, n. 60). For the text of the "Resolution on the National Movement and the Kuomintang" adopted by the Third National Congress of the CCP, see Zhonggong zhongyang wenjian xuanji (A Selected Collection of Documents of the Party Central of the Chinese Communist

Party）（Beijing: Zhonggong zhongyang dangxiao, 1989）, v. 1, pp. 146-148.

[18] One source indicated that the documents were shown to Zhang Ji and Xie Chi in Shanghai by a KMT member（Sun Jingya?）who had been a member of the CCP for half a year （Suqing, *op. cit.,* pp. 25 and 70）. Zeng Qi, the late leader of the China Youth Party, writes that he had come across the documents in Paris, but tried in vain to get veteran KMT members, including Wang Chonghui and others, to pass the information on to Sun Yat-sen. Just then Cao Renyuan, son-in-law of Xie Chi, was passing through Paris on his way back to China from Germany where he had completed his studies. Zeng entrusted the documents to Cao for delivery to Xie Chi in Shanghai（Zeng Qi, *Zeng Muhan xiansheng yizhu* （Posthumous Writings of Zeng Qi）（Taipei: Zhongguo qingniandang zhongyang zhixing weiyuanhui, 1954）, p. 475.

[19] Suqing, *op. cit.,* p. 15.

[20] *Ibid.*

[21] Allen S. Whiting, *Soviet Policies in China, 1917-1924*（New York: Columbia University Press, 1954）, p. 277.

[22] Suqing, *op. cit.,* pp. 16-17.

[23] *Ibid.,* pp. 18, 23, and 27.

[24] *Ibid.,* pp. 20-21.

[25] For the text of the impeachment proposal, see the sources cited in note 17.

[26] Suqing, *op. cit.,* p. 21.

[27] *Ibid.,* p. 24

[28] *Ibid.,* pp. 24-27.

[29] *Ibid.,* pp. 24 and 29-30. After arriving in Shanghai on June 20, Dai tendered his resignation to Sun Yat-sen as head of the Propaganda Department of the KMT, pleading incompetence and misunderstanding of his position by other KMT members（the text of his resignation letter was published in *KMT Weekly,* no, 29, July 13, 1924, p. 4）. In a letter to Chiang Kai-shek one-half year later, on December 13, 1925, Dai reiterated his reasons for resignation saying that squabbles among the KMT leaders and the communist expansion in the KMT had given the party a schizophrenic character fraught with the danger of having two sorts of discipline, and with the difficulty of coping with two philosophies in propaganda work. See Dai Jitao, *Dai Jitao xiansheng wencun*（Dai Jitao's Collected Works）（Taipei: Zhongguo guomindang zhongyang weiyuanhui, 1959）, v. 3, p. 982.

[30] Suqing, *op. cit.,* p. 25.

[31] *Ibid.,* pp. 32 and 34.

[32] *Ibid.,* pp. 34-35.

[33] Although none of the available sources indicates Sun's role in arranging the meeting, it seems most likely that he did so for the following reasons: (1) to let Borodin have a clearer appreciation of the anti-communist feelings among some of the KMT leaders, and (2) to give the impeachers an opportunity to question Borodin directly on communist activities in the KMT. Borodin could not have suggested such a meeting under the circumstances, and the impeachers could not have sought a meeting with Borodin without Sun's approval. Sun also was reported to have sent Sun Ke to the meeting as interpreter for Zhang Ji and Xie Chi (See Suqing, p. 32)

[34] *Ibid.*

[35] *Ibid.,* pp. 35-36. This suggestion was attributed to Hu Hanmin and Liao Zhongkai.

[36] A summary of the minutes was published in *KMT Weekly,* no. 30, July 20, 1924. The *Geming wenxian* (Documents of the Revolution) misidentifies this meeting as the 4th session of the CEC, obviously a typographical error (*Geming wenxian,* v. 9., p. 1286).

[37] For the text of the proclamation see *KMT Weekly,* no. 30, July 20, 1924, p. 6; also *Guofu quanji,* v. 1, pp. 893-904.

Shao Yuanchong, who made the initial draft of the proclamation with Wang Jingwei, was extremely upset with the liberty the CEC took in revising the draft at its meeting on July 7. He writes: "Arrived at 7 p.m. at the Military Headquarters for a meeting of the CEC. The many additions and deletions made by others in the proclamation draft rendered the document a mere perfunctory statement, reflecting a desire to speak out and yet not dare to do so. Alas! I consoled myself by scribbling down two verses from a T'ang poet: 'Abrim to the lips with imperial gossip, but not daring to breathe it in front of the parrots' (含情欲說宮中事鸚鵡頭前不敢言). At a time when the rats are running wild without fear, I can only endure the humiliation in hopes that things might gradually be cleaned up." See *Shao Yuanchong riji, op.cit.,* p.28.

[38] The texts of fifteen such petitions are reproduced in Suqing, *op. cit.,* pp. 59-84. Another fifteen are cited in Li Yunhan, *op. cit.,* pp. 319-323.

[39] *Supra.* p. 2, n. 4.

[40] Suqing, *op. cit.,* pp. 46, 50-51. Xie was reported to have fallen ill with a severe case of diabetes.

[41] *Supra,* p. 11.

[42] *KMT Weekly,* no. 29, July 12, 1924, p. 2.

[43] *Guofu Nianpu*（A Chronological Biography of Sun Yat-sen）（Taipei: Zhongguo guomindang Zhongyang dangshi shiliaobianji weiyuanhui, 1965）, v. 2, pp. 1031 and 1037.

[44] Following the disposition of the affairs involving Feng Ziyou, Xie Yingbo, Liu Chengyu, and Xu Qinghe（*supra*, p.2）, an overseas member, Xiao Focheng, was reported to have advised Sun Yat-sen that he（Sun）should not treat his old comrades so harshly, or else others would become so discouraged that the party would lose their support. To this Sun was reported to have replied that he had no choice but to suppress their opposition. He argued that in view of the gradually stabilized situation in the North, where the warlords were consolidating their position and control of the government, and also of the fact that the troops in Guangdong refused to fight without money, thus threatening his plans for a northern expedition, he had no recourse but to cooperate with the communists. See *Hua zi ribao*, February 28, 1924, p.3.

In July 1924, SunYat-sen also told Liu Chengyu that he was not unaware of Soviet designs on China, but in the face of British, American, and Japanese hostility toward the Canton government, his alliance with the Soviet Union was aimed at easing pressure from the other foreign powers. Should the relations between the Canton government and the foreign powers improve, he saw no reason why the Kuomintang should lean just toward the Soviet Union. He also maintained that he would treat the communists in the Kuomintang with sincerity and will attempt to transform them into genuine believers in his Three People's Principles. If they should step out of bounds of party regulations, he would have his own way of dealing with them. See Liu Chengyu, "Xian zongli jiude lu"（The Late Sun Yat-sen's Moral Teachings）, in *Guoshiguan guankan*（Bulletin of the Academia Historica）, no. 1 （December 1947）, pp. 53-54.

[45] A. I. Cherpanov, *Zhongguo guominjun di beifa – Yige zhu hua junshi guwen di zaji*（The Northern Expedition of the Chinese National Revolutionary Army — Notes of a Military Advisor in China）（Beijing: Zhongguo shehui kexueyuan chubanshe, 1984）, p. 114. This is a Chinese translation of the author's *Zapiski Voennogo Sovetnika v Kitae*（Moscow, 1976）, which is a revised and combined edition of the author's two earlier works: *Zapiski Voennogo Sovetnika: iz Istorii Pervoi Gradzhdanskoi Revolutsionnoi Voiny*, 1924-1927（Moscow, 1964）and *Severnyi Natsionalno Revolutsionnoi Armii Kitae Zapiski*（Moscow, 1968）.

[46] *Guofu nianpu*, v. 2, p. 1039. The six members were Hu Hanmin, Wang Jingwei, Liao Zhongkai, Tan Pingshan, Wu Chaoshu, and Shao Yuanchong. Tan resigned presently and

was replaced by another communist, Qu Qiubai *(ibid.,* v. 2, p. 1041).

[47] Jiang Yongjing, *"Hu Hanmin xiansheng nianpu gao"* (A Draft Chronological Biography of Hu Hanmin), in Wu Xiang-xiang, ed., *Zhongguo xiandaishi congkan* (A Collection of Writings on Modem Chinese History) (Taipei: Zhengzhong shuju, 1961), v. 3, pp. 201-202. Dai Jitao also supported the idea. See Li Yunhan, *op. cit.,* pp. 241-244.

[48] *Guofu nianpu,* v. 2, p. 1030.

[49] *Ibid.,* pp. 1049-1050.

[50] *Ibid.*

[50] *Ibid.*

[51] Li Yunhan, *op. cit.,* pp. 324-331. Li's account is sourced to the minutes of the Central Political Council meetings kept at the Kuomintang Archives. The minutes are not yet publicly available.

[52] *Guofu nianpu,* v. 2, p. 1054.

[53] Li Yunhan, *op. cit.,* p. 327.

[54] *Ibid.,* pp. 327-328.

[55] *Ibid.* Jiang Yongjing in his draft chronological biography of Hu Han-min, attributes this statement to Hu Hanmin. See Jiang Yongjing, *op. cit.,* p. 204.

[56] Li Yunhan, *op. cit.,* p. 329. The fifth member of the Central Supervisory Committee, Wu Zhihui, also declined to sign the impeachment proposal. However, following the purge of the communists from the KMT in 1927, he expressed regret that he had not done so, and gave two reasons for his decision: (1) he did not believe the Communist Party, as a revolutionary party dedicated to assisting other revolutionary parties, would practice deceit; and (2) he trusted Sun Yat-sen's judgement. See Wu's introduction to *Tanhe gongchandang liang da yaoan* (Two Important Cases of Impeachment of the Communist Party), which was officially published by the Central Supervisory Committee of the KMT in September 1927. Hu Han-min wrote the cover title of the publication in his calligraphy.

[57] Li Yunhan, *op. cit.,* p. 330. The names of those voting against the motion are not given.

[58] The draft of the statement was first published in *KMT Weekly,* no. 40, September 28, 1924, p. 5. The final version, with some changes, is reproduced in *Geming wenxian* (Documents of the Revolution), v. 16, pp. 2773-2776.

[59] Li Yunhan, *op. cit.,* p. 337.

[60] *Ibid.*

[61] Robert C. North, *Moscow and Chinese Communists,* 2nd ed. (Stanford: Stanford University

Press, 1963), p. 83; and Benjamin I. Schwartz, *Chinese Communism and the Rise of Mao* (Cambridge, Mass: Harvard University Press, 1961), p. 52.

[62] For an account of the Merchant Corps Incident, see C. Martin Wilbur, *Sun Yat-sen: Frustrated Patriot* (New York: Columbia University Press, 1976), pp. 250-264.

卷尾

向CEAL辭別

1997年亞洲學會東亞圖書館協會主席馬泰來頒發該會「傑出貢獻獎」
給吳文津。

　　謝謝你們贈給我這個獎牌。繼埃德・比爾（Ed Beal）和錢存訓之後我
接受這個榮譽，實在感激不盡。

　　你們都知道我做圖書館員已經好多年了，到退休時正好46年。先在胡
佛研究所工作，後在哈佛燕京圖書館服務。其間正逢北美東亞圖書館和東亞
圖書館協會（CEAL）蓬勃發展的時期。過去50年間能親歷東亞圖書館和其
前輩如何有效地引導東亞圖書館發展真是很幸運的事。

　　自從那個沒有傳真，沒有電郵，CEAL尚未成立各小組的時代，幾個人
在亞洲學會年會時聚集在某個人的旅館房間裡以來，CEAL已經完成了好多
大事：諸如大規模地修改美國圖書館協會和國會圖書館編目規則；國會圖書

館東方語文編目卡複製項目（LC's Oriental Card Reproduction Project）；在台北成立中文研究資料中心（Chinese Materials and Research Aids Service Center）；發動對東亞圖書館的統計調查；發行東亞圖書館協會通訊等等。在北美東亞圖書館的發展史上，CEAL扮演了關鍵性角色。要是沒有CEAL的領導，我們很難想像今日美國東亞圖書館是什麼樣子。在接受這個獎牌之際，我要向長期辛勤為美國東亞圖書館貢獻良多的裘開明、埃德·比爾、錢存訓、雷蒙德·納恩（Raymond Nunn）、迪克·霍華德（Dick Howard）以及常石道雄等等致敬。

近年由於自動化的出現，圖書館經費來源變更，CEAL不必再為北美東亞圖書館負責解決所有的問題。研究圖書館組織（RLG）有其東亞研究諮詢團體（East Asian Studies Advisory Group），連線電腦圖書館中心（Online Computer Library Center，簡稱OCLC）有其中日韓文用戶團體（OCLC CJK Users Group）。還有全國日文圖書館資源合作委員會（National Coordinating Committee on Japanese Library Resources）以及好些個合作採購中日韓文的聯盟組織。但是它們都各有其局限性，並沒有減低CEAL作為全國所有東亞圖書館組織的重要性。CEAL還是最理想最合適的組織來領導全國討論東亞圖書館面臨的困難。在採取那種最好的方法來解決這些困難上，可以幫助大家達到共識。

最近對拼音的討論就是個好例子。討論間提出了一個問題：有鑑於科技已經進步到可以處理中日韓文字，而用中日韓文字可以更好更容易地與在東亞的圖書館溝通，我們還應不應該繼續使用羅馬拼音呢？CEAL應該開始好好檢視這個問題。最近在討論將東亞字元代碼（EACC）更換成通用代碼，統一代碼（Unicode），在規範文件中增添中日韓文等全國關心的問題上，CEAL都扮演了重要的角色。

中日韓文的數位資料越來越多，東亞圖書館如何來採購這些資料？也是個最好從全國的角度來解決的問題。如何有效地使用有限的經費採購印刷品和數位資料而不失平衡？需不需要成立一個全國聯盟或者地區聯盟合作採購和利用這些資料？應不應該要求RLG和OCLC把這些數位資料放在其資料庫，費用由使用的圖書館分攤？（OCLC CJK Users Group已經開始和OCLC討論這個問題了。）數位資料這個問題無疑將來會更加複雜，CEAL對這個問題可以明白表達一個代表全體東亞圖書館的觀點，免得因為我們的無知錯失挑戰的良機。我們必須要趕快行動，但也要確定我們的目標是正確的。

國會圖書館和哈佛大學賴世和日本研究所（Reischauer Institute for Japanese Studies）的日本檔案中心（Japan Documentation Center）辦得很成功（最近匹茨堡大學也成立了這樣的中心），令我們感到中國研究和韓國研究也需要這樣的中心。CEAL也可以領導大家探討如何成立這樣的中心。

還有保存資料的問題。中日韓文傳統的線裝書，在西方受訓修補西文書刊的圖書館員是無法修補的。CEAL是否可能籌募經費從東亞邀請一位專家來美國舉辦短期培訓班，教導我們自己的圖書館員如何初步修補中日韓文資料？

最後要提到的是東亞圖書館員的培訓問題。多數的東亞圖書館都是在職訓練其工作人員，特別是如何使用電腦方面的工作。東亞圖書館一直缺少一套有系統的培養東亞圖書館員以及再教育的課程。大學裡提供強大的東亞研究課程並提供獎助培養博士生，但是卻沒有培養作為東亞圖書館員的課程。很多年前芝加哥大學圖書館學校和東亞研究系合作設立了博士課程，一度非常成功。但是由於圖書館學校的撤銷和錢存訓先生的退休，這個項目就沒有了。為了東亞圖書館長期健全地成長，CEAL可以探索在其他學校成立像芝加哥大學過去那樣課程的可能性，或者申請經費舉辦像多年前威斯康辛大學、華盛頓大學、芝加哥大學那樣的暑期培訓班。

當然你們還可以想到其他CEAL可以主持的項目。重要的是CEAL作為東亞圖書館和東亞圖書館館員的全國性組織，以其過去建立的輝煌成就所具有的條件足以繼續領導北美東亞圖書館。讓我們大家為CEAL下個50年更強壯更有效而努力。

謝謝你們，並祝大家成功。

注釋

1998年3月25日東亞圖書館協會贈與吳文津對東亞圖書館和東亞圖書館協會傑出服務獎牌時，本文為在全體會員大會上的致辭。載《東亞圖書館學報》（*Journal of East Asian Libraries*），第116期（1998年10月），頁2-4。

（胡嘉陽譯）

附件

向吳文津致敬

　　1998年3月25日東亞圖書館協會全體會員大會向哈佛燕京圖書館榮休館長吳文津，為他多年來對東亞圖書館界及該會作出的傑出貢獻致敬。密西根大學東亞圖書館館長萬惟英代表該會向他頒贈獎牌以為褒揚。刻文如下：

　　當您榮休之際東亞圖書館協會為吳文津四十年來在東亞圖書館界及東亞學術界的傑出成就及領導以及對本會所作出的眾多貢獻特予表彰並致敬意

　　萬館長並宣讀東亞圖書館協會獻詞如下：

　　　　四十年來您是推動發展現代及當代中國研究資料之主要動力。在胡佛研究所東亞圖書館館長及哈佛燕京圖書館館長任內，您主持了這兩所圖書館傑出收藏的發展，開啟了現代中國的研究。

　　　　當無法到中國大陸使用研究資料時，您獲取了異常寶貴的「陳誠特藏」*當亟需對現代及當代中國研究有關資料的書目資訊時，您與您的同僚編輯出版了《現代中國研究指南》，列舉世界各國圖書館及研究機構所收藏的有關資料。您走遍三大洲的調查，以及您的外交、學術和創業者的才幹導致了「中國研究資料中心」的成立，因而更進一步充實了學術研究的基礎。

　　　　在擔任亞洲學會東亞圖書館委員會會長任內，您發動對東亞圖書館面臨的各種問題的研討，引起全國廣泛的注意，並獲得經費資助來解決問題。在您諸多的成就中，還包括您在香港中文大學成立大學圖書館時所扮的腳色；您為亞洲區基督教高等教育聯合董事會在四川主持的圖書館工作研習會；和您始終不懈地與人分享資料和資訊的慷慨作風。

　　歷史上總是以榜樣、成就和對理想的表達這些因素來紀念領袖人物。我們為您在激勵他人的抱負，為您利人的成就，以及為您與人分享傳播知識的精神表示欽佩。東亞圖書館協會為表彰如此傑出的事業感到榮幸。

注釋

* 1960年吳文津任胡佛研究所東亞圖書館館長任內在台北監製自陳誠副總統石叟資料室所藏「江西蘇維埃共和國」檔案的縮微膠捲，約1,500餘件。

（胡嘉陽譯）

Farewell Speech

Thank you very much for this award. It's a great honor to follow Ed Beal and T. H. Tsien in receiving this recognition from CEAL, and I am deeply grateful.

As you know, I have been a librarian for a long time, 46 years to be exact, first with the East Asian Collection at the Hoover Institution and then with the Harvard-Yenching Library at Harvard. My service coincided with the development of East Asian libraries in North America and with the growth of CEAL. It's enormously gratifying to see how East Asian libraries have developed in the last fifty years, and how CEAL and its predecessor bodies have functioned effectively in guiding that development.

We have come a long way from the days when CEAL meetings were held in someone's hotel room at AAS meetings, and there were no CEAL committees and there was no fax or e-mail. But a lot of work was done, such as the wholesale revision of the ALA and LC cataloging rules, the Oriental Vernacular Card Reproduction Project at LC, the founding of the Chinese Materials Center in Taipei, the initiation of the statistical survey, the publication of the *CEAL Bulletin*, etc. The role CEAL played in the development of East Asian libraries in North America was so vital that it is difficult to imagine where we would be today without the leadership that has been provided by CEAL. In receiving this award, I would like to pay tribute to those who labored long and hard for the benefit of our field, people like Kaiming Chiu, Ed Beal, T.H. Tsien, Raymond Nunn, Dick Howard, and Warren Tsuneishi, just to name a few.

With the advent of automation and the changed funding pattern in recent years, the latter especially regarding Japanese library resources, CEAL no longer has to be responsible for everything that has to do with East Asian libraries in North America. RLG has its East Asian Studies Advisory Group, OCLC has the OCLC CJK Users Group, and there are the National Coordinating Committee on Japanese Library Resources and several consortia on the acquisition of Chinese, Japanese, and Korean materials. But each of these groups has its own constituency, and they do not reduce the importance of CEAL as the national organization of all East Asian libraries. CEAL is still ideally suited to lead the national discourse on many of the problems facing East Asian libraries, and to help reach a national consensus on how best to approach them.

The recent discussion on pinyin is a case in point. And one question that has been brought forth by the pinyin discussion is whether we should continue to use romanization at all, given the technological advances in dealing with the CJK scripts and the paramount importance of better and easier communication with libraries in East Asia which do not use romanization. CEAL should begin an examination of this question. The recent discussions on upgrading the EACC code, the Unicode, and the incorporation of CJK scripts in the authority file are all matters of national concern, and CEAL has an important role to play in all such discussions.

The increasing availability of electronic resources in CJK languages and their acquisition by our libraries poses another problem that can best be dealt with from a national perspective. With limited financial resources, what is the most cost-effective way to achieve a proper balance between print materials and electronic resources for our libraries? Should a national consortium, or regional consortia be formed for the collecting and sharing of such resources and their costs? Should RLG and OCLC be asked to mount these resources on their databases and pass on the costs to the user libraries? (The OCLC CJK Users Group has already begun discussions with OCLC on this question.) The problems involving electronic resources will undoubtedly become more complex in the future. CEAL can help articulate a national vision so that the opportunities presented by this new challenge will not run ahead of our understanding of them. We need to move quickly, but we also want to make sure we do not end up at the wrong place.

The success of the Japan Documentation Center at LC, at the Reischauer Institute for Japanese Studies at Harvard, and recently at the University of Pittsburg suggests the need for such centers for Chinese and Korean studies as well. CEAL can take the lead in exploring the issues involved in establishing them.

Similarly, there is the question of preservation. Traditional CJK publications in the stitch-bound format require special treatment which cannot be provided by conservators trained in dealing with Western-language materials. Might it be possible for CEAL to seek financial support to invite an expert book conservator from East Asia to conduct workshops in this country to train our own people in at least the rudiments of conserving CJK materials?

Finally, there is the question of training East Asian librarians. While a great deal of on-the-job training takes place at individual libraries, especially regarding the application of technology, East Asian libraries lack a systematic training program for those entering our field, or a program for continuing education. The academic side of East Asian studies maintains its vigor by training Ph.D. students, often with financial support, but East Asian libraries do not have such a system. Many years ago, the University of Chicago instituted a joint Ph.D. program between its Library School and its East Asian Studies Department, but that program, though quite successful, is now defunct with the demise of its Library School and the retirement of T.H. Tsien. For the long-term health of East Asian libraries, CEAL might want to explore the possibility of re-introducing the Chicago program elsewhere, or at least help solicit funds to conduct short-term summer institutes such as the ones that were held at the University of Wisconsin, the University of Washington, and the University of Chicago many years ago.

There is no doubt that you can think of other programs CEAL can do. The point is that CEAL, as the national organization of East Asian libraries and librarians, is the body that is best equipped to continue to guide the development of all East Asian libraries in North America. It has an impressive track record on which to build. Let's rededicate ourselves to making CEAL an even stronger and an even more effective organization for the next 50 years.

Thank you again, and I wish you continued success.

Notes

This was published in *Journal of East Asian Libraries*, no. 116 (Oct. 1998), pp. 2-4.

Tribute to Eugene Wu

On March 25, 1998, on the occasion of the Plenary Session of the Council on East Asian Libraries, Eugene Wu, recently retired as Librarian of the Harvard-Yenching Library, was honored for his many years of distinguished service to the field of East Asian librarianship CEAL. Weiying Wan, Head of the Asia Library at the University of Michigan, presented him with a plaque reading

On the occasion of your retirement
the Council on East Asian Libraries
wishes to recognize and salute
Eugene Wen-Chin Wu
for your four decades of
extraordinary achievement
and leadership
in the fields of
East Asian librarianship and scholarship
and your many contributions to CEAL

Citation

To Eugene Wen-Chin Wu, for his distinguished service to the profession and to the Council of East Asian Libraries.

For four decades you have been the dynamic leading force in the development of research sources for modern and contemporary China studies. As Curator of the East Asian Collection at Hoover Institution and as Librarian of Harvard-Yenching Library, you presided over the growth of two outstanding collections whose riches have made possible the coming of modern Chinese studies.

When there was little direct access to China, you obtained for Chinese studies the invaluable Chen Cheng Collection. When there was urgent need for bibliographic information on contemporary China research, you and your collaborators accepted the challenge by producing the invaluable bibliographic and research guide, *Contemporary China: A Research Guide*, based on the resources of libraries and research institutions around the world. Your survey of three continents, and your talents as scholar, diplomat, and entrepreneur, led to the establishment of the Center for Chinese Research Materials (CCRM), further enriching the base for scholarship.

As Chairman of the Committee on East Asian Libraries, you launched the study of the range of problems faced by our libraries, bringing national attention and new funding to their solution. Among your many other accomplishments have been your role in planning for the library of the Chinese University of Hong Kong, the library workshop conducted in Sichuan for the United Board of Christian Higher Education, and your unfailing generosity in sharing resources and information.

History remembers leaders for their exemplification, their accomplishments, and their expressions of ideals. We admire you for the aspiration you inspire in others, for your achievements which benefit others, and for your dissemination of knowledge shared with others. The Council on East Asian Libraries honors itself in recognizing so distinguished a career.

Notes

This was published in *Journal of East Asian Libraries*, no. 116 (Oct. 1998), pp. 1-2.

美國東亞圖書館發展史及其他

2016年6月初版　　　　　　　　　　　　　　　定價：新臺幣800元
有著作權·翻印必究
Printed in Taiwan.

著　　者	吳　文　津	
總　編　輯	胡　金　倫	
總　經　理	羅　國　俊	
發　行　人	林　載　爵	

出　版　者	聯經出版事業股份有限公司	叢書主編　沙　淑　芬
地　　　址	台北市基隆路一段180號4樓	校　　對　吳　美　滿
編輯部地址	台北市基隆路一段180號4樓	封面設計　李　東　記
叢書主編電話	(02)87876242轉212	
台北聯經書房	台北市新生南路三段94號	
電　　　話	(02)23620308	
台中分公司	台中市北區崇德路一段198號	
暨門市電話	(04)22312023	
台中電子信箱	e-mail：linking2@ms42.hinet.net	
郵政劃撥帳戶第0100559-3號		
郵撥電話	(02)23620308	
印　刷　者	世和印製企業有限公司	
總　經　銷	聯合發行股份有限公司	
發　行　所	新北市新店區寶橋路235巷6弄6號2樓	
電　　　話	(02)29178022	

行政院新聞局出版事業登記證局版臺業字第0130號

本書如有缺頁，破損，倒裝請寄回台北聯經書房更換。　ISBN　978-957-08-4761-1 (精裝)
聯經網址：www.linkingbooks.com.tw
電子信箱：linking@udngroup.com